Fodor's

THE COMPL
AFRICAN SAFARI
PLANNER

1st Edition

Fodor's Travel Publications New York, Toronto, London, Sydney, Auckland
www.fodors.com

Be a Fodor's Correspondent

Your opinion matters. It matters to us. It matters to your fellow Fodor's travelers, too. And we'd like to hear it. In fact, we need to hear it.

When you share your experiences and opinions, you become an active member of the Fodor's community. That means we'll not only use your feedback to make our books better, but we'll publish your names and comments whenever possible. Throughout our guides, look for "Word of Mouth," excerpts of your unvarnished feedback.

Here's how you can help improve Fodor's for all of us.

Tell us when we're right. We rely on local writers to give you an insider's perspective. But our writers and staff editors—who are the best in the business—depend on you. Your positive feedback is a vote to renew our recommendations for the next edition.

Tell us when we're wrong. We're proud that we update most of our guides every year. But we're not perfect. Things change. Hotels cut services. Museums change hours. Charming cafés lose charm. If our writer didn't quite capture the essence of a place, tell us how you'd do it differently. If any of our descriptions are inaccurate or inadequate, we'll incorporate your changes in the next edition and will correct factual errors at fodors.com immediately.

Tell us what to include. You probably have had fantastic travel experiences that aren't yet in Fodor's. Why not share them with a community of like-minded travelers? Maybe you chanced upon a beach or bistro or B&B that you don't want to keep to yourself. Tell us why we should include it. And share your discoveries and experiences with everyone directly at fodors.com. Your input may lead us to add a new listing or highlight a place we cover with a "Highly Recommended" star or with our highest rating, "Fodor's Choice."

Give us your opinion instantly at our feedback center at www.fodors.com/feedback. You may also e-mail editors@fodors.com with the subject line "The Complete African Safari Planner Editor." Or send your nominations, comments, and complaints by mail to The Complete African Safari Planner Editor, Fodor's, 1745 Broadway, New York, NY 10019.

You and travelers like you are the heart of the Fodor's community. Make our community richer by sharing your experiences. Be a Fodor's correspondent.

Happy Traveling!

Tim Jarrell, Publisher

FODOR'S THE COMPLETE AFRICAN SAFARI PLANNER
Editor: Alexis C. Kelly
Editorial Contributor: Deborah Kaufman

Editorial Production: Linda K. Schmidt
Writers: Kate Turkington (lead writer), Brian Berkman, Sanja Cloete-Jones, Karena du Plessis, Debra A. Klein, Jennifer Stern, Tara Turkington, Kristan Schiller
Maps & Illustrations: Henry Columb and Mark Stroud, Moon Street Cartography; Bob Blake, Rebecca Baer, and William Wu, *map editors*
Design: Fabrizio LaRocca, *creative director*; Guido Caroti, Siobhan O'Hare, *art directors*; Tina Malaney, Chie Ushio, Ann McBride, *designers*; Melanie Marin, *senior picture editor*; Moon Sun Kim, *cover designer*
Cover Photo: front (South Africa), Frank Herholdt/Stone/Getty Images; back, Thomas Dressler/age fotostock
Production/Manufacturing: Steve Slawsky

COPYRIGHT

Copyright © 2008 by Fodor's Travel, a division of Random House, Inc.

Fodor's is a registered trademark of Random House, Inc.

All rights reserved. Published in the United States by Fodor's Travel, a division of Random House, Inc., and simultaneously in Canada by Random House of Canada, Limited, Toronto. Distributed by Random House, Inc., New York.

No maps, illustrations, or other portions of this book may be reproduced in any form without written permission from the publisher.

First Edition

ISBN 978-1-4000-1928-1

ISSN 1941-0336

SPECIAL SALES

This book is available at special discounts for bulk purchases for sales promotions or premiums. Special editions, including personalized covers, excerpts of existing books, and corporate imprints, can be created in large quantities for special needs. For more information, write to Special Markets/Premium Sales, 1745 Broadway, MD 6-2, New York, New York 10019, or e-mail specialmarkets@randomhouse.com.

AN IMPORTANT TIP & AN INVITATION

Although all prices, opening times, and other details in this book are based on information supplied to us at press time, changes occur all the time in the travel world, and Fodor's cannot accept responsibility for facts that become outdated or for inadvertent errors or omissions. So **always confirm information when it matters**, especially if you're making a detour to visit a specific place. Your experiences—positive and negative—matter to us. If we have missed or misstated something, **please write to us.** We follow up on all suggestions. Contact the The Complete African Safari Planner editor at editors@fodors.com or c/o Fodor's at 1745 Broadway, New York, NY 10019.

PRINTED IN SINGAPORE
10 9 8 7 6 5 4 3 2 1

CONTENTS

AFRICAN SAFARIS IN FOCUS

CONTENTS

CONTENTS

CLOSE UPS

MAPS

ABOUT
THIS BOOK

Our Ratings

Sometimes you find terrific travel experiences and sometimes they just find you. But usually the burden is on you to select the right combination of experiences. That's where our ratings come in.

As travelers we've all discovered a place so wonderful that its worthiness is obvious. And sometimes that place is so experiential that superlatives don't do it justice: you just have to be there to know. These sights, properties, and experiences get our highest rating, **Fodor's Choice,** indicated by orange stars throughout this book.

Black stars highlight sights and properties we deem **Highly Recommended,** places that our writers, editors, and readers praise again and again for consistency and excellence.

By default, there's another category: any place we include in this book is by definition worth your time, unless we say otherwise. And we will.

Disagree with any of our choices? Care to nominate a place or suggest that we rate one more highly? Visit our feedback center at www.fodors.com/feedback.

Budget Well

Hotel and restaurant price categories from ¢ to $$$$ are defined in the opening pages of each chapter. For attractions, we always give standard adult admission fees; reductions are usually available for children, students, and senior citizens. Want to pay with plastic? **AE, DC, MC,** and **V** after restaurant and hotel listings indicate whether American Express, Diners Club, MasterCard, and Visa are accepted.

Restaurants

Unless we state otherwise, restaurants are open for lunch and dinner daily. We mention dress only when there's a specific requirement and reservations only when they're essential or not accepted—it's always best to book ahead.

Hotels

Hotels have private bath, phone, TV, and air-conditioning and operate on the European Plan (aka EP, meaning without meals), unless we specify that they use the Continental Plan (CP, with a continental breakfast), Breakfast Plan (BP, with a full breakfast), or Modified American Plan (MAP, with breakfast and dinner) or are all-inclusive (including all meals and most activi-

ties). We always list facilities but not whether you'll be charged an extra fee to use them, so when pricing accommodations, find out what's included.

Many Listings	
★	Fodor's Choice
★	Highly recommended
⊠	Physical address
⊹	Directions
🕮	Mailing address
☎	Telephone
🖷	Fax
⊕	On the Web
✑	E-mail
☜	Admission fee
⊘	Open/closed times
Ⓜ	Metro stations
▭	Credit cards

Hotels & Restaurants	
🏨	Hotel
⇥	Number of rooms
⚲	Facilities
⑩	Meal plans
✕	Restaurant
⚶	Reservations
⤩	Smoking
🍺	BYOB
✕🏨	Hotel with restaurant that warrants a visit

Outdoors	
🏌	Golf
⛺	Camping

Other	
☾	Family-friendly
⇨	See also
⊠	Branch address
☞	Take note

Your Safari

WHAT'S WHERE

The following numbers refer to chapters.

3 Kenya. Part of what's known as East Africa, you can expect golden lions, red-robed warriors, snowcapped mountains, pristine white beaches, orange sunsets, and coral-pink dawns. You'll also experience some of the world's most famous safari destinations—Masai Mara, Mt Kilimanjaro, the Rift Valley—and world class beach destinations like Diani Beach and the tiny Arab town of Lamu.

4 Tanzania. Tanzania, also part of East Africa, attracts far fewer tourists than Kenya and South Africa, which is remarkable especially since it boasts some of Africa's greatest tourist attractions—the Serengeti, the Great Migration, Olduvai Gorge, Ngorongoro Crater, Selous Game Reserve, and Lake Victoria.

5 South Africa. Africa's most developed country, at the very tip of the continent, is many worlds in one: modern bustling cities, ancient rock art, gorgeous beaches, fabulous game lodges, well-run national parks, mountain ranges, desert, and winelands. It's home to Kruger National Park and the Kwa-Zulu Natal reserves.

6 Botswana. Botswana itself is a natural wonder with terrains that vary from vast salt pans to the pristine waterways of the Okavango Delta. Expect lots of game, few tourists, and stars brighter than you'll ever see.

7 Namibia. From the Namib Desert—the earth's oldest—to the fog-enshrouded Skeleton Coast, from the great game park of Etosha to Damaraland's stark beauty and desert elephants, to bustling small cities with a fascinating mix of colonial and modern, you've never visited anywhere quite like Namibia.

8 Victoria Falls. Shared by Zambia and Zimbabwe, Vic Falls, as its fondly called, is one of the natural wonders of the world, unsurpassed by anything. Dr. Livingstone's description still holds good: "scenes so lovely must have been gazed upon by angels in their flight." The adventure center of Africa, adrenaline junkies can try everything from bungee jumping and white-water rafting, to canoeing, rappelling, and jet skiing.

SKELETON

NAMI

N

Swakopmund
Walvis Bay

COAS

Lude

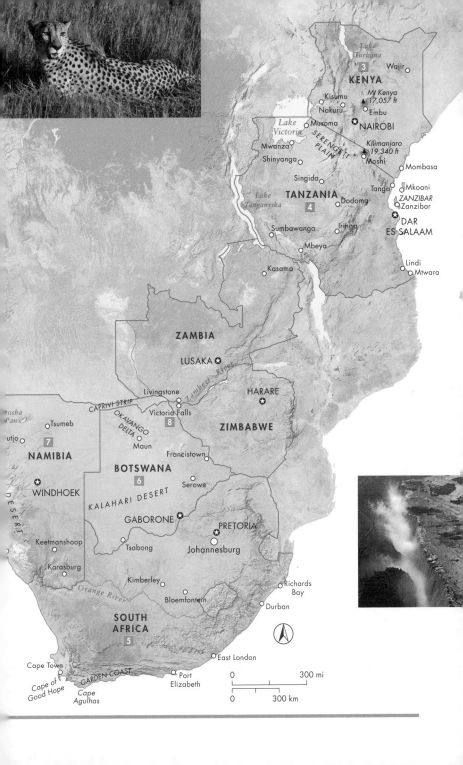

KENYA

3

Lake
Turkana

Wajir

Kisumu
Nakuru

Mt Kenya
▲ 17,057 ft
Embu

Musoma ✪ NAIROBI

Lake
Victoria

SERENGETI
PLAIN

Kilimanjaro
▲ 19,340 ft
Moshi

Mwanza

Shinyanga

Mombasa

Singida

Tanga

Mkoani
ZANZIBAR
Zanzibar

TANZANIA

4

Dodoma

Lake
Tanganyika

Sumbawanga

Iringa

✪ DAR
ES SALAAM

Mbeya

Lindi
Mtwara

Kasama

ZAMBIA

LUSAKA ✪

HARARE
✪

Zambezi River

Livingstone

Victoria Falls

CAPRIVI STRIP

ZIMBABWE

8

osha
Pan

Tsumeb

OKAVANGO
DELTA

Maun

Francistown

utjo

7

NAMIBIA

BOTSWANA

6

Serowe

WINDHOEK ✪

KALAHARI DESERT

GABORONE ✪

PRETORIA
✪

Keetmanshoop

Tsabong

Johannesburg

DESERT

Karasburg

Kimberley

Richards
Bay

Orange River

Bloemfontein

Durban

SOUTH
AFRICA

5

East London

Cape Town

GARDEN COAST

Port
Elizabeth

| 0 | | | 300 mi |

Cape of
Good Hope

Cape
Agulhas

| 0 | | | 300 km |

WHEN TO GO

You can visit the parks covered in this book most of the time. However, in the dry season (read: winter) vegetation is low and surface water is scarce making it easier to spot game. But it's much cheaper to travel in the low and shoulder seasons, when the bush looks much more beautiful—although you will encounter rain sometimes and it will be harder to spot game—and there are lots of baby animals. It also gets *very* hot everywhere from December to the end of February.

The Seasons

The seasons in sub-Saharan Africa are opposite of those in North America. Summer is December through March, autumn is April and May, winter in June through September, and spring is October and November.

Winter is usually high season throughout safari areas because it's the driest time of the year and game is easiest to spot. The exception is South Africa, where high season is linked with the summer vacation schedules of South Africans (December through mid-January).

When we say "Low season," we're saying that this is the rainy season. Although the rains are intermittent—often occurring in late afternoon—the bush and vegetation are high and it's more difficult to spot game. It can also get very hot and humid during this time. However, the upside is that there are far fewer tourists, lodge rates are much cheaper (often half-price), and the bush is beautifully lush and green. Plus there are lots of baby animals, and if you're a birder, all the migrant species are back from their winter habitats.

"High Season" refers to the winter months in East and Southern Africa when there is little to no rain at all. It's also called the Dry Season. Days are sunny and bright, but the nights are cool. In the desert, temperatures can plummet to below freezing, but you will be snug and warm in your tent wherever you stay. The landscape will be barren and dry (read: not very attractive), but it means that game is easy to spot. Because of the lack of surface water it also means that game must use permanent waterholes where it can be easily seen. This is the busiest tourist time when there are most visitors.

The "Shoulder Season" occurs between summer and winter; what we call "fall" in the states. The rains are just beginning, tourist numbers are decreasing, and the vegetation is starting to die off. Lodges will offer cheaper rates.

Seasonal Access to Parks

		Summer				Fall		Winter				Spring	
		Dec	Jan	Feb	Mar	Apr	May	Jun	Jul	Aug	Sep	Oct	Nov
BOTSWANA	The Okavango Delta	●	●	●	●	●	●	●	●	●	●	●	●
BOTSWANA	Moremi Wildlife Reserve	●	●	●	●	●	●	●	●	●	●	●	●
BOTSWANA	Chobe Nat'l Park	●	●	●	●	●	●	●	●	●	●	●	●
BOTSWANA	Kwando Game Reserve	●	●	●	●	●	●	●	●	●	●	●	●
KENYA	Masai Mara	●	●	●	●	●	●	●	●	●	●	●	●
KENYA	Amboseli Nat'l Park	●	●	●	●	●	●	●	●	●	●	●	●
KENYA	Tsavo Nat'l Park	●	●	●	●	●	●	●	●	●	●	●	●
KENYA	Laikipia Plateau	●	●	●	●	●	●	●	●	●	●	●	●
NAMIBIA	Namib Naukluft Park	●	●	●	●	●	●	●	●	●	●	●	●
NAMIBIA	Damaraland	●	●	●	●	●	●	●	●	●	●	●	●
NAMIBIA	Etosha Nat'l Park	●	●	●	●	●	●	●	●	●	●	●	●
SOUTH AFRICA	Kruger Nat'l Park	●	●	●	●	●	●	●	●	●	●	●	●
SOUTH AFRICA	Sabi Sands Game Reserve	●	●	●	●	●	●	●	●	●	●	●	●
SOUTH AFRICA	KwaZulu-Natal Parks	●	●	●	●	●	●	●	●	●	●	●	●
SOUTH AFRICA	Kgalagadi Transfrontier Park	●	●	●	●	●	●	●	●	●	●	●	●
TANZANIA	Serengeti Nat'l Park	●	●	●	●	●	●	●	●	●	●	●	●
TANZANIA	Ngorongoro Crater	●	●	●	●	○	○	●	●	●	●	●	●
TANZANIA	Lake Manyara Nat'l Park	●	●	●	●	●	●	●	●	●	●	●	●
TANZANIA	Selous Game Reserve	●	●	●	○	○	○	●	●	●	●	●	●
TANZANIA	Gombe Stream and Mahale Mountains Nat'l Parks	●	●	●	●	●	●	●	●	●	●	●	●

KEY: ● = Low Season, Park Open   ● = Shoulder Season Park Open   ● = High Season Park Open
○ = Low Season, Park Closed   ○ = Shoulder Season Park Closed   ○ = High Season Park Closed

IF YOU LIKE

Drop Dead Luxury

So you want the whole game experience but don't want to rough it? No problem. Our favorites will tempt you to defect from the real world and live like kings and queens.

Londolozi, South Africa. Hide yourself away at this gorgeous getaway, themed around huge granite boulders. It's all about location here.

Mala Mala, Mpumalanga, South Africa. One of the oldest and most distinguished of all southern African bush lodges, this is the haunt of royalty, celebs, and the jet set.

Mombo Camp, Botswana. The spacious, graciously decorated en-suite rooms of this legendary camp may have a tented feel, but they are ultraluxurious with great game-watching views.

Ngorongoro Crater Lodge, Tanzania. The theme here is Great Zimbabwe ruins meets SS *Titanic* baroque and your abode will be palatial and the game-viewing equally fabulous.

Ntwala Island Lodge, Namibia. This lodge, 80 km (50 mi) upstream from the Victoria Falls, comprises four spectacular art deco-meets-Africa chalets built on a cluster of islands linked by walkways.

Shompole Lodge, Kenya. You'll feel like you're a part of an Arabian Nights fantasy when you enter your multipeaked thatch roof tent and see your personal pool and the views of the Rift Valley's distant plains and mountains.

Thanda Main Lodge, Kwa-Zulu-Natal, South Africa. This exquisite lodge has beehive-shape dwellings that blend elements of royal Zulu with an eclectic pan-African feel. Shaka never had it this good.

The Out of Africa Experience

Turn back the clock to the great, glorious days of the early safaris, when Ernest Hemingway and Teddy Roosevelt stalked the golden grasses of the plains with the Big Five in their rifle sights. Forget the rifles, but shoot as much as you like—with cameras. We have the perfect spots.

Cottars 1920s Safari Camp, Kenya. For an original safari replay it doesn't get much better than this—claw-foot tubs, antique rugs, wrought-iron candlesticks, old gramophones, polished butlers' trays—all under white safari tents.

Finch Hattons, Kenya. Live your every African dream at this classy camp where you'll dine at a table sparkling with silver and crystal as strains of Mozart softly fill the African night.

Il Moran, Kenya. Situated where Kenya's first colonial governors used to twirl their handlebar moustaches and sip their G&Ts while on safari, enjoy the exclusive location, teeming game, and bygone elegance.

King's Pool, Botswana. From the ancient tree dominating the main deck to the lush accommodations, everything is on a regal scale—a tribute to the European royalty who used to hunt in this area.

Selati Lodge, South Africa. Formerly a private hunting lodge, the early-1900s ambience stems from genuine train memorabilia. Old leather suitcases, antique wooden chairs, and signals recall the days of a 1870s train line.

Serena Kirawira Camp, Tanzania. Any well-heeled Victorian traveler would feel at home in this elegant pioneer ambience—polished wooden floors, antique furniture, copper urns, and shining brass lamps.

To Interact with the Locals

Of course you want to see lots of game, but may want to meet the local people, too. Although many of the cultural and village visits are not entirely authentic given the need for tourist dollars, we've tried to find you the genuine article. Go with an open mind, a nonjudgmental approach, and a friendly smile.

Deception Valley Lodge, Botswana. At Central Kalahari's only lodge you'll meet the desert-dwelling Naru people, who built it entirely by hand. Expect pure magic during a three-hour walk with the Bushmen themselves.

Il'Ngwesi Lodge, Kenya. Learn about hunting, gathering honey, animal trapping with indigenous poisons, and fashioning beadwork at the nearby Masai village.

Kichwa Tembo Tented Safari Camp, Kenya. A visit to a nearby Masai village is a must at this sought-after camp. The tribe's young men will explain their culture in English learned at the local school.

Lake Manyara Serena Lodge, Tanzania. Take a guided walk to Mto wa Mbu, a small town that's home to more than 100 different tribes. Here you'll visit homes, a school, a church, the market, and a banana-leaf bar.

Ol Seki Mara Camp, Kenya. At this eco-friendly camp you'll visit authentic, nontouristy Masai villages, where you might be lucky enough to witness a genuine betrothal or post-initiation ceremony.

Serra Cafema, Namibia. Only the nomadic Himba people share this remote awesome area and a visit to a local village will be a life-changing experience.

To Bring the Kids

More and more families want their kids to share in their safari experience and more lodges are catering to kids with programs designed especially for them. Always find out in advance which camps welcome kids as many still don't allow kids under 12. Remember: good behavior is essential. You don't want to spoil someone's safari of a lifetime.

Berg-en-Dal, South Africa. Kids can explore in safety at this attractive, fenced camp, which has a great pool and curio shop. Get them to walk around the camp's perimeter and spot game.

Kwando, Botswana. Kids learn to track, make plaster casts of spoor, spot game, cook over the boma fire, tell stories, catch and release butterflies, make bush jewelry, and learn about ecology.

Ngorongoro Serena Lodge, Tanzania. Apart from game drives, there are picnic lunches, balloon trips, and guided walks to the crater's rim or along the nature trail around the lodge.

Okaukuejo, Namibia. The 24-hour floodlighted waterhole—regarded as one of the finest in Africa—will keep kids entranced for hours. They can sit, stand, or run (quietly) around.

Pafuri Camp, South Africa. This lovely camp in Kruger's far north has a superb children's program and special family accommodations that give everybody privacy. Kids will love Crooks Corner, where baddies-on-the-run used to hide.

Voi Wildlife Lodge, Kenya. This is a popular family destination (kids under 2 stay free, 2–12 at half price), so don't expect peace and tranquillity. There's a kids' play area, pool, DVDs, and wildlife games.

IF YOU LIKE

An Animal Encounter

If you've set your heart on one particular animal, read on because these camps will provide incredible, once-in-a-lifetime experiences.

Addo Elephant Back Safaris, South Africa. Be introduced to a small group of trained African elephants. Take a short elephant ride, go for a scenic walk through the bush with them, touch them, feed them, and watch them bathe.

Crocodile Camp, Kenya. Get your cameras clicking at the nightly crocodile feeding at the Galana River when staff members call individual crocs by name and throw food to them.

Greystoke Mahale, Tanzania. About 60 of the area's 1,000 or so wild chimpanzees live in the forest near this gorgeous lodge on a deserted beach, so you have an excellent chance of spotting them.

Londolozi, South Africa. This is the place to see leopards. The most beautiful and successful of all feline predators, watching a leopard move through the bush is a truly awesome sight.

Ol Kanyau Camp, Kenya. The focus is on elephants, which have been studied here for nearly 40 years. You'll never forget the thrill of your first nose-to-trunk introduction to one of the 52 great matriarchal herds.

Palmwag Rhino Camp, Namibia. If it's rhinos you're after, especially the rare black rhino, then this remote tented camp in the heart of the 400,000-hectare (one million acre) private Palmwag Reserve is a must.

To Get Out of the Vehicle

Game drives are thrilling and often action-packed but sometimes, particularly if you are a second-time visitor to Africa and have ticked off your Big Five, you'd like to get up close and personal with the African bush and its inhabitants. Here are some of the best ways to really get down to nature.

Footsteps Across the Delta, Botswana. Learn the secrets of the Okavango—on foot and by mokoro—with outstanding guides. Enjoy game drives, night drives, boat trips, and fishing as well.

Lewa Wilderness, Kenya. Game drives here are action-packed, but try game-spotting from a different angle—on top of a camel or from the back of a horse, or, on your own two feet.

Offbeat Safaris, Kenya. Horseback riding alongside thousands of plains game is a once-in-a-lifetime experience, but only if you're an experienced rider and fit enough to ride four or six hours a day.

Olduvai Tented Camp, Tanzania. Go walking in the Ngorongoro highlands with genuine Masai warriors at this no-frills camp that's just south of the Serengeti border.

Phinda Walking Safari, South Africa. Ambling through the forest or over the plains each morning for four or five hours might be just what you're looking for. You can follow it up by an evening game drive to rest your weary feet.

Rhino Walking Safaris, South Africa. You'll leave for morning guided walks from one of three tiny camps situated in central Kruger's pristine bushveld.

To See the Great Migration

No matter where you stay during the Great Migration, you'll be assured of unforgettable sights. But we've highlighted a few camps where sightings may be even more spectacular. Remember that world weather cycles are changing—there's no guarantee that at that particular place and time your game-viewing will always live up to the National Geographic TV Channel.

Grumeti River Camp, Tanzania. Watch out for galloping wildebeest at this exclusive camp on the banks of the famed Grumeti River, where you'll be perfectly positioned to witness one of the greatest shows on earth.

Little Governors' Camp, Kenya. A ferry ride across the Mara River and a short walk escorted by armed guides takes you to this lovely camp sited directly in the path of the wildebeest migration.

Mara Serena Safari Lodge, Kenya. If you get tired of looking at the endless grasslands where the migration takes place in front of your eyes, then spot game at the lodge's own busy waterhole.

Naibor Camp, Kenya. Situated in a particularly game-rich area 20 minutes away from one of the legendary migration river crossings, this is the perfect base for watching the migration.

Sayari Camp, Tanzania. This camp is perfectly poised for watching the Mara River crossing, when hundreds of thousands of wildebeest plunge into the crocodile-infested water on their journey north.

Serengeti Under Canvas, Tanzania. This luxury mobile camp follows the migration, staying put for a couple of months and then moving north with the herds. Not cheap but worth every penny.

To Get Away From the Crowds

We can't whisk you away from all civilization and people, but we know that if you choose any of the following camps and lodges you'll be assured of privacy and exclusivity.

Duba Plains, Botswana. Based deep in the Okavango Delta, this tiny camp on an isolated island has superb game-viewing. Only two 4x4 open game vehicles operate in the whole reserve so you're assured of exclusivity.

Jack's Camp, Botswana. If you're bold-spirited, reasonably fit, and enjoy a rugged pioneer experience, then Jack's is for you. Try quad-biking, sleeping out under the stars, or walking with the Bushmen.

Loliondo Mobile Camp, Tanzania. Get away from the big lodges and busy safari routes and put yourself in the expert hands of your guide, cooks, waiters, and camp attendants and experience a true old-style private safari.

Mnemba Island, Tanzania. For the ultimate beach escape where time stands still, where sand, sea, and horizon melt into each other, this exclusive lodge with only 20 guests is hard to beat.

Sand Rivers Selous, Tanzania. Above a wide bend of the Rufiji River—hundreds of miles away from touristy Africa—this lodge is just about as isolated and exclusive as you can get.

Sarara Tented Camp, Kenya. At this small remote tented camp below the Mathews Mountains in the 75,000 acre Namunyuk Wildlife Conservation Trust, the only strangers in the night you'll see are the wildlife residents.

IF YOU LIKE

!Xaus Lodge, South Africa. Located in one of South Africa's most remote parks, Xaus (pron. Kaus) provides great hospitality, game drives, desert walks, and introductions to the local bushmen.

To Stay in Eco-Lodges

Want to do a little good while you experience the trip of a lifetime? Never sacrificing luxury, these spots look after the environment, the local communities, and the wildlife so you can feel good while you're having fun.

Amboseli Porini Camp, Kenya. A silver ecoaward winner, this camp is co-owned with the local Masai community. You'll see very few visitors (numbers are limited to 12 per day), but lots of game including predators and elephants.

Campi ya Kanzi, Kenya. This was the first camp in Kenya to be gold-rated by Ecotourism Kenya for its efforts in sustainable tourism and is one of the most environmentally friendly camps in East Africa.

Delta Camp, Botswana. A major conservation plus for this enchanting camp set deep in the Okavango is that motorboats are not used; the emphasis is on preserving the purity of the environment.

Saruni Camp, Kenya. This exclusive eco-friendly lodge just outside the Masai Mara boasts the Masai Wellbeing Space, which uses local plants for its treatments and is considered one of the best spas in Kenya.

Vuyatela, Djuma, Sabi Sands, South Africa. This vibey camp mixes contemporary African township culture with modern Shangaan culture. Your hosts are husband-and-wife team Jurie and Pippa Moolman, who are passionate about the environment and ecology.

Wilderness Damaraland Camp, Namibia. A joint community venture with the local *riemvasmakers* (thong makers), this eco-friendly isolated camp has won numerous awards for its successful integration of local communities, the environment, and wildlife.

To Go to the Beach

Going on Safari isn't only about seeing game these days; it's also about where you're going to go before or after your safari to unwind. Luckily, there are plenty of beach resort options to pick from in this part of the world.

Alfajiri Beach Villa, Kenya. Near Diani Beach, these double-story villas are some of the most luxurious in the world; each has its own pool that borders the Indian Ocean. You can go on safari or hang out at the beach and play in the water—there are all sorts of water activities on offer.

Kiwayu Safari Village, Kenya. Located northeast of Lamu, this village is one of the most romantic spots in all of Kenya. The area is known for its deep-sea fishing, and the hotel is close to the Kiunga Marine National Reserve—a great place for snorkeling. Make sure you book far in advance.

Mnemba Island, Tanzania. For the ultimate beach escape head to this tiny island off the tip of Zanzibar. There are diving and snorkeling off a pristine coral reef, and you might just rub elbows with the rich and famous.

Ras Nungwi, Tanzania. You'll find this resort on the northern tip of Zanzibar overlooking the Indian Ocean's turquoise waters. The balmy breezes and numerous lounge areas beg you to just sit down and relax, but if you can't, there are water sports, a

spa, and local tours to Stone Town, spice plantations, and Jozani Forest.

Rocktail Bay Lodge, South Africa. If you're in the mood for pristine beaches, surf fishing, snorkeling, or sunbathing, then coming to this lodge nestled in the Maputaland Coastal Reserve will be the perfect beach getaway after your safari.

Zimbali Lodge, South Africa. With direct access to the beach, this lodge near Durban, is set in one of the last remaining coastal forests in the Kwa-Zulu Natal province. Play golf, go horseback riding, or swim in the pool on the beach.

Natural Wonders

Sub-Saharan Africa is home to amazing game, welcoming people, and awe-inspiring natural wonders.

The Great Migration. This annual journey of more than 2 million animals through Kenya and Tanzania is a safari-seeker's Holy Grail; some consider it to be one of the world's greatest natural wonders.

Mt. Kilimanjaro. Kili, as it's fondly called, is one of the continent's highest peaks and the tallest free-standing mountain in the world. It's one of the easier mountains to climb; about 12,000 people each year set out for the summit.

The Namibia Dunes. Located in Namib Naukluft Park, the largest game park in Africa, lie the mythical Nambia sand dunes. Said to be the highest dunes in the world, this is an adventure seekers dream.

The Ngorongoro Crater. Nearly 3 million years old, this World Heritage site in northern Tanzania is a haven for wild game. Though it does get busy during high season, your experiences far outweigh the annoyances.

Okavango Delta. At its peak, the world's largest inland delta covers some 16,000 square km (6,177 square mi) of northwest Botswana.

Skeleton Coast. Littered with the skeletons of old boats, this part of the Namibian coast is beautiful, but bleak. The Bushmen call it "The Land God Made in Anger."

Victoria Falls. More than 91 meters (300 feet) high and visible from 50 km (31 mi) away, the Falls are one of the world's seven natural wonders.

WHAT'S YOUR BUDGET?

When setting a budget, consider how much you want to spend and keep in mind three things: your flight, the actual safari costs, and extras. You can have a low-budget self-catering trip in one of South Africa's national parks or spend a great deal of money in one of the small, pampering, exclusive camps in Botswana. Almost every market has high-priced options as well as some economical ones.

Luxury Safaris

The most popular option is to book with a tour operator and stay in private lodges, which are owned and run by an individual or company rather than a government or country. Prices at these lodges include all meals and, in many cases, alcoholic beverages, as well as two three- to five-hour-long game-viewing expeditions a day. Occasionally high-end lodges offer extra services such as spa treatments, boat trips, or special-occasion meals served alfresco in the bush. Prices range from US$350 to US$1,600 per person per night sharing a double room. If you travel alone, expect to pay a single supplement because all safari-lodge rooms are doubles.

Safaris on a Shoestring

Don't let a tight budget deter you. There are many opportunities for big-game experiences outside the luxury lodges. Your least expensive option is to choose one of the public game parks—Kruger National Park in South Africa, for example—where you drive yourself and self-cater (shop for and prepare all meals yourself). The price of this type of trip is approximately one-tenth of that for private, fully inclusive lodges.

Mobile safaris are another option. Travel is by 4x4 (often something that looks like a bus) and you sleep in tents at public or private campsites. You need to be self-sufficient and bush-savvy to travel this way.

Rates for national park camps, called rest camps, start at about $34 a day for a two-bed *rondavel* (a round hut modeled after traditional African dwellings) and go up to $85 for a four-bed bungalow. Budget about $6 for breakfast, $8 for lunch, and $12 for dinner per person for each day on the trip. You also need to factor in park entry fees (usually a onetime fee of approximately $20 per person).

Booking a private lodge in the off-season also saves a bundle of money. Many lodges—South Africa's Sabi Sands area, for example—cost about US$800 per person per night during the high season but can drop to about US$500 a night during the slower months of July and August.

The Extras

Besides airfare and safari costs, make sure you budget for tips, medications, film, and other sundries. Plan to stay at a city hotel on your first and last nights in Africa—it'll help you adjust to jet lag and makes things altogether easier. Expect to pay from US$50 for basic accommodations to a maximum US$750 a night in the most luxurious hotels.

Plan to spend US$15 to US$25 a day (per traveler) on gratuities. In South Africa tips are on the higher end of this range and usually are paid in rand (the local currency); you may also use U.S. dollars for tips, however. Elsewhere in southern Africa, U.S. currency is preferred.

Not digital yet? Stock up on film before you head out into the bush; a roll costs about US$20 in a safari camp. ■TIP→ **Don't forget to save some money for souvenirs.**

SAFARI PLANNING TIMELINE

Six Months Ahead
■ Research destinations and options and make a list of sights you want to see.

■ Start a safari file to keep track of information

■ Set a budget.

■ Search the Internet. Post questions on bulletin boards and narrow your choices.

■ Contact a travel agent to start firming up details.

■ Choose your destination and make your reservations.

■ Buy travel insurance.

Three to Six Months Ahead
■ Find out which travel documents you need.

■ Apply for a passport, or renew yours if it's due to expire within six months of travel time.

■ Confirm whether your destination requires visas and certified health documents.

■ Arrange vaccinations or medical clearances.

■ Research malaria precautions.

■ Book excursions, tours, and side trips.

One to Three Months Ahead
■ Create a packing checklist. ⇨ *See our list in Chapter 9.*

■ Fill prescriptions for antimalarial and regular medications. Buy mosquito repellant.

■ Shop for safari clothing and equipment.

■ Arrange for a house and pet sitter.

One Month Ahead
■ Get copies of any prescriptions and make sure you have enough of any needed medicine to last you a few days longer than your trip.

■ Confirm international flights, transfers, and lodging reservations directly with your travel agent.

Three Weeks Ahead
■ Using your packing list, start buying articles you don't have. Update the list as you go.

Two Weeks Ahead
■ Purchase traveler's checks and some local currency. Collect small denominations of U.S. currency ($1 and $5) for tips.

■ Get ready to pack; remember bag size and weight restrictions.

One Week Ahead
■ Suspend newspaper and mail delivery.

■ List contact numbers and other details for your house sitter.

■ Check antimalarial prescriptions to see whether you need to start taking medication now.

■ Arrange transportation to the airport.

■ Make two copies of your passport's data page. Leave one copy, and a copy of your itinerary, with someone at home; pack the other separately from your passport. Make a PDF of these pages that can be accessed via e-mail.

A Few Days Ahead
■ Get pets situated.

■ Pack.

■ Reconfirm flights.

■ Buy snacks and gum for the plane.

One Day Ahead
■ Check destination weather reports.

■ Make a last check of your house and go through your travel checklist one final time.

WHO'S WHO

There's no substitute for a knowledgeable tour operator or travel agent who specializes in Africa. These specialists look out for your best interests, are aware of trends and developments, and function as indispensable backups in the rare instance when something goes wrong.

African safari operator. Also referred to as a ground operator, this type of outfitter is a company in Africa that provides logistical support to a U.S.–based tour operator by seeing to the details of your safari. An operator might charter flights, pick you up at the airport, and take you on game-viewing trips, for example. Some operators own or manage safari lodges. In addition, an operator communicates changing trends and developments in the region to tour operators and serves as your on-site contact in cases of illness, injury, or other unexpected situations.

African-tour operator. Based in the United States, this type of company specializes in tours and safaris to Africa and works with a safari outfitter that provides support on the ground. Start dates and itineraries are set for some trips offered by the operator, but customized vacations can be arranged. Travelers usually find out about these trips through retail travel agents.

Air consolidator. A consolidator aggressively promotes and sells plane tickets to Africa, usually concentrating on only one or a few airlines to ensure a large volume of sales with those particular carriers. The airlines provide greatly reduced airfares to the consolidator, who in turn adds a markup and resells them directly to you.

Retail travel agent. In general, a travel agent sells trip packages directly to consumers. In most cases an agent doesn't have a geographical specialty. When called on to arrange a trip to Africa, the travel agent turns to an African-tour operator for details.

Before you entrust your trip to an agent, do your best to determine the extent of his or her knowledge as well as the level of enthusiasm he or she has for the destination. There are as many travel companies claiming to specialize in Africa as there are hippos in the Zambezi, so it's especially important to determine which operators and agents are up to the challenge.

After choosing a tour operator or travel agent, it's a good idea to discuss with him or her the logistics and details of the itinerary so you know what to expect each day. Ask questions about lodging, even if you're traveling on a group tour. A lodge that is completely open to the elements may be a highlight for some travelers and terrifying for others, particularly at night when a lion roars nearby. Also ask about the amount of time you'll spend with other travelers. If you're planning a safari honeymoon, find out if you can dine alone when you want to, and ask about honeymoon packages.

Tour Operators

Outfitter	Location	Tel. no.	Website	Countries it covers
Abercrombie & Kent	USA	800/554-7016	www.abercrombiekent.com	Kenya, Tanzania, South Africa, Botswana, Namibia, Zambia, Zimbabwe
African Adventure Company	USA	800/882-9453	www.africa-adventure.com	Kenya, Tanzania, South Africa, Botswana, Namibia, Zambia, Zimbabwe
African Extravaganza	Namibia	26/61/37-2100	www.african-extravaganza.com	Namibia
Africa Serendipity	USA	212/288-1714	www.africaserendipity.com	Kenya, Tanzania
African Travel Resource	UK	0845/450-1520	www.africantravelresource.com	Kenya, Tanzania, South Africa, Botswana, Namibia, Zimbabwe
Big Five	USA	800/244-3483	www.bigfive.com	Kenya, Tanzania, South Africa, Botswana, Namibia, Zambia
CC Africa Safaris & Tours	South Africa USA	27/11/809-4300 888/882-3742	www.ccafrica.com	Kenya, Tanzania, South Africa, Botswana, Namibia, Zambia
Cheli & Peacock	Kenya	254/20/60-4053	www.chelipeacock.com	Kenya
Damaraland Trails & Tours	Namibia	061/23-4610	no web	Namibia
Desert & Delta Safaris	South Africa	27/11/706-0861	www.desertdelta.co.za	Botswana, Zambia, Zimbabwe
Fazendin Portfolio	USA	303/895-9583	www.fazendinportfolio.com	Kenya, Tanzania, South Africa, Zambia
Gamewatchers Safaris	Kenya	254/20/712-3129	www.porini.com	Kenya, Tanzania
Islands in Africa	South Africa	27/11/706-7207	www.islandsinafrica.com	Botswana, Namibia
Ker & Downey	USA	800/423-4236	www.kerdowney.com	Kenya, Tanzania, South Africa, Botswana, Namibia, Zambia
Micato Safaris	USA Kenya	800/642-2861	www.micatosafaris.com	Kenya, Tanzania, South Africa, Botswana, Namibia, Zambia
NatureFriend Safaris	Namibia	264/61/23-4793	www.naturefriendsafaris.com	Botswana, Namibia, Zambia
Orient Express	South Africa	27/11/481-6052 800/237-1236	www.orient-express-safaris.com	South Africa, Botswana, Namibia, Zambia
Premier Tours	USA	800/545-1910	www.premiertours.com	Kenya, Tanzania, South Africa, Botswana, Namibia, Zimbabwe
Sardius Tours	Kenya	254/20/201—5094	www.sardiustours.com	Kenya, Tanzania
Skeleton Coast Safaris	Namibia	264/61/22-4248	www.skeletoncoastsafaris.com	Namibia
Skyview of Africa	Kenya	254/20/375-1672	www.skyviewofafrica.com	Kenya, Tanzania
Tanzania Odyssey	UK	866/356-4691	www.tanzaniaodyssey.com	Tanzania
Thompsons Africa	South Africa	27/31/275-3500	www.thompsonssa.com	Kenya, Tanzania, South Africa, Botswana, Namibia, Zambia, Zimbabwe
Wilderness Safaris	South Africa	27/11/807-1800	www.wilderness-safaris.com	South Africa, Botswana, Namibia, Zambia, Zimbabwe

TOUR OPERATORS

Our list of tour operators hardly exhausts the number of reputable companies, but those listed were chosen because they are established firms that offer a good selection of itineraries ranging from overland safaris, walking and fly-in safaris, under-canvas safaris or safari lodges. Although various price options are offered, we suggest that where possible you go for all-inclusive packages, which will cover every aspect of your safari from flights and road transfers to game drives, guided game walks, food, drinks, and accommodation.

Abercrombie & Kent (⊠ *USA* ☎ *800/554–7016* ⊕ *www.abercrombiekent.com*) In business since 1962, this company is considered one of the best in the safari business and is consistently given high marks by former clients. From your first decision to go on safari to its successful conclusion, A&K offers seamless service. They have a professional network of local A&K offices in all their destination countries, staffed by full-time A&K experts. They are also renowned for their top tour directors and guides. Their head office in the states is located in Oak Brook, Illinois.

Africa Adventure Company (⊠ *USA* ☎ *954/491–8877* ⊕ *www.africa-adventure.com*) For more than 20 years this Florida-based company has planned safaris of all kinds. They also specialize in all sorts of tours that you can add on to your safari from exploring cities, gorilla trekking, and fishing, to diving, beaching, and lots more.

African Extravaganza (⊠ *Namibia* ☎ *264/61/372–100* ⊕ *www.african-extravaganza. com*) This company specializes in shuttle services (to and from destinations as well as pickups and drop offs at airports); scheduled safaris; charter tours and fly-ins; self-drive options; and day excursions. It offers

a three-day Windhoek/Sossusvlei excursion (which they call a shuttle) for N\$3,200 per person, which includes minibus transport via the scenic, serpentine Spreetshoogte Pass; accommodations at the Namib Naukluft Lodge; your own guide; all meals; and an excursion to Sesriem and Sossusvlei.

Africa Serendipity (⊠ *USA* ☎ *212/288–1714* ⊕ *www.africaserendipity.com*) This New York–based company has excellent Africa-based operators with more than 50 years experience. They offer top accommodations, top guides, and excellent service and always help you plan your safari, beach escape, city stay, or tour down to the last detail.

African Travel Resource (⊠ *UK* ☎ *0845/450–1520* ⊕ *www.africantravelresource.com*) This is a Web-based resource site that provides you with numerous trip possibilities. After you've browsed to your heart's content and made all the relevant the decisions, the operator will do the easy part and book the trip for you. So, if you're looking to plan a trip to Mt. Kilimanjaro, you can search through the huge resource base and choose your perfect trip.

Big Five (⊠ *USA* ☎ *800/244–3483* ⊕ *www. bigfive.com*) Offering more than 100 tours to Africa, this Florida-based operator promises its clients a trip of a life-time—if you're not happy with the tour choices, Big Five will custom-create one for you. You can be assured that whatever trip you do choose, your knowledge-able agent will be able to assist you from personal experience. Founded in 1973, Big Five focuses on low-impact, sustainable tourism and patronizes environmentally responsible lodgings.

CC Africa (⊠ *South Africa* ☎ *27/11/809–4300 in South Africa, 888/882–3742 in*

U.S. ⊕*www.ccafrica.com*) CC Africa is a highly experienced tour operator with 16 years of service to the safari-going public. They offer ready-made trips and tours to all parts of Southern or East Africa or can tailor one to your needs, from the budget-conscious to the lavish. They offer some of the best destinations and accommodations in Africa (read: they own and manage all their properties), from the Okavango to remote Indian Ocean islands. They specialize in honeymoon packages.

Cheli & Peacock (⊠*Kenya* ☎*254/20/60– 4053* ⊕*www.chelipeacock.com*) Based in Nairobi, Cheli & Peacock features small luxury camps and lodges in Kenya's top national parks and reserves. The variety of locations covers a broad selection of ecosystems, game, and conservation. Each agent creates a safari itinerary that best suits the likes and dislikes of each client producing once in a lifetime experiences.

Damaraland Trails and Tours (⊠*Namibia* ☎*264/61/23–4610*) If you've got your heart set on seeing Namibia, then seriously consider Damaraland as they specialize in tours of the country. Guided rock-art safaris, including a fully inclusive six-day hike in the Brandberg (you need a doctor's certificate of fitness), are conducted by Joe Walter. Few people know the Brandberg as intimately as Joe, who also has a wealth of knowledge on the rock art and flora of the mountain range.

Desert & Delta Safaris (⊠*South Africa* ☎*27/11/706–0861* ⊕*www.desertdelta. co.za*) has inclusive fly-in safari packages to its own camps such as Chobe Game Lodge, Okavango Camp, and Moremi Camp, plus lots of other destinations,

such as Victoria Falls. They are the only safari lodge company that is 100% Botswana owned.

Fazendin Portfolio (⊠*USA* ☎*303/993– 7906* ⊕*www.fazendinportfolio.com*) This Denver-based company is not a traditional operator, but rather a portfolio representing operators, lodges, and safari experiences. It was developed specifically with the needs and desires of North American travelers in mind. From luxury tented camping safari experiences to unique cultural adventures, you'll certainly find exactly what you're looking for and expecting out of this once-in-a-lifetime trip.

Gamewatchers Safaris (⊠*Kenya* ☎*254/ 20/712–3129* ⊕*www.porini.com*) This Nairobi-based safari company specializes in delivering tailored safaris to small camps and lodges in East Africa. They can also include beach getaways in your package. Every guest is guaranteed a personal, authentic travel experience and the opportunity to experience the magic of the African bush while helping protect Africa's wildlife, ecosystems, and cultures.

Islands in Africa (⊠*South Africa* ☎*27/ 11/706–7207* ⊕*www.islandsinafrica. com*) Delivering you to the islands of Africa for more than 14 years, with award-winning accommodation on tiny private islands on the Zambezi; "islands of sand" in unique destinations such as the Central Kalahari, and fishing lodges in Namibia.

Ker & Downey (⊠*Botswana* ☎*267/686– 0375* ⊕*www.kerdowney.com*) One of the oldest and most respected safari companies in Africa, Ker & Downey also has an office in Texas. The company utilizes its exclusive camps to provide traditional safari experi-

TOUR OPERATORS

ences. Accommodation options range from rustic to deluxe. Their three-day walking and interpretive Okavango tour "Footsteps Across the Delta" is the only one of its kind.

Micato Safaris (✉ *USA* ☎ *800/642–2861* ⊕ *www.micatosafaris.com*) Family-owned and -operated, this New York–based operator offers deliberately luxurious trips. Safari lodges enchant with such unadulterated luxuries as private plunge pools and personal butlers. Cultured safari guides educate, instruct, and amuse, while itineraries offer an irresistible array of experiences from the sophisticated pleasures of Cape Town to the celebrated savannahs of the Serengeti and the near spiritual beauty of the Kalahari.

NatureFriend Safaris (✉ *Namibia* ☎ *264/ 61/23–4793* ⊕ *www.naturefriendsafaris. com*) This dynamic Namibian company, which also operates Dune Hopper Air Taxis, has flexible fly-in packages from Windhoek or Swakopmund to the Sossusvlei area. It also offers a wide range of exclusive fly-in safaris (called wing-in by the operator) to other tourist destinations in Namibia, including Skeleton Coast, Damaraland, and Etosha.

Orient-Express Safaris (✉ *South Africa* ☎ *27/ 11/274–1800 in South Africa, 800/237– 1236 in U.S.* ⊕ *www.orient-express-safaris.com*) A member of the Small Luxury Hotels of the World organization, this operator owns three strategically located camps in some of Botswana's most diverse ecosystems and most desirable destinations: Chobe National Park, Moremi Wildlife Reserve, and the Okavango Delta. All the camps have identical thatch tented lodging with identical furnishings and plenty of bells and whistles.

Premier Tours (✉ *USA* ☎ *800/545–1910* ⊕ *www.premiertours.com*) Based in Philadelphia, but owned and operated by people from Africa, Premier specializes in adventure tours for anyone from 18 to 55. They are a founding member of the United Nations Environment Program's initiative on sustainable tourism development and offer consolidated airfares to Africa.

Sardius Tours (✉ *Kenya* ☎ *254/20/201– 5094 or 254/20/251–547* ⊕ *www.sardiustours.com*) One of the top tour and safari companies in East Africa, Sardius specializes in innovative lodgings and beach itineraries. They also offer mobile tented safaris that follow the migration.

Skeleton Coast Fly-In Safaris (✉ *Namibia* ☎ *264/61/22–4248* ⊕ *www.skeletoncoastsafaris.com*) This fly-in safari company runs superb four- and six-day trips to the Skeleton Coast that include visits with the Himba people, who, with their red-ocher body coverings, elaborate plaited hair, and intricate bead necklaces and leather aprons, live much as they have for centuries.

Skyview of Africa (✉ *Kenya* ☎ *254/20/375– 1672* ⊕ *www.skyviewofafrica.com*) Skyview offers memorable safaris in Kenya and Tanzania to international clients. Destinations include the Ngorongoro Crater, the Serengeti, Masai Mara, Amboseli, and even a Mt. Kenya climb.

Tanzania Odyssey (✉ *UK* ☎ *866/356–4691 in the U.S.* ⊕ *www.tanzaniaodyssey.com*) Based in London with offices in Arusha and Dar-es-Salaam, this knowledgeable company has spent more than 12 years creating tailor-made itineraries to suit every individual requirement, from safaris and beach holidays to honeymoons. They are the only company to have taken

extensive video footage of each and every lodge in Tanzania and Zanzibar.

Thompsons Africa (✉ *South Africa* ☎ *27/31/ 275–3500* ⊕ *www.thompsonssa.com*) Thompsons, which has been given awards for excellence by the South Africa Travel Industry and South African Airways, works with every budget to plan all types of tours including day trips and safaris. Agents are available 24 hours a day to answer your questions.

Wilderness Safaris (✉ *South Africa* ☎ *27/11/ 257–5000* ⊕ *www.wilderness-safaris.com*) One of Africa's most respected and innovative tour operators, you'll be assured of impeccable service, gorgeous destinations and accommodations, and game galore on any of their packages. They operate a seven-day fly-in safari from Windhoek, which covers most of the main tourist destinations in Namibia. It also owns the majority of lodges in Botswana and offers all kinds of packages, including a choice of "premier," "classic," "vintage," or "camping wild" camps in a great variety of locations and ecosystems, from the delta to the Kalahari Desert. It also offers mobile safaris and custom tours for all Botswana destinations. They specialize in honeymoon packages.

QUESTIONS TO ASK A SAFARI SPECIALIST

Don't forward a deposit to a safari specialist (a general term for a safari operator or African-tour operator) until you have considered his or her answers to these questions. Once you have paid a deposit, you're liable for a penalty if you decide to cancel the arrangements for any reason.

■ Do you handle Africa exclusively?

■ How many years have you been selling tours in Africa?

■ Are you or any of the staff native to the continent?

■ To which professional organizations do you belong? For example, the American Society of Travel Agents (ASTA) or the United States Tour Operators Association (USTOA)?

■ Has your company received any accolades or awards relating to Africa?

■ Can you provide a reference list of past clients?

■ How often do you and your staff visit Africa?

■ Have you ever visited Africa yourself?

■ What sort of support do you have in Africa?

■ Do you charge a fee? (Agents and operators usually make their money through commissions.)

■ What is your cancellation policy?

■ Can you handle arrangements from start to finish, including flights?

■ What is your contingency plan in case of war or terrorism?

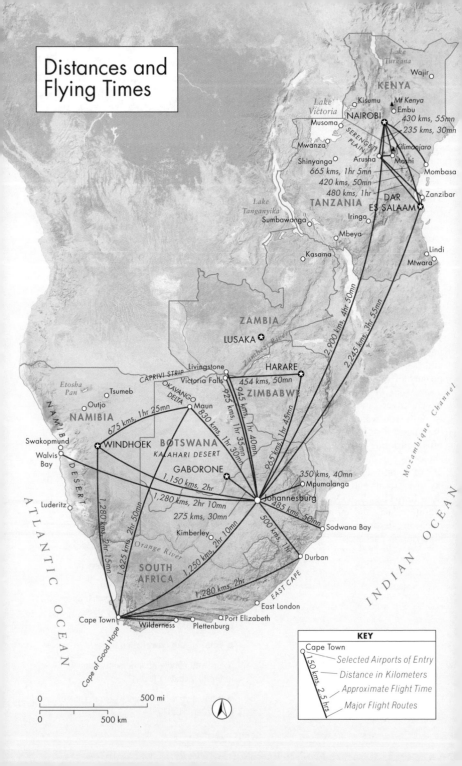

Distances and Flying Times

KENYA

Lake Turkana

Wajir

Kisumu

Mt Kenya ▲ Embu

Musoma

NAIROBI 430 kms, 55mn
235 kms, 30mn

Mwanza

Shinyanga Arusha Kilimanjaro Moshi

Mombasa

665 kms, 1hr 5mn
420 kms, 50mn
480 kms, 1hr

Lake Tanganyika

DAR ES SALAAM Zanzibar

Sumbawanga Iringa TANZANIA

Mbeya

Lindi

Kasama

Mtwara

ZAMBIA

LUSAKA Zambezi River

2,900 kms, 4hr 50mn

2,245 kms, 3hr 55mn

Livingstone

CAPRIVI STRIP

Victoria Falls HARARE 454 kms, 50mn

925 kms, 1hr 35mn

945 kms, 1hr 40mn

ZIMBABWE

965 kms, 1hr 45mn

Etosha Pan

Tsumeb

Outjo

OKAVANGO DELTA

675 kms, 1hr 25mn

Maun

830 kms, 1hr 30mn

NAMIBIA

Swakopmund WINDHOEK **BOTSWANA**

Walvis Bay KALAHARI DESERT

GABORONE 350 kms, 40mn

1,150 kms, 2hr Mpumalanga

Luderitz 1,280 kms, 2hr 10mn 485 kms, 50mn

275 kms, 30mn Johannesburg

1,625 kms, 2hr 50mn Sodwana Bay

Kimberley 500 kms, 1hr

Orange River

1,280 kms, 2hr 15mn 1,250 kms, 2hr 10mn Durban

SOUTH AFRICA

1,280 kms, 2hr

EAST CAPE

East London

Cape Town Wilderness Plettenburg Port Elizabeth

Cape of Good Hope

ATLANTIC OCEAN

INDIAN OCEAN

Mozambique Channel

0 ——— 500 mi

0 ——— 500 km

KEY

Cape Town — Selected Airports of Entry

—— Distance in Kilometers

—— Approximate Flight Time

1,150 kms, 2.5 hrs — Major Flight Routes

WHAT TO EXPECT
WHILE ON SAFARI

Your safari will be one of the most memorable trips you'll ever take, and it's essential that your African experience matches the one you've always imagined. Nothing should be left to chance, and that includes where you'll stay and how you'll get around.

If you already know what the term *bush* means, then you've read all the books and brochures and watched all the movies and TV shows about Africa and African safaris and are ready to book the real thing.

But what happens if the chalet you get is not what you expected it to be, or your game-viewing vehicle does not quite look like those you've seen in the movies?

Read on to figure out what you really can expect when booking lodging and safari options and which options will be best for you to make your African dreams a reality. After all, you should get the very best from your experience. This is a once-in-a-lifetime trip.

By the way, *bush* is a term used to describe the natural setting of your safari—be it in forests, plains, or on riverbanks. The expression "going to the bush" means going away from urban areas and into the wilderness.

Above: Making friends with giraffes in South Africa

LODGING

The days are long gone when legendary 19th-century explorer Dr. David Livingstone pitched his travel-stained tent under a tree and ate his sparse rations. But whether you go simple in a basic safari tent with an adjacent bucket shower and long-drop toilet, choose ultra-comfort in a mega-tent or canvas-and-thatch chalet, or go totally over-the-top in a glass-walled aerie-cum-penthouse with a state-of-the-art designer interior, you'll still feel very much part of the bush.

LUXURY LODGES

Kings Pool

Some would say that using the word *luxury* with *safari lodge* is redundant, as *all* such lodges fall into this category. But there's *luxurious*, and then there's *luxurious*. Options in the latter category range from *Out of Africa* accommodations with antique furniture, crystal, and wrought-iron chandeliers, to thatch-roofed stone chalets, Tuscan villas, and suites that wouldn't seem out of place in midtown Manhattan. In all, you can expect to find a/c; in many there will be a small library, a spa, a gift shop, and Internet service. You may even have your own plunge pool.

PERMANENT TENTED CAMPS

Think luxurious, oh-so-comfortable, and spacious...in a tent. This no ordinary tent, though. Each has its own bathroom, usually with an outdoor shower; a wooden deck with table and chairs that overlooks the bush; and carpet or wooden floors, big "windows," and an inviting four-poster (usually) bed with puffy pillows and fluffy blankets (for those cold winter months). The public space will comprise a bar, lounge, dining areas, viewing decks, usually a pool, and a curio shop. Some will have internet, a/c, and private plunge pools.

Severin Safari Camp

1

POTTY TALK

Using the bathroom in the bush will be an eye-opening experience for you. Most often, bathing will be via bucket shower, which is a hot water–filled canvas bucket dangling from a tree. And your toilet? Well that might be a long hole in the ground below a toilet seat—it's called a long-drop toilet. Picture a very rustic outhouse with canvas walls.

MOBILE TENTED CAMPS

CC Africa

This option varies enormously. You could have the original, roomy walk-in dome tent (complete with canvas bedrolls, crisp cotton bedding on GI stretchers, open-air flush toilets, and bucket showers) that's ready and waiting for you at day's end. Or you could have luxury tents (with crystal chandeliers, antique rugs, and shining silver) that stay in one place for a few months during peak seasons. They are all fully serviced (the staff travels with the tents), and you'll dine under the stars or sip coffee as the sun rises.

NATIONAL PARK ACCOMMODATIONS

What you'll get in this category depends on which park you're in and what type of lodgings you're looking for. Accommodations can vary from camp sites to simple one-room rondavels (round huts) with en-suite bathroom; safari tents to two- to four-bed cottages; or possibly a top-of-the-range guest house that sleeps eight people. With the exception of some camping sites, all national-park accommodations are fully serviced with staff to look after you.

Rondavels at Taita Hill Lodge, Kenya

TRANSPORTATION

Your safari transportation is determined by your destination and could range from custom-made game-viewing vehicles (full-service safari) to a combi or minivan (basic safari or self-drive). There shouldn't be more than six people per vehicle. To make sure you experience every view, suggest to your ranger that visitors rotate seats for each drive. Be warned if you're going it alone: roads in Africa range from superb to bone-crunching. Plan your route carefully, arm yourself with reliable maps, and get up-to-date road conditions before you go.

OPEN-SIDED LAND ROVERS

This is the most common game-viewing vehicle, usually a Land Rover or a Land Cruiser. Each vehicle seats six to eight people. Sit beside the ranger/driver if you're a bit unsteady, because you won't have to climb up into the rear. The back seats tend to be bumpy, but you get great views, and you'll hear every word the driver says if you choose the seats behind him. The more expensive the camp, the fewer people in the vehicle.

POP TOPS

Used mainly in East Africa, because of dirt, dust, and rain, these hard-topped minivans pop up so you can stand up, get a better view, and take photos in every direction. If you're claustrophobic or very tall, this might not be the vehicle for you, but there are outfitters that have larger vehicles that can "stretch." If it gets really hot outside, you'll be happy to close up and turn on the a/c. Make sure water and sodas are available.

SMALL PLANES

As many camps and lodges are inaccessible by land, or are in very remote places, you'll often fly in 6- to 10-seat plane. This is particularly true in Botswana's Okavango Delta. Always take a bottle of water with you (small planes can get very hot), and make sure you have medication ready if you're prone to motion sickness. Keep in mind the strictly enforced luggage restriction: 12 kg (26 lbs) of luggage in a soft bag that can squeeze into the plane's small hold. Flights can be bumpy, and landing strips are often just baked earth.

MINIVANS

It's unlikely that you'll use one of these unless you are on a very cheap safari or a self-drive—they are, however, perfect for the Namib Desert. The advantage is that they sit high off the ground and provide much better views; some outfitters offer vehicles that can expand. If you're self-driving, make sure you get a van with a/c and power steering. The farther north you go, check out your prospective vehicle's year and make sure it's as recent as possible.

WATERCRAFT

If your lodge is on or near a river, expect to go out in a boat. Options range from the big sunset safari boats with bar and bathroom on the Zambezi and Chobe rivers to a six- or eight-seater along the Okavango and smaller rivers, where your amenities include a cool box of drinks and snacks but no toilet. One of the highlights of your stay in the Okavango Delta will be gliding in a *mokoro* (a canoe) poled by an expert local waterman through papyrus-fringed channels where hippos and crocs lurk.

SPECIAL CONSIDERATIONS

Children on Safari

Most safari operators and private game reserves don't accept children under a certain age, usually under 8, but sometimes the age limit is as high as 12. This age limit is largely for safety reasons. Animals often respond, not in a positive manner, to something that is younger, slower, or smaller than they are. And even though you might think your six- or seven-year-old adores all sorts of animals and bugs, you'd be surprised how overwhelmed kids can become, out of the comfort of their home and backyard, by the size and multitude of African insects and wildlife.

Take into account, also, that when you're following a strange schedule and getting in and out of small planes, safari vehicles, boats, and the like with other people whom you probably won't know, there often is no time to deal with recalcitrant children—and fussing will, you can be guaranteed, annoy the other people in your plane or lodge, who have spent a great deal of money for what may be a once-in-a-lifetime safari trip.

One option, if you can afford it, is to book a private safari where no other people are involved and you dictate the schedule. Many private lodges will rent you the entire property for the length of your stay; this is often the only way these camps allow children under age 8 on safari. At the very least, a camp will require that you pay for a private safari vehicle and guide if you have children under 12. Be advised that, even if you're renting the whole camp, babies and toddlers still aren't allowed out on game-viewing trips.

One great family option is to stay with CC Africa, a safari operator with children's programs at several of their upscale camps throughout Southern and East Africa. While you follow your own program, your kids pursue their own wilderness activities; you all meet up later for meals and other activities.

A much cheaper alternative is also one of the most enjoyable for a safari as a family: a self-driving trip where you stay at national parks. No destination is better in this regard than Kruger National Park in South Africa, where there are comfortable accommodations and lots of other families around. You'll be able to set your own schedule, rent a cottage large enough for the entire family, and buy and prepare food you know your children will eat.

It's best not to visit malarial areas with children under age 10. Young kidneys are especially vulnerable to both the effects of malaria and the side effects of malaria prophylactics. You might opt to practice stringent nonchemical preventive measures, but know the risks: malaria's effects on young children are much worse than they are on older people.

Going on safari with babies also isn't recommended. Some lodges, such as those at Mala Mala, provide babysitting service for infants, but babies aren't allowed out in safari vehicles. The sound of an infant crying puts most predators on alert—dangerous to other passengers as well as the child. Keep in mind also that the bush is often a hot and dusty place with little in the way of baby-friendly amenities. You'd have to bring all your own supplies, and if something were to go wrong there would be no way to get immediate help until a flight could be arranged.

People with Disabilities

Having a disability doesn't mean you cannot go on safari. It's important, however, to plan carefully to ensure that your needs can be adequately met. South African lodges, especially the high-end private ones, are the easiest to navigate and have the fewest steps. Keep in mind that all-terrain 4x4 vehicles don't have seat belts, so you need enough muscle control to keep yourself upright while the vehicle bumps along the unpaved roads. Getting in and out of these elevated vehicles can also be challenging. Mala Mala Game Reserve in South Africa is completely accessible and even has specially equipped four-wheel-drive safari vehicles with harness seat belts.

Older Travelers

Safaris everywhere welcome older travelers. However, before you book a safari, find out as many details as possible about how taxing a trip might be both physically and mentally. Consider the types of accommodations (for example, find out whether a lodge is built on an incline or has many stairs, and whether bathrooms have grab bars) as well as how much time will be spent in the elements, such as in the hot sun where it's easy to dehydrate, and whether there are daily activities such as canoeing that are physically challenging. For travelers older than 55, Elderhostel arranges a number of annual educational trips to both East and Southern Africa that consider special needs.

SHOULD YOU TAKE THE KIDS?

Consider the following if you're thinking about bringing children to a private safari lodge:

■ **Are they afraid of the dark?** A safari camp that runs on generator-powered batteries will have minimal lights at night.

■ **Are they startled easily?** Large animals may come quite close to rooms or tents or near safari vehicles.

■ **Are they comfortable with strangers?** Most meals at safari lodges are at communal tables, and shared six-seat planes are the basic form of transportation between remote safari camps.

■ **Are they troubled by bugs?** The African bush can be filled with moths as big as small birds as well as a host of other flying and crawling insects.

■ **Are they picky eaters?** Meals are usually buffet style and food for camps is often ordered at least a month in advance, so your child's favorite food may not be available.

TYPES OF SAFARIS

Do you picture yourself zipping from camp to camp in a tiny Cessna, getting a bird's-eye view of a water hole? Or inspecting an animal track up close while on a multiday walk through the bush? Since there are many kinds of safaris, you should think hard about what approach suits you best. There are high- and low-end versions of each option, and you can always mix and match options to create your ideal itinerary.

Luxury Lodge–Based Safaris

The majority of safari-goers base their trips at luxury lodges, which pack the double punch of outstanding game-viewing and stylish, atmospheric accommodations. A lodge may be made up of stone chalets, thatch-roof huts, rondavels, or large suitelike tents. Mosquito nets, leather furnishings, and mounted trophies add to the ambience. Dinners are served in an open-air *boma* (traditional thatch dining enclosure). All have hot-and-cold running water, flush toilets, toiletries, laundry service, electricity, and, in most cases, swimming pools. Some lodges also have air-conditioning, telephones, hair dryers, and minibars. The most lavish places also have private plunge pools.

Make no mistake—you pay for all this pampering. Expect to spend anywhere from US\$400 to US\$1,300 per person per night, depending on the season. All meals, beverages, house wines, game drives, and walks are included. A three-night stay is ideal, but two nights are usually sufficient to see the big game.

The time you spend at a private lodge is tightly structured. With some exceptions, the lodges offer almost identical programs of events. There are usually two three- to four-hour game drives a day, one in the early morning and another in the evening. You spend a lot of time sitting and eating, and in the afternoon you can nap and relax. However, you can always opt for an after-breakfast bush walk, and many lodges now have spas and gyms. If you're tired after your night drive, ask for something to be sent to your room, but don't miss the bush *braai* (barbecue) and at least one night in the boma.

On game drives at bigger camps, rangers stay in contact with one another via radio. If one finds a rhino, for example, he relays its location to the others so they can bring their guests to have a look. It's a double-edged sword. The more vehicles you have in the field, the more wildlife everyone is likely to see. But don't worry, most lodges are very well disciplined with their vehicles and there are rarely more than three or four vehicles at a sighting. As your vehicle arrives, one already there will drive away. In choosing a game lodge, remember to check how much land a lodge can traverse and how many vehicles it uses. Try to go on a bush walk with an armed ranger—an unforgettable experience, as the ranger can point out fascinating details along the way.

All lodges arrange transfers from nearby airports, train stations, or drop-off points, as the case may be. In more remote areas most have their own private airstrips carved out of the bush and fly guests in on chartered aircraft at extra cost. If you're driving yourself, the lodge will send you detailed instructions, because many of the roads don't appear on maps and lack names.

Fly-In Safaris

The mode of transportation for fly-in safaris is as central to the experience as the accommodations. In places such as northern Botswana, where few roads are paved, or northern Namibia, where distances make road transfers impractical, small bush planes take you from lodge to lodge. These planes are usually six-seat Cessna 206 craft flown by bush pilots. The planes have no air-conditioning and in summer can very hot indeed, especially in the afternoon. But most flights are short—approximately 30 minutes or so—so bite the bullet or you'll miss out on some of the really fabulous destinations.

However, flying from destination to destination is a special experience. The planes stay at low altitudes, allowing you to spot game along the way: you might see elephant and buffalo herds lined up drinking along the edges of remote water holes, or large numbers of zebras walking across the plains. Fly-in safaris also allow you to cover more territory than other types of safaris. In Botswana, for example, the trip between the diverse game destinations of the Moremi Wildlife Reserve in the Okavango Delta and northern Chobe National Park is 40 minutes by plane; it would take six hours by vehicle, if a road between these locations existed.

Hopping from place to place by plane is so easy and fast that many travelers make the mistake of cramming their itineraries with too many lodges. Plan your trip this way and you'll spend more time at airstrips, in planes, and shuttling to and from the airfields than tracking animals or enjoying the bush. You will glimpse animals as you travel back and forth—sometimes you'll even see them on the airstrips—but you won't have time to

STAR STRUCK

You'll be awed by the brilliance of the night skies on safari, especially if you live in a city. To add romance and interest to your stargazing, study up on the southern skies and bring a star guide. Also most guides are knowledgeable about the stars, so ask questions.

stop and really take in the sights. If possible, spend at least two nights at any one lodge; three nights is even better.

The best way to set up a fly-in safari is to book an all-inclusive package that includes airfare. (It's impractical to try to do it yourself.) A tour operator makes all the arrangements, and many offer standard trips that visit several of its lodges. For example, in Botswana, Orient-Express Safaris has a package that includes three camps in three very different locations.

Lighten Up

The key to fly-in safaris is to pack light. In southern Africa the maximum weight allowed for luggage is 26 pounds (South Africa is the exception to this rule). Your bag should be a soft-sided duffel or something similar, so the pilot can easily fit it into the small cargo area. At most private lodges, laundry is included.

■ TIP➔ If your bag is over the weight limit, or if you weigh more than 220 pounds, you will be required to purchase an additional plane seat (usually about US$100).

TYPES OF SAFARIS

Walking Safaris

Many lodges offer walks as an optional way to view game. On a walking safari, however, you spend most, if not all, of your time in the bush on foot, accompanied by an armed guide. Because you're trekking through big-game country, there's an element of danger. But it's the proximity to wilderness that makes this type of trip so enchanting—and exciting. Of course, you can't stop every step of the way or you'd never get very far, but you will stop frequently to be shown something—from a native flower to spoor to animals—or to discuss some aspect of animal behavior or of tracking.

Walking treks take place on what are known as wilderness trails, which are natural tracks made by animals and are traversed only on foot, never by vehicle, to maintain their pristine condition. These trails usually lead into remote areas that you would never see on a typical safari. In most cases porters or donkeys carry the supplies and bags. Accommodation is usually in remote camps or occasionally in tents.

■ TIP→ **If you consider a walking safari, you must factor in your physical condition.** You should be in good health and be able to walk between 4 and 10 mi a day, depending on the scope of the trip. Some trips don't allow hikers under age 12 or over age 60. Also, you shouldn't scare easily. No guide has time for people who freeze up at the sight of a beetle, spider, or something more menacing up close; guides need to keep their attention on the wilds around them and on the group as a whole. The guides are armed, and they take great caution to keep you away from trouble. Your best insurance against getting in harm's way is to always listen to your guide and follow instructions.

Mobile & Overland Safaris

Most mobile-safari operations are expertly run but are aimed at budget-conscious travelers. They are mostly self-sufficient camping affairs with overnights at either public or private campgrounds, depending on the safari's itinerary and price. Sometimes you stay at basic lodges along the way. Travel is often by something that looks like a 4x4 bus.

For young people, or the young at heart, mobile safaris are a great way to see the land from ground level. You taste the dust, smell the bacon cooking, stop where and when you want (within reason), and get to see some of the best places in the region. Trips usually run 14 to 21 days, although you can find shorter ones that cover fewer destinations. Prices start at US$750 and climb to US$2,500 for all-inclusive trips. Not sure whether all-inclusive is right for you? Consider combining a mobile safari with a lodge-based one, which gives you the best of both worlds. A minimum of 10 nights is recommended for such an itinerary.

Self-Drive Safaris

A self-drive safari, where you drive yourself in your own rental vehicle, is a great option for budget travelers and for those who feel comfortable seeing the bush without a ranger at hand to search out game or explain what you're seeing. The two most popular and easiest-to-navigate options for this kind of trip are Kruger National Park in South Africa and Etosha National Park in Namibia. These two parks have paved, well-marked roads and a wide range of accommodations that include family-size chalets, small huts, tents, and camping sites. You may buy your own groceries and cook for yourself at all of these areas; some options,

especially in Kruger, have restaurants and stores on-site.

If possible, rent a van or a 4x4, since the higher off the ground you are the better your chances of spotting game (although a two-wheel-drive car is fine), and you can stop and start at your leisure; remember that you have to stick to marked roads. In addition to patience, you'll need drinks, snacks, and a ready camera. Keep your eyes and ears open and you may come across game at any time, in any place.

■ TIP→ Purchase a good park map that shows roads, watering holes, different ecozones, and the types of animals you can expect to find in each. It's no good driving around open grassland searching for black rhinos when the lumbering browsers are miles away in a woodland region. You can buy these maps when you enter a park or at rest-camp shops, and it would be foolish to pass them up.

When planning your day's game drive, plot your route around as many water holes and rivers as possible. Except during the height of the summer rains, most game must come to permanent water sources to drink. In winter, when the land is at its most parched, a tour of water holes is bound to reap great rewards. Even better, take a picnic lunch along and park at the same watering hole for an hour or two, especially in winter, when the car interior doesn't become too hot. Not only will you see plenty of animals, but you'll find yourself slipping into the drama of the bush. Has that kudu seen the huge crocodile? What's making the impala nervous? What's that sitting on my car?

THE CHANGING CONTINENT

This age-old proverb illustrates the intricate dance performed daily by countless species in the African bush. The continent is home to the greatest population of wildlife on the planet, but by 1986, Central Africa had lost about half of its wildlife habitats while the number of extinct plants in Southern Africa increased from 39 to 58 between 1980 and 1995 alone. More than 700 vertebrate species and about 1,000 species of trees are threatened with extinction in Africa. The balance between African wildlife and its environment—not to mention indigenous peoples—is delicate; it shifts unpredictably as Mother Nature plays her hand.

Poaching

Fueled by a growing demand in Asia as well as online sales in the United States, the killing of elephants for their tusks has reached levels not seen since 1989. Elephant populations are actually increasing across Southern Africa, but herds in Central and Western Africa continue to struggle.

The Convention on International Trade in Endangered Species of Wild Fauna and Flora (CITES), attended by 172 countries every two to three years, offers a chance for members to review conservation progress as well as make amendments to the list of endangered species. Today, CITES offers protection, in varying degrees, to more than 30,000 species of plants and animals worldwide. In 2007, there was good news for conservationists when the convention approved a decade-long suspension of trade in elephant ivory. Almost simultaneously, scientists announced a breakthrough procedure that matches the genetic profile of poached ivory to the region in Africa where the elephant came from. This promises to be an invaluable tool for antipoaching enforcement.

The victory for the elephants at CITES did not come without a price however. The approval of a one-off sale of stockpiled ivory by a handful of African nations was a compromise. Naturally, this raises concerns that any ivory sales will stimulate illicit markets. Other animals in high demand by poachers include crocodiles for their skins, rhinoceroses for their tusks, hippos for their teeth, monkeys for their pelts, and chimps for medical research.

The Many Consequences of War

Ironically, one of the most far-reaching causes of wildlife extinction on the African continent is one of the least obvious: the erosion of the environment caused by war and government instability. In the words of Kenyan environmentalist and Nobel Peace Prize Winner Wangari Mathai, we can only hope that "in a few decades, the relationship between the environment, resources and conflict may seem almost as obvious as the connection we see today between human rights, democracy, and peace."

In previously war-torn Angola many elephants migrating into the country have had their trunks and legs blown off by land mines, condemning them to excruciating deaths because without its trunk, an elephant can't eat. The situation is getting better and elephants are learning to navigate away from the land mines, though no one knows how or why they have the sense to do this. And in Southern Africa, during the 1970s, '80s, and '90s the South African Defense Force played a major role in the decimation of Africa's elephant and rhinoceros populations. Initially, this was undertaken as a way of helping to fund the wars in Angola and Mozambique with illicit ivory sales but it gradually became an organized ring for profiteering at very high levels of the Apartheid government.

There is hope. Bodies such as the African Union are fostering an open dialogue on conflicts, which may have once been viewed as regional and the African Ministerial Conference on the Environment has tried to foster discussions on land degradation and water resource management. By taking small steps, Africa has made considerable progress toward creating a healthier ecosystem for both humans and wildlife.

Global Climate Change

In 2006, an international coalition of "green groups" released a report that predicted climate change will hit Africa hardest. The report indicated that although climates across Africa have always been erratic, there will be new extremes in its near future if the effects of global warming are not reversed. Temperatures in the Nile basin are rising and are expected to continue to rise, while the famous icecap on Mount Kilimanjaro is fast disappearing.

WHAT'S BEING DONE?

Environmentalists from the international community are initiating training programs for local government officials, postgraduate courses at African universities, and regional workshops, which will help community members understand steps they can take to slow the effects of global warming. The United Nations Framework Convention on Climate Change, an international treaty aimed at reducing greenhouse gas emissions, has also launched a number of community-based initiatives in Africa that have helped raise awareness.

This will have serious implications for the rivers that depend on the ice melt for their flow, which in turn affects access to water by both human and animal populations. In addition, while the semi-arid regions of Southern Africa become drier, parts of equatorial Africa are getting wetter.

Although a lack of environmental regulations in Africa may be in some small way to blame, the greatest threat is caused by economic activity in the wealthier, industrial countries of the western world. It is believed that global greenhouse gas emissions will need to be cut by up to 90% in order to mitigate the detrimental effects of global warming in Africa. It is vital for every traveler to remember that when you return to your everyday life, what you do on a daily basis will affect the future of the creatures you just experienced. Though the situation may seem overwhelming, if each individual does his part in reducing his carbon footprint, progress can be made.

–Kristan Schiller

Flora & Fauna

FLORA & FAUNA PLANNER

Watching Dos & Don'ts

Observe animals silently. Talking loudly can frighten animals away and disturb their natural activities.

Never attempt to attract an animal's attention. Don't imitate animal sounds, clap your hands, pound the vehicle, or throw objects.

Show respect for your driver and guide's judgment. They have more knowledge and experience than you. If they say no, there's a very good reason.

Doing a self-drive? Always stay in the vehicle and drive slowly and carefully, keeping ample distance between you and the wildlife.

Walking Safaris. Stay downwind from the animals, keep noise to a bare minimum, and walk at an even stride. Don't make any quick or excited movements.

Never litter. Aside from the obvious disrespect for the environment, any tossed item can choke or poison animals.

Never attempt to feed or approach wild animals. This is especially important to remember near lodges and in campgrounds where animals may have become accustomed to human visitors.

Wildlife Safety & Respect

Nature is neither kind nor sentimental. Do not be tempted to interfere with the natural processes. The animals are going about the business of survival in a harsh environment, and you can unwittingly make this business more difficult. Don't get too close to the animals and don't try to help them cross some perceived obstacle; you have no idea what it's really trying to do, or where it wants to go. If you're intrusive, you could drive animals away from feeding and, even worse, from drinking at water holes, where they are very skittish and vulnerable to predators. That time at the water hole may be their only opportunity to drink that day.

Never feed any wild creature. Not a cute monkey, not an inquisitive baboon, not a baby tree squirrel, or a young bird out of its nest. In some camps and lodges, however, animals have gotten used to being fed or stealing food. The most common animals in this category are baboons and monkeys; in some places they sneak into huts, tents, and even occupied vehicles to snatch food. If you see primates around, keep all food out of sight, and keep your windows rolled up. (If a baboon manages to get into your vehicle, he will trash the interior as he searches for food and use it as a toilet.)

Never try to get an animal to pose with you. This is probably the biggest cause of death and injury on safaris, when visitors don't listen to or believe the warnings from their rangers or posted notices in the public parks. Regardless of how cute or harmless they may look, these animals are not tame. An herbivore impala, giraffe, or ostrich can kill you just as easily as a lion, elephant, or buffalo can.

Immersion in the African safari lands is a privilege. In order to preserve this privilege for later generations, it's important that you view wildlife with minimal disturbance and avoid upsetting the delicate balance of nature at all costs. You are the visitor, so act like you would in someone else's home: respect their space. Caution is your most trusted safety measure. Keep your distance, keep quiet, and keep your hands to yourself, and you should be fine.

2

Nighttime Safety

Never sleep out in the open in any area with wildlife. If you're sleeping in a tent, make sure it's fully closed as in zipped or snapped shut; if it's a small tent, place something between you and the side of the wall to prevent an opportunistic bite from the outside. Also, if you are menstruating, be sure to dispose of your toiletries somewhere other than in or near your tent. All in all, if you're in your tent and not exposed, you should be quite safe. Few people lose their lives to lions or hyenas. Malaria is a much more potent danger, so keep your tent zipped up tight at night to keep out mosquitoes.

Never walk alone. Nearly all camps and lodges insist that an armed ranger accompany you both during the day and at night, and rightly so.

Best Viewing Times

The best time to find game is in the early morning and early evening, when the animals are most active, although old Africa hands will tell you that you can come across good game at any time of day. Stick to the philosophy "you never know what's around the next corner," and keep your eyes and ears wide open all the time. If your rest camp offers guided night drives on open vehicles with spotlights—go for it. You'll rarely be disappointed, seeing not only big game, but also a lot of fascinating little critters that surface only at night. Book your night drive in advance or as soon as you get to camp.

Driving Directions

Approach animals cautiously and quietly and "feel" the response of the animals. As soon as an effect is noted slow down or stop, depending on the circumstances. Human presence among wild animals never goes unnoticed. In the Serengeti and Masai Mara, cheetah survival is being jeopardized by guides who try to drive too close to them, thereby giving up the cheetah's location to its prey or sometimes just chasing away the skittish cat, thus impacting the animal's ability to hunt, eat, and ultimately survive. Not all game guides and rangers are sensitive to this, their focus being on giving you the best sighting. But if you feel uncomfortable, say so.

A Voyage of Discovery

As you embark on your safari, consider how lucky you are to be witnessing these rare species in their natural habitat. The element of excitement in a safari is ever present: part of it, perhaps, is the potential for danger, but part is also the notion that you are on a voyage of discovery. To this day, researchers in Africa continue to unearth new species at alarming speed. In the summer of 2007, for example, a group of scientists on a two-month expedition in the eastern Democratic Republic of the Congo discovered six new species in a remote forest that had been previously off limits to scientists for almost 50 years (the new species included a bat, a rodent, two shrews, and two frogs). At that rate—almost one new species each week—one can't help but wonder what else is out there or who will find it and when.

Making a List, Checking It Twice

Many national parks have reception areas with charts that show the most recent sightings of wildlife in the area. To be sure you see everything you want to, stop at the nearest reception and ask about a spotting chart, or just chat with the other drivers, rangers, and tourists you may encounter there, who can tell you what they've seen and where.

FINDING THE BIG FIVE

The fauna that can be found on an African safari is as varied and vast as the continent's landscape. Africa has more large animals than anywhere else in the world, and is the only place on earth where vast herds still roam the planes.

		African Buffalo	Elephant	Leopard	Lion	Rhino
BOTSWANA	The Okavango Delta	●	●	●	●	●
	Moremi Wildlife Reserve	●	●	●	●	●
	Chobe Nat'l Park	●	●	●	●	●
	Kwando Game Reserve	●	●	●	●	○
KENYA	Masai Mara	●	●	●	●	●
	Amboseli Nat'l Park	●	●	●	●	●
	Tsavo Nat'l Park	●	●	●	●	●
	Laikipia Plateau	●	●	●	●	●
NAMIBIA	Namib Naukluft Park*	○	○	◑	◑	○
	Damaraland	○	●	○	○	●
	Etosha Nat'l Park	●	●	●	●	●
SOUTH AFRICA	Kruger Nat'l Park	●	●	●	●	●
	Sabi Sands Game Reserve	●	●	●	●	●
	KwaZulu-Natal Parks	●	●	●	●	●
	Kgalagadi Transfrontier Park	○	○	●	●	○
TANZANIA	Serengeti Nat'l Park	●	●	●	●	●
	Ngorongoro Crater	●	●	●	●	●
	Lake Manyara Nat'l Park	●	●	●	●	○
	Selous Game Reserve	●	●	●	●	●
	Gombe Stream and Mahale Mountains Nat'l Parks**	○	○	○	○	○

*This park is noted for its stunning scenic beauty - not game
**These parks are primarily for primate viewing - chimpanzees and monkeys
KEY: ● = yes ◑ = Rarely ○ = No

Continued on page 60

THE BIG 5

There's nothing quite like the feeling of first setting eyes on one of the Big Five—buffalo, elephant, leopard, lion, and rhino—in the African bush. Being just a few feet from these majestic creatures is both terrifying and exhilarating, even for the most seasoned safari-goer.

by Kristan Schiller

The Big Five was originally a hunting term referring to those animals that posed the greatest risk to hunters on foot—buffalo, elephant, leopard, lion, and rhino. Today it has become one of the most important criteria used in evaluating a lodge or reserve, though it should never be your only criterion.

THE AFRICAN BUFFALO

Often referred to as the Cape buffalo, this is considered by many to be the most dangerous of the Big Five because of its unpredictability and speed. Do not confuse them for the larger Asian water buffalo or, for that matter, with North American bison as this is an altogether heftier and more powerful beast. They have very few predators other than human hunters. Lion do prey on them, but it generally takes an entire pride or a large male lion to bring down an adult buffalo.

They can reach up to 1,800 pounds, and their lifespan is about 30 years, though they rarely make it to half that. Diets consist mainly of grass and water—they will not stay in a place where there is less than ten inches of rain per year.

Safari goers can expect to see Cape Buffalo in savannahs throughout sub-Saharan Africa, especially in Kenya, Tanzania, Botswana, Zambia, Zimbabwe, and South Africa. Herds generally number around a few hundred, however, buffalo have been known to gather in the Serengeti in the thousands during the rains. Herds mainly consist of females and their offspring. Males reside in bachelor groups, and the two come together only during the mating season. You shouldn't fear a herd, but do be on the look out for lone old males. Called dagha boys—dagha is the clay mixture used for building huts— they spend much of their days in mud wallows and are usually thickly coated in the stuff. While seemingly lethargic, these old guys can turn on a dime and run like lightening. If a buffalo charges you, run for the nearest cover. If it is upon you, your best bet is to lie flat on the ground; you can minimize the damage by playing dead.

THE ELEPHANT

The largest of the land animal, it once roamed the continent by the millions. Today, according to the World Wildlife Fund (WWF), the population, mainly found in Southern and Eastern Africa, is about 600,000. The continent's forest elephants (of central and West Africa) are still under severe threat.

African elephants are divided into two species. Savannah elephants are the largest, at 13 feet and 7 tons, and can be found by lakes, marshes, or grasslands. Forest elephants have an average height of 10 feet and weight of 10,000 pounds. They're usually found in central and West African rainforests.

An elephant's gestation period is 22 months—the longest of any land animal. The aver- age calf is 265 pounds. When calves are born, they are raised and protected by the entire herd—a group of about 10 females led by the oldest and largest. Males leave the herd after 15 years, often living with other males or alone.

When an elephant trumpets in a showy manner, head up and ears spread, it's a mock charge—frightening but not physically dangerous. If an elephant stomps the ground, holds its ears back and head forward, and issues a loud, high-pitched screech, this means real trouble. A charging elephant is extremely fast and surprisingly agile. If you're on foot make for the nearest big tree or embankment; elephants seldom negotiate these obstacles. If you're in a vehicle, hit the gas.

THE RHINO

There are two species of these massive, primeval-looking animals in Africa: the black, or hooklipped, rhino and the white, or square-lipped, rhino. Both species have poor eyesight and erratic tempers and will sometimes charge without apparent reason; the rhino is surprisingly agile for its size. Both the black and white rhino are about 60 inches tall at their shoulders, but their weight differs. A black rhino can weigh up to one and a half tons, while a white rhino can grow to over 2 tons. Though they do share habitats and feeding grounds (both are vegetarians and feed on everything from grass and bushes to trees), the black rhino, the more aggressive of the two, is found in areas of dense vegetation, while the larger white rhino (pictured here) resides mainly in savannahs with water holes or mud wallows.

More often than not, rhinos live in sanctuaries, or protected areas, where they are safe from poachers. You'll spot them in Kenya, Tanzania, Botswana, Zambia, Zimbabwe, and South Africa. The black rhino tends to be solitary while the white rhino is more likely to travel in a herd, or "crash." Calves are born after 16 months in the womb; this may explain why the relationship between a female rhino and her calf is extremely close—it can last up to four years. As the calves get older, they may leave their mother's side to join a crash, but will eventually wander off to live on their own.

Sadly, the survival of this incredible mammal is under serious threat from poaching. Their numbers are down 85% since 1970 alone—black rhino horns are traded on the black market as symbols of wealth, mainly in the Middle East—but serious efforts by conservationists are underway to help save them.

⚠ When a rhino is about to attack, it lowers its head, snorts, and launches into a swift gallop of up to 30 miles an hour.

THE LION

Known as the king of beasts—the Swahili word for lion, "simba," also means "king," "strong," and "aggressive"—this proud animal was once found throughout the world. Today, the majority of the estimated 23,000 lions are found in sub-Saharan Africa—a small population are also found in India—in grasslands, savannah, and dense bush.

Watching a lion stalk its prey can be one of the most exciting safari encounters. Females do most of the hunting, typically setting up a plan of attack, which is then carried out by the pride. Lionesses take turns hunting and this collective labor allows them to conserve their energy and survive longer in the bush. They are most active from dusk to dawn. A pride consists of about 15, mostly female, lions. The males, identified by their gorgeous golden-red manes, are often brothers who behave territorially; their main task is to pro-tect the females and the cubs. Typically, the females in the pride will give birth at approximately the same time, and the cubs will be raised together. Litters usually consist of two to three cubs that weigh about three pounds each. Sometimes, males that take over a pride will kill existing cubs so that they can sire their own with the lioness.

Lions can sleep for up to 18 hours a day. Lounging about in the grass, lions will often lick each other, rub heads, and purr contentedly. But don't be fooled by their charms. When a lion moves, it can do so with awesome speed and power—a charging lion can cover 330 feet in four seconds. If you come face to face with a lion, never, ever turn your back and try to run—that is your death warrant. Your best bet is to "play dead" and to protect your neck with an arm or stick to prevent a paralyzing bite.

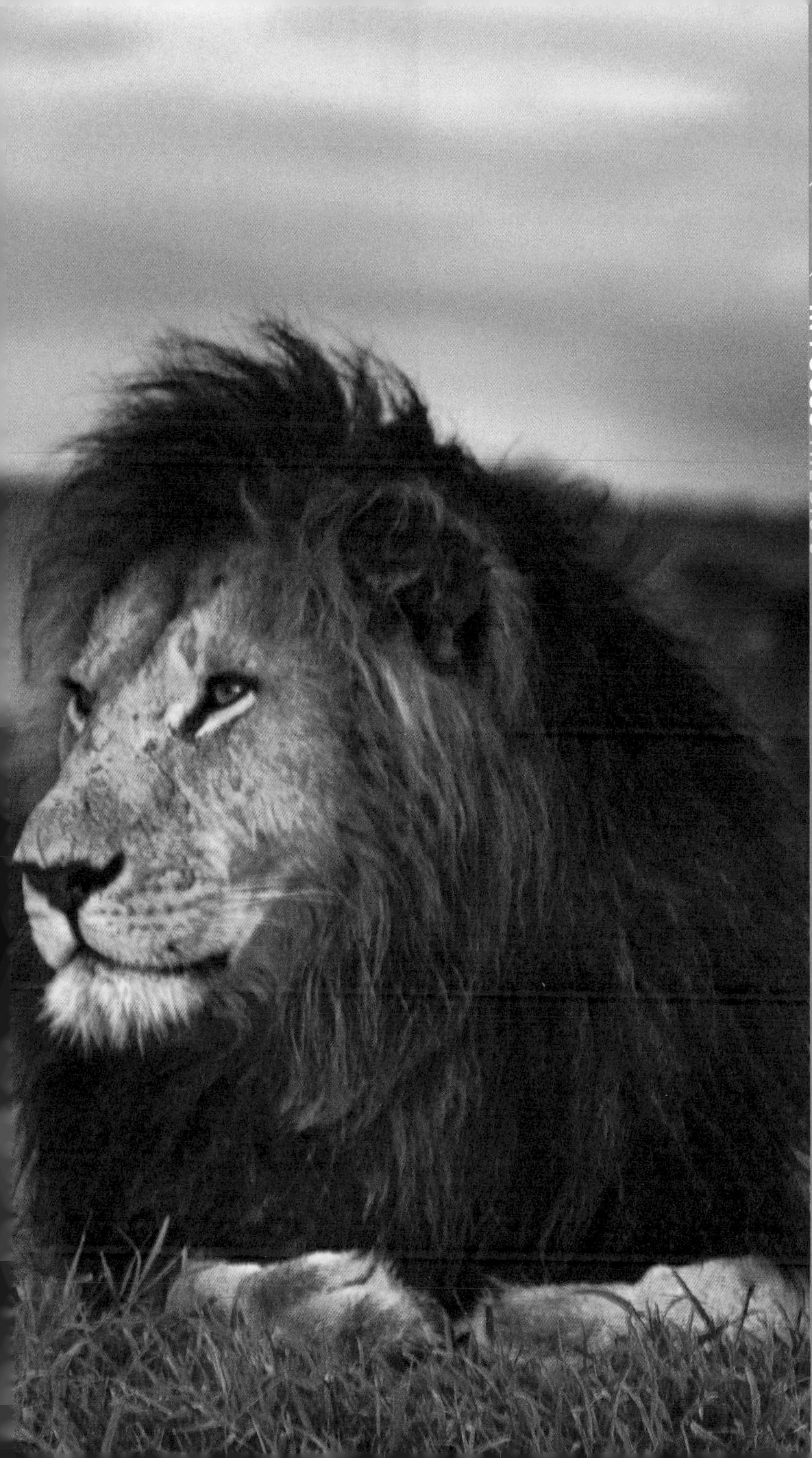

THE LEOPARD

Secretive and shrewd, leopard can live for about 10–15 years in the wild. They are extremely difficult to spot on safari, primarily because they are nocturnal and spend the daylight hours resting in tall trees or dense bush. Plus, they rarely stay in one area for more than a few days.

Leopard can vary in appearance, their coat ranging from a light tawny hue in dry areas to darker shades in the forest. Their spots, called rosettes, are round in East Africa, but square in Southern Africa. Leopard can also be found in India, China, Siberia, and Korea. The female leopard, whose litter usually ranges from about two to four cubs, will keep her young hidden for about two months after birth, then feed and nurse them for an additional three months or so until her cubs are strong enough to roam with her. What about dad? Male leopards play no part in rearing the cubs. In fact, the male is usually long gone by the time the female gives birth. He leaves her after they mate, although he has been known to return to kill the cubs, hence the reasoning behind keeping them hidden for the first few months of their lives.

Leopard use a combination of teeth and razor-sharp claws to kill their prey; it's not uncommon for a leopard's lunch to be taken away by lion or hyena. In order to avoid this, the leopard will often drag their larger kills into a tree where they can dine amongst the leaves in relative peace and quiet.

THE LITTLE 5

We've all heard of the Big Five, but keep a look out for the Little Five, a term given to the animals with names that include the Big Five: antlion, buffalo weaver, elephant shrew, leopard tortoise, and rhinoceros beetle.

RHINOCEROS BEETLE

The rhinoceros beetle grows up to two inches long. It has large spikes—similar in appearance to a rhino's tusks—that are used in battle with other rhino beetles, or for digging, climbing, and mating.

LEOPARD TORTOISE

The largest turtle in Africa, the leopard tortoise can grow up to two feet long and weigh up to 100 pounds. It lives in the grasslands of East and Southern Africa and doesn't mate until it's at least 12 years old. Its name stems from its black and yellow-spotted shell, which resembles a leopard's coat.

ELEPHANT SHREW

These ground-dwelling mammals range in size from that of a mouse to a large rabbit. They live in lowland forests, woodlands, rocky outcrops, and deserts and eat small fruits and plants. They get their name from their long nose, which resembles a miniature elephant's trunk.

ANTLION

Also known as a "doodlebug" because of the winding patterns it leaves in the sand when building traps, the antlion makes its home on dry, sandy slopes sheltered from the wind. Essentially larva, it eventually grows into an insect akin to a dragonfly.

BUFFALO WEAVERS

Similar in appearance to sparrows, buffalo weavers are found in East Africa. Their name comes from the way they weave their nests—found in the branches of tall trees—with grass, creating a complex maze of tunnels. Boasting a yellow plumage (sometimes with black), it lives in small groups where the bush is dry.

FAUNA

OTHER ANIMALS

You'll be amazed by how many visitors ignore a gorgeous animal that doesn't "rank" in the Big Five or lose interest in a species once they've checked it off their list. After you've spent a few days in the bush, you will hopefully understand the idiocy of racing about in search of five animals when there are 150 equally fascinating species all around you. Here are a few to lookout for.

Baboons

(A) These are the most adaptable of the ground-dwelling primates and can live in all manner of habitats as long as they have water and a safe place to sleep. Baboons travel in groups of about 40, sleeping, eating, and socializing together. Give them a wide berth. Like other animals, they are vicious when they feel threatened, and they have huge canine teeth. They eat mainly grass but will also consume small quantities of meat.

Cheetah

(B) Reaching speeds of 70 mph, Cheetahs are the world's fastest land animal—they have slender, muscular legs and special pads on their feet for traction. With its characteristic dark spots, the cheetah also has a distinctive black "tear" line running from the inside corner of its eye to the mouth. A solitary creature, cheetahs are found mainly in open savanna. Males and females can sometimes be seen together after mating, but usually the male is alone and females are with the cubs. Cheetahs generally prey on gazelle and impala. Sadly, this stunning cat is one of the most endangered animals due to shrinking habitat, loss of prey, and disease.

Giraffe

(C) Giraffe—the tallest living animals—are social creatures that live in loose herds without a lot of jockeying for power or territorial shows of strength. Young giraffes are usually left alone during the day while their mothers go off to feed, leaving them vulnerable to predators. According to the African Wildlife Foundation, only one-quarter of infant giraffes survive their first year. Highly sought after for its meat and hide, the giraffe is also vulnerable to poaching.

Hippo

(D) Though they may be comical looking, these are actually one of Africa's most dangerous animals. The most common threat display is the yawn, which is telling you to back off. When approaching hippos by boat, bang your paddle to alert them and give them a wide berth. Never get between a hippo and its water, as this will appear to them that you're trying to corner them and may result in an attack. Poaching is a great threat to hippos as their ivory tusks are still hunted, like the elephant's, to sell on the black market.

Impala

(E) One of the most populous animals in the African bush, impalas can be found in grasslands and wooded areas, usually near to water. Similar in appearance to a deer, impalas are reddish-brown with white hair inside the ears, over each eye and on the chin, throat, and rear. A thin black line runs along the lower back as well as on the back of each thigh. An herbivore, the impala eats grass and shrubs and doesn't have trouble with food shortage except in cases of extreme draught.

FAUNA

Springbok

(F) This cinnamon-color gazelle has a dark brown stripe on its flanks, a white underside, and short, slender horns. It often engages in a mysterious activity known as "pronking," a seemingly sudden spurt of high jumps into the air with its back bowed. Breeding takes place twice a year, and the young will stay with their mothers for about four months. These herbivores travel in herds, which range in number, although in general they contain a few territorial males, jockeying for the attention of available females.

Wild Dogs

(G) Also called the "painted dog" because of each dog's uniquely spotted coat, the wild dog is headed toward extinction. Once found in vast numbers throughout sub-Saharan Africa, it now numbers about 3,000 and shrinking. This highly social animal with batlike ears and a furry tail lives in small packs of about 15 and exhibits elaborate vocalizations such as barks, howls, and whines, especially at the outset of a hunt. Efficient, intelligent, and quick, wild dogs eat antelopes, warthogs, wildebeest, rats, and birds and both the male and female keep close watch over the pups.

Wildebeest

(H) Living on the savanna plains of Kenya and Tanzania, the wildebeest itself is an odd-looking creature with a large head and front end, curved horns, and slender body and rear. Mothers give birth to their young in the middle of the herd, and calves will be up and running within days. They feed on grass and tend to remain in one area as long as food is plentiful, though their habitat is being threatened.

Zebra

(I) There are three species in Africa: the Burchell's or common zebra, East Africa's Grevy's zebra (named after former French

president Jules Grevy), and the mountain zebra of South and Southwestern Africa. All three have striped coats and strong teeth for chewing grass and often travel in large herds. A baby zebra or foal will become quite close to both parents, mimicking the father in its behavior until it learns to live on its own.

Hyena

(J) Hyenas live in groups called clans, but they make their homes in dens. They mark their territory with gland secretions or droppings. Cubs are nursed for about 18 months, at which point they head out on hunting and scavenging sprees with their mothers. Both a strategic hunter and an opportunist, hyenas will feed on its kill as well as that of others. Despite its seemingly harmless nature, it is both aggressive and dangerous. African folklore links the hyena with witchcraft and legends, a fact that has been exacerbated in popular culture such as *The Lion King*.

Nile Crocodile

(K) Averaging about 16 feet and 700 pounds, the Nile crocodile can be found in sub-Saharan Africa, the Nile River, and in Madagascar's rivers. They eat mainly fish but will eat almost anything including a baby hippo or a human. Although fearsome in appearance and hunting reputation, they are unusually sensitive with their young, carefully guarding their nests until their babies are born. Their numbers have been seriously affected by poachers, who seek their skins and sell them for profit to designers shoe makers.

Bush Baby

(L) Found throughout East Africa, this tiny primate makes shrill cries similar to a human baby's. They live in tree hollows, nests, or manmade beehives and move in herds of mothers and offspring. Nocturnal creatures, they have excellent night vision and batlike ears that enable them to track insects. They generally stay in trees to avoid their main predators, eagles and snakes.

FAUNA

BIRDS

Many people come to Africa solely for the birds. There are thousands of winged beauties to oooh and ahhh over; we mention a few to look out for.

Bateleur Eagle

(A) This spectacular bird lives in trees and bush throughout Sub-Saharan Africa; it is probably one of the best known birds in Africa. Mainly black with a red back, legs, and beak and white underneath its wings, the Bateleur eagle can fly up to 200 mi at a time in search of prey, which includes antelope, mice, other birds, snakes, and carrion. They mate for life, staying with the nest for several years after the female gives birth.

Lappet-Faced Vulture

(B) Also known as the Nubian vulture, this scavenger feeds mainly on carrion and carcasses that have been killed by other animals. The most aggressive of the African vultures, it will also, on occasion, kill other, weaker birds or attack the nests of young birds as prey. The Lappet-faced vulture has a bald head and is pink in color with a wingspan of up to 8½ feet.

Lilacbreasted Roller

(C) A stunning-looking bird with a blue and lilac-colored breast, it calls the open woodland and savanna plains throughout sub-Saharan Africa and in the southern Arabian Peninsula home. It's usually found solo or in pairs in high places such as treetops or poles. Both parents nurture a young nest and are extremely territorial and aggressive when it comes to defending it. During mating, the male will fly to great heights in the sky then swoop down quickly making screeching cries.

Kori Bustard

(D) The world's heaviest flying bird is found all over Southern and Eastern Africa.

Reaching almost 30 pounds and about 3½ feet in length, the male is approximately twice as large as the female; both are gray in color with back crests and yellow legs. Although it does fly, the majority of its time is spent on land where it can find lizards and seeds. One male mates with several females, who then raise the young on their own.

Pel's Fishing Owl
(E) A large red-brown owl with no ears, bare legs, and dark eyes, it lives along the banks of the Limpopo River and several rivers in South Africa's KwaZulu Natal province. It's the only fishing owl in the world and emerges at night to fish with its sharp talons. The owls communicate with each other through synchronized hooting at night as they guard their stretch of riverbank.

Wattled Crane
(F) The rarest African crane calls Ethiopia, Zambia, Botswana, Mozambique, and South Africa home. A gray-and-white bird, it can reach up to 5 feet tall and, while mating, will nest in pairs along the shallow wetlands of large rivers. They eat water reeds, seeds, insects, and grain. Sometimes they wander onto farmlands where they are vulnerable to attack or poisoning by farmers. Recently, the crane has been added to the "endangered" list and is on South Africa's "critically endangered" list.

FLORA

Although the mammals and birds of Africa are spectacular, we'd be remiss if we didn't mention the amazing plant life that also calls this varied landscape home. The floral wealth of the African continent is astounding, with unique, endemic species growing in all parts—the South African Cape has one of the richest of the world's six floral kingdoms. There are also several species of non-native plants and trees in Africa that have become the subject of lively debate due to their effect on the environment.

TREES

African Mahogany

(A) Found in West Africa, primarily in Ivory Coast, Ghana, and Nigeria, this tree is a member of the Khaya genus. It requires significant rainfall in order to thrive and can reach up to 140 feet with a 6-foot trunk diameter. The tree is often used for furniture making due to the strength and hardness of its wood.

Baobab

(B) A quirky-looking tree that grows throughout mainland Africa and Madagascar, the baobab has a wide, hollow trunk with spiny-looking branches growing out at the top in all directions—it almost looks like it's upside down with the roots sprouting out at the top. Known for storing water in its trunk, the baobab lives in dry regions and can grow to be up to 400 years old; some even reach the thousands. A deciduous tree, it remains leafless during the dry season.

Fever

(C) The fever tree can be found along lakes and rivers in Kenya and South Africa, mainly in the lowland areas. It has a luminous, yellow-green bark that is smooth and flaky with white thorns and clusters of yellow flowers bloom from the ends of

2

its branches. (The bark is used in Africa to treat fevers and eye problems, hence the name.) Bees are attracted by the sweet smell of the flowers, and birds often nest in its branches as the thorns offer extra protection against predators.

Fig

(D) There are as many as 50 species of fig trees in Southern and East Africa, where they may reach almost gigantic proportions. Although figs provide nourishment for a variety of birds, bats, and other animals, they are most noted for their symbiotic relationship with wasps, which pollinate the fig flowers while reproducing. The fig seed is dispersed throughout the bush in the droppings of animals who feed on the fruit.

Jackalberry

(E) The jackalberry, also known as the African ebony, is found all over sub-Saharan Africa. It generally grows on top of termite mounds in savanna woodlands—the termites actually live in the roots of the tree. It can grow up to 80 feet tall and 16 feet wide. It bears white, fragrant flowers and a fleshy, yellow fruit that bush animals—impala, warthog, and baboons—love. The bark and leaves of the tree have long been used to stop infections and bleeding.

Sausage

(F) This unique tree, found in Southern Africa, bears sausagelike fruits that hang from ropelike stalks. The tree grows to be about 40 feet with fragrant, red flowers that bloom at night and are pollinated by bats, insects, and the occasional bird. The fresh fruit, which can grow up to 2 feet long and weigh as much as 15 pounds, is poisonous, but can be made into various medicines and an alcohol similar to beer.

FLORA

PLANTS

Magic Guarri Tree

This round shrub has dark green leaves and white or cream-color flowers. Its fruit is fleshy and purple with one seed in its center; the fruit can also be fermented to produce an alcoholic beverage. The guarri grows along floodplains and rivers and has many different uses: the bark is used as a dye in basket making; the root can be used as mouthwash; and the wood, sometimes used to make furniture, is said to have magical or supernatural powers and so is never burned as firewood.

Strelitzia Flower

(G) Also known as Bird of Paradise or the crane flower, the strelitzia is indigenous to South Africa. It grows up to 6½-feet tall with a beautiful fan-shape crown with bright orange and bluish purple petals that grow perpendicular to the stem giving it the appearance of a graceful bird.

Welwitschia mirabilis

(H) Though it's ugly to look at, this is one of the world's oldest plants; it's estimated that welwitschia live to about 1,500 years, though botanists believe some can live to be 2,000 years old. It's found in the Namib Desert and consists solely of two leaves, a stem base, and roots. The plant's two permanent leaves are leathery and wide, and they lie on the ground getting tattered and torn, with growth occurring during the summer months.

Wild Thyme

(I) Also called Creeping Thyme, it grows mainly in rocky soil and outcrops. Its fragrant flowers are purple or white, and its leaves are used to make herbal tea. Honeybees use the plant as an important source of nectar. There is also a species of butterfly whose diet consists solely of wild thyme.

Cape Fynbos

(J) There are six plant kingdoms—an area with a relatively uniform plant population—in the world. The smallest, known as the Cape Floral Kingdom or Capensis, is found in South Africa's southwestern and southern cape; it's roughly the size of Portugal or Indiana and is made up of eight different protected areas. In 2004 it became the sixth South Africa site to be named to the UNESCO World Heritage list. The Holarctis or Boreal Floral Kingdom is the largest, encompassing most of the northern hemisphere, north of the Tropic of Cancer.

Fynbos, a term given to the collection of plants found on the cape, accounts for four-fifths of the Cape Floral Kingdom; the term has been around since the Dutch settled the area. It includes no less than 8,600 plant species including shrubs, proteas, bulbous plants like gladiolus and lachenalias (in the hydrangea family), aloes, and grasslike flowering plants. Table Mountain alone hosts approximately 1,500 species of plants and 69 protea species—there 112 protea species worldwide.

From a distance, fynbos may just look like random clusters of sharp growth that cover the mountainous regions of the Cape, but up-close you'll see the beauty and diversity of this colorful growth.

Kenya

WELCOME TO KENYA

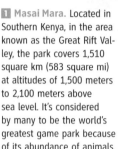

TOP REASONS TO GO

★ **The great migration.** Millions of plains game move in an endless cycle of birth and death from Tanzania's Serengeti to Kenya's Masai Mara.

★ **Eyeball big game.** Visiting Kenya's legendary national parks and game reserves guarantees that you'll see the Big Five as well as huge herds of plains animals and hundreds of colorful birds.

★ **Africa's fabled tribe.** The tall and dignified red-robed Masai have held explorers, adventurers, and writers in thrall for centuries.

★ **Beach escapes.** Miles of white sandy beaches line an azure ocean, and there are water sports galore.

★ **Turn back the past.** Check out ancient history along the coast where Arab traders and Vasco da Gama once sailed. In the World Heritage tiny town of Lamu you'll find an Arabic way of life unchanged for centuries.

1 **Masai Mara.** Located in Southern Kenya, in the area known as the Great Rift Valley, the park covers 1,510 square km (583 square mi) at altitudes of 1,500 meters to 2,100 meters above sea level. It's considered by many to be the world's greatest game park because of its abundance of animals.

2 **Amboseli National Park.** The snowcapped peak of Kilimanjaro and quintessential Kenyan landscape (open plains, acacia woodland, grasslands, bush, and marshland) greet you along the Tanzanian border.

3 **Tsavo National Park.** Once known for its legendary man-eating lions, Tsavo, which is made up of Tsavo East and West, is now home to peaceful prides and loads of other game. The park's close proximity to the coast makes it a great choice for those who want to combine beach and beasts in the rainy season.

SUDAN

Lotagipi Swamp

Lake Turkana

UGANDA

CHERANGANI HILLS

Mt. Oboa 3,063 m

Kakamega

Lake Victoria

Kisumu

GREAT RIFT VALLEY

Nakuru

Masai Mara Reserve

Lake Naivasha

Lake Nakuru

TANZANIA

4 **Laikipia Plateau.** Fast becoming Kenya's hottest game destination, the area is home to the Samburu National Reserve, which has more game per square mile than any other spot in the country, and some of its classiest camps and lodges.

GETTING ORIENTED

3

Kenya lies on Africa's east coast. It's bordered by Uganda to the west, Tanzania to the south, Ethiopia to the north, Somalia to the northeast, and the Indian Ocean to the southeast. It's a land of amazing diversity with extraordinary tourist attractions: great game reserves including Masai Mara and Samburu, the Great Rift Valley, fertile highlands, parched deserts, long pristine beaches and coral reefs, marine parks, mountains, and rivers and lakes. Its two major cities couldn't be more different. Nairobi, the capital, is a bustling city where colonial buildings rub shoulders with modern skyscrapers. Steamy Mombasa on the coast retains its strong Arabic influence and history as Kenya's largest and busiest port. Kenya is also home to the Masai, who've roamed the plains for centuries.

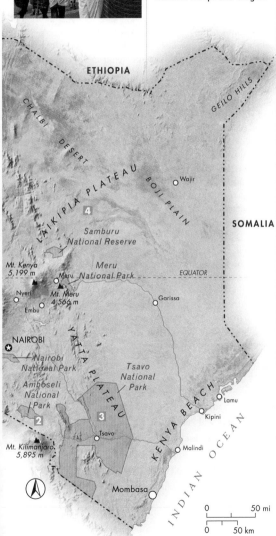

ETHIOPIA

CHALBI DESERT

GEILO HILLS

LAIKIPIA PLATEAU

BOJI PLAIN

O Wajir

4

Samburu National Reserve

SOMALIA

Mt. Kenya 5,199 m

Meru

Meru National Park

EQUATOR

Nyeri O

Mt. Meru 4,566 m

O Garissa

Embu O

NAIROBI

YATTA PLATEAU

Nairobi National Park

Tsavo National Park

Amboseli National Park

KENYA BEACH

O Lamu

2

3

O Kipini

Tsavo

Mt. Kilimanjaro 5,895 m

O Malindi

INDIAN OCEAN

Mombasa

0   50 mi

0   50 km

KENYA PLANNER

Important Details

Embassies United States (✉ *United Nations Ave., Gigiri, Nairobi* ☎ *020/363–6000*).

Emergencies Dial 999 for the ambulance and fire and police departments.

Money Matters The official currency is the Kenya Shilling. Available Notes are 50, 100, 200, 500, and 1,000 shillings. Available coins are 1, 5, 10, 20, and 40 shillings.

Passports & Visas Your passport must be valid up to six months after you leave Kenya. Single-entry visas (US$50), valid for three months, are available at Nairobi's Jomo Kenyatta International Airport (you can use US$, euros, or UK pounds sterling), and can be used to move freely between Kenya and Tanzania.

Visitor Information There's no official tourist office in Nairobi and the one in Mombasa isn't very good. Your best option is to consult the official Kenya destination Web site (⊕www. magicalkenya.com) before you leave home. Kenya Tourism Federation, which represents the private sector of the tourism industry has a good tourist help line (☎020/604–767), and the Web site for Kenya Wildlife Services (⊕www.kws. org) is a good source if you're going to a national park.

Health & Safety

You'll need full-cover medical travel insurance, and, if you're planning to dive, trek, or climb, make sure your insurance covers active pursuits. Check with your health care provider to see what vaccinations might be necessary for your destination(s). Always use sunscreen and bug repellent with DEET. HIV/Aids is rampant.

Mugging, purse-snatching, and pickpockets are rife in big towns. Leave your good jewelry and watches at home, and unless you're actually on safari, keep cameras, camcorders, and binoculars out of sight. Lock important items in the hotel or lodge safe. If you must carry valuables, use a money belt *under* your clothes; keep some cash handy so you don't reveal your money belt in public. Bring copies of all your important documents and stash them away from the originals. Carry extra passport photos in case you need new documents fast. Walk in a group during the day, and don't venture out on foot at night. Never take food or drink from strangers—it could be drugged.

Be on the lookout for common street scams like hard luck stories or appeals to finance a scholarship. Don't be fooled if a taxi driver announces upon arrival that the fee you negotiated was per person or that he doesn't have change for your large bills. Be polite but firm if you are stopped by police officers charging you with an "instant fine" for a minor infraction. If you request to go to the police station, the charges are often dismissed.

Fast Facts

Size 582,645 square km (224,960 square mi)
Number of National Parks 49
Number of Private Reserves Too many to count
Population of Country Approximately 32 million
Big Five You'll find them all here.
Language Kiswahili is the official language, but most people speak English.
Time Kenya is on EAT (East Africa Time), which is three hours ahead of Greenwich Mean Time and eight hours ahead of North America's Eastern Standard Time.

About the Camps & Lodges

There are more than 2,000 licensed hotels, camps, and lodges in Kenya. There are modern hotels in Nairobi, but some older establishments offer comparable service and comfort plus colonial ambience. Price categories in this chapter treat all-inclusive lodges differently from other lodgings (see chart below). Lodging, meals, and activities are included at private lodges; find out in advance if park fees (US$60 to US$100 per day) are included. There are no elevators in lodging facilities outside hotels in big cities, but most everything is at ground level. Children are not always welcome at lodges. Some camps, lodges, and coastal hotels are closed during rainy months; ask in advance.

Hotel prices usually include dinner and a full English breakfast. Many lodges and hotels offer special midweek or winter low-season rates. Camping really isn't an option unless you're a hardcore camper. There are all kinds of luxurious beach accommodations available, but these resorts get crowded during holiday season, so it's essential to book in advance.

Kenya prides itself on game meat, and the seafood, organically grown vegetables, and tropical fruits are excellent. Sample traditional Indian and Arab food when you're near the coast, and look for Kenyan-grown tea and coffee and Tusker beer, a local brew.

WHAT IT COSTS In U.S. dollars

	¢	$	$$	$$$	$$$$
SAFARI CAMPS & LODGES	under $199	$200–$450	$451–$750	$751–$1,000	over $1,000
LODGING	under $100	$101–$150	$151–$200	$201–$250	over $250
DINING	under $5	$6–$10	$11–$20	$21–$30	over $30

All prices refer to an all-inclusive per-person, per night rate including 12.5% tax, assuming double occupancy. Hotel prices are for a standard double room in high season. Restaurant prices are per person for a main course at dinner, a main course equivalent, or a prix-fixe meal.

When to Go

Generally speaking, Kenya, which straddles the equator, has one of the best climates in the world with sunny, dry days; daytime temperatures average between 20°C (68°F) and 25°C (77°F). The coast can get hot and humid, though sea breezes cool things down and the mountainous regions can get very cold—remember there's snow all year round on the highest peaks. Try to avoid the long rains of March and April or the short rains of October, November, and December because park roads can become impassable and mosquitoes are at their busiest and deadliest. Game viewing is at its best during the driest seasons (May–September, January, and February) because the lack of surface water forces game to congregate at waterholes. Safari high season is July–November when the annual wildebeest migration is in full swing, but it's much cheaper to go in the low season (April and May), because rates drop dramatically. High season at the coast is September through January (hottest time is December and January), but avoid Christmas and New Year periods as holiday resorts are packed. If you're a birder, aim to visit between October and April when the migrant species have arrived. **African Weather Forecasts** (⊕ *www.africanweather.net*) lists weather information for the entire continent.

By Kate
Turkington

Kenya is where "going on safari" started. A hundred years or so ago, visitors from all over the world, including Teddy Roosevelt, started traveling to Africa, lured by stories of multitudes of wild animals; there were more than 3 million large mammals in constant movement around East Africa's plains at the time. Today millions of international visitors continue to flock to this East African nation each year. Although humans have made their mark, Kenya still holds onto its pristine wilderness.

But Kenya's tourism industry, the main source of foreign revenue, is very susceptible to perceptions of tourist safety. Tourism declined in the late 1990s following a series of attacks on tourists and the terrorist bombing of the U.S. Embassies in Nairobi and Dar es Salaam in 1998, but the industry has seen a rise in visitor numbers in recent years, with record figures for the first half of 2007 showing a 30% increase. There seems to be no reason to consider Kenya unsafe as a tourist destination. Fingers are crossed that Kenya continues on her stable path and that the tourism industry continues to grow.

Kenya's human history dates back at least six million years. In 2001 the controversial Millennium Man was discovered near Lake Baringo in the northwest. This find and Richard and Mary Leakey's literally ground-breaking discovery of *Homo Habilis* in the '60s fuel ongoing excavations.

Today there are more than 70 ethnic groups in Kenya that range from the Masai, Samburu, Kikuyu, and Turkana tribes to the Arabs and Indians that settled on the coast and the descendants of the first white settlers in and around Nairobi and the Kenya highlands. In Nairobi, about 40% of the population is Kikuyu—a Bantu people numbering more than 6 million. Islam arrived along the coast in the eighth century, followed in the 15th century by Portuguese explorers and sailors who came looking for the sea route to India. During the rule of Seyyid

Said of Oman in the 1830s, German, British, and American merchants established themselves on the coast, and the notorious slave routes were created.

The British created what was then known as British East Africa in the late 1800s. After a much-publicized and often sensationalized struggle by native Kenyans against British rule in the 1950s, known as the Mau Mau era, Kenya finally won independence in 1963.

If there were animal karma some of Kenya's great parks, like the Masai Mara, would be an animal's nirvana, because this is food paradise. It's an abundantly stocked raptor restaurant that offers something for every predator's palate: a hyena hamburger place, a jackal fast-food joint, cheetah takeaways, banquets for bat-eared foxes, breakfast, lunch, and dinner for leopards, feasts for lions, and lush grazing for vegetarians.

Don't be put off by people who say that there are far too many tourists, which sometimes makes you feel like you're in a big zoo. Although the Masai Mara is much more crowded with visitors than neighboring Tanzania's Serengeti, you'll still get a superb year-round game experience, and your safari could be cheaper, too. Kenya has a compact and easily accessible tourist circuit, and the authorities are now limiting visitor numbers in national parks, as they do in South Africa's Kruger Park.

Kenya is not just about big game. It has a gorgeous tropical coastline with white sandy beaches, coral gardens, superb fishing, and snorkeling, diving, and vibey beach resorts. Traditional triangular-sailed dhows still ply their trade providing unforgettable seafood to the surrounding restaurants. You'll discover unique islands with ancient stone Arab buildings, where a donkey is the main means of transport, and where time really does seem to have stood still.

MUST-SEE PARKS

Unfortunately, you probably won't be able to see all of Kenya in one trip. So we've broken down the chapter by **Must-See Parks** (Masai Mara National Reserve, Amboseli National Park, Tsavo National Park, and Laikipia Plateau) and **If You Have Time Parks** (Nairobi National Park, Meru National Park, Lakes Nakuru, Turkana, and Naivasha), to help you better organize your time. We suggest though, that you research *all* of them before you make your decision.

MASAI MARA

Game
★★★★★

Park Accessibility
★★★★★

Ease of Getting
Around
★★★★★

Accommodations
★★★★★

Scenic Beauty
☆★★★★

The legendary Masai Mara Game Reserve ranks right up there with Tanzania's Serengeti National Park and South Africa's Kruger National Park in terms of the world's finest wildlife sanctuaries.

Established in 1961, some 275 km (171 mi) southwest of Nairobi, it covers an area of 1,800 square km (702 square mi) and is demarcated by the Serengeti in the south, the Loita Hills in the east, the Esoit Oloo-lolo escarpment in the west, and the Itong Hills in the north. It's also part of the Serengeti ecosystem that extends from northern Tanzania into southern Kenya. This ecosystem of well-watered plains supports one of the largest populations of numerous animal groups on earth. There are more than 2 million wildebeest; 250,000 Thompson's gazelle (arguably the prettiest of all antelope); 200,000 zebra; 70,000 impala; 30,000 Grant's gazelle; and a huge number of predators including lion (the largest population in Kenya), leopard, cheetah, jackal, hyena, and numerous smaller ones. There are also more than 450 species of birds, including 57 species of raptors. Every January, one of the greatest natural shows on earth begins, when the wildebeest start to move in a time-honored clockwise movement around the Serengeti toward the new fresh grazing in the Masai Mara. It's an unforgettable experience.

Local communities, not Kenya Wildlife Services, manage this reserve giving the Masai—who are pastoralists—the rights to graze their stock on the perimeters of the reserve. Although stock is lost to wild animals, the Masai manage to coexist peacefully with the game, and rely only on their own cattle for subsistence; in Masai communities wealth is measured by the number of cattle owned. You'll see the Masai's *manyattas*—beehive huts made of mud and cow dung—at the entrance to the reserve. The striking appearance of the Masai, with their red robes and ochre-dyed and braided hair, is one of the abiding images of Kenya. Many lodges offer visits to traditional Masai villages and homes, and although inevitably, these visits have become touristy, they are still well worth doing. Witnessing the dramatic *ipid,* a dance in which the *moran* (warriors) take turns in leaping high into the air, will keep your camera clicking nonstop. However, the future fate of the instantly recognizable Masai is inextricably bound up with the growth of tourism—it seems certain that their unique nomadic way of life in which they seasonally followed the new grazing with their flocks will be forced to change.

The Masai people named the reserve mara, which means spotted, but whether mara applies to the landscape, which is spotted with vegetation, or the hundreds of thousands of wildebeest and other game that spot the landscape, is anybody's guess. When you go, let us know what you think.

WHERE TO STAY

All prices have been quoted in high season rates, as most people will want to come during the migration. However, at low- and mid-season, rates can be considerably cheaper. Check for special offers, etc., before you book.

LUXURY LODGES

$$ ⛺ **Campi Ya Tembo.** You certainly won't come across another vehicle at this exclusively sited camp in the Masai Mara. Also owned and managed by Saruna, it has three comfortable Beduoin-looking tents with en-suite bathrooms with hot and cold running water and flush toilets. You can track elephants on foot or take action-packed night drives when you've more than a good chance of spotting a leopard as well as other nocturnal animals such as bushbabies and genets. ✐ *Box 304, Narok, Kenya* ☎ *254/734–764616 or 050/224–24* ⊕ *www.sarunicamp.com* ⇥ *3 tents* ⚲ *In-hotel: bar* ⊟ *AE, DC, MC, V* ⦿ *FAP.*

$$ ⛺ **Mara Serena Safari Lodge.** Perched high on a hill deep inside the reserve, attractive mud-color, domed huts, echo the style and shape of the traditional Masai manyattas. Each hut has rooms that echo the ethnic theme of the exteriors with soft, honey-color furnishings and a personal balcony that overlooks the plains and the distant Esoit Oloolo lolo escarpment—the views are spectacular. Though it's highly unlikely, if you do get tired of gazing out at the endless rolling grasslands where the migration takes place each year, then keep watch at the busy waterhole below the restaurant for a continuous wildlife show. Activities include ballooning (expensive but the trip of a lifetime), guided walks, bush barbecues, and game drives. After bouncing around in an open-sided game vehicle, it's great to enjoy a relaxing massage at the Maisha Spa. The Masai dancing is also spectacular. ✐ *Box 48690, Nairobi* ☎ *050/22059 or 020/284–2000* ⊕ *www.serenahotels.com* ⇥ *74 rooms* ⚲ *In-hotel: bar, restaurant, pool, spa* ⊟ *AE, DC, MC, V* ⦿ *FAP.*

$$ ⛺ **Saruni Camp.** This exclusive ecofriendly lodge lies just outside the ☾ Masai Mara National Reserve in a remote valley. Each of the six cottages has polished wooden floors and is furnished with handcarved cedarwood beds, Persian rugs, African art, colonial antiques, and comfortable chairs. You'll dine at a long table at Kuro House, the main lodge, which combines an eclectic mix of old-style Africa and modern design. The Italian cuisine here is superb, but there's also a wide

Fodor's Choice
★

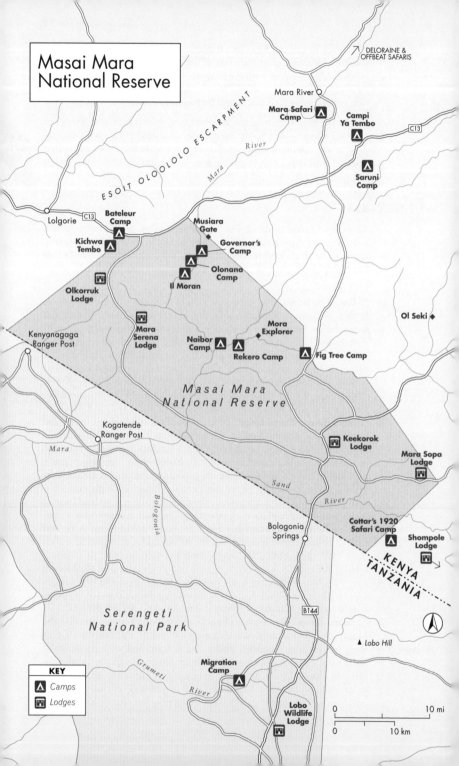

Masai Mara National Reserve

DELORAINE & OFFBEAT SAFARIS

Mara River

ESOIT OLOOLOLO ESCARPMENT

Mara River

Mara Safari Camp

Campi Ya Tembo

C13

Saruni Camp

Lolgorie

C13

Bateleur Camp

Kichwa Tembo

Musiara Gate

Governor's Camp

Olonana Camp

Il Moran

Olkorruk Lodge

Kenyanagaga Ranger Post

Mara Serena Lodge

Naibor Camp

Mora Explorer

Rekero Camp

Fig Tree Camp

Ol Seki

Masai Mara National Reserve

Kogatende Ranger Post

Mara

Keekorok Lodge

Mara Sopa Lodge

Sand River

Bologonia Springs

Cottar's 1920 Safari Camp

Shompole Lodge

KENYA
TANZANIA

Serengeti National Park

B144

▲ *Lobo Hill*

Grumeti River

Migration Camp

Lobo Wildlife Lodge

KEY

⛺ *Camps*

🏠 *Lodges*

0   10 mi

0   10 km

international menu available that uses fresh, locally grown, organic produce. You can also participate in a bush barbecue or dine alone by candlelight on your veranda. The library has a superb collection of Africana—it's definitely worth a visit. Children over eight are welcome. The tucked-away Masai Wellbeing Space, which uses local plants for its treatments, is run by one of Italy's most famous spas, Centro Benessere Stresa, and is considered one of the best spas in Kenya. All the guides are members of the Kenya Professional Safari Guides Association and Saruni supports the innovative Koyiaki Guiding School, which trains young Kenyans. Make sure you factor in the $45 per person, per day park fees into your expenses as this is not included in the lodge's fees. ⌂ *Box 304, Narok, Kenya* ☎*254/734–764616 or 050/224–24* ⊕*www.saruni camp.com* ⌖*6 cottages* ⌂*In-hotel: bar* ▤*AE, DC, MC, V* ⍯*FAP.*

WORD OF MOUTH

"Amboseli has a plethora of elephants and other animals. There are also some amazing views here of Mt. Kili in the background. They have slightly different vehicles here, with a "bait" seat at the front of the vehicle. I have to say sitting in this seat was amazing and thrilling. It was especially nice sitting there on the night drive, using the spotlight to spot animals."

–richardfh

PERMANENT TENTED CAMPS

$$$ ☖ **Bateleur Camp.** Who can forget the final scene in *Out of Africa* when two lions, symbolic of the Karen Blixen/Denys Finch-Hatton love affair, are silhouetted lying on a hill amid the African bush? If you're among the many who saw that movie and began fantasizing about your own African experience, then you'll be happy to know that this totally private and very romantic world-class camp is just below that famous hill. You may not get Robert Redford in the end, but you will be assured of celebrity status and service while you're here. The spacious tents are pitched under an A-frame wood structure with polished wooden floors and a wooden deck with steps leading down to the bush and encircling trees below. A massive four-poster bed dominates the tent's interior—a handy long padded stool, great for sitting on while putting on and taking off your boots after a game drive or bush walk, sits at the foot of the bed. The public areas—also made of wood and canvas—are decorated with old leather armchairs, antique Persian rugs, and a well-stocked, but small library. The game viewing will keep you busy by day and night, but do try to include a picnic on the edge of the Great Rift Valley—it will induce dreams of those who once hunted and gathered here millennia ago. ⌂ *CC Africa, Private Bag X27, Benmore 2010, South Africa* ☎*27/11/809–4300* ⊕*www.ccafrica.com* ⌖*40 tents* ⌂*In-hotel: bar, pool* ▤*AE, DC, MC, V* ⍯*FAP.*

$$ ☖ **Cottars 1920s Safari Camp.** If you want to turn back the clock and immerse yourself in the kind of original safari ambience that Ernest Hemingway enjoyed, then it doesn't get much better than this. From the superb and gracious service to the casual touches of antique luxury— claw-foot tubs, faded antique rugs, wrought-iron candlesticks, old gramophones, polished butlers' trays—all under authentic white safari

tents, the Cottar family's 80 years of experience certainly shows itself here. Sit outside your own spacious tent on a wooden rocking chair and watch the hills and valleys below; or relax in the deep red armchairs of the main tented lounge and admire the old photos and prints. At night as you sip a brandy snifter under the soft ambient glow of oil lamps by a blazing log fire, you'll forget all about the 21st century. The sweeping graceful tents with separate lounge and bedroom areas and floor level canvas decks, are in a huge, 250,000-acre exclusive concession between the Maasai Mara, Serengeti, and Loliondo reserves. Because it's a private concession you won't see the masses of other tourists that you can hardly help bumping into elsewhere in the Masai Mara itself. Because they operate just outside the reserve, Cottars' game vehicles are also allowed off-road, which means more freedom to follow game. (Try a bone-jolting ride in an ox wagon for a genuine early pioneer experience.) The legendary fourth-generation Kenyan Calvin Cottar could be your guide (at extra cost), but his experienced colleagues won't let you down either. Enjoy a quiet moment in the tented reading room, or rest in a hammock by the natural rock pool, or enjoy a complementary massage. ☐ Box 39806, Nairobi ☎020/603–090, 888/870–0903 toll-free in U.S. ⊕www.cottars.com ⇆6 tents ⚹In-hotel: bar, pool ▤AE, DC, MC, V ⦿FAP.

$ ▦ **Fairmont Mara Safari Club.** With newly refurbished interiors, this classy camp more than meets Fairmont Hotels & Resorts global reputation for luxury and excellent standards of service. The camp is surrounded on three sides by the croc- and hippo-filled Mara River, although you'll be safe and snug in your spacious wood-floored tent, which is set on stilts with its own private balcony. The bedspread of your four-poster mosquito-netted bed is made of the iconic red cloth used for Masai warrior robes, while brightly colored handwoven rugs, comfortable chairs, and big windows ensure your aprés-safari comfort. The main lodge is themed old-style safari with deep padded leather and fabric armchairs, beaded lamps, an open fireplace, and an inviting wood-paneled bar. Keep family and friends informed of your big-game adventures with Internet access in the library, or write in your journal on the spacious outside deck that leads to a heated pool, complete with bar and private massage tents. Game is plentiful, food and service excellent. Forego one morning game drive in favor of a hot air balloon safari over the Mara plains followed by a bush champagne breakfast—you'll thank us—or stroll in the footprints of the hippo-trodden path escorted by a Masai warrior. ☐ Box 58581, Masai Mara Reserve ☎020/216—940 ⊕www.fairmont.com ⇆50 tents ⚹In-hotel: bar, restaurant, pool, spa ▤AE, DC, MC, V ⦿FAP.

$ ▦ **Fig Tree Camp.** This attractive camp on the banks of the Talek River overlooks the plains and its location in the north end of the reserve gives it easy access to all the game areas. You'll stay in a safari tent or stone-and-thatch chalet, both furnished in African ethnic themes, but you should try for a tent with a river view; be sure to have taken your malaria *muti* (muti is the generic African word for medicine). Both tents and chalets are en-suite and have small verandas or balconies. The thatch-and-stone paved public areas are open and inviting, with two busy bars, an indoor and outdoor eating area, and a tree house coffee deck where you can watch the passing animal show. Don't expect the ultimate in luxury, but you'll get good value for money and also get to meet lots of international visitors. ■ TIP→ **If you need 24-hour hot water, then this is *not* the place for you.** There's only electricity 4–9 AM, noon–3 PM, and 6 PM–midnight. If you want a bit more luxury and exclusivity, go for one of the Ngaboli tents, where you'll sleep in a four-poster bed and have lots more room. Added bonuses for camp guests include lectures, a resident nurse, and an in-house medical clinic. Activities are extra: game drives are US$55 per drive or per day and night safaris, bush walks, champagne breakfasts, and bush dinners range in price US$55–US$100. ⬧ *Box 40683, Nairobi* ☎ *020/605–328* ⊕ *www. madahotels.com* ⇆ *38 tents, 27 chalets* ⚐ *In-hotel: bar, pool, restaurant, curio shop* ▭ *AE, DC, MC, V* ❑ *FAP.*

$$ ⬚ **Il Moran.** One of the famous Governors' Camps, Il Moran is where Kenya's first colonial governors used to twirl their handlebar moustaches and sip their gin and tonics while on safari—as you can imagine, it boasts an exclusive location that's teeming with game. Il Moran, which means warrior in Masai, sits on the edge of the plains, nestled in a private forest on the banks of the Mara river, so don't limit yourself to thrilling game drives because there's also great fishing. Once upon a time there were 20 tents here, but the owner decided to reduce the number of visitors so as to give you an even more exclusive experience. Today there are just 10 tents, imaginatively furnished with stunningly original furniture hand-carved from ancient olive trees, the antique Persian rugs that seem obligatory in so many safari accommodations, battered old leather suitcases, and glowing oil lamps. You'll feel like a pampered Victorian gentleman or lady as you soak in your clawfoot tub—the Victorian gentry would certainly approve of the bidet as well. There are once-in-a-lifetime game drives, moonlighted dinners, and guided bush walks, but treat yourself to the hot air balloon ride (an extra cost) with a champagne breakfast in the bush to follow. ⬧ *Box 48217, Nairobi* ☎ *020/273–4000 or 020/273–4001* ⊕ *www. governorscamp.com* ⇆ *10 tents* ⚐ *In-hotel: bar, pool, spa* ▭ *AE, DC, MC, V* ❑ *FAP.*

$ ⬚ **Kichwa Tembo Tented Safari Camp.** Kichwa Tembo, which means head
Fodor's Choice of the elephant in Kiswahili, is one of Kenya's most sought-after camps
★ in Africa. Perched on the edge of a riverine forest below the Oloololo Escarpment, the camp lies directly in the path of the migration. The en-suite tents are spacious and have seemingly never-ending views of the plains from the verandas. You'll be surrounded by the unforgettable sounds of the African night as you drift off to sleep. During the day you can take a dip in the shady pool between activities or just relax on your veranda while you fill out your bird and mammal lists. Don't forget to keep an eye out for passing animals: there'll be predators galore, as well as blue- and red-tailed monkeys, the mischievous banded mongoose, and if you're really lucky, the endangered black rhino. The candlelighted dinner on the banks of the Sabaringo River is a must-do for anyone. The staff here is attentive and charming, and the seductively stocked curio shop will have you swiping that credit card in

no time. ⌁CC *Africa, Private Bag X27, Benmore 2010, South Africa* ☎*27/11/809–4300* ⊕*www.ccafrica.com* ⇥*40 tents* ⚘*In-hotel: bar, pool, curio shop* ▤*AE, DC, MC, V* ⦿*FAP.*

$ ⛅**Little Governors' Camp.** Getting to this camp is an adventure in itself. First you take a ferry across the Mara River followed by a short, escorted—by armed guides—walk (you don't want to be lion's snack before your safari even starts) before arriving at this gorgeous little camp that was described by BBCTV as "the prime wild life real estate in the world." It was also rated the top safari camp in Kenya by the prestigious World Travel Awards for 2007. The accolades are not surprising, as you can be assured of superb service and comfortable accommodations. Each large tent is built on wooden platforms and has an en-suite bathroom with constant hot and cold running water and flush toilets—this may seem normal, but most places can only provide hot water at the end of the day (after solar power has heated it) or in the morning (after the donkey boiler has been lighted). Lighting, as at many of the traditional Masai Mara camps, is by gas, kerosene lantern, and candlelight giving an authentic original safari atmosphere to your surroundings. If you're lucky to be here during a full moon, you can watch the game come and go at the large waterhole in front of the camp. You'll eat superb home-cooked meals under a blue sky or at night in a candlelighted dining tent. If you need to stretch your legs after a muscle-clenching, nerve-wracking game drive, go on a guided walking safari, or visit a nearby Masai village and join in the *ipid* jumping dance with the warriors. One more detail to mention—the camp sits directly in the path of the wildebeest migration. ⌁*Box 48217, Nairobi* ☎*020/273–4000 or 020/273–4001* ⊕*www.governorscamp. com* ⇥*17 tents* ⚘*In-hotel: bar, pool* ▤*AE, DC, MC, V* ⦿*FAP.*

$$ ⛅**Mara Explorer.** At this intimate little camp, tucked in a riverine forest on a bend on the Talek River, you'll be able to watch elephants wading, hippos snorting, and all other sorts of game from your outdoor clawfoot bathtub that overlooks the river. Of course, a cocktail of choice from your personal butler makes the scene so much more appealing. Legendary explorer Dr. Livingstone never knew what he was missing. A handcrafted wooden bed dominates the en-suite tent, but there's still room for the bedside tables fashioned from logs, old chests, and weather-beaten tin trunks that serve as tables, and an old-fashioned rocking chair where you can sit and tick off your mammal and bird lists. Move a little farther outside and you can laze on your wooden deck, savoring every tranquil moment. You'll be truly awed by the numbers of predators you see—lion, leopard, cheetah, hyena—preying on the plains herbivores. All the Masai Mara activities are available, and you'll particularly enjoy the breakfast picnics where the lions can watch *you* feeding. You'll eat delicious meals in an open-air dining area, which looks out over the river, and there are a cozy lounge and small library for those moments when you want to sit still. ⌁*Box 74888, Nairobi* ☎*020/444–6651* ⊕*www.heritage-eastafrica.com* ⇥*10 tents* ⚘*In-hotel: bar* ▤*AE, DC, MC, V* ⦿*FAP.*

$$ ⛅**Naibor Camp.** Only 20 minutes away from one of the legendary migration river crossings, this stylish camp doesn't exclusively follow

the old traditional safari camp feel, but it aims for a fusion of old and new with specially designed pale khaki and white mesh tents, minimalist clean-lined hand-carved wooden furniture, roof-to-ceiling earth-color drapes, and plain-color couches and chairs that are highlighted with ethnic-patterned cushions. The whole camp lives up to its name—naibor means simplicity and space in Kiswahili—but you'll never lose that essential sense of being on an African safari. The spacious tents on the banks of the Talek River are furnished with handwoven straw mats, a hand-carved figwood bed, simple bedside tables with lots of surface space for books, flashlights, reading glasses, and all those other things you need at night. Soft white bed linen is complemented with brightly colored cushions and throws. There's a big private veranda from where you can catch the elephants going down to drink, or listen to and watch the myriads of birds. The game here is exceptionally good, but give yourself a break from that plethora of plenty and go for an all-day walk, try mountain biking, go honey-hunting, visit Lake Victoria for a day, or do what everybody *must* in the Mara, and take a balloon ride. ■ TIP➔The camp is closed April, May, and November. ⌂ *Box 74888, Nairobi* ☎ *020/444–6651* ⊕ *www.heritage-eastafrica.com* ⌁ *10 tents* ⌂ *In-hotel: bar* ▭ *AE, DC, MC, V* ⦿ *FAP.*

$$ ▦ **Olonana Camp.** Named after an honored Masai chief, this attractive ecofriendly camp in game-rich country rests on the western border of the reserve overlooking the Mara River and the Ooloolo escarpment. Feeling really lazy? Hibernate in your huge wooden-floor tent—it's more like a mini-pavilion than a tent—prop yourself up on pillows in your queen-size bed and watch the river below. There are floor-to-ceiling mosquito-proofed "windows" and stone-walled en-suite bathrooms with his and her basins and stools, and a roomy shower. Feeling energetic? Take a guided bush walk or hike up the escarpment. Don't let the lodge's manyatta-styled entrance fool you. Once inside the main lodge you'll find the understated luxury of hand-carved solid wooden furniture; cream, russet, and brown linens; handwoven African rugs; and a selection of indigenous art and artifacts. The reed-roofed main viewing deck overlooks a hippo pool with daylong entertainment from these overgrown clowns. The food is superb and you have the option to dine with your fellow guests or on your own veranda. There are an inviting pool, a small but good library, and excellent opportunities to observe the everyday lives of the Masai in the adjacent village. ⌂ *Box 59749, Nairobi* ☎ *020/695–0002 or 020/695–0244* ⊕ *www. olonana.com* ⌁ *12 tents* ⌂ *In-hotel: bar, pool, curio shop* ▭ *AE, DC, MC, V* ⦿ *FAP.*

$$ ▦ **Ol Seki Mara Camp.** This ecofriendly camp is in the pristine northern regions of the reserve. One of the reserve's newest properties, it was designed and built by the Allan family—one of Kenya's top safari operators for more than 37 years. Opened in 2005, it's named after the olseki or sandpaper tree, which is a Masai symbol of peace, harmony, and wealth. Set on round wooden platforms on a rocky outcrop that's surrounded by bird-filled indigenous trees, the 12-sided tents look as if they are sailing through the bush. Inside, it's all space and light, with simple stylish furnishings: a double and single bed, cream and

Ol Seki

Mara Explorer

Bateleur

earth-tone soft furnishings, straw mats, carefully planned lighting, and en-suite toilet and shower. The lean, clean effect is carried through to the attractive dining tent and library. There's a full range of activities including morning and night game drives with lots of game—you might get one of Kenya's only woman guides—bush picnics, star-gazer walks, botanical walks, and visits to authentic, nontouristy Masai villages, where you might be lucky enough to witness a genuine betrothal or postinitiation ceremony. ■ TIP➔ As this is a seasonal camp, it's only open June–March. ✉ *Box 15114, Nairobi* ☎ *020/89–1190 or 020/89–0375* ⊕ *www.olseki.com* ⇋ *6 tents* ♿ *In-hotel: bar, pool* ⊟ *AE, DC, MC, V* ⦿*FAP.*

$$ ⊞**Rekero Camp.** The Beaton family, owners of this seasonal tented camp, settled in Kenya more than a century ago and helped pioneer the country's conservation movement. The camp, tucked away in a grove of trees more than 40 km (25 mi) from the main tourist throng farther east, is beautifully situated on a river bank near the confluence of the Talek and Mara rivers. You'll sleep in one of only seven tents, each hidden from the other and all with great views of the plains and the river. There's an ancient wildebeest crossing practically on your doorstep, so you won't have to bounce around for hours in an open-sided game vehicle to find the game. But when you do find game, there won't be hordes of other visitors to spoil the sight. Tents are bright and comfortably furnished with a double bed, wood furniture, handwoven rugs, and en-suite bathrooms with flush toilets and canvas bucket showers. As the camp is unfenced, expect all kinds of game to wander past your tent, but don't worry, you'll be safe within your canvas walls and a Masai warrior will escort you to and from the main areas. ■ TIP➔ The camp is only open June–October and December–March. ✉ *Box 56923, Nairobi 2128* ☎ *No phone* ⊕ *www.rekerocamp.com* ⇋ *7 tents* ♿ *In-hotel: bar* ⊟ *AE, DC, MC, V* ⦿*FAP.*

BUDGET LODGING

$ ⊞**Keekorok Lodge.** This unpretentious lodge has rather basic accommodations, but it was the first lodge built in the Masai Mara. Though it's a bit gray at the temples, it's superb location—directly in the path of the wildebeest migration—means you won't have to leave camp to see animals galore. You'll stay in a Sand River stone chalet or A-frame wood-and-stone bungalow, both simply furnished with comfortable beds, mosquito nets, and an en-suite old-fashioned white-tiled bathroom with bath and overhead shower. Outside there's a small stone veranda with a rustic table and camping chairs. There's a 300-meter (984 feet) raised wooden walkway that leads to a viewing deck with great views of the plains and a hippo pool. The camp is unfenced, so you'll often see elephants and buffalos round its perimeter. Activities include lectures on the Masai culture, wildlife video viewings, hot air balloon rides, or tanning by the pool. ✉ *Box 42788, Nairobi* ☎ *050-22680 or 020/650–392* ⊕ *www.africanmeccasafaris.com* ⇋ *12 chalets* ♿ *In-hotel: bar, pool* ⊟ *AE, DC, MC, V* ⦿*FAP.*

$ ⋔**Offbeat Safaris.** A truly wonderful and unique way to see game and experience Kenya at close hand is to go on a horse safari; you should only do this if you're an experienced rider—you want to be able to gallop if you meet a hungry predator—and if you're fit enough to ride four or six hours a day. Your safari begins at Deloraine, the beautiful old colonial mansion owned by Tristan and Lucinda Voorspuy who keep more than 80 horses on the estate—Tristan served in the British Household Cavalry, so he really knows his oats. The estate, which has welcomed British royalty, is on the western edge of the Great Rift Valley on the lower slopes of Mount Londiani. When you choose the Mara safari, you'll stay at small rustic but comfortable tented camps along the way, sometimes spending two or three nights at the same camp, depending on which route you choose. But even if you get a bit saddle-sore, riding alongside hundreds of thousands of plains game is an once-in-a-lifetime experience. *Box 1146, Nanyuki, Kenya 10400 054/62–31081 www.offbeatsafaris.com AE, DC, MC, V FAP.*

¢   **Mara Sopa Lodge.** Located on a hillside near the Oloolaimutia Gate, this budget lodge (Sopa means welcome in the Masai language) is one of the most popular in the reserve. Even though it's always busy, the delightfully friendly and experienced staff will make you feel uniquely special. You'll sleep in a *rondawel* (small round thatch roof hut) that has a tiny veranda and is simply but pleasantly furnished in traditional African style with lots of earth-color soft furnishings. The brightly decorated public areas are nestled among profuse flowering plants and trees; notices telling you about meal times, balloon booking times, how to book a picnic and lots of other information are pasted throughout the main area. Don't expect all the bells and whistles of the luxury lodges—hot water is only available mornings and evenings—but the setting and the feeling of Africa on your doorstep more than compensates. Plus, there's a great pool to cool off in after a hot dusty game drive where African-theme events, such as Masai dancing or African food, are held. There's also a quaintly named "Wild Animals Viewing Deck" in camp. Because you're over 6,000 feet above sea level, you'll be cool in summer and will definitely need a jacket or sweater in winter. *Box 72630, Nairobi 020/375—0183 or 020/375-0235 www. sopalodges.com 77 rondawels, 12 suites, 1 presidential suite In-room: phone, minibar, TV. In-hotel: bar, restaurant, pool, curio shop AE, DC, MC, V FAP.*

NATIONAL PARKS ACCOMMODATIONS

For the foreign visitor, particularly for the first-time visitor, these campsites with no facilities are not really an option, unless you are an experienced camper, or hard core traveler.

BETWEEN MASAI MARA & AMBOSELI NATIONAL PARK

LUXURY LODGES

$ ▦**Shompole Lodge.** Midway between Masai Mara and Amboseli, not far from the Kenya/Tanzania border, is the exquisite Shompole Lodge, which looks out onto the Rift Valley's distant plains and mountains. The Shompole Conservancy, a group venture with the Masai, consists of 56,000 hectares (138,379 acres) teeming with game. Built on huge stilted wooden platforms above the surrounding wilderness, each brown-and-cream tent rests under a multipeaked thatch roof, which also shelters a spacious open living area built of local stone and wood. As you lie on your deck beside your personal pool, look out to the distant horizon. You'll feel as if you're taking part in an Arabian Nights fantasy. The main building continues the theme of light, space, water, and air. It'll be hard to drag yourself away, even for the amazing game drives, a breakfast in the fig tree forest, or a walk at Lake Natron to see the million plus flamingos. This lodge is Africa at its most innovative, beautiful, and best. ⌂*Box 10665, Nairobi* ☎*020/884–135* ⊕*www. shompole.com* ▭*AE, DC, MC, V* ❏|*FAP.*

AMBOSELI NATIONAL RESERVE

Game
☆☆★★★

Park Accessibility
★★★★★

Ease of Getting Around
★★★★★

Accommodations
★★★★★

Scenic Beauty
★★★★★

Amboseli National Reserve, immediately northwest of Mount Kilimanjaro and 240 km (150 mi) southeast of Nairobi on the Tanzanian border, is certainly one of the most picturesque places in the whole of Africa to watch game. Where else could you watch a great herd of elephants trudging slowly across a wide empty plain dominated by Africa's highest mountain, Kilimanjaro?

At dawn, as the cloud-cover breaks and the first rays of sun illuminate the snow-capped 19,340 feet (5,895 meters) peak, you'll be awed by the colors—rosy pinks and soft reds—of the sky that provide the perfect backdrop for the plains below. It gets even better at dusk, when the whole area is backlighted, and the mountain stands out in stark relief against the swiftly setting fiery sun. That's the pretty picture. The reality, though slowly improving, is that one of Kenya's most visited parks has become a dustbowl of overused tourist trails, traffic jams, and irresponsible off-road driving.

Amboseli has a checkered history. First established as a natural reserve in 1948, it was returned to Masai ownership and management in 1961, but soon became environmentally degraded with too many cattle and too many tourists. Some 10 years later, 392 square km (151 square mi) were designated a national park, and cattle-grazing was forbidden. This angered the mainly pastoral Masai, who took their revenge by killing a majority of the rhino population. Eventually peace was restored with some expedient land swapping, and today there's a responsible environmental program that controls the well-being of the game, puts limits on tourist numbers, and enforces a strict policy on off-road driving.

There are five different habitats in Amboseli: open plains, acacia woodland, thornscrub, swamps, and marshlands. To the west is the Ol Doinyo Orok massif and Lake Amboseli, which is usually dry, but when the heavy rains return so do the flamingos, and the whole surrounding area becomes green and lush again. Expect some impass-able roads at these times, as well as when the lake is completely dry, because the fine alkaline dust which blows up from the lake's surface is hell for tires.

Amboseli is filled with great game: zebra, warthog, giraffe, buffalo, impala, wildebeest, the long-necked mini-giraffelike gerenuks, and baboons galore. But your chances of seeing predators are much less than in the Masai Mara. Lions were almost hunted to the point of extinction by the Masai because they killed their herds of cattle. Those that survived are still skittish and often not comfortable with vehi-cles. If a predator is spotted, it is often surrounded by far too many vehicles, and put under great stress. Interestingly, the hunting meth-ods of cheetah within the park have changed dramatically because of tourist pressure. Accustomed to hunting at dawn and dusk, they've now resorted to hunting at midday—tourist siesta time—with poorer success rates, thus their numbers are decreasing. But if it's elephants you're after, then Amboseli is the place. Perhaps the oldest and most studied elephant population in sub-Saharan Africa lives here. There are more than 1,000 of these great pachyderms today, and because they are accustomed to visitors and vehicles you'll experience eyeball-to-knee-high close encounters.

Game-viewing is best around the main swamps of Enkongo Narok, which means black and benevolent, and the Amboseli landmark, Observation Hill. Enkongo Narok, in the middle of the park, is where you can see water seeping up from the lava rocks. Observation Hill provides a surefire opportunity to spot game, especially elephants, as it looks out over the plains.

Birdlife is also prolific, with more than 420 recorded species. There are dozens of birds of prey including more than 10 different kinds of eagles. In the swamp areas, which are fed by the melting snow of Kili-manjaro, there's a profusion of water birds including seasonal flamingo and more than 12 species of heron.

WHERE TO STAY

LUXURY LODGES

$ **Amboseli Serena Safari Lodge.** Situated plumb in the middle of the park, beside a natural flowing spring, this lodge enjoys spectacular views of Mount Kilimanjaro. Pink painted guest cottages (looking a lit-tle like colorful mushrooms) line narrow paved walkways, and although trees and shrubs give you a certain amount of privacy, they also take away your view. The food, cooked with homegrown fresh herbs and vegetables, is excellent, particularly the homemade pasta. Because the lodge is near the Enkongo Narok Swamp, there's always plenty of game around. Take a game drive, go walking with a Masai guide, enjoy a bush breakfast, and always remember to keep your doors and windows closed to keep out marauding vervet monkeys, which look cute but can make off with your belongings. (Toothpaste is a great favorite.) The rooms are small, and fairly basic, with a couple of twin beds with

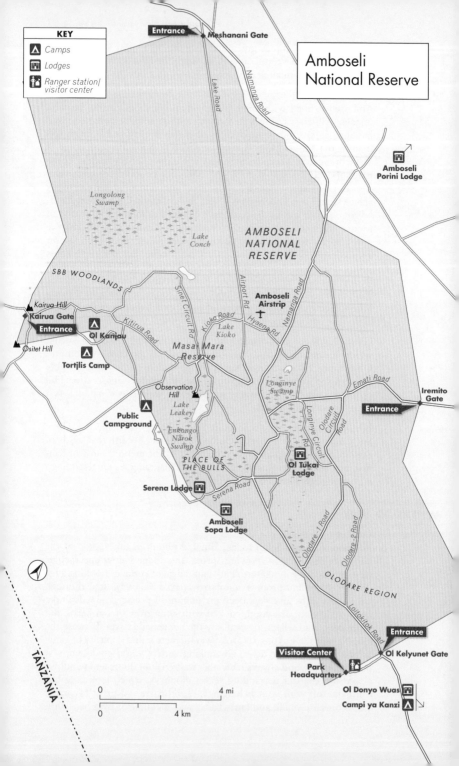

eye-catching pink and purple bedspreads, a small dressing table, and en-suite bathroom. There are no mosquito nets, so spray yourself liberally rather than depending on the provided insect wipes. There's a small pool, but don't hope to catch a tan because the trees surrounding it cast heavy shade. What the lodge lacks in luxury is more than made up by the friendly and helpful staff. ⬥ *Box 48690, Nairobi* ☎*050/22059 or 020/284–2000* ⊕*www.serenahotels.com* ⮑*96 rooms* ♿*In-hotel: bar, restaurant, pool* ▤*AE, DC, MC, V* ⦿*FAP.*

$ 🏨**Amboseli Sopa Lodge.** Although this attractive lodge wasn't around
☾ when Ernest Hemingway wrote *The Snows of Kilimanjaro*, he would have enjoyed much the same spectacular views and wildlife as you, because he stayed nearby while writing it. The lodge is in lush established gardens in the foothills of Mount Kilimanjaro near the Tanzanian border. You'll stay in roomy mud-and-thatch en-suite hut, gaily decorated in African styles with lots of wood, animal motifs, and brightly colored soft furnishings. Enjoy a hearty breakfast and lunch buffet inside in the big African-theme dining room, or eat out beside the pool where there's also a very pleasant poolside bar. In the evening sit down to a four-course meal where you can choose between European, African, or Asian dishes. There are a stunning lounge area and great viewing deck. It's also a great place for kids—there's plenty of room for them to run around, a lovely pool, and babysitters are always available if you want to be child-free for an evening. The lodge offers lots of activities, which are an additional cost, including game drives, guided walks, and trips to Masai villages. If you want to have a go at climbing Mount Kilimanjaro, the lodge can arrange that, too. ⬥*Box 72630, Nairobi* ☎*020/375–0183 or 020/375–0235* ⊕*www. sopalodges.com* ⮑*47 rooms* ♿*In-hotel: bar, restaurant, pool, curio shop* ▤*MC, V* ⦿*FAP.*

PERMANENT TENTED CAMPS

$$$ 🏨**Amboseli Porini Camp.** This exclusive, back-to-nature tented camp is far, far away from the madding crowd in the game-abundant Selenkay Conservancy, a few miles north of Amboseli National Park. A silver eco-award winner, the camp is co-owned with the local Masai community. Because the area is relatively new to tourism, you'll see few visitors (numbers are limited to 12 per day), but lots of game including lion, leopard, cheetah, and the ubiquitous Amboseli elephants. Birdlife is prolific with lots of raptors everywhere. Big, comfortably furnished tents are solar-powered and have en-suite bathrooms with a basin, shower, and flush toilet. You'll eat hearty home-cooked meals outside the mess tent, serenaded with birdcalls by day, and nocturnal animals by night. Game drives are taken in an open-sided safari vehicle—yours will be the only one for miles and miles. You'll visit a Masai village, take an informative walk in a dry riverbed, enjoy a picnic lunch in Amboseli itself, and at night, after an exhilarating night game drive, you'll return to your own little private spot in the African wilderness. The all-inclusive price includes roundtrip road transfers, Amboseli park fees, as well as conservancy fees, all game drives, sundowners, walks with Masai warriors, Masai village visits, full board, and free house wines, beer, and soft drinks. ⬥*Box 388, Village Market, Nai-*

robi ☎*020/712–2504 or 020/712–3129* ⊕*www.porini.com* ⊲*9 tents* ▭*MC, V* ⦿*FAP.*

$ ⊡**Tortillis Camp.** This multiaward-winning rustic bush camp is named after the flat-topped *acacia tortilis* trees that surround the camp. The main thatch roof open bar, lounge, and dining room overlook a waterhole and have superb views of Mount Kilimanjaro and Mount Meru in neighboring Tanzania. Your large tent snugly sits under a huge thatch canopy and is raised up on a wooden deck with wooden floors, a king-size bed, and an en-suite bathroom with hot showers and flush toilets. If you want to catch up on your journal or bird and mammal lists, then relax on the comfortable furniture on your

personal sitting area, or laze by the pool in between activities (the lodge provides these at an extra cost). There's a family house with a one double and one twin-bed room if you don't fancy splitting up between two tents. The mainly north Italian food is delicious and is whipped up from the owner's original family recipes. The food is made even tastier by homegrown herbs and vegetables. There's a minimum three-night-stay requirement. ⌂*Cheli & Peacock, Box 743, Uhuru Gardens, Nairobi* ☎*020/603–054 or 020/603–090/1* ⊕*www.tortilis.com* ⊲*17 tents, 1 family house* ⌂*In-hotel: bar, restaurant, pool, curio shop* ▭*MC, V* ⦿*FAP.*

SEASONAL TENTED CAMPS

$$ ⊡**Ol Kanjau Camp.** If you want to get up close and personal with the real Africa, then this tented camp at the foot of Mount Kilimanjaro will put you just a canvas tent flap away from the surrounding wilderness. Co-owned by long-term Kenyan conservationists and ecologists Mike and Judy Rainy and the neighboring Kisongo Masai, the camp is beside Amboseli National Park in the game-rich area of the Greater Amboseli region. You'll sleep in a big comfortable bed in a spacious tent, with a hot water bucket shower. There's electricity by day, but at night, softly glowing gas lanterns complement the classic safari experience. There's game of all kinds, but the focus here is on elephants (Ol Kanjau means elephants), which Mike and Judy have been studying for nearly 40 years. You'll never forget the thrill of your first nose-to-trunk introduction to one of the 52 great matriarchal herds. Take a game drive with a knowledgeable guide, go mountain biking, take a guided bush walk with a habituated baboon troop, a cultural visit to a Masai village, or just soak up quintessential Africa outside your tent. The camp is closed April, May, and November. ⌂*Box 56923, Nairobi* ☎*020/600–457 or 020/605–108* ⊕*www.olkanjau.com* ⊲*6 tents* ▭*MC, V* ⦿*FAP.*

3

Amboseli Serena Safari Lodge Bedroom interior

Camp ya Kanzi

Ol Donyo Wuas

BUDGET LODGING

¢ ✕🏨 **Ol Tukai Lodge.** Just 3 km (2 mi) east of Amboseli National Park,
☺ this is an ideal location to spot game including the famously studied
Amboseli elephants. In fact, Ol Tukai claims that this is the best place
in the world to watch elephants. Apart from the plains game and its
attendant predators, there are more than 400 species of birds to be
identified, and Ol Tukai offers specially designed bird walks through its
grounds for beginners and experts alike; it's a wonderful opportunity to
introduce yourself or the kids to the world of birds. This resort manages
to be modern and traditional at the same time—its facilities are world
class but its feel and ambience is unmistakably African. The resort is
set amid acres of well-kept lawns dotted with the familiar symbol of
the plains—*acacia tortilis* trees—and has a superb view of Mount Kilimanjaro. En-suite chalets, built of local stone and slate, are furnished
with handcrafted wooden furniture and colorfully decorated with faux
animal skin fabrics, rugs, and throws; each has a personal veranda.
Innovatively designed public areas are open and spacious; everywhere
you go you'll have a different view. For that special group celebration,
choose the three-bedroom stone and wood Kibo Villa, tucked away
in its own private 5 acres where you can self-cater or eat at the main
lodge. Babysitters are available. ■TIP→ **Game drives and other activities
are not included in the price.** ✉*Box 45403, Nairobi* ☎*020/444–5514*
⊕*www.oltukailodge.com* 🛏*80 chalets, 1 villa* ⚭*In-hotel: bar, restaurant, pool, curio shop* ▤*AE, DC, MC, V* ⋈*FAP.*

NATIONAL PARKS ACCOMMODATIONS

Public campsites are run by the local Masai communities, but there are
no facilities. Unless you're a hardcore camper, these are not really an
option for the first timer.

NEAR TO AMBOSELI & TSAVO EAST & WEST

$$ 🏨 **Ol Donyo Wuas.** Fancy the idea of being one of only 16 visitors with
☺ exclusive access to a quarter of a million acres of wilderness on the
slopes of the Chyulu Hills, northeast of Amboseli? Then these stone
and thatch cottages, with great views of the plains and Mount Kili-
manjaro, are perfect for you. Each cottage is furnished with handmade
wooden furniture, hand-woven rugs, comfortable chairs, and a huge
mosquito net draped over the beds Bedouin style. Ecofriendly solar
power fires up the lights and the hot water in your en-suite bathroom.
Bring the kids because three of the cottages have extra bedrooms. For
total privacy, book the Hide. Built on stilts, it overlooks a waterhole
and is set away from the other cottages. There are numerous activities
to choose from including game drives, guided walks, Masai cultural
visits, horseback riding on the plains (for beginners and experts alike),
and clay pigeon shooting. Excellent food and friendly, attentive service
are the norm. Meals are taken in the centrally positioned lounge and
dining room with a big open fireplace for those chilly nights. The hori-
zon pool has stunning views of Mount Kilimanjaro. ✉*Box 24133,
Nairobi* ☎*020/600–457 or 020/605–108* ⊕*www.oldonyowuas.com*
🛏*8 cottages* ⚭*In-hotel: bar, restaurant, pool* ▤*MC, V* ⋈*FAP.*

$ ⚏ **Campi ya Kanzi.** One of the most environmentally friendly camps in East Africa, this lovely camp, whose name means "Camp of the Hidden Treasure" in Kiswahili, is in the Kuku Group Ranch, the natural corridor between Amboseli and Tsavo National Parks. It was the first camp in Kenya to be gold-rated by Ecotourism Kenya for its efforts in sustainable tourism, and has won other prestigious international ecotourism awards. It's also co-owned by the Masai from the ranch area and Luca Belpietro and his wife Antonella Bonomi. The ranch itself stretches 1,036 square km (400 square mi) from the foothills of Mt. Kilimanjaro to the Chyulu Hills in the north, and because of the different altitudes, you'll find all sorts of habitats from wide plains and riverine bush to high mountain forests. You'll also find plenty of game—more than 50 mammals and 400 bird species—but few tourists, a welcome relief from the pop-top traffic jams of Amboseli. To see all this, choose between game drives (where the game is really wild and not used to vehicles), guided game walks, botanical walks, birdwatching, and cultural visits. Take your kids to the Masai school and open their eyes to a completely different side of life. The main lounge and dining areas built of lava rock and thatch are in Tembo (Elephant) House, which has superb views of Mount Kilimanjaro, the Taita Hills, and Chyulu Hills. All the tents have great views, as well as wooden floors, a veranda, and an en-suite bathroom with bidet, flush toilet, and hot and cold running water. The Hemingway and Simba tented suites boast king-size beds, a dressing room, en-suite bathroom with his and her washbasins, and verandas overlooking Mt. Kilimanjaro. Note that there is an additional US$70 per person, per day conservation fee, which goes entirely to the local Masai community. ⌂*Box 236, Mtito Andei, 90128 Kenya* ☎*720/461–300* ⊕*www.maasai.com* �){6 tents, 1 suite* ⌖*In-hotel: bar, restaurant* ▤*MC, V* ⦿*FAP.*

TSAVO NATIONAL PARK

Game
☆☆★★★

Park Accessibility
☆★★★★

Ease of Getting
Around
☆★★★★

Accommodations
☆★★★★

Scenic Beauty
☆★★★★

At almost 21,000 square km (8,108 square mi), Tsavo National Park is Kenya's largest park. It includes the areas of Tsavo East and Tsavo West. Both stretch for about 130 km (80 mi) along either side of Nairobi/Mombasa Highway, the main road from Nairobi to Mombasa. It's amazing that just a few miles away from the constant thunder of motor traffic on Kenya's busiest road is some of Kenya's best wildlife viewing.

TSAVO EAST

More inaccessible than its sister park, Tsavo East—11,747 square km (4,535 square mi)—is also one of Kenya's least visited parks. It's a fairly harsh landscape of scrubland dotted with huge baobab trees, but photographers will revel in the great natural light and the vast plains stretching to the horizon. There's lots of greenery along the banks of the Voi and Galana rivers, and the big Aruba Dam, built across the Voi, attracts game and birdlife galore. You'll see herds of elephant and buffalo, waterbuck, and all kinds of animals coming to drink at the dam. The Lugard Falls, on the Galana River, is more a series of rapids than actual waterfalls; walk along the riverbank to catch a glimpse of the water-sculpted rocks. Legend has it that the falls were named after the first British Pro-Consul, who volunteered for Kenya's Colonial Service to escape an unrequited love affair at home. Another fascinating feature in the park is the 290-km-long (180-mi-long) Yatta Plateau, one of the world's longest lava flows. It runs parallel to the Nairobi/Mombasa Highway and is 5 to 10 km (3 to 6 mi) wide and 305 meters (1,000 feet) high. Mudanda Rock, a 1.5-km (2-mi) outcropping, is a water catchment area. You'll see plenty of wildlife coming to drink at the dam below. There's plenty of game in this park including zebras, kongoni antelope, impala, lion, cheetah and giraffe, and rarer animals such as the oryx, lesser kudu, and the small klipspringer antelopes, which can jump nimbly from rock to rock because of the sticky suction pads under their feet. And yes, it's true. Those fat and hairy marmotlike creatures you see sunning themselves on the rocks—the hyraxes—are first cousins to elephants.

The park became infamous in the late 1890s when the Man Eaters of Tsavo, a pride of lions that specialized in human flesh, preyed on the Indian migrant laborers who were building the railway. More than 130 workers were killed; the incident was retold in the 1996 thriller, *The Ghost and the Darkness*, starring Val Kilmer. In the 1970s and '80s Tsavo became notorious once again for the widespread poaching that decimated the elephant population and nearly wiped out rhinos altogether. Today, thanks to responsible management, enlightened environmental vision, and proper funding, both elephant and rhino populations are on the rise.

> ### THE LEGEND OF THE BAOBAB
>
> Legend has it that when the gods were planting the earth, the baobab refused many locations. In anger, the gods threw them out of heaven and they landed upside down. Take a good look. When not in leaf, they look exactly as if their roots are sticking up into the air.

TSAVO WEST

Tsavo West covers 7,065 square km (2,728 square mi), which is a little less than a third of the total area comprising all of Kenya's national parks. It lies to the west of the Chyulu Hills—said to be the world's youngest mountains at only a few hundred years old—and with its diverse habitats of riverine forest, palm thickets, rocky outcrops and ridges, mountains and plains, is more attractive and certainly more accessible than Tsavo East. It's also a lot more crowded. In the north heavily wooded hills dominate; in the south there are wonderful views over the Serengeti Plains. Take a boat ride or go birding on Lake Jipe, one of the most important wetlands in Kenya. If you like birds, you'll be keen to get a glimpse of the whitebacked night heron, African skimmers, and palm-nut vultures. The lake, which lies in the park's southwest corner on the Kenya Tanzania border, is fed from the snows of Kilimanjaro and the North Pare mountains. There's evidence of volcanic activity everywhere in the park, especially where recent lava flows absorb the rainfall. In one spectacular spot, this rainfall, having traveled underground for 40 km (25 mi) or so, gushes up in a pair of pools at Mzima Springs, in the north of the park. There's a submerged hippo blind here, but the hippos have gotten wise to tourists and often move to the far side of the pools. Because of the fertile volcanic soil and abundance of water, the park is brimming with animal, bird, and plant life. You'll see lion and cheetah—especially in the dry season when the grass is low—spotted hyenas, buffalo, the beautiful Masai giraffes, and all kinds of antelope, including Thompson's and Grant's gazelle—the prettiest of the antelope.

WHERE TO STAY

TSAVO EAST

LUXURY LODGES

$$$$ ⌂ **Kilalinda Lodge.** This exclusive lodge is set in the Kilalinda Wildlife Conservancy, a private wildlife conservation area totaling 8,000 acres on the banks of the Athi River overlooking the Yatta Plateau; on a clear day you can see that famous mountain in the distance. En-suite cottages, each with its own veranda and unique furnishings—big four-poster bed, colorfully bordered mosquito nets, hand-woven woolen carpets and bedspreads, tiled floors, and sumptuous drapes—stretch out along the river bank where indigenous trees and shrubs guarantee you privacy. Sip a cool drink or watch birds and animals from your own little sandy beach—keep a sharp eye out for crocs and hippos, though it's very unlikely they'll trespass on your territory—or mingle with the other guests at the airy open clubhouse bar. At night, when the lodge is lighted by soft lantern light, you'll forget all about the real world. The food is delicious—home-baked bread, cakes and pastries, homemade pasta, and lots of homegrown fresh fruit and veggies round out the menu. Game drives are exhilarating, but for something a little different, take a guided walk along the riverbank, or go game and bird spotting out on the river in a rubber dinghy. (You don't have to paddle yourself!) ☐ *Box 6648, Nairobi* ☎ *020/605–349* ⊕ *www.kilalinda.com* ⌂ *6 cottages* ☐ *In-hotel: bar, restaurant, pool* ☐ *AC, DC, MC, V* ⦿ *FAP.*

$

Fodor's Choice

★ ⌂ **Galdessa Camp.** The ultimate in luxury, this stunningly beautiful camp is on the south bank of the Galana River and many consider it to be one of Kenya's best camps; we agree. Overlooking the Yatta Plateau upstream from the Lugard Falls, it's actually two lodges; the main lodge has 11 spacious *bandas* (thatch and canvas bungalows) including one honeymoon banda; the other smaller lodge has three bandas, also including a honeymoon one. Each lodge has its own lounge, dining area, and bar overlooking the river. The elegant and imaginatively decorated bandas are built on wooden platforms with an A-frame thatch roof and a private veranda that has breathtaking river views. The furnishings are African theme with huge hand-carved beds, wooden chests, deep-cushioned armchairs, hand-woven rugs, and wall hangings. There's an en-suite bathroom with flush toilet and bucket shower. If you want total privacy, then opt for the honeymoon bandas, which have separate verandas on stilts—perfect for canoodling to your heart's content under the stars. The quality and standard of the food is just what you would expect in this gorgeous camp—superb. Don't be surprised if you see a pride of lions strolling along the riverbank or a few black rhino; this area has the largest unfenced population of black rhino. ☐ *Box 714, Village Market, Nairobi* ☎ *020/712–1356 or 020/712–1074* ⊕ *www.galdessa.com* ⌂ *14 bandas* ☐ *In-hotel: bar, restaurant* ☐ *MC, V* ⦿ *FAP.*

¢ ⌂ **Rock Side Camp** (formerly Westermann's Safari Camp). Between Tsavo East and West, this former hunting camp is a great base to explore both parks. The Tozers, who live here permanently, have transformed this delightful getaway into a luxury destination that's simply but taste-

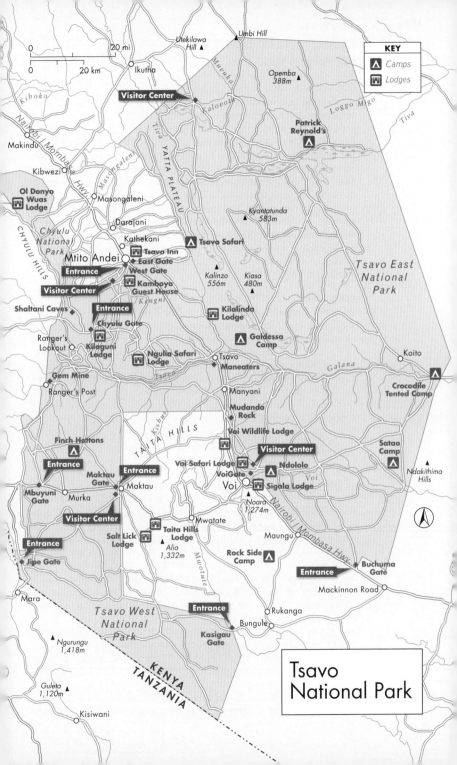

Tsavo
National Park

fully decorated with en-suite facilities. Accommodations are at the
foot of a rocky *kopje* (small hill)
that look out towards plains in the
foreground and mountains in the
background. It's all about personal
service and individual attention
here. The slate, stone, and thatch

> ## PARK ESSENTIALS
>
> If you are only here for a day, you
> can buy a day permit (US$40 per
> adult, US$20 per child).

bar and restaurant with rustic wooden furniture is surrounded by flowering plants and trees—you can't help but feel immediately at home
here. Food is homemade, often homegrown and delicious. The camp
doesn't offer game drives, but you can go for a walk in the bush, climb
up the kopje, or just sit with the tipple of your choice and watch the
spectacular sunsets. ■ TIP→The plus side? Rock Side is cheap because it's
not in the actual park. The down side? It doesn't offer activities. ⌂ *Box 5,
Voi, Kenya* ☎*043/30–028 or 043/30–233* ⊕*www.westermannssafa-
ricamp.com* ⇰*16 bandas, 5 cottages* ⼕*In-hotel: bar, restaurant, pool*
▤*AC, DC, MC, V* ⼌*FAP.*

PERMANENT TENTED CAMPS

$$ ⊡**Patrick Reynolds's Mobile Camp at Tiva River.** If you're looking for
personally conducted walking tours and game drives, then this small
tented camp—open from June to October—in the remote northern part
of the park will hit the spot. Seasoned safari guide Patrick Reynolds
will introduce you to the rich ecosystems along the river and delight
you with his seemingly bottomless store of knowledge and anecdotes.
Tents are comfortable and spacious with a wooden bed, camp chair,
shower, and toilet. While you're on the mobile safari you'll also be
comfortable on thick mattresses on fly camp beds. You'll enjoy simple,
home-cooked meals to the sound of the dawn chorus, or by flickering
flames under a star-studded sky. ⌂ *Box 56923, Nairobi* ☎*020/600–
457* ⊕*www.bush-and-beyond.com* ⇰*6 tents* ⼕*In-hotel: bar,* ▤*AC,
DC, MC, V* ⼌*FAP.*

$ ⊡**Crocodile Camp.** The main attraction at this tented camp, which is on
the outskirts of Tsavo East with a great view over the Galana River, is
the nightly crocodile feeding—staff members call individual crocs by
name and throw food to them. The tents, surrounded by well-tended
gardens, are small but comfortable with a/c (which you probably won't
need), twin beds, and en-suite bathroom. If you want a hot shower,
make sure you have it when there's electricity—5 PM until dawn. Suites
are roomier than the tents and have en-suite bathrooms and a veranda
with a view. Relax on the patio outside the attractive thatch bar and
dining area, or take a dip in the small pool. It can sometimes get cold
at night, so pack a jacket or sweater. This area along the river is green
and fertile and home to lots of game, from predators to herbivores,
and there are hundreds of bird species including lots of eagles. ⌂ *Box
90653, Mombasa* ☎*41/548–5520* ⊕*www.africansafariclub.com*
⇰*16 tents, 4 suites* ⼕*In-hotel: bar, restaurant, pool* ▤*AC, DC, MC,
V* ⼌*FAP.*

$ ⊡**Satao Camp.** This small and friendly camp, owned and run by Ann
☾ and Trevor Jennings, lies on a traditional migration route, so it's not

3

Galdessa

Salt Lick Safari Lodge

Galdessa

short of game. It's not short on comfort either. You'll stay in one of 20 tents (quite close to one another, so don't expect perfect privacy), each with its own veranda. All are built under individual thatch canopies and shaded by ancient tamarind trees. There's a handmade bed inside your green canvas tent, with lots of attractive African-patterned soft furnishings. The bathrooms are en-suite with flush toilet and a bucket shower, which the attentive staff makes sure is hot and ready when you are. The food is wholesome and fresh, and it's great to sit under the 200-year-old tamarind tree and watch the elephants at the waterhole. There's a thatch viewing deck on stilts where you can sit and read, catch up on your journal, or just watch, wait, and see what walks up. There's an attractive dining area under thatch, but lunch is usually taken alfresco under the trees. Kids under 2 stay free, and those 2–12 are only $38. ⌂ *Box 90653, Mombasa* ☎ *011/47–5074 or 011/47–5075* ⊕ *www.sataocamp.com* ⇥ *16 tents, 4 suites* ⌂ *In-hotel: bar, restaurant, pool* ▤ *AC, DC, MC, V* ⏀ *FAP.*

BUDGET LODGINGS

¢ 🏨 **Voi Safari Lodge.** You can't beat the view and the price at this rather characterless lodge. Situated on top of a hill with panoramic views of the surrounding wilderness, and, when there's water, of a very busy waterhole where elephants come to drink, bathe, and play. If they are there, you'll get a great view of the tuskers (a colloquial name for elephants) from the underground blind. Rooms are small and basic, with two beds, mosquito nets, and an en-suite shower and flush toilet. The buffet food is pleasant with a good choice of dishes. The bar area is built on different levels providing for great views of the plains. There's plenty of game in the surrounding areas, so forget about the rather dull accommodations—after a day chasing over the plains all you'll want is a cold beer and a clean comfortable bed, and that's what you'll get. ⌂ *Tsavo Safari Camp East, Nairobi 30471* ☎ *020/233–6858* ⊕ *www. africanmeccasafaris.com* ⇥ *52 rooms* ⌂ *In-hotel: bar, restaurant, pool* ▤ *AC, DC, MC, V* ⏀ *FAP.*

¢ 🏨 **Voi Wildlife Lodge.** Set in 25 acres on the boundary of Tsavo East
♻ National Park, this resort lodge—only 5 km (3 mi) off Nairobi/Mombasa Highway, a four-hour drive from Nairobi, and a two-hour drive from Mombasa—is a good place to combine with a beach holiday. Don't expect perfect peace and tranquility though, as it's a popular family destination (kids under 2 stay free, 2–12 at half price). Apart from the obligatory game drives, which are extra but always action-packed and fruitful, there's plenty to do at the lodge. The viewing deck is a great place to spot game any time of day and night. If you're feeling active, there are pool, badminton, and table tennis, a pool with a poolside Jacuzzi, and aerobics classes at the inviting spa. Bringing the kids? Ask about the babysitting services. There are also a children's play area outside and a discovery room inside with wildlife DVDs and games. Accommodations include comfortable African-theme en-suite rooms or an en-suite tent that'll give you the feeling of camping. There are specially designed rooms for physically handicapped people near the lobby. ⌂ *Box 63048, Nairobi* ☎ *020/273–7133* ⊕ *www.voi*

wildlifelodge.com ⤲*72 rooms* &*In-hotel: bar, restaurant, pool, spa, curio shop* ▭*AC, DC, MC, V* |○|*BP.*

NATIONAL PARKS ACCOMMODATIONS

There are public campsites at the main gate of the park, but they don't have facilities. Visitors must bring everything with them from camping gear to water. Unless you're a hardcore camper they are not really an option.

TSAVO WEST

LUXURY LODGES

$ 🍴**Kilaguni Lodge.** Recently renovated, this lovely old lodge has a special place in Kenya's safari history as it was Kenya's first lodge to be built in a national park. Timber, stone, and thatch buildings complement the natural wilderness surroundings and when it's not wreathed in clouds, there's a good view of Mt. Kilimanjaro. You can watch game and birds from any one of several viewing decks, or enjoy a drink in the bar carved out of rocks. En-suite rooms are decorated in the ubiquitous African-theme fabrics, but are comfortable and spacious. Buffet meals with plenty of variety are way above the average. You can book all sorts of activities at the lodge including morning and afternoon game drives, bush breakfasts and dinners, and guided walks. ⌂*Box 48690, Nairobi* ☎*050/22059 or 020/284–2000* ⊕*www.serenahotels. com* ⤲*56 rooms* &*In-hotel: bar, restaurant, pool* ▭*AE, DC, MC, V* |○|*FAP.*

$ 🍴**Sarova Salt Lick Game Lodge.** Set in the Taita Hills just outside the park is this uniquely designed lodge—it looks like something the Hobbits might have created, but aboveground not below it. Honey-color rondawels with dark brown thatch roofs looking a little like overgrown pepper pots sit high above the ground on stilts and overlook a chain of small floodlighted waterholes. You may feel you're in the middle of a fantasy, but this is real Africa—there is a lot of big game just outside your door. After dark, when everyone is safely inside the resort, a wooden drawbridge is ceremoniously drawn up—suddenly it's no longer Hobbits but Lord of the Rings. The en-suite round rooms are comfortably if basically furnished, but it's the experience you're here for not the room decor, although the public areas are sumptuously decorated with rugs, batiks, and a number of authentic African artifacts. Request a top room or one over a waterhole for a close-up encounter with elephants, buffalos, and lots of other game. Be sure to visit the underground viewing room at night, because you've a better chance of spotting nocturnal animals like civets, porcupine, and maybe even a leopard. The food is excellent with lots of fresh homegrown vegetables. ⌂*Taita Hills Wildlife Sanctuary, Box 30624, Nairobi* ☎*43/30270 or 43/30250* ⊕*www.saltlicklodge. com* ⤲*96 rooms* &*In-hotel: bar, restaurant, pool, shop* ▭*AE, DC, MC, V* |○|*FAP.*

> **PARK ESSENTIALS**
>
> If you are only visiting for the day, you can buy a permit (US$40 per adult, US$20 per child).

PERMANENT TENTED CAMPS

$$ ⊡ **Finch Hattons.** If you saw the movie *Out of Africa,* then you'll have some idea, even if it's rather over-romanticized, of who Denys Finch Hatton was. At the turn of the 20th century he left his native England and fell in love not only with Karen Blixen, but also with Kenya. A big game hunter and host extraordinaire, he soon cultivated a reputation for leading classy, exclusive safaris for British and American tycoons and British royalty, among others. His legend lives on in this superb tented camp—frequently voted "Best Tented Camp in Africa" by top writers and travelers—where your every whim is catered to, your every dream of Africa comes true, and where you'll dine at a table sparkling with silver and crystal as strains of Mozart (Denys's favorite composer) softly fill the African night. The camp is in groves of old acacia trees near the Kenya/Tanzania border. The tents are elegantly and luxuriously furnished with antique furniture, wooden chests, and even a daybed on your personal veranda. Save your pennies, it's expensive, but this lodge is worth it. ⌂ *Box 24423, Nairobi* ☎ *20/553–237 or 20/351–8391* ⊕ *www.finchhattons.com* ⇔ *50 tents* ⌂ *In-hotel: bar, restaurant, pool* ▤ *AE, DC, MC, V* ⋈ *FAP.*

BUDGET LODGING

¢ ⊡ **Ngulia Safari Lodge.** High on the edge of the Ndawe escarpment with
⟳ panoramic views of the plains below, this unassuming but attractive lodge offers all the generic game park activities (not included) plus spacious en-suite rooms all overlooking the wide savanna. Thatch and wood bandas raised just above ground level, each with its own veranda, blend in aesthetically with the bush environment. Inside they have tiled floors and snazzy brightly colored soft furnishings. There are an inviting pool surrounded by flowering shrubs and trees, two inviting bars, and a restaurant with good home-cooked food. Because the lodge is in the park, you don't have to travel far to see lots of big game: lions, cheetahs, a leopard if you're lucky, elephants, buffalos, and hundreds of pretty little gazelles. ⌂ *Box 82082, Mombasa* ☎ *866/527–4281 U.S. toll-free reservations* ⊕ *www.africanmeccasafaris.com* ⇔ *52 rooms* ⌂ *In-hotel: bar, restaurant, pool* ▤ *AE, DC, MC, V* ⋈ *FAP.*

NATIONAL PARKS ACCOMMODATIONS

Public campsites are run by the local Masai communities, but because there are no facilities this is really not an option, unless you're a hard-core camper.

$ ⊡ **Kamboyo Guest House.** This reasonably priced, self-catering government guesthouse is 8 km (5 mi) from the Mtito Andei Gate, an easy 240-km (149-mi) drive from Nairobi. Built of red brick and red tiles, it has three clean, sparsely furnished bedrooms. Linens and basic kitchen implements are provided; bring drinking water and firewood. You are allowed up to 10 guests; it's a bit of a squash, but worth it for the proximity to attractions such as Mzima Springs. Book early at the lodge or Kenya Wildlife Service. ⌂ *The Senior Warden, Box 71, Mtito Andei, Kenya* ☎ *0456/22483* ⊕ *www.kws.org* ⇔ *1 guesthouse* ⌂ *In-hotel: kitchen* ▤ *AE, DC, MC, V* ⋈ *Self-catering.*

3

LAIKIPIA PLATEAU

Game

☆★★★★

Park Accessibility
☆★★★★

Ease of Getting
Around
☆☆★★★

Accommodations
☆☆★★★

Scenic Beauty

☆★★★★

Stretching all the way to Ethiopia and the Sudan, Laikipia Plateau, gateway to Kenya's little-visited northern territory, is not in itself a national park or reserve, but it has become one of Kenya's most recent conservation successes. This is primeval Eden without hordes of game vehicles and flashing, whirring cameras.

Amid spectacular scenery, traditional ways of pastoral life continue side by side with an abundance of free-roaming game. Comprising a series of privately owned farms and ranches in an area roughly half the size of Wales, it's rapidly becoming a major tourist destination. In 1992 the Laikipia Wildlife Forum (⊕ *www.laikipia.com*) was formed to combine the interests and efforts of both the privately owned ranches and the communal landowning local communities. Local communities banded together to form their own big ranches and have managed to keep up a traditional way of life as well as embracing tourism. A rewarding by-product of this development has been to foster both cultural identity and community solidarity. This is high country, with altitudes from 1,700 meters (5,577 feet) to 2,600 meters (8,530 feet), so bring those sweaters and jackets. Habitats range from arid semi-desert, scrubland, and sprawling open plains in the north and south, to the thick forests of cedar and olive trees in the east. Two rivers, the Ewaso Ng'iro and Ewasa Narok, dominate the area, which also includes the Laikipia National Reserve and the Lewa Wildlife Conservancy. The area around the Laikipia National Reserve has one of the biggest and most diverse mammal populations in Kenya—only the Masai Mara can boast more game. The Big Five, including black and white rhino, are all present, plus the wide-ranging wild dogs; there's even a chance of seeing the rare aquatic sitatunga antelope. Also keep an eye out for Grevy's zebra, which is more narrowly striped than its southern cousin. It was once hunted almost to extinction for its fine desirable skin, but is reestablishing itself well in the area with a growing population. If you can, a visit to one of Kenya's last great true wilderness areas is a must before it becomes as crowded as some of the better-known reserves and parks farther south.

SAMBURU NATIONAL RESERVE

In the far north of the Plateau, north of Mount Kenya, is the remote Samburu National Reserve. It's highly regarded by experienced travelers and old Africa hands alike as perhaps the best reserve in Kenya. The drive from the foothills of Mount Kenya into the semi-desert is awesome, and where the road follows the river, you'll be treated to the unusual spectacle of riverine bush and forest on the one side, and desert on the other. Again, there's game galore, if you don't spot at least one lion, cheetah, or leopard, or even all three—in addition to giraffe, hippo, antelope, elephant, baboons, vervet monkeys, oryx, and zebra—you might want to get your eyes tested because this whole area hasn't yet become as commercialized as those along the Kenya/Tanzanian border. You'll be privy to a genuine traditional way of life as you watch the red-robed Samburu tribesmen, former kin to the Masai, bringing their cattle down to the river to drink. The lives of the Samburu, like their kinsmen, are centered round their livestock, their traditional source of wealth. After initiation, boys become *morans* (warriors) whose role it is to protect both humans and livestock from drought, famine, and predators. In Samburu don't be surprised to come across the native camels padding along through the arid savanna.

Unless you've lots and lots of time, however, it's not a good idea to attempt these far northern areas on your own. Choose one of the many superb private lodges instead, which will look after your transport arrangements from Nairobi. All this exclusivity and abundance of game doesn't come cheap, but it's worth spending more to experience more—your game viewing will be personal, intimate, and extremely rewarding.

WHERE TO STAY

LUXURY LODGES

$$ 🏠 **Laragai House.** For a once-in-a-lifetime experience of doing things like the Old Colonials once did, then consider booking this opulent thatch-and-stone family home that's furnished with antiques, imported furniture, fine china and crystal, and beautiful paintings and is surrounded by gorgeous manicured gardens. The staff is hard to better in terms of service and friendliness. Alas you can only stay here when the owners are not in residence, but it's worth waiting for. It sleeps 12 people in ultimate luxury, and there's extra room if necessary for kids and guides. ⌂ *Box 24133, Nairobi* ☎ *020/600–457 or 020/605–108* ⊕ *www.borana. co.ke* 🛏 *10 rooms* 🏊 *In-hotel: pool* ☰ *MC, V* ⦿ *Self-catering.*

> **WORD OF MOUTH**
>
> "Samburu is a very arid region in northern Kenya, not far from the Somalia border. The fauna there is quite unique. You can see Grevy's zebra, reticulated giraffes, gerenuk, and oryx. The reticulated giraffe are really the most beautiful—their body markings and colors make them so elegant."
>
> –Mohammed

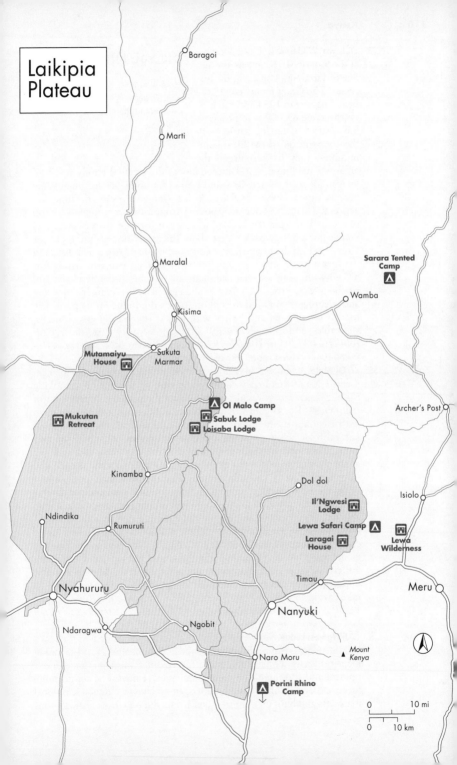

Laikipia
Plateau

Baragoi

Marti

Maralal

Sarara Tented
Camp

Wamba

Kisima

Mutamaiyu
House

Sukuta
Marmar

Ol Malo Camp

Sabuk Lodge

Loisaba Lodge

Archer's Post

Mukutan
Retreat

Kinamba

Dol dol

Isiolo

Il'Ngwesi
Lodge

Ndindika

Rumuruti

Lewa Safari Camp

Laragai
House

Lewa
Wilderness

Nyahururu

Timau

Meru

Ndaragwa

Ngobit

Nanyuki

Naro Moru

Mount
Kenya

Porini Rhino
Camp

0   10 mi

0   10 km

$$ ⊡ **Lewa Wilderness.** Lewa Downs, at the foot of Mt. Kenya, is another one of Laikipia's conservation successes. The Craig family emigrated from England in 1924 and still lives on the same 65,000-acre property, but instead of raising cattle, with the cooperation of the local communities, they have returned the

> **DID YOU KNOW?**
>
> More than three-quarters of all Kenya's game is found on private land, not in the national parks and reserves.

area to a wildlife haven. Descendants of the original family will lead you on all sorts of activities and claim that you'll see as much game here as almost anywhere else in Africa. Game drives are thrilling and action-packed, but try game-spotting from a different angle—on top of a camel or from the back of a horse, or on your own two feet. (If you've got a dodgy back forget about the camel riding.) Look out for Grevy's zebra, the more elegant cousin of the regular plains zebra, and the rare aquatic sitatunga antelope. The cottages are attractively furnished with a big wooden bed, hand-carved chests, comfy chairs and an en-suite bathroom. Hot water and electricity are available morning and evening; if you need to cool off, take a dip in the lovely pool. The food is wholesome and hearty with lots of organically grown herbs, vegetables, and fruit. ⌂ *Lewa Wildlife Conservancy, Box 10607, Nairobi* ☎ *64/31405 or 20/607–197* ⊕ *www.lewa.org* ⊅ *8 cottages* ⚐ *In-hotel: tennis court, pool* ▭ *MC, V* ⊙ *FAP.*

$$ ⊡ **Ol Malo.** Choose a luxurious tent or a thatch cottage perched on
☾ a cliff edge at this lovely camp to the west of Samburu overlooking Mount Kenya. You'll find yourself under the personal supervision of the owners, Rocky and Colin Francombe. Spacious and elegant tents with elephant-theme interiors have en-suite bathrooms made out of natural rock, while the stone and thatch cottages, some built on two levels, have king-size beds and baths that you can lie in and look out at the passing wildlife. The main lodge also built of natural rock and olive wood is cozy and comfortable. There's also a huge pool, which clings to the rock edge, spilling its waters to the rocks below. Drives are extremely rewarding with game galore, but for something a little different try a camel ride (not for bad backs), a nature walk, an overnight stay in the Look Out Hut—a little wooden hut in the bush—or go camping under the stars. Horseback riding is a fascinating way to spot game: there are also safe and friendly ponies for kids, and children's gift packs on arrival, plus other activities for kids. There's also the opportunity to meet and mix with the local Samburu people and to take part in some of their activities. ⌂ *Box 30 Rumuruti, Kenya 20321* ☎ *20/600–457* ⊕ *www.olmalo.com* ⊅ *4 cottages, 2 tents* ⚐ *In-hotel: bar, restaurant, pool* ▭ *AE, DC, MC, V* ⊙ *FAP.*

$ ⊡ **Il'Ngwesi Lodge.** Situated on a rocky outcrop in the north of the Lewa Wildlife Conservancy, this intimate and environmental award–winning lodge prides itself on its successful efforts to integrate community development and sustainable environmental management. The comfortably furnished open-walled bandas with open-air showers are made of local materials and built on a slope—their fronts rest on wooden stilts—thus

3

Sabuk

Sabuk

Il'Ngwesi Lodge

giving uninterrupted views of the surrounding wilderness. Make sure you take the opportunity to sit out at the main lodge and watch the waterhole below or cool off in the horizon pool, which gently flows down into the bush below; water is gravity-piped from a nearby natural spring. You'll see plenty of game including lion, leopard, cheetah, hyena, the elusive wild dog, and large herds of elephant and buffalo, plus the plains game. Learn about hunting, gathering honey, animal trapping with indigenous poisons, or fashioning beadwork with the local Masai at the nearby Masai Cultural Manyatta. You won't want to miss the dancing of the warriors and maidens—it's the genuine article. ✉ *Box 263, Timau 1042, Kenya* ☎ *62/31–830* ⊕ *www.ilngwesi.com* 🛏 *6 bandas* ♿ *In-hotel: bar, pool, restaurant* ▭ *MC, V* ⦿ *FAP.*

$ ⛶ **Loisaba Lodge.** This lodge sits plumb in the middle of the game-rich Laikipia Plateau on a 300-meter (984-foot) plateau that looks south to Mt. Kenya with stunning views of the Laikipia plains. Built of cedar, stone, and wood, this lovely lodge is nestled among gardens of aloes, succulents, and flowering trees. From the veranda of your en-suite room, gaze out at the dizzying views or just watch the waterhole below with its passing show of animals. If you fancy something even more special, opt for one of the Star Beds (closed in November), which have been created with the local community. Don't expect a meager stretcher under the stars. You'll stay in an en-suite room with thatch roof, handcrafted furniture, and wooden floors set among big rocks overlooking waterholes. Every evening your friendly and attentive Laikipia Masai attendants will wheel out your double bed onto the platform under the star-studded clear night sky, where carefully shrouded under a mosquito net, you can watch the world turn. If you're looking for something even more different, go for a quad bike ride. It's not only a thrilling experience but also contributes directly to sponsoring a classroom for the local kids. ✉ *Cheli & Peacock, Box 743, Uhuru Gardens, Nairobi* ☎ *020/603–054 or 603–090* ⊕ *www.loisaba.com* 🛏 *7 rooms, 8 star beds* ♿ *In-hotel: bar, pool, spa, tennis court* ▭ *AE, DC, MC, V* ⦿ *FAP.*

$ ⛶ **Mukutan Retreat.** If you read and cried over Kuki Gallman's best seller *I Dreamed of Africa,* then you'll recognize the name of this lovely lodge on the Mukutan River in the northwest of the Laikipia Plateau. You're ensured of privacy for that romantic getaway or special occasion in one of only three cottages built of stone, wood, and papyrus, with uniquely designed interiors set among lush gardens. The homegrown food is delicious, choose from an Italian or classic Indian vegetarian cuisine, then relax in the elegant, luxurious main building, also built of organic local materials. Take a yoga or meditation class in between your game drives where you're likely to see the rare black rhino as well as lots of other game. ✉ *Box 45593, Nairobi* ☎ *020/520–799* ⊕ *www.gallmannkenya.org* 🛏 *3 cottages* ♿ *In-hotel: pool, spa* ▭ *AE, DC, MC, V* ⦿ *FAP.*

$ ⛶ **Mutamaiyu House.** This family-owned house is at the northern end of the Laikipia Plateau on the 49,000-acre Mugie Ranch. It garners rave reviews from its guests, many of whom are repeat visitors. You'll stay in one of four thatch and stone cottages brightly furnished with handmade rugs and bedspreads, original African artifacts and flagstone floors. The food is first class, made with lots of homegrown ingredients. The comforting and inviting spacious main lounge has a crackling log fire on those chilly nights; when the sun is shining relax by the big pool and look out over the far-stretching wilderness. On your game drives you could see all of the Big Five, including the endangered black rhino, which has been successfully reintroduced to the area. ⌂ *Box 30, Rumuruti, Kenya 20321* ☎*062/31–043* ⊕*www.mutamaiyu.com* ⌖*4 cottages* ⌂*In-hotel: bar, pool* ⊟*AE, DC, MC, V* ⎮⊙⎮*FAP.*

$ ⬚**Sabuk Lodge.** This lodge organically created out of local thatch, stone, and wood clings to a hillside on the northwest of the Laikipia Plateau. Overlooking the ever-flowing Ewaso N'giro River you'll enjoy spectacular views and great hospitality. In between activities, lie on your uniquely designed handcrafted big bed in your charming open-fronted room and gaze out at the river below. If you can't tear yourself away from the view, then just move into the bathroom, slip in the deep stone bath, flip water over the edge to the rocks below and stay gazing. The comfortable main open-sided lodge ensures you're never far away from those memorable views. On chilly nights a roaring log fire keeps you cozy and warm. Food is plentiful, fresh, and delicious with superb breakfasts on the viewing deck. Spend a night out under the stars at a fly camp after a day's camel safari (no camel-riding for dodgy backs), go walking, birding, or fishing or try tubing down the river. Game is plentiful and you should see elephants, lions, leopards, giraffe, Grevy's and plains zebras, and much, much more. Because there are no fences, the game can wander at will. ■TIP➙ **The camp is closed from Easter until the end of May.** ⌂*Cheli & Peacock, Box 743, Uhuru Gardens, Nairobi* ☎*020/603–054 or 020/603–090/1* ⊕*www.sabuklodge.com* ⌖*5 cottages* ⌂*In-hotel: bar, pool* ⊟*AE, DC, MC, V* ⎮⊙⎮*FAP.*

PERMANENT TENTED CAMPS

$$$ ⬚**Porini Rhino Camp.** Opened in summer 2007, this delightful eco-
★ friendly tented camp is nestled among Kenya's ubiquitous *acacia tortilis* trees in a secluded valley in the Ol Pejeta Conservancy. This 90,000-acre stretch of game-rich wilderness lies between the snow-capped Mt. Kenya and the foothills of the Aberdares. This location treats guests to a double whammy—abundant game including the Big Five and the endangered black rhino and superb views across the open plains. Each beautifully placed tent has stunning views from its personal veranda, and inside there's an en-suite bathroom with flush toilet and bucket shower with hot water heated by solar power. Sip sundowners from a carefully chosen vantage point, and then take a spectacular night drive. By day stretch your legs on a guided bush walk with a Masai guide or have your heartstrings tugged at the nearby Sweetwaters Chimpanzee Sanctuary. If you're feeling extra energetic and really want to walk on the wild side, then the camp also offers walking safaris. ⌂*Box 388, Village Market 00621, Nairobi* ☎*020/712–2504 or 020/712–3129* ⊕*www.porini.com* ⌖*6 tents* ⊟*MC, V* ⎮⊙⎮*FAP.*

$$ ⬚**Lewa Safari Camp.** If it's rhinos you're after, then this delightful, but small tented camp in the 65,000-acre Lewa Conservancy, right where the old Rhino Sanctuary headquarters used to stand, is for you. There's

a comfortable main building for eating and relaxing, but to see all those rhino, sit out on the wide veranda and watch them come to drink at the waterhole along with elephants and lots of other game. Spacious tents protected by a sturdy thatch roof have comfortable beds, a desk for keeping up on those precious journal notes, a personal veranda that looks out over lush green lawns. The food, as elsewhere in the conservancy, is homegrown and tasty. Bird-watching is spectacular in this area, but it's possible that while you're watching out for feathered friends, you're likely to spot big game as well, including lions. Burn up some calories and have a unique experience at the same time by going on a guided game walk. 🖾 *Lewa Wildlife Conservancy, Box 10607, Nairobi* 🕾*64/31405 or 20/607–197* ⊕*www.lewa.org* 🛏*9 cottages* ⚘*In-hotel: pool* ▤*MC, V* ♨*FAP.*

> ## BRINGING UP THE CHIMPS
>
> In 1993 Lonrho Africa, the Kenya Wildlife Services, and the Jane Goodall Institute opened the Sweetwaters Chimpanzee Sanctuary to house three chimps orphaned by the bush meat trade. Today, the sanctuary, located in the Ol Pejeta Conservancy, has 40 chimps in its protection. The primates are housed in two areas: the eastern side (96 acres) for the older chimps and the western side (151 acres) for the young ones. It costs about $6,000 a year to take care of each chimpanzee. To find out how you can visit the sanctuary or help to support them, visit ⊕ www.olpejetaconservancy.org.

$$ 🖾**Sarara Tented Camp.** This small, tented camp lies below the peaks of the Mathews Mountains in the 75,000-acre Namunyuk Wildlife Conservation Trust, a community project between landowners and the local Samburu people. Accommodation is in five spacious tents, sited under pole-supported thatch roofs with flush toilets and open-air showers. The main banda sits on stilts overlooking a busy waterhole and natural rock pool—yes, you swim here but it's not close to the waterhole and you are quite safe—with stunning views of the Mathews Mountains. Game is plentiful with resident lion and leopard, and there's an excellent chance of seeing wild dog as there are two packs in the area. Look out for the attractive colobus monkeys when you go for a guided hike in the forest. Go donkey-trekking in the mountains, or take a camel safari with an overnight stop at a fly camp. ■TIP➜**The camp is closed April 15 through the end of May, as well as November.** 🖾*Bush-and Beyond, Box 10607, Nairobi* 🕾*020/600–457* ⊕*www.lewa.org* 🛏*5 tents* ⚘*In-hotel: pool* ▤*AE, DC, MC, V* ♨*FAP.*

NATIONAL PARKS ACCOMMODATIONS

There's a campsite next to Samburu Lodge, but as elsewhere in Kenya, campsites have few or no facilities and are not really an option for a visitor with time restrictions or first timers.

IF YOU HAVE TIME

Although we've gone into great detail about the must see parks in Kenya, there are many others to explore if you have time. Here, we mention a few good ones to explore.

NAIROBI NATIONAL PARK

The most striking thing about Nairobi National Park, Kenya's oldest national park, is not a mountain or a lake, but the very fact that it exists at all. This sliver of unspoiled Africa survives on the edge of a city of almost 3 million people. Where else can you get a photo of animals in their natural habitat with skyscrapers in the background? As you travel into the city from Jomo Kenyatta International Airport, you're likely to see gazelles grazing near the highway.

A 20-minute drive from downtown Nairobi (7 km [4 mi]) the park is tiny compared to Kenya's other game parks and reserves; it covers only 117 square km (44 square mi). It's characterized by open plains that slope gently from west to east and rocky ridges that are covered with rich vegetation. Seasonal streams run southeast into the Mbagathi Athi River, which is lined with yellow fever and acacia trees. In the west the river runs through a deep gorge where rocky outcrops are the favored habitat of leopards.

Fences separate the park from the nearby communities of Langata and Karen, but they do not always prevent the occasional leopard or lion from snacking on a dog or horse. This is because of an open corridor to the south that allows wildebeest and other animals to move to other areas in search of food; researchers believe the annual migration in this area was once as spectacular as that in the Serengeti.

Despite the urban pressures, the park contains a good variety of wildlife especially during the dry season. Animals migrate here from other areas knowing that there's always a source of permanent water. You can see the Big Five, minus elephants as the area is not big enough to support them. ■TIP➜ If you want to see baby elephants, visit the David Sheldrick Elephant Orphanage close to the main entrance of the park. Zebras, elands, impalas, and Grant's and Thomson's gazelles are well represented. Warthogs and ostriches are common on the open plains. Larger game includes Masai giraffes, which browse in the woodland, and a herd of 50 black rhinos, sometimes found in the light bush around the forest area; black rhinos have been particularly successful here because it has been easier to keep track of and control poachers. Hippos can be spied in the larger pools of the Mbagathi Athi River as well as from a nature trail in the eastern section of the park. In the extreme western border of the park, a low ridge covered by a stand of hardwood trees is home to herds of bushbucks and impalas as well as some of the park's olive baboons. Impala Point, at the edge of the ridge, makes a good vantage point to scan the plains with binoculars for concentrations of game.

Predators include about 30 resident lions—you've an excellent chance of seeing a lion kill—and cheetahs. Rangers keep a careful note of the movements of the larger animals, so it is worth asking at the gate where to look for lions or rhinos.

More than 500 species of permanent and migratory birds have been spotted in the park. Around the dams used to create marshes you will find Egyptian geese, crowned cranes, yellow and saddle-billed storks, herons, African spoonbills, sacred ibis, hammerkops, Kittlitz's sand plovers, and marabou storks. In the plains look for secretary birds, vultures, helmeted guinea fowls, bustards, yellow-throated sand grouse, larks, pipits, and Jackson's widow birds, which display their long tails and attractive plumage during the long rains in May and June. The forests hold cuckoo shrikes, sunbirds, waxbills, flycatchers, and warblers.

The park's network of paved and all-weather dirt roads can be negotiated by cars and vans, and junctions are generally signposted and clearly marked on the official park map, which you can pick up at the gate or any bookstore or tourist office. Open-roof hatches are not permitted in the park. Do not leave your vehicle except where permitted, as unsuspecting tourists have been mauled by lions and attacked by rhinos. ■TIP➜There are no accommodations inside the park. ⌂Kenya Wildlife Service, Box 40241, Nairobi ☎02/501–081 ⊕www.kws.org ✉$40 ⊙Daily 6 AM–7 PM.

MERU NATIONAL PARK

Situated 370 km (230 mi) northeast of Nairobi and west of Mount Kenya, this little-visited park (1,810 square km [699 square mi]) offers some of Kenya's wildest country, but was taken off the mainstream safari circuit and deleted from safari operators' destination lists because of the lawless poachers who wiped out the white rhino population in the 1980s. Although the Kenyan government has gotten grips on the security situation, the park still finds it difficult to shake off its negative image. But rest assured that all is now well and the park is a safe and fulfilling destination—after all, this is the place where wildlife champions Joy and George Adamson hand-reared Elsa the lioness made famous by the 1966 film, *Born Free*.

A successful rehabilitation program reintroduced elephants and rhinos to the park in 2001; both populations are doing well. There is a lot of other game here, including buffalo, lion, leopard, cheetah, hippo, lesser kudu, hartebeest (grassland antelope), Grevy's and Burchell's zebra, the gerenuk (a mini-giraffe), the reticulated or Somali giraffe, waterbuck, oryx, and Grant's gazelle. The park is part of an ecosystem that includes Kora National Park and Mwingi, Rahole, and Bisanadi reserves. It straddles the equator and is home to a great variety of habitats including scrubland dotted with baobab trees, lush green grasslands, and riverine forests. Tana, Kenya's longest river, is fed by 13 rivers that create a superb habitat for bird life as well. Check out the Somali ostrich, raptors such as the red-necked falcon and the palmnut

Continued on page 122

Blue wildebeest in Tanzania's Serengeti National Park

THE GREAT MIGRATION

by Kate
Turkington

Nothing will prepare you for the spectacle that is the Great Migration. This annual journey of more than 2 million animals is a safari-seeker's Holy Grail, the ultimate in wildlife experiences. Some say it's one of the world's greatest natural wonders.

The greater Serengeti ecosystem, which includes Kenya's Masai Mara (north) and Tanzania's Serengeti (south), is the main arena for this awesome sight. At the end of each year during the short rains—November to early December—the herds disperse into the southeast plains of Tanzania's Seronera. After calving early in the new year (wildebeests drop up to 8,000 babies a day), huge numbers of animals start the 800-km (497-mi) trek from these now bare southeast plains to lush northern pastures. On the way they will face terrible, unavoidable danger. In June and July braying columns—40-km (25 miles) long—have to cross the crocodile-infested Grumeti River. Half of the great herds which successfully survive the crossing will stay in northern Tanzania, the other half will cross over into Kenya's Masai Mara. In early October the animals begin their return journey back to Seronera and come full circle, only to begin their relentless trek once again early the following year.

WHO'S MIGRATING

What will you see during the migration?

More than **2 million** wildebeest
250,000 Thompson's gazelle
200,000 zebra
70,000 impala
30,000 Grant's gazelle

In addition, huge numbers of predators follow the herds. You're likely to see lion, leopard, cheetah, jackal, hyena, and numerous smaller predators.

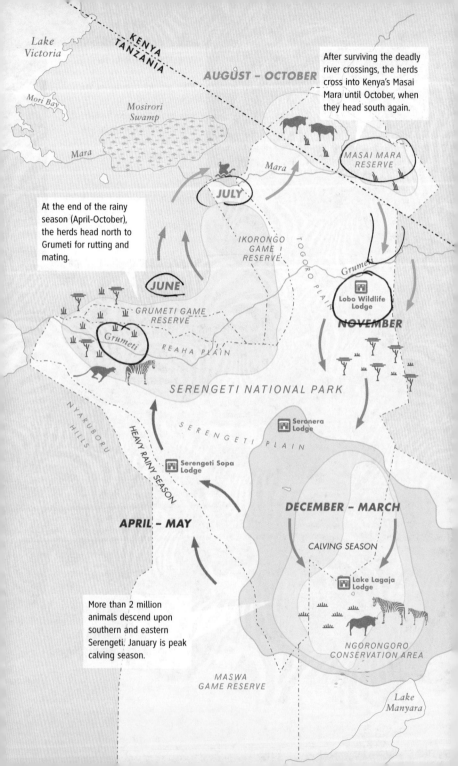

Lake Victoria

Mori Bay

KENYA
TANZANIA

Mara

Mosirori Swamp

AUGUST – OCTOBER

After surviving the deadly river crossings, the herds cross into Kenya's Masai Mara until October, when they head south again.

MASAI MARA RESERVE

Mara

JULY

At the end of the rainy season (April-October), the herds head north to Grumeti for rutting and mating.

IKORONGO GAME RESERVE

TOGORO PLAIN

JUNE

Grumeti

Lobo Wildlife Lodge

NOVEMBER

GRUMETI GAME RESERVE

REAHA PLAIN

Grumeti

SERENGETI NATIONAL PARK

NYARUBORU HILLS

SERENGETI PLAIN

Seronera Lodge

HEAVY RAINY SEASON

Serengeti Sopa Lodge

DECEMBER – MARCH

CALVING SEASON

APRIL – MAY

More than 2 million animals descend upon southern and eastern Serengeti. January is peak calving season.

Lake Lagaja Lodge

MASWA GAME RESERVE

NGORONGORO CONSERVATION AREA

Lake Manyara

DRIVEN BY DINNER

WHERE THE MAGIC HAPPENS

The Serengeti more then lives up to its awesome reputation as an amazing spot to see wildlife and it's here that the Great Migration begins and ends. The park's ecosystem supports some of the most abundant mammal populations left anywhere on earth and it covers almost 15,000 square km (9,320 square mi) of seemingly endless plains, riverine bush, forest and scrubland roughly the size of Northern Ireland or Connecticut. It stretches between the Ngorongoro highlands, Lake Victoria, and Tanzania's northern border with Kenya. It was named a UNESCO World Heritage Site in 1978 and an International Biosphere Reserve (a UNESCO international conservation area) in 1981.

WHEN TO GO

Because rainfall patterns are unpredictable, it's difficult to anticipate timings for the migration. But usually, by the beginning of each year, the grazing on the southeast plains of Serengeti's Seronera is exhausted and the herds start to move northwest into Tanzania's West-

WASHED UP

In 2007, because of heavy rains, rivers became swollen and almost impassable. Disoriented, the wildebeest mistimed the crossings and over 10,000 drowned. Bloated bodies washed up on the river banks for weeks afterwards and crocodiles were so sated they could hardly move.

ern Corridor. The actual crossing of the Grumeti River, usually between June and July, when an unrivalled bloody spectacle of terrified frantic wildebeest and huge lashing crocodiles unfolds, is a gruesome, unforgettable spectacle. You'll see hundreds of thousands of animals between March and November, including predators. Seronera in March, April and May is an ideal time for a safari because there are huge concentrations of predators preying on all the baby animals. Safaris are much cheaper between April and June, and although you may not witness the actual river crossings, you'll still be privy to prime game-viewing experiences. Plus there will be far fewer vehicles.

..ture, and that mega-score on serious birder's life list, the Pel's fishing owl, which hides in the huge ancient trees along the rivers. ⌂ *Kenya Wildlife Service, Box 11, Maua* ☏ *020/604–767* ⊕ *www. kws.org* ✉ *US$20 per day* ⊙ *Daily* 6AM–6 PM.

WHERE TO STAY

LUXURY LODGES

$$ 🏨 **Elsa's Kopje.** This camp was built on the same hill where George Adamson built Elsa's Camp, his first camp, which was named after the lioness he raised with his wife, author Joy Adamson. It's a strikingly attractive lodge both for its elevated position and for its imaginatively designed thatch cottages. Each cottage is unique, with boulders for walls, trees growing through the roof, lots of flowing water, and spacious interiors furnished with handcrafted furniture, hand-woven rugs, and earth-toned cushions, throws, and bedspreads. All the cottages have privacy, but if you're on honeymoon or want to be alone, choose the two cottages separated from the others by a suspension bridge. Watch the plains game ambling through the grasslands from your veranda, or go hunting predators or rhinos in open-sided game vehicles before sundowners at the palm-fringed hippo pools. The home-cooked, homegrown food is principally northern Italian, but if you're not a pasta person, there's plenty more to choose from. ⌂ *Box 39806, Nairobi* ☏ *20/60–4053* ⊕ *www.chelipeacock.com* 🛏 *9 cottages* △ *In-hotel: pool* ▤ *AE, DC, MC, V* ⦿ *FAP.*

$ **Leopard Rock Lodge.** Antique furniture, Persian rugs, and understated elegance characterize this exclusive lodge, which sprawls out along the banks of the Murera River. You'll stay in one of the thatch and wood bandas, with his-and-her en-suite bathrooms; or a family cottage or suite: all have stunning views. The food is superb even by high Kenyan standards, and there's a great wine list and open-air kitchen. The lodge offers a pottery workshop and an unforgettable pool that allows you to come safely nose-to-nose—there's a glass panel between the river and the pool—with crocs in the river. There's also a pool bar and Jacuzzi. ⌂ *Box 34464, Nairobi* ☏ *20/600–031* ⊕ *www. leopardmico.com* 🛏 *15 cottages, 5 family cottages, 10 suites* △ *In-hotel: pool, library* ▤ *AE, DC, MC, V* ⦿ *FAP.*

THE LAKES OF KENYA

In addition to its great game parks, Kenya is home to huge beautiful lakes that are often covered with uncountable flocks of flamingos. Here's just a snapshot of four of them.

3

LAKE NAIVASHA

One of the Rift Valley's few freshwater lakes, Lake Naivasha is a popular spot for day trips and weekends away from Nairobi as it's only about an hour and half by car. The pleasant forested surroundings, which are a far cry from the congestion and noise of Nairobi, are another big draw. Keep an eye out for the yellow fever trees, and the abundant populations of birds, monkeys, and hippos. Such an attractive location lured a group of settlers to build their homes on its shores. Known collectively as "White Mischief," these settlers were internationally infamous for their decadent, hedonistic lifestyle. A 1987 movie of the same name, starring Greta Schacci, was based on a notorious society murder set during this time.

Cross over by boat to Crescent Island Wildlife Sanctuary, where you can see giraffes, zebras, and other plains herbivores, but absolutely no predators. Need a pick-me-up or a place to stay while you're here? La Belle Inn (☎050/202–1007 ✉labelleinn@kenyaweb.co) is a great place for breakfast or a terrace sundowner. It also has a business center with Internet access. The Crater Lake Tented Camp (⊕www.heritage-eastafrica.com) is a classy place to stay with great views of the lake and the Lake Naivasha Simba Lodge (⊕www.marasimba.com), though primarily a conference center, has lovely grounds, big rooms, and loads of facilities.

LAKE NAKURU

If it's birds and flamingos you're after, then Lake Nakuru, 230 km (143 mi) northwest of Nairobi, hits the spot. You will find millions—yes, millions—of these engaging birds to gaze upon. From the air, and even when you see them from far off, the flamingos color the lake bright pink. There are also more than 400 other bird species here, plus incredible game including leopard, the endangered black rhino, and lots of plains game. The lake is in Lake Nakuru National Park, which you can drive around it in a few hours. The main road, which circles the lake, has the best game viewing. If you'd like to do an overnight, Lake Nakuru Lodge (⊕www.lakenakurulodge.com) and Sarova Lion Hill Game Lodge (⊕www.sarovahotels.com) are both on the lake. ☏Kenya Wildlife Service, Box 40241, Nairobi ☎020/600–800 ⊕www.kws.org ✉$40 ☺Daily 6 AM–6 PM.

LAKE TURKANA

The tip of Lake Turkana, in Kenya's northwest, runs into the Ethiopian highlands, but the rest of Kenya's biggest lake stretches for 250 km (155 mi) south. Sometimes called the Jade Lake because of its vivid

Kenya's Tribes

Kikuyu men and women with spears and traditional garb at Thompson's Falls.

KIKUYU

The Kikuyu account for almost 25% of the country's total population. Most Kikuyu live around Mount Kenya and because of the fertility of the land there, they have become largely a pastoralist people, farming the rich fields around the mountain and up in the Kenyan highlands.

The Mau Mau Rebellion (1952–58) was a sad time in Kikuyu—and Kenyan—history, with frustrations among Kenyan tribes towards the colonizing British resulting in guerilla warfare. During this time, many Kikuyu were killed and detained in British camps. This difficult era spurred the move towards independence and in 1964 Jomo Kenyatta, a Kikuyu, became Kenya's first president. Kenya's third president, Mwai Kibaki, is also Kikuyu, as is Nobel Peace prize winner and Greenbelt Movement Founder Wangari Maathai.

LUO

Mainly in Western Kenya, the Luo tribe is one of the country's largest accounting for about 15% of the population. Most members make their living through fishing and farming. The culture is rich in musical traditions and the sounds and melodies common in their music are said to be the basis for Kenya's modern pop music.

Today, the most well-known Luo is probably Raila Odinga, the top opposition party leader who ran against Mwai Kibaki in the much disputed 2007 presidential election. Odinga and Kibaki entered into a power-sharing government in early 2008.

MASAI

Known to be great warriors, the Masai are also largely associated with Kenya. This red-clad tribe is mainly found in Southern Kenya and Tanzania. To find out more about this ethnic group, *see* Tanzania's Tribes box *in* Chapter 4 green color, it's a shallow alkaline lake in the Great Rift Valley that has been drying up alarmingly over the past decade. Surprisingly, it's still home to the legendary giant Nile perch, huge herds of hippos and more Nile crocodiles than anywhere else in the world—more than 20,000 reside here. There's abundant birdlife with many European migrants wintering around its shores. Lobolo Camp (⊕www.bush-and-beyond. com) makes a good base and boats can be hired for US$250 per day. ⌖*Kenya Wildlife Service, Box 40241, Nairobi* ☎ ⊕*www.kws.org.*

LAKE VICTORIA

Kenya shares Africa's biggest freshwater lake with its neighbors, Uganda and Tanzania. Tanzania has the lion's share: 49%; Uganda has 45%; Kenya only 6%. The lake is so huge (68,000 square km [26,000 square mi]) that it has its own weather system with unpredictable storms, squalls, and high waters just like the ocean. The dhow was first introduced to Lake Victoria by Arab slave traders, and the local Luo shipbuilders quickly adopted the shape and lateen sail. You'll see fishing fleets of white-sailed dhows all over the lake, fishing mainly for the delicious Nile perch. These fish, which can reach the size of a fully grown shark, now account for about 80% of the fish in the lake. Their presence still arouses controversy. On the one hand, they are the basis for a multimillion dollar processing and export industry; on the other, scientists say they are destroying the lake's ecosystem. Kisumu, on Lake Victoria's shore, is the main town of Western Kenya, and Kenya's third largest, although it lacks the postindependence prosperity and development of Mombasa and Nairobi. It's got a bit of a run-down feel reminiscent of some of the small towns on the Indian Ocean coast. If you're a birder, head for Ndere Island National Park (⊙*Daily 6–6* ⊞*US$5*) or the Kisumu Bird Sanctuary (⊙*Dawn–dusk* ⊞*No fee*), both breeding grounds for hundreds of water birds. April to May is the best season. Mfangano Island Camp (⊕www.governorscamp.com) and Rusinga Island lodge (⊕www.rusinga.com) are top-of-the-range luxury lodges.

GATEWAY CITY

As Nairobi is Kenya's capital city and the main hub for visitors, it's very likely that you'll be spending an overnight in Nairobi between flights. The following information will help you plan those hours productively and safely.

NAIROBI

Updated by
Kate Turkington

The starting point for safaris since the days of Teddy Roosevelt and Ernest Hemingway, Nairobi is still the first stop for many travelers headed to the wildlife parks of East Africa. Just over a century ago Nairobi was little more than a water depot for the notorious "Lunatic Express." Every railhead presented a new nightmare for its British builders. Work was halted by hungry lions (a saga portrayed in the film *The Ghost and the Darkness*) as well as by masses of caterpillars that crawled on the tracks, spoiling traction and spinning wheels. Nearsighted rhinos charged the noisy engines. Africans fashioned jewelry from the copper telegraph wires, leading to a head-on collision between two engines after the communication wires were cut. The budget ballooned to £9,500 ($19,685) a mile, an enormous amount of money in 1900.

Nairobi, which means "cool water" in the language of the Masai, wouldn't remain a backwater for long. In her 1942 memoir, *West with the Night*, aviatrix Beryl Markham wrote that less than three decades after it was founded, the city "had sprung from a collection of corrugated iron shacks serving the spindly Uganda Railway to a sprawling welter of British, Boers, Indians, Somalis, Abyssinians, natives from all over Africa and a dozen other places." Its grand hotels and imposing public buildings, she wrote, were "imposing evidence that modern times and methods have at last caught up with East Africa."

Today Nairobi's skyline surprises first-time visitors, whose visions of the country are often shaped by wildlife documentaries on the Discovery Channel or news reports about poverty on CNN. Since it was founded little more than a century ago, Nairobi has grown into one of the continent's largest capitals. Some early architecture survives here and there, but this city of almost 3 million people is dominated by modern office towers.

This is not to say the city has lost all its charm—the venerable Norfolk and Stanley hotels recall the elegance of an age long since past, and the big black taxis from London lend a sense of style. Sometimes you can even describe the city as beautiful. After a good rain the city seems to have more green than New York or London. Brilliant bougainvillea line the highway from the airport, flame trees shout with color, and, in October, the horizon turns lavender with the blossoms of jacaranda.

But Nairobi has more than its share of problems. This city that grew too fast has paralyzing traffic jams, with many unsafe or overloaded vehicles on the road, and no hint of emissions control. Crime is on the rise, and stories about muggings and carjackings have led to the capital's moniker "Nairobbery." In addition, there is a growing disparity between rich and poor. Private estates on the edge of Nairobi resemble those of Beverly Hills or Boca Raton, with elaborate wrought-iron fences surrounding opulent mansions with stables, tennis courts, and swimming pools. The upper crust is known as the *wabenzi*, with "wa" a generic prefix for a people or tribe and "benzi" referring to the ubiquitous Mercedes-Benz cars lining the driveways. Not far away you can glimpse vast mazes of tin shacks, many with no electricity or running water.

These problems have pushed many travelers to the sanctuary of the suburbs. The Ngong Hills, consisting of "four noble peaks rising like immovable darker blue waves against the sky," mark the southwestern boundaries of Nairobi, embracing the townships of Langata and Karen. The latter is named after Baroness Karen Blixen, who wrote under the pen name Isak Dinesen about her life on a coffee farm here. Purple at dusk, the Ngong Hills are a restful symbol of *salaam*, Swahili for "peace." Here people take a deep breath, toast the setting sun, and discuss the remains of the day.

Exclusive guest homes, such as the Giraffe Manor and the House of Waine, provide a sense of peace in the suburban bush. Some of the better boutiques selling everything from antiques to art are found in Karen and Langata. The suburb of Langata lies on the edge of the Nairobi National Park, a great introduction to the magnificent wildlife of Kenya. No wonder many visitors return here year after year. They discover how Blixen felt when she wrote in one of her letters: "Wherever I may be in future, I will always wonder whether there is rain on the Ngongs."

GETTING ORIENTED

Nairobi National Park is to the south of the city, with Jomo Kenyatta International Airport and Wilson Airport on the park periphery. Karen and Langata, suburbs of Nairobi, are southwest of the city center, and the Ngong Hills, on the edge the Great Rift Valley, are beyond them. Muthaiga, Gigiri, and Limuru are to the north.

WHAT TO SEE

CITY CENTER

❶ **City Market.** Designed in 1930 as an aircraft hangar, this vast space is a jumble of color, noise, and activity. Head to the balcony to view the

To Go or Not to Go

Violence erupted in Kenya after the country's much flawed December 2007 election. The incumbent president, Mwai Kibaki, was declared the victor in a much debated win over the top opposition leader, Raila Odinga. Election officials stated that voter fraud was evident on both sides. Immediately following the tally, rioters took to the streets in the cities of Kisumu, Kericho and Eldoret to protest the results; Nairobi's slums did not escape the violence.

More than 1,000 people were killed and more than 60,000 people were displaced in the ensuing violence. The main conflict revolved around the incumbent president's tribe, the Kikuyu, and the Luo tribe, that of the opposition leader. Numerous African heads-of-state and influential people visited the country to try to help broker peace talks between the two sides. In early 2008, Kibaki and Odinga entered into a power-sharing government. Though the political future of Kenya is uncertain, the magnitude and beauty of Kenya has not changed.

So, is it safe to travel to Kenya? A lot depends on your own comfort level. When you're traveling to Africa you must check in on what's going on politically and culturally. This is not the first time violence has erupted around an election; rioting occurred in Kenya after the 1992 elections as well. Sign up for news briefings from web sites like AllSafe Travels (www.allsafetravels. com) that send daily updates on your future travel destination(s).

flower, fruit, and vegetable stands on the main level. Outside the market entrance is Biashara Street, where you'll find all sorts of tailors, haberdashers, and seamstresses. Look for kikois and kangas, traditional fabrics worn by Kenyan women. They make for colorful sarongs that are good for wearing over a bathing suit or throwing over a picnic table. They're half the price here than in the hotel shops. ⊠ *Muindi Mbingu St.* ☎ *No phone* 💲 *Free* ⊙ *Mon.–Sat. 8–4.*

❻ David Sheldrick Orphanage for Rhinos and Elephants. Take a morning excursion, which you can book through your tour guide or hotel concierge, to this amazing rescue center that was set up by Daphne Sheldrick after the death of her husband David, who was famous for his anti-poaching activities in Tsavo National Park. You'll be able to watch baby elephants at play or having a bath, knowing that one day when they're old enough they will be successfully reintroduced into the wild. It's an absolutely unmissable and heartwarming experience. Make a donation, however small, or go for gold and adopt your own baby elephant. Reservations are essential. ⊠ *Entrance is at Maintenance Gate on Magadi Rd.* ☎ *020/891–996* ⊕ *www.sheldrickwildlifetrust.org* 💲 *Donation* ⊙ *Daily 11 AM–noon.*

❷ Kenya National Museum. On Museum Hill off Chiromo Road, this interesting museum has good reproduction rock art displays and excellent prehistory exhibits of the archaeological discoveries of Richard and Mary Leakey. When working near Lake Turkana in the 1960s the Leakeys discovered the skull and bones of Homo habilis, believed to be the ancestor of early humankind. Their findings established the Rift Valley as the possible Cradle of Humankind, although both South Africa's Sterkfontein Caves and Ethiopia's Hadar region claim the same distinction. There are also excellent paintings by Joy Adamson, better known as the author of *Born Free,* and a good collection of Kenya's birds and butterflies. The Kenya Museum Society takes guided bird walks every Wednesday morning at 8:45. There are some good craft shops and a museum shop, and it's worthwhile popping in to the Kuona Trust, the part of the museum that showcases young Kenyan artists. ⊠*Museum Hill, off Chiromo St., Nairobi* ☎*020/0930–1800* ⊕*www.museums. or.ke* 🖾*Free* ⊙*Daily 8:30–4:30.*

❹ **Nairobi National Park.** *See If You Have Time, above for more information about this park.*

❸ **Railway Museum.** Established to preserve relics and records of East African railways and harbors, this museum is great fun for children of all ages. You can see the rhino catcher that Teddy Roosevelt rode during his 1908 safari and climb into the carriage where Charles Ryall, a British railroad builder, was dragged out a window by a hungry lion. There are great photos and posters, plus silver service from the more elegant days of the overnight train to Mombasa. Rides on steam trains take place on the second Saturday of each month. ⊠*Station Rd. near Uhuru Hwy.* ☎*020/221–211* 🖾*US$3* ⊙*Daily 9:30–6.*

SUBURBS

❺ **Karen Blixen Museum.** *Out of Africa* author Karen Blixen lived in this estate from 1913 to 1931. This is where she threw a grand dinner party for the Prince of Wales and where she carried on a torrid relationship with aviator Denys Finch Hatton. The museum contains a few of her belongings and some of the farm machinery she used to cultivate the land for coffee and tea. There's also some of her furniture, but most of it is found in the McMillan Library in Nairobi. There is a magnificent view of the surrounding hills from her lawn, which is dominated by euphorbia, the many-armed plant widely known as the candelabra cactus. On the way to the museum you may notice a signpost reading NDEGE. On this road, whose Swahili name means "bird," Finch Hatton once landed his plane for his visits with Blixen. After his plane crashed in Voi, he was buried nearby in the Ngong Hills. Guides will take you on a tour of the garden and the house, but there is little reference to the literary works by Blixen, who wrote under the pen name Isak Dinesen. ⊠*Karen Rd., Karen* ☎*02/882–779* ⊕*www.museums.or.ke* 🖾*Ksh 200* ⊙*Daily 9–6.*

OFF THE BEATEN PATH

Olorgesailie. Set in the eastern branch of the Great Rift Valley, Olorgesailie is one of Kenya's best-known archaeological sites. Discovered in 1919 by geologist J. W. Gregory, the area was excavated by Louis and Mary Leakey in the 1940s. They discovered tools thought to have been made by residents of the region more than a half million years ago. A small museum shows some of the axes and other tools found nearby. The journey here is unforgettable. As you drive south on Magadi Road, you'll find that past the town of Kiserian the route climbs over the southern end of the Ngong Hills, affording fine views of the entire

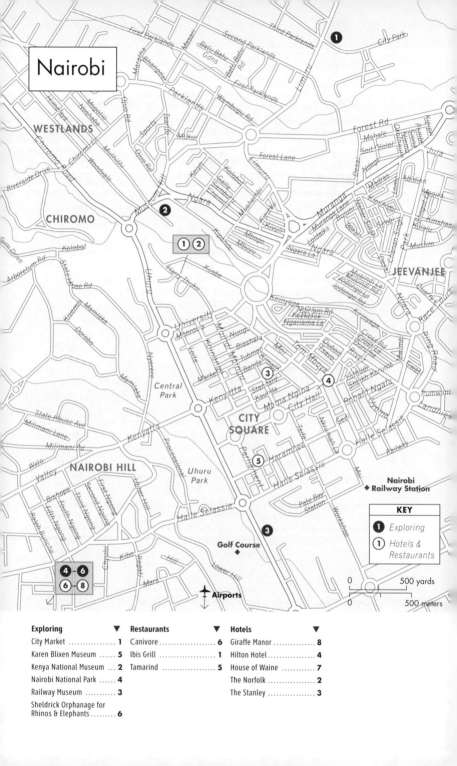

Nairobi

WESTLANDS

CHIROMO

JEEVANJEE

Central Park

CITY SQUARE

NAIROBI HILL

Uhuru Park

Golf Course ◆

Nairobi ◆ Railway Station

KEY

❶ *Exploring*

① *Hotels & Restaurants*

0	500 yards
0	500 meters

✈ **Airports**

Exploring ▼	Restaurants ▼	Hotels ▼
City Market **1**	Canivore **6**	Giraffe Manor **8**
Karen Blixen Museum **5**	Ibis Grill **1**	Hilton Hotel **4**
Kenya National Museum ... **2**	Tamarind **5**	House of Waine **7**
Nairobi National Park **4**		The Norfolk **2**
Railway Museum **3**		The Stanley **3**
Sheldrick Orphanage for Rhinos & Elephants **6**		

valley. Volcanic hills rise out of the plains as the road drops into dry country where the Masai people graze their herds. ✉*65 km (40 mi) south of Nairobi* ☎*02/742-131* ⊕*www.museums.or.ke* 🎫*Ksh 300* ⊙*Daily 9–6.*

WHERE TO STAY

The two landmark lodgings in the capital, the Norfolk Hotel and the Sarova Stanley Hotel have thrown their doors open to visitors for more than a century. Both have been beautifully renovated and now have everything from health clubs to business centers. Newer luxury hotels, including such landmarks as the Nairobi Hilton (⊕*www.hilton.com*) are giving them a run for their money.

Although corporate travelers may need to stay in Nairobi, those wishing to get away from the hustle and bustle can head to the distilled air of the Ngong Hills, which prompted Karen Blixen to write "here I am, where I ought to be." Many visitors feel the same affinity with this landscape where several country establishments offer more peaceful surroundings.

$$$$ **Giraffe Manor.** Yes, giraffes really do pop their heads through the windows and bat their improbable eyelashes at you at this stately old look-alike gabled Scottish hunting lodge. Built of honey-color sandstone and set in a forest in the Nairobi suburb of Karen, it's 20 minutes by road from the town's center. It's a haven of peace and tranquillity, unless you reckon curious giraffes and snuffling warthogs as stressful. Rare endangered Rothschild's giraffes roam freely through the estate, and you can find out more about the species at the adjacent Giraffe Centre. If possible, choose a honeymoon master bedroom with an art deco bathroom. There's also a family suite with two rooms and the Karen Blixen annex that's decorated with the author's original furniture and paintings. Because it's high on the "places to stay" list of global movers and shakers you never know who might be sitting next to you at dinner. ⌂*Koitobos Rd., Karen, Nairobi* ☎*020/89-1078 or 020/89-0949* ⊕*www.giraffemanor.com* 🛏*4 rooms* ⌂*In-hotel: pool, restaurant, library* ☰*AE, DC, MC, V* ⚬*FAP.*

$$$$ **House of Waine.** You'll find nostalgia, history, and romantic surroundings at this family-owned boutique hotel. Set in lush gardens, it's 20 minutes from downtown Nairobi in the quiet suburb of Karen. It was here that the notorious Danish womanizer, man-about-town, and wannabe coffee farmer, Baron Bror von Blixen-Finecke, brought his lovely young wife Karen. It was also here that Karen met and fell hopelessly and helplessly in love with the English hunter and adventurer Denys Finch Hatton—their tragic romance was brought vividly to life in the movie *Out of Africa* starring Meryl Streep and Robert Redford. Colonial ambience mixes comfortably with modern luxury in the beautifully appointed guest suites, each uniquely decorated in vivid colors with elegant furniture and a marble en-suite bathroom. Kids under 2 are free and those 2–11 are half-price. The Karen Blixen Museum is just next door if you want to find out more about this extraordinary woman writer. ⌂*Box 25035, near junction of Masai La. and Bogani Rd., Nairobi* ☎*20/89-1820 or 20/89-1553* ⊕*www.houseofwaine.*

com ⬐*11 suites* ⬧*In-room: a/c, TV, safe, minibar, Internet. In-hotel: bar, restaurant, heated pool* ▭*AE, DC, MC, V* ⎮◯⎮*FAP.*

$$$$ 🏨 **The Norfolk Hotel.** This grand old colonial lady will take you back to the heady early days when settlers, adventurers, colonial officers, and their ladies arrived in the capital to make their names and their fortunes. Built in 1904, the Norfolk was one of Nairobi's first hotels and quickly became the meeting place and watering hole for everybody who was anybody in the colony. The original mock Tudor facade and colonial opulence still remain, so you can easily imagine yourself back in the early days as you sip your G&T—it's always called G&T, *never* gin and tonic—or an excellent local Tusker beer on the terrace or in the leather-chaired bar. 🏠*Box 58581, Harry Thuku Rd., Nairobi* ☎*020/221–6940, 866/840–8208 toll-freein U.S.* ⊕*www.fairmont. com* ⬐*129 rooms, 18 suites, 6 luxury cottages* ⬧*In-room: safe. In-hotel: bar, restaurant, pool, shops* ▭*AE, DC, MC, V* ⎮◯⎮*BP.*

$ 🏨 **Hilton Hotel.** Centrally located, this circular building has become a city landmark. There's nothing much to distinguish it from other Hilton hotels anywhere in the world, apart from some African-theme decor, but it's comfortably predictable. ✉*Mama Ngina St., Nairobi* ☎*020/25–0000* ⊕*www.hilton.com* ⬐*287 rooms* ⬧*In-room: a/c, TV, safe, minibar. In-hotel: bar, restaurant, heated pool, gym, spa, business center* ▭*AE, DC, MC, V* ⎮◯⎮*BP.*

$ 🏨 **The Sarova Stanley.** Also one of Nairobi's oldest hotels, the Stanley was named after the journalist Henry Morton Stanley who immortalized himself by discovering a long-lost Scots explorer with one of the best sound bites in history: "Dr. Livingstone, I presume?" At the hotel's famous outdoor Thorn Tree Café, named for the acacia tree at its center, early travelers would pin notes and messages for fellow travelers to the tree. Today, there's an Internet café where the communication tradition continues and you can get light meals and live music. 🏠*Box 30680, corner Kenyatta Ave. and Kimati St., Nairobi* ☎*020/–316377* ⊕*www.sarova.co.ke* ⬐*217 rooms* ⬧*In-room: minibar, safe, Internet. In-hotel: bar, restaurant, gym, pool, shops* ▭*AE, DC, MC, V* ⎮◯⎮*BP.*

WHERE TO EAT

$$ ✕**Carnivore.** One of the most famous restaurants in Kenya, Carnivore is
★ known for serving wild game—buffalo, giraffe, gazelle, impala, wildebeest, zebra, or even crocodile—grilled over a vast charcoal fire. Waiters carry the sizzling meat to your table on long skewers and carve whatever you wish onto the cast-iron platters that serve as plates. Only when you offer a little white flag of surrender do they stop carving. Various sauces, such as a garlic fruit salsa, tempt the taste buds. As strange as it may seem, there are also many excellent choices for vegetarians. The house drink is called *dawa,* a Swahili word for "medicine," and the secret blend of vodka, honey, and lime is prepared by a smiling man in a poncho of colorful kikoi cloth. Sunday night is Africa night, with live music. ✉*Langata Rd., between Nairobi and Langata* ☎*02/60–2990* ⊕*www.tamarind.co.ke* ⬧*Reservations essential* ▭*AE, DC, MC, V.*

$$ ✕**Ibis Grill.** Run by Eamon Mullan, one of the country's finest chefs,
★ this restaurant in the Norfolk Hotel reflects his talent for producing contemporary cuisine with a Kenyan twist. Specialties change daily,

but you can't go wrong starting with the "taste of three soups," which recently included ostrich consommé, seafood chowder scented with Pernod, and creamy asparagus soup with a dumpling filled with spicy cream cheese. For your entrée move on to grilled giant prawns with mango-mint relish and garlic dip or mignons of ostrich fillet with black pudding served with a juniper berry glaze. The atmosphere is cool and sophisticated, with pink-linen tablecloths and heavy silverware. French doors open onto a lovely courtyard. The Norfolk also offers one of the best buffet breakfasts in town for residents and nonresidents alike. ⊠*Norfolk Hotel, Harry Thuku Rd.* ☎*20/250–900* ✍*Reservations essential Jacket required* ▭*AE, DC, MC, V.*

$$ ✕**Tamarind.** Hands down the finest seafood restaurant in town, Tama-
★ rind is famous for its deep-fried crab claws, ginger crab, and *piri piri* (spicy, buttery prawns grilled over charcoal). Everything is flown up daily from the coast, including the Malindi sole and the Kilifi oysters, tiny but very flavorful and served either raw or as classic oysters Rockefeller. Try the delicious *kokonda,* based on a famous dish from Fiji—raw fish and shrimp are marinated in lime juice, coconut cream, fennel, mustard seed, and local chili peppers. The setting is quite lovely, with stained glass by renowned Kenya artist Nani Croze. Reservations essential. ⊠*National Bank of Kenya, Harambee Ave.* ☎*20/251–811* ⊕*www.tamarind.co.ke* ✍*Reservations essential* ▭*AE, DC, MC, V.*

NAIROBI ESSENTIALS

TRANSPORTATION

BY AIR

Most major European airlines fly into Jomo Kenyatta Airport, Kenya's major airport, as do African airlines such as South African Airways, EgyptAir, Ethiopian Airlines, and Kenya Airways. Unfortunately, there are no direct flights from the U.S. to Kenya at the time of this writing. Airport departure tax is included in your scheduled flight tickets, but check before you leave home. If not, US$40 in hard currency is payable upon departure from Kenyan airports. Departure tax for internal flights is Ksh 100.

Air Travel Resources in Kenya Kenya Airports Authority (⊕ *www.kenyaairports.co.ke*).

AIRPORTS Jomo Kenyatta International Airport is 15 km (9 mi) from the city. The airport has several banks with ATMs, and Bureaux de Change where you can change money. Barclays Bank, National Bank of Kenya, and Transnational Bank have branches and 24-hour money changing daily. You can also use the ATMs, although some accept only Visa. It takes about 40 minutes to drive from the airport to the city center by taxi (about US$15; always negotiate first) or regular shuttle bus. Many hotels have shuttle service; be sure to organize this when you book your room.

Wilson Airport 6 km (4 mi) south of the city on the Langata Road is Nairobi's second airport. It's used for domestic, charter, and some international flights.

International Airports **Jomo Kenyatta International Airport** (*NBO* ☏ *020/822–111* ⊕ *www.kenyaairports.co.ke*). **Wilson Airport** (*WIL* ☏ *020/501–943* ⊕ *www.kenyaairports.co.ke*).

FLIGHTS Most major European and African airlines fly into Jomo Kenyatta Airport. There are no direct flights from the U.S. to Kenya at the time of this writing. Flying via London, Amsterdam, or Dubai is a popular option. There are plenty of cheap and efficient domestic flights available, including daily flights on Air Kenya between Nairobi and Mombasa, Lamu and Kisungu. Air Kenya also flies daily to Amboseli, Kiwayu, Lamu, Nanyuki, Malindi, the Masai Mara, and Meru. As tourist numbers grow, more flights are added all the time. There are also numerous charter flights available from Nairobi to the major tourist destinations and individual lodges and camps. When you book your safari, it's a good idea to ask your accommodation destination to book your internal flights for you as part of your package.

International Airlines **South African Airways** (☏ *020/227–486* ⊕ *www.flysaa.com*). **Kenya Airways** (☏ *020/320–74747* ⊕ *www.kenya-airways.com*).

Domestic Airlines **KenyaAirways** (☏ *020/320–74747* ⊕ *www.kenya-airways.com*). **Air Kenya** (☏ *020/605745* ⊕ *www.airkenya.com*).

TRANSFERS Taxis and *matatus* (passenger minivans carrying 15 passengers) are available all over the city, and are now much more safe and reliable than in the past. There's an 80 km (50 mi) per hour speed limit, and it's compulsory to buckle up. Always negotiate the price before setting out. A taxi should cost you about US$30 from the airport to center city.

Tuk tuks, motorized three-wheel buggies, are fun if you can bear the fumes; confirm the price beforehand. If you want a bus, look for green City Hoppers, but beware of pickpockets. A taxi or your own two feet are the safest means of transportation.

Contacts at Wilson Airport **Safarilink** (☏ *020/600–777* ⊕ *www.safarilink-kenya.com*). **CHS Aviation** (☏ *020/501–408*). **Eagle Aviation** (☏ *020/606–015*). **Equator Airlines** (☏ *020/501–360*). **Ibis Aviation** (☏ *020/602–257*).

BY CAR
You're probably only in Nairobi overnight or for a few hours, so you definitely won't need a car. Take a taxi.

CONTACTS & RESOURCES

BUSINESS SERVICES & FACILITIES
Most big hotels offer these, and there are also Internet cafés everywhere. Ask at your hotel for the nearest reliable one. Post offices are open 8–12:30 and 2–5. Ask your concierge for the nearest location.

Contacts **Cybercafes** (⊕ *www.cybercafes.com*) lists more than 4,000 Internet cafés worldwide.

EMERGENCIES
Police in general are friendly and helpful to tourists. There are two private hospitals (avoid the government hospitals) with excellent staff and

facilities, which have 24-hour pharmacies. There are plenty of pharmacies all over downtown Nairobi. Consult your concierge or host.

Contacts **Central Police Station** (⊠ *University Way* ☏ *020/222–222 or 020/717–777, dial 999 for all emergencies).***Aga Khan Hospital** (⊠ *Parklands Ave., Parklands* ☏ *020/746–309).* **Nairobi Hospital** (⊠ *Argwings Kodhek Rd.* ☏ *020/272–2160).*

HOLIDAYS
If a public holiday falls on a Sunday, it will be observed the next day, Monday. Muslim festivals are timed according to local sightings of various phases of the moon and dates vary accordingly. During the lunar month of Ramadan that precedes Eid al-Fitr, Muslims fast during the day and feast at night and normal business patterns may be interrupted. Many restaurants are closed during the day and there may be restrictions on smoking and drinking.

HOURS OF OPERATION
Banking hours are weekdays from 9 AM to 2 PM and on the first and last Saturday of the month from 9 to 11 AM. Some banks in Mombasa and Nairobi stay open later on weekdays. Some banks at Jomo Kenyatta International Airport are open 24 hours. Government offices are open weekdays from 8 or 8:30 AM to 1 PM and 2 to 5 PM. Private businesses follow similar hours. Some may be open on Saturday mornings.

MONEY
Only change money at banks, Bureaux de Change, or authorized hotels. Don't be tempted to change money on the street, however good a deal you are being offered. There are ATMs at most banks throughout the country and credit cards are accepted mostly everywhere (not in the markets or small shops). Visa, MasterCard, Plus, and Cirrus cards are universally accepted, but not always American Express and Diners Club. Most guides are more than happy to accept US$ as tips. If you're bringing dollars with you, bring only notes printed after 1995, and avoid torn or very dirty ones. It's a good idea to have a small stash of lower denomination dollars. Travelers' checks are widely accepted.

RESTROOMS
Use only hotel or restaurant restrooms. You'll find them clean and efficient. When you're on safari, discuss with your guide before the drive what arrangements there will be, usually just a bush. Never leave paper in the wilderness. If necessary scrape a little hole or bury it under a pile of dirt, stones, and sticks.

Find a Loo **The Bathroom Diaries** (⊕ *www.thebathroomdiaries.com*) is flush with unsanitized info on restrooms the world over—each one located, reviewed, and rated.

BEACH ESCAPES

Guided by a captain's sinewy foot on the rudder, the graceful dhow is a common sight in the shimmering waters off the Kenya Coast. These triangular-sailed boats symbolize a region where the culture of Arabia fused with that of Africa. Sultry languor prevails in places like Mombasa, Malindi, and Lamu, enticing you to trade your safari shorts for a soft sarong, then to shed that to slip into the warm sea.

THE KENYAN COAST

Updated by
Kate Turkington

Intricately carved doorways studded with brass and white walls draped with bougainvillea distinguish the towns that dot Kenya's coastline. Arab traders who landed on these shores in the 9th century brought their own culture, so the streets are dominated by a different style of dress and architecture from what you see in other parts of Kenya. Men stroll the streets wearing traditional caps called *kofias* and billowing caftans known as *khanzus*, while women cover their faces with black veils called *bui-buis* that reveal only their sparkling eyes.

The creation of Swahili, a combination of Arabic and African Bantu, came about when Arab traders married African women. Swahili comes from the Arabic words *sahil*, meaning "coast," and *i*, meaning "of the." As seductive as the rhythm of the sea, Swahili is one of the most melodic tongues on earth. The coastal communities of Lamu, Malindi, and Mombasa are strongholds of the language that once dominated communities from Somalia to Mozambique.

Mombasa, the country's second-largest city, was once the gateway to East Africa. Karen Blixen described people arriving and departing by ship in the book *Out of Africa*. Mombasa's harbor still attracts a few large cruise ships, but nothing like the hundreds that sailed here before World War I. In Lamu, a Swahili proverb prevails: *Haraka haraka haina baraka* (Haste, haste, brings no blessing). The best-preserved Swahili town in Kenya, Lamu, has streets hardly wide enough for a donkey cart. Narrow, winding alleyways are lined with houses set tight against one another. It is said that the beautifully carved doors found here are built first, then the house constructed around them. By the same token, a mosque is built first, and the town follows. Due north—the direction of Mecca—is easy to discern because of the town's orientation.

Azure waters from Lamu to Wasini are protected by the 240-km (150-mi) coral reef that runs parallel to the coast. Broken only where rivers cut through it, the reef is home to hundreds of species of tropical fish. The beaches themselves have calm and clear waters that hover around 27°C (80°F). As Ernest Hemingway put it, "The endless sand, the reefs, the lot, are completely unmatched in the world."

Mombasa has an international airport, but many travelers deplane at Nairobi, then make their way to the coast. Others fly directly to Lamu. However you get here, don't miss putting your foot in this ivory white sand.

GETTING HERE & AROUND

Getting to the towns along the Kenya Coast is easier than ever. Once, nearly every traveler to the region had to travel through Mombasa, but this is no longer the case. Expanded service means you can fly directly to once-isolated towns such as Malindi and Lamu. Travel by car around Mombasa is fairly safe, but the road to Lamu has been plagued by armed robberies. Avoid this route if at all possible.

EAT RIGHT, SLEEP WELL

The excellent cuisine reflects the region's rich history. Thanks to Italians, basil is everywhere, along with olive oil, garlic, and fresh lettuce. The Portuguese introduced tomatoes, corn, and cashews. Everything is combined with pungent spices such as coriander and ginger and the rich coconut milk often used as a cooking broth.

The Indian Ocean delivers some of the world's best fishing, so marlin, sailfish, swordfish, kingfish, and many other types of fish are on every menu. Not surprisingly, sashimi made from yellowtail tuna is favored by connoisseurs (and was listed on menus here as "fish tartare" before the rest of the world discovered Japanese cuisine). Prawns can be gargantuan, and wild oysters are small and sweet. Diving for your own lobster is an adventure, but you will easily find young boys happy to deliver fresh seafood to your door. Sometimes they simply march from door to door laden with fresh pineapples, bananas, mangos, and papayas. You can even place your order for the next day.

Accommodations along the Kenya Coast range from sprawling resorts with several restaurants to small beach houses with kitchens where you can prepare your own meals. To really get a sense of the region consider staying in a private home. Most accommodations along the coast can arrange snorkeling, windsurfing, waterskiing, and deep-sea fishing.

MOMBASA

You may well find yourself in Mombasa for a few hours or an overnight stop. The city is a strange mixture of culture, religion, and history—it's the second oldest trade center with Arabia and the Far East. Today it still plays an important role as the main port for Kenya. Although it lacks the beautiful beaches of the north and south, it has a rich fascinating history. Visit the Old Town with its Arab influence, narrow streets lined with tiny shops and souks (markets), where you can watch an appealing array of traditions and maybe see a belly dancer performing her rhythmic enticing talents in one of the numerous cafés. The Old Harbour, frequented by numerous dhows, is an ideal place to arrange a short cruise on one of these local boats that have plied the oceans for centuries. Fort Jesus, designed by an Italian and built by the Portuguese in the late 16th century, is a major visitor draw and well worth a visit. In summer there's an impressive sound and light show.

WHAT TO SEE

4 Anglican Cathedral. Built in the early part of the last century, the cathedral is a memorial to Archbishop James Hannington, a missionary who was executed in 1885. The influence of Middle Eastern Islamic architecture is clear in the frieze, the dome, and the tall, narrow windows. The paneling behind the high altar is reminiscent of the cathedral in Stone Town. ⊠ *Nkrumah Rd. and Cathedral Rd.*

2 Basheikh Mosque. Like other Swahili towns, Mombasa probably had a Muslim community from the time it was founded. This mosque, painted cream and white, is said to be built on a foundation dating from the 11th century. The purposeful square facade of this mosque reflects the best in Islamic architecture. ⊠ *Old Kilindini Rd. at Kibokoni Rd.*

3 Fort Jesus. This massive edifice was built in the late 16th century by the
★ Portuguese, who were keen to control trade in the region. When the Omanis captured the fort at the end of the 17th century, they made some adjustments. The walls were raised to account for the improved trajectory of cannons mounted aboard attacking ships. By the end of the 18th century, turrets were erected. For water, the garrison relied on wells. There is a large pit cistern in the center of the compound, which some guides say was the bath of the harem—an intriguing notion. The captain's house retains some traces of the Portuguese—note the outline of the old colonnade. The exhibits at the museum include an important display on ceramics of the coast, beautiful carved doors studded with brass, and the remains of a Portuguese gunner, *San Antonio de Tanna*, which sank outside the fort at the end of the 17th century. Objects from the ship—shoes, glass bottles, a powder shovel, and cannon with its muzzle blown away—bring the period to life. There are also exhibits of finds from archaeological excavations at Gedi, Manda, Ungwana, and other sites. ⊠ *End of Nkrumah Rd.* 🖭 *Ksh 400* 🕓 *Daily 8:30–6.*

6 Moi Avenue. Like to shop? The city's most popular shopping strip, Moi Avenue is Mombasa's equivalent of New York's 5th Avenue. Here you'll find prominent landmarks such as the Tusks. ⊠ *Moi Ave.*

1 New Burhani Bohra Mosque. The elaborate facade and soaring minaret of this mosque overlook the Old Harbor. Built in 1902, it's the third mosque to occupy this site. ⊠ *Buchuma Rd.*

5 Tusks. Dominating Moi Avenue are the famous elephant tusks that cross above the roadway. They were erected to commemorate the 1952 visit of Britain's Princess Elizabeth, now Queen Elizabeth II. ⊠ *Moi Ave. at Uhuru Gardens.*

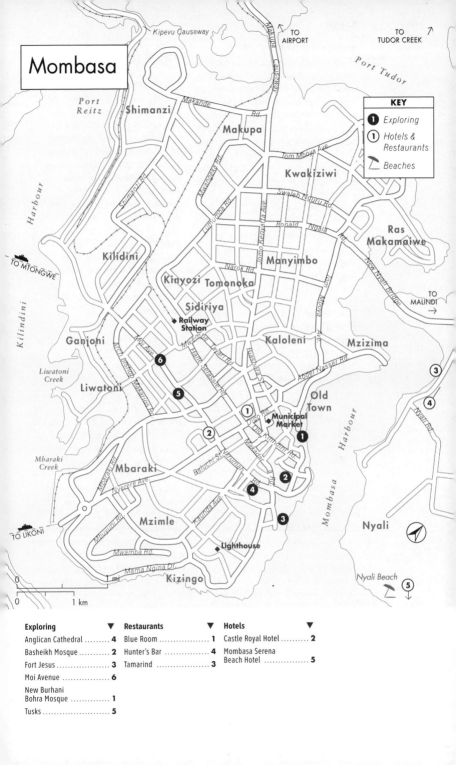

Mombasa

KEY

1️⃣ Exploring

① Hotels & Restaurants

⛱ Beaches

Exploring ▼

Anglican Cathedral **4**

Basheikh Mosque **2**

Fort Jesus **3**

Moi Avenue **6**

New Burhani
Bohra Mosque **1**

Tusks **5**

Restaurants ▼

Blue Room **1**

Hunter's Bar **4**

Tamarind **3**

Hotels ▼

Castle Royal Hotel **2**

Mombasa Serena
Beach Hotel **5**

WHERE TO STAY & EAT

$$$$ ✕**Tamarind.** What the Carnivore restaurant does for meat in Nairobi, this fine restaurant does for seafood in Mombasa. A 15-minute drive from downtown and a welcome house cocktail—a *dawa* made of lime, vodka, honey, and crushed ice—will introduce you to a memorable meal and unforgettable experience. Overlooking a creek flowing into the sea, the restaurant is designed like an old Moorish palace with fountains, high arches, and tiled floors. If you love seafood, you'll be in heaven. You can take a lunch- or dinner-dhow cruise around Tudor Creek and soak up some sun and sea air by day, or watch the moon rise over Mombasa Old Town by night as soft Swahili music makes the food and wine go down even better. ⊠*Silo Rd., Nyali* ☎*041/474–600* ⊕*tamarinddhow.com* ☐*AE, DC, MC, V* ⊗*12:30–2:30* PM, *7–10:30* PM.

> **ARCHITECTURE**
>
> The region's architecture is characterized by arcaded balconies and red-tile roofs. One of the great concepts of coastal interiors is the *baraza*, an open sitting area with cushions perfect for parties or intimate conversations. Lamu furniture, with its deep brown color, provides a compelling contrast to the white walls. Local decorations can include fish traps made of palm rib or bamboo and—the latest thing—items made of old dhow wood. This decor has become so fashionable that East African interiors grace houses and apartments from Manhattan to Mayfair.

$$$ ⊞**The Mombasa Serena Beach Hotel.** This gorgeous resort at Nyali Beach was built to resemble a 13th-century Arab town. A visit here will transport you to another time and place with its courtyards brimming with fountains, narrow twisty lanes, handcarved balconies and busy market squares. Spacious rooms have an old Arab ambience with handcarved wooden furniture and handwoven rugs, all in deep browns. Set in lush tropical gardens next to an improbable blue sea, you won't have to leave home to enjoy a full-on beach holiday. Food is excellent with lots of fresh fish, seafood, and vegetables flown in daily from Lake Naivasha and Timau in Nanyuki. There's plenty to do here including day excursions to crocodile farms, Shimba National Park, the Arabuko Sokoke forest, the Kipepeo Butterfly Farm, or the haunted ruins of the ancient town of Gedi. There are all manner of water activities available, too, but a trip in a glass-bottomed boat to the nearby coral reef is a must. ⊡*Box 48690, Nairobi* ☎*050/22059 or 020/284–2000* ⊕*www.serenahotels.com* ⇥*166 rooms* ⌂*In-room: a/c, safe. In-hotel: business center, bar, restaurant, pool, tennis court* ☐*AE, DC, MC, V* ⏺*MAP.*

$$ ✕**Hunter's Bar.** This small, intimate international restaurant is one of Mombasa's best, very popular with foreign visitors and Mombasa's expatriates. With trophy animals mounted on the walls, the place resembles a hunting lodge. Although it serves a wide range of dishes including excellent seafood and venison, Hunter's best known for its mouthwatering steaks and homemade desserts like apple pie. It's also a good place to stop for a cold beer. ⊠*M. Komani Rd., Nyali.* ☎*011/471–771* ☐*DC, V* ⊗*Closed Sun.*

¢–$ ✕**Blue Room.** Famous for its *bhajias* (deep-fried pastries filled with vegetables), this family-owned Indian restaurant has been in business for more than 50 years. It seats more than 140 people, making it one of the largest restaurants in the city. The menu features more than 65 items of both Western and Indian origin, and its bright clean interior with tiled floors and plenty of chairs and tables keeps people coming. The curries and Indian vegetarian dishes are especially good, as are the tasty snacks. Try the samoosas, kebabs, or even fish and chips. There's also an ice-cream parlor and DVD rental shop. You'll also find a cybercafé inside, where you can send an e-mail back home. ⊠*Intersection of Haile Selassie Rd. and Digo Rd.* ☎*011/224–021* ⊕*www.blueroomonline.com* ⊟*No credit cards* ⊘*Daily 9* AM*–10* PM.

¢ 🏨**Castle Royal Hotel.** Originally built in 1919, and recently refurbished, this gleaming white old colonial building is in Mombasa's town center only a short distance away from the old town and Fort Jesus. Rooms are small but comfortable with wrought-iron bedheads, colorful soft furnishings, and big picture windows. Front rooms have a balcony. The Long Bar, reminiscent of the cool colonnaded colonial bars of Singapore and India, is a great place for a drink as you watch the sun set, and there's a good terrace restaurant. ⊠*Moi St., Central Mombasa* ☎*20/315–680* ⊕*www.castlemsa.com* ⟲*48 rooms* ⚑*In-room: a/c, TV, safe. In-hotel: restaurant, bar, pool* ⊟*AE, DC, MC, V* ⦿*BP.*

MOMBASA & MALINDI ESSENTIALS

TRANSPORTATION

BY AIR   Kenya Airways has seven daily flights between Nairobi and Mombasa, as well as daily flights between Mombasa and Zanzibar. There are flights to Malindi three times a week, and daily to Lamu.

Contacts **AirKenya** (☎*020/320–4747* ⊕*www.airkenya.com*). **Kenya Airways** (☎*020/642–2000 in Nairobi, 041/227–616041 in Mombasa* ⊕*www.kenya-airways.com*).

BY BIKE & MOPED   Fredlink delivers bikes as far north as Malindi and as far south as Diani Beach for an extra charge of Ksh 2,000. It also rents scooters and motorbikes. It also offers motorbike and four-wheel-drive tours.

Contacts **Fredlink Tours** (⊠*Diani Sea Resort Shops, Diani Beach Rd., Mombasa 80100* ☎*403/300–064* ⊕*www.motorbike-safari.com*).

BY BUS   There are lots of bus companies that go to Nairobi including Connection and Akamba—you'll see their kiosks on Jomo Kenyatta Avenue opposite the Islamic cemetery. There are plenty of buses between Mombasa and Malindi. They take about three hours and cost approximately US$2.

In Mombasa and Malindi, as well as up and down the coast, transport is provided by *matatus* (minibuses named for the pennies that used to be the fare). Matatus are numerous and cheap, but have people jammed in the aisles and pop music blaring through loudspeakers. And the names of the matatus—such as Rambo Jet and Rocket Rover—are a clue these are not the safest way to travel.

Contacts **Akamba** (⊠*Kitui Rd, Off Kampala Rd., Nairobi* ☎*020/556–062*).

BY TAXI   Taxis in Mombasa and Malindi are inexpensive. The drivers are friendly and helpful and will wait or return to collect you if you ask. For journeys north to Malindi or other destinations, check out the shared taxis, which come in the form of Peugeot station wagons.

Taxis are also available to pick you up at the airport, phone the office and they will radio call a taxi to pick you up at the airport.

Contacts **Kenatco Taxis Ltd** (⊠ *Ambalal House, Mombasa Trade Centre, Nkrumah Rd.* ☎ *041/222-7503*).

BY TRAIN   The Mombasa Express—sometimes referred to as the Nairobi–Mombasa overnight train or the Jambo Kenya Deluxe—departs every evening from Mombasa at 7 PM, pulling into Nairobi at just past 9 AM the next morning. Once a rather elegant experience, it is no longer that as service is sometimes canceled at the last minute, parts of the train have deteriorated, and the ride is a bit rough. Many independent travelers still consider the journey a highlight of their trip to Kenya though, as you get to see lots of beautiful scenery and it's quite inexpensive. The trip will cost you about Ksh 3,370 ($50). The Mombasa Railway Station is on Haile Selassie Road.

There is no train to Malindi.

Contacts **East Africa Shuttles and Safaris** (☎ *722/348-656* ⊕ *www.eastafricashuttles.com*). **Kenya Railway** (☎ *020/221-211*). **Kuja Safaris** (☎ *020/313-371* ⊕ *www.kujasafaris.com*).

CONTACTS & RESOURCES

EMERGENCIES   Emergency Numbers **Emergency Hotline** (☎ *999 from a Kenyan landline, 112 from a mobile phone*). **Mombasa Central Police Station** (☎ *041/225-501*). **Tourist 24 hour Helpline** (☎ *020/604-767 or 020/605-485*).

Hospitals **Aga Khan Hospital** (⊠ *Vanga Rd., Kizingo, Mombasa* ☎ *041/222-7710*). **Pandya Memorial Hospital** (⊠ *Dedan Kimathi Rd.* ☎ *041/314-140*).

Pharmacy **Makadara Chemists** (☎ *041/222-4197or 041/222-6814*). **Buhani Pharmacy.** (⊠ *Uhuru St., near Uhuru Gardens, Malindi* ☎ *041/20-490*).

MAIL &   The main post office on Digo Road, Mombasa is open weekdays 8–6
SHOPPING   and Saturday 9–noon.

Contacts **Mombasa Post Office** (⊠ *GPO Building, Digo Rd.* ☎ *041/222-7705*).

MONEY   Barclay's Bank has several ATMs in Mombasa. There's one on Malindi
MATTERS   Road, on Kenyatta Avenue near Digo Road, on Nkrumah Road near Fort Jesus, and on the main road out of Mombasa to Nairobi. If you want to change money, Forex Bureau has exchange shops on Digo Road near the Municipal Market and near the entrance of Fort Jesus.

If you're in Malindi, there's an ATM at the Barclay's Bank.

Contacts **Barclays Bank** (⊠ *Lamu Rd., Malindi* ☎ *042/20-656*). **Fort Jesus Forex Bureau** (⊠ *Opposite Fort Jesus Museum, Ndia Kuu Rd., Mombasa* ☎ *041/223-0116*). **Pwani Forex Bureau** (⊠ *Abdel Nasser Rd, Opposite Mackinon Market,*

Mombasa ☎*041/222–1727).* **Standard Chartered Bank** (✉*Lamu Rd., Malindi* ☎*042/20–130).*

SAFETY The best way to see Mombasa and Malindi is on foot, but you should not walk around at night. If you take a taxi at night, make sure it delivers you all the way to the door of your destination. Purse snatchers are all too common. Beware of people who might approach you on Mombasa's Moi Avenue offering to become your guide. Tell them "Hapana, asante sana" ("No, thank you") and move on.

TELEPHONES The international code for Kenya is 254. The city code for Mombasa is 041. If you are calling from outside Kenya, drop the "0" when dialing.

VISITOR INFORMATION Mombasa Coast Tourist Information (MCTA), near the Tusks, sells books on city sights such as Fort Jesus. It's open weekdays 8–noon and 2–4:30, and Saturday 8–noon. The best map is *The Streets of Mombasa Island*, which sells for Ksh 500 ($7.50).

Contacts Malindi Tourist Office (✉*Malindi Complex, Lamu Rd., Malindi* ☎*No phone* ⊕*www.malindikenya.com).*

Mombasa Coast Tourism Association (✉*Moi Ave.Mombasa* ☎*041/222–5428* ✐*mcta@africaonline.co.ke).* **Tourist 24-hour Helpline** (☎*041/222–5428).*

SOUTHERN BEACHES

Kenya's coast south of Mombasa contains some of the country's most beautiful beaches. The highway from Mombasa runs all the way to the Tanzania border, providing easy access to a string of resorts.

Diani Beach. Once a true tropical Eden with gorgeous weather and equally gorgeous scenery this 20-km (12-mi) stretch of sand, 30 km (19 mi) south of Mombasa, is the most developed along the southern coast. One reason that it's so popular is that the reef filters out the seaweed, so the sandy shores are truly pristine. If you stay in one of the private cottages, local fishermen will take your order and deliver lobsters and other delicacies of the deep to your door.

Shimoni. Just 60 km (37 mi) south of Diani, on the tip of a peninsula known for its excellent deep-sea fishing you'll find the village of Shimoni, which means "place of the holes." Ocean currents dug out a maze of coral caves, one of them 11 km (7 mi) long. This catacomb was used as an underground tunnel for loading slaves onto dhows. You can see iron shackles that still remain on the cave walls.

WHAT TO SEE

Mwana Mosque. This well-preserved 16th-century mosque stands at the mouth of the Mwachema River. The high-ceilinged prayer room is still used regularly by worshippers. The Mosque is surrounded by baobab trees, which grow to great size here since there are no elephants to root them out. ■TIP➔ It's respectful for lady visitors to cover their heads, shoulders, and knees in whatever mosque they visit. A good tip is to carry a scarf and a kekoi to wrap around the body if necessary. ✉*In baobab grove between Diani and Tiwi.*

Jadini Forest. You'll find the remains of the Jadini Forest, which once covered the whole of the coastal area, at the southern end of Diani. It's home to vervet monkeys, troops of baboons, and endangered Angolan black-and-white colobus monkeys, as well as butterflies and birds. It's a great place for a picnic with lots of nature trails, but watch out for thieving monkeys! One-hour guided primate walks (US$5) are offered as well as 1½-hour night walks (US$7) where you can see bush babies as well as monkeys. ☒ *Close to Papillon Beach* ☎ *040/320–3519* ☎ *US$5* ⊘ *Mon.–Sat. 8–5.*

★ **Kisite-Mpunguti Marine National Park.** A few miles off the coast, this 28-square-km (11-square-mi) national park is known for its beautiful coral gardens. More than 40 varieties of coral have been identified, including staghorn, brain, mushroom, and pencil. More than 250 species of fish have been spotted feeding around the reef, including butterfly fish, parrot fish, and angelfish. Humpback dolphins are a common sight, as are big schools of bonitos and frigate mackerels. The entire protected area, just past Wasini Island, is in shallow water and can be easily reached by motor boat or dhow. ☒ *4–8 km (2–5 mi) from Shimoni* ⊕ *www.kws.org* ☎ *$6.*

Wasini Island. Take a walk to the ancient Arab settlement near the modern village of Wasini Island. Here you'll find the ruins of 18th- and 19th-century houses and a Muslim pillar tomb inset with Chinese porcelain. If you're into snorkeling or diving, make this a definite stop. The boat from Shimoni costs $4 one-way. ☒ *1 km (½ mi) from Shimoni* ⊕ *www.wasini-island.com* ☎ *$6.*

WHERE TO STAY & EAT

$$$ ✕**Ali Barbour's Cave.** You can dine in a naturally formed cave deep underground or on an outdoor terrace at this popular seafood restaurant. You can't go wrong with the crab salad marinated with lemon and chilies. You can also choose excellent French food. There is a shuttle bus that will pick up people staying in the Diani Beach area. ☒ *Between Diani Sea Lodge and Trade Winds* ☎ *040/320–2033* ☞ *Reservations essential* ⊟ *AE, DC, MC, V.*

$$ ✕**African Pot.** This relaxed beachfront restaurant, made of thatch and wood, is in front of the Coral Beach cottages on Shimoni Beach. It serves excellent Swahili food, including the traditional *ugali*—some say it's the inspiration for grits—greens, and gumbo. Live African music is occasionally featured here. ☒ *Near entrance to Coral Beach Cottages, near Shimoni* ☎ *040/320–3890* ⊟ *No credit cards.*

$ ✕**Sundowner.** This cheap, but cheerful thatch bar and eatery is a five-minute walk from the Diani Beach Chalets. It serves good seafood, including grilled and fried fish, tasty local food and curries, and an excellent English breakfast. Local beer and drinks are also cheap here. ☒ *Southern end of Diani Beach* ☎ *040/320–2138* ⊟ *No credit cards.*

$$$$ ⊡**Alfajiri Beach Villa.** Built of stone and thatch, these double-story villas
ℭ are some of the most luxurious villas in the world. Elegantly furnished
★ with the wit and style you would expect of owner and host Marika Molinaro, one of Kenya's top interior designers. You can choose between the Garden Villa, the Cliff Villa, or the Beach Villa (book

months in advance for the later) where Marika has put together handmade furniture—made on the property—and comfortable beds, chairs, and sofas that complement her husband Fabricio's global collection of fascinating artifacts. Each villa has two en-suite bedrooms with extra rooms for the kids, wide balconies and verandas, and a geometric-shape pool that borders the Indian Ocean. The service is superb and so is the Mediterranean cuisine. Go for a safari, enjoy all the beach and water activities, or leave the kids with a nanny and be alone for a while. *Box 454, Ukundu, Diani, Kenya 040/320–2630 www.alfajirivillas.com 3 villas In-hotel: bar, restaurant, pool AE, DC, MC, V FAP.*

SELF-CATERING ACCOMMODATIONS

Not interested in staying in a hotel? There's a large variety of cottages and houses for rent along the beach. Most come with a cook and housekeeper, all you have to do is provide your own food—which is easy to do as there are nearby stores and supermarkets. Check out the following Web sites to start your search: *www.kenyaholidayvillas.com*, *www.kenyasafarihomes.com*, *www.dianibeach.com*.

$$$$ **Diani Reef Beach Resort and Spa.** This luxurious resort will make sure you get the best out of your beach break. There are stylishly decorated, well-equipped rooms each with a balcony or terrace, all the sporting and entertainment facilities you could wish for, and 300 meters (984 feet) of lovely palm-fringed beach front. Choose a garden room overlooking lush greenery and flowering plants, or a deluxe room with its own Jacuzzi. Fresh delicious food is served at four restaurants including a seafood and an Asian one. Or pig out on mouthwatering oven-fresh goodies from the pastry shop. There's a huge range of activities from tennis, squash, pool, and table tennis, to water skiing, scuba diving, snorkeling, windsurfing, and sailing. A ride in a glass-bottomed boat out to the coral reef is mandatory. Don't pass up the chance to get a massage at the Maya Spa. At the end of the day watch a movie in the state-of-the-art cinema, or try your luck in the glitzy casino. There's a great kids' program that will entertain the tots while you do your own thing. *Box 35, Ukundu, Diani, Kenya 040/320–2723 or 040/320–3308 www.dianireef.com 300 rooms In-room: a/c, safe, minibar, Internet. In-hotel: business center, bar, restaurant, pool, tennis court AE, DC, MC, V MAP.*

$$$$ **Indian Ocean Beach Club.** This classy beachfront resort stretches for 500 meters (1,640 feet) along the Indian Ocean amid 10 hectares (25 acres) of indigenous gardens. The white Moorish-style main lodge has high arches, terra-cotta tiled floors, lots of space and offers a cool, inviting respite from the sand, sea, and sun. There's also plenty of space in the sea-facing whitewashed thatch clubrooms each with a veranda and attractively furnished with soft white curtains, blue-and-white bedspreads, russet-color tiled floors, and hand-carved furniture. The resort also has a huge freeform pool plus three plunge pools, three bars, and three restaurants. Sit beside the sea in the Bahari Cove restaurant and eat delicious fresh fish and seafood, or try the exotic Asian

cuisine at Spices. Go deep-sea fishing, scuba diving, snorkeling, wind-surfing, or sailing or just chill out on the beach and watch the waves lapping on the white sandy shore. ⌂ *Box 73, Ukundu, Diani, Kenya* ☎ *040/320–3730* ⊕ *www.jacarandahotels.com* ⤢ *100 rooms* ⌂ *In-room: a/c. In-hotel: 3 restaurants, 3 bars, pool, tennis court* ▤ *AE, DC, MC, V* ⋈ *MAP.*

¢ 🔲 **Nomad Beach Hotel.** You'll get excellent value-for-money at this small family-owned hotel nestled in the heart of a coconut plantation at the edge of a natural forest. The charming wood and thatch bands are only a coconut shy from the white sandy beach, where you can swim, sunbathe, snorkel, or dive to your heart's content. After a day full of activity, you can relax in the attractive thatch bar that overlooks the Indian Ocean. Listen to a live band afternoons and evenings, and eat delicious seafood at the very reasonably priced restaurant. It's famous for its Sunday lunches, so make sure you get there early to get a table. ⌂ *Box 1, Akuni, Diani, Kenya* ☎ *040/320–2155* ⤢ *21 bandas and cottages* ⌂ *In-room, fan, safe. In-hotel: bar, restaurant, pool* ▤ *AE, DC, MC, V* ⋈ *MAP.*

SOUTHERN BEACH ESSENTIALS

TRANSPORTATION

BY AIR Most people fly into Mombasa's Moi International Airport and make their way down the coast by taxi, rental car, or hotel shuttle. There is an airstrip at Ukunda for charter flights.

BY BUS From the southern side of the Likoni Ferry terminal there are KBS buses heading south every 20 minutes from 7 to 7, less frequently in the evening. It takes about a half hour to reach Diani Beach.

Contacts **KBS** (✉ *Jomo Kenyatta Ave.* ☎ *011/224–851*).

BY FERRY You must take the Likoni Ferry to travel south of Mombasa. Two ferries run simultaneously, departing about 20 minutes apart, with fewer departures late in the day and in the evening. Vehicles are charged by length, usually about Ksh 45 per car. Pedestrians ride free. Matatus leave the city center (in front of the Post Office) on a regular basis down to the Ferry Terminal.

CONTACTS & RESOURCES

MAIL & The region's largest post office is south of the Ukunda Road junction
SHIPPING headed for Diani Beach. It's open from Monday through Saturday 8–5.

MONEY Barclay's Bank has an ATM in Ukunda, north of the junction headed for Diani Beach.

SAFETY If you take a taxi at night, make sure it delivers you all the way to your destination. Tourist Police officers patrol beaches, but don't tempt fate by bringing jewelry, cameras, or cash. Women should not walk alone on the beach.

If you are walking from Tiwi to Diani, consult the tidal chart beforehand. A creek that you must swim across at high tide is known as "Panga Point," after the machete used as a weapon by muggers.

Drink plenty of bottled water and wear sunscreen. It's a good idea to wear a thick T-shirt to protect your back from sunburn when snorkeling.

TELEPHONES The city code for Diani Beach and the surrounding communities is 040. If you are calling from outside Kenya, drop the "0" in the city code.

VISITOR INFORMATION Contacts **Ukuna Tourism** (⊠ *Private Safaris Bldg., Ukunda Rd.*).

LAMU

Designated a UNESCO World Heritage Site in December 2001, Lamu Old Town is the oldest and best-preserved Swahili settlement in East Africa. Some 260 km (162 mi) north of Mombasa—and just two degrees below the Equator—Lamu is separated from the mainland by a narrow channel that's fringed with thick mangroves protected from the sea by coral reefs and huge sand dunes. You won't find any motorized vehicles in this tiny medieval town—only donkey and handcarts ply the quiet narrow winding streets. A stronghold of Islam for many centuries, you'll see men in *kofias* and *khanzus and* women in *bui-buis*.

There are many old mosques (not all will allow Westerners to visit) and Arab houses with beautiful handcarved mahogany and cedar doors. There's so much to look at in the town itself, including the Hindu Temple in Mwagogo Road that it might be hard to tear yourself away. But if you can bear to leave, take a dhow cruise to visit the 14th-century ruins on the Pate and Manda islands.

Lamu has also become a hot destination for global glitterati: Princess Caroline of Monaco has a house here along with any number of other notables. But nothing and nobody can destroy the ambience of this lovely little town. Small boys with backs against ancient walls chant verses from the Koran, light-sounding drums beat, a flute plays, donkeys bray, a muezzin calls from a stone tower atop a small mosque, palm trees wave in the soft sea breezes, and a white-sailed dhow sails past on the bluest of seas.

It gets very sticky and hot, so either find a cool rooftop veranda to sip a fresh juice as cool sea breezes blow, or take tea with some of the locals as you potter about the little shops and stores set in massive stone buildings with thick coral rag walls. Lamu Museum right on the seafront is also a cool refuge, where you can admire the 18th-century Kidaka plasterwork and some old carved throne chairs. As the sun goes down, head to the small battlements of the Lamu Fort, formerly a fortification and a prison, before another cool drink at the café overlooking the town's main square.

GETTING HERE & AROUND

Lamu is a very easy town to get around because it is so small. The cobbled streets are laid out in a grid fashion with the main street, Harambee Avenue, running parallel to the harbor.

WORD OF MOUTH

"I was just in Lamu. It was quite peaceful, probably the most peaceful place I've ever been."

–saridder

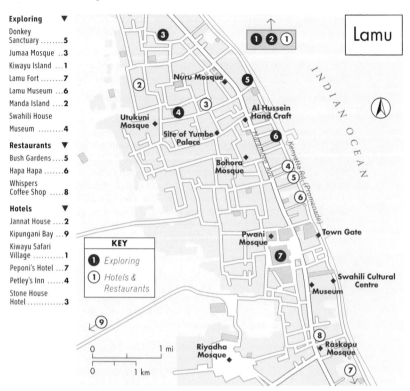

WHAT TO SEE

❺ Donkey Sanctuary. Donkeys are the main transport in Lamu, and the Sanctuary was started in 1987 by Elisabeth Svendsen, a British doctor, to protect and look after the working donkeys. It's now managed and run in conjunction with the KSPCA (Kenya Society for the Protection and Care of Animals). There's a treatment clinic where locals can get their donkeys wormed, a training center, and a resting place for a few of the old animals that can no longer work. If you don't want to go inside, you can eyeball a few donkeys over the low wall in front of the yard. An annual prize is given to the Lamu donkey in the best physical condition. ⊠*Kenyatta Rd.* ⊕*www.thedonkeysanctuary.org.uk* 🖼*Donations accepted* ⊙ *Weekdays 9–1.*

❸ Jumaa Mosque. Located in the north of the town, just off Harambee Avenue, Jumaa is the second oldest mosque in Lamu. It dates from 1511, and was used up until the late 1800s for trading slaves. ⊠*Off Harambee Ave.*

❶ Kiwayu Island. This strip of sand is 50 km (31 mi) northeast of Lamu. The main attraction of Kiwayu Island is its proximity to Kiunga Marine National Reserve, a marine park encompassing Kiwayu Bay. The confluence of two major ocean currents creates unique ecological conditions that nurture three marine habitats—mangroves, sea-grass beds, and coral reefs. Here you have a chance of catching a glimpse of the most endangered mammal in Kenya, the manatee. Because of its tasty flesh, this gentle giant has been hunted to near extinction all along Africa's eastern coast. The best way to get here is to charter a dhow from Lamu. If you can muster a group of six people, it should cost you about US$15–US$20 per person including food, water, and snorkeling equipment. Otherwise, your lodge or hotel will arrange the trip for you.

> **A GOOD TIP**
>
> Ask at your hotel or lodging for a local guide to take you aaround the city. Make sure you agree to a price before you head out, and then let him introduce you to the history of this remarkable little town. You'll walk round it in a couple of hours with lots of cold drink stops on the way. And you won't need a map or a guidebook. Plus you'll get the real inside story.

❼ Lamu Fort. This imposing edifice, which was completed in 1821, marks the southern corner of the town. It was used as a prison from 1910 to 1984, when it became part of the country's museum system. Today, it is a central part of the town as it hosts conferences, exhibits, and theater productions. If you have a few moments, climb up to the battlements for some great views of Lamu. ✉ *Kenyatta Rd.* ⊕ *www.museums.or.ke* ✆ *Free* ◷ *Daily 8–6.*

❻ Lamu Museum. You enter the museum through a brass-studded door that was imported from Zanzibar. Inside there are archaeological displays showing the Takwa Ruins excavations, some wonderful photos of Lamu taken by a French photographer from 1846 to 1849 (you'll be amazed at how little has changed in Lamu), some intricately carved Lamu headboards and throne chairs, and a good bookshop. In the Balcony Room upstairs is a fascinating display of musical instruments including the famed Siwa Horns, made of brass and resembling elephant tusks. Dating from the 17th-century they're reputed to be the oldest surviving musical instruments in Sub-Saharan Africa. ✉ *Kenyatta Rd.* ⊕ *www.museums.or.ke* ✆ *$3* ◷ *Daily 8–6.*

❷ Manda Island. Just across the channel from Lamu, the mostly uninhabited Manda Island once held one of the area's largest cities. The once-thriving community of Takwa was abandoned in the 17th century, and archaeologists have yet to discover why. Reached by taking a dhow up a baobab tree-lined creek, the ruins are a popular day trip from Lamu and Shela. ✉ *10 min by boat from Lamu.*

❹ Swahili House Museum. This beautifully restored Swahili merchant's house has original period furniture. Notice the traditional beds with woven bases of rope, and the fine carved Kalinda screen in the main room. There's a garden full of flowering tropical shrubs and trees and the original well. ✉ *A few blocks south of Juma Mosque, Old Town* ⊕ *www.museums.or.ke* ✆ *$2* ◷ *Daily 8–6.*

WHERE TO STAY & EAT

¢–$$ ✕ **Bush Gardens.** Service isn't the fastest in the world at this lively waterfront eatery, but it's worth waiting for the delicious seafood and fresh fish—definitely try the tuna, shark, or snapper. Entrées are served with coconut rice or french fries. If you stop by for breakfast, make sure to try the fresh fruit juices. ⊠ *Harambee Ave., south of main jetty, Lamu* ☎ *No phone* ◷ *Daily 7 AM–10 PM* ⊟ *No credit cards.*

$ ✕ **Hapa Hapa.** With a name that is Swahili for "Here, Here," Hapa Hapa is known for its outstanding seafood. Make sure to try the barracuda. This restaurant is on the waterfront, making it a great spot to watch the fishing boats heading out into the Indian Ocean. ⊠ *Harambee Ave., south of main jetty, Lamu* ☎ *042/633–145* ⊟ *No credit cards.*

¢ ✕ **Whispers Coffee Shop.** Located in the same building as the Baraka Gallery, which has gifts and souvenirs, this upscale café has a pretty courtyard where you can sip the excellent cappuccino and munch a delicious homemade pastry. ⊠ *Harambee Ave., Lamu* ☎ *No phone* ⊟ *No credit cards.*

¢–$ ✕▦ **Petley's Inn.** Established by the eccentric Englishman Percy Petley in 1862, this small hotel is on the waterfront, next to the Lamu Museum. The two nicest en-suite rooms face the sea. The rooftop restaurant offers a range of excellent seafood. There's a swimming pool on the first floor, and the rooftop bar can be lively in the evening because it's one of the few places in Lamu town to serve a cold mug of Tusker. ⊠ *Box 421, Lamu* ☎ *042/633–272* ⇨ *11 rooms* ✑ *islands@africaonline. co.ke* ⟁ *In-room: a/c. In-hotel: bar, pool* ⊟ *MC, V* ⊺⊙⊺ *FAP.*

¢ ✕▦ **Jannat House.** This 18th-century former Arab merchant's house is decorated with hand-carved wooden furniture, tiles floors, and colorful linens. The food is fresh and good, and the hotel serves alcohol—a rarity in this Muslim area. Another rarity, the hotel has a pool in the garden. Enjoy a cold beer or juice on the rooftop terrace as you gaze out toward Manda Island. ⊠ *Box 195, Lamu* ☎ *042/633–414* ⇨ *16 rooms* ⊕ *www.jannathouse.com* ⟁ *In-room: a/c. In-hotel: bar, pool* ⊟ *MC, V* ⊺⊙⊺ *BP.*

¢ ✕▦ **Stone House Hotel.** You'll feel like a member of the old Arab aristocracy when you say in this lovely 18th-century house in the heart of Old Lamu. The large en-suite rooms are decorated with old furniture, wooden beams, and colorful linens. Cool off in the breezy rooftop restaurant, where you'll hear the calls to prayer (Muslims pray five times a day) and donkeys braying as you gaze out across the rooftops of the town. ⚠ **The hotel does not have hot water.** ✑ *Box 193, Lamu, Kenya* ☎ *042/633–544* ⇨ *10 rooms, 4 share bath* ⟁ *In-room, fan. In-hotel: bar, restaurant, pool* ⊟ *AE, DC, MC, V* ⊺⊙⊺ *BP.*

$$$$ ▦ **Kipungani Bay.** On the southern tip of Lamu Island, this lodge is for anyone who's looking for a truly secluded getaway. The immense thatch and reed cottages—a half-hour trip by speedboat from Lamu and just a stone's throw from the gentle Indian Ocean—feel removed from the rest of the world. There's not much to do here but take walks on the sandy beach, snorkel at the nearby reef, or charter a boat to go deep-sea fishing. Excursions take you to Lamu for shopping or to Matondoni for a glimpse at the ancient art of crafting a dhow. From the freeform saltwater pool you have a stunning view of the sunset. ⊠ *Kipungani* ☎ *020/444–2115* ⇨ *15 cottages* ⊕ *kipungani.heritage-eastafrica.com* ⟁ *In-hotel: restaurant, bar, pool* ⊺⊙⊺ *BP.*

$$$$ ⚐Kiwayu Safari Village. Fifty kilometers (31 mi) northeast of Lamu you'll find one of the most romantic destinations in Kenya. The Village is a collection of thatch-roof bandas that face the northern tip of Kiwayu Island. The cottages are vast, with views of the lagoon from the hammocks hanging on the private verandas. For dinner, sample local delicacies such as giant mangrove crabs or sweet rock oysters. The area is known for its deep-sea fishing—record-setting sailfish, marlin, and tuna have been caught here. The hotel is very near the Kiunga Marine National Reserve, where coral reefs offer great snorkeling. Book far in advance for holidays. In addition to the per person, per day rate, expect to pay a $30 per day conservation fee. ⊠*Kiwayu Island* ☎*020/600–107 or 020/600–891* ⊕*www.kiwayu.com* ⌨*18 cottages* ⚒*In-hotel: restaurant, bar* ▭*AE, DC, MC, V* ⊘*Closed Apr.–June.*

$$$$ ⚐Peponi's Hotel. Peponi's is well known for its beachfront location, lovely accommodations, and superb food. Owned and run by descendants of original Happy Valley settlers, there's an atmosphere of total laid-back charm. Anything goes here, but don't be fooled, the hotel is impeccably run and organizes everything from your water sports to your day excursions. You'll sleep in a sea-facing room with polished honey-color mud floors, whitewashed ceilings with beams of old black wood, a massive four-poster bed, kelim rugs, and old Zanzibar settles (wooden couches). On your sea-facing veranda, get comfortable on lie-out chairs and watch the boats bobbing out to sea. The food is legendary. There are no bells and whistles, just simply cooked food that's fresh and totally unforgettable—try the giant prawns in butter sauce. If you want to go for something other than seafood, eat Swahili-style as you sit round a big brass platter on the floor. The hotel is closed May and June. ⌂*Box 7543, Nairobi* ☎*042/633–421 or 042/633–154* ⊕*www.peponi-lamu.com* ⌨*24 rooms* ⚒*In-room, fan, safe. In-hotel: bar, restaurant, pool* ▭*AE, DC, MC, V* ⎤*MAP.*

LAMU ESSENTIALS

TRANSPORTATION

BY AIR Kenya Airways has daily flights from Nairobi. AirKenya has frequent flights to Lamu and Kiwayu from Nairobi, Mombasa, and Malindi. It also offers hops from Lamu to Kiwayu.

Carriers AirKenya (⊠*HBaraka House, near Whispers Restaurant, Lamu* ☎*042/633–063*). **Kenya Airways** (⊠*Ground floor, Casuarina Guest House, Waterfront, Lamu* ☎*0042/632–040*).

BY BOAT & DHOW Most hotels can arrange for a trip by dhow from Lamu to Shela or Matondoni. Find out the going price from your accommodations and confirm with the captain before setting out. You can also head to neighboring islands such as Manta, Manda Moto, and Pate. More distant destinations, such as Kiwayu, are more expensive.

CONTACTS & RESOURCES

FESTIVALS & SEASONAL EVENTS The Maulidi festival, marking the birth of Muhammad, has been celebrated on Lamu for more than a century. Dhow races, poetry readings, and other events take place around the town's main mosques. Maulidi, which takes place in the spring, attracts pilgrims from all over Kenya.

HOLIDAYS   October 10 is Moi Day, and October 20, Kenyatta Day. December 12 is Jamhuri (Independence Day). The period of Ramadan may cause some places to be closed until sunset. The date of Ramadan is decided by the lunar calendar, and the fasting period begins 11 days earlier every year. Try to get here toward the end of Ramadan, when a huge feast and party, the Eid al Fitr, brings everyone out to the streets.

INTERNET   A few hotels have Internet but the service is slow and unreliable. You can e-mail from the post office.

MAIL & SHIPPING   The main post office in Lamu is south of the jetty on Harambee Avenue. It's open weekdays 8–12:30 and 2–5, Saturday 9–noon.

Post Offices Lamu (✉ *Harambee Ave.*).

MONEY   The Standard Chartered Bank on the waterfront has terribly slow service and is open weekdays 9–3 and Saturday 9–11. You're better off cashing traveler's checks at your hotel.

SAFETY   The best way to see Lamu town is on foot, but you should not walk alone at night. Crime is rare in this part of Kenya, but it's better to be on the safe side.

TELEPHONES   You'll find public phones in front of the post office on Harambee Avenue. The area code for Lamu is 040. If you are calling Lamu from outside Kenya, dial the country code, 254, the area code, 040, and the local number.

MALINDI

Malindi, the country's second-largest coastal town, is 120 km (75 mi) north of Mombasa and has been an important port for hundreds of years. In ancient Chinese documents, "Ma Lin De" is referred to as a stop on the trade route. The town battled with Mombasa for control of the coast, which explains why Portuguese explorer Vasco da Gama received such a warm welcome when he landed here in 1498 but was given the cold shoulder in Mombasa. The Vasco da Gama Cross, made from Portuguese stone, sits on a promontory on the southern tip of the bay. Malindi, with its narrow streets, beautiful houses, and colonial hotels, is certainly worth a visit. It's a much more laid-back place than Mombasa and is an attractive place for an after-safari beach break. Lots of expatriates, particularly Italians, have made their home here, so you can expect a fair degree of sophistication in the hotels, resorts, eating places, and shops. The Old Town is still a great place to hunt for colorful fabrics and antiques, and the beach is clean and attractive, although it gets a bit seaweedy in spring. The coastal town has two nearby parks, Malindi and Watamu. These are marine parks where you can watch fish and corals from a glass bottom boat or snorkel, but the collection or destruction of shells is strictly forbidden. It also offers deep-sea fishing and other water sports. It's an easy place to get around because there are lots of tuk tuks and boda bodas (bicycle taxis), which are everywhere day and night.

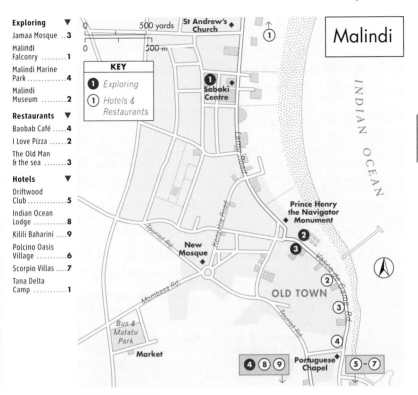

WHAT TO SEE

❸ Jamaa Mosque. The 14th-century tombs beside this mosque are among the oldest in Malindi. It was here in the 1800s that slaves were auctioned weekly until 1873. ✉*Near Uhuru Park.*

❶ Malindi Falconry. If you're into birds, you'll have a ball here. A knowledgeable guide tells you all about the resident birds of prey. You'll see rare creatures, such as the southern banded snake eagle, and can watch a bird safari where the birds strut their stuff for visitors. ✉*Behind the Malindi Complex* ☎*No phone* ☐*US$10* ⊙*Daily 10–6.*

❹ Malindi Marine Park. Home to an impressive variety of colorful coral, you'll find two main reefs here that are separated by a deep sandy-bottom channel. There's very little commercial fishing in the area, which means the kingfish found here are trophy size. The water ranges from 25°C (77°F) to 29°C (84 °F), making this a particularly pleasant place to snorkel or scuba dive. If you want to stay dry, try one of the glass-bottom boats. ✉*Offshore from Malindi* ⊕*www.kws.org* ☐*US$12 for boat, US$8 entry fee* ⊙*Dawn–dusk.*

❷ Malindi Museum. Delve into some of Malindi's fascinating history at this museum, which was once the home of a 19th-century trader. You'll find it on the seafront near the Malindi jetty and the fish market. It has temporary exhibitions and also serves as a visitor information center. ⊕*www.museums.or.ke* ⌦*$3* ⊘*Daily 8–6.*

WHERE TO STAY & EAT

$ ✕**The Old Man and the Sea.** Near the fishing jetty, this stylish former
★ Arab house has been lovingly restored and is known as one of the best places in town noted for its fresh seafood. Sticking with the Hemingway theme, its sister restaurant north of town is called The Sun Also Rises. ⊠*Vasco da Gama Rd.* ☎*042/31106* ⌦*Reservations essential* ▱*AE, MC, V.*

✕**Baobab Cafe.** Eat breakfast, lunch, or dinner or just have a beer or
¢ juice at this friendly, cheerful restaurant. The fish curry is particularly good. ⊠*On sea front, close to Portuguese Church* ☎*042/31699* ▱*AE, MC, V.*

¢ ✕**I Love Pizza.** Overlooking the bay, this good-value place is famous for its, you guessed it, pizza. You can also order fresh seafood. The calamari salad is excellent. ⊠*Vasco da Gama Rd.* ☎*042/20672* ▱*AE, MC, V.*

$ ✕▦**Driftwood Club.** In an attractive garden, these Swahili-style individual bandas, each with a thatch roof and small veranda, are seconds away from the pool and beach. Comfortable rooms have cool white tiled floors, colorful cushions and bedspreads, and sturdy wooden furniture. The staff, always eager to see to your needs, can arrange for any type of water sports. The restaurant serves excellent seafood, and the pub is considered the best in town. If you've always wanted to dive, the Club will set up lessons for you as well as catering for experienced divers. ⊠*3 km (2 mi) south of Malindi, Box 63* ☎*042/20155* ⊕*www. driftwoodclub.com* ⇝*37 rooms* ⏃*In-room: a/c, safe. In-hotel: restaurant, bar, pool* ▱*AE, V* ⎮◯⎮*BP.*

$$$$ ▦**Indian Ocean Lodge.** This Arab-style mansion near Casuarina Point is within a walled garden overflowing with bougainvillea on a property that forms the northern boundary of the Marine National Reserve. Furnished with kilims, brass ornaments, and four-poster beds, the enormous suites have sitting rooms and private balconies. Elegant meals with fine wines are served outdoors, within earshot of the private beach. The hotel will arrange excursions to Gẹdi, bird-watching in the Arabuko–Sokoke Forest, snorkeling, or fishing trips. ⊠*Point Casuarina* ☎*020/331–684* ⊕*www.savannahcamps.com* ⇝*8 rooms* ⏃*In-hotel: pool, minibar* ▱*AE, DC, MC, V* ⊘*Closed Apr.–May* ⎮◯⎮*FAP.*

$$$$ ▦**Tana Delta Camp.** Although its location at the mouth of the Tana River is remote, once you are here, you won't want to leave. You'll be transported to the camp from Malindi by 4x4 and boat and will most likely spot hippos along the way. They won't be the last animals you see— hike by the river to spy bushbuck, yellow baboons, and vervet monkeys, or canoe past herons, kingfishers, and bee-eaters. Shaded by tamarind trees, the tents all have pri-

> ## WORD OF MOUTH
>
> "We took a trip out to the Malindi Marine park, which has been in existence since Kenya's independence in 1963. We saw cowries, corals, a vast variety of reef fish and even an octopus."
>
> –acabot

vate baths and running water. The dining tent is built atop a huge sand dune, providing a view of the ocean. ⊠*Bush Homes of East Africa, Box 56923, Nairobi* ☎*020/600–457 or 020/609–699* ⊕*www.bush-homes. co.ke* ⚲*6 tents* ⚓*In-hotel: pool, beachfront* ☰*AE, V* ⦿*FAP.*

$$ ⬛ Kilili Baharini.$$ ★ This elegant resort, much favored by Italians, is in large grounds amid a profusion of tropical flowering plants 4 km (2½ mi) from Malindi. Spacious airy rooms, mostly decorated in white, have classy antique furniture, complemented by the dark browns of the rugs, bedspreads, and lamps. A private furnished veranda looks out onto the pool where your breakfast is served each morning. Even the Romans hardly had it so good. The excellent food is mainly Italian, but if you're not a pasta person there are all sorts of other delicious dishes from seafood to steaks. ⊠*Casuarina Rd., Box 93, Malindi, Kenya* ☎*042/20169* ⊕*www.kililibaharini.com* ⚲*29 rooms, 6 suites* ⚓*In-room: a/c, minibar, safe. In-hotel: pool, bar, restaurant, spa* ☰*AE, V* ⊗*Closed May–July* ⦿*FAP.*

¢ ⬛**Polcino Oasis Village.** These white thatch-roof en-suite apartments with kitchenette sleeping one to three people are right on Silver Sands beach, 3 km (1.8 mi) from town. It's not the quietest place but offers good value for money with a big pool, Internet café, bar, and restaurant. ⊠*Tourist Rd.* ☎*042/31995* ⊕*www.holidays-kenya.com* ⚲*130 cottages* ⚓*In-hotel: bar, restaurant, pool, Internet* ☰*AE, V* ⦿*BP.*

¢ ⬛**Scorpio Villas.** Thatch-roof cottages filled with handcrafted furniture such as huge Zanzibar beds and day couches are scattered around the exotic gardens of this resort near the Vasco da Gama Cross. Your cottage will have a kitchen staffed with your own cook, although you are free to join the other guests in the restaurant. There are three pools, and the beach is a short walk down a narrow path. ⊠*Box 368, Harambee Rd., Malindi* ☎*042/20194* ⊕*www.scorpiovillas.co.ke* ⚲*25 villas* ⚓*In-hotel: restaurant, bar, 3 pools* ☰*MC, V* ⦿*FAP.*

KENYA ESSENTIALS

TRANSPORTATION

BY AIR

When booking flights, check the routing carefully as some involve stopovers or require you to change airlines. Several flight options from America require long layovers in Europe before connecting to Nairobi or Mombasa. This is especially true for the cheaper flight options.

Airports Jomo Kenyatta International Airport *(JKIA)* (⊠ *Nairobi* ☎ *020/661–1000 or 020/822–111).* Moi International Airport *(MBA)* (⊠ *Mombasa* ☎ *041/343–3211 or 041/343–4021).* Wilson Airport (⊠ *Nairobi* ☎ *020/603–260).*

Air Travel Resources in Kenya Kenya Airports Authority (⊕ *www.kenyaairports.co.ke).*

FLIGHTS

Kenya Airways offers flights directly to Moi International in Mombasa from a variety of European and African destinations. Kenya Airways and Thomsonfly fly from Mombasa to London, and Condor flies to Frankfurt from Mombasa.

If you are flying from New York (JFK) or Washington (Dulles) your best option is to fly to Nairobi and take an internal flight to Mombasa. Emirates offers flights to Jomo Kenyatta International Airport (JKIA) in Nairobi via Dubai. British Airways offers direct flights to Nairobi. KLM flies from Atlanta (ATL) to Nairobi. Virgin Atlantic Airways flies directly from London Heathrow to Nairobi. Connections to Mombasa from Nairobi can be made several times a day using AirKenya or Kenya Airways.

Kenya Airways has seven daily flights between Nairobi and Mombasa, as well as daily flights between Mombasa and Zanzibar. AirKenya has flights twice a day between Nairobi and Mombasa and continuing flights to Malindi (three times a week) and Lamu (daily).

Several of the airlines operating from Moi International Airport have charter flights that are organized externally by tour operators. If you don't want to book flights yourself, check that your tour operator's flight prices are not too expensive and that there are no hidden costs.

Airlines British Airways (☎ *020/327–7400, (44)870/850–9850 in U.K.* ⊕ *www. britishairways.com).* **Condor** (☎ *(49)180/570–7202 in Germany* ⊕ *www.condor. com).* **Emirates** (☎ *020/327–4747, 800/777–3999 in U.S.* ⊕ *www.emirates.com).* **KLM** (☎ *020/329–0000* ⊕ *www.klm.com).* **Thompsonfly** *(Corsair)* (☎ *(44)870/190– 0737 in U.K.* ⊕ *www.thomsonfly.com).* **Virgin Atlantic Airlines** (☎ *020/396–9500, (44)870/380–2007 in U.K.* ⊕ *www.virgin-atlantic.com).*

Domestic Airlines AirKenya (☎ *020/606–539* ⊕ *www.airkenya.com).* **Kenyan Airways** (☎ *020/642–2000* ⊕ *www.kenya-airways.com).*

AIRLINE TICKETS

The least expensive airfares to Kenya are priced for round-trip travel and must usually be purchased in advance. Cheaper air flights may also have longer layovers. Airlines generally allow you to change your return date for a fee; most low-fare tickets, however, are nonrefundable. To determine when it's best to buy tickets so you can save money, check out FareCompare.com, which has historical and current airfares, and Farecast.com, which predicts fare changes based on historical data. Unlike other sites, AirfareWatchDog.com includes rates for budget airlines.

If your charter flights are being booked with tour operators, make sure you are aware of the price and check to make sure extra costs have not been added on.

Keep abreast of fares even after buying tickets. Some airlines give you credit for the value of the price reduction if the airfare goes down later (ask about this when booking). The innovative Web site Yapta.com monitors drops in airfares for just this purpose. You'll often have to pay a fee to rebook your flight, but if the fare drops substantially, the charge may be worth it.

AIR PASS

The Star Alliance African Airpass can only be purchased by international passengers arriving to Africa on a Star Alliance carrier (United, Air Canada, US Airways, South African Airways, etc.) and is good for 4 to 10 flights. The flights are sold in segments, priced by the distance between cities. These are only economy class seats and can be expensive when compared to the discount airline pricing within South Africa, but they are a bargain for the longer routes, such as Nairobi to Johannesburg for under $272. If your itinerary includes more than two of the 25 cities served in Africa, this may be a good choice.

■ TIP➔ Please note that The Star Alliance African Airpass only connects to Nairobi, and a flight to Mombasa will have to be independently booked with Kenya Airways or Air Kenya. Also, all flights within Africa on the Airpass are on South African Airways.

For island-hoppers, it is worth noting that Air Seychelles, Air Mauritius, and Air Austral offer an Indian Ocean Airpass that makes island-hopping easy for those with enough vacation time to wait out infrequent flights between airports in Comores, Mauritius, Madagascar, Maldives, Rodrigues, Reunion, and the Seychelles. The minimum purchase is three segments, and they do represent a savings over à la carte flights. Air Mauritius usually gives the fastest response.

Air Pass Contact Info **Air Mauritius** (☎ *020/224–0024* ⊕ *www.airmauritius.com*). **Lufthansa** (☎ *800/645–3880 in U.S.* ⊕ *www.lufthansa.com*) is the member airline for Star Alliance in Kenya. **Star Alliance** (⊕ *www.staralliance.com*).

CHARTER FLIGHTS

Charter companies are a common mode of transportation when getting to safari lodges and remote destinations throughout Southern and East Africa. These aircraft are well-maintained and are almost always booked by your lodge or travel agent. The major charter companies run daily shuttles from Jomo Kenyatta International Airport and Wilson Airport to popular tourism destinations, such as Mombasa and the national parks. On-demand flights, those made at times other than those scheduled, are very expensive for independent travelers, as they require minimum passenger loads. If it is just two passengers, you will be charged for the vacant seats. Keep in mind that you probably won't get to choose the charter company you fly with. The aircraft you get depends on the number of passengers flying and can vary from very small (you will sit in the co-pilot's seat) to a much more comfortable commuter plane. Those with a severe fear of small planes might consider road travel instead.

Due to the limited space and size of the aircraft, charter carriers observe strict luggage regulations: luggage must be soft sided and weigh no more than 15 kg (33 lbs).

CHARTER COMPANIES

African Sky Charters (☎020/601–467) has its main office at Wilson Airport. It flies to numerous destinations in East Africa including safari spots, Mombasa, and Nairobi. You can book your flights directly with them.

East African Air Charter (☎020/603–858) has its main office at Wilson Airport. The charter flies to safari destinations as well as other major destinations in East Africa. You can book your flights directly with them or through a travel agency.

Phoenix Aviation (☎020/604–048) has its main office at Wilson Airport. It also flies to numerous destinations in East Africa including safari spots, Mombasa, and Nairobi. You can book your flights directly with them.

Safarilink (☎020/600–777 or 020/600–787 ⊕www.safarilink-kenya.com) has its main office at Wilson Airport. The charter flies to main safari destinations such as Masai Mara, Amboseli, as well as Mt. Kilimanjaro. You can book your flights directly with Safarilink or through a travel agency.

BY CAR

The first thing you will have to remember is that Kenyans drive on the left-hand side of the road. That may be confusing at first, but having the steering wheel on the right might help to remind you that the driver should be closer to the middle of the road. You'll get used to it very quickly once you start. The most dangerous maneuver is turning onto an empty road, without oncoming traffic to orient you. Be careful not to lapse and veer to the right side.

Carjackings can and do occur with such frequency that certain high-risk areas are marked by permanent carjacking signs. Kenya Police (⊕www.kenyapolice.go.ke) recommend following safety tips such as ensuring your vehicle is locked, removing all visible valuables, driving during the day and with other people in the car, and keeping your eyes open for suspicious characters approaching or staring at your car. They also recommend keeping your gas tank half-full at all times, mapping out your route beforehand, driving the speed limit, and checking to make sure that any vehicle that requests you to stop has the official designation of the Kenyan Police.

If you rent a car, ask for two spare tires as well as a jack for possible punctures you might experience on some of the more poorly maintained roads. If you plan to go on a long drive, make sure you have maps that you are familiar with or get a GPS system, if available. To check road conditions of different routes visit the Automobile Association of Kenya's Web site (⊕ *www.aakenya.co.ke*), which is regularly updated.

AUTO CLUBS

Visitors to Kenya can get a temporary membership that lasts for six months and costs Ksh1,500 ($23). In the case of a collision or breakdown, you should immediately phone the Automobile Association of Kenya's (KAA) emergency numbers.

In Kenya **Automobile Association of Kenya** (☎ *020/825–060 in Nairobi, 041/249–2431 in Mombasa, or 072/022–7267 24-hour emergency line* ⊕ *www. aakenya.co.ke*).

GASOLINE

Most major credit cards are accepted at petrol stations, and nearly all gas stations are equipped with ATMs. There are no self-service stations; attendants pump the gas, check the oil and water, and wash the windows. According to the KAA it is not customary to tip the petrol attendants. Kenya has a choice of unleaded or leaded gasoline, and many vehicles operate on diesel—be sure you get the right fuel. Older vehicles run on leaded fuel. Check when booking a rental car as to what fuel to use. Gasoline is measured in liters, and the cost works out to about Ksh 70 ($1) a liter, though this is subject to extreme change. When driving long distances, check your routes carefully, as the distances between towns—and hence gas stations—can be as much as 200 km (120 mi). It's better to fill a half-full tank than to try to squeeze the last drop out of an unfamiliar rental car.

ROAD CONDITIONS

Kenya roads, especially the highways, have improved over the past few years with continuous upgrades; however, some roads are still poorly maintained and may have potholes that make for difficult driving conditions. Check out any routes you may take beforehand by going onto the Automobile Association of Kenyan's Web site, or phoning them to ask about the road you plan on driving on. If you are concerned about carjacking, ask the police about the areas that experience the highest levels of carjacking. The Kenyan Roads Board (⊕ *www.krb.go.ke*) also publishes information and updates on roadwork and road conditions in Kenya.

If it's safe to do so, it's courteous for slow vehicles to move over onto the shoulder, which is separated from the road by a solid yellow line. (In built-up areas, however, road shoulders are occasionally marked by red lines. This is a strict "no-stopping" zone.) The more aggressive drivers expect this and will flash their lights at you if you don't. Where there are two lanes in each direction, remember that the right-hand lane is for passing. If you're not concentrating, you might end up dawdling along in the right lane, annoying faster drivers.

It's dangerous to drive at night in some rural areas, as roads are not always fenced and domestic or wild animals often stray onto the road. In very remote areas only the main road might be paved, whereas many secondary roads are of high-quality gravel. Traffic is often light in these areas, so be sure to bring extra water and carry a spare, a jack, and a tire iron (your rental car should come with these).

In towns, minibus taxis (matatus) can be quite unnerving, swerving in and out of traffic without warning to pick up customers. Stay alert at all times, and expect the unexpected. Many cities use mini-traffic circles that look like giant fried eggs in lieu of four-way stops. These can be dangerous, particularly if you're not used to them. In theory, the first vehicle to the circle has the right-of-way; otherwise, yield to the right. In practice, keep your wits about you at all times. In most cities traffic lights are on poles at the side of the street. The Kenyan Police also keep a list of "Accident Hotspots" on their Web site.

RULES OF THE ROAD

If you are planning traveling by car in Kenya, it is advisable to buy a road map before you depart as the Kenyan Automobile Association of Kenya doesn't seem to sell maps. Check with your home automobile club, as many provide international maps and other resources, or online.

Throughout the country, the speed limit on highways is 80 kph (50 mph) for pickups, 110 kph (68 mph) for normal cars and 65 kph (40 mph) for big trucks. The speed limit in towns is 50 kph (about 31 mph) in towns. Of course, many people drive far faster than that. Wearing seat belts is required by law, and the legal blood-alcohol limit is 0.08 mg/100 ml, which means about one glass of wine puts you at the limit. It is illegal to talk on a handheld mobile phone while driving.

But the most important thing for Americans and Canadians to remember is to drive left, and look right.

RENTAL CARS

The decision to rent a car in a foreign country depends on many factors: whether you get nervous when you get lost or see it as an adventure; whether you enjoy going off the beaten path, or would rather do the tried-and-true itinerary. You should always ask for the best route, where it's safe to park and, as Kenyan crime can be unpredictable, safety tips and suggested places to stop, if need be. Make sure you have your destination's contact information with you, as well as that of the hotel you just left.

Make sure that a confirmed reservation guarantees you a car. Agencies sometimes overbook, particularly for busy weekends and holiday periods.

Because some of the roads in Kenya are in poor condition, car rental may be more expensive than in other countries. Make sure to check the insurance your rental company provides. Some companies charge more on the weekend, so it's best to get a range of quotes before booking your car. Request car seats and extras such as GPS when you book, and ask for details on what to do if you have a mechanical problem or other emergency.

In order to rent a car you need to be 23 years or older and have held a driver's license for three years. Younger international drivers can rent from some companies, but will pay a premium. Most companies allow additional drivers, yet some charge. Get the terms in writing before you leave on your trip.

Leave ample time to return your car when your trip is over. You shouldn't feel rushed when settling your bill. Be sure to get copies of your receipt.

Car Rental Resources **Avis** (⊠ *Moi International Airport, Moi Ave., Southern House, Mombasa* ☎ *041/222–4485*). **Payless Car Hire** (⊠ *Jomo Kenyatta Ave., Mombasa* ☎ *041/249–6012*).

CONTACTS & RESOURCES

CUSTOMS & DUTIES

Visitors may bring in new or used gifts and souvenirs up to a total value of Ksh 5,000 (about $75) duty-free. For additional goods (new or used) over Ksh 5,000, duty fees are applicable depending on the assessment of customs. In addition, each person may bring cigarettes, cigars, and tobacco not exceeding 250 grams in weight, 2 liters of wine, 1 liter of other alcoholic beverages, perfume and toilet water not exceeding 500 ml, of which not more than 25% may be perfume, into Kenya or other East African countries. The tobacco and alcohol allowance applies only to people 18 and over.

The United States is a signatory to CITES, a wildlife protection treaty, and therefore does not allow the importation of living or dead endangered animals, or their body parts, such as rhino horns or ivory. If you purchase an antique that is made partly or wholly of ivory, you must obtain a CITES preconvention certificate that clearly states the item is at least 100 years old. The import of zebra skin or other tourist products also requires a CITES permit.

Information in Kenya **Kenya Customs Service Department** (⊕ *www.kra. go.ke*).

U.S. Information **U.S. Customs and Border Protection** (⊕ *www.cbp.gov*). **U.S. Fish and Wildlife Service** (⊕ *www.fws.gov*).

ELECTRICITY

The electrical current is 220 volts, 50 cycles alternating current (AC); wall outlets in most of the region take 15-amp plugs with three round prongs (the old British system), but some take the straight-edged three-prong plugs, also 15 amps.

If your appliances are dual-voltage, you'll need only an adapter. In remote areas (and even in some lodges) power may be solar or from a generator; this means that delivery is erratic both in voltage and supply. In even the remotest places, however, lodge staff will find a way to charge video and camera batteries, but you will receive little sympathy if you insist on using a hair dryer or electric razor.

HEALTH

The CDC provides up-to-date information on health risks and recommended vaccinations and medications for travelers to Southern and East Africa. Check with the CDC's traveler's health line regarding the regions you'll be visiting. For up-to-date, local expertise, contact SAA Netcare Travel Clinics.

The Web site Travel Health Online is a good source to check out before you travel because it compiles primarily health and some safety information from a variety of official sources, and it's done by a medical publishing company.

The Flying Doctors Service offered by AMREF provides air evacuation services for medical emergencies in Kenya, Tanzania, and Uganda or anywhere within a 1,000 km (621 mi) radius of Nairobi. The planes fly out of Nairobi's Wilson Airport 24 hours a day, 365 days a year. They also provide transportation between medical facilities, fly you back to Europe, Asia, or North America, or provide you with an escort if you're flying on a commercial carrier.

Health Warnings **National Centers for Disease Control & Prevention** (*CDC* ☎ *877/394–8747 international travelers' health line* ⊕ *www.cdc.gov/travel*). **Travel Health Online** (⊕ *www.tripprep.com*). **World Health Organization** (*WHO* ⊕ *www.who.int*).

Medical-Assistance Companies **The Flying Doctors Service** (☎ *020/315–454 landline, 073/363–9088 mobile* ⊕ *www.amref.org*).

OVER-THE-COUNTER REMEDIES

You can buy over-the-counter medication in pharmacies and supermarkets. Your body may not react the same way to the Kenyan version of a product, even something as simple as a headache tablet, so bring your own supply for your trip and rely on pharmacies just for emergency medication.

For information about medication and for a list of licensed pharmacies and pharmacists in Kenya, visit the Pharmacy and Poisons Board's Web site (⊕ *www.pharmacyboardkenya.org*).

MAIL

There is a post office in Nairobi and Mombasa. Both are open weekdays 8–6 and Saturday 9–noon.

Kenya has more than 100 registered postal and courier firms and franchises, including DHL. Internet cafés and post and courier offices are in convenient places like shopping malls and are open late.

All overseas mail costs the same. A postcard is about Ksh 55 (80¢), and a letter will run you about Ksh 95 ($1.40), depending on size and weight.

SHIPPING PACKAGES

If you make a purchase, try your best to take it home on the plane with you, even if it means packing your travel clothes and items into a box and shipping those to your home, or buying a cheap piece of luggage and paying the excess weight fees. If you buy something from a store accustomed to foreign visitors, they will likely already have a system for getting your items to you, often in a surprising few weeks' time.

Most courier services offer speed and overnight services. The postal corporation of Kenya (Posta) has an Expedited Mail Service that offers next-day delivery to the U.K. and three-day delivery to the U.S. (maximum weight, 31.5 kg [70 lbs.]) at more competitive prices than courier companies. G4S couriers in Kenya partners with DHL and offers international courier services for extremely valuable parcels. FedEx is represented by Easy Africa Courier Limited in Kenya.

Express Services DHL Kenya (☎020/692–5120 ⊕ www.dhl.co.ke). **East Africa Courier Limited** (☎020/211–307). **G4S** (☎020/698–2000 or 020/532–360 ⊕ www.g4s.co.ke). **Posta** (☎020/243–434 in Nairobi, 041/222–7705 in Mombasa ⊕ www.posta.co.ke).

MONEY

ATMS & BANKS

Banks open at 9 on weekdays and close at 3; on Saturday they open at 9 and close at 11. Banks are closed on Sunday. Many banks can perform foreign-exchange services or international electronic transfers. Try to avoid banks at their busiest times—at 9 and from noon to 2 on Friday, and at month's end—unless you're willing to arrive early and lineup with the locals. Major banks in Kenya are Barclay's, Kenya Commercial, and Standard Chartered.

Major international credit cards such as Visa and MasterCard are accepted at Kenyan banks and by ATMs. It is wise to bring two ATM cards for different accounts whenever traveling abroad, both in case one is stolen or "eaten" by a machine, and to give yourself an option in case a machine takes only one or the other type. Most ATMs accept Cirrus, Plus, Maestro, Visa Electron, and Visa and MasterCard.

The best place to withdraw cash is at an indoor ATM, preferably one guarded by a security officer. If you're unsure where to find a safe ATM, ask a merchant. If anyone approaches you while you're using an ATM, immediately press cancel.

CREDIT CARDS

Throughout this guide, the following abbreviations are used: **AE**, American Express; **DC**, Diners Club; **MC**, MasterCard; and **V**, Visa.

It's a good idea to inform your credit-card company before you travel, especially if you're going abroad and don't travel internationally very often. Otherwise, the credit-card company might put a hold on your card owing to unusual activity—not a good thing, halfway through your trip. Record all your credit-card numbers—as well as the phone numbers to call if your cards are lost or stolen—in a safe place, so you're prepared should something go wrong. MasterCard, Visa, and American Express all have general numbers you can call collect if you're abroad.

MasterCard, Visa, and American Express are accepted almost everywhere, whereas Diners Club is not quite as widely accepted. Discover is not recognized.

Reporting Lost Cards **American Express** (☎ *800/528-4800 in U.S., 336/393-1111 collect from abroad* ⊕ *www.americanexpress.com*). **Diners Club** (☎ *800/234-6377 in U.S., 303/799-1504 collect from abroad* ⊕ *www.dinersclub.com*). **MasterCard** (☎ *800/627-8372 in U.S., 636/722-7111 collect from abroad* ⊕ *www.mastercard. com*). **Visa** (☎ *800/847-2911 inU.S., 866/654-0162 collect from Kenya* ⊕ *www. visa.com*).

CURRENCY & EXCHANGE

At this writing, the schilling was trading at about Ksh 65 to US$1. It is still relatively inexpensive given the quality of lodgings, which cost probably two-thirds the price of comparable facilities in the United States. Though some hotels in the cities have been known to charge expensive rates for tourists.

To avoid administrative hassles, keep all foreign-exchange receipts until you leave the region, as you may need them as proof when changing any unspent local currency back into your own currency.

Currency Information **Central Bank of Kenya** (✉ *Haile Selassie Ave., Nairobi* ☎ *020/286-1000* ⊕ *www.centralbank.go.ke*).

TRAVELER'S CHECKS

Some consider this the currency of the cave man, and it's true that fewer establishments accept traveler's checks these days. Nevertheless, they're a cheap and secure way to carry extra emergency money, particularly on trips to urban areas. Only bring American Express traveler's checks if coming from the United States, as Amex is well known and widely accepted; you can also avoid hefty surcharges by cashing Amex checks at Amex offices. Whatever you do, keep track of all the serial numbers in case the checks are lost or stolen.

Traveler's checks in either schillings or other major denominations (U.S. dollars, euros, and sterling) are readily accepted by most lodgings, though most people use credit cards.

Contacts **American Express** (☎ *888/412-6945 in U.S., 801/945-9450 collect outside of U.S. to add value or speak to customer service* ⊕ *www.american express.com*).

PHONES

CALLING WITHIN KENYA

Local landline calls are quite cheap and administered by Telkom Kenya. Hotels add hefty surcharges to phone balls. Prepaid cards for public telephone booths can be purchased at cafés, newsstands, convenience stores, and telephone company offices. City codes are (0)41 for Mombasa and (0)20 for Nairobi; include the first 0 when you dial within the country. When making a phone call in Kenya, always use the full 10-digit number, including the area code, even if you're in the same area. Telkom Kenya now offers VoIP calling card services, for cheap international calls at Ksh 15 per minute.

Directory inquiries numbers are different for each cell-phone network. Safaricom is 191 and Celtel is 111. These calls are charged at normal rates, but the call is timed only from when it is actually answered. You can, for an extra fee, get the call connected by the operator.

Contacts **Directory Assistance** (☎ *020/323-2000*). **Telkom Kenya** (⊕ *www. telkom.co.ke*).

CALLING OUTSIDE KENYA

The country code for the United States is 1.

When dialing out from Kenya, dial 000 before the international code. So, for example, you would dial 000 (0001) for the United States. Other country codes are 00044 for the United Kingdom, 00027 for South Africa, and 00033 for France.

If you really want to save on international phone calls, the best advice is to provide a detailed itinerary back home and agree upon a schedule for calls. Even if they call your "free" cell phone, they'll be paying on the other end, so speak quickly or keep in touch via the Internet.

Access Codes **MCI WorldPhone** (☎ *0800/220-111 from Kenya*).

MOBILE PHONES

The biggest mobile phone service providers in Kenya are Celtel Kenya (formerly KenCell) and Safaricom.

The least complicated way to make and receive phone calls is to obtain international roaming service from your cell phone service provider before you leave home, but this can be expensive. Cell phones can be rented by the day, week, or longer from the airport on your arrival, but this is an expensive option, too.

If you have brought your cell phone to Kenya, you can activate inbound roaming on Celtel's network by selecting "settings" in your phone menu, then "phone Settings," followed by "network selection," then "manual selection," and then "Celtel" or 63903 or "yes."

Safaricom also has partnerships with service providers in a number of countries that can set up international roaming on your phone.

Contacts **Kenya Celtel** (☎ *0733/100-710 or 0733/100-700* ⊕ *www.ke.celtel. com*). **Cellular Abroad** (☎ *800/287-5072* ⊕ *www.cellularabroad.com*) rents and sells GMS phones and sells SIM cards that work in many countries, but cost a lot more than local solutions. **Safaricom** (☎ *020/427–2100 24-hour helpline* ⊕ *www. safaricom.com*). **Mobal** (☎ *888/888–9162* ⊕ *www.mobalrental.com*) rents mobiles and sells GSM phones (starting at $49) that will operate in 140 countries. Per-call rates vary throughout the world. **Planet Fone** (☎ *888/988–4777* ⊕ *www.planet-fone.com*) rents cell phones, but the per-minute rates are expensive.

SAFETY

Kenya is a relatively poor country and crime is a reality for residents and tourists alike. Kenya is attracting growing numbers of tourists every year, and is making a concerted effort to educate tourists about crime in the country and encourage the practice of basic safety precautions.

Try to keep your valuables in a hotel safety box, and do not take valuables with you while you are sightseeing or walking around. Mugging is one of the most frequent crimes committed, and this can be thwarted by not carrying valuables, particularly cell phones, passports, identification, or expensive jewelry. Keep a little money for spending, or if you are carrying your credit card, keep it safe on your person (not, for example, in your back pocket). Tourist authorities do not recommend chasing or running after pickpocketers, as they have been known to lead tourists into areas where other members of a gang wait.

Crime is a problem particularly in major cities, and visitors should take precautions to protect themselves. Do not walk alone at night, and exercise caution even during the day. Avoid wearing jewelry (even costume jewelry), don't invite attention by wearing an expensive camera around your neck, and don't flash a large wad of cash. If you are toting a handbag, wear the strap across your body; even better, wear a money belt, preferably hidden from view under your clothing. When sitting at airports or at restaurants, especially outdoor cafés, make sure to keep your bag on your lap or between your legs—otherwise it may just quietly "walk off" when you're not looking. Even better, loop the strap around your leg, or clip the strap around the table or chair. Beware of thieves posing as tourist guides, taxi drivers, or police. Always ask for official identification.

Don't drive alone, especially at night or in areas that you don't know well. Drive carefully and slowly and look out for errant pedestrians. Carjacking is another problem, with armed bandits often forcing drivers out of their vehicles at traffic lights, in driveways, or during a fake accident. Always drive with your windows closed and doors locked, don't stop for hitchhikers, and park in well-lighted places. At traffic lights, leave enough space between you and the vehicle in front so you can pull into another lane if necessary. In the unlikely event you are carjacked, don't argue, and don't look at the carjacker's face. Just get out of the car, or ask to be let out of the car. Do not try to keep any of your belongings—they are all replaceable, even that laptop with all that data on it. If you are not given the opportunity to leave the car, try to stay calm, ostentatiously look away from the hijackers so they can be sure you can't identify them, and follow all instructions. Ask again, calmly, to be let out of the car.

Many places that are unsafe in Kenya will not bear obvious signs of danger, so always be aware. Kenyan police also publish information and details about crime "hot spots" on their Web site. Make sure you know exactly where you're going. Purchase a good map and obtain comprehensive directions from your hotel, rental car agent, or a trusted local. Taking the wrong exit off a highway into a rural or deserted area could lead you straight to disaster. Many cities are ringed by "no-go" areas. Learn from your hotel or the locals which areas to avoid. If you sense you have taken a wrong turn, drive toward a public area, such as a gas station, or building with an armed guard, before attempting to correct your mistake, which could just compound the problem. When parking, do not leave anything visible in the car; stow it all in the trunk. As an added measure, leave the glove box open, to show there is nothing of value inside (take the rental agreement with you).

Before setting out on foot, ask a local, such as your hotel concierge, or a shopkeeper, which route to take and how far you can safely go. Walk with a purposeful stride so you look like you know where you're going, and duck into a shop or café if you need to check a map, speak on your mobile phone, or recheck the directions you've been given.

Lone women travelers need to be particularly vigilant about walking alone and locking their rooms. Harassment does occur. If you do attract someone who won't take a firm but polite no for an answer, appeal immediately to the hotel manager, bartender, or someone else who seems to be in charge. If you have to walk a short distance alone at night, such as from the hotel reception to your room in a dark motel compound, or back from a café along a main street, have a plan, carry a whistle, or know what you will do if you are grabbed.

Street kids in Kenya sometimes form gangs and can be dangerous. Tourist groups recommend ignoring or walking away from one or a group of boys if they harass you. Don't give money to the children, as it is often spent on drugs; donating a meal is a better idea.

TAXES

In Kenya the value-added tax (V.A.T.), currently 16%, is included in the price of most goods and services, including accommodations and food. To get a V.A.T. refund, foreign visitors must present receipts at the airport and carry purchased items with them or in their luggage. Fill out Form V.A.T. 4, available at the airport V.A.T. refund office. Make sure that your receipts are original tax invoices, containing the vendor's name and address, V.A.T. registration number, and the words tax invoice. Refunds are paid by check, which can be cashed immediately at an airport bank or refunded to your credit card with a small transaction fee. Visit the V.A.T. refund desk in the departures hall before you go through check-in, and organize receipts as you travel. Officials will go through your receipts and randomly ask to view purchases.

Airport taxes and fees are included in the price of your ticket.

Contacts **Kenya Revenue Authority** (☎ *020/281–7700* ⊕ *www.kra.go.ke*).

GREEN LODGINGS IN KENYA

Being a responsible ecotourist is important. But how can you be sure you're traveling green? We've given you a few places you can stay on safari that are ecoconscious. Of course our list is not exhaustive, but it's a starting place.

Though the folks at **Cottars 1920s Safari Camp** (above) tread lightly on the environment, this camp remains one of the most exclusive and luxurious in Africa. Perhaps that's because this place knows what it's doing, and has been doing so since 1919. Cottars offers bush picnics, walks, and even night drives. The owners of Cottars have paid the local Masai community for use of their land, and have also helped finance the building of a local school and medicine for nearby clinics so that the camp and its activities are seen as a part of—not an intrusion on—the surrounding land and its people. *See Permanent Tented Camps, in Masai Mara for more information about the camp.*

CONTACT INFORMATION

Cottars 1920s Safari Camp: 020/603–090 or 888/870–0903 (toll-free in U.S.); www.cottars.com

Il Ngwesi Camp: 62/31–830; www.ilngwesi.com

Porini Rhino Camp: 020/712–2504 or 020/712–3129; www.porini.com

Il Ngwesi Camp (below) is a shining example of how a safari lodge can reduce poverty and strengthen partnerships between the tourist trade and local communities in Africa. Built only with local materials, the camp is completely solar-powered and its water comes from a nearby spring and is gravity-fed to the lodge. The local Masai community helped build and continues to run the camp through a communal group. *See Luxury Lodges, in Laikipia Plateau for more information about the camp.*

Opened in 2007, **Porini Rhino Camp** (top right) is the largest black rhino sanctuary in East Africa with more than 70 black rhinos. The camp has no permanent structures and is strategically constructed around trees and shrubs to minimize the human footprint on the natural landscape. The camp uses solar power for electricity and water is heated with ecofriendly, sustainable charcoal briquettes; there is no generator. The conservancy is owned by the local Masai, and the camp is run with the aim of creating income for the tribe. *See Permanent Tented Camps, in Laikipia Plateau for more information about the camp.*

HOW GREEN IS YOUR TOUR OPERATOR?

You don't want to travel with a company that has hijacked the "eco" label with false aims, you want to travel with a company that truly adheres to and believes in green travel. Before you book your trip, question several tour operators about their relationship to the communities where their safaris take place. Ask about the company's philosophies on recycling, energy efficiency, water conservation, and waste management. Also find out whether the company, or the lodges it uses, provides economic opportunities for local communities. Many reputable outfitters have established foundations that make donations to local peoples or wildlife, to which you can contribute. Some will even arrange trips for guests to nearby schools, orphanages, or neighborhoods during off-peak game-viewing hours.

Tanzania

ME TO
NIA

TOP REASONS
TO GO

★ **The great migration.**
This annual movement is
one of the great natural
wonders of the world.

★ **Big-game adventures.**
You'll be amazed at how
close up and familiar you
get not only with the Big
Five but with thousands
of other animals as well.

★ **Sea, sand, and sun.**
Tanzania's sun-drenched,
but deserted beaches are
lapped by the turquoise
blue waters of the Indian
Ocean. Swim, snorkel,
scuba dive, sail, fish, or
just chill on soft white
sands under waving
palm trees.

★ **Ancient cultures.**
From the traditional red-
robed, bead-bedecked no-
madic Masai in the north to
the heady mix of Arab and
African influences in Zanzibar, you'll encounter unique
peoples and cultures just
about everywhere you go.

★ **Bird-watching.** Stay
glued to your binoculars
in one of the finest bird-
watching destinations
in the world. You'll see
hundreds of species in
a variety of habitats.

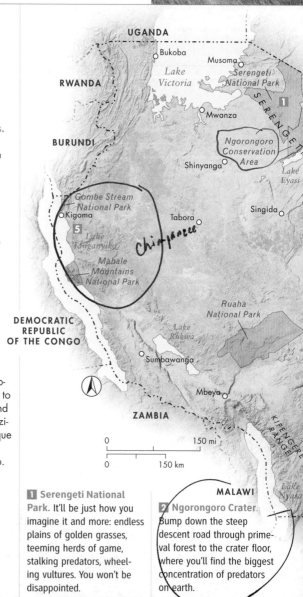

1 **Serengeti National
Park.** It'll be just how you
imagine it and more: endless
plains of golden grasses,
teeming herds of game,
stalking predators, wheel-
ing vultures. You won't be
disappointed.

2 **Ngorongoro Crater.**
Bump down the steep
descent road through primeval forest to the crater floor,
where you'll find the biggest
concentration of predators
on earth.

3 **Lake Manyara National Park.** Tree-climbing lions, huge troops of baboons, elegant giraffes, harrumphing hippos, myriad birds, ancient forest, lakeside plains, and towering cliffs characterize this enchanting, little-visited park.

4 **Selous Game Reserve.** Escape the tourist crowds in the world's second-largest conservation area, where you can view game on foot, by boat, or from your vehicle.

5 **Gombe Stream and Mahale Mountains National Parks.** Follow in the footsteps of world-famous primatologist Jane Goodall and come face to face with wild chimpanzees. It's an unforgettable wildlife encounter.

GETTING ORIENTED

Covering an area of 886,037 square km (342,100 square mi), which includes the islands of Mafia, Pemba, and Zanzibar, Tanzania is about twice the size of the state of California. It's bordered by the Indian Ocean in the east, Kenya to the north, and Mozambique to the south. The country is also home to some of the most coveted tourist destinations in the world: Serengeti; Ngorongoro Crater; Zanzibar; Lakes Victoria, Tanganyika, and Malawi; and Mt. Kilimanjaro, Africa's highest freestanding mountain. Tourism doesn't come cheap, but you'll be rewarded with spectacular views, legions of game, and unique marine experiences. The area also has more than 1,130 bird species. Traveling distances are vast, so be prepared for lots of trips in different-sized planes, or bite the bullet and face the notoriously bad potholes and seriously bumpy dirt roads.

KENYA

Ngorongoro Crater
Mt. Meru
4,566 m
Mt. Kilimanjaro
5,895 m
Arusha
Lake Manyara
Moshi
Arusha National Park
3
Lake Manyara National Park
Tarangire National Park
MASAI STEPPE
Dodoma
Tanga
Wete
PEMBA
Mkoani
Mkokotoni
Koani
Stone Town
ZANZIBAR
Morogoro
Kibaha
DAR ES SALAAM
Iringa
MAFIA
Selous Game Reserve
4
Mohoro
INDIAN OCEAN
Lindi
Mtwara
Songea

MOZAMBIQUE

4

TANZANIA PLANNER

Fast Facts

Number of National Parks 15

Number of Private Reserves
Too many to count.

Population In 2007 it was
39,384,223.

Big Five All the Big Five including Black and White rhino.

Language Official languages
are Kiswahili and English.

Time Tanzania is on EAT (East
Africa Time), which is three
hours ahead of Greenwich Mean
Time and eight hours ahead of
Eastern Standard Time.

Tipping

If you've been given good service, tip accordingly. For a two-
or three-night stay at a lodge
or hotel tip a couple of dollars
for small services, US$2–US$5
per day for room steward and
waiter. Your guide will expect
a tip of US$10–US$15 per day
per person; if he's gone out of
his way for you, then you may
wish to give him more. It's a
good idea to carry a number of
small denomination bills. U.S.$
are acceptable almost everywhere, but if you're planning to
go to more remote places, then
shillings are preferred.

Health & Safety

Malaria is the biggest health threat in Tanzania, so be vigilant about taking anti-malarials and applying bug spray.
Consult with your doctor or travel clinic before leaving
home for up-to-date anti-malarial medication. At time of
writing HIV/AIDS is less a risk than in some other African
countries, but the golden rule is *never* to have sex with a
stranger. It's imperative to use strong sunscreen: remember
you are just below the Equator where the sun is at its hottest. Stick to bottled water and ensure that the bottle seal is
unbroken. Put your personal medications in your carry-on
and bring copies of prescriptions. If you develop flulike
symptoms after you return home—headaches, fever, joint
pains—consult your doctor immediately and inform him or
her that you've been in a tropical diseases area.

The same safety rules apply wherever you are in Africa:
leave expensive jewelry and watches at home. Lock valuables away wherever and whenever possible. Carry only
the money you need on a daily basis. Keep copies of all
your documents in your luggage away from the originals.

Important Details

Embassies United States (⊠ *686 Old Bagamoyo Rd., Dar
es Salaam* ☎ *022/266–8001*).
Emergencies Police Hotline (☎ *999 or 111*).
Money Matters The official currency is the Tanzania Shilling. Notes are 500, 1,000, 2,000, 5,000, and 10,000.
Passports & Visas Most visitors require a visa to enter
Tanzania. You can buy one upon arrival—make sure you
have at least $100 cash as the visa price has recently
increased and does so all the time and two passport
pictures—but get one ahead of time if possible. Visas
are valid for three months and allow multiple entries.
Passports must be valid for 6 months after your planned
departure date from Tanzania.
Visitor Information The Tanzanian Tourist Board (TTB)
(☎ 022/211-1244 ⊕ www.tanzaniatouristboard.com) has
offices in Dar es Salaam and Arusha. The tourist board's
Web site is a great online source for pretrip planning.

About the Camps & Lodges

You'll find the ultimate in luxury at many of the safari camps, lodges, and coastal resorts and hotels. We highly recommend that you opt for a private camp or lodge if possible, because everything is usually included—lodging, transport to and from the lodge, meals, beverages including excellent house wines, game drives, and other activities. Check in advance whether park fees are included in your rate as these can get very expensive if you have to pay them daily. The southern safari circuit is cheaper in general, but you will need to factor in the cost of transport. Many lodges and hotels offer low-season rates. If you're opting for a private game lodge, find out whether they accept children (many specify only kids over 12), and stay a minimum of two nights, three if you can. If you're traveling to the more remote parks, allow for more time. National park accommodations are few and very basic. Unless you are a hardcore camper, we advise that you stick with another type of accommodation. It's essential to note that more often than not, there will not be an elevator in your lodge—which are usually one story—and because of the rustic locations, accommodations are not wheelchair-friendly. You'll encounter lots of steps, rocky paths, dim lighting, and uneven ground.

Food in the lodges is plentiful and tasty, and if you head to the coast, you'll dine on superb seafood and fish with lots of fresh fruit and vegetables. All places now have at least one vegetarian course on the menu. The price categories used for lodging in this chapter treat all-inclusive lodges differently from other lodgings; see the price chart below for details.

WHAT IT COSTS In U.S. dollars

	¢	$	$$	$$$	$$$$
SAFARI CAMPS & LODGES	under $199	$200–$450	$451–$750	$751–$1,000	over $1,000
LODGING	under $100	$101–$150	$151–$200	$201–$250	over $250
DINING	under $5	$6–$10	$11–$20	$21–$30	over $30

All prices refer to an all-inclusive per-person, per night rate including 12.5% tax, assuming double occupancy. Hotel prices are for a standard double room in high season. Restaurant prices are per person for a main course at dinner, a main course equivalent, or a prix-fixe meal.

When to Go

There are two rainy seasons: the short rains (*mvuli*) October through December; and the long rains (*masika*) from late February to early May. Given the influence of global warming, these rains are not as regular or intense as they once were. It's best to avoid the two rainy seasons because many roads become impassable. Ngorongoro Crater is open all year, but the roads become extremely muddy and difficult to navigate during the wet seasons. High season is January to the end of September, but prices are much higher during this time. Make sure you find out in advance when the lodge or destination of your choice is closed as many are open only during the dry season. The coast is always pretty hot and humid, particularly during the rains, but is much cooler and more pleasant the rest of the year. The hottest time is December just before the long rains. In high-altitude areas such as Ngorongoro highlands and Mt. Kilimanjaro temperatures can fall below freezing. The Web site for **African Weather Forecasts** (⊕ *www.africanweather. net*) lists weather information for the entire continent.

4

By Kate
Turkington

Tanzania is the quintessential, definitive Africa of your dreams. And who wouldn't want to visit a place where the names of its legendary travel destinations roll off the tongue like an incantation: Zanzibar, Serengeti, Olduvai Gorge, Mt. Kilimanjaro, Lake Tanganyika, Lake Victoria, the Rift Valley, the Ngorongoro Crater, Olduvai Gorge, the Cradle of Humankind.

Great plains abound with legions of game, snow-capped mountains soar above dusty valleys, rain forests teem with monkeys and birds, beaches are covered in sand as soft and white as talcum powder, and coral reefs host myriads of jewel-like tropical fish. Although Tanzania is one of the poorest countries in the world—its economy depends heavily on agriculture, which accounts for almost half of its GDP—it has more land (more than 25%) devoted to national parks and game reserves than any other wildlife destination in the world. Everything from pristine coral reefs to the crater highlands, remote game reserves, and the famous national parks are protected by government law and placed in trust for future generations.

The East African coast appears to have first been explored by the Phoenicians in approximately 600 BC. Bantu peoples arrived about 2,000 years ago and a few 4th-century Roman coins have turned up at the coast. We can tell from ancient writings that the Romans certainly knew about Mt. Kilimanjaro and the great inland lakes, but nobody is quite sure how they came by this knowledge. By 100 AD trade with India and the Middle East was well established, and many city-states ruled by local sultans sprang up along the coast. The Portuguese first arrived at the end of the 15th-century looking for a trade route to India, but their hold on the country was shattered when the Sultan of Oman captured Mombasa in 1698; 150 years later he transferred his

DID YOU KNOW?

Tanzania is one of the world's largest producers of cashews, exporting 110,231 tons of raw nuts each year.

capital here from Oman. The slave trade dominated the coast and the interior from the early 1800s. It was only finally eradicated after the passionate first-hand accounts given by Dr. Livingstone in the 1850s proposing the abolition of the slave trade came to fruition in 1918 when the British took control of Tanzania. This was followed in the Scramble for Africa by German rule. Germany was determined to make the colony self-sufficient by planting coffee and cotton, efforts which failed. Tanzania returned to British hands after World War I and finally won its independence in 1964. It's now a stable multi-party democracy. Dar es Salaam is still the country's capital, but the legislative offices have been transferred to the central city of Dodoma, which was been chosen to be the new national capital in 1973; the transfer is slow moving because of the great expense. The National Assembly already meets there on a regular basis.

Tanzania has always been the poor relation of Kenya in terms of tourist numbers, but in recent years numbers of visitors are increasing along with a better infrastructure and tourist facilities.

There are two circuits you can follow in Tanzania: the conventional northern tourist circuit, which includes the Serengeti and Ngorongoro Crater or the lesser-traveled southern tourist circuit of Selous Game Reserve and Ruaha, Mahale, and Gombe national parks among others. You'll be amply rewarded for the often lengthy traveling to these southern locations by having the places much more to yourself and usually at cheaper rates.

Serengeti *is* all it's cracked up to be with endless plains of golden grasses (Serengeti means "endless plain" in the Masai language), teeming game, abundant bird life, and an awe-inspiring sense of space and timelessness. Ngorongoro Crater justly deserves its reputation as one of the natural wonders of the world. The ride down onto the crater floor is memorable enough as you pass through misty primeval forest with wild orchids, swinging vines, and chattering monkeys, but once on the floor you could well be in the middle of a National Geographic TV program. You can follow in the footsteps of legendary hunters and explorers when you visit Selous Game Reserve in the south. Although it's the second largest conservation area in the world after Greenland National Park, only 5% of the northern part is open to tourists; but don't worry, you'll see all the game and birds you could wish for with the advantage of seeing it by boat and on foot. If it's chimpanzees you're after, then Gombe Stream and Mahale Mountains national parks are the places to head for. A lot of traveling (much of it by boat) is required, but the experience is well worth the effort and you'll join only a small community of other privileged visitors who have had the unique experience of coming face-to-face with wild chimpanzees.

The animals aren't the only wonders Tanzania has to offer. There are the island of Zanizibar, Pemba, and Mafia, as well as Mt. Kilimanjaro, Mt. Meru, and the three great lakes of Victoria, Tanganyika, and Lake Malawi. Wherever you go, you are guaranteed travel experiences that you'll remember for the rest of your life.

MUST-SEE PARKS

Unfortunately, you probably won't be able to see all of Tanzania in one trip. So we've broken down the chapter by **Must-See Parks** (Serengeti National Park, Ngorongoro Conservation Area, Lake Manyara National Park, Selous Game Reserve, Gombe Stream and Mahale Mountains National Parks) and **If You Have Time Parks** (Arusha National Park, Tarangire National Park, and Ruaha National Park) to help you better organize your time. We suggest though, that you read about all of them and then choose for yourself.

DID YOU KNOW?

According to the Tanzania Tourist Board the Top 10 Tanzania destinations are:

1. Ngorongoro Crater

2. Serengeti National Park

3. Zanzibar and Pemba islands

4. Tarangire National Park

5. Lake Manyara National Park

6. Mt. Kilimanjaro

7. Selous Game Reserve

8. Ruaha National Park

9. Mafia Island

10. Mt. Meru

SERENGETI NATIONAL PARK

Game
★★★★★

Park Accessibility
★★★★★

Ease of Getting Around
★★★★★

Accommodations
★★★★★

Scenic Beauty
☆★★★★

The very name Serengeti is guaranteed to bring a glint to even the most jaded traveler's eye. It's up there in that wish list of legendary destinations alongside Machu Picchu, Angkor Wat, Kakadu, Killarney, and the Great Pyramid of Giza. But what distinguishes Serengeti from all its competitors is its sheer naturalness.

It's 15,000 square km (5,791 square mi) of pristine wilderness and that's it. Its Masai name *Serenget,* means Endless Plain. A primeval Eden par excellence, named a World Heritage Site in 1978 and an International Biosphere Reserve in 1981, Serengeti is all it's cracked up to be. You won't be disappointed.

This ecosystem supports some of the most plentiful mammal populations left anywhere on earth and the animals here seem bigger, stockier, stronger, and sturdier than elsewhere in Africa. Even the scrub hares are bigger than their southern neighbors, loping rather than scampering over the tussocks and grassy mounds. Hyenas are everywhere and raptors are in perpetual motion—tawny eagles, kestrels, harriers, kites, buzzards, and vultures. Expect to see at least one baby wildebeest that has fallen by the wayside lying alone encircled by patient, voracious vultures or prowling hyenas.

But let's put you right in the picture. You'll probably land at a busy landing strip, maybe near Ntuti, where a dozen open-sided vehicles wait to pick up the new arrivals. Don't worry about lots of vehicles. In your few days driving around the Serengeti you'll certainly see others, but not too many. As you leave the airstrip, your vehicle will weave its way through herds of zebra and gazelle. Rufous-tailed weavers, endemic to Northern Tanzania, flutter up from the sandy road. The plains stretch endlessly with misty mountains faint in the distance. At first the plains are ringed by trees, but then only an occasional and solitary tree punctuates the golden grasses. Wherever you stay, you'll be

CLOSE UP

Writer Snapshot

We came upon a pride of 14 lions dozing languidly (as only lions can) in the long grass. The 4 adults and 11 cubs have finished stuffing themselves on a wildebeest. Heavy breathing permeates the air and flies buzz round the blood-stained muzzles. Suddenly, as if she has just remembered something, a lioness bloated with food, yawns, stretches, shakes the flies off, and begins to stalk purposefully off through the long grass. She is intent, focused. We follow in our vehicle and watch her golden body flowing through the long grass for just over a kilometer. There is one solitary tree on the horizon. As we all reach it together—vehicle and lioness—a huge male, unseen before he lifts up his heavy head, gives a little moan of recognition. Her 6-month-old cub rushes up to her, nearly knocking her over with his enthusiastic welcome. She turns around, cub trotting beside her, and begins to make her way back to the food source. The male puts his head between his paws and goes back to sleep. Babysitting over for the time being.

looked after royally, with comfortable accommodation, good food, a dawn chorus of bubbling birdsong, and an evening serenade of whooping hyenas with a backing group of softly calling lions.

What will you remember about the Serengeti? The unending horizons and limitless plains. The sheer space. The wildebeest. The oh-so-beautiful Thompson's and Grant's gazelles. The bat-eared foxes playing in the early morning sun. Lions galore, and in particular, the one that may wander past your tent one night and roar under the blazing stars. The hosts of water birds by the streams, lakes, and rivers. The ancient flat-topped acacia trees, ancient guardians of this windswept wilderness. The quiet. The Big Country. Knowing how small is your place in the interconnectedness of all things. And how privileged you are to be able to experience the wonder of it all…

WHERE TO STAY

LUXURY LODGES

$$$$ ☷ **Sasakwa Lodge.** This is one of three camps in the Grumeti Reserve, a 350,000-acre concession in Serengeti's Western Corridor. If you're at all familiar with the Singita name, you'll know it is associated in South Africa with some of the most luxurious and elegant lodges in the Sabi Sands Private Reserve in South Africa. This superlative lodge, built in the style of a 1920s East African ranch house, adds more luster to the Singita name. You'll stay in one of seven honey-color stone cottages, each elegantly furnished with hand-carved furniture, cream and white throws, cushions, and lamps, and copies of antique animal prints lining the high walls. Need some down time? Sit out on your deck and watch for game, luxuriate in your own heated pool, or laze in your lounge and listen to the state-of-the-art sound system. There are game drives here—the game is as good as it gets—but there are also horseback riding and mountain biking, all with an armed guard in

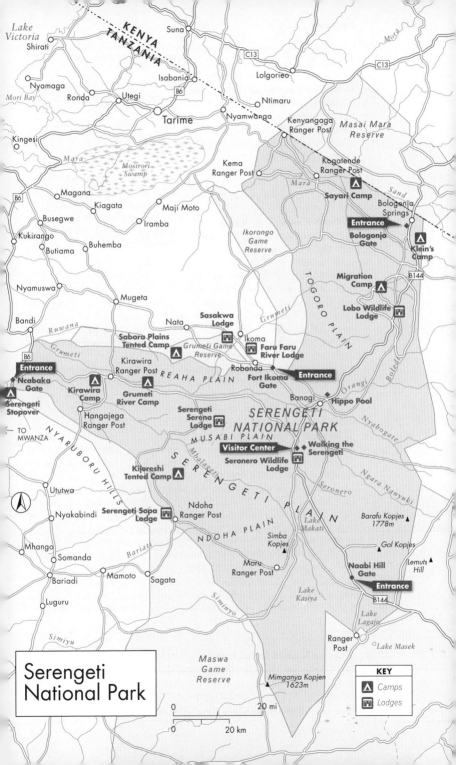

Serengeti National Park

attendance. Enjoy a massage before a fine dinner served with crystal and silver. ■TIP→ No children under 10 are allowed and the lodge is closed April and May. *Singita Central Reservations, Claremont, Cape Town 7735, South Africa* ☎021/683–3424 ⊕*www.singita.com* ➬*7 cottages* ⋄*In-room: a/c, minibar, safe, pool. In-hotel: bar, restaurant, pool, spa, Internet, TV, library, tennis courts* ☰*AE, MC, V* ⦿*FAP.*

$$$ ☖**Klein's Camp.** This lovely little camp, named after the 1920s American big game hunter Al Klein, is built on the crest of the Kuka Hills with 360-degree panoramic views. Because it lies just outside the national park on a 24,710-acre private conservancy leased from the local Ololosokwan community, you can go on unrestricted game drives and three-hour bush walks—night drives are particularly thrilling. A visit with your Masai guide to his village will be another highlight. Stone and thatch cottages have en-suite bathrooms and a private veranda with great views over the Grumeti River valley. The separate dining and lounge area and very comfortable large bar have stunning views. Game is very good, especially along the river. *CC Africa, Private Bag X27, Benmore 2010, South Africa* ☎27/11/809–4300 ⊕*www.kleinscamp.com* ➬*10 cottages* ⋄*In-hotel: bar, pool, curio shop* ☰*AE, DC, MC, V* ⦿*FAP.*

$$ ☖**Serengeti Serena Lodge.** Situated high on a hill with superb views over the central Serengeti, the two-story thatch cottages are shaped like Masai huts and are among indigenous trees. Each is individually decorated with handcrafted African furniture and colorful Africa-theme soft furnishings. If you need to unwind, head to your wooden balcony and gaze far out over the plains. You'll get lost in your thoughts and the view. If you're in a sociable mood, head to the huge bar and dining area, also rondawel-shaped, which is supported by tall carved figures of Masai maidens and warriors. The food here is tasty and plentiful, and there's a gorgeous horizon pool with another great view. All the Serengeti activities are on offer and are included, but it's worth spending those extra pennies on an exclusive balloon safari and champagne breakfast. *Serena Central Reservations, Arusha, Tanzania* ☎027/250–6304 ⊕*www.serenahotels.com* ➬*66 rooms* ⋄*In-hotel: bar, restaurant, pool* ☰*AE, DC, MC, V* ⦿*FAP.*

PERMANENT TENTED CAMPS

$$$$ ☖**Serena Kirawira Camp.** Turn back the clock and stay at a camp that any well-heeled Victorian traveler would have felt completely at home in. Colonial comfort meets Africa in this gorgeous tented camp overlooking the Western Corridor just west of Seronara. Kirawira is a member of the Small Luxury Hotels of the World group, but that won't

> ### WORD OF MOUTH
>
> "We drove through the western corridor of Serengeti and saw wildebeest—truly a spectacle. We saw a huge herd of elephants—80 or 100 in number—wandering in the plains. On our last day, we ran into a lion and a lioness whose cubs were hidden in some grass right next to the dirt road. What a sight! We had our picnic lunch 5 feet away from that family. I got my best pictures at that location"
>
> –dhruvgupta

surprise you as the elegant pioneer ambience—polished wooden floors, gleaming antique furniture, handmade patchwork bedspreads, copper urns, and shining brass lamps—wraps itself around you. Your spacious double en-suite tent faces the endless plains where you can go for exhilarating game-packed drives and guided walks. Venture farther afield to go fishing or sailing on Lake Victoria. A crocodile safari—brave souls go out at night to track and watch crocs—by the Grumeti River will be a highlight, as will your meals; the food here is some of the Serengeti's finest. ⏷*Serena Central Reservations, Arusha, Tanzania* ☎*027/250–6304* ⏷*www.kirawiracamp.com* ⏷*25 tents* ⏷*In-hotel: bar, restaurant, pool* ⊟*AE, DC, MC, V* ⏷*FAP.*

$$$ ⏷**Faru Faru River Lodge.** The third camp in the Grumeti concession in Serengeti's Western Corridor—it joins Sabora Plains Tented Camp and Sasakwa Lodge—is sprawling but intimate and is built in the style of a classic East African safari camp under sycamore trees on a hill that overlooks a gorgeous pool and the bush beyond. Local rock, wood, and thatch dominate the main buildings but you'll sleep in a classic East African tented suite from where you can watch the game at the waterhole below from your Victorian-style claw-foot tub or from your veranda. Buffalo, elephant, topi (an East African antelope), and giraffe all come to drink as do predators, while black-and-white colobus monkeys scream and swing in the trees along the river. The Great Migration moves through the reserve between June and August, although there's plenty of game all year round. Bird life is prolific with more than 400 species including lots of raptors. Viewing decks and public areas jut out over the rock pool and overlook the Grumeti River making imaginative use of local stone and wooden poles; although the effect is rustic, there is nothing rustic about the elegantly furnished tents and superb service. Dine alone with your personal waiter in attendance, or mingle with the other guests and swap fireside stories after a day's game-viewing. ■TIP→ No children under 10 are allowed and the lodge is closed April and May. ⏷*Singita Central Reservations, Claremont, Cape Town 7735, South Africa* ☎*021/683–3424* ⏷*www.singita.com* ⏷*6 tented suites* ⏷*In-room: a/c, minibar, safe, pool. In-hotel: bar, restaurant, pool, spa, Internet, TV, library, tennis courts* ⊟*AE, MC, V* ⏷*FAP.*

$$$ ⏷**Grumeti River Camp.** Situated on the banks of a Grumeti River tributary, this is one of the most exclusive tented camps in the Serengeti. En-suite tents are furnished much like you would see on the set of a Hollywood movie trying to do Africa chic. There are handmade wooden beds decorated with metal posts and bedheads, deep blue chairs with Ghanaian Kente (hand-woven fabric from Ghana) cloth cushions, handblown Kenyan glass, colorful rugs, and woven tables. The service is flawless, and there's an abundance of birdlife and game with resident hippos munching outside the tents at night. This is CC Africa at its best. ⏷*CC Africa, Private Bag X27, Benmore 2010, South Africa* ☎*27/11/809–4300* ⏷*www.ccafrica.com* ⏷*10 tents* ⏷*In-hotel: bar, pool, curio shop* ⊟*AE, DC, MC, V* ⏷*FAP.*

$$$ ⏷**Sabora Plains Tented Camp.** It's not often that you'll stay in a marquee-shape tent elegantly furnished with silk curtains, antique furniture, a/c, and stylish African artifacts, but that's what you'll get at this ultraluxu-

Grumeti River Camp, Serengeti National Park

Grumeti River Camp, Serengeti National Park

Klein's Camp, Serengeti National Park

Klein's Camp, Serengeti National Park

rious camp set among green lawns adjacent to the Great Migration route. The game-abundant terrain ranges from open plains and rocky outcrops to riverine forest and woodlands in this 350,000-acre Grumeti concession in Serengeti's Western Corridor. At night, glowing gas lamps transform the tents raised on polished wooden platforms into a bush fairyland, although the only winged creatures you see will be the night birds and the fluttering moths. If you're an experienced rider, galloping across the plains with zebra and wildebeest is an unforgettable experience. For a more soothing experience, have a spa treatment on your veranda as you gaze out at the never-ending plains. At night, enjoy the brilliance of the night sky before or after a superlative meal. ■TIP➡ **No children under 10 are allowed, and the lodge is closed April and May.** ⌂ *Singita Central Reservations, Claremont, Cape Town 7735, South Africa* ☎ *021/683–3424* ⊕ *www.singita.com* ⇌ *6 tents* ⌂ *In-room: a/c, minibar, safe, pool. In-hotel: bar, restaurant, pool, spa, Internet, TV, library, tennis courts* ☰ *AE, MC, V* ⍐ *FAP.*

$ ⊞ **Migration Camp.** Because this lovely camp is sited in northeast Serengeti among the rocky Ndasiata Hills you won't see as many vehicles as you would nearer Seronara in the center of the park, but the game is all here. It's hard to believe that the accommodation is actually tented because it looks so luxurious. Spacious tents with hand-carved wooden furniture, big windowlike screens, en-suite bathroom, and a veranda facing the Grumeti River give you a ringside seat of the migration. The main areas with their deep leather chairs, sofas, handsome rugs, and elegant fittings seem more like a gentlemen's club you'd find in London or Washington, DC, than a tent. Game is good all year round, but when the migration passes through it is awesome. Take a guided game walk from the camp, laze at the pool, or catch up on your reading in the small library. Too fast paced for you? May we suggest sitting on your veranda to watch what's happening game-wise in the surrounding wilderness. Food and service match the surroundings and accommodation in quality and style. Elewana recommends that you book through a safari specialist rather than directly. *See the Tour Operators chart in Chapter 1, Your Safari for operator suggestions.* ⌂ *Elewana Lodges, Arusha, Tanzania* ☎ *027/254–0630 or 027/254–0630* ⊕ *www.elewana.com* ⇌ *20 tents* ⌂ *In-hotel: bar, restaurant, pool, Jacuzzi* ☰ *AE, MC, V* ⍐ *FAP.*

$ ⊞ **Sayari Camp.** Overlooking the Mara River in Serengeti's northwest, where the park borders Kenya's Masai Mara National Park, this small tented camp is perfectly poised for watching the river crossing—hundreds of thousands of wildebeest plunge into the crocodile-infested water on their relentless journey north. The unforgettable sightings of this natural wonder of the world (between July and November) often exceed those of next-door Masai Mara. The spacious en-suite tents with hot water safari showers and flush toilets, colorfully decorated with handwoven rugs and wall-hangings are only a few hundred meters away from the river, so you can sit and relax in comfort while the herds build up on the bank. Then, at the appropriate moment, you can make your move and start clicking away. The Wedge, a nearby plain, is home to permanent spring-fed water and attracts thousands of antelope and other plains animals. Because this area of Serengeti is less visited than the west and south but still has an abundance of game and birdlife, you may not see another vehicle—always a huge bonus. Get there before the word gets out—you'll feel at the end of the world. ⌂ *Asilia Lodges, Arusha, Tanzania* ☎ *027/250–2799* ⊕ *www.asilialodges.com* 📞 *8 tents* 🛁 *In-hotel: bar, restaurant* ⊟ *AE, MC, V* ⊙ *FAP.*

MOBILE TENTED CAMPS

$$$
★ **Tanzania under Canvas.** CC Africa's mobile camp follows the migration beginning (usually in March) in Serengeti's northeast near Lake Ntutu on a small bluff with splendid acacia trees overlooking a small river. The camp stays put for a couple of months at a time and then moves northward with the herds. Comfortable walk-in tents (Tanzania's largest) with chandeliers that tinkle in the breeze (yes, there's even electricity) have en-suite bucket showers, copper washbasins, a flush toilet, deep, comfortable beds with crisp linen and fluffy mohair blankets, Indian rugs, a dawn chorus of joyous birdsong, and an evening serenade of whooping hyenas with back vocals by softly calling lions. If you want to rough it in the bush, then don't come to a CC Africa mobile camp because you'll be pampered at every turn. But, you're never cocooned away from the surrounding natural wonders. This is the most marvelous way to experience the migrations, the wonders of Serengeti and Africa. It's certainly not cheap, but it definitely every penny. ⌂ *CC Africa, Private Bag X27, Benmore 2010, South Africa* ☎ *27/11/809–4300* ⊕ *www.ccafrica.com* 📞 *6 tents* ⊟ *AE, DC, MC, V* ⊙ *FAP.*

$$
Nduara Loliondo. If you want to do your own thing away from the big lodges and busy safari routes, then this small intimate mobile camp, formerly Loliondo Mobile Camp, is for you. Taking up to eight travelers at a time, the "pack up and go" camp is run by Nomad Tanzania, a fitting name for a company that specializes in moving you to the game at the right place at the right time. Put yourself in the expert hands of your guide, cooks, waiters, and camp attendants to experience a true old-style safari. Accommodation is in one of four comfortable tents with hot bucket showers, bush toilet, and a big mess tent where you'll get together at the end of a hot dusty day. Your own vehicle and knowledgeable driver-guide stays with you for the length of your safari and can choose to do what you want, where you want. After a day's activities you'll enjoy sipping a glass of chilled white wine by the roaring campfire as you relive your experiences. Nomad operates several mobile camps in Tanzania, but they do not take direct bookings or publish their rates, so you'll need to contact your own safari operator for more information. *See the Tour Operators chart in Chapter 1, Your Safari, for operator suggestions.* ⌂ *Nomad Tanzania, Arusha, Tanzania* ⊕ *www.nomad-tanzania.com* 📞 *4 tents.*

BUDGET ACCOMMODATIONS

¢ **Kijereshi Tented Camp.** This small, budget camp, popular with independent travelers as well as those traveling in groups, lies on the western border of Serengeti. Furnished en-suite tents and bungalows are basic but comfortable, and there's a good restaurant, bar, lounge, and pool.

There's also a campsite 1 km (½ mi) from the lodge with cold water and bush toilet, however, campers may use the lodge facilities, that is, hot water and flush toilet. *See the Tour Operators chart in Chapter 1, Your Safari, for operator suggestions.* ⇆*12 tents, 2 family units* ⌁*In-hotel: bar, restaurant, pool, curio shop* ⊟*AE, MC, V* ❏*FAP.*

¢ ⌂**Serengeti Stop Over.** If you're coming by road from Mwanza, this is a convenient stopover just outside the national park. Accommodation is in clean basic en-suite bandas, and there's a small restaurant and bar. Friendly knowledgeable staff can arrange safaris into the park, fishing and boating trips to Lake Victoria, and cultural visits to nearby villages. Lake Victoria is within walking distance. If available, you can hire a safari vehicle for US$150 per day. ⌖*Box 2099, Arusha, Tanzania* ☎*028/262–2273 or 0748/422–359* ⊕*www.serengetistopover.com* ⇆*10 rooms* ⌁*In-hotel: bar, restaurant* ⊟*AE, MC, V* ❏*BP.*

¢ ⌂**Seronera Wildlife Lodge.** Although this big popular lodge is attractively located around huge rocks and boulders that are next to a number of waterholes, it's also plumb in the middle of Serengeti—an ideal place for superb wildlife viewing. But don't expect the levels of service and luxury you would get from some of the smaller, more exclusive camps. However, it's cheap and cheerful, with small rather drab en-suite rooms with king-size beds and big windows, and a cafeteria-style restaurant and bars that come alive in the evenings when the day's game viewing or ballooning experiences are shared. (You're only five minutes from balloon lift-off here.) The food is hearty and wholesome with a tasty evening buffet, often accompanied by the snorts and har-rumphing of the nearby hippos. You'll certainly see lots of game at close quarters, but lots of other visitors and vehicles, too. ⌖*Box 2633, Arusha, Tanzania* ☎*027/254–4595* ⊕*www.hotelsandlodges-tanzania.com* ⇆*75 rooms* ⌁*In-hotel: bar, restaurant, pool, TV, curio shop* ⊟*AE, MC, V* ❏*FAP.*

NATIONAL PARKS ACCOMMODATIONS

A resthouse at Seronera Park headquarters has basic accommodation with breakfast. There are several campsites in Serengeti including six in the Seronera area, one each at Lobo and Kirawira and one near the Ndabaka Gate. You don't have to prebook, just show up with all your provisions, camping gear, and water. Facilities include a long-drop bathroom and if you're lucky, a cold shower. Unless you're a hardcore camper, stick to the camps and lodges.

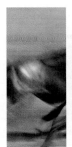

NGORONGORO CRATER

Game
★★★★★

Park Accessibility
★★★★★

Ease of Getting
Around
☆★★★★

Accommodations
★★★★★

Scenic Beauty
★★★★★

Ngorongoro Crater ranks right up there among Africa's must visit wildlife destinations: Serengeti, Masai Mara, Etosha, Kruger Park, and the Okavango Delta. Almost every would-be safari-goer wants to come here, and rightly so. One of only three UNESCO World Heritage sites in Tanzania (together with the Serengeti and the Selous Game Reserve), the crater is often called the Eighth Wonder of the World.

It lies in the Biosphere Reserve of the Ngorongoro Conservation Area, which covers 8,300 square km (3,204 square mi) in northern Tanzania. This reserve was specifically planned to accommodate both the traditional Masai communities and tourists. You'll see Masai villagers grazing their sheep and cattle all over.

The Ngorongoro Crater lies in a cluster of other volcanoes (sometimes seen rather ominously smoking) that borders the Serengeti National Park to the north and west. It's actually a collapsed volcano or *caldera*. The original volcano, which may have been higher than Kilimanjaro, collapsed in on itself over time and now forms a perfect basin. Once inside you'll feel like you're at the bottom of a deep soup bowl with very steep sides. The basin, measuring 18 km (11 mi) in diameter, lies 500 meters (1,640 feet) below the rim which towers above it at about 2,200 meters (7,217 feet) above sea level.

Believed to have formed some 2 million years ago, the crater har-

PARK ESSENTIALS

Entrance fees increase all the time, but in 2007 it cost US$30 per person to enter the Ngorongoro Conservation area. If you want to go down into the crater (aka crater service), it will cost you US$100 per vehicle per half day. Only 4x4s are allowed in the crater.

Keep in Mind

Although the crater is one of the most spectacular places on earth there are a few drawbacks to this Eden. Avoid April and May as these months are particularly wet in the crater. Also, because there is no restriction on the number of vehicles, there can be well over a 100 at one time in the high season. It's amazing to have a close-up encounter with some of Africa's finest game, but not if you're surrounded by other vehicles and often very noisy, boisterous tourists. It's best to go down as early as possible (the gates open at 6:30) to avoid the later traffic jams. But the crater is a once-in-a-lifetime experience so grit your teeth, ignore all the other tourists, and enjoy one of the world's most spectacular destinations.

bors an astonishing variety of landscapes—forests, peaks, craters, valleys, rivers, lakes, and plains—including the world-famous Olduvai Gorge where some of our earliest human ancestors once hunted and gathered. *See the Cradle of Mankind box, below.*

The very steep and bumpy drive into the crater—don't be surprised if you encounter at least one vehicle with a puncture—begins high up in the forest. At dawn thick mist drifts through the trees and visibility is next to nothing. Although this lush highland forest looks exactly like a rain forest, it's not. It's a *mist* forest, which depends on a regular and abundant amount of mist and drizzle. If you look closely enough, you'll see the particles of mist swirling like raindrops among the ancient trees. The aptly named pillarwood trees stand sentinel over the strangler figs, the croton trees, the highland bersama (a local plant), and purple flowers of the wild tobacco. The tree trunks and branches are home to thousands of epiphytes—specialized plants such as arboreal orchids and ferns—which cling to their hosts and absorb moisture with their own aerial roots. Watch out for the delicate white orchid flowers among the curtains of Old Man's Beard, or hanging tree moss.

Monkeys, bushbuck, bush pigs, and elephants frequent the forest, although it's unlikely you'll see them. What you will see if you are staying in one of the crater lodges are well-mown lawns, which are not the result of hardworking gardeners but that of zebras and buffaloes, which after dark seek sanctuary from predators here. It's not dogs you hear barking after sundown but the warning calls of vigilant zebras and baboons. The crater floor, dominated by a huge flamingo-filled alkaline lake, holds the highest concentration of predators in the world—lions, hyenas, jackals, leopards. Cheetahs can occasionally be seen but fall prey to lions and hyena, which the nervous and fragile cheetah is no match for. Big herds of plains game such as Thompson's and Grant's gazelle, impala, giraffe, zebra, and wildebeest are easy meat for the thoroughly spoiled predators that need to expend very little energy to score a megameal. You'll probably see at least one pride of bloated lions lying on their backs, paws in air, stuffed and totally damaging

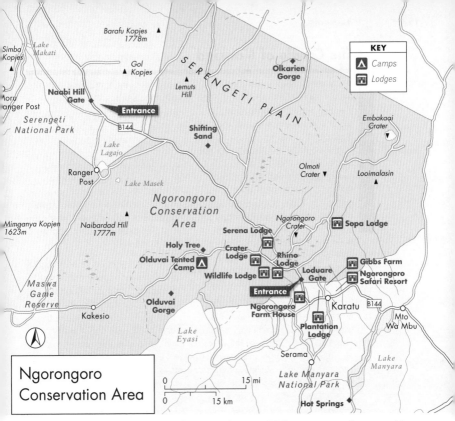

Ngorongoro Conservation Area

KEY

▲ Camps

🏠 Lodges

their noble image as the King of Beasts. Make sure you ask your guide to point out a black or white rhino if he spots one. This is also a great place to take a boat safari down one of the hippo-dense rivers.

Birdlife is also spectacular with some endemic species: the Rufous-tailed weaver, Schalow's wheatear, and large flocks of the incredibly beautiful Crowned cranes. Because this is a continuous killing ground you'll quickly become a vulture expert. If you're a birder, ask for a guide who knows his birds well because not all the guides do.

WHERE TO STAY ON THE CRATER RIM

LUXURY LODGES

$$$$ 🏠 **Ngorongoro Crater Lodge.** Imagine walking into a Hollywood film set where the spectacular setting is literally "Great Zimbabwe ruins meets SS *Titanic* baroque." Clusters of stilted rooms with woven conical banana-leaf domes and fancifully carved stone chimneys cling to the crater's rim and somehow blend in with the natural surroundings. Your palatial abode has polished wooden floors, leather armchairs, and a dramatic mix of furniture and styles including crystal chandeliers and hand-wrought local lamps. Ceiling-high swaths of silk taffeta drapes frame a small veranda with some of the world's most awesome views.

CLOSE UP

The Cradle of Mankind

If you're interested in evolution and human origins, Olduvai Gorge, a World Heritage Site, is a definite must. It's about a 90-minute drive from the Ngorongoro Crater and is only accessible via a badly maintained road. The gorge, about 48 km (30 mi) long, is part of the Great Rift Valley, which stretches along eastern Africa. It has played a key role in palaeoanthropologists' understanding of the history of humanity providing clues dating from about 2.5 million years ago. There is a small museum at the gorge, but it doesn't really do justice to the magnitude of fossil discoveries made here.

Locals actually call Olduvai "Oldupai," which is the Masai name for a sisal plant, *Sansevieria ehrenbergii,* which grows all over in the area. The view overlooking the gorge is spectacular, and for a few extra shillings or dollars, your guide will be easily persuaded to take you down into the gorge where important fossils were found.

It's all a rather makeshift affair, and the guides aren't all fluent in English, so you may struggle to understand explanations inevitably filled with the Latin names of fossils.

Archaeological rock stars like the Leaky family have made some of these important discoveries:

■ *Paranthropus boisei* dating back 2.5 million years. These hominids had massive jaws and large, thickly enameled molars suitable for crushing tough vegetation. Their bite was several times more powerful than that of modern humans.

■ The first specimens of *Homo habilis,* which lived about 2 million to 1.6 million years ago. This is the earliest known named species of the Homo genus. Scientists believe that *Homo habilis* was one of the first hominid species that could make and use stone tools, enhancing our ancestors' adaptability and chances of long-term survival.

■ The world's oldest stone tools dated about 2 million years old, which are very primitive—basically just crude tools fashioned from pebbles.

By Tara Turkington

Hand-carved doors lead to a massive bathroom with fresh cut roses, a freestanding tub, and a tessellated tile shower straight out of a Roman villa. The main dining room has a 1920s ocean liner stateroom feel, but the adjacent lounge comes straight from an old English country house. It's a daring glamorous mix of competing styles and themes that somehow works. However, the standards of food and service don't quite match the boldness of the architecture and opulence of the interiors. ⓓ *CC Africa, Private Bag X27, Benmore 2010, South Africa* ☏ *27/11/809–4300* ⊕ *www.ccafrica.com* ✐ *30 rooms* ⌂ *In-hotel: Internet, bar, pool, spa, safari shop* ▱ *AE, DC, MC, V* ⍟ *FAP.*

$$ ⍒ **Ngorongoro Serena Lodge.** This inviting lodge, built of river stone ☾ and covered with indigenous creepers, is tucked along the lip of the crater—evoking similarities to Hobbit dwellings. Comfortable rooms with honey-color walls and blue, red, and gray soft furnishings are accessed by a wooden walkway guarded by the roots of ancient trees. Hand-painted bushman art motifs on the walls complement the hand-carved wooden furniture. Each room has a rock-hewn veranda with

awesome views. Keep warm on those chilly crater nights in the cozy lounges and by day, after the mist has cleared, enjoy more spectacular views from the split-level bar and dining room where the food is wholesome and hearty. The lodge will arrange your excursions including trips to a Masai village, ballooning, game drives, and picnic lunches (not included in quoted price). Amble along the nature trail that winds around the lodge or take a guided walk to the crater's rim. After the bone-jolting ascent and descent in the crater, a back rub or an herbal massage at the spa are just what the doctor ordered. Kids under 12 are half price, if sharing with an adult and children under 2 are free. ⌂Serena Central Reservations, Arusha, Tanzania ☎027/250–6304 ⊕www.serenahotels.com ⇦75 rooms ⌂In-hotel: Internet, bar, restaurant, pool, spa, safari shop ☰AE, DC, MC, V ⦿FAP.

$ ⍨**Ngorongoro Sopa Lodge.** The best thing about this acceptable but rather shabby lodge on the eastern edge of the crater is the spectacular sunset views from the bar lounge, the dining room, the gardens, swimming pool, and some of the guest rooms. Not all the rooms have great views, however, so try for a room on the top floor in the higher numbers. Some rooms in the lower level have no view at all. Rooms are big with simple but rather outdated furnishings and dim lighting but regard it as 1970s retro and then it becomes fun. Hot water is only available at certain hours so check with the desk when you arrive. The public areas where you meet up with your safari guides each morning are big and noisy until the safaris leave, but if you're looking for peace and quiet then stay behind and just enjoy the views. Food is plentiful and varied, and the hotel has a relaxed welcoming atmosphere and friendly staff. If you're a birder, you will particularly enjoy the lodge's forested grounds full of many different species. A bonus is the lodge's private ascent and descent road, which takes hours off traveling into the crater. ⌂Box 1823, Arusha, Tanzania ☎027/250–0630 or 027/250–0639 ⊕www.sopalodges.com ⇦96 rooms ⌂In-hotel: bar, restaurant, pool, curio shop ☰MC, V ⦿FAP.

$ ⍨**Ngorongoro Wildlife Lodge.** The first lodge to be built in the Ngorongoro Crater, it still retains a rather 1970s government feel with its natural stone and wood buildings and sparsely furnished motel-like rooms. En-suite bathrooms may have old-fashioned fittings, but the water is hot and all the rooms have huge floor-to-ceiling windows with views over the fever tree forest and crater floor that more than compensate for the spartan interiors. The public areas also retain the 1970s ambience, but you're not going to be sitting around for long, so who needs luxury? The food is unmemorable but palatable, and the friendly staff will organize your game-viewing excursions to the crater floor (not included in quoted price). If you're into archaeology and the evolution of humankind, then a day visit to the Olduvai Gorge is a must, plus nearby Laetoli, where hominid footprints are preserved in volcanic rock 3.6 million years old. ⌂Box 2633, Arusha, Tanzania ☎027/254–4595 or 027/254–4807 ⊕www.hotelsandlodges-tanzania.com ⇦72 rooms ⌂In-hotel: bar, restaurant, pool, curio shop ☰MC, V ⦿FAP.

WHERE TO STAY IN THE NGORONGORO CONSERVATION AREA

LUXURY LODGING

$ ☷ **Gibbs Farm.** If it weren't for the profusion of tropical flowering plants and trees and idyllic sunny weather, you could believe yourself in an English country house at this lovely working organic coffee farm midway between Lake Manyara

> **DID YOU KNOW?**
>
> A white rhino baby follows its mother, but a black rhino's baby walks in front of its mother.

and the Ngorongoro Crater. The 1929 original farmhouse has managed to retain its old-fashioned charm with a wide veranda, intimate lounges, inviting reading nooks, and a bar and dining room that look much as they must have done almost a 100 years ago. Small but luxurious guest cottages with en-suite bathrooms are scattered throughout the gardens and provide a perfect base to explore the Crater and Lake Manyara National Park as well as a perfect retreat from the hurly-burly of exhilarating game drives. Expect delicious home-cooked food served with organic veggies and fruit from the farm's own gardens. The coffee is superb. Take advantage of the genuine Masai health and beauty treatments developed by a third generation Masai healer at the farm's Living Spa in the Oseru Forest Clinic. ☐ *Box 280, Karatu, Tanzania* ☎ *027/253–4397* ⊕ *www.gibbsfarm.net* ☞ *20 rooms* ♿ *In-hotel: bar, restaurant, pool, curio shop* ☰ *AE, MC, V* ⧖ *MAP.*

$ ☷ **Ngorongoro Farm House.** Once the home and coffee plantation of a 19th-century German settler, this beautifully renovated property facing the Oldeani volcano now consists of three intimate camps of 40 spacious cottages built and decorated in old colonial style. Cottages and the thatched-roof main farmhouse are set in lovely gardens only 5 km (3.1 mi) from the Ngorongoro Lolduare gate. You'll sleep under a thatched roof in a large airy bedroom tastefully decorated with handmade wooden furniture, hand-woven rugs, polished floors, and an en-suite bathroom and veranda. The main farmhouse has a bar, library, restaurant, and lounge, all perfect for relaxing after a busy day out. The food is delicious and uses lots of organic vegetables and herbs from the farm's own gardens. Dinner by lamp and candlelight capture the charm of a long lost era. If you're looking for some down time, spend some time by the pool or just wander round the gardens and spot birds. Excursions include trips to the crater and conservation area as well as face-to-face encounters with local communities (not included in the quoted price). ☐ *Box 8276, Arusha, Tanzania* ☎ *7027/250–4093* ⊕ *www.africawilderness.com* ☞ *40 rooms* ♿ *In-hotel: bar, restaurant, pool, curio shop* ☰ *AE, MC, V* ⧖ *MAP.*

$ ☷ **Plantation Lodge.** Traditional Africa meets contemporary classic in the stylish interiors of this exquisite lodge set in established gardens amid coffee plantations only 4 km (2½ mi) from the Ngorongoro Crater. Cottages are furnished in a clean uncluttered style that employs African motifs, prints, and artifacts complemented by the creams, browns, and whites of the soft furnishings, the wooden furniture, and terra-cotta tiled floors. Dr. Livingstone never had it so good. Beautiful en-suite tiled bathrooms continue the theme of space and light, as do the public

4

Gibb's Farm

Gibb's Farm

Ngorongoro Crater Lodge

areas where you can dine in style at a massive long wooden table with your fellow guests, or have a romantic candlelit dinner à deux in the garden or on your private veranda. Food is homegrown and tastily prepared, and there's a wine list of good South African wines *See the South African Wine primer, in Chapter 5, South Africa, for more information about these great wines.* The lodge can arrange your entire safari for you, or just your daily activities; neither is included in the quoted price. The lodge has many repeat guests and the guestbook echoes the word *Paradise* written over and over again. ✉ *Box 34, Karatu, Tanzania* ☎ *027/253–4405* ⊕ *www.plantation-lodge.com* ⇆ *18 rooms* ⅃ *In-hotel: bar, restaurant, pool, curio shop* ☰ *AE, MC, V* ⭾ *MAP.*

PERMANENT TENTED CAMPS

$ ⛺ **Olduvai Tented Camp.** You'll have the opportunity to go walking in the Ngorongoro highlands with genuine Masai warriors at this no-frills, but untouristy camp. Built within a circle of kopjes (rocky outcrops) just south of the Serengeti border in the Ngorongoro Conservation Area, the camp operates in complete harmony with the Masai. It's the closest camp to the Olduvai Gorge, which is only a 40-minute drive from the Ngorongoro Crater. The food is not the greatest, but the location and feeling of being in genuine contact with the wild more than compensate for the very basic cuisine. The game is particularly abundant December through May, and guests have been kept awake all night during the migration by the snuffling and snorting of thousands of wildebeest. Tents have wooden floors and thatch roofs with basic chemical toilets and bucket showers, but that's much more than the ancient humans who walked these plains nearly 4 million years ago had. There are two thatch rondawels for eating and sitting, and an open fire-pit where you'll reminisce after the day's activities, which can include a variety of superb walking safaris, game drives, or a trip to the Olduvai museum. All activities are included. ✉ *Dorking, UK* ☎ *866/6–SAFARI from U.S.* ⊕ *www.africatravelresource.com* ⇆ *16 tents* ⅃ *In-hotel: bar, restaurant, curio shop* ☰ *MC, V* ⭾ *FAP.*

BUDGET LODGING

¢ ⛺ **Ngorongoro Safari Resort.** If you're looking for something cheap and cheerful and don't mind being on the main road next to a garage and a very popular campsite, then this well-run property will hit the spot. Set in pleasant gardens in the middle of the lively little town of Karatu, the resort's rooms are retro 1970s with satin flounced bed frills, print curtains, wooden dressing tables, and big windows, but they are also clean and comfortable with en-suite hot showers and complementary bottled drinking water. The resort is ideally situated along the main road to the Ngorongoro Crater, Olduvai Gorge, Lake Eyasi, and Serengeti. There are a couple of very interesting daily excursions, including a visit the Iraqw people of the Ngorongoro highlands and a guided walk with superb views which meanders through forest highlands to a nearby waterfall. ✉ *Box 159, Karatu, Tanzania* ☎ *027/253–4287* ⊕ *www.ngorongorocampandlodge.com* ⇆ *32 rooms* ⅃ *In-hotel: bar, restaurant, pool, curio shop* ☰ *AE, MC, V* ⭾ *BP.*

LAKE MANYARA NATIONAL PARK

Game
☆☆★★★

Park Accessibility
★★★★★

Ease of Getting
Around
☆☆★★★

Accommodations
☆☆★★★

Scenic Beauty
☆★★★★

In the Great Rift Valley south of Serengeti and the Ngorong-oro Crater lies the Cinderella of Tanzania's parks—the often overlooked and underrated Lake Manyara National Park. When Ernest Hemingway faced the rusty-red rocks of the almost 2,000-feet-high rift valley escarpment that dominates the park, he called this area "the loveliest place I have seen in Africa."

Lake Manyara National Park is small, stretching only some 330 square km (127 square mi) along the base of the escarpment with two-thirds of its surface taken up by shallow alkaline Lake Manyara. This serene flat lake is one of the so-called "Rift Lakes" that stretch like jewels along the floor of the Rift Valley.

The park may be small, however, but what it lacks in size it makes up for in diversity. Its range of ecosystems at different elevations makes for dramatic differences in scenery. At one moment you are traveling through a fairy-tale forest (called groundwater forest) of tumbling, crystal-clear streams, waterfalls, rivers, and ancient trees, the next you're bumping over flat grassy plains that edge the usually unruffled lake, pink with hundreds of flamingos.

In the deep forest where old tuskers still roam, blue monkeys swing among huge fig and tamarind trees, giant baobabs and mahoganies, using their long tails as an extra limb. They've got orange eyes, roman noses, and wistful expressions. In the evenings as motes of dusty sunlight dance in the setting sun, there's an excellent chance of spotting troops of more than 300 olive baboons (better looking and furrier than their Chacma cousins) sitting in the road, grooming each other, chatting, and dozing, while dozens of naughty babies play around them and old granddaddies look on with knowing eyes.

The thick, tangled evergreen forest eventually gives way to acacia woodlands with tall, flat-topped acacias and fever trees and finally to open plains where hundreds of elephants, buffalo, and antelope roam, accompanied by Masai giraffes so dark they look as if they have been dipped in chocolate. This is a great place to see hippos at close hand as they lie on the banks

of the lake, or as they begin to forage as dusk approaches. The park is known for its tree-climbing lions, not common to see, but you can be sure if one vehicle glimpses them then the bush telegraph will quickly reach your truck, too. No one really knows why they climb and roost in trees, but it's been suggested by one former warden of the park that this unusual behavior probably started during a fly epidemic when the cats climbed high to escape the swarms of biting flies on the ground. He suggests that the present ongoing behavior is now part of their collective memory.

If you're a birder then put this park on your must-visit list. Because of the great variety of habitats there is a great variety of birds; more than 400 species have been recorded. As you drive through the forest you'll hear the Silvery-cheeked hornbills long before you see them flapping noisily in small groups among the massive trees braying loudly as they fly. The edges of the lake as well as its placid surface attract all manner of water birds large and small. Along the reed-fringed lakeshore you'll see huge pink clouds drifting to and fro. These "clouds" are flocks of flamingos, not so prolific as they once were before the El Niño floods of the late '90s, but now building up steadily again year by year. White-backed pelicans paddle through the water as the ubiquitous African fish eagle soars overhead. Other water birds of all kinds congregate—waders, ducks, geese, storks, spoonbills, egrets, and herons. In the thickets at the base of the red escarpment overlooking the lake, which angles up dramatically at 90 degrees, watch out for Nubian woodpeckers, the very pretty and aptly named Silver birds (flycatchers), Superb, Ashy, and Hildebrand's starlings, Yellow wagtails, trilling cistocolas, Red-cheeked cordon bleus, Peter's twinspots, Bluenecked mousebirds, and every cuckoo in Christendom. The Red-and-yellow barbet is known as the "Bed and Breakfast bird" for its habit of living where it eats—in termite mounds. The park is also a raptor's paradise, where you can spot up to 51 daytime species including dozens of Augur Buzzards, small hawks, and harriers. Deep in the forest you might be lucky enough to see Africa's most powerful eagle, the Crowned eagle, which is strong enough to carry off young antelope, unwary baboons, and monkeys. At night listen for up to six different kinds of owl, including the Giant Eagle owl and the diminutive but very vocal African Scops owl.

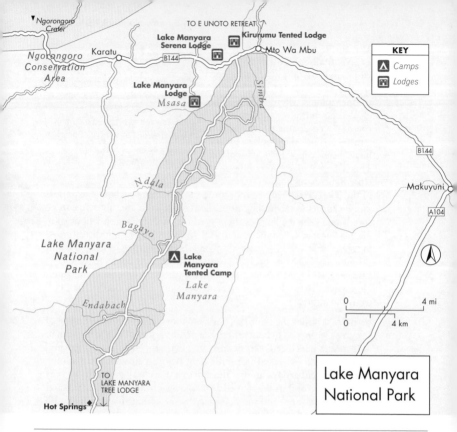

Lake Manyara
National Park

WHERE TO STAY

LUXURY LODGES

$$$ **Lake Manyara Tree Lodge.** The 10 tree houses of the camp—the only one in Lake Manyara National Park—are cradled in the boughs of giant mahogany trees. It's a Swiss Family Robinson setting without the DIY aspect. You'll be greeted at forest floor level entrance by an array of upturned wooden canoes before climbing up to the main areas built under ancient branches heavy with foliage, fruit, and flowers. Your huge wooden thatch bedroom decorated with dangling looped ropes of palm fronds (don't do a Tarzan and swing through the trees) has its own lounge area and en-suite bathroom where you can relax in a bubble bath as birds flit past the big window. Take time to sit on your wooden deck suspended above the forest floor as old elephants silently browse beneath you and tumultuous birdsong chokes the air. There's fine dining by soft gas lamps as owls call. Bush picnics, game drives, and bird-watching trips are all part of the memorable experience at this enchanting camp. ⌂ *CC Africa, Private Bag X27, Benmore 2010, South Africa* ☎ *27/11/809–4300* ⊕ *www.ccafrica.com* ➥ *10 rooms* ⌂ *In-hotel: bar, pool, curio shop* ☰ *AE, DC, MC, V* ⏣ *FAP.*

$$ 🏨 **Lake Manyara Serena Lodge.** Although not situated in the actual park, this lodge scores major points for its breathtaking views. On the edge of the escarpment overlooking the lake, the cluster of comfortably furnished en-suite double-story rondawels celebrates the area's legendary birdlife with its avian theme of sweeping cone-shape thatch roofs and interior brightly colored "winged" frescoes. A stream that attracts all kinds of bird life runs through the property adding to the

WORD OF MOUTH

"Are you planning on a night game drive at Lake Manyara? This was a real highlight for us on our safari last October. We saw hippo, porcupine, bush babies, genets, a pride of lions and an aardvark. The daytime drive we had in Lake Manyara was good, too, but the night drive was out of this world!"

–MyDogKyle

avian ambience. Another big bonus for this attractive but not very private lodge is the program of varied activities. You can choose from a microlite plane ride to look at the Great Rift Valley from 1,500 feet up; take an hour-long gentle nature walk; or if you're more energetic, hike in the forest and clamber over rivers, navigate thickly forested hillsides, and get spectacular views over the lake. Exhilarating mountain-bike rides take you down the Rift Valley escarpment and to the lakeshore. A very special outing is a village walk to the nearby town of Mto wa Mbu, which is home to more than 100 different tribes, although estimates vary according to whom you're talking with. However many there are, it's certain that there are dozens of different languages being spoken—this is apparently one of the richest linguistic mixes in Africa. You'll visit individual homes, a school, a church, and the market and end up at a banana-leaf bar with a fruit tasting. ✍*Serena Central Reservations, Arusha, Tanzania* ☎*027/250–6304* ⊕*www.serenahotels.com* 🛏*54 rooms* ♿*In-hotel: bar, restaurant, pool* ⊟*AE, DC, MC, V* ⊘*FAP.*

$ 🏨 **E Unoto Retreat.** Overseen by its American vice-president who lives
♨ on the property, this stylish "Tanzania Masai luxury lodge," which lies at the foot of the Rift Valley escarpment has attractive Masai-theme bungalows. Interiors boast hand-carved, funky, king-size wooden beds with colorful local beadwork complemented by hand-woven rugs and woven lampshades. Outside, your personal balcony has bird's-eye views over Lake Miwaleni and the lofty escarpment. There are four honeymoon suites and, rare for safari lodges, another four are wheelchair-friendly. There's a lively outdoor bar, and an excellent international cuisine, complete with a great kids' menu, is served in the open-air restaurant. The very friendly and knowledgeable staff will arrange your excursions such as game drives in the park, mountain biking, or walking with a Masai guide to the nearby village to find out more about the local Masai people. ✍*Box 15234, Arusha, Tanzania* ☎*0744/360–908* ⊕*www.maasaivillage.com* 🛏*25 cottages* ♿*In-hotel: bar, restaurant, pool* ⊟*AE, DC, MC, V* ⊘*FAP.*

PERMANENT TENTED CAMPS

$ ⛺**Kirurumu Tented Lodge.** The 20 secluded double tents of this highly regarded intimate camp set among indigenous bush high on the escarpment will make you feel much closer to Africa than some of the bigger lodges. Spacious thatched roof tents each with its own veranda are built on wooden platforms with great views overlooking Lake Manyara. Gaily decorated with animal motif soft furnishings, woven straw circular mats, and carved bedside lamps, all tents have an en-suite bathroom with flush toilet and ceramic hand basins. Larger family tents are also available with plenty of room for the kids. Known for its excellent food and friendly service the camp is an ideal base for game drives in the park, mountain biking, horse riding, hiking, and bird-watching. For something very special go fly-camping in the forest, but fix this with the lodge in advance. After an action-packed day, sip your sundowner in the attractive open-sided bar before enjoying a memorable meal in the restaurant with stunning views over the Rift Valley floor. ⌑*Box 2047, Arusha, Tanzania* ☎*027/250–7011 or 027/250–7541* ⊕*www.kirurumu.com* ↩*22 tents* ⌂*In-hotel: bar, restaurant* ▤*AE, DC, MC, V* ⏐⊙⏐*FAP.*

BUDGET ACCOMMODATION

¢ ⛺**Lake Manyara Lodge.** The accommodations are spartan, but stunning views over the Rift Valley from this former government property make up for the lack of luxury. Double-story rooms are clean and adequate, and all have superb views from individual balconies. Situated in a garden that is a magnet for birds, the lodge arranges all kinds of activities for you. ⌑*Box 2633, Arusha, Tanzania* ☎*027/254–4595 or 027/254–807* ⊕*www.hotelsandlodges-tanzania.com* ↩*100 rooms* ⌂*In-hotel: bar, restaurant, pool* ▤*AE, DC, MC, V* ⏐⊙⏐*FAP.*

¢ ⛺**Lake Manyara Tented Camp (aka Migunga Forest Camp).** The main attraction of this secluded bush camp, apart from its reasonable price, is its location in an indigenous forest just 2 km (1.2 mi) from the town of Mto wa Mbu. En-suite tents with hot-water showers are basic and comfortable, and meals are included in the price. There's a pleasant bar and restaurant, and the friendly staff will arrange game drives and other activities for you. ⌑*Box 207, Arusha, Tanzania* ☎*027/250–8424* ⊕*www.swalasafaris.com* ↩*9 tents* ⌂*In-hotel: bar, restaurant* ▤*AE, DC, MC, V* ⏐⊙⏐*FAP.*

¢ ⛺**National Parks Accommodations.** There are two campsites comprising 10 thatch-roof en-suite huts with water, toilets, and showers near the main gate. Hot water is rare, and you need to bring supplies. You can buy basic foodstuffs at Mto wa Mbo. Not recommended unless you're a hardcore camper. ⌑*Tanzania National Parks Head office, Dodoma Rd., Arusha, Tanzania* ☎*027/250–3471* ⊕*www.tanzaniaparks.com* ▤*No credit cards.*

4

Lake Manyara Tree Lodge

Lake Manyara Tree Lodge

SELOUS GAME RESERVE

Game
☆☆★★★

Park Accessibility
☆★★★★

Ease of Getting
Around
☆★★★★

Accommodations
☆☆★★★

Scenic Beauty
☆★★★★

Most visitors come away from Selous (sel-oo) Game Reserve acknowledging that this is Africa as it is—not as tourism has made it. Selous National Park is one of only three World Heritage sites in Tanzania. A true untamed wilderness, the reserve covers 50,000 square km (19,305 square mi) and comprises 5% of Tanzania, Selous Game Reserve is the largest national park in Africa and the second largest in the world.

Only Greenland National Park at 972,000 square km (375,398 square mi), which is larger than England and France combined beats Selous. But before you get too excited over the statistics, although Selous is still arguably the biggest area of protected pristine wilderness left in Africa, most of it is off-limits to tourists. The reserve is bisected from west to east by Tanzania's biggest river, the Rufiji, and only the area north of the river is open to visitors. So, although it's teeming with game, it forms only about 5% of the total park.

The other 95% is mainly leased to hunting concessions. Hunting is still a very contentious issue and although both sides passionately argue a plausible case it's still hard for many people to accept that shooting some of Africa's most beautiful and precious animals just for fun is ethically acceptable. However, hunting is under fairly strict government control and half of each substantial hunting fee is

A GOOD TIP

Take the train down to Selous from Dar es Salaam. It's a 5½-hour comfortable scheduled train journey that travels through the Selous as well as past many rural villages. On the way back, you can fly directly to Zanzibar and skip Dar. Ask your lodge to make all arrangements or contact Tanzania Zambia Railways Authority ☎022/26-2191 for more information.

put back into the management and conservation of the reserve. It's possible that without this money the Selous would not exist and rampant poaching would take over.

The visitor area of Selous north of the Rufiji River stretches for about 1,000 square km (386 square mi) and will provide you with great game viewing and bird-watching opportunities. This is still unspoiled Africa, where Tarzan himself might have swung through the trees or swum fearlessly through the crocodile-infested river. The fact that there are very few lodges adds to the area's exclusivity. These are along and beside the Rufiji River, which rises in Tanzania's highlands then flows 250 km (155 mi) to the Indian Ocean. The Rufiji boasts the highest water-catchment area in East Africa. A string of five small lakes—Lake Tagalala, Lake Manze, Lake Nzerekea, Lake Siwando, and Lake Mzizimia—interlinked by meandering waterways gives something of an Okavango Delta feel to the area and the birdlife—more than 400 recorded species—is prolific as are the huge crocodiles and lumbering hippos.

> ## SELOUS'S NAMESAKE
>
> Captain Frederick Courtenay Selous (sel-oo) was a famous English explorer and Great White Hunter who roamed the area in the late 1800s. Considered by many to be the greatest hunter of all time he recounted his adventures in best-selling books of the day, and his safari clients included none other than Teddy Roosevelt. He was killed by a German sniper at Beho Beho in 1917 while scouting for the British against the German *Schutztruppe* (a mixed force of German troops and local Africans) during World War I. His grave lies where he fell.

There are major advantages to visiting this park. First, although tourist numbers are now creeping up, there's no chance whatsoever that you'll be game viewing in the middle of a noisy bunch of vehicles. Because only a handful of tourists to Tanzania ever come to this lovely reserve, you'll see very few other visitors. Our advice is to get here quickly before the jungle telegraph spreads the news of its many attractions.

Another major draw is that much of your game viewing and bird-watching will be done from the water. Because Selous is a game reserve, not a national park, a larger range of activities are permitted, so you can walk, camp, and go on a boat safari. There's nothing quite like watching a herd of elephants showering, playing, and generally having fun as you sit in a boat in the middle of a lake or river. As you watch, lots of other game including buffalo and giraffe will also amble down to the banks to quench their thirst. If giraffes are your favorite animals, Selous will delight you because it is one of the few places in Africa where you can see big herds of up to 50.

Another Selous bonus, especially if you've been bouncing about in a game vehicle for days in other parks, is that you can walk in the Selous, not alone but with an armed ranger. Although the game can be skittish as it is not as habituated as in Serengeti or Ngorongoro, walking through the bush or beside a river is a rare opportunity to get up close with nature, and you never know what's around the next corner. Your lodge will organize a short three-hour walk, or if you want to camp out in the bush, an overnight safari.

In the past Selous had a major problem with rampant poaching, which decimated the elephant population and all but made the biggest herd of black rhino in the world extinct. In the 1980s the number of black rhino, previously estimated at 3,000, fell alarmingly to almost none. Today, thanks to the efforts of international and local conservation organizations, the black rhino has been pulled back from almost

PARK ESSENTIALS

If you are brave enough to go it alone in the park, you will need a 4x4 and very good driving skills. Don't even attempt to visit during the rainy season (March–May), as roads are impassable. Permits cost US$30 per person per day plus US$30 per vehicle. If you are camping, you will be required to hire an armed guard at US$15–US$20 per day. You can also hire a guide for about US$15–US$20 per day.

certain extinction to approximately 150 individuals, and together with other game numbers are increasing all the time. There are now approximately 65,000 elephants, 8,000 sable antelope, and an estimated 50,000 puku antelope, but you'll be lucky to see either sable or puku as they tend to stick to the thick bush or inaccessible areas of the park. What you almost certainly will see is the endangered African wild dog. Selous has up to 1,300 individuals in several wide-ranging packs: double that of any other African country. Three packs range north of the Rufiji so there's a good chance of spotting these "painted wolves," especially from June to August when they are denning and stay put for a few months.

Selous is a birder's mecca with more than 400 species. Along the river with its attendant baobab trees and borassus palms, expect to see different species of herons from the aptly named Greenback heron to the Malagasy squacco heron which winters here. Storks, skimmers, and little waders of all kinds fossick in the mud and shallow water, while at dusk you may get a glimpse of the rare ginger-color Pel's Fishing Owl, which screeches like a soul in torment. In summer, flocks of hundreds of brightly colored Carmine bee-eaters flash crimson along the banks where they nest in holes, and kingfishers of all kinds dart to and fro.

WHERE TO STAY

LUXURY LODGES

$$$ **Sand Rivers Selous.** Deep in the southwest corner of Selous this lodge is just about as isolated and exclusive as you can get. Sited in the Sand River area above a wide bend of the Rufiji River, the stone-and-thatch lodge and chalets are literally and metaphorically hundreds of miles away from tourist Africa with its ubiquitous curio shops and gawking tourists. Your open-fronted en-suite chalet has a king-size bed, elegant wooden furniture, elegant cream and white soft furnishings, carefully chosen African artifacts, and great river views. In front of the main lodge, which is shaded by a 1,500-year-old baobab tree, there's a stone

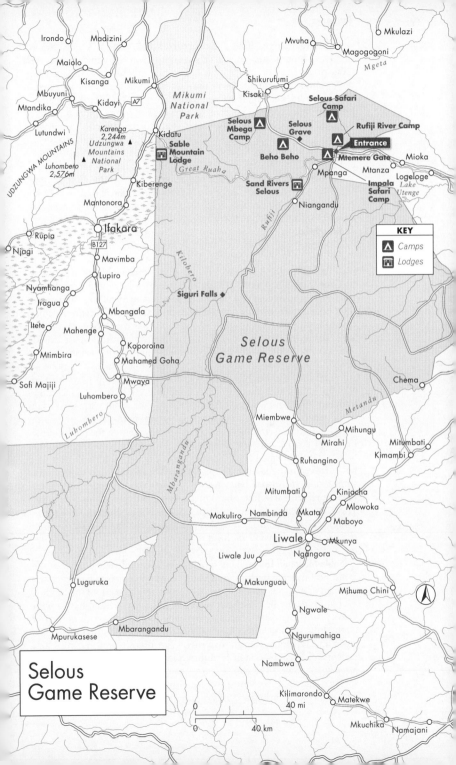

Selous
Game Reserve

walkway that curves along the riverbank where you can sit and watch cavorting hippos and dozing crocs. Apart from its game drives, the lodge prides itself on its walking safaris; you don't have to be super fit, but a ramble through the surrounding wilderness with some of Tanzania's best guides is something you'll never forget. Watch birds and game from a gently chugging boat, or spend a night fly-camping beside Lake Tagalala to a soundtrack of lions roaring, chortling hippos and splashing crocs. The boat trip through Stiegler's Gorge (named after a Swiss explorer who got taken out here by an elephant in 1907) is your best chance of seeing a leopard. The lodge does not take direct bookings. *See the Tour Operators chart, in Chapter 1, Your Safari, for operator suggestions.* ⌂*Nomad Tanzania, Arusha, Tanzania* ☎*022/286–5156* ⊕*www.nomad-tanzania.com* ⇨*8 chalets* ♿*In-hotel: bar, restaurant, pool* ⊟*AE, DC, MC, V* ��*FAP.*

$$ ⓣ**Beho Beho.** Regarded by many safari aficionados as being one of the best in East Africa for its accommodation, superb views over the floodplains, fine dining, and impeccable service this ultraluxurious camp was the first in the Selous to be built in the cool highlands northwest of Lake Tagalala. Lake Tagalala is reputed to have more crocodiles than almost anywhere else in Africa. You'll see why as you chug along on a boat safari. Eight stone-and-thatch chalets with private en-suite bathrooms, a dressing room, and two verandas overlooking the wide floodplains are beautifully decorated with travel-worn leather trunks and suitcases, African artifacts, old maps and prints, writing desks, hand-carved wooden furniture, and comfortable Zanzibari day beds. Although not on the river, a pool in front of the camp plays host to buffalo, hippo, and whatever game happens to be in the area including lion, elephant, and wild dog. You'll visit the hot sulfur springs of Maji Moto where you can swim in the deep natural pools. If you stay more than four nights, seize the opportunity to camp out on the banks of the dry Beho Beho River. After first walking through a remote part of the Selous with an armed guide for an hour or two, you'll think that you have strayed into an Arabian Nights fantasy as you catch sight on the sumptuously furnished tents at Bush Camp. No kids under 12. Closed mid-March to early June. Bookings are made through the U.K.'s Bay Travel or other reputable operators. *See the Tour Operators chart, in Chapter 1, Your Safari, for operator suggestions.* ☎*44/193/226–0618 in U.K., 022/260–0352 in Tanzania* ⊕*www.behobeho.com* ⇨*8 chalets* ♿*In-hotel: bar, restaurant, pool* ⊟*AE, DC, MC, V* ⓘ*FAP.*

$ ⓣ**Sable Mountain Lodge.** This intimate little camp nestled deep in the forest and riverine bush offers superb value for money. Choose to stay in an en-suite stone cottage with its own veranda overlooking the forest built into the Beho Beho hillside, or a spacious tented banda with views over the riverbed. Separate bars and restaurants—two at the top of the hills, two near the base—serve the cottages and bandas. Cottages and tents are simply furnished with brightly colored rugs and bedspreads, rustic wooden furniture, plenty of storage space, and 24-hour solar power. The camp's pure clean water comes from a nearby spring. There's a tree house where you can sit and watch the birds and game—it overlooks a busy waterhole—as well as a star-gazing platform. Activities include game drives, walking, water safaris, birding, and fly camping and although there's an abundance of game, an additional bonus is the scarcity of other vehicles. It's very unlikely that you'll ever encounter another vehicle on your full-day's game drive. This is also a perfect honeymoon spot to destress after a hectic

WORD OF MOUTH

"The boat game drives to us were what really set off this park/ reserve from the others. What a nice change of pace and the means to get close to both land and aquatic wildlife."—rsnyder

wedding. Two gorgeous bandas built on high wooden stilts are sited away from the rest of the camp, giving you total privacy and stunning views. You can lie in your big double bed and gaze out at untamed Africa. ⌂ *A Tent with a View Safaris, Box 40525, Dar es Salaam, Tanzania* ☎ *022/211–0507* ⊕ *www.saadani.com* ⇌ *8 cottages, 5 tents* ⌂ *In-hotel: bar, restaurant, pool* ▤ *AE, DC, MC, V* ⏍ *FAP.*

PERMANENT TENTED CAMPS

$$ ⊡**Selous Impala Camp.** This attractive small camp on Lake Mzizimia's shores nestles among borassus palms and riverine bush with great views over the Rufiji. Tents on wooden platforms raised on stilts, each with its own en-suite bathroom and private veranda, have comfortable African-theme soft furnishings and rustic handmade wooden furniture. Join other guests in the main thatch lounge or on the viewing deck overlooking the river for meals and sundowners. If you're here in the dry season between June and October, you'll see plains game galore as the animals come to drink at the perennial river. As well as elephant, buffalo, hippos, antelope of all kinds, and the always lying-in-wait crocodiles, there's a good chance of spotting lion and wild dog. Selous boasts more than 400 species of birds, so keep that bird-spotting list nearby at all times. Go for a guided game walk with an armed ranger, a game drive, or a boat safari, visit Stiegler's Gorge or the Maja Moto hot springs, or just chill out at this comfortable and unpretentious camp. ■TIP➡ There are some very good deals available if you fly in with Coastal Aviation which operates the camp. ⌂ *Tanzanian Odyssey, Box 3052, Dar es Salaam, Tanzania* ☎ *022/211–7959 or 022/211–7960* ⊕ *www.tanzaniaodyssey.com* ⇌ *7 tents* ⌂ *In-hotel: bar, restaurant, pool* ▤ *AE, DC, MC, V* ⏍ *FAP.*

$$ ⊡**Selous Safari Camp.** In the middle of the riverine bush on the banks of Lake Nzerakera this luxuriously appointed camp comprises nine tents built on wooden platforms which blend in graciously with the surrounding wilderness. The open-sided spacious tents each with two verandas are tastefully decorated in creams, browns, and whites with a big bed, antique wooden chests, hand-carved settles, and colorful rugs. An en-suite bathroom with his-and-her brass hand basins and an open-air hot-water shower overlooks the bush. Public palm-thatch areas of polished wood platforms ringed with rope and wood rails have comfortable cane furniture, African artifacts, camp chairs, and elegant pieces of furniture from a bygone age. The camp is unfenced, so be prepared for all sorts of game to wander past your tent or the main viewing deck. At night the camp takes on a fairytale atmosphere when

it is lit by dozens of softly glowing gas lanterns. Activities include game drives and guided walks, boating, bird watching, or just relaxing on the veranda. ⌂ *Box 23443, Dar es Salaam, Tanzania* ☎ *022/212–8485* ⊕ *www.selous.com* ⟿ *9 tents* ⌂ *In-hotel: bar, restaurant, pool* ☰ *MC, V* ⓄⒾ *FAP.*

$ ⬚ **Rufiji River Camp.** This unpretentious great-value-for-the-money camp
★ is the oldest in the reserve and it shows; the friendly owner and his experienced staff have got things absolutely right. On a wide bend on the Rufiji at the end of the eastern sector of the reserve, you'll stay in one of 20 spacious no-frills but comfortable en-suite tents spread out along the river. The home-cooked Italian cuisine is excellent, but if you're not a pasta fan, there are plenty of other options. Depending on the length of your stay you can choose any or all of the activities on offer including game drives, boat safaris, and overnight fly-camping. This camp also stays open throughout the rainy season (March–May), but you will need to book well in advance if you intend to visit then. Game is prolific, you won't have to leave camp to see elephants, buffalo, and all sorts of other game, including a good chance of seeing wild dog. Sit out on the sunset deck and wait for Africa's wildlife to come to you. ⌂ *Box 13824, Nyumba Ya Sanaa, Dar es Salaam, Tanzania* ☎ *022/212–8663* ⊕ *www.rufijirivercamp.com* ⟿ *20 tents* ⌂ *In-hotel: bar, restaurant, pool* ☰ *AE, DC, MC, V* ⓄⒾ *FAP.*

BUDGET ACCOMMODATION

¢   ⬚ **Selous Mbega Camp.** This comfortable and affordable camp is just outside the border of the Selous Game Reserve under a canopy of trees in its own private 14.8-acre riverine forest reserve. You'll stay in a large safari tent raised on stilts with a palm-thatch roof, a tiny en-suite bathroom, and a wooden deck. The main areas also under thatch and facing the Rufiji River are built round a giant African mahogany tree where all kinds of monkeys play and call. A camp "special" is the Angolan black-and-white colobus monkey called Mbega in Kiswahili whence the camp gets its name. Food is far from gourmet but is interesting and palatable, including venison, fresh fish, and homegrown veggies. All the Selous activities are on offer including game walks and drives, boat safaris, birding safaris, and visits to the hot springs. Don't miss out on a trip to the local village and school. Kids under 4 free, 4–11 half-price accommodation only. ⌂ *Box 23443, Dar es Salaam, Tanzania* ☎ *022/265–0250* ⊕ *www.selous-mbega-camp.com* ⟿ *13 tents* ⌂ *In-hotel: bar, restaurant* ☰ *AE, DC, MC, V* ⓄⒾ *FAP.*

Sand Rivers Selous

Beho Beho Safari Lodge

Selous Safari Camp

GOMBE STREAM & MAHALE MOUNTAINS NATIONAL PARKS

Game
☆☆☆☆★

Park Accessibility
☆☆☆★★

Ease of Getting
Around
☆☆☆☆★

Accommodations
☆☆☆★★

Scenic Beauty
★★★★★

If your heart is set on tracking our nearest animal relatives—the intriguing, beguiling, and oh-so-human chimpanzees—then take the time and effort to get to one or both of these rarely visited but dramatically beautiful parks. You'll meet very few other visitors, and very few other people on earth will share your experience.

The best time to see chimps is toward the end of the dry season: July–October when they come out of the forest and lower down the slopes—sometimes even to the beach.

Don't go trekking if you have a cold, flu, or any other infectious diseases. Chimps are highly susceptible to human diseases, and you certainly wouldn't wish to reduce the chimp population even further.

GOMBE STREAM NATIONAL PARK

Bordering Burundi to the west, Tanzania's smallest national park—only 52 square km (20 square mi)—is easily one of the country's loveliest. It's tucked away on the shores of Africa's longest and deepest lake, Lake Tanganyika, 420 mi long and 30 mi wide. The lake is a veritable inland sea, the second deepest lake in the world after Russia's Lake Baikal. This small gem of a park 3.5 km (2.2 mi) wide and only 15 km (9.3 mi) long stretches from the white sandy beaches of the blue lake up into the thick forest and the mountains of the Rift escarpment behind.

Though the area is famous for its primates, don't expect Tarzan-like rain forest because the area is mainly covered with thick *brachystegia* woodland. There are also strips of riverine bush alongside the many streams that gouge out steep valleys as they make their way from the highlands to flow down into the lake.

You've got to be determined to get here because Gombe is only accessible by boat. But you'll be amply rewarded with one of the most exciting animal encounters of a close kind that is still possible on our planet. You'll hear the chimps long before you see them. A series of hoots and shrieks rising to a crescendo of piercing whoops sounds like a major primate battle is about to begin. But it's only the members of the clan identifying one another, recognizing one another, and finally greeting one another.

PARK ESSENTIALS

Entry fees for Gombe are US$120 per 24 hours, the highest of any park in Tanzania. The Mahale entry fee is US$100. Your guide will cost US$25. No kids under 7. Because of the traveling time you will need to spend at least two nights in either or both of the parks.

Gombe became famous when Brit Jane Goodall came to the area in 1960 to study the chimpanzee population. At the time she wasn't known or recognized as the world-renowned primatologist she would later become. Sponsored by the legendary paleontologist Louis Leakey of Olduvai Gorge, Goodall came to Gombe as an eager but unqualified student of chimpanzees. At first many of her amazing unique studies of chimp behavior were discounted because she young, unknown, and not a respected scientist. How could a chimpanzee be a hunter and meat-eater? How could a chimpanzee possibly use grass stalks and sticks as tools? Whoever had heard of inter-troop warfare? Today her ground-breaking work is universally acknowledged. Read more about her and her experiences at Gombe in her bestselling book *In the Shadow of Man*. You'll also be able to meet descendants of those chimpanzees she studied and made famous. Fifi, who was only three when Goodall arrived at Gombe in 1960, survived to the millennium.

But be warned—to follow in Jane or Fifi's footsteps you need to be fairly fit. Keeping up with a group of feeding and moving chimpanzees as they climb hills and forage in deep valleys can be very strenuous work. But the effort will be worth it—there's nothing on earth quite like coming face to face with a chimpanzee or accompanying a group as they make their way through the forest.

MAHALE MOUNTAINS NATIONAL PARK

Just south of Gombe on the shores of Lake Tanganyika lies Tanzania's most remote national park. Thirty times bigger than Gombe, Mahale is a stunningly beautiful park with crystal-clear streams, soaring forested mountains, and deserted white sandy beaches. Mount Nkungwe at 2,460 meters (8,070 feet) dominates the landscape. More than 700 chimpanzees live in the area and are more accessible and more regularly seen than at Gombe.

In 1965 the University of Kyoto in Japan established a permanent chimpanzee research station in Mahale at Kisoge, about a kilometer from the beach. It's still going strong and remains highly respected.

There are no roads in Gombe or Mahale: all your game viewing and chimpanzee tracking is done on foot. If you're a couch potato, stick with the National Geographic TV channel. What else will you see other than chimpanzees? You'll almost certainly see olive baboons, vervet monkeys, red-, blue-, and red-tailed colobus monkeys, and some exciting birds. More than 230 bird species have been recorded here, so look out for crowned eagles, the noisy trumpeter hornbills, and the "rasta" birds (the crested guinea fowls with their black punk hairdos). Don't expect to see big game; although there are roan antelope, elephant, giraffe, buffalo, lion, and wild dog in the eastern savanna and woodland, these areas are largely inaccessible. But you're not here for big game. You're here to meet your match.

WHERE TO STAY

LUXURY LODGES

$$$$
★   **Greystoke Mahale.** If you were a castaway, this would be heaven. It's difficult to imagine almost anywhere on earth that's wildly beautiful and remote as this exotic camp on the eastern shore of Lake Tanganyika. Six wood-and-thatch bandas nestle on the forest rim. Behind them thickly wooded mountains rise almost 2,500 meters (8,200 feet); in front of them white sands stretch to the peaceful azure waters of the lake. Tarzan, of course, was really Lord Greystoke, so this aristocrat of camps is well-named. Your banda has furniture of bleached dhow wood, a rustic toilet and shower, and a lower and upper wooden deck with views over the lake. The main building is loosely based in the style of a Tongwe chief's hut, although many of your meals will be taken on the beach, at night by glowing lanterns. It's not easy to get here: a four-hour flight from Arusha followed by a two-hour boat ride. But once here you won't ever want to leave. About 60 of Mahale's 1,000 or so wild chimpanzees live in the forest near Greystoke, so you have an excellent chance of spotting them. Go snorkeling, birding, or just chill. Bookings are made only through reputable tour operators. *See the Tour Operators chart in Chapter 1, Your Safari, for operator suggestions.* ⊠ *Tanzania* ⊕ *www.greystoke-mahale.com* ⤳ *6 bandas* ⚐ *In-hotel: bar, restaurant* ⊟ *AE, DC, MC, V* ⑩ *FAP.*

¢   **Kigoma Hilltop Hotel.** On a hill overlooking the lake about 2 km (1.2 mi) from Kigoma's town center, this hotel makes an ideal base for your chimpanzee trekking. You'll stay in a comfortable no-frills cottage with a/c, a mini-refrigerator, satellite TV, and an en-suite bathroom. What puts the hotel above any other in the area is that it not only arranges your excursions for you, but also has all kinds of water-sports equipment for hire. Go snorkeling, fishing, swimming or just chill out on the private beach. There are also a gym, business services, and a large pool. Try delicious Indian food at the restaurant, or stay conventional and stick with Western food. No alcohol is sold, but you can bring your own. ⌂ *Box 1160, Kigoma, Tanzania* ☎ *028/280–4435 or 028/280–4436* ⊕ *www.chimpanzeesafaris.com* ⤳ *8 tents* ⚐ *In-hotel: restaurant* ⊟ *AE, DC, MC, V* ⑩ *BP.*

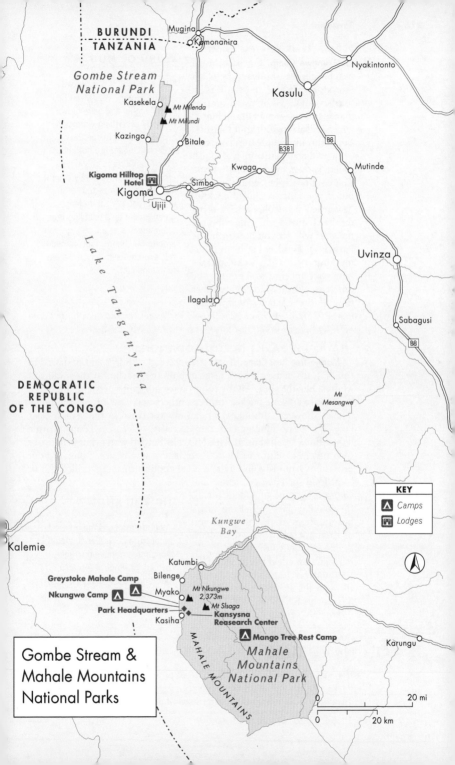

BURUNDI
TANZANIA

Mugina

Kamonanira

Nyakintonto

*Gombe Stream
National Park*

Kasulu

Kasekela

▲ Mt Milenda
▲ Mt Milundi

Kazinga

Bitale

B381

B8

Kwaga

Mutinde

**Kigoma Hilltop
Hotel**

Kigoma

Simbo

Ujiji

Lake Tanganyika

Uvinza

Ilagala

Sabagusi

B8

DEMOCRATIC
REPUBLIC
OF THE CONGO

Mt
Mesangwe ▲

*Kungwe
Bay*

KEY

▲ *Camps*

▥ *Lodges*

Kalemie

Katumbi

Bilenge

Greystoke Mahale Camp

Myako

Nkungwe Camp

Park Headquarters

Kasiha

Mt Nkungwe ▲
2,373m
▲ Mt Sisaga

**Kansysna
Reasearch Center**

▲ **Mango Tree Rest Camp**

Karungu

*Mahale
Mountains
National Park*

MAHALE MOUNTAINS

Gombe Stream &
Mahale Mountains
National Parks

20 mi

0

0   20 km

PERMANENT TENTED CAMPS

$ ⊡**Nkungwe Camp.** On a secluded beach about midway between Greystoke Mahale and the Kasiha tourist camp, Nkungwe Camp is managed by Kigoma Hilltop Hotel, which will arrange all your logistics. You'll stay in a simply furnished tent on a wooden platform with flush toilet, shower and a small deck. There's a beach hut with sun beds, but if you fancy a chilled cocktail be warned: no alcohol is sold. Bring the hard stuff with you, although the staff will get you beer from the Park HQ. Food is far from gourmet, but after a day's chimp trekking your appetite won't notice the difference. Open March–November only. ⊡ *Box 1160, Kigoma, Tanzania* ☏*028/280–4435 or 028/280–4436* ⊕*www.chimpanzeesafaris.com* ⇝*8 tents* ⌂*In-hotel: restaurant* ⊟*AE, DC, MC, V* ⏃*FAP.*

NATIONAL PARKS ACCOMMODATIONS

¢ ⊡**Mango Tree Rest Camp.** If you are on a tight budget and prepared to rough it, this national park rest camp on the beach near the middle of Mahale hits the spot. All the rooms have mosquito nets and are clean. Some have en-suite bucket showers, others make use of the communal bucket showers, although you can always swim in the crystal clear lake. There's no running water or electricity—kerosene lamps provide light—but a small shop at Park HQ sells bottled water (but bring your own just in case of shortages), beer, and a few basics. Bring all your provisions from Kigoma. Hire a local cook to rustle up grilled fish or local food such as rice, beans, and *chapattis* (a type of Indian bread) for you. Pay park fees at the park's headquarters at the northern end of the park where you disembark before coming to the camp. Bookings can be made through any of the Kigoma travel agencies or directly through the senior park warden if he answers his phone. ☏*028/280–2586* ⊟*No credit cards.*

> ### DID YOU KNOW?
>
> Illegal trafficking is the greatest threat to Tanzania's endangered chimpanzee population. Highly coveted for medical research, zoos, and as pets, baby chimps are taken by force resulting in the death of many protective adults.

IF YOU HAVE TIME

If you still have time after you've explored our picks for Must See Parks, put the following parks on your list, too: Arusha National Park, Tarangire National Park, Ruaha National Park.

Continued on page 224

MOUNT KILIMANJARO
by Debra Bouwer

Kilimanjaro, a dormant volcano on the roof of Africa, is one of the closest points in the world to the sun (Chimborazo in the Andes is the closest). It's also the highest peak on the continent and the tallest free-standing mountain in the world. So great is her global attraction that approximately 12,000 people from around the world attempt to reach her mighty summit each year.

Rising to an incredible height of 5,895 meters (19,336 feet) above sea level, Mt. Kilimanjaro is a continental icon. She towers over the surrounding Amboselli plains and covers an area of about 750 sq km (290 sq mi). On a clear day, she can be seen from 150 km (93 mi) away. Thousands attempt to reach Kilimanjaro's highest peak, but only about 64% will officially make the summit, known as Uhuru Peak. Many reach the lower Stella Point at 5,745 meters (18,848 feet) or Gilmans' Point, at 5,681 meters (18,638 feet), which earns them a certificate from the Kilimanjaro Parks Authority.

The origin of the name Kilimanjaro has varying interpretations. Some say it means "Mountain of Greatness," others believe it to mean "Mountain of Caravans." There is a word in Swahili, "kilima" which means top of the hill and an additional claim is that it comes from the word "kilemakyaro" which, in the Chagga language, means "impossible journey." Whatever the meaning, the visual image of Kilimanjaro is of a majestic peak.

Top: Southern Giraffe with Mt. Kilimanjaro in the background, as seen from Amboseli National Park in Kenya

IS KILIMANJARO EASY TO CLIMB?

Kilimanjaro is one of the few high peaks in the world that can be climbed without any technical gear. Most climbers head up her flanks with the aid of trekking poles, while others abandon their poles for a camera and a zoom lens. Don't let the ease fool you though, the lack of oxygen near the summit radically slows down one's ascent. Here, oxygen levels in the air decrease to about 60% of levels at the coast. A simple act of rolling up a sleeping bag can wear you out. Walking and ascending slowly will help your body adapt to these diminished oxygen levels.

About 12,000 thrill seekers arrive on the mountain each year, each accompanied by an entourage of 4 to 6 people that include porters, guides, and a cook.

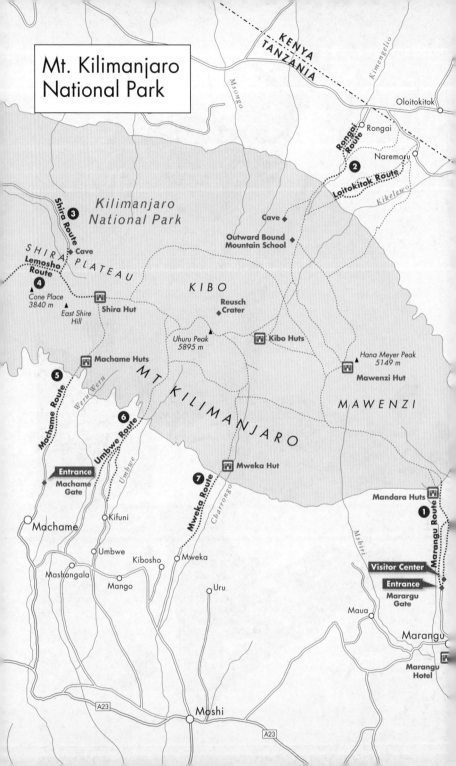

Mt. Kilimanjaro National Park

KENYA
TANZANIA

Oloitokitok

Rongai Route
Rongai

❷ Naremoru
Loitokitok Route

Msongo

Kimengelio

Kikelewo

Kilimanjaro
National Park

❸ Shira Route

Cave

Outward Bound
Mountain School

SHIRA PLATEAU

Cave

Lemosho Route

❹ Cone Place
3840 m

East Shire Hill

Shira Hut

KIBO

Reusch Crater

Uhuru Peak
5895 m

Kibo Huts

Hana Meyer Peak
5149 m

Mawenzi Hut

❺ Machame Route

Machame Huts

Weru Weru

MT KILIMANJARO

MAWENZI

❻ Umbwe Route

Umbwe

Mweka Hut

❼ Mweka Route

Charrongo

Entrance
Machame Gate

Machame

Kifuni

Umbwe

Kibosho

Mweka

Mango

Uru

Mshiri

Marangu Route

Mandara Huts ❶

Visitor Center
Entrance
Marargu Gate

Mashangala

Maua

Marangu

A23

Moshi

A23

Marangu Hotel

TREKKING KILI

Up, up, and away. Hikers ascend Kilimanjaro.

WHERE TO START

Most treks head out from Moshi, a bustling town at the mountain's base whose streets are lined with tourist stalls, tailors, banks and restaurants. Here you'll find registered guides and accredited trekking companies that will arrange your climb. We like Nomadic Adventure (⊕ *www.nomadicadventures.co.za*) because they offer great personal service, have climbed the mountain many times themselves, and get involved in the big Kilimanjaro Cleanup, a project that hauls thousands of pounds of waste off the mountain each year.

WHEN TO GO

The warmest, clearest trekking days are mid-December to February or September and October. June, July, and August are superb trekking months too, but evening temperatures tend to be colder. The wettest months are November, early December, April, and the start of May, which brings some snow.

Daytime temperatures range from 28°C (85°F) to 38°C (100°F) in the forest, but plummet to a frigid -2°C (28°F) to -16°C (3°F) at the summit. A general rule of thumb: with every 200 meters gained, the temperature drops by one degree.

THE ROUTES

There are seven routes to the summit: Marangu, Rongai, Shira, Lemosho, Machame, and Umbwe—all have long drop toilets. ❶ **Marangu** is the shortest (it takes a minimum of 5 days) and thus most popular route with accommodations in huts equipped with bunk beds, public dining areas, and flush toilets. Some even have solar heated showers. The other routes, which take at least six days to trek, require camping. ❷ **Rongai** (or **Loitokitok**) is the quietest as it heads out close to the Kenyan border, a far distance from Moshi. Along with Marangu, Rongai is classified as an easier route. ❸ **Shira**, ❹ **Lemosho** and ❺ **Machame** are steep and difficult, but also more scenic as they head through the distinct geographical zones: forest, shrub land, alpine desert, and snow fields. ❻ **Umbwe** is the steepest, but also the most direct ascent to the summit. ❼ **Mweka** can only be used as a descending route from the western side.

GEOLOGY & TERRAIN

Mount Kilimanjaro has five different types of terrain that you'll encounter while trying to reach the summit.

Forests

Cultivated Farmlands: Around the outskirts of Moshi near the base of the mountain are endless subsistence plantations of maize and banana. Small villages line the routes up to the various starting points on Kilimanjaro, and small children play in the fields.

Forests: The forest zone spreads around the base of the mountain; it is hot, humid, and generally wet. Starting at about 5,900 feet—there's cultivated farmland below this—the forest reaches up to 2,800 meters (9,186 feet) and is home to a myriad of small creatures and primates, including the black-and-white colobus monkey. Tall trees reach for the sunlight, their feet firmly anchored into a maze of roots on which cling mosses and brightly colored flowers including the rare and exotic impatiens Kilimanjari flower, unique to this mountain. Lichens hang in sheets and small birds dart to and fro.

Shrubland/Heath Zone

Shrubland or Heath Zone: At the edge of the forest zone, the vegetation suddenly changes to shrubland that's full of flowers, shrubs like the 6 meters (20 feet) high erica arborea, and daisy bushes that grow as big as pompoms. This zone extends up to about 12,467 feet where the landscape turns into alpine desert.

Alpine Desert

Alpine Desert: As the shrubs of the heath zone diminish in size, one enters the alpine desert, full of gnarled volcanic lava rock. Small burrows shelter the hyrax and field mice that eke out a living in this desert moonscape. Large white-naped ravens scavenge among the sand and stone.

Glaciers

Glaciers and Summit: As the desert rises to 16,404 feet, the summit of the mountain looms above, her flanks covered in ashen scree. Massive age old glaciers, hanging as though suspended in time, are slowly receding as the planet warms. Here among these towing blocks of ice at 19,340 feet, is Uhuru Peak, the summit of Kilimanjaro.

Summit

While other mountains are taller, Kilimanjaro is at the equator making it one of the closest to the sun.

KILIMANJARO VERSUS EVEREST

	Kilimanjaro	Everest
How tall from sea level?	19,340 feet	29,035 feet
Temperatures at the summit?	Below 0°C (32°F) to as much as -20°C (-4°F) with wind chill factor	From -15°C (5°F) to -100°C (-148°F) in extreme conditions
How many deaths occur each year from people trying to climb to the top?	Guides estimate about 12 a year, though there are no official figures	6 in 2005; 10 in 2006
How long does it take to climb to the top?	A minimum of 5 days	Between two and three months depending on which route you take
What is the most treacherous stretch?	There really isn't a treacherous stretch, but rather the Barranco Wall, which is a steep rock section climbed when doing the Machame, Shira, Lemosho and Umbwe Routes, is the trickiest	Any section above 24,606 feet is classified as the Death Zone

TIPS

1) Check out the internet or trekking magazines for tour operator suggestions

2) Choose an operator that is registered, has registered guides, has porters' interests at heart, an environmental policy, etc.

3) Communicate any health problems to your tour operator when you book

4) Choose your route according to what you want: scenery, challenge, type of accommodation, size of group

5) For a quiet climb on a well travelled route, avoid the full moon, as this is when the summit night is the busiest

6) Train about 2 months before you leave—this also helps to "train your brain" that you are heading off for a challenge. Squats, lunges and lots of hill walking with a pack are essential

7) Fly with your boots on— that way you won't lose them if your luggage gets lost

8) Read up on altitude sickness and symptoms and take the necessary medication with you

9) Drink 3-5 liters of water a day. The rule is 1 liter per 1,000 meters (3,280 feet) ascent

10) Add in acclimatisation days if possible or consider climbing Mt. Meru first

11) Take only photos; leave only footprints

ARUSHA NATIONAL PARK

Don't overlook the tiny Arusha National Park. Though it only covers 137 square km (58 square mi), it has more to see than many much larger reserves. You'll find three distinct areas within the park: the forests that surround the Ngurdoto Crater, the brightly colored pools of the Momella Lakes, and the soaring peaks of Mt. Meru. And with the city of Arusha only a 32 km (20 mi) drive to the northeast, it's easy to see the park in a day.

Established in 1960, the park was originally called Ngurdoto Crater National Park, but after the mountain was annexed in 1967 it became known as Mt. Meru National Park. Today it is named for the Warusha people who once lived in this area. The Masai also lived here, which is why many of the names for sights within the park are Swahili. ⓘ *Tanzania National Parks, Box 3134, Arusha* ☎ *027/255–3995* ⊕ *www.tanzaniaparks.com* 💲 *$25* ⊙ *Daily 6:30–6:30.*

NGURDOTO FOREST & CRATER

After entering the park through the Ngurdoto Gate, you'll pass through the fig, olive, and wild mango trees of the Ngurdoto Forest. Farther along is the Ngurdoto Crater, which is actually a caldera, or collapsed crater. Unlike the nearby Ngorongoro Crater, this caldera appears to have had two cones. There are no roads into the crater itself, so the buffalo and other animals that make their homes in the swampy habitat remain protected. You can drive around the rim, where you'll find a misty landscape covered with date palms, orchids, and lichens. The grasslands to the west are known as Serengeti Ndogo ("Little Serengeti") and boast a herd of Burchell's zebras, thriving because there are no lions nearby.

Many baboons and other monkeys are found in the Ngurdoto Forest. Elegant black-and-white colobus monkeys spend most of the morning basking in the sun in the highest parts of the forest canopy, then later move lower in the branches to feed on the tender vegetation. Colobus monkeys do not drink water but get all their moisture from their food. They are endangered because their lovely fur was prized by humans.

MOMELLA LAKES

From Ngurdoto Crater drive northeast to the Momella Lakes. Reedbuck and waterbuck are common sights near the dirt road. There are numerous observation points along the way for getting a closer look at the more than 400 species of birds that have been spotted in the area. The lakes were created by lava flow from nearby Mt. Meru; each is a distinct color because of the varying mineral content in the water. Each lake, therefore, attracts different types of birds. Keep an eye out for the flamingos that feed on the algae.

> **WORD OF MOUTH**
>
> "Arusha National Park is a nice park to start a safari. It's sort of like an introductory experience before visiting some of the other larger parks." —Traveller88

MT. MERU

From the Momella lakes the road toward Mt. Meru leads into a forest with a profusion of wildflowers. Here you'll encounter dik-diks and red forest duikers. Rangers can accompany you on walks to the rim of Meru Crater, where you'll have a breathtaking view of the sheer cliffs rising to the summit. Keep an eye out for a diminutive antelope called the klipspringer.

Because it is not as well known, the slopes of Mt. Meru are blissfully uncrowded. Although Meru looks diminutive alongside Kilimanjaro, do not underestimate what it takes to climb to the top. You must be in good shape, and you need to allow time to acclimatize. Climbing Mt. Meru itself takes at least three days. The route begins at the Momella Gate, on the eastern side of the mountain. Huts along the way sleep 24–48 people, but inquire beforehand whether beds are available; if not, you should bring a tent. You can arrange for no-frills journeys up the mountain through the park service, or book a luxury package through a travel company that includes porters to carry all your supplies. Either way you'll be accompanied by an armed guard to protect you from unfriendly encounters with elephant or buffalo.

TARANGIRE NATIONAL PARK

Although this lovely 2,600-square-km (1,004-square-mi) park is an easy drive from Arusha—just 118 km (71 mi) southwest—and adjacent to Lake Manyara, it has continued to be something of a well-kept secret. This relative secrecy is odd because during the dry season it's part of the migratory movement and is second only to Ngorongoro Crater in concentration of wildlife. The best time to visit is July through September, when thousands of parched animals flock to the watering holes and thousands more make their long way to the permanent water of the Tarangire River.

GAME-VIEWING

During the dry season, huge herds of elephants, elands, oryx, zebras, buffalo, wildebeest, eland, giraffe, and impala roam the park. Hippos are plentiful and pythons can sometimes be seen in trees near the swamps. If you want to spot waterbuck or the mini-giraffe, the gerenuk, head for the Mkungero Pools. Tarangire is much more densely wooded than Serengeti with acacia, mixed woodland, and the ubiquitous baobab trees, although you'll find grasslands on the southern plains where cheetahs hunt.

There are more than 500 species of birds in Tarangire National Park, including martial and bateleur eagles. Especially good bird-watching can be had along the wetlands of the Silale Swamp and around the Tarangire River. Yellow-collared lovebirds, hammerkops, helmeted guinea fowl, long-toed lapwings, brown parrots, white-bellied go-away birds, and a variety of kingfishers, weavers, owls, plovers, and sandpipers make their homes here. A shallow alkaline lake attracts flamingos and pelicans in the rainy season. Raptors are plentiful including the palm-nut vulture and lots of eagles. You may hear a cry that sounds quite similar to the American Bald Eagle, but is in fact its look-alike cousin the African Fish eagle.

ANCIENT ART

Kolo, just south of Tarangire, is where you'll find some of the most accessible Kondoa rock paintings. From the last stage of the Stone Age, these illustrations on cave walls depict hunting scenes using stylized human and animal figures. These fragile documents of an era long past were studied by Mary Leakey, who wrote a book about them called *Africa's Vanishing Art*. At a nearby site Leakey discovered "pencils" in which ocher and other pigments had been ground and mixed with grease. Later excavations revealed that some were 29,000 years old. ⌂ *Tanzania National Parks, Box 3134, Arusha* ☎ *027/250–1930* ⊕ *www.tanzaniaparks.com* ◷ *Weekdays 9–5, Sat. 9–noon* ☒ *$35.*

RUAHA NATIONAL PARK

Remote and rarely visited, Ruaha is Tanzania's second largest park—10,300 square km (3,980 square mi). Oddly enough, it attracts only a fraction of the visitors that go to Serengeti, which could be because it is less well-known and is difficult to access. But East Africa Safari aficionados claim it to be the country's best-kept secret. There are huge concentrations of buffalos, elephants, antelope, and more than 400 bird species.

Classified as a national park in 1964, it was once part of the Sabia River Game Reserve, which the German colonial government established in 1911. Ruaha is derived from the word "great" in the Hehe language and refers to the mighty Ruaha River, which flows around the park's borders, and it's only around the river that the park is developed for tourism with a 400-km (249-mi) road circuit. The main portion of the park sits on top of a 1,800-meter (5,900 foot) plateau with spectacular views of valleys, hills, and plains—a wonderful backdrop for game-viewing. Habitats include riverine forest, savanna, swamps, and acacia woodland. The best time to visit is May through December, because although even in the wet season the all-weather roads are passable, it's incredibly difficult to spot game at that time because of the lush, tall vegetation.

GAME-VIEWING

There are elephant, buffalo, lion, spotted hyena, gazelle, zebra, greater and lesser kudu, and giraffe roaming this park. If you're lucky, you might even see roan and sable antelope or witness a cheetah hunt on the open plains in the Lundu area. Lion are well habituated to vehicles so you would be very unlucky not to spot at least one pride, and if you've set your heart on seeing wild dogs, then try to come in June or July when they are denning; this makes them easier to spot than at other times because they stay in one place for a couple of months. There are also lots of crocs and hippos in the river areas. Bird "specials" include the lovely little Eleonaora's falcon (December through January is the best time to spot one), Pel's Fishing owl, Pale-billed Hornbill, and the Violet-crested hornbill.

> **RUAHA ESSENTIALS**
>
> There's an entrance fee of US$25 per person, per 24-hour visit, and it must be paid in cash. Ask at your lodge for a copy of the Ruaha booklet which has maps, checklists, and hints on where to look for particular species.

ANIMAL THREATS

Poaching has been a serious problem in this park as the rhino was at one point hunted to near-extinction. But in 1988, the Tanzanian government joined with the WWF (the World Wildlife Foundation) to initiate the Selous Conservation Programme, which has eased the problem considerably. The international ban on ivory in the 1990s has also contributed to increasing elephant numbers.

WHERE TO STAY

LUXURY LODGES

$$ **Jongomero Tented Camp.** This is the only camp in the southwest corner of Ruaha National Park. If you've come to see animals, but no other trucks or people, then this is your place. The tents, which have furniture that was made from the wood of old dhows, are perched along the banks of the (sometimes dry) Jongomero River—when you're at the lodge's bar, check out the bowl filled with handmade nails that were collected as the boats were dissembled. Take your morning or afternoon tea out on your veranda, you might catch a glimpse of a few passing animals. The food is excellent and there is always something packed away for you when you're out on your drives. The pool is a great place to relax and ponder all that you've seen during your day, and the view of the setting sun is incredible. If you're interested, game walks with your own personal armed national parks guard, can be arranged. *Selous Safari Camp, Box 23443, Dar es Salaam, Tanzania* 022/212–8485 *www.selous.com* 8 tents *In-hotel: pool, bar, restaurant* MC, V FAP.

$$ **Ruaha River Lodge.** Comfortably furnished stone cottages with spacious interiors and en-suite bathrooms sit on a rocky hillside overlooking a series of rapids in the Ruaha River. This charming and very scenic camp is also Ruaha's oldest. It's divided into two camps of 12 rooms each; both camps have their own bar and restaurant. You don't have to jump in a game vehicle to see some amazing wildlife as game is plentiful in and around the camps. There's a resident hippo in the river, elephants regularly pass through camp on their way to drink, and lots of other animals browsing along the river banks. *Foxes African Safaris, Box 10270, Dar es Salaam, Tanzania* 01452–862288 *in U.K., 023/244–0194 in Tanzania* *www.tanzaniasafaris.info* 24 rooms *In-hotel: bar, restaurant* DC, MC, V FAP.

$ **Tandala Camp.** Because Tandala is in a private conservancy 13 km (8 mi) outside the entrance gate, guests can take guided night drives, early morning game walks, or go fly camping—all of which you can not do within the park. There are no frills here, but it's very comfortable and you stay in an en-suite tent that's built on a wooden platform that overlooks a seasonal river. There's an attractive restaurant and bar area beside the small swimming pool. A nearby waterhole attracts game at all times, particularly during the dry season, although elephants are hanging around most of the time. ⌂ *Dar es Salaam, Tanzania* ☎ *026/270–3425* ✉ *tandalacamp@yahoo.com* ⇨ *10 tents* ⌂ *In-hotel: bar, restaurant* ▭ *DC, MC, V* ⚄ *FAP.*

GATEWAY CITY

4

Updated by
Kate Turkington

Many visitors to Tanzania will find themselves with a layover in Dar es Salaam or Arusha before or after their safari. For some ideas and suggestions to help determine where you should stay, eat, and if you have time, some sights to visit, read on.

DAR ES SALAAM

Dar es Salaam means "haven of peace" in Arabic, and paradoxically that's just what you'll find in this bustling port city on the Indian Ocean. Although it has grown to become Tanzania's most important commercial center, Dar es Salaam still recalls its origins as a fishing village. The reason is the city's inhabitants, who go out of their way to make newcomers feel at home. When someone says *"Karibu!"* when you meet, they are saying "Welcome!" Although Dar has transformed itself in the last decades into a modern bustling city its mix of Arabic, German, English, Asian, and Swahili cultures gives it great charm, albeit a scruffy charm. Situated almost midway between Kenya in the north and Mozambique in the south at the edge of the sparkling blue Indian Ocean, Dar es Salaam's harbor is crowded with the hand-hewn canoes and triangular-sailed dhows that have distinguished the region for centuries. The palm-lined shore is lively with men selling freshly caught fish, mending giant nets, and scrubbing down their boats, while women nearby are roasting crayfish over open fires or stirring pots of soup. As with Zanzibar, one of your most abiding memories will be of the pungent scents and heady aromas of spices, food, and tropical flowers.

Now the graceful triangular-sailed dhows which have plied these seas

IF YOU HAVE TIME

Travel 70 km (43 mi) north to the historically fascinating town of Bagamoyo where old buildings such as the Catholic Museum in the grounds of the Holy Ghost Mission, and the Old Fort are well worth visiting. At the Old Fort, once an Arab trader's slave prison, you can see the underground tunnel along which slaves were herded to waiting dhows. The damp walls bore witness to the most terrible human suffering. It was in Bagamoyo that Henry Morton Stanley arrived after his three-year journey across Africa.

for centuries share the harbor with mammoth tankers, as the sleepy village has been transformed into one of East Africa's busiest ports, second only to Kenya's Mombasa. The country's major commercial center, Dar es Salaam has also become its largest city, home to more than 3.5 million inhabitants. Dar es Salaam also serves as the seat of government during the very slow move to Dodoma, which was named the official capital in 1973. The legislature resides in Dodoma, but most government offices are still found in Dar es Salaam.

In the early 1860s, Sultan Seyyid Majid of Zanzibar visited what was then the isolated fishing village of Mzizima, on the Tanzanian coast. Anxious to have a protected port on the mainland, Majid began constructing a palace here in 1865. The city, poised to compete with neighboring ports such as Bagamoyo and Kilwa, suffered a setback after the sultan died in 1870. His successor, his half-brother Seyyid Barghash, had little interest in the city, and its royal buildings fell into ruins. Only the Old Boma, which once housed royal guests, still survives.

The city remained a small port until Germany moved its colonial capital here in 1891 and began constructing roads, administrative offices, and many of the public buildings that remain in use today. The Treaty of Versailles granted Great Britain control of the region in 1916, but that country added comparatively little to the city's infrastructure during its 45-year rule.

Tanzania gained its independence in 1961. During the years that followed, President Julius Nyerere, who focused on issues such as education and health care, allowed the capital city to fall into a decline that lasted into the 1980s. When Benjamin William Mkapa took office in 1985, his market-oriented reforms helped to revitalize the city. The city continues to evolve—those who visited only a few years ago will be startled by the changes.

Dar es Salaam itself continues to grow and prosper with new hotels and restaurants mushrooming almost overnight and is now luring visitors that once might have scurried past on their way to the Serengeti. It doesn't hurt that the city has a bustling waterfront, interesting neighborhoods, and sights like the National Museum, which contains the famous fossil discoveries by Richard and Mary Leakey including the 1.7 million-year-old hominid skull discovered by Mary Leakey in the Olduvai Gorge in 1959.

GETTING HERE & AROUND

To find your way around Central Dar es Salaam, use the Askari Monument, at the intersection of Samora Avenue and Azikiwe Street as a compass. Most sights are within walking distance. Four blocks northeast on Samora Avenue you'll find the National Museum and Botanical Gardens; about seven blocks southwest stands the Clock Tower, another a good landmark. One block southeast is Sokoine Drive, which empties into Kivukoni Front as it follows the harbor. Farther along Kivukoni Front becomes Ocean Road.

Dar es Salaam

INDIAN OCEAN

UPANGA

Golf Course

KISUTU

Botanical Gardens

MCHAFUKOGE

Madaraka

Kivukoni Front

Harbour

KARIAKOO

Kariako Market

Clock Tower

Malindi Wharf

KIGAMBONI

Kurusini Creek

Main Quay

Bandari

KEY
- **1** *Exploring*
- **(1)** *Hotels & Restaurants*

| 0 | | 500 yards |
| 0 | | 500 m |

Exploring ▼	Restaurants ▼	Hotels ▼
Askari Monument **1**	Bandari Grill **4**	Royal Palm Hotel **2**
Tanzania National	Sawasdee **5**	The Souk **1**
Museum **2**	Serengeti **3**	

Along Samora Avenue and Sokoine Drive you'll find banks, pharmacies, grocery stores, and shops selling everything from clothing to curios. Northwest of Samora Avenue, around India Street, Jamhuri Street, and Libya Street, is the busy Swahili neighborhood where merchants sell all kinds of items, including Tanzania's best kangas. Farther west you'll find the large Kariakoo Market.

BEACHES

The pristine beaches north and south of Dar es Salaam are irresistible for those seeking the calm, cool waters of the Indian Ocean. Kunduchi Beach and Oyster Bay, just north of Dar es Salaam, offer a range of lodgings from thatch-roof bungalows to luxury high-rises. Open-air bars, cafés, and restaurants sit so close to shore you can feel the sea breeze. When you tire of swimming, you can snorkel around the coral reefs or sail in dhows to small islands such as Bongoyo and Mbudya.

A REAL GEM

Looking for that one-of-a-kind gift or keepsake? How about jewelry with Tanzanite in it? Given by Masai fathers to mothers upon the birth of their child, this deep blue stone, discovered in 1967, is unique to Tanzania. And though you can purchase the gems just about anywhere these days, you can't beat the prices or the bargaining you'll find in the shops of Arusha and Dar es Salaam—you'll be able to purchase loose stones, existing pieces, or customize your own design. ⚠ Do not buy any Tanzanite from street vendors. Nine times out of ten it will be a fake stone.

WHAT TO SEE

❶ Askari Monument. This bronze statue was erected by the British in 1927 in memory of African troops who died during World War I. (The word *askari* means "soldier" in Swahili.) It stands on the site of a monument erected by Germany to celebrate its victory here in 1888. That monument stood only five years before being demolished in 1916. ⊠ *Samora Ave. and Azikiwe St.*

❷ Tanzania National Museum. Apart from the Leakey fossil discoveries, which are some of the most important in the world, there are also good displays of colonial exploration and German occupation. ⊠ *Near Botanical Gardens, between Samora Ave. and Sokoine Dr.* ☎ *212– 2030 or 211–7508* ☞ *US$3* ☉ *Daily 9:30–6.*

WHERE TO STAY

$$$ 🏨 **Royal Palm Hotel.** Dar's classiest hotel (formerly the Sheraton) is surrounded by pleasant gardens and is next to a golf course. It's got all the bells and whistles one would expect from a five-star quality hotel including a business center, several restaurants, a large pool and a fitness center. ⊠ *20 Ohio St.* ☎ *211–2416* ⊕ *www.moevenpick-hotels. com* ⇆ *230 rooms* ⚏ *In-room: safe, Internet, a/c. In-hotel: restaurant, room service bar, pool, gym, sauna* ☰ *AE, DC, MC, V* ⊙*BP.*

¢ 🏨 **The Souk.** Located in the Slipway, a shopping and leisure complex in a converted boatyard, the Souk is a great place for an overnight or base for exploration from Dar. The rooms are simple, but comfortable— they are a respite from the craziness of Dar in calming shades of blue and white. A few of the rooms have views of the Msasani Bay, which is a nice touch. The complex has a book store, supermarket, a playground for the kids, four restaurants, and numerous curio shops including a great craft market that sells everything from Tinga Tinga paintings and jewelry to leather sandals and beaded creations. Transportation can be arranged to and from the airport and there are regular tours of Bongoyo island, Tanzania's first marine reserve, as well as fishing trips and cruises to Mafia, Pemba, and Zanzibar islands. ✉ *The Slipway, Chole Rd., Msasani Peninsula* ☎ *022/260–0893* ⊕ *www.slipway.net* ⃗*20 rooms* ⌂ *In-room: safe, minibar, a/c. In-hotel: bar, 4 restaurants, Internet, curio shops* ☰ *AE, MC, V* ⍾*BP.*

WHERE TO EAT

You can spend days sampling Dar es Salaam's remarkably varied cuisine. There's no need to spend a lot, as *hotelis* (cafés) offer heaping platefuls of African or Indian fare for less than Tsh 5,000 ($5). Typical *chakula* (food) for an East African meal includes *wali* (rice) or *ugali* (a slightly damp mound of breadlike ground corn) served with a meat, fish, or vegetable stew. A common side dish is *kachumbari,* a mixture of chopped tomatoes, onions, and cucumbers. Even less expensive are roadside stalls, such as those that line the harbor, offering snacks such as chicken and beef kebabs, roast corn on the cob, and *samosas,* triangular pastries stuffed with meat or vegetables. If you're in the mood for something sweet, try a doughnutlike *mandazi.* Wash it all down with a Tusker or Safari, local beers, or with *chai,* a hot tea served with milk, sugar, and various spices.

Should you be in the mood for something fancier, upscale hotels offer cosmopolitan meals and elaborate buffets for as much as $30. Even at the toniest of restaurants, reservations are rarely required. Restaurants in hotels generally are open until at least 10:30 PM, even on Sunday, although the hours of local restaurants vary.

$$ ✕ **Sawasdee.** With a name that means "welcome" in Thai, Sawasdee
★ has a peaceful atmosphere and attentive service that make it one of the best eateries in the city. Tanzania's first Thai restaurant, Sawasdee serves authentic dishes—duck in brown sauce, fish in ginger, chicken in green curry—prepared by a highly esteemed chef from Bangkok. The restaurant on the ninth floor of the New Africa Hotel overlooks the sparkling lights of the harbor. ✉ *New Africa Hotel, Azikiwi St. and Sokoine Dr.* ☎ *022/211–7050* ☰ *AE, MC, V* ⊗ *No lunch weekdays.*

$$ ✕ **Serengeti.** Sumptuous buffets have made this restaurant on the ground
★ floor of the Royal Palm Hotel a favorite among tourists as well as business executives. The cuisine changes nightly—Monday, Thursday, and Sunday are reserved for Asian fare; Tuesday, Wednesday, and Friday are the nights to go for European-style meals. Saturday the chef turns his attention to the foods of East Africa. The restaurant is also open for lunch and dinner, including the champagne breakfast which is a Sunday morning ritual among regular patrons. ✉ *Ohio St. and Ali Hassan Mwinyi Rd.* ☎ *022/211–2416* ☰ *AE, MC, V* ⊗ *Daily 6–10:30 PM.*

$ ✕ **Bandari Grill.** Long one of Dar es Salaam's best values, this place attracts the city's movers and shakers. Many business deals are cut over the "power lunch" served on the mezzanine. The seemingly endless buffet features traditional Tanzanian cuisine as well as selections from other countries. The beef tenderloin tips with king prawns is always a favorite. There's also a sports bar where executives kick back after a long day. Enjoy live music most evenings or stop by for breakfast or lunch. ⊠*Azikiwe St. and Sokoine Dr.* ☎*022/211–7050* ▤*AE, MC, V* ☉*Daily 7–11:30* PM.

DAR ES SALAAM ESSENTIALS

TRANSPORTATION

Do not buy tickets for transport, especially on ferries, trains, or buses, from anyone other than an accredited ticket seller.

BY AIR Many airlines fly directly to Dar es Salaam from Europe, but there are no direct flights from the United States.

KLM offers the only daily flights to Dar es Salaam. Other airlines that fly here frequently are Air India, Air Zimbabwe, Air Tanzania, British Airways, Egypt Air, Emirates, Ethiopian Airlines, Kenya Airways, South African Airways, and Swissair. British Airways has one flight daily from Dar es Salaam to London and Air Tanzania has daily flights to Dar es Salaam from destinations within East Africa. Air Tanzania, Precision Air, and Bank Air have several daily flights to Zanzibar.

Julius Nyerere International Airport, formerly Dar es Salaam International Airport, is about 13 km (8 mi) from the city center. Plenty of white-color taxis are available at the airport and will cost you about Tsh 15,000 to the city center. This can usually be negotiated. Most hotels will send drivers to meet your plane, if arranged in advance.

Airports **Julius Nyerere International Airport** (⊠*Kipawa, Off Nyerere Rd.* ☎*022/284–4211 or 022/284–4212* ⊕*www.tanzaniairports.com*).

BY FERRY Ferries operated by Sea Ferries Express to Zanzibar depart daily at 7:15, 10:30, 1, and 4:15 from the Zanzibar Ferry Terminal. The two-hour journey costs about Tsh 45,500 ($40). The Kigamboni ferry to the southern beaches runs continuously throughout the day and departs from the southern tip of the city center, where Kivukoni Front meets Ocean Road. The 10-minute ride costs about Tsh 100 ($1) one way.

Contacts **Sea Ferries Express** (⊠*Sokoine Dr., Dar es Salaam* ☎*022/213–7049*). **Zanzibar Ferry Terminal** (⊠*Sokoine Dr., Dar es Salaam*).

BY TAXI Taxis are the most efficient way to get around town. During the day they are easy to find outside hotels and at major intersections, but at night they are often scarce. Ask someone to call one for you. Taxis don't have meters, so agree on fare before getting in. Fares run about Tsh 2,000 within the city.

CONTACTS & RESOURCES

DAY TOURS As tour operators come and go and management and itineraries change, we advise you to check with your accommodations for recommendations or go to the Tanzania Tourist Board for information. *See Visitor Information below for the tourist board's contact information.*

EMBASSIES **Contacts** **American Embassy** (⊠*686 Old Bagamoyo Rd.Msasani* ☎*022/266–8001* ⊕*tanzania.usembassy.gov*).

HOURS OF OPERATION Shopping hours can vary, but usually they are 8:30–1 and 2–4:30. However, some of the tourist and curio shops stay open later.

MAIL & SHIPPING Postal service in Dar es Salaam is generally reliable. The main post office is downtown near the Askari Monument. Hotels will sell stamps and deliver mail to the post office. If you are sending something valuable, try DHL Worldwide Express.

Overnight Services DHL Worldwide Express (✉ *Nyerere St.* ☎ *022/286–1000* ⊕ *www.dhl.co.tz* ⊙ *Weekdays 8–6, Sat. 8–1*).

Post Office Main Post Office (✉ *Opposite CREB Azikiwe Bank, Azikiwe St.* ☎ *022/212–4952* ⊕ *www.tanpost.com* ⊙ *Weekdays 8–1, weekends 9–noon*).

> ## SHOPPING
>
> If you haven't yet picked up your gifts and curios, then stop by Arusha's Cultural Heritage Centre (✉ *Serengeti Rd.*). It's one of the best curio shops in Tanzania and is only 3 km (1.8 mi) out of town. You can buy carvings, jewelry, including the gemstone Tanzanite, colorful African clothing, local music, and much more. The King and Queen of Norway and Bill Clinton and his daughter Chelsea have all stopped to pick up last minute gifts and souvenirs.

SAFETY Dar es Salaam is among the safest cities in East Africa. It's fine to wander around by yourself during the day, but after dark it's best to stick with your companions. Because taxis are cheap, it's a good idea to use them at night. The area with the most street crime is along the harbor, especially Kivoni Front and Ocean Road.

Foreign women tend to feel safe in Dar es Salaam. But remember, women in Dar never wear clothing that exposes their shoulders or legs. You should do the same. You'll feel more comfortable in modest dress.

Read up on travel tips before your trip. Check out ⊕ *www.fodors.com* for stories from other travelers about their experiences with crime, scams, or the best service they've received in a country. You should also visit the Web site of your embassy in Tanzania. Find out where they are located, and ask them about travel requirements or information you might need.

VISITOR INFORMATION The Tanzania Tourist Board's Head Office is in Dar-es-Salaam. It has maps and information on travel to dozens of points of interest around Tanzania and is very helpful. The staff will discuss hotel options with you and assist you in making reservations.

Contacts Tanzania Tourist Board (✉ *3rd fl., IPS Building, corner of Azikiwe St. and Samora Ave.* ☎ *022/213–1555 information, 022/211–1244 head office* ⊕ *www. tanzaniatouristboard.com* ⊙ *Weekdays 9–5, Sat. 9–noon*).

ARUSHA

Arusha could be any small town in sub-Saharan Africa—dusty, crowded, and forgettable. A couple of pleasant features do distinguish it, however: potted plants line the pot-holed streets (put there by the plant nurseries just behind the sidewalks), and on a clear day, you can

Tanzania's Tribes

The Masai are a semi-nomadic people from Kenya and northern Tanzania whose distinct customs and dress have given them relative notoriety in the Western world. The Masai women wear colorful beaded jewelry, and men and women often wear bright red blankets over their shoulders. The tribe is patriarchal in structure and Masai elders make important decisions for each tribe. A famous rite of passage for Masai boys involves the circumcision of the penis without anesthetic: this process is a painful one, but in order to become warriors the boys are meant to endure it without any display of discomfort. Masai culture also dictates that boys must kill a lion before being circumcised.

Although this practice is less common these days, Masai who hunt lion rarely face any legal consequence. Wealth is measured in terms of cattle in the Masai community, and thus, cattle are considered sacred; they believe that cows are a gift from God. Since the Masai move about so much, their homes—also called *inkajijik*, or *boma*—are made from materials they find in their surroundings. They are generally constructed of mud, sticks, grass, and cow dung and are circular in shape. A typical Serengeti scene (and a beautiful one, if you are lucky enough to come across it) is a wide savannah peppered with baobab trees and earthen Masai boma.

see Mt. Meru, Africa's fifth-highest mountain at 4,556 meters (14,947 feet) looming in the distance.

The town is bisected by the Nauru River. The more modern part is to the east of the river where most of hotels, safari companies, and banks are located; west of the river is where the bus station and main market are. Most people spend an overnight here either coming or going. There's not really much to see and do in Arusha. If you do go out, you'll be accosted by safari touts.

WHERE TO STAY & EAT

$$ ✕**Stiggy's.** Long one of Arusha's most popular dining spots, this authentic Thai restaurant is run by a husband and wife team from Australia and Thailand, respectively. Expect to dine on authentic Thai cuisine amid a lively atmosphere. But take a taxi if you plan to go here—it's not safe to walk in the area. ✉*Old Moshi Rd.* ☎*0744/895–525* ▤*AE, MC, V* ☾*Tues.–Sun. noon–midnight.*

$$ ✕▥**Arusha Coffee Lodge.** Being 5 km (3 mi) from town and five minutes ☾ from Arusha Airport makes this a great option for pre- or post-safari layovers. Situated in the middle of what is claimed to be Tanzania's largest coffee plantation and designed around the original plantation homes, the split-level chalets are furnished in Victorian style, with big balconies and your own coffee percolator to try out the local produce. There's a first-class restaurant (US$10–US$35) and the service is impeccable. Wines are from South Africa and Chile. ✉*Serengeti Rd., Airport vicinity* ☎*027/254–0630* ⊕*www.elewana.com* ⇆*18 rooms* ♿*In-room: safe, minibar. In-hotel: restaurant, bar, pool* ▤*MC, V* ⦿*BP.*

$$$–$$$$ ▥**The Arusha Hotel.** Bang in the middle of town, opposite the clock tower, this recently refurbished hotel built in 1894 retains a colonial feel, with elegantly decorated rooms and lovely gardens running down to the Themi River. It's also home to a gift shop, a bookshop, and a casino. ✉*Main Rd.* ☎*027/250–7777* ⊕*www.thearushahotel.com* ⇆*86 rooms* ♿*In-room: a/c, safe, minibar, Internet. In-hotel: spa, restaurant, bar, pool, business center* ▤*MC, V* ⦿*BP.*

¢ ▥**Moivaro Coffee Plantation Lodge.** There are stunning views of the changing colors of Mt. Kilimanjaro from the grounds of this coffee plantation. You can explore nearby Mt. Meru by horseback or mountain bike, play a few games of tennis, or relax in the pool. Simple stone cottages, each with a private veranda, are warmed by fireplaces for the cool nights. ✉*6 km (4 mi) east of Arusha* ☎*027/255–3243* ⊟*027/255–3242* ⊕*www.moivaro. com* ⇆*25 rooms* ♿*In-hotel: spa, restaurant, tennis court* ▤*MC, V.*

ARUSHA ESSENTIALS

TRANSPORTATION

BY AIR There are no direct flights from the United States. Generally you need to connect through a city on the mainland, the easiest being Dar es Saalam.

Visitors from the United States and Europe require visas to enter Tanzania, which are available at your airport of arrival.

Airlines Air Tanzania (☎*027/250–3201* ⊕*airtanzania.com*). **Coastal Air** (☎*027/250–0087* ⊕*www.coastal.cc*). **Ethiopian Airlines** (☎*027/250–6167* ⊕*www.ethiopianairlines.com*). **Kenya Airways** (☎*027/254–8062* ⊕*www.kenya-airways.com*). **Precision Air** (☎*027/250–6903* ⊕*www.precisionairtz.com*). **South African Airways** (☎*027/250–3201* ⊕*ww2.flysaa.com*).

Airports Arusha Airport *(ARK)* (☎*027/741–530 or 027/744–317* ⊕*www. tanzaniairports.com*).

BY TAXI You will be approached immediately after you land by taxi drivers. Be sure to agree on a price before getting in, as taxis do not have meters. The fare to downtown Arusha is approximately US$25.

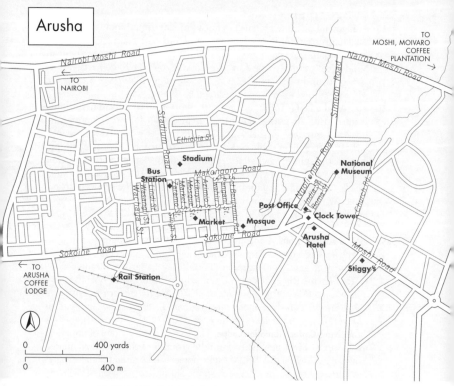

CONTACTS & RESOURCES

BUSINESS SERVICES & FACILITIES EMERGENCIES

There are a number of Internet cafés in the city as well as in major hotels and lodges, that charge around Tsh 1,000–Tsh 5,000 ($1–$5) for an hour. This is probably the best form of communication in Arusha.

Hospitals AICC Hospital (✉ *Old Moshi Rd., Arusha* ☎ *027/254-4392*).

SAFETY

It's unlikely that you would want to explore Arusha at night, but if you do, take a taxi to and from your destination. As in any East African city muggings and purse-snatching are common.

VISITOR INFORMATION

The Tanzanian Tourist Board (TTB) has an Arusha office where you can pick up maps and brochures for the area. Tanzania National parks also has an office here that can help you book accommodations or answer any of your safari questions.

Contacts Arusha Tourist Information Center (✉ *Boma Rd.* ☎ *057/503-843* ⊕ *www.tanzaniatouristboard.com*). **Tanzania National Parks** (✉ *Opposite Cultural Heritage Centre, Serengeti Rd.* ☎ *027/250-1930* ⊕ *www.tanzaniaparks.com*).

BEACH ESCAPES

4

Looking for a little R&R after your safari? Tanzania has 1,424 km (883 mi) of beautiful, pristine coastline just waiting for you to explore. Looking for an island getaway? Tanzania has those, too. Zanzibar and Mnemba Island are perfect spots to kick back and relax.

ZANZIBAR

Updated by Kate Turkington

This ancient isle once ruled by sultans and slave traders served as the stepping stone into the African continent for missionaries and explorers. Today this jewel in the Indian Ocean attracts visitors intent on discovering its sandy beaches, pristine rain forests, or boldly colored coral reefs. Once known as the Spice Island for its export of cloves, Zanzibar has become one of the most exotic flavors in travel, better than Bali or Mali when it comes to beauty that will make your jaw drop.

Separated from the mainland by a channel only 35 km (22 mi) wide, and only six degrees south of the equator, this tiny archipelago—the name Zanzibar also includes the islands of Unguja (the main island), Pemba, and Mnemba—in the Indian Ocean was the launching base for a romantic era of expeditions into Africa. Sir Richard Burton and John Hanning Speke used it as their base when searching for the source of the Nile. It was in Zanzibar that journalist Henry Morton Stanley, perched in an upstairs room overlooking the Stone Town harbor, began his search for David Livingstone.

The first ships to enter the archipelago's harbors may have belonged to the Phoenicians, who are believed to have sailed in around 600 BC, and since then every other great navy in the eastern hemisphere has dropped anchor here at one time or another. But it was Arab traders who left an indelible mark. Minarets punctuate the skyline of Stone Town, where more than 90% of the residents are Muslim. In the harbor you will see dhows, the Arabian boats with triangular sails. Islamic women with their faces covered by black boubou veils scurry down alleyways so narrow their outstretched arms could touch buildings on both sides. Stone Town received its odd name because most of its buildings were made of limestone, which means exposure to salty air has eroded many foundations. Flat rooftops, perfectly suited for the deserts where many of the oldest inhabitants originated, merely collected rain. After more than a few roofs collapsed from the standing pools, residents started changing their construction methods. As you gaze out upon the rooftops in the evening, you may now notice vaulted A-frames, the better to drain the water during monsoons.

The first Europeans who arrived here were the Portuguese in the 15th century, and thus began a reign of exploitation. As far inland as Lake Tanganyika, slave traders captured the residents outright or bartered for them from their own chiefs, then forced the newly enslaved to march toward the Indian Ocean carrying loads of ivory tusks. Once at the shore they were shackled together while waiting for dhows to collect them at Bagamoyo, a place whose name means "here I leave my heart." Although it's estimated that 50,000 slaves passed through the Zanzibar slave market each year during the 19th century, many more died en route.

Tanganyika and Zanzibar merged in 1964 to create Tanzania, but the honeymoon was brief. Zanzibar's relationship with the mainland remains uncertain as calls for independence continue. "Bismillah, will you let him go," a lyric from Queen's "Bohemian Rhapsody," has become a rebel chant for Zanzibar to break from Tanzania. The archipelago also has tensions of its own. Accusations of voting irregularities during the elections in 2000 and 2005 led to violence that sent scores of refugees fleeing to the mainland. Calm was quickly restored. As the old proverb goes, the dogs bark and the caravan moves on.

Zanzibar's appeal is apparent to developers, who are intent on opening restaurants, hotels, and even water-sapping golf courses. But so far the archipelago has kept much of its charm. It retains the allure it had when explorer David Livingstone set up his expedition office here in 1866.

Zanzibar Island, locally known as Unguja, has amazing beaches and resorts, incredible dive spots, acres and acres of spice plantations, the Jozani Forest Reserve, and Stone Town. Plus, it's only takes a little more than an hour to fly there. It's a great spot to head for a post-safari unwind.

Stone Town, archipelago's major metropolis, is a maze of narrow streets lined with houses featuring magnificently carved doors studded with brass. And though it can rightly be called a city, much of the western part of the larger island is a slumbering paradise where cloves, as well as rice and coconuts, still grow.

Jozani Forest Reserve is home to the rare Kirk's red colobus monkey, which is named after Sir John Kirk, the British consul in Zanzibar from 1866 to 1887. The species is known for its white whiskers and rusty coat. Many of the other animals that call this reserve home are endangered because 95% of the original forests of the archipelago have been destroyed. Reserves have been established to harbor such species as the

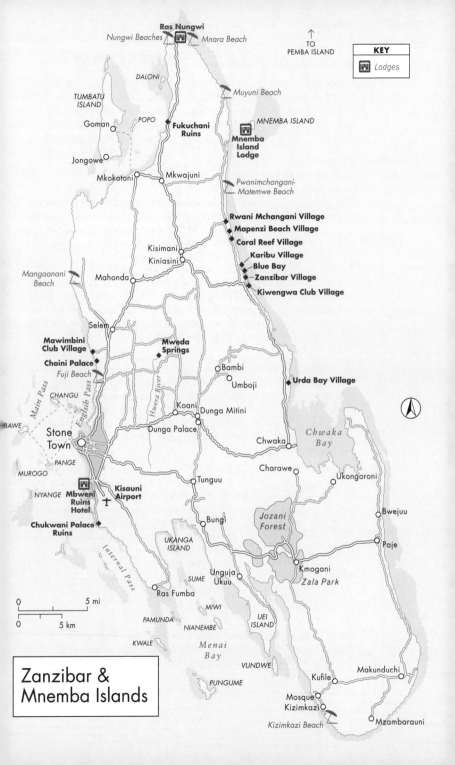

Ras Nungwi
Nungwi Beaches ⌂ ← *Mnara Beach*

↑
TO
PEMBA ISLAND

KEY
⌂ *Lodges*

DALONI

TUMBATU ISLAND

POPO

← *Muyuni Beach*

MNEMBA ISLAND

Goman

Jongowe

Mkokotoni Mkwajuni **Fukuchani Ruins**

⌂ **Mnemba Island Lodge**

Pwanimchangani-Matemwe Beach

◆ **Rwani Mchangani Village**
◆ **Mapenzi Beach Village**
◆ **Coral Reef Village**
Kisimani ◆ **Karibu Village**
Kiniasini ◆ **Blue Bay**
Mangaanani Beach ↖ Mahonda ◆ **Zanzibar Village**
◆ **Kiwengwa Club Village**

Selem

Mawimbini Club Village ◆
Mweda Springs
Choini Palace ◆
Fuji Beach ◆ Bambi

Main Pass *English Pass* *Hwera River* Umboji ◆ **Urda Bay Village**

CHANGU

BAWE Koani ◆ Dunga Mitini

Stone Town Dunga Palace ◆ Chwaka *Chwaka Bay*

PANGE

MUROGO Charawe Ukongoroni
NYANGE **Mbweni Ruins Hotel** **Kisauni Airport** ✈ Tunguu

Chukwani Palace Ruins ◆ Bungi *Jozani Forest* Bwejuu

Internal Pass *UKANGA ISLAND* Paje

SUME Unguja Ukuu Kmogani
Ras Fumba *Zala Park*

MIWI
PAMUNDA *NIANEMBE* *UEI ISLAND*

KWALE *Menai Bay* *VUNDWE* Makunduchi

PUNGUME Kufile

0   5 mi
0   5 km

Mosque ☂
Kizimkazi
Kizimkazi Beach ↖ Mzambarauni

Zanzibar & Mnemba Islands

blue duiker, a diminutive antelope whose coat is a dusty bluish-gray.

Although the main island of Unguja feels untouched by the rest of the world, the nearby islands of Pemba and Mnemba offer retreats that are even more remote. For many years Arabs referred to Pemba as Al Khudra, or the Green Island, and indeed it still is, with forests of king palms, mangos, and banana trees.

The 65-km-long (40-mi-long) island is less famous than Unguja except among scuba divers, who enjoy the lush coral gardens with colorful sponges and huge fans. Archaeology buffs are also discovering Pemba, where sites from the 9th to the 15th centuries have been unearthed. At Mtambwe Mkuu coins bearing the heads of sultans were discovered. Ruins along the coast include ancient mosques and tombs. In the 1930s Pemba was famous for its sorcerers, attracting disciples of the black arts from as far away as Haiti. Witchcraft is still practiced, and, oddly enough, so is bullfighting. Introduced by the Portuguese in the 17th century, the sport has been improved by locals, who rewrote the ending. After enduring the ritual teasing by the matador's cape, the crowds drape the bull with flowers and parade him around the village.

Beyond Pemba, smaller islands in the Zanzibar Archipelago range from mere sandbanks to Changu, once a prison island, and Mnemba, a private retreat for guests who pay hundreds of dollars per day to get away from it all. To the west of Pemba, Misali Island reputedly served as a hideout for the notorious Captain Kidd, which makes visitors dream of buried treasure. In reality it is the green sea turtles that do most of the digging.

June through October is the best time to visit Zanzibar because the temperature averages 26°C (79°F). Spice tours are best during harvest time, July and October, when cloves (unopened flower buds) are picked and laid out to dry. Zanzibar experiences a short rainy season in November, but heavy rains can fall from March until the end of May. Temperatures soar during this period, often reaching over 30°C (90°F). Most travelers come between June and August and from mid-November to early January. During these periods many hotels add a surcharge.

Zanzibar observes Ramadan for a month every year. During this period Muslims are forbidden to eat, drink, or smoke between sunrise and sunset. Although hotels catering to tourists are not affected, many small shops and restaurants are closed during the day. If you plan to arrive during Ramadan, aim for the end, when a huge feast called the Eid al-Fitr (which means "end of the fast") brings everyone out to the streets.

WHAT TO SEE

Anglican Cathedral. This was the first Anglican cathedral in East Africa and its crucifix was carved from the tree under which explorer David Livingstone's heart was buried in the village of Chitambo. Built in 1887 to mark the end of the slave trade, the cathedral's high altar was constructed on the site of a whipping post. Nothing of the slave market remains, although nearby are underground chambers in which slaves were forced to crouch on stone shelves less than 2 feet high. Ask to take the stairs up to the tower, which affords a bird's-eye view of Stone Town. ⊠ *Off Creek Rd.* ☎ *No phone* 🎫 *Tsh 1,000* ⊘ *Daily 8–6.*

Beit al-Sahel. This structure was known as the People's Palace, but for a long time the name was a bitter irony. It was here that sultans and their families lived from the 1880s until the revolution of 1964. It now exhibits collections of furniture and clothing from the days of the sultans. A room is dedicated to Princess Salme, daughter of Sultan Said, who eloped with a German businessman in the 19th century. On the grounds outside are the tombs of Sultan Said and two of his sons. ⊠ *Mizingani Rd.* ☎ *No phone* 🎫 *US$3* ⊘ *Tues.–Sat. 10–8.*

Beit el-Ajaib. Known as the House of Wonders because it was the first building in Zanzibar to use electric lights, this four-story palace is still one of the largest buildings in the city. Built in the late 1800s for Sultan Barghash, it was bombarded by the British in 1886, forcing the sultan to abdicate his throne. Today you'll find cannons guarding the beautifully carved doors at the entrance. Check out the marble-floored rooms, where you'll find exhibits that detail the country's battle for independence. ⊠ *North of Old Fort* ☎ *No phone* 🎫 *US$2* ⊘ *Weekdays 9–6, weekends 9–3.*

Darajani Market. This gable-roofed structure built in 1904 houses a sprawling fruit and vegetable market. Goods of all sorts—colorful fabrics, wooden chests, and all types of jewelry—are sold in the shops that line the surrounding streets. To the east of the main building you'll find spices laid out in colorful displays of beige, yellow, and red. On Wednesday and Saturday there's an antiques fair. The market is most active in the morning between 9 and 11. ⊠ *Creek Rd., north of New Mkunazini St.* ☎ *No phone* 🎫 *Free* ⊘ *Daily 8–6.*

Dhow Harbor. The scent of cloves hangs heavy in the air as stevedores load and unload sacks of the region's most valuable crops. Every day you'll spot dhows arriving from the mainland with deliveries of flour and other goods not available on the islands. Fishermen deposit their catch here early in the morning. This is a seedy area, so be cautious. ⊠ *Malindi St., north of Malawi St.*

Forodhani Gardens. This pleasant waterfront park is a favorite spot for an evening stroll. Dozens of venders sell freshly grilled fish under the light of gas lanterns. ⊠ *Mizingani St.*

Hamamni Baths. Built in the late 19th century by Sultan Barghash, these public baths still retain the grandeur of a past era. Although they are now closed, you can get the key from the shopkeeper next door (don't forget to pay him the entrance fee) and explore the maze of marble-floored rooms leading to the ornately tiled tubs. ⊠ *Hamamni St.* ☎ *No phone* 🖅 *Tsh 500.*

A GOOD TIP

Many tour operators offer a guided walking tour of Stone Town for approximately US$20–US$25. Ask your hotel for guide suggestions.

Old Dispensary. With intricately carved wood balconies that make it resemble a wedding cake, this former dispensary shines again after being renovated by community groups. Built at the turn of the last century, it was donated to the city by an Indian merchant named Tharia Topan. Today it houses shops, galleries, and a small café. ⊠ *Mizingani Rd., near Malindi Rd.* ☎ *No phone* 🖅 *Free* ⊙ *Daily 9–6.*

★ **Old Fort.** Built by the Portuguese in 1560, this bastioned fortress is the oldest structure in Stone Town. It withstood an attack from Arabs in 1754. It was later used as a jail, and prisoners who were sentenced to death met their ends here. It has undergone extensive renovation and today is headquarters for many cultural organizations, including the Zanzibar International Film Festival. Performances of traditional dance and music are staged here several times a week. The Neem Tree Café is a good place to stop for lunch. ⊠ *Creek Rd. and Malawi Rd.* ☎ *No phone* 🖅 *Free* ⊙ *Daily 10–6.*

St. Joseph's Cathedral. Built by French missionaries more than a century ago, this ornate church is based on the basilica of Notre Dame de la Garde, in Marseilles, France. It's now one of the city's most recognizable landmarks, with twin spires that will be one of the first sights you'll see as you arrive in Stone Town. ⊠ *Cathedral St. near Gizenda St.* ☎ *No phone.*

WHERE TO STAY

BEACH RESORTS
$$–$$$

🖼 **Ras Nungwi.** You may ask yourself, "Where exactly am I going." But the more than hour drive from the airport through local towns and over bumpy roads will be worth it once you arrive. You'll feel as if you've stepped into another world when you're greeted by balmy breezes, swaying palms, and a nice cool drink. Request one of the rooms with water views, it may be more expensive, but it's lovely to wake up and see the turquoise waters. The rooms immediately say island getaway: the handcrafted four-poster beds are draped in mosquito netting, the tiled floors are cooling to walk on, and your own veranda is a perfect place to jot in your journal or write home. If you're looking for an adventure, the resort offers snorkeling, scuba diving, dhow cruises, and deep sea fishing, as well as tours of Nungwi—the local town—Stone Town, Jozani Forest, and spice plantations. If you want to relax, the pool beckons, the beach is gorgeous to walk along, and the Peponi Spa, which opened in 2007, offers a full spa menu. Kids are welcome. ■ TIP➔ **The resort is closed in April and May.** ⊠ *Nungwi Peninsular, North Region* ☎ *024/224–0487* ⊕ *www.rasnungwi.com* 🛏 *32 rooms* ⌂ *In-room: a/c, safe. In-hotel: spa, Internet, restaurant, bar, pool, curio shop* ☰ *MC, V* ⏉ *MAP.*

$$ ⊞**Mbweni Ruins Hotel.** Ten minutes from the airport and Stone Town, this historic—great-value-for-the-money—hotel was once an Anglican Girl's School for slave trade orphans. It sits right on the beach amid its own botanical gardens with more than 650 plant species. Some of the original plants were brought here from London's Kew Gardens in the late 1800s and the cousin of English novelist William Makepeace Thackeray, Miss Caroline Thackeray, was Headmistress here for 25 years starting in 1877. En-suite rooms are small but comfortable with a tiny lobby, beamed ceilings, hand-carved high wooden four-poster beds with a picture of a stern Victorian lady above them, and a tiled balcony with Moorish arches where you can sit and hear the waves lapping gently on the mangrove-fringed shore. The bar and restaurant face the ocean and are full of attractive Zanzibari furniture and lamps. ⊠*20 Battery Beach, Box 10690, Marine Parade 4056* ☎*223–5478* ⊕*www. mbweni.com* ⤶*13 rooms* ⌂*In-room: a/c, safe. In-hotel: restaurant, bar, pool* ⊟*AE, DC, MC, V* ⦿*BP.*

IN STONE   ⊞**The Zanzibar Serena Inn.** Regarded as one of Tanzania's best hotels
TOWN and a member of Small Luxury Hotels of the World, this gorgeous hotel
$$$$ is in two restored historic buildings integrated into a single property. Superbly situated on the Stone Town seafront, you'll live like a sultan in its luxuriously decorated interiors with genuine antiques, Persian rugs, old Zanzibari carved doors, fretwork screens, chandeliers, and carved staircases. ∎**TIP➔It's worth paying an extra US$40 per night to get a prime view.** ⊠*Shangani St., Shangani* ☎*024/223–3051* ⊕*www. serenahotels.com* ⤶*51 rooms* ⌂*In-room: a/c, minibar, safe. In-hotel: restaurant, bar, pool* ⊟*MC, V* ⦿*FAP.*

¢–$$$ ⊞**Beyt al Chai.** Also known as the Stone Town Inn, this former tea house recalls days gone by. The ornate wooden staircase takes you to the guest rooms and the lounge—a great place to read a book, write postcards, or sip a cool drink. The rooms have high ceilings, thick walls and small windows which keep out the heat. The carved wooden four poster beds are draped in mosquito netting adding a sense of relaxation. ⊠*Kelele Square, Shangani* ☎*0774/444–111* ⊕*www. stonetowninn.com* ⤶*6 rooms* ⌂*In-room: a/c. In-hotel: safe, phone, restaurant* ⊟*MC, V* ⦿*BP.*

WHERE TO EAT

Zanzibar was the legendary Spice Island, so it's no surprise the cuisine here is flavored with lemongrass, cumin, and garlic. Even the beverages have an extra kick; cinnamon enlivens tea and coffee, while ginger flavors a refreshing soft drink called Tangawizi. Zanzibar grows more than 20 types of mangos, and combining them with bananas, papayas, pineapples, and passion fruit makes for great juices. When it comes to dinner, seafood reigns supreme. Stone Town's seaside fish market sells skewers of kingfish and tuna. Stop by in the early evening, when the catch of the day is hauled in and cleaned. Make sure to try the prawn kebabs, roasted peanuts, and corn on the cob at the outdoor market at Forodhani Gardens. Try the vegetarian Zanzibar pizza for breakfast; it's more like an omelet.

Gratuities are often included in the bill, so ask the staff before adding the usual 10% tip. Credit cards are not widely accepted, so make sure you have enough cash. Lunch hours are generally from 12:30 to 2:30, dinner from 7 to 10:30. Dress is casual for all but upscale restaurants, where you should avoid T-shirts, shorts, and trainers.

$$$–$$$$ ✕**Tower Top.** With stunning views past the city's minarets to the harbor where dhows are setting out to sea, this rooftop restaurant is a great place to watch the sun sink into the Indian Ocean. It only holds about 20 people, who dine on fish or chicken accompanied by spice-scented rice while reclining on soft cushions. At weekends traditional music and dance accompany the delicious food. You'll feel more a part of the scene if you wear something loose-fitting, perhaps even the local caftans known as *khanzus*. Dinner only. ⊠*Hurumzi St.* ☎*024/223–0171* ⊕*www.emerson-green.com* ◿*Reservations essential* ⊟*No credit cards.*

$$$ ✕**The Spices Rendez-Vous.** Considered to be the finest Indian food on the island stop by for delicious Tandoori Chicken and Prawn Curry. There's African music and dancing on Tuesday evenings. ⊠*Intersection of Kenyatta and Vuga Rds.* ☎*024/223–4241* ◷*Daily 2–10* PM ⊟*No credit cards.*

¢–$$$ ✕**Archipelago.** The breezy, open layout of this BYOB restaurant adds to the casual feel. You'll find tourists and locals alike dining upon the fresh seafood. Check out the dry erase board for the daily specials. The also serve breakfast and lunch. ⚠ You will have to climb up one flight of stairs to get here. ⊠*Hurumzi St., Shangani* ☎*024/223–0171* ⊟*No credit cards* ◷*Daily 6–10:30* PM.

$$ ✕**Monsoon Restaurant.** For great Swahili food check out this atmospheric restaurant. The inside is decorated in a North African vibe. There are low tables with cushions to sit on the floor. If you'd rather have views of the ocean and Fordhani Gardens, choose the veranda instead. Some nights there's traditional Tarab music. Check out the chalkboard by the front door for the daily specials. ⊠*Hurumzi St.* ☎*024/223–3076* ◷*Daily 10* AM–*midnight* ⊟*No credit cards.*

$ ✕**Mercury's.** As you might expect this trendy waterside hangout, named after Queen lead singer Freddie Mercury born just a couple of blocks away, is one of Zanzibar's vibiest places. There are great seafood, pizzas, pasta, and steaks and the wooden terrace overlooking the ocean is ideal for those sunset drinks. ⊠*Hurumzi St.* ☎*024/223–3076* ◷*Daily 10* AM–*midnight* ⊟*No credit cards.*

MNEMBA ISLAND, OFF ZANZIBAR

Fodor'sChoice   For the ultimate beach escape where time stands still, where sand, sea,
★   and horizon melt into each other, where there is exclusivity, total relaxation, and impeccable food and service it would be hard to find almost anywhere in the world as alluring as Mnemba Island Lodge on CC Africa's privately owned Mnemba Island; the guest list includes royalty, celebrities, pop stars, business tycoons, and international honeymooners. You'll be transported from Zanzibar by 4x4 and speed boat to this ultimate desert island and as you arrive the "Wow!" factor immediately

kicks in. Your huge beach house Swiss Family Robinson deluxe— one of only ten on the island—hidden between strips of coastal forest faces a turquoise colored sea that would have challenged even the palette of Van Gogh. Coconut matting covers the walls and floors of your bedroom, dressing room, en-suite bathroom, and covered veranda furnished with handmade Zanzibari furniture and cream and white soft furnishings. A feature of this superlative lodge is its imaginative use of recycled glass. Check out the blue glass bead shower curtain, your soap dish, or your champagne flute. Diving and snorkeling off a pristine coral reef just a few feet from shore is a perfect 10, and if you've always wanted to dive, then this is the place to fulfill that dream with two ultra-experienced Belgian dive masters and state-of-the-art equipment. The nonstop cooing of doves will soothe even the most savage breast as the tiniest antelopes in the world, the rare suni, scamper happily past you on twiglike legs as you sit on the beach under your private canopy and sip sundowners. Mix with fellow guests from all over the world or dine alone a few feet from the soft surf under pulsing stars by glowing lantern light. Heaven can't be better than this. Make sure you book well in advance as Mnemba Island is a legendary and much-sought after destination. ☝CC Africa, Private Bag X27, Benmore 2010, South Africa ☎27/11/809–4300 ⊕www.ccafrica.com ⋟10 beach chalets ⚭In-hotel: bar, restaurant, safari shop ▤AE, DC, MC, V ⚭FAP.

> ## WORD OF MOUTH
>
> "We did a snorkel trip to Mnemba Island. You go by dhow which was great, and a bargain at $20. Lots of healthy corals and masses of fish; the visibility was fair to good. It was a full moon when we were there and the tides were very extreme (this was a show in itself)."
>
> –Jocilen

ZANZIBAR ESSENTIALS

TRANSPORTATION

BY AIR There are no direct flights from the United States. Generally you need to connect through a city on the mainland, the easiest being Dar es Saalam. From Dar es Saalam to Stone Town, there are regular flights in small twin-engine aircraft operated by Precision Air and Coastal Air. The flight takes around 20 minutes. From Nairobi and Mombasa, you can fly to Stone Town on Kenya Airways.

You can also hop between the two main islands of Zanzibar. Zan Air, a local charter company, flies between Stone Town and Chake Chake three times a week. The flights take 20 minutes, and give you a spectacular aerial view of the islands and the coral reefs. Coastal Air flies every day except Saturday from Dar es Salaam to Stone Town to Chake Chake.

Visitors from the United States and Europe require visas to enter Tanzania. Zanzibar is a semi-autonomous state within Tanzania, so you don't need a separate visa to visit, but you do need to show your passport.

Airlines **Coastal Air** (☎024/223–3112 ⊕www.coastal.cc). **Precision Air** (☎024/223–4521 ⊕www.precisionairtz.com). **Zan Air** (☎024/223–3670 ⊕www.zanair.com).

Airports **Zanzibar Airport** (☎ *024/223–3979* ⊕ *www.zanzibar-airport.com*).

BY BIKE OR MOPED — Bikes can be rented from shops near Darajani Market. Mopeds and motorcycles are another great way to get about the island.

BY BOAT — Several hydrofoil ferries travel between Dar es Salaam and Stone Town. The fastest trips, lasting about 75 minutes, are on hydrofoils operated by Sea Express and Azam Marine. Sea Express has daily departures from Dar es Salaam at 7.30, 10, noon, 2:30, and 4:30, with returns at 7, 10, noon, 2:30, and 4:30. Azam Marine departs from Dar es Salaam at 8, 1:15, and 4, returning at 7, 1:30, and 4.

Tickets can be purchased on the spot or in advance from the row of offices next to the port in Dar es Saalam. Timetables and prices are displayed on boards outside each office. Tickets for nonresidents range from $40 for first class (Tsh 45,000) to $35 (Tsh 40,000) for second class. The harbor is quite busy so keep an eye on your possessions and if you don't want help from a porter, be firm.

Contacts **Azam Marine** (☎ *022/212-3324 in Dar es Salaam, 022/223-1655 in Zanzibar*). **Sea Express** (✉ *Sokoine Dr.* ☎ *022/213-7049*).

BY TAXI — When you arrive you will be approached by taxi drivers. Be sure to agree on a price before getting in, as taxis do not have meters. The fare to Stone Town should be around Tsh 11,000 (around $10–$15). Your driver may let you out several blocks before you reach your hotel because the streets are too narrow. Ask the driver to walk you to the hotel. Be sure to tip him if he carries your luggage.

CONTACTS & RESOURCES

BUSINESS SERVICES & FACILITIES — There are a number of Internet cafés in the city as well as in major hotels and resorts, that charge around Tsh 1,000–Tsh 5,000 ($1–$5) for an hour. This is probably the best form of communication on the island.

DAY TOURS — Spice tours are a very popular way to see Zanzibar. Guides take you to farms in Kizimbani or Kindichi and teach you to identify plants that produce cinnamon, turmeric, nutmeg, and vanilla. A curry luncheon will undoubtedly use some of the local spices. Any tour company can arrange a spice tour, but the best guides are those who work for Mr. Mitu, a renowned guide who has his own agency and a battalion of guides trained by him. The average price for a spice tour is $15, including lunch. Most depart around 9:30 AM from Stone Town.

Fisherman Tours is an experienced operator based in Stone Town that offers general city tours. There are many types of tours available. John da Silva, a local artist, gives tours of the architecture in Stone Town. If you cannot reach Mr. Da Silva or Mr. Mitu on the below numbers, enquire at a local tour operator or at the Tourist Information Centre as to where you can get hold of them.

Contacts **Fisherman Tours** (✉ *Vuga Rd., near Magestic Cinema, Stone Town* ☎ *024/223-8791*). **John da Silva** (✉ *Stone Town* ☎ *024/223-2123*). **Mr. Mitu** (✉ *Stone Town* ☎ *024/223-1020*).

EMERGENCIES Zanzibar Medical & Diagnostic Center provides 24-hour emergency services. Ask for Dr. Mario Mariani. The main hospital in Stone Town is the state-run Mnazi Mmoja Hospital.

Hospitals **Mnazi Mmoja Hospital** (✉ *Kaunda Rd., Stone Town* ☎ *024/223–1071*). **Zanzibar Medical & Diagnostic Center** (✉ *Vuga Rd., near Makunazini St., Stone Town* ☎ *024/223-3113, 741/750–0040 24-hour emergency hotline*).

HEALTH Visitors to Zanzibar are required to have a yellow fever vaccination certificate; some Web sites also recommend polio, Hepatitis A, and typhoid vaccinations. You should also talk with your doctor about a malaria prophylactic. The best way to avoid malaria is to avoid being bitten by mosquitoes, so make sure your arms and legs are covered and that you wear plenty of mosquito repellent. Always sleep under a mosquito net; most hotels and guesthouses provide them. The sun can be very strong here, so make sure to slather yourself with sunscreen as well. Antihistamine cream is also quite useful for when you do get bitten, to stop the itch. Drink bottled water, and plenty of it—it will help you avoid dehydration. Avoid raw fruits and vegetables that may have been washed in untreated water.

MAIL & SHIPPING Stone Town's main post office is east of town near Amani Stadium. A more convenient branch office is on Kenyatta Road in the Shangani District. On Pemba Island, the post office at Chake Chake is on the main road toward the police station. International post can take up to three weeks or longer.

MONEY There are handy currency exchange booths in Stone Town that offer good rates. The best rates are at Forex Bureau around the corner from Mazson's Hotel on Kenyatta Road, and the Malindi Exchange across from Cine Afrique. Mtoni Marine Center, also in Stone Town, will give a cash advance on your Visa or MasterCard. It charges a commission as well as a processing fee. Currency exchange offices can also be found on Pemba in Chake Chake and in Wete. Most people will except U.S. dollars, but be aware of the exchange rate and make sure you are not being overcharged.

SAFETY Although the best way of experiencing Stone Town is to wander around its labyrinthine streets, you should always be on your guard. Don't wear jewelry or watches that might attract attention, and keep a firm grasp on purses and camera bags. Leave valuables in the safe at your hotel. Always take a taxi when traveling at night.

Muggings have been reported at Nungwi and other coastal resorts, so never carry valuables onto the beach.

As Zanzibar is a largely conservative, Muslim state, it is advisable for women to dress modestly.

Homosexuality is frowned upon in Zanzibar, and displays of public affection can be prosecutable.

TAXES The 20% value-added tax is not always included in the quoted price of goods and services, so be sure to inquire. A $5 harbor tax is required when buying ferry tickets.

TELEPHONES The regional code for Zanzibar is 024.

TIPPING Tips are often included in restaurant bills; inquire if your bill does not make it clear. If not, 10% is sufficient. Many tour operators include tips for hotel staff in their packages; otherwise, porters should be tipped Tsh 1,000 ($1). If you stay in a private home, it is customary to tip the cooks, maids, and gardeners about Tsh 1,000 ($1) a day. Taxi drivers do not expect a tip unless they carry your luggage or serve as a guide.

VISITOR INFORMATION The free tourist magazine *Recommended in Zanzibar*, found in hotels and shops, lists cultural events, as well as tide tables that are very useful for divers. There is a tourist information center north of Stone Town. Although not very useful for information about the city, it does book rooms in inns in other parts of the island.

Contacts **Zanzibar Tourist Information Center** (☎ *024/223-3485*). **Zanzibar Tourist Corporation** (☎ *024/223-8630* ⊕ *www.zanzibartouristcorporation.com*).

TANZANIA ESSENTIALS

TRANSPORTATION

BY AIR

When booking flights, check the routing carefully as some involve stopovers or require you to change airlines. Several flight options from America require long layovers in Europe before connecting to Dar es Salaam or Arusha. This is especially true for the cheaper flight options.

Most travelers arrive in Tanzania through Dar es Salaam airport. Many airlines fly directly to Dar es Salaam from Europe, but there are no direct flights from the United States.

KLM offers the only daily flights to Dar es Salaam from Amsterdam's Schipol airport. Other airlines that fly here frequently are Air India, Air Zimbabwe, Air Tanzania, British Airways, Egypt Air, Emirates, Ethiopian Airlines, Kenya Airways, South African Airways, and Swissair. British Airways has one flight daily from Dar es Salaam to London. Air Tanzania has daily flights to Dar es Salaam from destinations within East Africa. Air Tanzania has several daily flights to Zanzibar.

Airlines **Air India** (☎ *022/215-2642* ⊕ *www.airindia.com*). **Air Tanzania** (☎ *022/211-8411* ⊕ *www.airtanzania.com*). **Air Zimbabwe** (☎ *022/212-3526* ⊕ *www.airzimbabwe.com*). **British Airways** (☎ *022/211-3820* ⊕ *www.britishairways.com*). **Emirates** (☎ *022/211-6100* ⊕ *www.emirates.com*). **Ethiopian Airlines** (☎ *022/211-7063* ⊕ *www.ethiopianairlines.com*). **Kenyan Airways** (☎ *022/211-9377* ⊕ *www.kenya-airways.com*). **KLM** (☎ *022/213-9790* ⊕ *www.klm.com*). **South Africa Airways** (☎ *022/211—7044* ⊕ *www.flysaa.com*). **Swiss Air** (☎ *022/211—8870* ⊕ *www.swiss.com*).

AIRPASS The Star Alliance African Airpass can only be purchased by international passengers arriving to Africa on a Star Alliance carrier (United, Air Canada, US Airways, South African Airways, etc.) and is good for 4 to 10 flights. The flights are sold in segments, priced by the distance between cities. These are only economy class seats and can be expensive when compared to the discount airline pricing within South Africa, but they are a bargain for the longer routes, such as Nairobi to Johannesburg for under $300. If your itinerary includes more than two of the 25 cities served in Africa, this may be a good choice.

Contact Info **Star Alliance** (⊕ www.staralliance.com).

AIRPORTS & Dar es Salaam International Airport (Julius Nyerere International Air-
TRANSFERS port) is about 13 km (8 mi) from the city center. Plenty of white-color taxis are available at the airport and will cost you about Tsh 15,000 to the city center. This can usually be negotiated. Most hotels will send drivers to meet your plane, if arranged in advance.

Airports **Arusha Airport** (☎ 027/741–530 or 027/744–317 ⊕ www.tanzani airports.com). **Dar es Salaam International Airport** (☎ 022/284–4212 ⊕ www. tanzaniairports.com). **Kilimanjaro International Airport** (☎ 027/255–4252 ⊕ www.kilimanjaroairport.co.tz). **Zanzibar Airport** (☎ 024/223–3979 ⊕ www. zanzibar-airport.com).

CHARTER Charter companies are a common mode of transportation when getting
FLIGHTS to safari lodges and remote destinations throughout East Africa. These aircraft are well-maintained and are almost always booked by your lodge or travel agent. The major charter companies run daily shuttles from Dar es Salaam to popular tourism destinations, such as Serengeti. On-demand flights, those made at times other than those scheduled, are very expensive for independent travelers, as they require minimum passenger loads. If it is just two passengers, you will be charged for the vacant seats. Keep in mind that you probably won't get to choose the charter company you fly with. The aircraft you get depends on the number of passengers flying and can vary from very small (you will sit in the co-pilot's seat) to a much more comfortable commuter plane. ■TIP➔ Those with a severe fear of small planes might consider road travel instead.

Due to the limited space and size of the aircraft, charter carriers observe strict luggage regulations: luggage must be soft sided and weigh no more than 44 lbs (20 kg).

Charter Companies **Coastal Air** (✉ Stone Town ☎ 024/233–489). **Flightlink** (✉ Dar es Salaam ☎ 022/284–3073). **Precision Air** (☎ 022/212–1718 ⊕ www.precisionairtz.com). **Tanzanair** (✉ Dar es Salaam ☎ 022/284–3131 or 022/211–3151). **Sky Aviation** (✉ Dar es Salaam ☎ 022/284–4410).

CONTACTS & RESOURCES

CUSTOMS & DUTIES
You can bring in a liter of spirits or wine and 200 cigarettes duty fee.

The CITES (Convention of International Trade in Endangered Species of Wild Fauna and Flora) was established to prevent trafficking in endangered species. The United States is a signatory to CITES and therefore does not allow the importation of living or dead endangered animals, or their body parts, such as rhino horns or ivory. If you purchase an antique that is made partly or wholly of ivory, you must obtain a CITES preconvention certificate that clearly states the item is at least 100 years old. The import of zebra skin or other tourist products also requires a CITES permit. Although you can buy curios made from animal products in Tanzania, your home country may confiscate them on arrival. Don't buy shells or items made from sea turtles.

U.S. Information U.S. Customs and Border Protection (⊕ *www.cbp.gov*). **U.S. Fish and Wildlife Service** (⊕ *www.fws.gov*).

ELECTRICITY

The electrical current is 220 volts, 50 cycles alternating current (AC); wall outlets in most of the region take 15-amp plugs with three round prongs (the old British system), but some take the straight-edged three-prong plugs, also 15 amps.

If your appliances are dual-voltage, you'll need only an adapter. In remote areas (and even in some lodges) power may be solar or from a generator; this means that delivery is erratic both in voltage and supply. In even the remotest places, however, lodge staff will find a way to charge video and camera batteries, but you will receive little sympathy if you insist on using a hair dryer or electric razor.

HEALTH

The CDC provides up-to-date information on health risks and recommended vaccinations and medications for travelers to Southern and East Africa. Check with the CDC's traveler's health line regarding the regions you'll be visiting.

The Web site, Travel Health Online, is a good source to check out before you travel because it compiles primarily health and some safety information from a variety of official sources, and it's done by a medical publishing company.

The Flying Doctors Service offered by AMREF provides air evacuation services for medical emergencies in Kenya, Tanzania, and Uganda or anywhere within a 1,000 km (621 mi) radius of Nairobi. The planes fly out of Nairobi's Wilson Airport 24 hours a day, 365 days a year. They also provide transportation between medical facilities, fly you back to Europe, Asia, or North America, or provide you with an escort of you're flying on a commercial carrier.

Medical-Assistance Companies The Flying Doctors Service (☎ *020/315–454 landline, 254/733/639–088 mobile* ⊕ *www.amref.org*).

OVER-THE-COUNTER REMEDIES You can buy over-the-counter medication in pharmacies and supermarkets in the larger towns only. Bring your own supply for your trip and rely on pharmacies just for emergency medication.

SHOTS &
MEDICATIONS
Be up-to-date on yellow fever, polio, tetanus, typhoid, meningococcus, rabies, and hepatitis A. It's not necessary to have a cholera jab, but if you are visiting Zanzibar it's sensible to get a cholera exception form from your GP or travel clinic. Visit a travel clinic 8 to 10 weeks before you travel to find out your requirements. If you are coming to Tanzania for a safari, chances are you are heading to a malarial game reserve. Millions of travelers take oral prophylactic drugs before, during, and after their safaris. It is up to you to weigh the risks and benefits of the type of antimalarial drug you choose to take. If you are pregnant or traveling with small children, consider a nonmalarial region for your safari.

The CDC provides up-to-date information on health risks and recommended vaccinations and medications for travelers to East Africa. The Web site, Travel Health Online, is a good source to check out before you travel because it compiles primarily health and some safety information from a variety of official sources, and it's done by a medical publishing company.

Health Warnings National Centers for Disease Control & Prevention (*CDC* ☎ *877/394–8747 international travelers' health line* ⊕ *www.cdc.gov/travel*). **Travel Health Online** (⊕ *www.tripprep.com*). **World Health Organization** (*WHO* ⊕ *www.who.int*).

MAIL

The mail service in Tanzania is reasonably reliable, but mail can take weeks to arrive, and money and other valuables may be stolen from letters and packages. You can buy stamps from your hotel or the postcard shop. Post offices are chaotic and crowded.

SHIPPING
PACKAGES
If you make a purchase, try your best to take it home on the plane with you, even if it means packing your travel clothes and items into a box and shipping those to your home, or buying a cheap piece of luggage and paying the excess weight fees. If you buy something from a store accustomed to foreign visitors, they will likely already have a system for getting your items to you, often in a surprising few weeks' time.

FedEx and DHL have offices in the major towns. Check addresses on the Web before you leave home or ask at your hotel.

Express Services DHL (⊕ *www.dhl.co.za*). **FedEx** (⊕ *www.fedex.com*).

MONEY

Tanzania's notorious black market no longer exists, but tourists are occasionally approached by strangers to change money. Don't be tempted, even if it sounds like a good deal. Undercover policemen have been known to approach tourists on streets to catch them out. They'll give you a warning, but you might not get your money back. Banks and change bureaus buy dollars at similar rates. Hotel exchange rates are often significantly lower.

The regulated currency is the Tanzanian shilling (Tsh). Bargaining, especially at market places, is part of the shopping experience. But always be aware of the exchange rate and pay appropriately—you don't want to underpay, but you also don't want to be charged exorbitant "tourist" prices.

ATMS & BANKS   There are banks in all major cities and ATMs. It is wise to bring two ATM cards for different accounts with you whenever traveling abroad, both in case one is stolen or "eaten" by a machine and to give yourself an option in case a machine takes only one or the other type. Most ATMs accept Cirrus, Plus, Maestro, Visa Electron, Visa, and MasterCard.

The best place to withdraw cash is at an indoor ATM, preferably one guarded by a security officer. If you're unsure where to find a safe ATM, ask a merchant. Most machines will not let you withdraw more than the equivalent of about $150 at a time. If anyone approaches you while you're using an ATM, immediately press cancel.

CREDIT CARDS   Visa is the most widely accepted credit card, followed by MasterCard and Diners Club. American Express does not enjoy the popularity it does in other parts of the world. Discover is not recognized. Hotels, shops, and airlines may tell you that using a credit card will add a percentage to your cost, then ask if you would rather pay in cash. Most large hotels only accept U.S. dollars; some budget hotels will also accept Tanzanian shillings. You can draw cash directly from an ATM in Dar es Salaam, Arusha and Mwanza.

Throughout this guide, the following abbreviations are used: **AE**, American Express; **DC**, Diners Club; **MC**, MasterCard; and **V**, Visa.

It's a good idea to inform your credit-card company before you travel, especially if you're going abroad and don't travel internationally very often. Otherwise, the credit-card company might put a hold on your card owing to unusual activity—not a good thing halfway through your trip. Record all your credit-card numbers—as well as the phone numbers to call if your cards are lost or stolen—in a safe place, so you're prepared should something go wrong. MasterCard, Visa, and American Express all have general numbers you can call collect if you're abroad.

Reporting Lost Cards American Express (☎ *800/528–4800 in U.S., 336/393–1111 collect from abroad* ⊕ *www.americanexpress.com*). **Diners Club** (☎ *800/234–6377 in U.S., 303/799–1504 collect from abroad* ⊕ *www.dinersclub.com*). **MasterCard** (☎ *800/627–8372 in U.S., 636/722–7111 collect from abroad* ⊕ *www.mastercard. com*). **Visa** (☎ *800/847–2911 in U.S., 410/581–9994 collect from abroad* ⊕ *www. visa.com*).

CURRENCY &
EXCHANGE   At this writing, the exchange rate was about Tsh 1,163 to US$1.

To avoid administrative hassles, keep all foreign-exchange receipts until you leave the region, as you may need them as proof when changing any unspent local currency back into your own currency at the airport as you leave. Better still, don't leave yourself with any Tsh—you won't be able to change them outside of Tanzania.

TRAVELER'S
CHECKS   Some consider this the currency of the cave man, and it's true that fewer establishments accept traveler's checks these days. Nevertheless, they're

a cheap and secure way to carry extra emergency money, particularly on trips to urban areas. Only bring American Express traveler's checks if coming from the United States, as Amex is well known and widely accepted; you can also avoid hefty surcharges by cashing Amex checks at Amex offices. Whatever you do, keep track of all the serial numbers in case the checks are lost or stolen.

Traveler's checks in either rand or other major denominations (U.S. dollars, euros, and sterling) are readily accepted by most lodgings, though most people use credit cards.

Contacts **American Express** (☎ *888/412–6945 in U.S., 801/945–9450 collect outside of U.S. to add value or speak to customer service* ⊕ *www.americanexpress.com*).

SAFETY

GOVERNMENT ADVISORIES State Department warnings often do not pertain to street crime, but rather large demonstrations, or ongoing conflicts, such as wars or regional clashes. Check newspapers and Web sites and even travel forums for details about events on the ground.

The Web site for AllSafeTravels gathers safety information from government Web sites as well as news media and even users; sorts it; and posts it in a very searchable, user-friendly way. For a small fee they will send you customized e-mail alerts to any destination to which you're planning to travel. The upshot? You'll get a very full picture of where you'll be traveling.

General Information & Warnings **U.S. Department of State** (⊕ *www.travel.state.gov*). **AllSafeTravels** (⊕ *www.allsafetravels.com*).

TAXES

All Tanzanian hotels pay a bed tax, which is included in quoted prices.

Airport taxes and fees are included in the price of your ticket.

TELEPHONES

The "0" in the regional code is used only for calls placed from other areas within the country. To call from abroad, dial the international access number 00, then the country code 255, then the area code 24, and then the telephone number, which should have six or seven digits. If you run across a number with only five digits, it's a remnant of the old system that was changed in 1999. Because telephone communications are difficult, many people in the travel business have mobile phones.

GREEN LODGINGS IN TANZANIA

Our list of Tanzania's ecoconscious lodgings is not exhaustive, but it's a starting place that will hopefully inspire you to travel green. Remember to minimize the negative impact on your surroundings, while nurturing the cultural integrity of indigenous peoples.

CONTACT INFORMATION

Chumbe Island: 024/223–1040; www. chumbeisland.com

Sand Rivers Selous: 022/286–5156; www. nomad-tanzania.com

Tanzania Under Canvas: 011/809–4300; www. ccafrica.com

Chumbe Island, (opposite top & bottom) between the Tanzanian coast and the islands of Zanzibar, is the country's first marine national park. It's home to 400 species of coral, 200 species of fish, and a boutique luxury hotel. The island's ecotourism concept was the brainstorm of a German conservationist who, since the early 1990s, has succeeded in developing it as one of the world's foremost marine sanctuaries. Seven thatched bungalows with specially built roofs catch rainwater that is funneled into bathrooms through a tank in the floor. Electricity is solar-powered, and toilets are doused in sweet-smelling compost and later cleaned. Scuba diving, snorkeling, island hikes guided by expert rangers, and outrigger boat rides leave you with plenty to do while you absorb the lesson of sustainability at Chumbe.

Set within 31,000 mi of Tanzania wilderness in the Selous Game Reserve, **Sand Rivers Selous** might be the closest you'll get to nature in all of Africa. Seven cottages made of stone and thatch are raised on stakes above the Rufiji River; the cottages have open fronts that look out over the surrounding woodlands and river. Perhaps most important for green travelers, though, is Sand Rivers Selous's involvement in the Selous Rhino Trust. In partnership with the Tanzania Division of Wildlife, the owners and a few dedicated partners have identified 16 black rhino in the region—a triumph for a part of the world that was once supported at least 3,000 of these great beasts. Today, the black rhino numbers at no more than a handful in Tanzania and the rest of Africa, but the trust is steadily working to change this with constant monitoring and conservation support at Sand Rivers Selous. *See Luxury Lodges, in Selous Game Reserve for more information about the camp.*

Think no electricity, no running water, and vast plains. Now think hot bucket showers, romantic canvas tents, Indian rugs, and fine cuisine. Top it off with the knowledge that you're contributing to the welfare of the local Masai communities and you've got a stay at **Tanzania Under Canvas,** (opposite) a camp within the Kleins Camp Private Concession in Northern Tanzania. Tanzania Under Canvas is part of the CC Africa group of camps that works to implement education and AIDS awareness programs in local communities through the Africa Foundation, a nonprofit rural development organization focused on sustainable development. Tanzania Under Canvas also offers guests night drives, visits to local Masai settlements, and interpretive bush walks, which also contribute to the immersing international travelers in indigenous cultures for the mutual benefit of both. *See Mobile Tented Camps, in Serengeti National Park for more information about the camp.*

QUESTIONING AN OPERATOR'S INTEGRITY?

So you've decided to go the green route and stay in an ecolodge while you're on safari. We commend you. But how do you make sure that your operator is true to his/her word and practices green as well? Inquire with a watchdog agency such as Tourism Concern (⊕ *www. tourismconcern.org.uk*) or Green Globe (⊕ *www. greenglobe.org*), or with a conservation organization such as World Wildlife Fund (⊕ *www.worldwildlife.org*) or the African Wildlife Foundation (⊕ *www.awf.org*), both of which have been actively promoting clarity in standards for green tourism.

South Africa

WELCOME TO SOUTH AFRICA

TOP REASONS TO GO

★ **Big game.** You're guaranteed to see big game—including the Big Five—in national parks and at many private lodges.

★ **Escape the crowds.** South Africa's game parks are rarely crowded. You'll see more game with fewer visitors here than you will almost anywhere else in Africa.

★ **Luxury escapes.** Few other sub-Saharan countries offer South Africa's high standards of accommodation, service, and food amid gorgeous surroundings of bush, beach, mountains, and desert.

★ **Nature's playground.** Love to play? You've come to the right place. There's everything from big-game adventures and bird-watching to golfing and hiking, surfing and scuba diving.

★ **Beyond the parks.** After you take in the animals you can hit Cape Town, one of the most stylish cities in the world; the nearby Winelands; the inspiring scenery of the Garden Route; the vibrant port of Durban; and soft white-sand beaches.

Map labels:
BOTSWANA
Kgalagadi Transfrontier Park
4
Bokspits
NAMIBIA
Tswalu Kalahari Reserve
Kimberley
Vioolsdrif
Orange River
NAMAQUALAND
GREAT KAROO
Laaiplek
Addo Elephant Park
Wellington
CAPE FOLDED MOUNTAINS
Cape Town
GARDEN ROUTE
Wilderness
Plettenberg
Port Elizabeth
Cape of Good Hope
Mossel Bay
Cape Agulhas
ATLANTIC OCEAN

1 Kruger National Park. A visit to Kruger, one of the world's great game parks, may rank among the best experiences of your life. With its amazing diversity of scenery, trees, amphibians, reptiles, birds, and mammals, Kruger is a place to safari at your own pace, choosing between upscale private camps and simple campsites.

2 Sabi Sands Game Reserve. The most famous and exclusive of South Africa's private reserves, this 153,000-acre park is home to dozens of private lodges, including the world-famous Mala Mala and Londolozi. With perhaps the highest game density of any private reserve in Southern Africa, the Sabi Sands fully deserves its exalted reputation.

GETTING ORIENTED

South Africa lies at the foot of the continent, where the Atlantic and Indian oceans meet. Not only geographically and scenically diverse, it's a nation of more than 47 million people of varied origins, cultures, languages, and beliefs. Its cities and much of its infrastructure are thoroughly modern—Johannesburg, for example, could pass for any large American city. It's only when you venture into the rural areas or come face to face with the Big Five that you see an entirely different South Africa.

3 KwaZulu-Natal Parks. Hluhluwe-Umfolozi is less than 6% of Kruger's size but delivers the Big Five plus all the plains game. It also has about 1,250 species of plants and trees—more than you'll find in some countries. Mkuze and Itala are even smaller but worth the visit, and if you're looking for the ultimate in luxury, stay at Phinda or Thanda private reserves.

4 Kgalagadi Transfrontier Park. Together with its neighbor, Botswana's Gemsbok National Park, this park covers more than 38,000 square km (14,670 square mi)—one of very few conservation areas of this magnitude left in the world. Its stark, desolate beauty shelters huge black-maned Kalahari lions among other predators and provides brilliant birding, especially birds of prey.

SOUTH AFRICA PLANNER

Fast Facts

Size 1,221,037 square km (471,442 square mi)

Number of National Parks 22: Addo Elephant, Agulhas, Augrabies Falls, Bontebok, Camdeboo, Golden Gate Highlands, Karoo, Kruger, Mapungubwe, Marakele, Mokala, Mountain Zebra, Namaqua, Table Mountain, Tankwa Karoo, Tsitsikamma, West Coast, and Wilderness National Parks; Ais/Richtersveld and Kgalagadi Transfrontier Parks; Knysna National Lake Area; uKhahlamba/Drakensberg Park.

Number of Private Reserves Hundreds, including Sabi Sands and KwaZulu-Natal's Phinda and Thanda.

Population Approximately 47.9 million.

Big Five The gang's all here.

Language South Africa has 11 official languages: Afrikaans, English, Ndebele, North and South Sotho, Swati, Tsonga, Tswana, Venda, Xhosa, and Zulu. English is widely spoken.

Time SAST (South African Standard Time), seven hours ahead of North American Eastern Standard Time.

Health & Safety

HIV and AIDS are endemic. Beyond these, the most serious health problem is malaria, which occurs in the prime game-viewing areas of Mpumalanga and Limpopo provinces (home to Kruger, Sabi Sands) and northern KwaZulu-Natal (site of Hluhluwe-Umfolozi, Mkuze, and Itala game reserves, and Phinda and Thanda private reserves). Travelers heading to malaria-endemic regions should consult a health-care professional at least one month before departure for advice on antimalarial drugs. As the sun goes down, wear light-color long-sleeve shirts, long pants, and shoes and socks, and apply mosquito repellent generously. Always sleep in a mosquito-proof room or tent, and keep a fan going. If you're pregnant or trying to conceive, avoid malaria areas if at all possible.

Important Details

Embassies The **American Embassy** (⊠ 877 Pretorius St., Arcadia ☎ 021/431–4000) is in Tshwane.

Emergencies Europ Assistance (☎ 0860/635–635 ⊕ www.europassistance.co.za) arranges emergency evacuation. For a general emergency, dial the **South Africa Police Service** (SAPS ☎ 10111 from landline, 112 from mobile phone ⊕ www.saps.gov.za). For an ambulance, call the **special ambulance number** (☎ 10177) or SAPS.

Money Matters The unit of currency is the rand (R), with 100 cents (¢) equaling R1. Bills, which are differentiated by color, come in R10, R20, R50, R100, and R200 denominations. Coins are minted in R5, R2, R1, 50¢, 20¢, 10¢, 5¢, 2¢, and 1¢ denominations.

Passports & Visas A valid passport (for infants as well as adults) with two blank facing visa pages is needed to enter South Africa for visits of up to 90 days. Your passport must be valid for at least six months after your return date, or you will be denied entry. There is no visa fee for Americans.

About the Camps & Lodges

Accommodations range from fairly basic huts to the ultimate in luxury at most of the private camps. The advantage of a private lodge (apart from superb game-viewing) is that often everything is included—lodging, meals, beverages including excellent house wines, game drives, and other activities. You'll also be treated like royalty. (Indeed, you may well brush shoulders with royals and celebs of all kinds.) The price categories used for lodging in this chapter treat all-inclusive lodges differently than other lodgings (see the price chart below for details). Note that there are no elevators in any safari lodging facility in Kruger.

At most establishments, prices include a three- to five-course dinner plus a full breakfast. Most places now have at least one vegetarian course on the menu. Many lodges and hotels offer special midweek or winter low-season rates. If you're opting for a private game lodge, find out whether they accept children (many specify only kids over 12), and stay a minimum of two nights, three if you can.

In most national parks you have a choice between budget self-catering huts from R250 per couple per night and much more expensive (but worth it) self-catering cottages in the more remote and exclusive bush camps that range from R600 to R1100. Visit the South African National Parks Web site (⊕ www.sanparks.org) to get information and book accommodations. ■TIP→ **Bookings open every September 1 for the following year. Make sure you book well in advance and, if possible, avoid July, August, and December, which are South African school vacations.** Note: If you can, book by phone. It's quicker and your booking will be confirmed (and paid for, if you wish) on the spot.

WHAT IT COSTS In South African rand

	¢	$	$$	$$$	$$$$
DINING	under R50	R50–R75	R75–R100	R100–R125	over R125
LODGING	under R500	R500–R1,000	R1,000–R2,000	R2,000–R3,000	over R3,000
FULL-SERVICE SAFARI LODGING	under R2,000	R2,000–R5,000	R5,000–R8,000	R8,000–R12,000	over R12,000

Restaurant prices are per person for a main course at dinner, a main course equivalent, or a prix-fixe meal. Hotel and lodging prices are for a standard double room in high season, including 12.5% tax.

When to Go

The best time to go on safari is in winter, May through September. The vegetation is sparse so it's easier to spot game, and water is scarce so game congregates around photo-friendly water holes. However, although it's very hot in summer (October through April), the bush looks its best; there will be lots of young animals, and the summer bird migrants will have returned. That said, keep in mind that hotel prices rise dramatically and accommodations are at a premium November through March. At most private game lodges you'll see game year-round.

Johannesburg has one of the best climates in the world. Summers are sunny and hot (never humid), with short afternoon thunderstorms. Winter days are bright and sunny, but nights can be frosty. Although November through January is Cape Town's most popular time, with glorious sunshine and long, light evenings, the best weather is between February and March. Cape winters (May through August) are unpredictable with cold, windy, rainy days interspersed with glorious sun. The coastal areas of KwaZulu-Natal are warm year-round, but summers are steamy and hot. The ocean water is warmest in February, but it seldom dips below 17°C (65°F).

For weather forecasts for the whole country, check out **South Africa Weather Service** (⊕ www.weathersa.co.za).

5

By Kate
Turkington

Since 1994, when Nelson Mandela spearheaded its peaceful transition to democracy, South Africa has become one of the fastest-growing tourist destinations in the world. And it's not difficult to see why. The country is stable and affordable, with an excellent infrastructure; friendly, interesting, amazingly diverse people; and enough stunning sights, sounds, scenery, and attractions to make even the most jaded traveler sit up and take notice. And nearly everybody speaks English—a huge bonus for international visitors.

South Africa has always teemed with game. That's what drew the early European explorers, who aimed to bring something exotic home with them. After all, as Pliny the Elder, one of Africa's earliest explorers, wrote almost two thousand years ago, *ex Africa semper aliquid novi*—out of Africa always comes something new. Sometimes it was a giraffe, a rhinoceros, a strange bird, or an unheard-of plant.

In the latter half of the 19th century, Dr. Livingstone, Scotland's most famous Christian missionary, opened up much of the interior on his evangelizing expeditions, as did the piratical Englishman Cecil John Rhodes, who famously made his fortune on the Kimberley diamond mines and planned an unsuccessful Cape-to-Cairo railway line. About the same time, lured by the rumors of gold and instant fortunes, hundreds of hunters came to the lowveld to lay their hands on much-sought-after skins, horns,

TIPS FOR TIPPING

Plan to give the local equivalents (U.S. dollars are also fine) of about US$10 per person per day to the ranger and US$5 per day to the tracker, plus an additional tip of US$25 for the general staff. If someone has done something special for you—a safari ranger who went all out to show you the Big Five in one game drive, or arranged a special moonlight treat—you can certainly give more. Envelopes are provided in safari rooms and tents for tipping.

and ivory. Trophy hunters followed, vying with each other to see how many animals they could shoot in one day—often more than 100 each.

Paul Kruger, president of the Transvaal Republic (a 19th-century Boer country that occupied a portion of present-day South Africa), took the unprecedented visionary step of establishing a protected area for the wildlife in the lowveld region; in 1898 Kruger National Park was born.

CHOOSING A FIELD GUIDE

Arm yourself with specialized field guides on mammals and birds rather than a more general one that tries to cover too much. Airports, lodges, and camp shops stock a good range, but try to get hold of one in advance, and do a bit of homework.

South Africa has 22 national parks covering deserts, wetland and marine areas, forests, mountains, scrub, and savanna. Hunting safaris are still popular but are strictly controlled by the government, and licenses are compulsory. Although hunting is a controversial issue, the revenue is substantial and can be ploughed into sustainable conservation, and the impact on the environment is minimal. Increasingly, wildlife conservation is linked with community development; many conservation areas have integrated local communities, the wildlife, and the environment, with benefits for all. Londolozi, Mala Mala, Phinda, and Pafuri Camp are internationally acclaimed role models in linking tourism with community-development projects.

Although the "Big Five" was originally a hunting term for those animals that posed the greatest risk to hunters on foot—buffalo, elephants, leopards, lions, and rhinos—it is used today as the most important criterion for evaluating a lodge or reserve. But don't let the lure of the Big Five turn your safari into a treasure hunt, or you'll miss the overall wilderness experience. Don't overlook the bush's other treasures, from desert meerkats and forest bush babies to antelopes, the handsome caracal, and spotted genets. Add to these hundreds of birds, innumerable insects, trees, flowers, shrubs, and grasses. Don't forget to search for the Little Five: the buffalo weaver, elephant shrew, leopard tortoise, lion ant, and rhinoceros beetle. A guided bush walk may let you see these little critters and more.

MUST-SEE PARKS

Unfortunately, you probably won't be able to see all of South Africa in one trip. So we've broken down the chapter by **Must-See Parks** (Kruger National Park, Sabi Sands Game Reserve, KwaZulu-Natal Parks, Kgalagadi Transfrontier Park) and the **If You Have Time Parks** (Tswalu Kalahari Reserve, Pilanesberg National Park, uKhahlamba/Drakensberg Park, Addo Elephant Park, Shamwari Game Reserve) to help you better organize your time. We suggest that you read about *all* of them and then choose for yourself.

KRUGER NATIONAL PARK

Game
★★★★★

Park Accessibility
★★★★★

Ease of Getting Around
★★★★★

Accommodations
★★★★★

Scenic Beauty
☆★★★★

There's no getting away from it, and it's worth repeating: visiting Kruger is likely to be one of the great experiences of your life. Founded in 1898 by Paul Kruger, president of what was then the Transvaal Republic, the park is a place to safari at your own pace, choosing from upscale private camps or simple campsites.

Kruger lies in the hot lowveld, a subtropical section of Mpumalanga and Limpopo provinces that abuts Mozambique. The park cuts a swath 80 km (50 mi) wide and 320 km (200 mi) long from Zimbabwe and the Limpopo River in the north to the Crocodile River in the south. It is divided into 16 macro ecozones, each supporting a great variety of plants, birds, and animals, including 145 mammal species and almost 500 species of birds, some of which are found nowhere elsewhere in South Africa.

How and where you tackle Kruger will depend on your time frame. With excellent roads and accommodations, it's a great place to drive yourself. If you don't feel up to driving or self-catering, you can choose a lodge just outside the park and take the guided drives—but it's not quite the same as lying in bed and hearing the hyenas prowling round the camp fence or a lion roaring under the stars. Plan if you can to come in winter (May–September), when the vegetation is sparse and it's much easier to spot game. The shoulder months of April and October are also good, and less crowded. If you can stand the heat, then visit in summer, when the park looks its best, there are young animals everywhere, and the migrant birds return.

If you can spend a week here, start in the north at the very top of the park at the Punda Maria camp; then make your way leisurely south to the very bottom at Crocodile Bridge Gate or Malelane Gate. With only three days or fewer, reserve one of the southern camps such as Berg-en-Dal or Lower Sabie, and just plan to explore these areas. No matter where you go in Kruger, be sure to plan your route and accommodations in advance (advance booking is essential). Game-spotting is not an exact science: you might see all Big Five, plus hundreds of other animals, but you could see much less. Try to plan your route to include water holes and rivers, which afford your best opportunity to see game. Old Africa hands claim that the very early morning,

PARK ESSENTIALS

It's worth renting an eight-seater *combi* (van) or SUV. Though more expensive than a car, they provide more legroom, and you'll probably have better luck spotting and observing game from your lofty perch. Always reserve well in advance.

when the camp gates open, is the best time for game-viewing, but it's all quite random—you could see a leopard drinking at noon, a breeding herd of elephants mid-morning, a lion pride dozing under a tree in the middle of the afternoon. You could also head out at dawn and find no wildlife at all. Be sure to take at least one guided night drive; you won't likely forget the thrill of catching a nocturnal animal in the spotlight.

Maps of Kruger are available at all the park gates and in the camp stores, and gas stations are at the park gates and at the major camps. Once in the park, observe the speed-limit signs carefully (there are speed traps): 50 kph (31 mph) on paved roads, 40 kph (25 mph) on dirt roads. Leave your vehicle only at designated picnic and viewing sites, and if you do come across animals on the road, allow them to pass before moving on. Sometimes you have to be very patient, especially if a breeding herd of elephants is blocking your way. ■TIP→ **Animals always have the right-of-way.** Always be cautious. Kruger is not a zoo; you are entering the territory of wild animals, even though many may be habituated to the sights and sounds of vehicles.

There are information centers at the Letaba, Skukuza, and Berg-en-Dal rest camps. There is a daily conservation fee, but Wild Cards, available at the gates or online, are more economical for stays of more than a few days. Reservations for all accommodations, bush drives, wilderness trails, and other park activities must be made through **South African National Parks.** *Box 787, Pretoria 0001* *012/343–1991* *www.sanparks.org* *R120 daily conservation fee* *Gates Apr.–Sept., daily 6–5:30; Oct.–Mar., daily 5:30 AM–6:30 PM, but sometimes vary.*

WILDERNESS TRAILS

Spend a few days hiking through the wilds of Africa and you may never again be satisfied with driving around a game reserve. On foot you gain an affinity for the animals and the bush that's impossible in the confines of a vehicle. Kruger has seven wilderness trails, each accommodating eight people. You need to be walking-fit and reasonably adventurous. Led by an armed ranger and local tracker, you'll go out in the morning for a few hours, come back at lunchtime for a meal and a siesta, and head out again in the early evening before returning to the same trail camp to relive the day's adventures around a cheerful campfire. These are not military-style marches but slow meanders, the point being to learn about your surroundings: the medicinal uses of

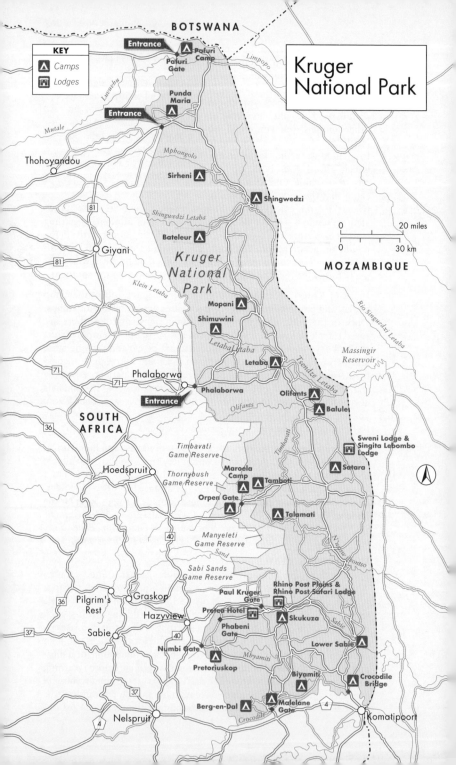

Kruger National Park

KEY
⛺ Camps
🏠 Lodges

BOTSWANA

Entrance
Pafuri Gate
Pafuri Camp

Limpopo

Entrance
Punda Maria

Luvuvhu

Mutale

Thohoyandou

Mphongolo

Sirheni

Shingwedzi

Shingwedzi Letaba

Bateleur

Kruger National Park

81

Giyani

81

Klein Letaba

Mopani

Shimuwini

Letaba Letaba

Letaba

Phalaborwa

71

71

Phalaborwa

Entrance

Olifants

SOUTH AFRICA

36

Olifants

Balule

Tsendze Letaba

Massingir Reservoir

Rio Singuedzi Letaba

MOZAMBIQUE

0   20 miles
0   30 km

Sweni Lodge & Singita Lebombo Lodge

Timbavati Game Reserve

Hoedspruit

Thornybush Game Reserve

Maroela Camp

Tamboti

Satara

Orpen Gate

Talamati

Timbavati

N'waswitshaka

36

40

Manyeleti Game Reserve

Sand

Sabi Sands Game Reserve

Pilgrim's Rest

36

Graskop

Hazyview

37

Sabie

40

Numbi Gate

Rhino Post Plains & Rhino Post Safari Lodge

Paul Kruger Gate

Protea Hotel

Phabeni Gate

Skukuza

Sabie

Lower Sabie

Mbyamiti

Pretoriuskop

Biyamiti

Crocodile Bridge

37

Berg-en-Dal

Malelane Gate

4

Crocodile

Komatipoort

Nelspruit

4

trees and plants, the role of dung beetles and wasps in the ecology, and ways to recognize animals by their spoor. In general, you don't get as close to animals on foot as you can in a vehicle. You will see animals, though, and many hikers can recount face-to-face encounters with everything from rhinos to elephants and lions.

> ### WORD OF MOUTH
>
> "If you are spending two to three weeks in South Africa, for game-viewing you are best served to go to Kruger and neighboring private reserves."
>
> –HariS

Hikes last three nights and two days (starting on Sunday and Wednesday), and you should be prepared to walk as far as 19 km (12 mi) a day, although this will depend on the consensus of the group. Don't be afraid to make your wishes heard; have a group chat with your ranger on the first night and decide on the walking agenda. No one under 12 or over 60 is allowed, although if you book the whole trail and produce a doctor's certificate, over-60s are allowed. Hikers sleep in rustic A-frame two-bed huts and share a reed-wall bathroom with flush toilets and bucket showers. Meals are simple bush fare, including stews and barbecues; you provide your own booze and soft drinks (which you can purchase from the camp where you meet before the trail). In summer the trails are often cheaper (it is uncomfortably hot to walk at this time); in winter, nights can be freezing, so bring very warm clothes and an extra blanket. These trails are incredibly popular; try to reserve 13 months in advance, when bookings open. The cost is approximately R2,350 per person per trail.

Bushman Trail. In the southwestern corner of the park, this trail takes its name from the San rock paintings and sites found in the area. The trail camp lies in a secluded valley dominated by granite hills and cliffs. Watch out for white rhinos, elephants, and buffalo. Check in at Berg-en-Dal.

Metsi Metsi Trail. The permanent water of the nearby N'waswitsontso River makes this one of the best trails for winter game-viewing. Midway between Skukuza and Satara, the trail camp hunkers in the lee of a mountain in an area of gorges, cliffs, and rolling savanna. Check in at Skukuza.

Napi Trail. Sightings of white rhinos are common on this trail, which runs through mixed bushveld between Pretoriuskop and Skukuza. Other frequent sightings include black rhinos, cheetahs, leopards, and elephants. If you're lucky, you may also see the nomadic wild dogs. The trail camp is tucked into dense riverine forest at the confluence of the Napi and Biyamiti rivers. Check in at Pretoriuskop.

★ **Nyalaland Trail.** If it's pristine wilderness and remoteness you're after, then this camp in the far north of the park is for you. The camp sits among ancient baobab trees near the Luvuvhu River, and you'll walk at the foot of huge rocky gorges as well as in dense forest. Some highly sought-after birds, such as Bohm's spinetail, crested eagle, and Pel's fishing owl, can be found in this birding hot spot of huge baobabs and sinister-looking slime-green fever trees. You're almost certain to see hippos, crocodiles, elephants, buffalo, and the strikingly colored nyala antelope, with its dark fur, white spotted nose, and yellow "soccer stockings." Check in at Punda Maria.

Olifants Trail. With one of the most spectacular sites of all trail camps, this camp sits on a high bluff overlooking the Olifants River and affords regular sightings of elephants, lions, buffalo, and hippos. You'll walk through landscape varying from riverine forest to the rocky foothills of the Lebombo Mountains. Check in at Letaba.

Sweni Trail. East of Satara, this trail camp overlooks the Sweni Spruit and savanna dotted with marula and knobthorn trees. The area attracts large herds of zebras, wildebeests, and buffalo with their attendant predators: lions, spotted hyenas, and, if you're very lucky, wild dogs. Check in at Satara.

Wolhuter Trail. If you want to come face-to-face with a white rhino, choose this trail midway between Berg-en-Dal and Pretoriuskop. The undulating bushveld, interspersed with rocky kopjes, is an ideal habitat for these tremendous, somehow anachronistic beasts, but you're also likely to see elephants, buffalo, and lions. Check in at Berg-en-Dal.

WHERE TO STAY

It's impossible to recommend just one camp in Kruger. One person might prefer the intimacy of Kruger's oldest camp, Punda Maria, with its whitewashed thatch cottages; another might favor big, bustling Skukuza. A great way to experience the park is to stay in as many of the camps as possible. The SANParks Web site (⊕ www.sanparks.org) has a comprehensive overview of the different camps. The bushveld camps are more expensive than the regular camps, but offer much more privacy and exclusivity—but no shops, restaurants, or pools. If you seek the ultimate in luxury, stay at one of the private luxury lodges in the concession areas, some of which also have walking trails.

LUXURY LODGES

The lodges that follow are in private concession areas within Kruger.

$$ ☆ **Singita Lebombo Lodge.** Taking its name from the Lebombo mountain ★ range and ecodriven in concept, Singita Lebombo, winner of numerous international accolades, has been built "to touch the ground lightly." It hangs seemingly suspended on the edge of a cliff, like a huge glass box in space. Wooden walkways connect the aptly named "lofts" (suites), all of which have an uncluttered style and spectacular views of the river and bushveld below. Outdoor and indoor areas fuse seamlessly. Organic materials—wood, cane, cotton, and linen—are daringly juxtaposed with steel and glass. This is Bauhaus in the bush, with a uniquely African feel. Public areas are light, bright, and airy, furnished with cane furniture, crisp white cushions, comfy armchairs, and recliners. Service is superb, as is the food, and nothing is left to chance. At the classy Trading Post, you can buy African art and artifacts, or enjoy a beauty treatment at the spa. ✆ *Box 650881, Benmore 2010* ☎ *011/234–0990*

⊕*www.singita.co.za* ⮌*15 suites* ♿*In-room: a/c, safe, refrigerator. In-hotel: bar, pool, gym, spa, Internet* ▤*AE, DC, MC, V* ⦿*FAP.*

$$ ▦**Sweni Lodge.** Built on wooden stilts, Sweni is cradled on a low riverbank amid thick virgin bush and ancient trees. More intimate than its sister camp, Lebombo, it has six huge river-facing suites glassed on three sides, wooden on the other. At night khaki floor-to-ceiling drapes lined with silk divide the living area from the bedroom, which has a king-size bed with weighted, coffee-color mosquito netting and a cascade of ceramic beads. Hanging lampshades of brown netting fashioned like traditional African fish traps, cream mohair throws, and brown leather furniture enhance the natural feel and contrast daringly with the gleam of stainless steel in the living room and bathroom. You can relax in a wooden rocking chair on your large reed-shaded deck while watching an elephant herd drink, or spend the night under the stars on a comfy, mosquito-net-draped mattress. ⌂*Box 650881, Benmore 2010* ☏*011/234–0990* ⊕*www.singita.co.za* ⮌*6 suites* ♿*In-room: a/c, safe, refrigerator. In-hotel: bar, pool, gym, spa, Internet* ▤*AE, DC, MC, V* ⦿*FAP.*

PERMANENT TENTED CAMPS

The camps of Rhino Post Plains Camp and Rhino Post Safari Lodge are situated in about 30,000 acres of pristine bushveld in the Mutlumuvi area of Kruger, 10 km (6 mi) northeast of Skukuza, the heart of Kruger Park; the area can be easily accessed by road or air. The concession shares a 15-km (9-mi) boundary with Mala Mala, in the Sabi Sands Game Reserve, and there's plenty of game movement between the two.

$ ▦**Rhino Post Plains Camp.** Overlooking a water hole amid an acacia knobthorn thicket deep in the heart of the Timbitene Plain, Plains Camp has comfortably furnished tents with wooden decks and great views of the plains. A deck with a bar and plunge pool is great for post-walk get-togethers, and there's a small tented dining area. The camp is simple, unpretentious, and very friendly, and has great food. ⌂*Box 1881, Juskei Park 2153* ☏*011/467–1886* ⊕*www.zulunet.co.za* ⮌*4 tents* ♿*In-hotel: bar, pool* ▤*AE, DC, MC, V* ⦿*FAP.*

$ ▦**Rhino Post Safari Lodge.** This lodge comprises eight spacious suites on stilts overlooking the Mutlumuvi riverbed. Each open-plan suite built of canvas, thatch, wood, and stone has a bedroom, private wooden deck, bathroom with a deep freestanding bath, his-and-her sinks, a separate toilet, and an outdoor shower protected by thick reed poles. ⌂*Box 1881, Juskei Park 2153* ☏*011/467–1886* ⊕*www.zulunet.co.za* ⮌*8 suites* ♿*In-hotel: bar, pool* ▤*AE, DC, MC, V* ⦿*FAP.*

¢ ▦**Pafuri Camp.** This gorgeous lodge stretches for more than a kilometer along the banks of the Luvuvhu River in Kruger's far north. The 240-square-km (93-square-mi) area embraces an amazing variety of landscapes and is one of the few places on earth where fever-tree and baobab forests intermingle. At Crooks Corner, where baddies-on-the-run of days-gone-by once lurked, a wide swath of sand stretching as far as the eye can see links Mozambique, South Africa, and Zimbabwe. There's great game plus ancient history—more than 1.5 million years ago, early humans lived here, and the area holds stone-age tools, rock engravings, and rock paintings. Pafuri also has the best birding in Kruger: this is the place to spot the rare and elusive Pel's fishing owl. There's a superb children's program, and special family accommodations provide privacy for parents and kids. The tented rooms face the river. ☐ *Wilderness Safaris, Box 5219, Rivonia 2120* ☎*011/807–1800* ⊕*www.pafuri.com* ↩*20 rooms* ♿*In-room: safe. In-hotel: restaurant, bar, pool, airport shuttle* ☐*AE, DC, MC, V* ◎*MAP.*

NATIONAL PARK ACCOMMODATIONS

Reservations for the following accommodations should be made through **South African National Parks** (☐*Box 787, Pretoria 0001* ☎*012/343–1991* ⊕*www.sanparks.org* ☐*AE, DC, MC, V*) . At this writing, some of the national park accommodations in Kruger were undergoing refurbishment, including the addition of air-conditioning; if this is an important amenity for you, call or check the Web site to confirm its availability in the accommodation of your choice.

¢ 🏠**Balule.** On the banks of the Olifants River, Satara's rustic satellite camp differs radically from the others because it really is simple, appealing to those who don't mind roughing it a bit and want to experience the true feel of the bush. There are no shops or restaurants—so bring your own food—and there's no electricity either (only lanterns). Accommodations are in basic three-bed huts with no windows (vents only); the shared bathroom facilities have running water. You must check in at Olifants, 11 km (7 mi) away. ↩*15 campsites, 6 huts.*

¢ 🏠**Berg-en-Dal.** This rest camp lies at the southern tip of the park, in
☾ a basin surrounded by rocky hills. Berg-en-Dal is known for its white
★ rhinos, leopards, and wild dogs, but it lacks the tremendous game intensity of some of the camps to its north. A dam (often nearly dry in winter) by one side of the perimeter fence offers good game-viewing, including a close look at cruising crocodiles and munching elephants. One of the more attractive camps, it has thoughtful landscaping, which has left much of the indigenous vegetation intact, making for more privacy. It has an attractive pool and well-stocked grocery–curio shop, and kids can run around safely here. ↩*63 chalets, 23 family cottages, 2 guesthouses, 70 campsites* ♿*In-room: kitchen (some). In-hotel: restaurant, pool, laundry facilities.*

¢ 🏠**Crocodile Bridge.** In the southeastern corner of the park, this superb small rest camp (it has won several awards for good service) doubles as an entrance gate, which makes it a convenient stopover if you arrive near the park's closing time and thus too late to make it to another camp. Although the Crocodile River provides a scenic backdrop, any sense of being in the wild is quickly shattered by views of power lines and farms on the south side. The road leading from the camp to Lower Sabie is famous for sightings of general game as well as buffalo, rhinos, cheetahs, and lions, but it's often crowded on weekends and holidays and during school vacations. A hippo pool lies just 5 km (3 mi) away. Two of the bungalows are geared toward travelers with disabilities. ↩*20 bungalows, 8 safari tents, 12 campsites* ♿*In-room: kitchen (some). In-hotel: laundry facilities.*

¢ ⚇ **Letaba.** Overlooking the frequently dry Letaba River, this lovely camp sits in the middle of elephant country in the central section of the park. There's excellent game-viewing on the roads to and all around the Englehardt and Mingerhout dams: be careful in the early morning and as the sun goes down that you don't bump a hippo. The camp itself has a real bush feel: all the huts are thatch (ask for one

overlooking the river), and the grounds are overgrown with apple-leaf trees, acacias, mopane, and lala palms. The restaurant and snack bar, with attractive outdoor seating, look out over the broad, sandy riverbed. Even if you're not staying at Letaba, stop at the superb elephant exhibit at the Environmental Education Centre and marvel at just how big elephants' tusks can get. Campsites, on the camp's perimeter, offer lots of shade for your tent or trailer. ➾*8 bungalows, 5 huts, 10 guest cottages, 2 guesthouses, 20 safari tents, 35 campsites ♿In-room: kitchen (some). In-hotel: restaurant, laundry facilities.*

¢ ⚇ ★ **Lower Sabie.** This is one of the most popular camps in Kruger for good reason: it has tremendous views over a broad sweep of the Sabie River and sits in one of the best game-viewing areas of the park (along with Skukuza and Satara). White rhinos, lions, cheetahs, elephants, and buffalo frequently come down to the river to drink, especially in the dry winter months when there is little surface water elsewhere. Long wooden walkways that curve around the restaurant and shop are particularly attractive; you can sit here and look out over the river. Half the safari tents have a river view. The vegetation around the camp is mainly grassland savanna interspersed with marula and knobthorn trees. There are lots of animal drinking holes within a few minutes' drive. Don't miss the H10 road from Lower Sabie to Tshokwane, where you'll almost certainly see elephants. ➾*30 huts, 62 bungalows, 24 safari tents, 1 guest cottage, 1 guesthouse, 33 campsites ♿In-room: kitchen (some). In-hotel: restaurant, pool, laundry facilities.*

¢ ⚇ **Malelane.** Small and intimate, this camp offering privacy and that close-to-the-bush feeling is ideal for backpackers and do-it-yourselfers. If you need supplies, a swim, or a bit more sophistication, you can head over to Berg-en-Dal, just a few kilometers away. A bonus is that you're within easy driving distance of good game areas around and toward Lower Sabie. Guided bush drives are also on offer. You check in at Malelane Gate, from which the camp is managed. ➾*5 bungalows, 15 campsites ♿In-room: kitchen (some).*

¢ ⚇ **Maroela.** Orpen's small, cozy satellite campsite is just 3 km (2 mi) away from the Orpen Gate. It can be hot, dry, and dusty at any time of the year, but you'll feel close to the bush among thorn and maroela (marula) trees. A small hide (blind) overlooks a water hole, and there's lots of excellent game in the vicinity, including cheetahs, lions, and rhinos. ➾*24 campsites (20 with power hook ups).*

¢   🔲 **Mopani.** Built in the lee of a rocky kopje overlooking a lake, this camp in the northern section is one of Kruger's biggest. The lake and the camp are an oasis for both animals and people amid not very attractive surrounding mopane woodlands. If it's hippos you're after, sit on your veranda overlooking the lake and feast your eyes on a cavalcade of these giants mating, frolicking, or just mooching about. Constructed of rough stone, wood, and thatch, the camp blends well into the thick vegetation. Shaded wooden walkways connect the public areas, all of which overlook the lake, and the view from the open-air bar is awesome. The à la carte restaurant (reserve before 6 PM) serves better food than most of the other camps, and the cottages are better equipped and larger than their counterparts elsewhere in Kruger. Ask for accommodations overlooking the lake when you book. Mopani lacks the intimate charm of some of the smaller camps, and the surrounding mopani woodland doesn't attract much game, but it's a really comfortable camp to relax in for a night or two if you're driving the length of the park. *45 bungalows, 12 cottages, 45 guest cottages, 1 guesthouse   In-room: kitchen. In-hotel: restaurant, bar, pool, laundry facilities.*

¢   🔲 **Olifants.** Olifants, in the center of Kruger, has the best setting of all the camps: high atop cliffs on a rocky ridge with panoramic views of the distant hills and the Olifants River below. A lovely thatch-sheltered terrace allows you to sit for hours with binoculars and pick out the animals below. Lions often make kills in the river valley, and elephants, buffalo, giraffes, kudu, and other game come to drink and bathe. Try to book one of the thatch *rondawels* (huts) overlooking the river for at least two nights (you'll need to book a year in advance) so you can hang out on your veranda and watch Africa's passing show below. It's a charming old camp, graced with wonderful indigenous trees like sycamore figs, mopane, and sausage trees—so called because of the huge, brown, sausage-shape fruits that weigh down the branches. The only drawback, particularly in the hot summer months, however, is that it has no pool. *97 rondawels, 2 guesthouses   In-room: kitchen. In-hotel: restaurant, laundry facilities.*

¢   🔲 **Orpen.** Don't dismiss this tiny Cinderella rest camp in the center of the park because of its proximity to the Orpen Gate. It may not be a particularly attractive camp—the rooms, arranged in a rough semicircle around a large lawn, look out toward the perimeter fence, about 150 feet away—but there's a permanent water hole, where animals come to drink, and plenty of game is in the vicinity, including cheetahs, lions, and rhinos. The two-bedroom huts are a bit sparse, with no bathrooms or cooking facilities (although there are good communal ones), but there are three comfortable family cottages with bathrooms and kitchenettes. And it's a blissfully quiet camp, as there are so few accommodations. *12 huts, 3 guest cottages   In-room: kitchen (some).*

¢   🔲 **Pretoriuskop.** This large, bare, nostalgically old-fashioned camp, conveniently close to the Numbi Gate in the southwestern corner of the park, makes a good overnight stop for new arrivals. The rocky kopjes and steep ridges that characterize the surrounding landscape provide an ideal habitat for mountain reedbuck and klipspringers—antelope not always easily seen elsewhere in the park. The area's sourveld (so named because its vegetation is less sweet and attractive to herbivores than other kinds of vegetation) also attracts browsers like giraffes and kudu, as well as white rhinos, lions, and wild dogs. There's not a lot of privacy in camp—accommodations tend to overlook each other—but there is some shade, plus a great swimming pool. ↘*82 rondawels, 52 bungalows, 6 cottages, 45 campsites &In-room: kitchen. In-hotel: restaurant, pool, laundry facilities.*

¢ ⊡ **Punda Maria.** It's a pity that few foreign visitors make it to this lovely little camp in the far north end of the park near Zimbabwe, because in some ways it offers the best bush experience of any of the major rest camps. It's a small enclave, with tiny whitewashed thatch cottages arranged in terraces on a hill. The camp lies in sandveld, a botanically rich area notable for its plants and birdlife. This is Kruger's best birding camp: at a tiny, saucer-shape, stone birdbath, just over the wall from the barbecue site, dozens of unique birds come and go all day. A nature trail winds through and behind the camp—also great for birding, as is the Punda/Pafuri road, where you can spot lots of raptors. A guided walking tour from here takes you to one of South Africa's most interesting archaeological sites—the stone Thulamela Ruins, dating from 1,250 to 1,700. Lodging includes two-bed bungalows with bathrooms and, in some cases, kitchenettes, plus fully equipped safari tents. There are also two very private six-bed family bungalows up on a hill above the camp; they're visited by an amazing variety of not-often-seen birds and some friendly genets. Reservations are advised for the restaurant (don't expect too much from the food), and only some of the campsites have power. ↘*18 2-bed bungalows, 2 family bungalows, 7 safari tents, 50 campsites &In-room: kitchen (some). In-hotel: restaurant.*

¢ ⊡ **Satara.** Second in size only to Skukuza, this camp sits in the middle of the hot plains between Olifants and Lower Sabie, in the central section of Kruger. The knobthorn veld surrounding the camp provides the best grazing in the park and attracts large concentrations of game. That in turn brings the predators—lions, cheetahs, hyenas, and wild dogs—which makes this one of the best areas in the park for viewing game (especially on the N'wanetsi River Road, also known as S100). If you stand or stroll around the perimeter fence, you may see giraffes, zebras, and waterbucks and other antelope. Despite its size, Satara has far more appeal than Skukuza, possibly because of the privacy it offers (the huts aren't all piled on top of one another) and because of the tremendous birdlife. The restaurant and cafeteria are very pleasant, with shady seating overlooking the lawns and the bush beyond. Accommodations are in large cottages and two- or three-bed thatch rondawels, some with kitchenettes (no cooking utensils). The rondawels, arranged in large circles, face inward onto a central, open, grassy area. Campsites are secluded, with an excellent view of the bush, although they don't have much shade. ↘*153 rondawels, 10 guest cottages, 3 guesthouses, 74 campsites &In-room: kitchen (some). In-hotel: restaurant, laundry facilities.*

¢ ⊡ **Shingwedzi.** Although this camp lies in the northern section of the park, amid monotonous long stretches of mopane woodland, it benefits enormously from the riverine growth associated with the Shingwedzi River and Kanniedood (Never Die) Dam. As a result, you'll probably find more game around this camp than anywhere else in the region—especially when you drive the Shingwedzi River Road early in the morning or just before the camp closes at night (but don't be late—you'll face a hefty fine). The roof supports of thatch and rough tree trunks give the camp a rugged, pioneer feel. Both the à la carte restaurant and the outdoor cafeteria have views over the Shingwedzi River. Accommodations are of two types: A and B. Try for one of the A units, whose steeply pitched thatch roofs accommodate an additional two-bed loft; some also have fully equipped kitchenettes. The huts face one another across a fairly barren expanse of dry earth, except in early spring, when the gorgeous bright pink impala lilies are in bloom. ⤖ *24 huts, 54 bungalows, 1 cottage, 1 guesthouse, 50 campsites △ In-room: kitchen (some). In-hotel: restaurant, pool, laundry facilities.*

¢   **Skukuza.** It's worth popping in to have a look at this huge camp. More like a small town than a rest camp, it has a gas station, police station, airport, post office, car-rental agency, grocery store, and library. It's nearly always crowded, not only with regular visitors but with busloads of noisy day-trippers, and consequently has lost any bush feel at all. Skukuza is popular for good reason, though. It's easily accessible by both air and road, and it lies in a region of thorn thicket teeming with game, including lions, cheetahs, and hyenas. The camp itself sits on a bank of the crocodile-infested Sabie River, with good views of thick reeds, dozing hippos, and grazing waterbuck. Visit the worthwhile museum and education center to learn something about the history and ecology of the park. However, if you're allergic to noise and crowds, limit yourself to a stroll along the banks of the Sabie River before heading for one of the smaller camps. ⤖ *199 bungalows, 16 cottages, 15 guest cottages, 7 guesthouses, 20 safari tents, 80 campsites △ In-hotel: restaurant, pool.*

¢   **Tamboti.** Kruger's first tented camp, a satellite of Orpen and very close to the Orpen Gate, is superbly sited on the banks of the frequently dry Tamboti River, among sycamore fig and jackalberry trees. Communal facilities make it a bit like an upscale campsite, but nevertheless it's one of Kruger's most popular camps, so book well ahead. From your tent you may well see elephants digging in the riverbed for water just beyond the barely visible electrified fence. Each of the walk-in, permanent tents has its own deck overlooking the river, but when you book, ask for one in the deep shade of large riverine trees—worth it in the midsummer heat. All kitchen, washing, and toilet facilities are in two shared central blocks. Just bring your own food and cooking and eating utensils. ⤖ *30 safari tents.*

BUSHVELD   Smaller, more intimate, more luxurious, and consequently more expen-
CAMPS   sive than regular rest camps, Kruger's bushveld camps are in remote wilderness areas of the park that are often off-limits to regular visitors. Access is limited to guests only. As a result you get far more bush and fewer fellow travelers. Night drives and day excursions are available in most of the camps. There are no restaurants, gas pumps, or grocery stores, so bring your provisions with you (though you can buy wood for your barbecue). All accommodations have fully equipped kitch-

ens, bathrooms, ceiling fans, and large verandas, but only Bateleur has air-conditioning and TV, the latter installed especially for a visit by South Africa's president. Cottages have tile floors, cheerful furnishings, and cane patio furniture and are sited in stands of trees or clumps of indigenous bush for maximum privacy. Many face directly onto a river or water hole. There are only a handful of one-bedroom cottages (at Biyamiti, Shimuwini, Sirheni, and Talamati), but it's worth booking a four-bed cottage and paying the extra, even for only two people. The average cottage price for a couple is R850, with extra people (up to five or six) paying R180 each. If you have a large group or are planning a special celebration, you might consider reserving one of the two bush lodges, which must be booked as a whole: **Roodewal Bush Lodge** sleeps 19, and **Boulders Bush Lodge** sleeps 12. Reservations should be made with **South African National Parks** ⌂ *Box 787, Pretoria 0001* ☎ *012/343–1991* ⊕ *www.sanparks.org* ☰ *AE, DC, MC, V.*

$ ⌂ **Bateleur.** Hidden in the northern reaches of the park, this tiny camp, the oldest of the bushveld camps, is one of Kruger's most remote destinations. Shaded by tall trees, it overlooks the dry watercourse of the Mashokwe Spruit. A raised platform provides an excellent game-viewing vantage point (don't forget to apply mosquito repellent if you sit here at dawn or dusk), and it's only a short drive to two nearby dams, which draw a huge variety of animals, from lions and elephants to zebras and hippos. The main bedroom in each fully equipped cottage has air-conditioning; elsewhere in each cottage there are ceiling fans, a microwave, and a TV. ⇥ *7 cottages* ⌂ *In-room: a/c, kitchen.*

$ ⌂ **Biyamiti.** Close to the park gate at Crocodile Bridge, this larger-than-average, beautiful, sought-after bush camp overlooks the normally dry sands of the Biyamiti River. It's very popular because it's close to the southern gates, and the game is usually prolific. A private sand road over a dry riverbed takes you to the well-sited camp, where big shade trees attract a myriad of birds and make you feel truly cocooned in the wilderness. The vegetation is mixed combretum woodland, which attracts healthy populations of kudu, impalas, elephants, lions, and black and white rhinos. After the stars come out you're likely to hear lions roar, nightjars call, and jackals yipping outside the fence. ⇥ *15 cottages* ⌂ *In-room: kitchen.*

¢   ⌂ **Shimuwini.** Birders descend in droves on this isolated, peaceful camp set on a lovely dam on the Letaba River. Towering jackalberry and sycamore fig trees provide welcome shade, as well as refuge to a host of resident and migratory birds. Away from the river, the riverine forest quickly gives way to mopane woodland; although this is not a particularly good landscape for game, the outstandingly beautiful roan antelope and handsome, rare black and white sable antelope move through the area. Resident leopards patrol the territory, and elephants frequently browse in the mopane. Be sure to visit the huge, ancient baobab tree on the nearest loop road to the camp—Shimuweni is the Shangaan word for "Place of the Baobab," and there are lots of these striking, unusual trees in the surrounding area. Cottages have one, two, or three bedrooms. One disadvantage is that the camp is accessed by a single road, which gets a bit tedious when you have to drive it every time you leave or return to the camp. ↩*15 cottages* ♿*In-room: kitchen.*

¢   🏨**Sirheni.** The most remote of all the bushveld camps and one of the
★   loveliest, Sirheni, another major bird-watching camp, sits on the edge of the Sirheni Dam, in an isolated wilderness area in the far north of the park. It's a long drive to get here, but well worth the effort. Because there is permanent water, game—including lions and white rhinos—can often be seen at the dam, particularly in the dry winter months. Keep your eyes open for the resident leopard, who often drinks at the dam in the evening. A rewarding drive for birders and game spotters alike runs along the Mphongolo River. You can watch the sun set over the magnificent bush from one of two secluded viewing platforms at either end of the camp, but be sure to smother yourself with mosquito repellent. ↩*15 cottages* ♿*In-room: kitchen.*

¢   🏨**Talamati.** On the banks of the normally dry N'waswitsontso River in Kruger's central section, this peaceful camp in the middle of a wide, open valley has excellent game-viewing. Grassy plains and mixed woodlands provide an ideal habitat for herds of impalas, zebras, and wildebeests, as well as lions, cheetahs, and elephants. You can take a break from your vehicle and watch birds and game from a couple of raised viewing platforms inside the perimeter fence. The accommodations are well-equipped and comfortable, with cane furniture and airy verandas. ↩*15 cottages* ♿*In-room: kitchen.*

BUDGET LODGING

¢   🏨**Protea Hotel Kruger Gate.** Set in its own small reserve 110 yards
☺   from the Paul Kruger Gate, this comfortable hotel gives you a luxury alternative to the sometimes bare-bones accommodations of Kruger's rest camps. The hotel has two major advantages: fast access to the south-central portion of the park, where game-viewing is best, plus the impression that you are in the wilds of Africa. Dinner, heralded by beating drums, is served in a *boma*, a traditional open-air reed enclosure around a blazing campfire. Rangers lead guided walks through the surrounding bush, and you can even sleep overnight in a tree house, or you can book a guided game drive (note that all these activities cost extra). Rooms, connected by a raised wooden walkway that passes through thick indigenous forest, have Spanish-tile floors and standard hotel furniture. Self-catering chalets sleep six. Relax on the pool deck overlooking the Sabie river, have a cocktail in the cool bar, or puff on a cheroot in the sophisticated cigar bar while the kids take part in a fun-filled Prokidz program (during school vacations only). ✉*Kruger Gate, Skukuza 1350* ☎*013/735–5671* ⊕*www.proteahotels.co.za* ↩*96 rooms, 7 chalets* ♿*In-room: a/c, refrigerator. In-hotel: restaurant, bar, pool* ▭*AE, DC, MC, V* ⫲*MAP.*

South Africa's Tribes

ZULU

South Africa's largest tribe, about 10 million Zulu (pictured above) live in the KwaZulu-Natal province, where they migrated over a thousand years ago. Because of the bloody clashes with British forces, Zulus are often stereotyped as a war-mongering people, but this is far from true. While the Zulu have historically proven to be highly adept in battle, it's not because of some biological ferocity, but rather an ability to plan and strategize. Today, it's their musical prowess that has had a major impact on popular culture. Kwaito, for example, is a style of music blending dance, hip-hop, and rap music; it's dominated by Zulu musicians. More traditional Zulu music has been incorporated into the music of western musicians, including Paul Simon and the soundtrack for the Broadway musical *The Lion King*. One of the more famous Zulu singing groups today is Ladysmith Black Mambazo, who has toured the world with their popular collection of traditional Zulu anthems.

XHOSA

The Xhosa people have lived in the Eastern Cape Province since the 15th century, when they migrated here from east and central Africa. They are the country's second most populous tribe (about 8 million people). A typical Xhosa village is made up of several kraals, or cattle enclosures, surrounded by family huts. In the 18th century, the Xhosa clashed with the Boers over land. Eventually, the Boers and British colonizers united in a policy of white rule, confining black South Africans to 13% of the land with the passage of the Native Land Act of 1913. This laid the foundation for Apartheid, which similarly restricted blacks to areas called Homelands. The Homelands were difficult to farm, overcrowded, and disease-ridden, and remain to this day a shameful part of South Africa's Apartheid past. It was not until Xhosa tribesman Nelson Mandela was elected president of South Africa in 1994 that the Homelands were abolished.

Singita Lebombo Lodge, Kruger National Park

Sweni Lodge, Krugerr National Park

Protea Hotel Kruger Gate, Kruger National Park

Rhino Post Plains Camp, Kruger National Park

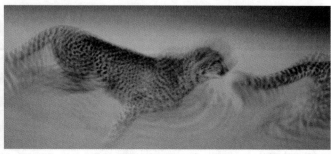

SABI SANDS GAME RESERVE

Game
★★★★★

Park Accessibility
★★★★★

Ease of Getting
Around
★★★★★

Accommodations
★★★★★

Scenic Beauty
☆☆★★★

This is the most famous and exclusive of South Africa's private reserves. Collectively owned and managed, the 153,000-acre reserve near Kruger is home to dozens of private lodges, including the world-famous Mala Mala and Londolozi. The Sabi Sands fully deserves its exalted reputation, boasting perhaps the highest game density of any private reserve in southern Africa.

Although not all lodges own vast tracts of land, most have traversing rights over most of the reserve. With an average of 20 vehicles (from different camps) watching for game and communicating by radio, you're bound to see an enormous amount of game and almost certainly the Big Five, but since only three vehicles are allowed at a sighting at a time, you can be assured of a grandstand seat. The Sabi Sands is the best area for leopard sightings. It's a memorable experience to see this beautiful, powerful, and often elusive cat—the most successful of all feline predators—padding purposefully through the bush at night, illuminated in your ranger's spotlight. There are many lion prides, and occasionally, the increasingly rare wild dogs will migrate from Kruger to den in the Sabi Sands. You'll also see white rhinos, zebras, giraffes, wildebeests, and most of the antelope species, plus birds galore.

If you can afford it, a splurge on a Kruger SKI ("spend the kids' inheritance") vacation could be the experience of a lifetime. Staying for two or three nights (try for three) at a private game lodge combines superb accommodations, service, and food with equally excellent game-viewing. Exclusivity on game drives (most lodges put only six people in a vehicle, along with a dedicated ranger and tracker) almost guarantees sightings of the Big Five. Words like "elegance," "luxury," and "privacy" are overused when describing the accommodations, but each lodge is unique. One place might have chalets done in modern chic, another lodges with a colonial feel, and a third open-air safari tents whose proximity to the bush makes up for what they lack in plushness. At all of them you'll be treated like royalty, with whom you may well rub shoulders.

Many accommodations have air-conditioning, minibars, room safes, a ceiling fan, and luxurious en-suite bathrooms. If mainline phone reception is available, there are room telephones. Cell-phone reception is patchy (depending on the area), but never take your cell phone on a game drive (or at least keep it turned off) to avoid disturbing the animals and annoying fellow passengers. All camps have radio telephones in case you need to make contact with the outside world. Chartered flights to and from the camps on shared private airstrips are available, or lodges will collect you from Hoedspruit airport or KMIA.

The daily program at each lodge rarely deviates from a pattern, starting with tea, coffee, and muffins or rusks (Boer biscuits) before an early-morning game drive (usually starting at dawn, later in winter). You return to the lodge around 10 AM, at which point you dine on a full English breakfast or brunch. You can then choose to go on a bush walk with an armed ranger, where you learn about some of the minutiae of the bush (including the Little Five), although you could also happen on giraffes, antelopes, or any one of the Big Five. But don't worry—you'll be well briefed in advance on what you should do if you come face-to-face with, say, a lion. The rest of the day, until the late-afternoon game drive, is spent at leisure—reading up on the bush in the camp library, snoozing, or swimming. A sumptuous afternoon tea is served at 3:30 or 4 before you head back into the bush for your night drive. During the drive, your ranger will find a peaceful spot for sundowners (cocktails), and you can sip the drink of your choice and nibble snacks as you watch one of Africa's spectacular sunsets. As darkness falls, your ranger will switch on the spotlight so you can spy nocturnal animals: lions, leopards, jackals, porcupines, servals (wildcats), civets, and the enchanting little bush babies. You'll return to the lodge around 7:30, in time to freshen up before a three- or five-course dinner in an open-air boma around a blazing fire. Often the camp staff entertains after dinner with local songs and dances—an unforgettable experience. Children under 12 are not allowed at some of the camps; others have great kids' programs (though no children under five or six are allowed to take part in game activities).

WHERE TO STAY

LUXURY LODGES

DJUMA   Djuma, Shangaan for "roar of the lion," is in the northeast corner of the Sabi Sands Game Reserve. It was the first game reserve in Africa to place permanent cameras at water holes and on a mobile vehicle so that Web surfers (⊕www.africam.com) can watch the goings-on in the African bush without leaving home. Your hosts are husband-and-wife team Jurie and Pippa Moolman, who are passionate about their work (Jurie has a bachelor's degree in ecology). Although there's a good chance of seeing the Big Five during the bush walk after breakfast and

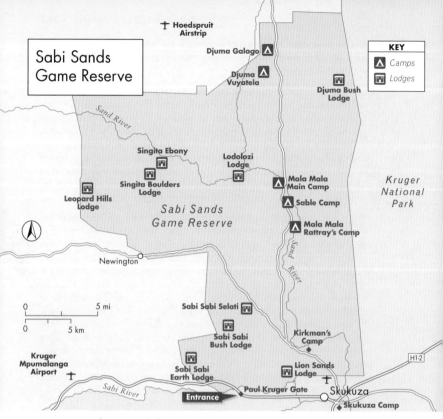

Sabi Sands
Game Reserve

KEY
△ Camps
▣ Lodges

Hoedspruit Airstrip

Djuma Galago △

Djuma △
Vuyatela

Djuma Bush Lodge ▣

Sand River

Singita Ebony ▣

Lodolozi Lodge ▣

Singita Boulders Lodge ▣

Mala Mala △
Main Camp

Kruger National Park

Leopard Hills Lodge ▣

Sable Camp △

Sabi Sands Game Reserve

Mala Mala △
Rattray's Camp

Sand River

Newington

0   5 mi
0   5 km

Sabi Sabi Selati ▣

Kirkman's Camp △

Sabi Sabi Bush Lodge ▣

Kruger Mpumalanga Airport

Sabi Sabi Earth Lodge ▣

Lion Sands Lodge ▣

H1-2

Sabi River

Entrance

Paul Kruger Gate

Skukuza

Skukuza Camp ◆

the twice-daily game drives, Djuma also caters to those with special bushveld interests, such as bird-watching or tree identification. Djuma's rangers and trackers are also adept at finding seldom-seen animals, such as wild dogs, spotted hyenas, and genets. You'll find none of the formality that sometimes prevails at the larger lodges. For example, members of the staff eat all meals with you and join you around the nighttime fire. In fact, Djuma prides itself on its personal service and sense of intimacy. Your dinner menu is chalked up on a blackboard (try ostrich pâté with cranberry sauce for a starter), as is the evening cocktail menu (how about a Screaming Hyena or African Sunrise?). *Box 338, Hluvukani 1363* ☎ *013/735–5118* ⊕ *www.djuma.com* ⊟ *AE, DC, MC, V* ⦿ *FAP.*

$ ▣ **Bush Lodge.** Sitting in a lush grove of tamboti trees and overlooking a water hole, this homey safari camp contains thatch chalets with rugged wooden furniture and faux-animal-skin fabrics. Don't miss out on a trip to the local villages (the real thing—not tourist traps) of Dixie and Utah, where you'll be introduced to the families of the people looking after you at camp. ⇥ *8 chalets* ⚘ *In-room: a/c. In-hotel: bar, pool.*

$ ▣ **Vuyatela.** Djuma's vibey, most upscale camp mixes contemporary African township culture with modern Shangaan culture, making it very different from most of the other private camps. Bright colors, trendy designs, hand-painted napkins, and candy-wrapper place mats combine with traditional leather chairs, thatch, and hand-painted mud walls. Look out for some great contemporary African township art, both classic and "naïf" artifacts, and especially for the chandelier made with old Coca-Cola bottles above the dining table. The camp is unfenced, and it's quite usual to see kudu nibbling the lawns or giraffes towering above the rooftops.

Accommodations are in beautifully decorated chalets with private plunge pools. For something different in between drives, why not have your hair braided in funky African style at the Comfort Zone, the in-camp spa? ⌦ *8 suites* ⌂ *In-room: a/c. In-hotel: bar, spa.*

¢ 🖼 **Galago.** A delightful and affordable alternative to the upscale lodges, Galago, which means "lesser bush baby" in Shangaan, is a converted U-shape farmhouse whose five rooms form an arc around a central fireplace. There's a big, shady veranda where you can sit and gaze out over the open plain before cooling off in the plunge pool. You can bring your own food and do your own cooking for less than half the all-inclusive price, or you can bring your own supplies and hire the camp's chef (R300 per day) to cook it for you. Game drives and walks are led by your own ranger. This is a perfect camp for a family safari or friends' reunion. ⌦ *5 rooms* ⌂ *In-room: a/c. In-hotel: pool.*

LEOPARD HILLS Owned by the Kruger family, whose distant family member Paul Kruger, president of the former Transvaal Republic, founded Kruger National Park in 1898, this hilltop lodge was built 100 years after the park's founding and is one of the newer luxury lodges bordering the Sabi Sands Game Reserve. Managed and run by the ultra-experienced Duncan and Louise Rodgers, the lodge has grown from its original five suites to the current complex of eight suites, private heated plunge pools, gym and *sala* (outdoor covered deck), library, and traditional Shangaan boma. As with many lodges in the area, Leopard Hills gives back to the community, and its on-site junior school provides an excellent education for the children of lodge staff throughout the Sabi Sands area. Expect to see the Big Five, take a guided bush walk, fly over the awesome Blyde River canyon in a helicopter, or visit the local village to meet the people and see how they live. 🗀 *Box 612, Hazyview 1242* 🖀*013/737–6626 or 013/737–6627* 🌐*www.leopardhills.com* ▤*AE, DC, MC, V* 🍽*FAP.*

$$ 🖼 **Leopard Hills Lodge.** Renowned for its relaxed and informal atmosphere, Leopard Hills is one of the premier game lodges in the Sabi Sands area. Set on a rocky outcrop with panoramic views of the surrounding bushveld, this small lodge offers privacy and luxury. Its main draw is its spectacular game-viewing; during a two-night stay you're almost guaranteed to see the Big Five at close quarters. Rangers are

eager to share their knowledge and quick to rush guests off to see big game. The décor has an authentic bush theme, which gels well with the surroundings. Each double room has its own private heated pool (in addition to the main pool) and deck overlooking the bushveld. Bathrooms have his-and-her showers both indoors and out. Attention to detail is manifested in the leopard tracks and similar African motifs that appear in walkways, bedrooms, and bathrooms; check out the ceramic chameleon around the dressing table. *8 rooms In-room: a/c, safe, refrigerator. In-hotel: bar, pool, gym, spa, Internet, no kids under 10.*

LION SANDS   Guests of the Lion Sands Private Game Reserve can take direct scheduled flights to the Mala Mala airfield through SA Airlink *(⇨ South Africa Essentials, below).* *Box 30, White River 1240* 013/735–5330 *www.lionsands.com* *AE, DC, MC, V* FAP.

$$ **Ivory Lodge.** If you seek the ultimate in luxury, privacy, and relaxation, look no further than this gorgeous, exclusive lodge. Only a focused giraffe could see into any of the six simple, uncluttered, elegant suites decorated in contemporary African-European style; the suites operate as villas with private entrances and superb views overlooking the Sabi River and Kruger beyond. Relax with intimate dinners and on-the-spot spa treatments, sample some of South Africa's finest wines in the on-site cellar, or head out on a game drive in a private vehicle with your own personal ranger. You'll also have a personal butler and plunge pool. You won't even know if Brangelina or Ewan is in the next villa. *6 suites In-room: a/c, safe, refrigerator. In-hotel: spa.*

$ **River Lodge.** This friendly lodge is set on one of the longest and best stretches of river frontage in Sabi Sands. You can watch the passing animal and bird show from your deck or from the huge tree-shaded wooden viewing area that juts out over the riverbank facing Kruger National Park. Although the guest rooms are small, they are comfortable and attractively Africa themed, with honey-color stone floors with pebble inlays, cream wooden furniture, embroidered white bed linens, and lamps and tables of dark indigenous wood. The food is imaginative and tasty (try kudu stuffed with peanut butter with a mushroom-and-Amarula sauce), the young staff cheerful and enthusiastic, and the rangers highly qualified. After an exhilarating game drive, take a leisurely bush walk, go fishing, sleep out under the stars, or relax with a beauty treatment at Lalamuka Spa (*Lalamuka* means "unwind" in Shangaan). Public spaces are large and comfortable and lack the African designer clutter that mars some other lodges. There's a resident senior ecologist, plus a classy and interesting curio shop. *20 rooms In-room: a/c, safe, refrigerator. In-hotel: bar, pool, spa.*

LONDOLOZI   Formerly a family farm and retreat since 1926, Londolozi today is synonymous with South Africa's finest game lodges and game experiences. (*Londolozi* is the Zulu word for "protector of all living things.") Dave and John Varty, the charismatic and media-friendly grandsons of the original owner, Charles Varty, put the lodge on the map with glamorous marketing, superb wildlife videos, pet leopards and lions, visiting celebrities, and a vision of style and comfort that grandfather Charles could never have imagined. Now, the younger generation, brother-and-sister team Bronwyn and Boyd Varty, are bringing their own creative stamp to the magic of Londolozi with a mission to reconnect the human spirit with the wilderness and to carry on their family's quest to honor the animal kingdom. Game abounds; the Big Five are all here, and the leopards of Londolozi are world famous. (You are guaranteed to see at least one.) There are five camps, each representing a different element in nature: Pioneer Camp (water), Tree Camp (wood), Granite Suites (rock), Varty Camp (fire), and Founders Camp (earth). Each is totally private, hidden in dense riverine forest on the banks of the Sand River. The Varty family live on the property, and their friendliness and personal attention, along with the many staff who have been here for decades, will make you feel part of the family immediately. The central reception and curio shop are at Varty camp. ✉ *Londolozi, Box 41864, Hyde Park 2024* ☎ *011/280–6655* ⊕ *www.londolozi.com* 🖃 *AE, DC, MC, V* ⏹*FAP.*

$$$ ⬚**Granite Suites.** Book all three private suites or just hide yourself away from the rest of the world like the celebrities and royals who favor this gorgeous getaway. Here, it's all about location, location, location. Huge, flat granite rocks in the riverbed, where elephants chill out and bathe, stretch almost to the horizon in front of your floor-to-ceiling picture windows, and the elephant prints and furnishings done in velvets and silvers, grays and browns, echo the shifting colors and textures of the mighty pachyderms. Bathe in your own rock pool. At night, when your suite is lighted by scores of flickering candles, you may truly feel that you're in wonderland. ➥*3 suites* ⛁*In-room: a/c, safe, refrigerator. In-hotel: bar, pool, Internet.*

$$ ⬚**Founders Camp.** This camp takes you back to the early days of Londolozi, before ecotourism was invented—when it was more important to shoot a lion than to take the perfect shot of it. The stone-and-thatch chalets sit amid thick riverine bush and are linked to the other chalets by meandering pathways. Each has its own wooden viewing deck and is decorated in classic black-and-cream ticking fabric, with compass safari lamps, military chests, and faded family documents. Relax on the thatch split-level dining and viewing decks that jut out over a quiet backwater of the Sand River, and watch the mammals and birds go by. After your game drive or walk, cool off in the tree-shaded swimming pool, which also overlooks the river. ➥*5 chalets* ⛁*In-room: a/c, safe, refrigerator. In-hotel: bar, pool, Internet.*

$$ ⬚**Pioneer Camp.** Pioneer Camp and its cottage suites are a loving tribute to the early days and legendary characters of Sparta, the original name of the Londolozi property. Channel into a past world through faded sepia photographs, old hunting prints, horse-drawn carts, gleaming silverware, and scuffed safari treasures, taking you back to a time when it took five days by ox wagon to get to Londolozi. In winter sink deeply into your comfortable armchair in front of your own blazing fireplace; in summer sit outside in your outdoor dining room and listen to Africa's night noises. Keep your ears and eyes open for the resident female leopard as she hunts at night. The public rooms comprise a small, intimate boma, inside and outside dining areas, viewing decks,

and a gorgeous S-shape pool nestling in the surrounding bush, where after your dip you can laze on padded lie out chairs and be lulled to sleep by the birdsong. ⇨6 *cottages* ⟳*In-room: a/c, safe, refrigerator. In-hotel: bar, pool, Internet, no kids under 12.*

$$ ☷ **Tree Camp.** The first Relais & Chateaux game lodge in the world, this ★ gorgeous camp, now completely rebuilt and redesigned (think leopards, lanterns, leadwoods, and leopard orchids), is shaded by thick riverine bush and tucked into the riverbank overlooking indigenous forest. Dave Varty has built more than 20 lodges around Africa, and he feels that this is his triumph. The lodge is themed in chocolate and white, with exquisite leopard photos on the walls, airy and stylish interiors, and elegant yet simple furnishings. Huge bedrooms, en-suite bathrooms, and plunge pools continue the elegance, simplicity, and sophistication, and all suites have their own plunge pools. From your spacious deck you look out onto a world of cool green forest dominated by ancient African ebony and marula trees. Treat yourself to a bottle of bubbly from the Champagne Library and then dine with others while swapping bush stories, or alone on your private sala. ⇨6 *suites* ⟳*In-room: a/c, safe, refrigerator. In-hotel: bar, pool, Internet.*

$ ☷ **Varty Camp.** This camp's fire has been burning for more than 80 ☾ years, making this location the very soul and center of Londolozi. It's also the largest of Londolozi's camps, centered on a thatched A-frame lodge that houses a dining room, sitting areas, and lounge. Meals are served on a broad wooden deck that juts over the riverbed and under an ancient jackalberry tree. The thatch rondavels, which were the Varty family's original hunting camp, now do duty as a library, a wine cellar, and an interpretive center, where you can listen to history and ecotourism talks—don't miss the Londolozi Leopard presentation. If you're looking for romance, have a private dinner on your veranda and go for a moonlight dip in your own plunge pool. In suites, the pool leads right to the riverbed. All rooms are decorated in African ethnic chic—in creams and browns and with the ubiquitous historic family photographs and documents—and have great bushveld views. Families are welcome, and the fascinating kids' programs should turn any couch potato into an instant wannabe ranger. ⇨2 *suites, 8 chalets* ⟳*In-room: a/c, safe, refrigerator. In-hotel: bar, pool, Internet.*

MALA MALA This legendary game lodge, which along with Londolozi put South
Fodor's Choice African safaris on the international map, has been tops in its field for
★ more than 40 years, delighting visitors with incomparable personal service, superb food, and discreetly elegant, comfortable accommodations where you'll rub shoulders with aristocrats, celebrities, and returning visitors alike. Mike Rattray, a legend in his own time in South Africa's game-lodge industry, describes Mala Mala as "a camp in the bush," but it's certainly more than that, although it still retains that genuine bushveld feel of bygone days. Both the outstanding hospitality and the game-viewing experience keep guests coming back. Mala Mala constitutes the largest privately owned Big Five game area in South Africa, and includes an unfenced 30-km (19-mi) boundary with Kruger National Park, across which game crosses continuously. The variety of habitats ranges from riverine bush, favorite hiding place of the leopard,

to open grasslands, where cheetahs hunt. Mala Mala's animal-viewing statistics are probably unbeatable: the Big Five are spotted almost every day. At one moment your well-educated, friendly, articulate ranger might fascinate you by describing the sex life of a dung beetle, as you watch the sturdy male battling his way along the road, pushing his perfectly round ball of dung with wife-to-be perched perilously on top; at another, your adrenaline will flow as you follow a leopard stalking impala in the gathering gloom. Along with the local Shangaan trackers, whose eyesight rivals that of the animals they are tracking, the top-class rangers ensure that your game experience is unforgettable. ✒️*Box 55514, Northlands 2116* 📠*011/268–2388* ⊕*www.malamala.com* ⊟*AE, DC, MC, V* 🍴*FAP.*

$$ 🏨**Rattray's on Mala Mala.** The breathtakingly beautiful Rattray's merges original bushveld style with daring ideas that run the risk of seeming out of place, but instead work wonderfully well. Eight opulent *khayas* (think Tuscan villas) with spacious his-and-her bathrooms, dressing rooms, and private heated plunge pools blend well with the surrounding bush. Each villa's entrance hall, with art by distinguished African wildlife artists such as Keith Joubert, leads to a huge bedroom with a wooden four-poster bed, and beyond a lounge liberally scattered with deep sofas, comfy armchairs, padded ottomans, writing desks (for those crucial nightly journal entries), antique Persian rugs, and a dining nook. Bird and botanical prints grace the walls. Floor-to-ceiling windows with insect-proof sliding doors face the Sand River and lead to massive wooden decks where you can view the passing wildlife. The main lodge includes viewing and dining decks, an infinity pool, lounge areas, and tantalizing views over the river. In the paneled library, with plush sofas, inviting leather chairs, old prints and photographs, and battered leather suitcases, the complete works of Kipling, Dickens, and Thackeray rub leather shoulders with contemporary classics and 100-year-old bound copies of England's classic humorous magazine *Punch*. After browsing the Cellar's impressive fine wines, have a drink in the bar with its huge fireplace, antique card table, and polished cherrywood bar. ➮*8 villas* ⚒*In-room: a/c, safe, refrigerator, Internet, TV, DVD. In-hotel: bar, pool, gym, no kids under 16.*

$$ 🏨**Sable Camp.** This fully air-conditioned, exclusive camp at the southern end of Main Camp overlooks the Sand River and surrounding bushveld. With its own pool, library, and boma, it's smaller and more intimate than Main Camp, but it shares the same magnificent all-around bush and hospitality experience. ➮*7 suites* ⚒*In-room: a/c, safe, refrigerator. In-hotel: bar, pool, gym, Internet, no kids under 12.*

$ 🏨**Main Camp.** Ginger-brown stone and thatch air-conditioned rondawels with separate his-and-her bathrooms are decorated in creams and browns and furnished with cane armchairs, colorful handwoven tapestries and rugs, terra-cotta floors, and original artwork. Public areas have a genuine safari feel, with plush couches, animal skins, and African artifacts. Shaded by ancient jackalberry trees, a huge deck overlooks the Sand River and its passing show of animals. Browse in the air-conditioned Monkey Room for books and wildlife videos, sample the magnificent wine cellar, sun yourself by the pool, or stay fit in the well-appointed gym. The food—among the best in the bush—is delicious, wholesome, and varied, with a full buffet at both lunch and dinner. Children are welcomed with special programs, activities, and goody-filled backpacks; kids under 12 are not allowed on game drives unless they're with their own family group, and children under 5 are not allowed on game drives at all. One guest room is geared toward travelers with disabilities. ⤳*18 rooms* &*In-room: a/c, safe, refrigerator. In-hotel: bar, pool, gym, children's programs, Internet.*

SABI SABI Founded in 1978 at the southern end of Sabi Sands, Sabi Sabi was one of the first lodges, along with Londolozi, to offer photo safaris and to link ecotourism, conservation, and community. Superb accommodations and the sheer density of game supported by its highly varied habitats draw guests back to Sabi Sabi in large numbers. There's a strong emphasis on ecology: guests are encouraged to look beyond the Big Five and to become aware of the birds and smaller mammals of the bush. ✏*Box 52665, Saxonwold 2132* ☎*011/483–3939* ⊕*www. sabisabi.com* ☰*AE, DC, MC, V* ⧉*FAP.*

$$ ⛺**Earth Lodge.** This avant-garde ecofriendly lodge was the first to break away from the traditional safari style and strive for a contemporary theme. It's a cross between a Hopi cave dwelling and a medieval keep, but with modern luxury. On arrival, all you'll see is bush and grass-covered hummocks until you descend a hidden stone pathway that opens onto a spectacular landscape of boulders and streams. The lodge, rated among the world's top 52 hot spots by *Condé Naste Traveler,* has rough-textured, dark brown walls encrusted with orange seeds and wisps of indigenous grasses. The mud-domed suites are hidden from view until you're practically at the front door. Surfaces are sculpted from ancient fallen trees, whereas chairs and tables are ultramodern or '50s style. Your suite has huge living spaces with a sitting area, mega bathroom, private veranda, and plunge pool. A personal butler takes care of your every need, and there's a meditation garden. Dine in a subterranean cellar or in the boma, fashioned from roots and branches and lighted at night by dozens of lanterns. ⤳*13 suites* &*In-room: a/c, safe, refrigerator. In-hotel: bar, pool, spa.*

$ ⛺**Bush Lodge.** Bush Lodge overlooks a busy water hole (lions are frequent visitors) and the dry course of the Msuthlu River. The thatch, open-sided dining area, observation deck, and pool all have magnificent views of game at the water hole. Thatch suites are connected by walkways that weave between manicured lawns and beneath enormous shade trees where owls and fruit bats call at night. All have a deck overlooking the dry river course (where you may well see an elephant padding along) and outdoor and indoor showers. Chalets at this large lodge are older and smaller—although more intimate in a way—but still roomy; they are creatively decorated with African designs and have a personal wooden deck. ⤳*21 chalets, 5 suites* &*In-room: a/c, safe, refrigerator. In-hotel: bar, pool, spa.*

$ ⛺**Little Bush Camp.** This delightful family camp combines airiness and ⟳ spaciousness with a sense of intimacy. At night glowing oil lanterns lead you along a wooden walkway to your comfortable thatch-roof suite decorated in earthy tones of brown, cream, and white. After your action-packed morning game drive—during which you'll see game galore—and your delicious brunch, relax on the wooden deck overlooking the bush, have a snooze in your air-conditioned bedroom, or laze away the time between activities at the pool area. In the evening you can sip a glass of complimentary sherry as you watch the stars—if you're a city slicker, you may never have seen such bright ones. ⊲76 *suites* ⬧ *In-room: a/c, safe, refrigerator. In-hotel: bar, pool, spa.*

$ ★ ⊞ **Selati Lodge.** For an *Out of Africa* feel, you can't beat Selati, an intimate, stylish, colonial-style camp that was formerly the private hunting lodge of a famous South African opera singer. The early-1900s atmosphere is created by the use of genuine train memorabilia—old leather suitcases, antique wooden chairs, nameplates, and signals—that recall the old Selati branch train line, which once crossed the reserve, transporting gold from the interior to the coast of Mozambique in the 1870s. At night the grounds of this small, secluded lodge flicker with the lights of the original shunters' oil lamps. Dinner is held in the boma, whereas brunch is served in the friendly farmhouse kitchen. Members of the glitterati and European royalty have stayed at the spacious Ivory Presidential Suite, with its Persian rugs and antique furniture. ⊲78 *chalets, 1 suite* ⬧ *In-room: a/c, safe, refrigerator. In-hotel: bar, pool, no kids under 10.*

SINGITA   Although Singita (Shangaan for "the miracle") offers much the same bush experience as the other lodges, its huge public areas, extravagant and enormous accommodations, and superb dining help set it apart. Enjoy a riverside breakfast, picnic lunch, or starlighted supper in the bush; browse in the reading rooms and wine cellar, which has a superb stock of vintage wines; relax in your huge, private suite; or shop at the Trading Store for African artifacts, bush clothes, handmade jewelry, and ostrich-skin purses. ⬠ *Box 650881, Benmore 2010* ☎*011/234–0990* ⊕*www.singita.co.za* ▤*AE, DC, MC, V* ⦿*FAP.*

$$ ★ ⊞ **Boulders Lodge.** The style is traditional African at this ultraluxurious camp, whose exterior echoes the great Zimbabwe ruins. Large ponds guard the entrance to the public areas, where decor combines modern with bushveld. An entrance hall with a fully stocked bar and pantry welcomes you into your enormous suite, where a freestanding fireplace dominates a glass-sided lounge. Dark brown, cream, and pale blue fabrics complement leather and wicker armchairs, a zebra-skin ottoman, and antique pieces from owner Luke Bailes's original family home. Occasional touches of steel—candleholders, mirrors, and lamps—provide a nice contrast. A herd of impalas could easily fit into the bathroom, which has dark stone floors, a claw-foot tub, his-and-her sinks, and massive indoor and outdoor showers. All the doors in the suite lead directly onto a wooden deck with mattresses, chairs, and a bubbling infinity pool with views of the surrounding bushveld. ⊲79 *suites* ⬧ *In-room: a/c, safe, refrigerator. In-hotel: bar, pool, spa.*

$$ ⊞ **Ebony Lodge.** Gardens, well-worn polished terra-cotta tiles and mud floors, deep comfy armchairs and sofas, and antiques make you feel like a houseguest in somebody's old family lodge. The cozy library

with its leather-bound books, period prints, leather armchairs, and silver trophies is a little gem. The bright yellow and orange walls in the suites contrast surprisingly well with the soft colors of the bush outside. Each suite has a double-sided fireplace, separate living room, enormous veranda, and bathroom with indoor and outdoor showers, plus a personal deck and plunge pool. ⮐9 *suites* ♿ *In-room: a/c, safe, refrigerator. In-hotel: bar, pool, spa.*

5

Leopard Hills Lodge, Sabi Sands Game Reserve

Bush Lodge, Sabi Sands Game Reserve

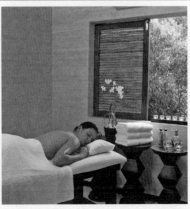

River Lodge, Sabi Sands Game Reserve

KWAZULU-NATAL PARKS

Game
☆★★★★

Park Accessibility
★★★★★

Ease of Getting
Around
★★★★★

Accommodations
★★★★★

Scenic Beauty
☆★★★★

The province of KwaZulu-Natal is a premier vacation destination for South Africans, with some of the finest game reserves in the country, including the Hluhluwe-Umfolozi Game Reserve. The reserve is small compared to Kruger, but here you'll see the Big Five and plenty of plains game, plus an incredibly biologically diverse mix of plants and trees. The nearby Mkuze and Itala game reserves are even smaller, but are still worth a visit for their numerous bird species and game.

KwaZulu-Natal's best private lodges, including Phinda and Thanda private reserves, lie in northern Zululand and Maputaland, a remote region close to Mozambique. These lodges put you sufficiently close to one another and Hluhluwe-Umfolozi Game Reserve to allow you to put together a bush experience that delivers the Big Five and a great deal more, including superb bird-watching opportunities and an unrivaled beach paradise. Malaria does pose a problem, however, and antimalarial drugs are essential. Summers are hot, hot, hot. If you can't take heat and humidity, then autumn, winter, and early summer are probably the best times to visit.

HLUHLUWE-UMFOLOZI GAME RESERVE

Reputedly King Shaka's favorite hunting ground, Zululand's Hluhluwe-Umfolozi (pronounced shloo-*shloo*-ee im-fuh-*low*-zee) incorporates two of Africa's oldest reserves: Hluhluwe and Umfolozi, both founded in 1895. In an area of just 906 square km (350 square mi), Hluhluwe-Umfolozi delivers the Big Five plus all the plains game and species like nyala and red duiker that are rare in other parts of the country. Equally important, it boasts one of the most biologically diverse habitats on the planet, a unique mix of forest, woodland, savanna, and grassland. You'll find about 1,250 species of plants and trees here—more than in some entire countries.

The park is administered by Ezemvelo KZN Wildlife, the province's official conservation organization, which looks after all the large game reserves and parks as well as many nature reserves. Thanks to its conservation efforts and those of its predecessor, the highly regarded Natal Parks Board, the park can take credit for saving the white rhino from extinction. So successful was the park at increasing white rhino numbers that in 1960 it established its now famous Rhino Capture Unit to relocate rhinos to other reserves in Africa. The park is currently trying to do for the black rhino what it did for its white cousins. Poaching in the past nearly decimated Africa's black rhino population, but as a result of the park's remarkable conservation efforts, 20% of Africa's remaining black rhinos now live in this reserve—and you won't get a better chance of seeing them in the wild than here.

Until 1989 the reserve consisted of two separate parks, Hluhluwe in the north and Umfolozi in the south, separated by a fenced corridor. Although a road (R618) still runs through this corridor, the fences have been removed, and the parks now operate as a single entity. Hluhluwe and the corridor are the most scenic areas of the park, notable for their bush-covered hills and knockout views, whereas Umfolozi is better known for its broad plains.

Compared with Kruger, Hluhluwe-Umfolozi is tiny—less than 6% of Kruger's size—but such comparisons can be misleading. You can spend days driving around this park and still not see everything, or feel like you're going in circles. Probably the biggest advantage Hluhluwe has over Kruger is that game-viewing is good year-round, whereas Kruger has seasonal peaks and valleys. Another bonus is its proximity to Mkuze Game Reserve and the spectacular coastal reserves of Greater St. Lucia Wetland Park. The park is also close enough to Durban to make it a worthwhile one- or two-day excursion.

KZN Wildlife can provide information about the park and help you book hikes on wilderness trails. ✉ *KZN Wildlife, Box 13069, Cascades, Pietermaritzburg 3202* ☎ *033/845–1000* ⊕ *www.kznwildlife.com.*

BUSH WALKS Armed rangers lead groups of eight on two- to three-hour bush walks departing from Hilltop or Mpila Camp. You rarely spot much game on these walks, but you do see plenty of birds and you learn a great deal about the area's ecology and tips on how to recognize the signs of the bush, including animal spoor. Walks depart daily at 5:30 AM and 3:30 PM (6 and 3 in winter) and cost R200. Reserve a few days in advance at Hilltop Camp reception (☎ *035/562–0848*).

GAME DRIVES A great way to see the park is on game drives led by rangers. These drives (R200 per person) hold several advantages over driving through the park yourself: you sit high up in an open-air vehicle, with a good view and the wind in your face; a ranger explains the finer points of animal behavior and ecology; and your guide has a good idea where to

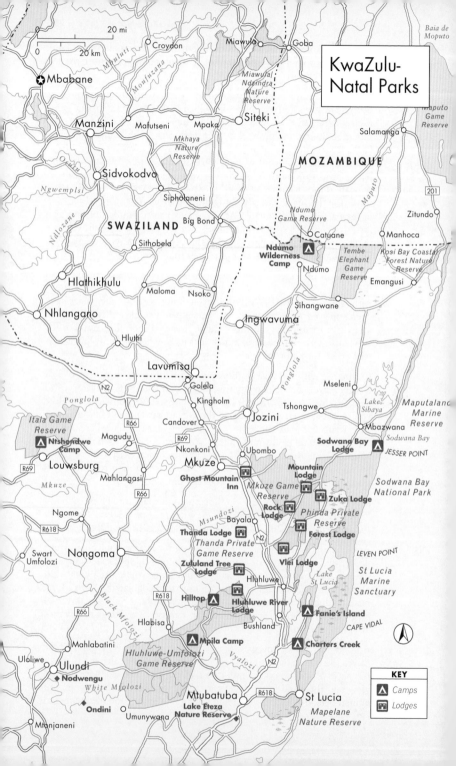

find animals like leopards, cheetahs, and lions. Game drives leave Monday–Saturday at 5:30 AM in summer, 6:30 AM in winter. The park also offers three-hour night drives, during which you search for nocturnal animals with powerful spotlights. These three-hour drives depart at 7, and you should make advance reservations at Hilltop Camp reception (☎035/562–0848).

WILDERNESS TRAILS

The park's **Wilderness Trails** are every bit as popular as Kruger's, but they tend to be tougher and more rustic. You should be fit enough to walk up to 16 km (10 mi) a day for a period of three days and four nights. An armed ranger leads the hikes, and all equipment, food, and baggage are carried by donkeys. The first and last nights are spent at Mndindini, a permanent tented camp. The other two are spent under canvas in the bush. While in the bush, hikers bathe in the Umfolozi River or have a hot bucket shower; toilet facilities consist of a spade and toilet-paper roll. Trails, open March–November, are limited to eight people and should be reserved a year in advance (R2,700 per person per trail).

Fully catered two- or three-night **Short Trails** involve stays at a satellite camp in the wilderness area. You'll sleep in a dome tent, and although there's hot water from a bucket shower, your toilet is a spade.

If that sounds too easy, you can always opt for one of the four-night **Primitive Trails.** On these treks hikers carry their own packs and sleep out under the stars, although there are lightweight tents for inclement weather. A campfire burns all night to scare off animals, and each participant is expected to sit a 90-minute watch. A ranger acts as guide. The cost is R1,800 per person per trail.

A less rugged wilderness experience can be had on the **Bushveld Trails,** based out of the tented Mndindini camp, where you're guaranteed a bed and some creature comforts. The idea behind these trails is to instill in the participants an appreciation for the beauty of the untamed bush. You can also join the Mpila night drive if you wish. Participation is limited to eight people and costs about R1,800 per person per trail.

WHERE TO STAY

NATIONAL PARK ACCOMMODATIONS IN HLUHLUWE-UMFOLOZI

Hluhluwe-Umfolozi offers a range of accommodations in government-run rest camps, with an emphasis on self-catering (only Hilltop has a restaurant). (The park also has secluded bush lodges and camps, but most foreign visitors can't avail themselves of these lodgings, as each must be reserved in a block, and the smallest accommodates at least eight people.) Conservation levies are R80 per person.

¢ **Hilltop Camp.** It may be a government-run camp, but this delightful lodge in the Hluhluwe half of the park matches some of South Africa's best private lodges. Perched on the crest of a hill, it has panoramic views over the park, the Hlaza and Nkwakwa hills, and Zululand. Thatch and ocher-color walls give it an African feel. Scattered across the crown of the hill, self-contained chalets have high thatch ceilings, rattan furniture, and small verandas. If you plan to eat all your meals in the restaurant or sample the evening *braai* (barbecue), forgo the more expensive chalets with fully equipped kitchens. If you're on a tight budget, opt for a basic rondawel with two beds, a basin, and a refrigerator; toilet facilities are communal. In addition to an à la carte restaurant, an attractive pub, a convenience store, and a gas station are on-site. Go for a stroll along a forest trail rich with birdsong, or take a bottle of wine to Hlaza Hide and join the animals as they come for their sundowners. ⌖*KZN Wildlife, Box 13069, Cascades, Pietermaritzburg 3202* ☎*033/845–1000* ⊕*www.kznwildlife.com* ✆*20 rondawels, 49 chalets* ⌂*In-room: kitchen (some). In-hotel: restaurant, bar* ⊟*AE, DC, MC, V.*

¢ 🏨**Mpila Camp.** In the central Umfolozi section of the park, Mpila is humbler than the classy Hilltop Camp and more reminiscent of some of Kruger's older camps. Choose among one-room huts sharing communal facilities, two- and three-bedroom cottages, chalets, an en-suite safari tent, or three secluded lodges. Gas is available, but you can only buy curios and sodas at the camp shop, so stock up with groceries before you arrive. Be sure to book your bush walks and game drives on arrival, as they work on a first-come, first-served basis. ⌖*KZN Wildlife, Box 13069, Cascades, Pietermaritzburg 3202* ☎*033/845–1000* ⊕*www.kznwildlife.com* ✆*12 huts, 2 cottages, 6 chalets, 9 safari tents, 3 lodges* ⌂*In-room: kitchen (some)* ⊟*AE, DC, MC, V.*

**NATIONAL PARK ACCOMMODATIONS
NEAR HLUHLUWE-UMFOLOZI**

¢ 🏨**Hluhluwe River Lodge.** Overlooking False Bay Lake and the Hluhluwe
☺ River flood plain, this luxurious, good-value, spacious, family-owned lodge set in indigenous gardens is the ideal base for visiting the game reserves and the Greater St. Lucia Wetland Park. After a day spent game-viewing, canoeing, bird-watching, boating, fishing, or walking in the pristine sand forest, you can relax in a terra-cotta-color A-frame chalet with cool stone floors, wood and wicker furniture, and cream-and-brown decor and furnishings. Alternatively, sit out on your wooden deck overlooking the bush, the floodplain, and the lake. This lodge is the only one with direct access to the lake, and as you chug along through bird-filled papyrus channels decorated with water lilies en route to the broad expanses of the main body of water, you might easily feel as though you're in Botswana's Okavango Delta. Water activities are dependent on the seasonal rains, so check with the lodge in advance. The food is excellent—wholesome country cooking with lots of fresh vegetables and good roasts. ✉*Follow signs from Hluhluwe village* ⌖*Box 105, Hluhluwe 3960* ☎*035/562–0246* ⊕*www.hluhluwe. co.za* ✆*12 chalets* ⌂*In-room: a/c. In-hotel: restaurant, bar, pool* ⊟*AE, DC, MC, V* ⍐*MAP.*

¢ 🏨**Zululand Tree Lodge.** About 16 km (10 mi) from the park, this lodge lies in a forest of fever trees on the 3,700-acre Ubizane Game Reserve, a small park stocked with white rhinos and plains game. It makes a great base from which to explore Hluhluwe, Mkuze, and St. Lucia. Built of thatch and wood, the open-sided lodge sits on stilts overlooking the Mzinene River. Rooms are in separate cottages, also on stilts, along the riverbank. The rooms themselves are small, but tastefully decorated with mosquito nets covering old-fashioned iron bedsteads made up with fluffy white duvets, African-print cushions, wicker, and reed matting. If you want the experience of sleeping alfresco, fold back the huge wooden shutters dividing the bedroom from the open deck. A qualified ranger will take you for a bush walk or a game drive (which is included in your stay) through the small reserve or a little farther afield for a game drive in nearby Hluhluwe-Umfolozi. At the nearby Illala Weavers you can buy superb handwoven Zulu baskets. ⊠ *Hluhluwe Rd.* ⬡ *Box 116, Hluhluwe 3960* ☎ *035/562–1020* ⊕ *www.zululandtreelodge. co.za* ⬡ *24 rooms* ⬡ *In-hotel: restaurant, bar, pool* ⊟ *AE, DC, MC, V* ⊙ *MAP.*

MKUZE GAME RESERVE

This 88,900-acre reserve in the shadow of the Ubombo Mountains, between the Mkhuze and Msunduze rivers, makes up the northwestern spur of the Greater St. Lucia Wetland Park, now a World Heritage site. (The park itself is one of the most important coastal and wetland areas in the world with five interlinked ecosystems: a marine system, a coastal dune system, lake systems, swamps, and inland savanna woodlands. It is this often-pristine diversity that makes it both important and amazingly beautiful.) Mkuze is famous for its birds: more than 400 bird species have been spotted here, including myriad waterfowl drawn to the park's shallow pans in summer. Several blinds, particularly those overlooking Nsumo Pan, offer superb views. Don't miss out on the amazing 3-km (2-mi) walk through a spectacular rare forest of towering, ancient fig trees, some as big as 82 feet tall and 39 feet around the base. Although only a fraction of Kruger's size, this is the place to find rhinos; there's a healthy population of both black and white rhinos. You won't find lions, buffalo, or elephants, but the low-lying thornveld supports lots of other game, including zebras, giraffes, kudus, and nyalas. The reserve is 48 km (30 mi) north of Hluhluwe-Umfolozi. Note that there are variant spellings of Mkuze in the area; you may also see Mkuzi or Mkhuzi. ⊠ *Off N2* ☎ *035/573–9004* ⬡ *R35 per vehicle, R35 per person* ⊙ *Daily 6–6.*

WHERE TO STAY

¢ 🏨 **Ghost Mountain Inn.** Swaths of scarlet bougainvillea run riot in the lush gardens of this family-owned country inn near Mkuze. It was here that Rider Haggard wrote some of his adventure stories, inspired perhaps by the mysterious lights and elusive flickering flames that give the mountain its spooky name. Rooms, each with a small veranda, are tastefully furnished in understated creams and browns with interesting historical prints. Large, invitingly restful public areas have terra-cotta tiles and comfortable cane furniture, and the cozy African lounge makes you feel like you've slipped back to the past. Don't miss the enthusiastic Zulu dancing before a succulent barbecue under the stars. At first light, wander down to the lake and watch the waterbirds wake up, or, later in the day, sit in the blind and watch them come home to roost. There's an excellent curio shop. The friendly staff can arrange tours to the neighboring game reserves and cultural sights, or will fix you up to go bird-watching or fishing. ⊠*Fish Eagle Rd., Mkuze* ☎*Box 18, Mkuze 3965* ☎*035/573–1025* ⊕*www.ghostmountaininn.co.za* ⟿*33 rooms* ♿*In-room: a/c. In-hotel: restaurant, bar, pool* ⊟*AE, DC, MC, V* ⊚*BP.*

ITALA GAME RESERVE

In northern KwaZulu-Natal Province, close to the Swaziland border, Itala (sometimes spelled "Ithala"), at 296 square km (114 square mi), is small even compared with the relatively compact Hluhluwe-Umfolozi. Its size and its dearth of lions are probably why this delightful park 221 km (137 mi) northwest of Hluhluwe-Umfolozi is usually bypassed, even by South Africans—although they clearly don't know what they're missing. The other four of the Big Five are here—it's excellent for black and white rhinos—and the park is stocked with cheetahs, hyenas, giraffes, and an array of antelopes among its 80 mammal species. It's also an excellent spot for birders. The stunning landscapes and the relaxed game-viewing make this area a breath of fresh air after the Big Five melee of Kruger.

The reserve, founded in 1972 and run by KZN Wildlife, is a rugged region that drops 3,290 feet in just 15 km (9 mi) through sandstone cliffs, multicolor rocks, granite hills, ironstone outcrops, and quartz formations. Watered by nine small rivers rising in its vicinity and covered with rich soils, Itala supports a varied cross section of vegetation, encompassing riverine thicket, wetland, open savanna, and acacia woodland. Arriving at its Ntshondwe Camp is nothing short of dramatic. The meandering road climbs from open plains to the top of a plateau dotted with granite formations, which at the last minute magically yield the rest camp at the foot of pink and russet cliffs.

KZN Wildlife can provide more information about the reserve. ⊠*KZN Wildlife, Box 13069, Cascades, Pietermaritzburg 3202* ☎*033/845–1000* ⊕*www.kznwildlife.com.*

WHERE TO STAY

NATIONAL PARK ACCOMMODATIONS
Although Itala has several exclusive bush camps, these are booked up months in advance by South Africans, making the chalets at its main camp the only practical accommodations for foreign visitors. Two people sharing a two-bed unit at Ntshondwe will pay about R350 per person per night.

¢ ★ 🖫 **Ntshondwe Camp.** In architecture, landscaping, and style, this beautiful government run rest camp, 69 km (43 mi) from Vryheid, comes closer than any other in the country to matching the expensive private lodges. Built around granite boulders and vegetation lush with acacias, wild figs, and giant cactuslike euphorbias, airy chalets with steep thatch roofs blend perfectly with the surroundings. Its two-, four-, and six-bed units can accommodate a total of 200 guests. Each self-catering chalet has a spacious lounge simply furnished with cane

> **SELF-GUIDED TRAILS**
>
> An unusual feature of Itala is its self-guided walking trails, in the mountainside above Ntshondwe Camp. The trails give you a chance to stretch your limbs if you've just spent hours cooped up in a car. They also let you get really close to the euphorbias, acacias, and other fascinating indigenous vegetation that festoon the hills. Ask at the camp reception for further information.

chairs, a fully equipped kitchen, and a large veranda surrounded by indigenous bush. Keep an eye open for eagles soaring above the pink and russet sandstone cliffs. A magnificent game-viewing deck juts out over a steep slope to provide views of a water hole and extensive panoramas of the surrounding valleys. Take a guided game drive (R150) or guided walk (R140), hike a self-guided trail, or follow one of the well-laid-out drives with markers at points of interest. Picnic at one of the many scenic picnic spots, all of which have barbecue facilities and toilets. A gas station, a store (with great curios), and a good restaurant are all on the premises. ☐ *KZN Wildlife, Box 13069, Cascades, Pietermaritzburg 3202* ☎ *033/845–1000 or 034/983–2540* ⊕ *www.kznwildlife.com* ⬙ *39 chalets* ☐ *In-room: kitchen. In-hotel: restaurant, bar, pool* ▤ *AE, DC, MC, V.*

PHINDA PRIVATE GAME RESERVE

Established in 1991, this flagship CC Africa reserve is a heartening example of tourism serving the environment with panache. Phinda (*pin-duh*) is Zulu for "return," referring to the restoration of 54,360 acres of overgrazed ranchland in northern Zululand to bushveld. It's a triumph. You may find it impossible to believe the area wasn't always the thick bush you see all around you. The Big Five have established themselves firmly, and Phinda can claim a stunning variety of seven different ecosystems: sand forest (which grows on the fossil dunes of an earlier coastline), savanna, bushveld, open woodland, and verdant wetlands.

Phinda can deliver the Big Five, although not as consistently or in such numbers as its sister lodge, Londolozi, in Mpumalanga. Buffalo, leopards, lions, cheetahs, spotted hyenas, elephants, white rhinos, hippos, giraffes, impalas, and the rare, elusive, tiny Suni antelope are all here, and rangers provide exciting interpretive game drives for guests. Birdlife is prolific and extraordinary, with some special Zululand finds: the pink-throated twin spot, the crested guinea fowl, the African broadbill, and the crowned eagle. Where Phinda also excels is in the superb quality of its rangers, who can provide fascinating commentary on everything from local birds to frogs. It's amazing just how enthralling the love life of a dung beetle can be! There are also Phinda adventures (optional extras) down the Mzinene River for a close-up look at crocodiles, hippos, and birds; big-game fishing or scuba diving off the deserted, wildly beautiful Maputaland coast; and sightseeing flights over Phinda and the highest vegetated dunes in the world.

WHERE TO STAY

For all reservations, contact **CC Africa** 🕭 *Private Bag X27, Benmore 2010* ☎*011/809–4300* ⊕*www.phinda.com* ▭*AE, DC, MC, V* ⏣*FAP.*

LUXURY LODGING

$$$$
☯ **Phinda Zuka Lodge.** An exclusive, single-use lodge for a family or small group of friends, Zuka (Zuka means "sixpence" in Zulu) is a couple of miles from the bigger lodges. Thatch cottages overlook a busy water hole, and you'll be looked after by the camp's personal ranger–host, butler, and chef. Children are welcome. ⌫*4 cottages (which must be rented as one unit)* ⚒*In-hotel: a/c, bar, pool.*

$
★ **Forest Lodge.** Hidden in a rare sand forest, this fabulous lodge overlooks a small water hole where nyalas, warthogs, and baboons frequently come to drink. The lodge is a real departure from the traditional thatch structures so common in South Africa. It's very modern, with a vaguely Japanese Zen feel thanks to glass-paneled walls, light woods, and a deliberately spare, clean look. The effect is stylish and very elegant, softened by modern African art and sculpture. Suites use the same architectural concepts as the lodge, where walls have become windows, and rely on the dense forest (or curtains) for privacy. As a result, you'll likely feel very close to your surroundings, and it's possible to lie in bed or take a shower while watching delicate nyalas grazing just feet away. ⌫*16 suites* ⚒*In-room: a/c. In-hotel: pool.*

$
☯ **Mountain Lodge.** This attractive thatch lodge sits on a rocky hill overlooking miles of bushveld plains and the Ubombo Mountains. Wide verandas lead into the lounge and bar, graced with high ceilings, dark beams, and cool tile floors. In winter guests can snuggle into cushioned wicker chairs next to a blazing log fire. Brick pathways wind down the hillside from the lodge to elegant split-level suites with mosquito nets, thatch roofs, and large decks overlooking the reserve. African baskets, beadwork, and grass matting beautifully complement the bush atmosphere. Children are welcome, although those under 5 are not allowed on game drives and 6- to 11-year-olds are permitted only at the manager's discretion. ⌫*20 suites, 7 chalets* ⚒*In-room: a/c. In-hotel: bar, pool.*

$ 🏠**Rock Lodge.** If you get tired of the eagle's-eye view of the deep valley below from your private veranda, you can write in your journal in your luxurious sitting room or take a late-night dip in your own plunge pool. All of Phinda's activities are included—twice-daily game drives, nature walks, riverboat cruises, and canoe trips along the Mzinene River. Scuba diving, deep-sea fishing, and spectacular small-plane flights are extras. Don't miss out on one of Phinda's legendary bush dinners: hundreds of lanterns light up the surrounding forest and bush, and the food is unforgettable. ↩6 *suites* ♿*In-room: a/c. In-hotel: bar, pool.*

$ 🏠**Vlei Lodge.** Accommodations at this small and intimate lodge are nestled in the shade of the sand forest and are so private it's hard to believe there are other guests. Suites—made of thatch, teak, and glass—have a distinct Asian feel and overlook a wet marshland on the edge of an inviting woodland. The bedrooms and bathrooms are huge, and each suite has a private plunge pool (one visitor found a lion drinking from his) and outdoor deck. The lounge–living area of the lodge has two fireplaces on opposite glass walls, a dining area, and a large terrace under a canopy of trees, where breakfast is served. The bush braai, with its splendid food and fairy-tale setting, is a memorable occasion after an evening game drive. ↩6 *suites* ♿*In-room: a/c. In-hotel: bar, pool.*

¢ 🏠**Phinda Walking Safari.** This unusual experience is a delightful way to get close to the bush. Your home for three nights is a spacious safari tent (with bathroom) in the middle of a rare sand forest. Here crowned eagles may survey you as you take a postprandial nap in a hammock under giant fig trees, or a fishing owl may call as you swap safari stories under the stars. Each morning (depending on the consensus of the group) you amble through the forest or over the plains for four or five hours; then it's back to camp for a presunset walk and game drive. An armed security guard ranger makes sure you get home safely, and the camp chef keeps the calories coming. The walking safari is not offered in summer because of the heat. ↩4 *luxury tents* ♿*In-hotel: bar, no kids under 16* ⊘*Closed Dec.–Feb.*

THANDA PRIVATE GAME RESERVE

Located in a wildly beautiful part of northern Zululand, Thanda is one of KwaZulu-Natal's newer game reserves. Like its neighbor Phinda did in the '90s, the 37,000-acre reserve is restoring former farmlands and hunting grounds to their previous pristine state, thanks to a joint venture with local communities and the king of the Zulus, Goodwill Zweletini, who donated some of his royal hunting grounds to the project. Game that used to roam this wilderness centuries ago has been reestablished, including the Big Five. Thanda (tan-duh) is Zulu for "love," and its philosophy echoes just that: "for the love of nature, wildlife, and dear ones." Rangers often have to work hard to find game, but the rewards of seriously tracking lions or rhinos with your enthusiastic and very experienced ranger and tracker are great. Because its owner is passionately committed not only to the land but also to the local people, there are many opportunities to interact with them. Don't miss out on Vula Zulu, one of the most magical and powerful

Zulu experiences offered in South Africa. After exploring the village, including the chief's kraal and the hut of the *sangoma* (shaman), where you might have bones thrown and read, you'll be treated to the Vula Zulu show, a memorable blend of narration, high-energy dance, song, and mime that recounts Zulu history. The lodge can also arrange golf, scuba diving, snorkeling, whale-watching, and fishing expeditions.

WHERE TO STAY

For all reservations, contact **Thanda.** Both the tented camp and the main lodge have kids' programs and a customized Junior Ranger's course. ⌂*Box 652585, Benmore 2010* ☎*011/704–3115* ⊕*www.thanda.com* ▭*AE, DC, MC, V* ⍾*FAP.*

$ 　ᵔ**Thanda Main Lodge.** There's a palpable feeling of earth energy in this
☾ magical and exquisite lodge that blends elements of royal Zulu with
★ an eclectic pan-African feel. Beautiful domed, beehive-shaped dwellings perch on the side of rolling hills and overlook mountains and bushveld. Inside, contemporary Scandinavian touches meet African chic—from the "eyelashes" of slatted poles that peep out from under the thatch roofs to the embedded mosaics in royal Zulu red and blue that decorate the polished, honey-color stone floors. Creative light fixtures include chandeliers made of handcrafted Zulu beads and lamps of straw or filmy cotton mesh. A huge stone fireplace divides the bedroom area from the comfortable and roomy lounge. Each chalet has a different color scheme and is decorated with beaded, hand-embroidered cushions and throws. Dip in your personal plunge pool after an exciting game drive, sunbathe on your private deck, or commune with the surrounding bushveld in your cool, cushioned *sala* (outdoor covered deck). Later, after a meal that many a fine restaurant would be proud to serve, come back to your chalet to find a bedtime story on your pillow, marshmallows waiting to be toasted over flickering candles, and a glass of Amarula cream. Or dine alone in your private boma by the light of the stars and the leaping flames of a fragrant wood fire. The spacious, uncluttered public areas—dining decks, bomas, library, and lounge—are decorated in restful earth tones accented by royal Zulu colors, beads from Malawi, Ghanaian ceremonial masks, and Indonesian chairs. ⌑*9 chalets* ⌂*In-room: a/c. In-hotel: bar, pool, spa, children's programs (ages 5–15).*

$ 　ᵔ**Thanda Tented Camp.** Perfect for a family or friends' reunion, this
☾ intimate camp deep in the bush brings you into close contact with your surroundings. You might wake up in your spacious safari tent with en-suite bathroom and private veranda to find a warthog or nyala grazing outside. The camp has its own vehicle, ranger, and tracker, and a huge sala with pool and sundeck. ⌑*4 tents* ⌂*In-hotel: bar, pool, spa, children's programs (ages 5–15).*

5

Hilltop Camp, Hluhluwe Game Reserve,

Impala Camp, Hluhluwe Game Reserve

Interior of Chalet, Hilltop Camp, Hluhluwe GR

Left: Rock Lodge; Right: Phinda Zuku Lodge, Phinda Private Game Reserve

Mountain Lodge, Phinda Private Game Reserve

Top: Vlei Lodge; Bottom; Forest Lodge

KGALAGADI TRANSFRONTIER PARK

Game
☆★★★★

Park Accessibility
☆☆★★★

Ease of Getting
Around
★★★★★

Accommodations
☆★★★★

Scenic Beauty
★★★★★

If you're looking for true wilderness, remoteness, and stark, almost surreal landscapes and you're not adverse to forgoing the ultimate in luxury and getting sand in your hair, then this amazing, uniquely beautiful park within the Kalahari Desert is for you.

In an odd little finger of the country jutting north between Botswana in the east and Namibia in the west lies South Africa's second-largest park after Kruger. Kgalagadi was officially launched in 2000 as the first transfrontier, or "Peace Park," in southern Africa by merging South Africa's vast Kalahari Gemsbok National Park with the even larger Gemsbok National Park in Botswana. The name Kgalagadi (pronounced kala-hardy) is derived from the San language and means "place of thirst." It is now one of the largest protected wilderness areas in the world—an area of more than 38,000 square km (14,670 square mi). Of this awesome area, 9,600 square km (3,700 square mi) fall in South Africa, and the rest in Botswana. Passing through the Twee Rivieren Gate, you will encounter a vast desert under enormous, usually cloudless skies and a sense of space and openness that few other places can offer.

The Kgalagadi Transfrontier is less commercialized and developed than Kruger. The roads aren't paved, and you will come across far fewer people and cars. There is less game on the whole than in Kruger, but because there is also less vegetation, the animals are much more visible. Also, because the game and large carnivores are concentrated in two riverbeds (the route that two roads follow), the park offers unsurpassed viewing and photographic opportunities. Perhaps the key to really appreciating this barren place is in understanding how its creatures have adapted to their harsh surroundings to survive—like the gemsbok, which has a sophisticated cooling system allowing it to tolerate extreme changes in body temperature. There are also insects in the park that inhale only every half hour or so to preserve the moisture that breathing expends.

5

The landscape—endless dunes punctuated with blond grass and the odd thorn tree—is dominated by two dry riverbeds: the Nossob (which forms the border between South Africa and Botswana) and its tributary, the Auob. The Nossob flows only a few times a century, and the Auob flows only once every couple of decades or so. A single road runs beside each riverbed, along which windmills pump water into man-made water holes, which help the animals to survive and provide good viewing stations for visitors. There are 82 water holes, 49 of which are along tourist roads. Park management struggles to keep up their maintenance; it's a constant battle against the ele-

> **PARK ESSENTIALS**
>
> You can buy Styrofoam coolers at Pick 'n Pay in Upington (or at any large town en route to the park) and then leave them behind for the camp staff when you exit the park. Pack ice and frozen juice boxes to keep your perishables chilled between camps. Ziplock bags are indispensable for keeping dust out of food (and for storing damp washcloths and swimsuits). You're not allowed out of your vehicle between camps, so keep your snacks and drinks handy inside the passenger area and not in the trunk.

ments, with the elements often winning. Similarly, the park constantly maintains and improves tourist roads, but again it's a constant battle. A third road traverses the park's interior to join the other two. The scenery and vegetation on this road change dramatically from the two river valleys, which are dominated by sandy banks, to a grassier escarpment. Two more dune roads have been added, and several 4x4 routes have been developed. From Nossob camp a road leads to Union's End, the country's northernmost tip, where South Africa, Namibia, and Botswana meet. Allow a full day for the long and dusty drive, which is 124 km (77 mi) one-way. It is possible to enter Botswana from the South African side, but you'll need a 4x4. The park infrastructure in Botswana is very basic, with just three campsites and mostly 4x4 terrain.

The park is famous for its gemsbok and its legendary, huge, black-maned Kalahari lions. It also has leopard, cheetah, eland, blue wildebeest, and giraffe, as well as meerkats and mongooses. Rarer desert species, such as the desert-adapted springbok, the elusive aardvark, and the pretty Cape fox, also make their home here. Among birders, the park is known as one of Africa's raptor meccas; it's filled with bateleurs, lappet-faced vultures, pygmy falcons, and the cooperatively hunting red-necked falcons and gabar goshawks.

The park can be superhot in summer and freezing at night in winter (literally below zero, with frost on the ground). Autumn—from late February to mid-April—is perhaps the best time to visit. It's cool after the rains, and many of the migratory birds are still around. The winter months of June and July are also a good time. It's best to make reservations as far in advance as possible, even up to a year or more if you want to visit at Easter or in June or July, when there are school vacations.

The park's legendary night drives (R110) depart most evenings about 5:30 in summer, earlier in winter (check when you get your camp), from Twee Rivieren Camp, Mata Mata, and Nossob. The drives set out just as the park gate closes to everyone else. You'll have a chance to see rare nocturnal animals like the brown hyena and the bat-eared fox by spotlight. The guided morning walks—during which you see the sun rise over the Kalahari and could bump into a lion—are also a must. Reservations are essential and can be made when you book your accommodations.

PARK ESSENTIALS

Winter or summer, bring a range of suitable clothing: shorts, T-shirts, and sunhats for the day, warm clothes for night. If you're going on a night drive (which is a must), then you'll need to wrap up with hats, scarves, coats, and blankets. You can boil and use park water for all cooking, but as it tastes very brackish (it has a high salt and mineral content), it's best to bring your own drinking water. You can fill up at the gateway town of Upington, or buy water from the camp shops.

Kgalagadi Transfontier National Park is approximately 250 km (155 mi) north of Upington in the far northern Cape and 904 km (560 mi) west of Johannesburg. If you drive from Johannesburg you have a choice of two routes: either via Upington (with the last stretch a 60-km [37-mi] gravel road) or via Kuruman, Hotazel, and Vanzylrus (with about 340 km [211 mi] of gravel road). The gravel sections on both routes are badly corrugated, so don't speed.

Upington airport is the nearest airport to the park and has car-rental facilities. It's also possible to reserve a rental car through an agency in Upington and then pick up the car from the Twee Rivieren camp. Under normal circumstances (no excessive rain, for example), a passenger car will be fine in Kgalagadi (except on the 4x4 routes). However, a 4x4 will give you greater access in the park, and as you sit higher up, better game-viewing.

There is a daily conservation fee, but Wild Cards, available at the gates or online, are more economical for stays of more than a few days. Reservations for all accommodations, bush drives, wilderness trails, and other park activities must be made through **South African National Parks** (⌂ *Box 787, Pretoria 0001* ☎ *012/426–5000 Pretoria, 021/552–0008 Cape Town* ⊕ *www.sanparks.org*). Don't forget to take antimalarial drugs and use a mosquito repellent, especially during the summer. ✉ *Park reception at Twee Rivieren rest camp* ☎ *054/561–2000.*

WHERE TO STAY

LUXURY LODGING

¢ 🖼 **!Xaus Lodge.** If you want to experience one of South Africa's most
FodorśChoice beautiful and isolated parks without hassle, then this luxury lodge
★ owned by the Khomani San and Mier communities and jointly managed with SANParks is the place for you. You'll be picked up in a 4x4 from Twee Rivieren, fed, watered, taken on game drives and desert

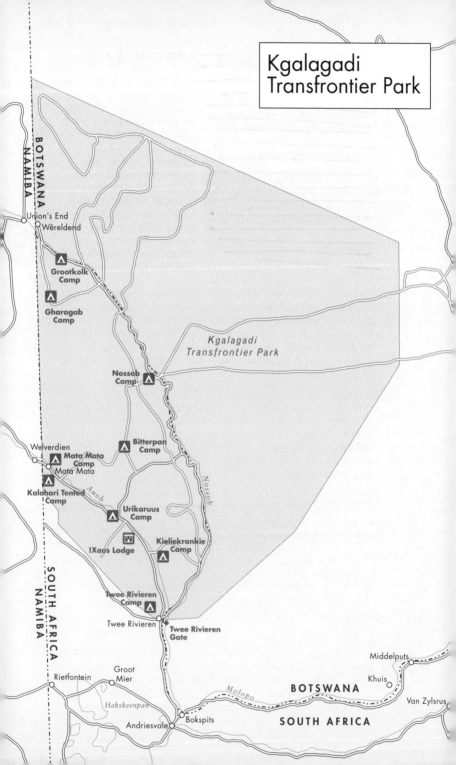

San Culture & Language

Also called the /Xam, the hunter-gatherer San (Bushmen) have a culture that dates back more than 20,000 years, and their genetic origins are more than 1 million years old, contemporary humans' oldest. Fast-forward a few years—about 2,000 years ago, to be inexact—when Korana or Khoi (Khoe) herders migrated south, bringing their livestock and settling along the Orange (Gariep/Garieb), Vaal, and Riet rivers. During the 18th and 19th centuries the Griquas—thought to be part Khoi and part slave—moved into the Northern Cape with their cattle and sheep.

At one time 20–30 languages pertaining to various clans flourished, but colonialism brought with it devastating results for the San's native tongue.

It lost out to Tswana and Afrikaans. In the nick of time in the 1870s, British doctor Wilhelm Bleek (who spoke /Xam) and Lucy Lloyd recorded the last activities of /Xam culture and tradition. (Some of these records can be found at the McGregor Museum in Kimberley.)

Still thousands of Northern Cape residents today acknowledge an ancestral connection to the largest San or /Xam group of the 18th and 19th centuries. The two biggest remaining groups are the !Xu and Khwe, who live at Schmidtsdrift, 80 km (50 mi) from Kimberley. Among the best-known groups in South Africa today are the Khomani San, some of whom still speak the ancient Nu.

5

walks, and introduced to the local San. Located deep in the desert 32 km (20 mi) from the Auob River road along a track that crosses the red dunes of the Kalahari, this enchanting lodge overlooks an amazingly scenic pan. The twin-bed en-suite chalets perch on sand dunes overlooking a water hole; each chalet has a private deck. A fan will keep you cool in summer, and a gas heater, hot-water bottle, and warm sheets will help you stay warm winter nights. A welcome swimming pool is set in a deck overlooking the pan. The attractive rustic furniture and eye-catching artwork throughout this delightful, unique lodge are all made by local craftspeople and artists. Activities include game drives in an open safari vehicle, walks with San trackers, and a chance to watch San artists at work. At night the stars and planets are bright and clear; a telescope brings ancient tradition and modern technology together as the San interpret for you their legends of the night sky. But !Xaus (pronounced kaus) comprises so much more than its activities: it is solitude, peace, and silence as you "listen" to day turn into night, plus interaction with the cheerful and willing staff, the majority of whom come from the surrounding local communities. Negotiations are ongoing to establish a private airstrip nearby. ⌂ *Box 30919, Tokai, Cape Town 7966* ☎ *021/701–7860* ⊕ *www.xauslodge.co.za* ⇔ *24 chalets* ⌂ *In-room: fan. In-hotel: restaurant, bar, pool* ⊟ *AE, DC, MC, V* ⊙ *FAP.*

NATIONAL PARK ACCOMMODATIONS

Accommodations within the park are in three traditional rest camps and several highly sought-after wilderness camps (try to reserve these if possible), which are spread around the park. All of the traditional rest camps have shops selling food, curios, and some basic equipment, but Twee Rivieren has the best variety of fresh fruit, vegetables, milk, and meat, and is the only camp with a restaurant. Twee Rivieren is also the only camp with telephone and cell-phone reception (although cell-phone reception quickly disappears as you head into the dunes) and 24-hour electricity; the other camps have gas and electricity, but the electricity runs only part of the day, at different times in each camp.

For all national park accommodations, contact **South African National Parks,** or you can reserve directly through the park (☎054/561–2000) if you happen to be there and would like to stay a night or add another night onto your stay. *✉ Box 787, Pretoria 0001 ☎012/426–5000 Pretoria, 021/552–0008 Cape Town ⊕www.sanparks.org ▭AE, DC, MC, V.*

REST CAMPS

¢ ▦**Mata Mata.** This camp, 120 km (74 mi) from Twee Rivieren on the Namibian border, has good game-viewing due to the proximity of the water holes. The camp's facilities are not as modern as those at Twee Rivieren, although there is a small shop stocking basics. *◄2 6-person cottages, 3 4-person cottages, 1 5-person mobile home, 2 3-person mobile homes ⌂In-room: kitchen.*

¢ ▦**Nossob.** In the central section of the park, this camp is on the Botswana border, 166 km (103 mi) from Twee Rivieren. Basic brick chalets come with an outside braai and real bush atmosphere and sleep from three to six people. Guesthouses have showers but no tubs. Most of the chalets are less than 50 yards from the fence, and there's also a stunning blind overlooking the water hole. You can see game without even leaving camp, but watch out for marauding jackals here; although they're not dangerous or aggressive, they're always on the lookout for unattended food. A small shop sells the basics. There's no electricity in the camp, and the generators are turned off at 11. *◄15 chalets, 1 cottage, 2 guesthouses ⌂In-room: kitchen.*

¢ ▦**Twee Rivieren.** On the Kgalagadi's southern boundary, this camp is home to the park's headquarters. It's the biggest of the camps and has the most modern facilities; all units have fully equipped kitchens, and the camp shop here is the best. You can choose among a couple of types of accommodations, from a two-bedroom, six-bed family cottage to

Bitterpan Lodge, Kgalagadi

a bungalow with two single beds and a sleeper couch. Try for units 1–16, which look out over the dunes. Take a guided morning walk *and* a night drive—worth every penny. There are educational exhibits on the Kalahari's animal and plant life. From Upington to Twee Rivieren is 260 km (161 mi) on a relatively good road; only the last 52 km (32 mi) is gravel. ⮕*1 cottage, 30 bungalows* ⌂*In-room: kitchen, no TV. In-hotel: restaurant, bar, pool.*

CAMPING   There's a limited number of campsites (R110) at Mata Mata (20), Nossob (20), and Twee Rivieren (24). All campsites have a braai and access to electricity and water, and there are communal bathroom facilities and a basic communal kitchen. Before you arrive, be sure to arm yourself with the "blue camping plug"—available from any camping–caravanning shop—and a long extension cord. Try to find a shady spot.

WILDERNESS   Kgalagadi is the first national park to provide accommodation deep
CAMPS   in the wilderness, where several unfenced wilderness camps with their own water holes for game-viewing put you deep in the heart of the Kalahari. These enchanting camps are very popular, so make your reservations well in advance—a year ahead, if possible. Each camp is slightly different, but all have the same facilities and are similarly priced. All have an equipped kitchen with a gas-powered refrigerator, solar-powered lights, gas for hot water, and a deck with braai facilities. You do need to supply your own water and firewood.

As all of these camps are unfenced (which is part of their desirability and charm), you should *never* walk outside your accommodation at night—you don't want to come face-to-face with a hungry lion or scavenging hyena!

¢   ⛺**Bitterpan.** This camp overlooks an enormous expanse of sand and a water hole, where you can watch game come and go from your deck or from the communal areas. Four double cabins with their own bathrooms border a narrow walkway that leads to a large communal kitchen, dining room, and braai area. Bitterpan is accessible only by 4x4, and only guests here may use the road from Nossob to Urikaruus. ⮕*4 cabins.*

¢   ⛺**Gharagab.** Although you'll need a 4x4 to negotiate the two-track road to Gharagab, it's worth every dusty mile for the chance to feel like you're the only person on earth. Situated in the far northern region of the park close to the Namibian border, this camp provides stunning elevated views of Kalahari dunes and the thornveld savanna. Although the game isn't as abundant as in the Grootkolk area, you're likely to have unusual or even rare sightings, such as a honey badger, eland, or an aardvark, and the feeling of splendid isolation is unforgettable. You may never again feel this alone. Each long tent built on wooden stilts has a kitchen, bedroom, and bathroom, plus a wooden deck (with a braii) overlooking a water hole. ⮕*4 cabins* ⌂*In-room: kitchen.*

¢   ⛺**Grootkolk.** Surrounded by camelthorn trees and close to the Nossob River bed, this lovely camp has good game-viewing, with lions, cheetahs, hyenas, and lots of antelope, including oryx and springbok. All four well-sited rustic desert cabins have a good view of the water hole, which is spotlighted for a couple of hours every night. Although the road to Grootkolk is heavily corrugated, you can negotiate it with a two-wheel-drive vehicle. ↪ *4 cabins* ♿ *In-room: kitchen.*

¢ ⛺**Kalahari Tent Camp.** Many visitors say that this good game-viewing camp overlooking the Auob River bed and water hole is one of the most beautiful places in the park, so try to stay for more than one night. Your accommodation consists of a large walk-in tent with a spacious and attractive bedroom, shower, and toilet. There's a separate, fully equipped kitchen tent, also suitable as a dining room, and the terrace between these two tents has excellent views over the riverbed and its wildlife. At night, look out for jackals, lions, a resident family of meerkats, and spare-wheel-cover-eating hyenas around the tents—just be sure to stay in your tent at night and avoid walking around. The secluded honeymoon unit has a king-size bed and a bath and shower. The camp is near the Mata Mata shop and gas station. ↪ *10 tents, 4 family tents, 1 honeymoon tent* ♿ *In-room: kitchen.*

¢ ⛺**Kieliekrankie.** Perched high on a big sand dune only 8 km (5 mi) from the game-rich Auob River road, this small camp overlooks seemingly infinite red Kalahari sands, creating an amazing sense of space and isolation. To be among the red dunes at full moon is an unforgettable experience. The four cabins have stunning views over the desert and come with a kitchen tent, bedroom, bathroom, and deck and braai. A huge bonus is that you can start your game drives before residents of the other camps reach this area, so you get the animals to yourself for a time. Situated in the Twee Rivieren region, the camp can be easily reached with a two-wheel-drive vehicle. ↪ *4 cabins* ♿ *In-room: kitchen.*

¢ ⛺**Urikaruus.** Four cabins with kitchens, bedrooms, and bathrooms are built on stilts among camelthorn trees overlooking the Auob River. You'll easily spot game as it comes to drink at the water hole close to the cabins, plus you'll have the surrounding area all to yourself on early-morning and late-afternoon game drives. On-site wardens will help you interpret the spoor you find around your cabin. Set in the Mata Mata region, Urikaruus is accessible by two-wheel-drive vehicles. ↪ *4 cabins* ♿ *In-room: kitchen.*

IF YOU HAVE TIME

We've given you detailed information on the must-see parks and private reserves of South Africa. If you've got extra time to spare, here are a few more worth exploring.

TSWALU KALAHARI RESERVE

Near the Kgalagadi Transfrontier Park is the malaria-free Tswalu, which at 900 square km (347 square mi) is the biggest privately owned game reserve in Africa; it's the perfect place to photograph a gemsbok against a red dune and an azure sky. Initially founded as a conservation project by the late millionaire Stephen Boler primarily to protect and breed the endangered desert rhino, it's now owned by the Oppenheimer family. Today it spreads over endless Kalahari dunes covered with tufts of golden veld and over much of the Northern Cape's Korannaberg mountain range. Its initial population of 7,000 animals has grown to more than 12,000, and it's now home to lions, cheetahs, buffalo, giraffes, and many species of antelope. It's the best place in Africa to see rhino—the reserve has more than 50 white and 20 black rhinos, which have amazingly adapted to living in the desert. Other rare species include roan and sable antelope, black wildebeest, and mountain zebra. There's not so much game as in some of Mpumalanga's private reserves because the land has a lower carrying capacity (the annual rainfall is only about 9¾ inches). But when you do see the animals, the lack of vegetation makes sightings spectacular. And the fact that only about three open-sided game vehicles traverse an area two-thirds the size of the entire Sabi Sands makes your escape all the more complete.

This is one of the most child-friendly game reserves in Southern Africa. Children are welcomed and well catered for, with lots of freedom and special activities.

WHERE TO STAY

Tswalu. The emphasis at Tswalu is on exclusivity, which is why the entire reserve can accommodate no more than 30 people at a time. Nothing is left wanting at this exclusive Relais & Châteaux property. Children 12 and under stay free with adults, and there are discounted rates for older kids. Road transfers from Kimberley or Upington can be arranged, or you can book a charter flight from Johannesburg. ⬤ *Box 1081, Kuruman 8460* ☎ *086/187-9258* ⊕ *www.tswalu.com* ▤ *AE, DC, MC, V* ⦿ *FAP.*

FLORA SAFARIS

There are some fascinating plant-viewing safaris in national parks you could try if you have the time. On a plant safari in Ai-Ais/Richtersveld Transfrontier Park you'll encounter some of the world's rarest and strangest plants. In August and September Namaqua National Park hosts one of the largest natural displays of wildflowers in full bloom anywhere in the world—a good time for a plant-viewing safari. Contact **South African National Parks** ⬤ *Box 787, Pretoria 0001* ☎ *012/343-1991* ⊕ *www.sanparks.org* for more details on these three- to five-day specialty safaris.

LUXURY LODGES

$$$$ ⛺ **Tarkuni.** In a private section of Tswalu, Tarkuni is an exclusive, self-
☺ contained house decorated similarly to Motswe and offering a comparable level of luxury. Perfect for small groups and families, Tarkuni
sleeps eight and comes with its own chef, game vehicle, and tracker.
The food almost matches the scenery in memorability, and every meal
is served in a different location: on a lantern-lighted dune or alongside
a crackling fire in the lodge's boma. Apart from guided walks and
drives, horseback trails (not included in the rate) that you traverse with
a qualified guide offer close encounters with wildlife. Two sets of bunk
beds, plus an adjoining nanny's quarters, are geared toward children.
↪*1 house* ☺*In-hotel: a/c, bar, restaurant, pool.*

$ ⛺ **Motswe.** Motswe, the Tswana word for village, is Tswalu's main
☺ lodge, made up of freestanding thatch-and-stone suites clustered
around a large main building with a heated natural-color pool and
a floodlighted water hole. The decor—in keeping with the unusual
and unique Tswalu experience—is minimalist and modern, echoing the
landscape in colors and textures. There's a special children's room, and
babysitting services and nannies are available. ↪*9 suites* ☺*In-hotel:*
a/c, bar, restaurant, pool, spa.

PILANESBERG NATIONAL PARK

This 150,000-acre park 150 km (93 mi) northwest of Johannesburg is
centered on the caldera of an extinct volcano dating back 1.3 billion
years that may well have once been Africa's highest peak. Concentric
rings of mountains surround a lake filled with crocodiles and hippos.
Open grassland, rocky crags, and densely forested gorges provide ideal
habitats for a wide range of plains and woodland game, including rare
brown hyenas, sables, and gemsbok. Since the introduction of lions
in 1993, Pilanesberg (pronounced pee-luns-berg) can boast the Big
Five—lions, elephants, rhinos, leopards, and buffalo. It's one of the
best places in the country to see rhinos; it's also ideal for bird-watching, thanks to its numerous grassland species, waterbirds, and birds of
prey. A huge plus is that the reserve is in a malaria-free area, unlike
many of the reserves in Mpumalanga. You can drive around the park
in your own vehicle or join guided safaris with Pilanesberg Mankwe
Safaris. The entertainment and resort complex of Sun City is nearby.
☎*014/555–5354 or 014/555–5357* ⊕*www.pilanesberg-game-reserve.*
co.za ☜*R16 per vehicle, R20 per person* ☉*Mar., Apr., Sept., and*
Oct., daily 6 AM*–6:30* PM*; May–Aug., daily 6:30–6; Nov.–Feb., daily*
5:30 AM*–7* PM*.*

WHERE TO STAY

LUXURY LODGES

$$ ⛺ **Tshukudu Game Lodge.** The most stylish option in the area, Tshukudu
★ is built into the side of a steep, rocky hill and overlooks open grass-
land and a large water hole where elephants bathe. If you watch long
enough, you can probably see most of the Big Five from your veranda.
Winding stone stairways lead up the hill to thatch cottages with private
balconies, wicker furniture, African materials, and black-slate floors.

Fireplaces and mosquito nets are standard, and sunken bathtubs have spectacular views of the water hole. It's a long, 132-step climb to the main lodge on the summit, making this an impractical choice for those with mobility problems. At night you can use a spotlight to illuminate game at the water hole below. ⊠ *Pilanesberg National Park, Box 6805, Rustenburg 0300* 🕾 *014/552–6255 lodge, 011/806–6888 reservations* ⊕ *www.legacyhotels.co.za* 🛏 *6 cottages* ♿ *In-hotel: restaurant, pool, no elevator* ▤ *AE, DC, MC, V.*

$ 🏨 **Kwa Maritane.** The greatest asset of this hotel, primarily a time-
☾ share resort, is its location: in a bowl of rocky hills on the edge of
★ the national park. The resort has a terrific blind overlooking a water hole and connected to the lodge via a tunnel; from your hotel room you can watch a TV channel dedicated to filming what's there round-the-clock. Guest rooms have high thatch ceilings and large glass doors that open onto a veranda. It's best to secure a unit far from the noise of the reception, dining, and pool areas. You can pay to go on day or night game drives in open-air vehicles or to go on guided walks with an armed ranger—both worthwhile. The breakfasts at the restaurant are legendary. ⊠ *Pilanesberg National Park* ☏ *Box 39, Sun City 0316* 🕾 *014/552–5100 hotel, 011/806–6888 reservations* ⊕ *www.legacyho-tels.co.za* 🛏 *90 rooms* ♿ *In-room: a/c, kitchen. In-hotel: restaurant, bar, pools, no elevator* ▤ *AE, DC, MC, V* ❘◎❘ *BP.*

¢–$ 🏨 **Bakubung.** Abutting the national park, this lodge sits at the head of a long valley with terrific views of a hippo pool that forms the lodge's central attraction—it's not unusual to have hippos grazing 100 feet from the terrace restaurant. Despite this, the lodge never really succeeds in creating a bush feel, perhaps because it's such a big convention and family destination. Its brick buildings feel vaguely institutional. Nevertheless, the guest rooms, particularly the executive studios, are very pleasant, thanks to light pine furniture, colorful African bedspreads, and super views of the valley. The lodge conducts game drives in open-air vehicles, as well as ranger-guided walks. A shuttle bus (R40 round-trip) runs to Sun City, 10 km (6 mi) away. ⊠ *Bakubung Gate, Pilanesberg National Park* ☏ *Box 294, Sun City 0316* 🕾 *014/552–6000 lodge, 011/806–6800 reservations* ⊕ *www.legacyhotels.co.za* 🛏 *76 rooms, 56 time-share chalets* ♿ *In-room: a/c. In-hotel: restaurant, bar, tennis court, pool, no elevator* ▤ *AE, DC, MC, V* ❘◎❘ *BP.*

BUDGET LODGING

¢ 🏨 **Manyane.** This resort is in a thinly wooded savanna east of Pilanes-berg's volcanic ridges. Offering affordable accommodations in the Sun City area, Manyane is simple but well located, efficiently run, and clean. Thatch roofing helps soften the harsh lines of bare tile floors and brick. You can choose from a two- or four-bed chalet with a small, fully equipped kitchen and bathroom; the camping facilities are also very popular. Self-guided nature trails lead from the chalets, providing interesting background on the geology and flora of the park. You can also take advantage of the outdoor chess and trampoline. ⊠ *Pilanes-berg National Park, Rustenburg 0300* 🕾 *014/555–1000* ⊕ *www.gold-enleopard.co.za* 🛏 *30 4-bed chalets, 15 2-bed chalets* ♿ *In-room: a/c, kitchen. In-hotel: restaurant, bar, pools* ▤ *AE, DC, MC, V.*

CLOSE UP

San Paintings

Besides the hiking opportunities and the sheer beauty of the mountains, the other great attraction of the Berg is the San (Bushman) paintings. The San are a hunter-gatherer people who once roamed the entire country from 8,000 years ago to the 1800s. With the arrival of the Nguni peoples from the north and white settlers from the southwest in the 18th century, the San were driven out of their traditional hunting lands and retreated into the remote fastnesses of the Drakensberg and the Kalahari Desert. San cattle raiding in Natal in the late 19th century occasioned harsh punitive expeditions by white settlers and local Bantu tribes, and by 1880 the last San had disappeared from the Berg. Today only a few clans remain in the very heart of the Kalahari Desert. More than 40,000 of their paintings are sprinkled in scores of caves and on rock overhangs throughout the Berg in more than 550 known San rock-art sites—probably the finest collection of rock paintings in the country. They tell the stories of bygone hunts, dances, and battles as well as relating and representing spiritual beliefs and practices. Images of spiritual leaders in a trance state, their visions, and their transformation of themselves into animals have now been studied and written about, although some of the meanings are still not fully understood. For more information on viewing rock-art sites, contact **Ezemvelo KZN Wildlife** (☎ *033/845–1999* ⊕ *www.kznwildlife. com*), the province's official conservation organization.

5

UKHAHLAMBA/DRAKENSBERG PARK

Although you don't come here for big game, or much game at all, it's well worth visiting this World Heritage site, the first in South Africa to be recognized for both its natural and cultural attractions, with some of the finest rock art in the world.

Afrikaners call them the Drakensberg: the Dragon Mountains. To Zulus they are uKhahlamba (pronounced Ooka-hlamba)—"Barrier of Spears." Both are apt descriptions for this wall of rock that rises from the Natal grasslands, forming a natural fortress protecting the mountain kingdom of Lesotho. The Drakensberg is the highest range in southern Africa and has some of the most spectacular scenery in the country. The blue-tinted mountains seem to infuse the landscape, cooling the "champagne air"—as the locals refer to the heady, sparkling breezes that blow around the precipices and pinnacles. It's a hiker's dream, and you could easily spend several days here just soaking up the awesome views.

The Drakensberg is not a typical mountain range—it's actually an escarpment separating a high interior plateau from the coastal lowlands of Natal. It's a continuation of the same escarpment that divides the Transvaal Highveld from the hot malarial zones of the lowveld in Mpumalanga. However, the Natal Drakensberg, or Berg, as it is commonly known, is far wilder and more spectacular than its Transvaal counterpart. Many of the peaks—some of which top 10,000 feet—are the source of crystalline streams and mighty rivers that have carved out myriad valleys and dramatic gorges. The Berg is a natural watershed, with two of South Africa's major rivers, the Tugela and the Orange, rising from these mountains. In this untamed wilderness you can hike for days and not meet a soul, and the mountains retain a wild majesty missing in the commercially forested peaks of Mpumalanga.

If possible plan your visit to the Berg during the spring (September and October) and late autumn (late April–June), because although summer sees the Berg at its greenest, it's also the hottest and wettest time of the year. Vicious afternoon thunderstorms and hailstorms are an almost-daily occurrence. In winter the mountains lose their lush overcoat and turn brown and sere. Winter days in the valleys, sites of most resorts, are usually sunny and pleasant, although there can be cold snaps, sometimes accompanied by overcast, windy conditions. Nights are chilly, however, and you should pack plenty of warm clothing if you plan to hike high up into the mountains or camp overnight. Snow is common at higher elevations.

> ## PARK ESSENTIALS
>
> The Natal Drakensberg is not conducive to traditional touring because of the nature of the attractions and the limited road system. It's best to check into a hotel or resort for two or three days and use it as a base for hiking and exploring the immediate area. If you decide to stay at one of the self-catering camps, it's best to do your shopping in one of the bigger towns, such as Winterton or Harrismith for Tendele, and Bergville or Estcourt for Giant's Castle, Kamberg, and Injasuti. For more information on touring the area, visit the Drakensberg Tourism Association Web site (⊕ *www.drakensberg.org.za*).

WHERE TO STAY

LUXURY LODGES

$ 　**Cleopatra Mountain Farmhouse.** It would be difficult to find better lodging or dining anywhere in Southern Africa than at this enchanting hideaway tucked away at the foot of the Drakensberg Range. The lodge overlooks a trout-filled lake and is encircled by mountains and old trees. Richard and Mouse Poynton, legendary South African chefs and hosts, have renovated the 1936 family fishing farm and created a perfect combination of comfort, tranquillity, style, and exceptional food. Homemade biscuits, hand-painted and stenciled walls, lovingly embroidered cushions and samplers, fluffy mohair blankets, and heated towel racks are just a few of the details you'll find here. Don't even mention the word diet in a place where rich, natural, superb food rules the day. You'll eat truly sumptuous meals with ceremony but no pretension in an intimate dining room warmed on cold days by a blazing log fire. ⌖*Box 17, Balgowan 3275* ☎*033/267–7243* ⊕*www.cleomountain.com* ⇒*6 rooms, 3 suites* ⊟*AE, DC, MC, V* ⏀*MAP*.

FodorśChoice ★

BUDGET LODGING

¢ 　**Cathedral Peak Hotel.** You'll get breathtaking views from almost every spot in this friendly, delightful hotel nestled among the mountains. Ideal for families, the resort has something for everyone: you can amble along a horse trail, go mountain biking, follow bird-watching trails, play a round of golf, or just soak up the heady mountain air. Accommodations run from basic singles to slightly bigger family units and various suites. Best for families is a deluxe suite with adjacent rooms and connecting door. You'll get excellent value here; prices include breakfast and hearty dinner buffets as well as most activities. And whether you're mildly active or a seasoned mountain hiker or climber, trained and experienced guides take you on daily walks and trails through the Berg. There's a children's dining room, plus babysitting service. ⊠ *Cathedral Peak Rd., 43 km (18 mi) from Winterton 3340* ☎ *036/488–1888 or 036/488–1889* ⊕ *www.cathedralpeak.co.za* ⟿ *96 rooms* ⚲ *In-hotel: restaurant, room service, bars, golf course, tennis courts, pool, gym, spa* ⊟ *AE, DC, MC, V* ⫿⊙⫿*MAP.*

¢ 🛏 **Tendele Hutted Camp.** In a truly spectacular setting smack in the middle of Royal Natal National Park, which contains some of the most stunning mountain scenery in the Drakensberg, this very popular camp makes a great base for long hikes into the mountains. Accommodations are in a variety of bungalows, cottages, and chalets, each with excellent views of the Amphitheatre, a sheer rock wall measuring 5 km (3 mi) across and more than 1,500 feet high. You must bring all your own food, although you can purchase staples and frozen meat at the main visitor center. In the bungalows and cottages all food is prepared by camp staff, but you can do your own cooking in the chalets. There is one lodge, which accommodates six people. ⓓ *KwaZulu-Natal Nature Conservation Service, Box 13069, Cascades 3202* ☎ *033/845–1000* ⟿ *26 chalets, 2 cottages, 1 lodge* ⚲ *In-room: kitchen (some)* ⊟ *AE, DC, MC, V.*

ADDO ELEPHANT PARK

Smack in the middle of a citrus-growing and horse-breeding area 72 km (45 mi) north of Port Elizabeth, this lovely little park is home to 450 elephants, 400 buffalo, 48 black rhino, hundreds of kudu and other antelopes, and six lions. At present the park has about 300,000 acres, but it's expanding all the time and is intended to reach a total of about 890,000 acres. But Addo is a work in progress: not all of the land is contiguous, and parts of the land are not properly fenced in yet. The four most accessible parts of the park are the original, main section and the Colchester, Nyati, and Zuurberg sections. The original section of Addo still holds most of the game, and is served by Addo Main and Gorah camps. The Colchester section, in the south, which has one SANParks camp, is contiguous with the main area but is not properly fenced yet so there's not much game there. The scenic Nyati section is separated from the main section by a road and railway line (which will eventually be covered by huge land bridges); there are two luxury lodges in the Nyati section, and the game-viewing is excellent. Just north of Nyati is the mountainous Zuurberg section, which does not have great game but is particularly scenic, with fabulous hiking trails and horse trails. It is also the closest section of the park to Addo Elephant Back Safaris.

You can explore the park in your own vehicle, in which case you need to heed the road signs that claim DUNG BEETLES HAVE RIGHT OF WAY...seriously. Addo is home to the almost-endemic and extremely rare flightless dung beetle, which can often be seen rolling its unusual incubator across the roads. Instead of driving you could take a night or day game drive with a park ranger in an open vehicle from the main camp. A more adventurous option is to ride a horse among the elephants. Less-experienced riders may ride along the fence line. Warning: no citrus fruit may be brought into the park, as elephants find it irresistible and can smell it for miles. ☎*042/233–0556* 🌐*www.addoelephantpark.com* *R80* ⏲*Daily 7–7 (may vary with seasons).*

WORD OF MOUTH

"The green and wildflower-strewn scene at Addo Elephant Park came as a shock. Seeing elephants in fields of daisies is quite a ways from seeing them dining on dry twigs and tree roots. We seriously enjoyed Addo and would strongly suggest it as a low-energy and quite easy introduction into game viewing and reserves."

–Gardyloo

★ **Addo Elephant Back Safaris** lets you get up close and personal with a small group of trained African elephants. You get to do a short elephant ride and then go for a scenic walk through the bush with them. You can touch them, feed them, and watch them as they bathe themselves with sand, water, or both (i.e., mud). The whole experience lasts about 2½ hours. You can also arrange for a fly-in day trip from Port Elizabeth. ☎*042/235–1400 or 083/283–2359* 🌐*www.addoelephantbacksafaris.co.za* *R650* ⏲*Visits by appointment.*

WHERE TO STAY

LUXURY LODGES

$$$ ★ **Gorah Elephant Camp.** A private concession within the main section of Addo, this lodge centers on an old farmhouse that has been restored and filled with antiques. Roaring log fires warm chilly winter nights, and the wide veranda provides cool shade in the heat of the day. The lodge overlooks a water hole where various animals come to drink, the stars of which are the elephants. Accommodations are in huge tents with private baths, shaded under thick thatch. Mosquito nets are more for effect than necessity, as this is a malaria-free area. Keep in mind that although this is a luxury lodge, there is no electricity, so you won't find hair dryers in the rooms. Meals are taken alfresco on the veranda or in the dining room. Cuisine and service are equal to the best in Africa. The lodge operates three game drives per day and/or escorted walks. ✉*Addo Elephant National Park* *Box 454, Plettenberg Bay 6600* ☎*044/532–7818* 🌐*www.gorah.com* *11 tents* *In-room: safe, no TV. In-hotel: bar, pool, no elevator, laundry service, Internet, airport shuttle, no kids under 10, no-smoking rooms* *AE, DC, MC, V* *FAP.*

$$ ★ **River Bend Country Lodge.** A private concession within the Nyati section of Addo, River Bend perfectly balances the idea of a sophisticated, comfortable country house with all the facilities of a game lodge. The

spacious public rooms, filled with antiques and comfy couches, are in a beautifully renovated farmhouse and outbuildings. The guest rooms are in individual cottages dotted around the lovely gardens; each is uniquely decorated with a different color scheme. In addition to the usual game drives, you can tour the adjacent citrus farm and a small game sanctuary, where you may see animals not found in Addo—giraffes, white rhinos, blue wildebeest, nyala, and impala. ✉ *On R335, about 70 km (43 mi) north of Port Elizabeth* ☎ *042/233–8000* 🌐 *www.riverbendlodge.co.za* *8 rooms* *In-room: a/c, safe, refrigerator, DVD. In-hotel: room service, bar, pool, laundry service, Internet, airport shuttle, no-smoking rooms* 💳 *AE, DC, MC, V* 🍴 *FAP.*

¢ Fodor'sChoice ★ **Hitgeheim Country Lodge.** This lovely lodge is set on a steep cliff overlooking the Sundays River and the town of Addo. Classically decorated rooms, graced with lovely antiques, are in separate thatch buildings, all with verandas overlooking the river. The bathrooms are spacious and luxuriously appointed with large tubs and enormous shower stalls. Some rooms have indoor and outdoor showers. Birds frolic in the natural vegetation that has been allowed to grow up to the edge of the verandas, and tame buck often wander around the garden. Hitgeheim (pronounced *hitch*-ee-hime) is a working ostrich, citrus, and buffalo-breeding farm, and you can walk through the game areas to look at the buffalo, eland, sable, and other antelope. The food is fabulous, and most guests opt to stay for the six-course dinners (R220). ✉ *18 km (11 mi) from Addo Main Gate on R335, and then follow R336 to Kirkwood* *Box 95, Sunland 6115* ☎ *042/234–0778* 🌐 *www.hitgeheim-addo.co.za* *8 rooms* *In-room: a/c, no phone, refrigerator, no TV. In-hotel: bar, pool, laundry service, Internet, airport shuttle, no kids under 12, no-smoking rooms* 💳 *AE, DC, MC, V* 🍴 *BP.*

NATIONAL PARK ACCOMMODATION

¢ **Addo Elephant National Park Main Camp.** Typical of SANParks rest camps, this location has comfortable chalets with cooking facilities and a shop that sells basic supplies as well as souvenirs. An à la carte restaurant is open for all meals, and a floodlighted water hole is nearby. Prices are calculated according to a complicated SANParks formula, which works out to anything from R140 to R480 per person sharing. Camping ranges from R40 to R60 per person. *Box 787, Pretoria 0001* ☎ *012/428–9111* 🌐 *www.addoelephantpark.com* *53 chalets, 5 tents, 20 campsites* *In-room: a/c (some), kitchen, no TV* 💳 *AE, DC, MC, V.*

SHAMWARI GAME RESERVE

This Eastern Cape reserve is, in every sense of the word, a conservation triumph. Unprofitable farmland has been turned into a successful tourist attraction, wild animals have been reintroduced, and alien vegetation has been, and is still being, eradicated. The reserve is constantly being expanded and now stands at about 54,400 acres. Its mandate is to conserve not only the big impressive animals, but also small things: the plants, buildings, history, and culture of the area. Shamwari has been awarded the Global Nature Fund Award for Best Conservation Practice, and wildlife manager Dr. Johan Joubert was voted one of South Africa's top 10 conservationists by the Endangered Wildlife Trust. ☎041/407–1000 or 042/203–1111 ⊕www.shamwari.com.

Ⓒ   About 7,400 acres have been set aside as **Wilderness Area,** where only Fodor'sChoice escorted walking safaris are allowed. You carry all your own stuff, and ★ head off into the wilds with a ranger to sleep under the stars. A two-night, all-inclusive package is R950 per person. Part of the reserve has been set aside as the **Born Free Centres** (there's one in the northern part and one in the southern part of the reserve). Here African animals rescued from around the world are allowed to roam in reasonably large enclosures for the rest of their lives, as they cannot safely be returned to the wild. Although these are interesting tourist attractions, the main purpose is educational, and about 500 local school children tour the centers every month.

WHERE TO STAY

LUXURY LODGES

$$$ 🛏**Bayethe Tented Lodge.** Huge air-conditioned safari tents under thatch create characterful, comfortable accommodations, and private decks with plunge pools overlook the Buffalo River. One tent is wheelchair accessible. Suites, which are separated from the other rooms by the reception area and a walk of a hundred yards or so, are huge and impressive. Gleaming light-wood floors, fireplaces, and an enormous deck with the most beautiful loungers all contribute to a sense of restrained style and opulence. ⌂Box 113, Swartkops, Port Elizabeth 6210 ☎041/407–1000 ⊕www.shamwari.com ♠9 rooms, 3 suites ♿In-room: a/c, safe, refrigerator, no TV (some). In-hotel: bar, pool, laundry service, concierge, airport shuttle, no kids under 12 ▭AE, DC, MC, V ⏐◯⏐FAP.

$$$ 🛏**Eagles Cragg.** Very different from the other Shamwari options, this Fodor'sChoice sleek, modern lodge makes use of light wood, pale sandstone, and ★ stainless-steel finishes. It's light and airy and gives a sense of space. All rooms have indoor and outdoor showers and private decks with plunge pools. Glass walls fold away to bring the feel of the bush into the room. ⌂Box 113, Swartkops, Port Elizabeth 6210 ☎041/407–1000 ⊕www.shamwari.com ♠9 rooms ♿In-room: a/c, safe, refrigerator, no TV. In-hotel: bar, spa, no elevator, laundry service, concierge, airport shuttle, no kids under 16 ▭AE, DC, MC, V ⏐◯⏐FAP.

$$$ 🛏**Lobengula Lodge.** Rooms are set around a central lawn and pool ★ area but face outward for privacy. Thatch roofs and earth tones are part of the African decor. All rooms have outdoor and indoor showers and open onto a private veranda. Two rooms and the suite have private plunge pools. Meals are served around a fireplace, and you may choose wines from the extensive cellar. ⌂Box 113, Swartkops, Port Elizabeth 6210 ☎041/407–1000 ⊕www.shamwari.com ♠5 rooms, 1 suite ♿In-room: a/c, safe, refrigerator. In-hotel: bar, pool, gym, spa, laundry service, concierge, airport shuttle, no kids under 16 ▭AE, DC, MC, V ⏐◯⏐FAP.

Continued on page 330

AFRICAN MUSIC & DANCE

Talking drums echo in the forests and over the plains. The pounding of hands on taut animal-skin–covered logs is heard and interpreted by tribes' versed in jungle telegraphy. This form of dialogue is outlawed, but the art survives and modern African music is born. The beat is the essential component of the music, and by extension, of African dance.

African music and dance are all about conveying moods and emotions. They're also an integral part of ritual and ceremony. Rhythm is the key. Interlocking rhythms follow a time-honored, prescribed pattern. Drumming as a spiritual release and a team-building exercise has now become cool in Europe and the United States. African singing is easily recognized for its polyphony, where several parts, or voices, take turns producing wonderful harmonies. African choirs, like the Soweto Gospel Choir (above), are world-famous. Praise-singers are common in ceremonies where high-ranking African dignitaries are present. Dance is polycentric—different parts of the body are used independently—and conveys images of love, war, coming of age, welcome, and rites of passage.

Musicologists lament that traditional forms of indigenous music and dance are being replaced by Western genres, but fortunately, African rhythms are eternal.

THE SOUNDS OF AFRICA

When you think traditional African music, think percussion (drums and xylophones), strings (the mouth bow), and winds (horns and whistles). You should also think of trumpets, guitars, pianos, or saxophones, as these have been absorbed into African jazz.

DJEMBE DRUMS

Djembe drums, originally from Mali, come in various sizes and are copied and manufactured all over the world.

TALKING DRUMS

These drums are among the oldest instruments in Western Africa. They are typically hourglass-shaped, with goat- or lizard-skin drum heads. The two heads are joined by strings or thongs, and their sound can be manipulated. The player, who puts the drum under his shoulder and beats the drum with a stick, can also tighten or loosen the connectors to create a sound similar to speech. Messages can thus be conveyed over considerable distances.

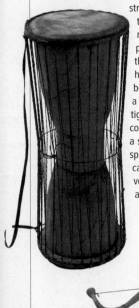

MBIRA

The *mbira*, or thumb-piano, has been played for more than 1,000 years at religious and social events. It consists of 22 to 28 metal keys or strips mounted atop a resonating box or shell.

KHOISAN MOUTH BOW
Derived from the hunting bow of the Kalahari Bushmen, the instrument dates back more than 40,000 years. You can still find them—usually as tourist souvenirs—all over the continent.

CONCERTINA
Though the concertina arrived with European settlers, it was absorbed into township music, as well as Boeremusiek (Afrikaans folk music). Present-day Afrikaans dance bands use the instrument in *sakkie-sakkie*, a style of music that accompanies sakkie, a South African dance.

MARIMBAS
Marimbas, or African xylophones, are found all over Southern and East Africa; the bigger the instrument, the deeper the sound. Originally part of the Lozi and Chopi tribal traditions in Zambia and Mozambique, they're now used in everything from pop songs to national anthems.

KUDU HORN
Made from the horn of the male greater kudu antelope, this instrument was originally used in hunting. Today you'll probably hear it only when you're called to meals at your safari lodge.

PENNYWHISTLE
The tin or pennywhistle, once used by cattle herders, is now an integral part of African music, specifically *kwela* (street music with jazz undertones).

5

IN FOCUS AFRICAN MUSIC & DANCE

MUSICIANS

Music and political activism have always gone hand in hand in South Africa. Under Apartheid, black music was ignored by music companies and radio stations, though it continued to thrive underground. American swing jazz had a huge influence on the music community in the 1950s, which soon evolved into an African jazz form known as *mbaqanga*, or "home-made."

In the 1960s, radio exposure forced the government to restrict lyrics and censor all songs considered subversive. This resulted in many jazz musicians leaving the country, among them Hugh Masekela and Miriam Makeba. After the collapse of Apartheid in the '90s, many of the exiled artists finally returned home. Today South Africa's Yvonne Chaka Chaka is one of the country's best known vocalists, singing everything from disco to R&B; her fans call her Princess Africa.

LADYSMITH BLACK MAMBAZO
Formed in 1964 by Joseph Shabalala, the Grammy-award–winning vocal group (*above*) came to world prominence when it joined Paul Simon on his 1986 album *Graceland*. The group performed at Nelson Mandela's inauguration in 1994 and continues to record and perform today, spreading a message of peace, love, and harmony.

MIRIAM MAKEBA
Miriam Makeba (*below*) began her professional career in the 1950s when she joined the Manhattan Brothers and later started her own, all-female group, the Skylarks. Her international hits "Pata Pata" and "The Click Song" focused world attention on South Africa's Apartheid policy. She's performed with Harry Belafonte and Paul Simon and has become known worldwide as Mama Africa.

HUGH MASEKELA
After much musical success in the 1950s, Masekela (*left*) fled South Africa in 1961 and studied music in London and New York. He had several hits in the United States, including "Grazin' in the Grass," which sold four million copies in 1968. Maseleka has performed with everyone from Louis Armstrong to Paul Simon and is considered by many to be a master of African music.

AFRICAN DANCING

Gumboot dancers perform during a New Year's eve carnival in Johannesburg, South Africa

Wherever groups of people come together in Africa, be it at weddings, funerals, or parties, you can be sure that there will be dancing. It's an essential part of the African psyche, one that is a form of expression and release for many Africans. The South Africa protest dance, the *toi-toi*, is synonymous with marches and strikes. Dancing is also synonymous with rhythm, and rhythm means drums. The drum symbolizes life and emotion; it beats as the heart of the community.

GUMBOOT DANCING

Gumboot dancing started in the late 1800s as a form of communication between mine workers. Today this ground-stomping dance is a spectacular art form that's performed all over Southern Africa. The dance is a specialty of Black Umfolozi, a troupe from Zimbabwe, and "Gumboots," a track from Paul Simon's *Graceland* album, featured South Africa's Boyoyo Boys.

KWAITO DANCING

The 1990s and the release of Nelson Mandela saw the creation of *kwaito*, a form of hip-hop music cre-ated on computers and synthesizers. It's widely known as the voice of the ghetto. The hugely popular kwaito dance, a kind of synchronized group tap-dancing, soon followed.

South Africa's leading kwaito group, Mandoza, performs before thousands of fans on the sand at Durban's North Beach

GATEWAY CITIES

South Africa's two hub cities are Johannesburg and Cape Town. It's almost certain that you will arrive and leave the country from one of these two cities. Make the most of your time in transit—there's a lot you can do in 24 hours, or even less.

JOHANNESBURG

Johannesburg epitomizes South Africa's paradoxical make-up—it's rich, poor, innovative, and historical. Traders hawk *skop* (boiled sheep's head, split open and eaten off newspaper) in front of polished glass buildings, as taxis jockey for position in rush hour. *Sangomas* (traditional healers) lay out herbs and roots next to the pavement tents of roadside barbers, and you never seem to be far from a woman selling *vetkoek* (dollops of deep-fried dough), beneath billboards advertising investment banks or cellphones.

Jo'burg was born as a mining camp, and its downtown area—the oldest part—is a jumbled grid of one-way streets heading in opposite directions reflecting its hasty start to life. While the city center is experiencing a revival, it's not somewhere that all visitors choose to visit close-up. The attractions in or close to the city center include the Nelson Mandela Bridge, MuseuMAfrica and the SAB World of Beer in the Newtown area, the Johannesburg Art Gallery, the Standard Bank Gallery and Diagonal Street in the downtown area, and Constitution Hill, the Civic Theatre, and the Johannesburg Planetarium in Braamfontein.

About 20 km (12 mi) to the south of downtown Johannesburg lies the vast township of Soweto, where you can take a township tour and visit the Hector Pieterson Museum. Between Soweto and the city are Gold Reef City and the Apartheid Museum.

■ TIP→ If you only have 24 hours, spend the evening at Newtown, and the next day take any one of the numerous half-day or day tours on offer.

WHAT TO SEE

❷ **Apartheid Museum.** The Apartheid Museum leaves no stone unturned, black or white, as it takes you on a journey through South African apartheid history—from the entrance, where you pass through a turnstile according to your assigned skin color, to the myriad historical, brutally

Fodor's Choice
★

honest, and sometimes shocking photographs, video displays, films, documents, and other exhibits. It's an emotional, multilayered journey. As you walk chronologically through the apartheid years and eventually reach the country's first steps to freedom, with democratic elections in 1994, you experience a taste of the pain and suffering with which so many South Africans had to live. A room with 121 ropes with hangman's knots hanging from the ceiling—one rope for each political prisoner executed in the apartheid era—is especially chilling. ⊠*Northern Pkwy. and Gold Reef Rd., Ormonde* ☎*011/309–4700* ⊕*www.apartheidmuseum.org* ⊠*R25* ☉*Tues.–Sun. 10–5.*

❶ Cradle of Humankind. The original Cradle of Humankind World Heritage Site (excluding Taung and the Makapans Valley, which lie farther away and were included in the World Heritage Site declaration in 2005) stretches over an area of about 470 square km (181 square mi) with about 300 caves. Inside these caves, palaeoanthropologists have discovered thousands of fossils of hominids and other animals, dating back about 4 million years. The most famous of these fossils are "Mrs Ples," a skull more than 2 million years old, and "Little Foot," a skeleton more than 3 million years old. While the Cradle does not have the world's oldest hominid fossils, it has the most complete fossil record of human evolution of anywhere on earth, and has produced more hominid fossils than anywhere else.

Fodor'sChoice ★

Archaeological finds at the Cradle of Humankind include 1.7-million-year-old stone tools, the oldest recorded in southern Africa. At Swartkrans, near Sterkfontein, a collection of burned bones tells us that our ancestors could manage fire more than 1 million years ago.

Not all the fossil sites in the Cradle are open to the public, but a tour of the Sterkfontein Caves and the visitor center (☎*011/668–3200* ⊕*www.maropeng.co.za*) provides an excellent overview of the archaeological work in progress, and a trip to Maropeng (☎*011/956–6342 or 0800/204–177* ⊕*www.maropeng.co.za*), a much larger visitor center 10 km (6 mi) from the Sterkfontein Caves, provides even more background. Special tours to fossil sites with expert guides can be booked at either of the visitor centers.

❸ Gold Reef City. This theme park lets you step back in time to 1880s Johannesburg and see why it became known as the City of Gold. One of the city's most popular attractions (avoid it on public holidays or weekends), it has good rides, and is based on the real history of Jo'burg.

In addition to riding the Anaconda, a scary roller coaster on which you hang under the track, feet in the air, you can descend into an old gold mine (additional fee), see molten gold being poured, or watch a gumboot dance, a riveting dance developed by black miners. The reconstructed streets are lined with operating Victorian-style shops and restaurants. And for those with money to burn, the large, glitzy Gold Reef Village Casino beckons across the road. ⊠*Gold Reef Rd., Ormonde* ☎*011/248–6800* ⊕*www.goldreefcity.co.za* ⊠*R100* ⊙*Tues.–Sun. 9:30–4; mine tours 10–4 every 30 min.*

❹ Hector Pieterson Memorial and Museum. Opposite Holy Cross Church, a stone's throw (literally, in those days) from the Tutu and Mandela homes, the Hector Pieterson Memorial and Museum is a crucial landmark. Pieterson, a 14-year-old student, was the first victim of police fire on June 16, 1976, when schoolchildren rose up to protest their second-rate *Bantu* (black) education system. The memorial is a paved area with benches for reflection, an inscribed stone and simple water feature, but in the museum are grainy photographs and films that bring that fateful day to life. Small granite blocks in the museum courtyard are a tribute to the 350 children among the more than 500 people who died during this violent time. *Khumalo and Phela Sts., Orlando West* ☎ *011/536–0611* ⊠*R15* ⊙ Mon.–Sat. 10–5, Sun. 10–4

WHERE TO STAY

Many of the hotels are linked to nearby malls and are well policed. Boutique hotels have sprung up everywhere, as have bed-and-breakfasts from Melville to Soweto. Hotels are quieter in December and January, and their rates are often cheaper over this period. Generally, the busy months in Jo'burg are from June to August. Most, if not all, of the good hotels are now in the northern suburbs. The Johannesburg Tourism Company (☎011/214–0700 ⊕*www.joburg.org.za*) has an excellent Web site with tons of useful information.

SANDHURST

$$

Fodor'sChoice

★

Saxon. Located in the exclusive suburb of Sandhurst, adjacent to the commercial and shopping center of Sandton, Saxon was voted the World's Leading Boutique Hotel by the prestigious World Travel Awards from 2001 to 2006 consecutively. Heads of state have stayed here, including Nelson Mandela, who came here after his release from prison and to work on his autobiography, *Long Walk to Freedom.* There's a sense of anticipation as you pass through the imposing gates. An azure pool adjoins the sleek modern building, located in expansive gardens. Inside, the feeling is calm and classical, though with an African touch—such as the extensive collection of African art hanging on the walls. Rooms are huge, light, and airy and have big bay windows overlooking the gardens or pool. Large-screen TVs, DVD players, and surround sound, and a workstation with a fast Internet connection are standard. The delightful restaurant has a wonderful setting and tasteful African decor. ⊠36 *Saxon Rd., Sandhurst* ☎011/292–6000 ⊕*www. thesaxon.com* ⊠27 *suites* △*In-room: minibar, data ports, Interne. In-hotel: restaurant, bar, 2 pools (1 heated), gym, spa, concierge.* ⊟*AE, DC, MC, V* ⌷⊙|*BP.*

ROSEBANK
$$$
▦**The Grace.** Most of the visitors to the Grace are businesspeople drawn to the old-world elegance behind the towering brick facade and concrete columns. It's also in the center of Rosebank and linked to the nearby mall and African crafts market. Travelers rave about the breakfast, and the restaurant, called simply the Dining Room, has established itself as one of Johannesburg's culinary centers. One of the hotel's finest features is the rooftop garden and pool area, which has amazing views of the northern suburbs' greenery. Thoughtful extras include transportation within a 10-km (6-mi) radius and tea and cake served in the lounge. ⊠*Bath and Tyrwhitt Aves., Rosebank 2196* ☏*011/280–7200* ⊕*www.thegrace.co.za* ➟*60 rooms, 15 suites* ⌂*In-hotel: restaurant, bar, pool, gym, spa, airport shuttle* ▭*AE, DC, MC, V* ℻*BP.*

$$
▦**Clico.** This small, upmarket guesthouse in central Rosebank is housed in a 60-year-old Cape Dutch house with a gracious garden and offers perhaps the best value for money in an area known for its expensive accommodation. Its decor is an engaging mix of old and new—from the original Oregon pine floorboards and antique inlaid-wood side tables from Morocco, to custom-made comfortable couches and the modern, whimsical sculptures like one of a woman floating above water by Anton Smit. The furnishings and bedroom suites are luxurious, and the service is slick yet personal. The superb food has a strong French influence though often with a local twist, and the chef adapts his menu daily to whatever fresh ingredients he can purchase. ⊠*27 Sturdee Ave., at Sturdee and Jellicoe, Rosebank 2196* ☏*011/252–3300* ⊕*www.clicoguesthouse.com* ➟*9 suites including 1 room self-catering* ⌂*In-room: refrigerator, safe, Wi-Fi. In-hotel: pool, airport shuttle, no elevator* ▭*DC, MC, V* ℻*BP.*

DUNKELD
WEST
$$$
▦**Ten Bompas.** This is a hotel-cum-restaurant and art gallery. It's small and luxurious, and the decor is minimalist, with carefully chosen African art. Suites, each done by a different interior designer, have separate lounges and bedrooms, fireplaces, complimentary minibars, satellite TV, and sound systems. You can also ogle brochures for the hotel's partner game lodges in the far north of Kruger National Park. Sides, the restaurant, turns in consistently good reviews. Its menu changes with the seasons. The food is exciting and fresh: roasted artichoke, mozzarella, and olive salad and roast-duck-and-orange risotto, for example. It also has a well-stocked wine cellar. ⊠*10 Bompas Rd., Dunkeld West* ☏*011/325–2442* ⊕*www.tenbompas.com* ➟*10 suites* ⌂*In-hotel: restaurant, bar, pools* ▭*AE, DC, MC, V* ℻*BP.*

WHERE TO EAT

Jo'burgers love eating out and there are thousands of restaurants scattered throughout the city to satisfy them. Some notable destinations for food include Melrose Arch, Parkhurst, Sandton, the South (for its Portuguese cuisine), Melville, and Chinatown in the CBD (Central Business District). Also check out the restaurants recommended on the official Johannesburg Web site (⊕*www.johannesburg.gov*). "Smart casual" dress is usually a good bet as is making reservations. Most places are open for lunch and dinner, though many establishments are closed on Sunday night and Monday as well as Christmas.

Park Ln.

Doris St. J. L. De Villiers Park

York St.

Paul Nel St.

Barnato St.

Yad Vashem Memorial Hall

Saunders St.

Alec Gerschel Park

Alexandra St.

Minors Jolly St.

Joel Rd.

Harley St.

Joel Rd.

Olivia Rd.

Hendon St.

Abel Road

Percy St.

Pretoria Street

South St.

HILLBROW

Soper Rd.

Donald Mackay Park

O'Reilly Rd.

Prospect Rd.

Gordon Ter.

Primrose Ter.

Charlton Terrace

Hadfield Rd.

Saratoga Avenue

DOORN-FONTEIN

Dora St.

Ellis Park

Beit St.

Leyds St.

Bok St.

Koch St.

Hancock St.

Currey St.

Noord St.

End Street Park

De Villiers St.

Rockey Street

Prein St.

JOHANNESBURG

Moseley St.

Charles St.

Beeson Rd.

President St.

Bezuidenhout Ave

Market Street

Commissioner St.

Commissioner Street

Fox St.

ABSA Group Museum

Main St.

Marshall Street

CITY & SUBURBAN

Park St.

Anderson Street

Albert St.

Durban St.

Albert St.

City & Suburban Rd.

Metrose St.

Durban St.

Grahamstown St.

Cornelius St.

Meikle St.

School St.

Wemmer Jubilee Rd.

5

DOWNTOWN
$–$$

✕ **Gramadoelas at the Market Theatre.** Crossing the threshold here is like stepping into some strange museum from another time—African artifacts and mirrors litter the huge room. Established in 1967, Gramadoelas has hosted an impressive list of guests including Nelson Mandela, Elton John, the Queen of England, Bill and Hillary Clinton, and many others. The restaurant specializes in the food of ordinary South Africans but also has a few dishes from farther north in the continent. Try *umngqusho* (beans and whole corn) or, if you're feeling adventurous, *mogodu* (unbleached ox tripe) or *masonja* (mopane worms). Cape Malay food is the mainstay, such as rich *bredie* (lamb casserole in a tomato sauce) and *bobotie* (a casserole of minced lamb). Meat lovers will like the selection of game meats such as the kudu panfried with dried fruit and spices. The popular buffet, serving a wide variety of dishes including starters, main courses, and desserts, is available most evenings, for R150. ⊠ *Market Theatre, Margeret Mcingana St., Newtown* ☏ *011/838–6960* ⊕ *www.gramadoelas.co.za* ▤ *AE, DC, MC, V* ⊗ *Closed Sun. No lunch Mon.*

¢–$$

✕ **Shivava Café.** Although not in the same league as the more famous Nambitha's and Wandie's traditional township restaurants in Soweto, the Shivava Café in Newtown is popular and easier to get to. Jazz music vies for attention with the rather boisterous crowd, and the place has the feel of a *shebeen* (township bar), making the experience that much more authentic. A specialty is pap (a traditional South African maize-meal porridge that is white and stiff) and mogudo (tripe), which is something of an acquired taste. The food is speedily prepared, and is a good example of black South African cuisine. If you want to be here just for the vibe, contemporary meals like steak are also served—with a certain African panache. ⊠ *1 President St., at Miriam Makeba and Jeppe St., Newtown* ☏ *011/834–8037 or 072/449–2199* ▤ *AE, DC, MC, V* ⊗ *Closed Mon.*

SANDTON
$$$–$$$$
Fodor'sChoice
★

✕ **Linger Longer.** Set in the spacious grounds of a grand old home in Wierda Valley, in the business center of Sandton, Linger Longer has an air of gracious elegance. The wooden floors, colorful walls, and striped curtains give this restaurant a wedgewood-like quality. Diners can reserve a table in the newly built conservatory. Though upmarket, this restaurant has a warm atmosphere and the hospitable staff and personal service of Chef Walter Ulz attracts local and international diners. The menu is varied and includes an array of seasonal specials. For starters the prawn firecracker is a good choice. Popular main dishes include the Asian split duck and the lamb rack cooked with crushed chermoula, a North African spice mix. The delicious portini ravioli is the best choice on the vegetarian main menu, and a good finale is the trio of sorbet. There's a good wine list. Reservations are essential. ⊠ *58 Wierda Rd., Wierda Valley, Sandton* ☏ *011/884–0465* ▤ *AE, DC, MC, V* ⊗ *Closed Sun. and public holidays. No lunch Sat.*

$–$$$

✕ **The Butcher Shop and Grill.** This is a good place for hungry carnivores. It specializes in prime South African meat aged to perfection by Alan Pick, the butcher/owner. An operating butchery features prominently in the restaurant, and special cuts can be ordered for the meal or to take home. Kudu, springbok, ostrich, and other game are often on the specials' list, and only the tenderest cuts are served. For lighter appetites, try the chicken or line fish. Jelly and custard pudding is a favorite with regulars. Pick has an excellent wine cellar. ✉*Nelson Mandela Sq., Sandton* ☎*011/784–8676* ⊕*www.thebutchershop.co.za* ▭*AE, DC, MC, V.*

THE SOUTH &
SOWETO
$
★

✕**Wandie's Place.** Wandie's isn't the only good township restaurant, but it's the best-known and one of the most popular spots in Jo'burg. The decor is eclectic township (a bit makeshift), and the walls are adorned with signatures and business cards of tourists that have crossed its path. The waiters are smartly dressed in bow ties, and the food is truly African. Meat stews, imifino (a leafy African dish), sweet potatoes, beans, corn porridge, traditionally cooked pumpkin, chicken, and tripe is laid out in a buffet in a motley selection of pots and containers. The food is hot, the drinks are cold, and the conversation flows. You may be unlucky and end up here with a tour bus, but it's big enough to cope and Wandie's now has an on-the-property guesthouse in case the alcohol flows too much. It's not that difficult to find and parking is safe, but it's probably better to organize a visit on a guided trip. ✉*618 Makhalamele St., Dube* ☎*011/982–2796* ⊕*www.wandies.co.za* ▭*AE, DC, MC, V.*

NIGHTLIFE

Fodor'sChoice
★

Johannesburg comes alive after dark, and whether you are a 24-hour visitor, rebellious punk rocker, or a suave executive in search of a classy lounge, there is always something to do. A great place to visit is the Newtown Cultural Precinct, an old area that started as a produce market, but has undergone a successful rejuvenation. Now safe, clean, and brightly lighted, it's home to the Market Theatre complex, restaurants, bars, jazz clubs, and shops. The area is also home to **Carfax** (✉*39 Pim St., Newtown* ☎*011/834–9187*), a converted factory building that hosts some of the city's biggest parties. Performance art, dance events with guest DJs, and rock shows draw a selection of the town's more interesting people.

SHOPPING

Across the street from the Market Theatre, **Newtown Market Africa** is a good option for African art and artifacts. Craftspeople from as far away as Cameroon and Zaire sell their masks, wooden artworks, decorative cloths, and blankets, often at prices that are cheaper than elsewhere in town. This is a good place to try to bargain a little. ✉*Bree and Wolhuter Sts., Newtown* ☎*083/732–0302* ◷*Sat. 9–5.*

Rosebank's **Rooftop Market** has become a Sunday tradition in the city. More than 600 stalls sell African and Western crafts, antiques, books, food, art, trinkets, CDs, jewelry, and clothes. Frequently African musicians, dancers, and other entertainers delight the roving crowds. ✉*Rosebank Mall, 50 Bath Ave., Rosebank* ☎*011/442–4488* ◷*Sun. 9–5.*

CAPE TOWN

If you're lucky enough to find yourself in Cape Town, make the most of it. Sheltered beneath the familiar shape of Table Mountain, this historic city is instantly recognizable, and few cities in the world possess its beauty and style.

A stroll through the city center reveals Cape Town's three centuries as the sea link between Europe and the East. Elegant Cape Dutch buildings, characterized by big whitewashed gables, often a thatch roof, and shuttered windows, abut imposing monuments to Britain's imperial legacy. In the colorful Bo-Kaap neighborhood the call to prayer echoes from minarets while the sweet tang of Malay curry wafts through the cobbled streets. At the vibrant Victoria & Alfred Waterfront, also referred to as the V&A Waterfront or simply the Waterfront, expensive hotels and plush apartments line the water's edge, and enthusiastic buskers perform in the walkways and public squares. And everywhere, whether you're eating outdoors at one of the country's best restaurants or sipping wine atop Table Mountain, you sense—correctly—that this is South Africa's most urbane, civilized city.

As impressive as all this is, though, what you will ultimately most likely recall about Cape Town is the sheer grandeur of its setting—Table Mountain rising above the city, the sweep of the bay, and mountains cascading into the sea. You may spend more time marveling at the views than anything else. Francis Drake wasn't exaggerating when he said this was "the fairest Cape we saw in the whole circumference of the earth," and he would have little cause to change his opinion today. You could spend a week exploring just the city and peninsula—and a lifetime discovering the nearby wonders of the Western Cape, including the Winelands, one of the great highlights of a trip to South Africa.

THE WINELANDS

No stay or stopover in Cape Town would be complete without a trip to the historic Cape Winelands, which lie in the city's backyard. They produce fine wine amid the exquisite beauty of rocky mountains, serried vines, and elegant Cape Dutch estates. By South African standards, this southwestern region of the Cape is a settled land, with a sense of continuity lacking in much of the rest of the country. Here farms have been handed down from one generation to another for centuries, and old-name families like the Cloetes and Myburghs have become part of the fabric of the region. But the whole Western Cape is an alluring province: a sweep of endless mountain ranges, empty beaches, and European history dating back more than three centuries and anchored by Cape Town in the southwest. The cultures of the indigenous Khoekhoen and San people—the first inhabitants of this enormous area—also contribute to the region's richness. In less than two hours you can reach most of the province's highlights from Cape Town—including the wine centers of Stellenbosch, Franschhoek, and Paarl—making the city an ideal base from which to explore. If your time is limited in the Cape Town area, you might want to join one of the many tours to the Winelands (*See* Cape Town Tours in Johannesburg & Cape Town Essentials, below).

WHAT TO SEE

6 **Boulders Beach.** This series of small coves lies among giant boulders on
★☺ the outskirts of Simon's Town. Part of the Table Mountain National Park, the beach is best known for its resident colony of African penguins. You must stay out of the fenced-off breeding beach, but don't be surprised if a wandering bird comes waddling up to you to take a look. Penguin-viewing platforms, accessible from either the Boulders Beach or Seaforth side, provide close-up looks at these comical birds. When you've had enough penguin peering, you can stroll back to Boulders Beach for some excellent swimming in the quiet coves. This beach is great for children because it is so protected and the sea is warm and calm. It can get crowded in summer, though, so go early. Without traffic, it takes about 45 minutes to get here from town, less from the Southern Suburbs. ⊠*Follow signs from Bellvue Rd., Simon's Town* ☎*021/786–2329* ⊕*www.sanparks.org* ⊠*R25* ☺*Daily 8–6:30.*

7 **Buitenverwachting.** Once part of Dutch governor Simon van der Stel's original Constantia farm, Buitenverwachting (which means "beyond expectation" and is roughly pronounced "bait-in-fur-wagh-ting") has an absolutely gorgeous setting. An oak-lined avenue leads past the Cape Dutch homestead to the thatch but modern cellar. Acres of vines spread up hillsides flanked by more towering oaks and the rocky crags of the Constantiaberg mountain. Buitenverwachting's wine is just as good as the view. The largest seller is the slightly dry Buiten Blanc, an easy-drinking blend of a few varietals. The best red is Christine, a blend of mostly cabernet sauvignon and merlot. The winery's eponymous restaurant is also worth a visit. ⊠*Off Klein Constantia Rd.* ☎*021/794–5190* ⊠*Tastings free* ☺*Weekdays 9–5, Sat. 9–1.*

1 **Greenmarket Square.** You can find African jewelry, art, and fabrics, plus good deals on clothing, handcrafted silver jewelry, and locally made leather shoes in this cobbled square that historically served as a forum for public announcements. In addition to being one of the best spots in town to purchase gifts, it's a lively and fun destination. More than half the stalls are owned by people from outside South Africa—political and economic refugees from Ethiopia, Eritrea, Zimbabwe, and the Democratic Republic of Congo—trying to eke out a living. Bargain, but do so with a conscience. ⊠*Longmarket, Burg, and Shortmarket Sts., Cape Town Central* ☎*No phone* ☺*Mon.–Sat. 9–4:30.*

8 **Kirstenbosch National Botanic Gardens.** Spectacular in each season, these
☺ world-famous gardens showcase stunning South African flora in a
Fodor'sChoice magnificent setting, extending up the eastern slopes of Table Moun-
★ tain and overlooking the sprawling city and the distant Hottentots Holland Mountains. No wonder the gardens are photographed from every angle. They aren't just enjoyed by out-of-town visitors, however; on weekends Capetonians flock here with their families to lie on the lawns and read their newspapers while the kids run riot. Walking trails meander through the gardens, and grassy banks are ideal for a picnic

5

Cape Town

Victoria Basin

Cruise Ship Terminal

South Arm
South Arm

Victoria & Alfred
Waterfront Information
Center

Duncan

Breakwater Blvd

Beach

South African
Maritime Museum

Portswood

Dock

Western Blvd

Main

Vesperdene

Table Bay Blvd

D.F. Malan

Hertzog Blvd

Oswald Pirow

Eastern Boulevard

Cape Town
Railway
Station

Adderley

St George's Mall

Cape Town Tourism
Information Office

Gold of Africa
Museum

CAPE
TOWN
CENTRAL

DE
WATERKANT

Castle of
Good Hope

General
Post Office

❹

❶

❷

❸

❸

5

KEY

1 *Exploring*

① *Hotels & Restaurants*

▶ **Exploring**

Boulders Beach **6**
Buitenverwachting **7**
Greenmarket Square **1**
Kirstenbosch National
Botanic Gardens **8**
Long Street **2**
Robben Island **4**
Table Mountain **5**
Two Oceans Aquarium **3**

▶ **Restaurants**

Africa Café **3**
Cape Colony Restaurant ..**8**
Haiku **6**
Noon Gun Tearoom
& Restaurant **4**
Panama Jack's **2**

▶ **Hotels**

Cape Grace **1**
Daddy Long Legs
Boutique Hotel **7**
Mount Nelson Hotel **9**
Townhouse Hotel **5**

or afternoon nap. The plantings are limited to species indigenous to Southern Africa, including fynbos—hardy, thin-leaf plants that proliferate in the Cape. Among these are proteas (including silver trees and king proteas), ericas, and *restios* (reeds). Magnificent sculptures from Zimbabwe are displayed around the gardens, too. ⊠ *Rhodes Ave., Newlands* ☎ *021/799–8783* ⊕ *www.sanbi.org* ⊠ *R30* ⊙ *Apr.–Aug., daily 8–6; Sept.–Mar., daily 8–7.*

② **Long Street.** The section of Long between Orange and Wale streets is lined with magnificently restored Georgian and Victorian buildings. Wrought-iron balconies and fancy curlicues on these colorful houses evoke the French Quarter in New Orleans. In the 1960s Long Street played host to bars, prostitutes, and sleazy hotels, but today antiques dealers, secondhand bookstores (Clarke's is a must), pawnshops, the Pan-African Market, and funky clothing outlets make this the best browsing street in the city. Lodgings here range from backpackers' lodges to the more exclusive Metropole hotel. At the mountain end is Long Street Baths, an indoor swimming pool and old Turkish *hammam* (steam bath). ⊠ *Cape Town Central.*

④ **Robben Island.** Made famous by its most illustrious inhabitant, Nelson Rolihlahla Mandela, this island, whose name is Dutch for "seals," has a long and sad history. At various times a prison, leper colony, mental institution, and military base, it is finally filling a positive, enlightening, and empowering role in its latest incarnation as a museum. Declared a World Heritage site on December 1, 1997, Robben Island has become a symbol of the triumph of the human spirit. Tours of the island are organized by the Robben Island Museum. (Other operators advertise Robben Island tours but just take visitors on a boat trip *around* the island.) As a result of the reconciliation process, most tour guides are former political prisoners. It can get pretty crowded, so reserve in advance, and take sunglasses and a hat in summer. ■ **TIP→ You are advised to tip your guide only if you feel that the tour has been informative.** ☎ *021/413–4220, 021/413–4221 for information, 021/413–4209, 021/413–4210, or 021/413–4211 for reservations, 021/413–4217, 021/413–4219 for ticket sales* ⊕ *www.robben-island.org.za* ⊠ *R150* ⊙ *Summer, daily 7:30–9; winter, daily 7:30–6; last boat generally leaves island at 8 in summer and 5 in winter (opening times and boat departures can vary, so phone ahead to check).*

Fodor'sChoice
★

⑤ **Table Mountain.** Along with Victoria Falls on the border of Zimbabwe and Zambia, Table Mountain is one of southern Africa's most beautiful and impressive natural wonders. The views from its summit are awe-inspiring. The mountain rises more than 3,500 feet above the city, and its distinctive flat top is visible to sailors 65 km (40 mi) out to sea. It's possible to climb the mountain, thought it'll take two to three hours, depending on your level of fitness. There is no water along the route; you *must* take at least 2 liters (½ gallon) of water per person. Table Mountain can be dangerous if you're not familiar with the terrain. Many paths that look like good routes down the mountain end in treacherous cliffs. Do not underestimate this mountain. It may be in the middle of a city, but it is not a genteel town park. Wear sturdy shoes or hiking boots; always take warm clothes, such as a Wind-breaker, and a mobile phone; and let someone know of your plans. Also be aware that in light of occasional muggings here, it's unwise to walk alone on the mountain. It's recommended that you travel in a group or, better yet, with a guide. Consult the staff at a Cape Town Tourism office for more guidelines. Another way to reach the summit is to take the cable car, which affords fantastic views. Cable cars depart from the Lower Cable Station, which lies on the slope of Table Mountain near its western end; the station is a long way from the city on foot, and you're better off traveling by car, taxi, or *rikki* (a small, low-tech minibus). *Table Mountain Aerial Cableway* ✉*Tafelberg Rd.* ☎*021/424–8181* ⊕*www.tablemountain.net* ✍*R120 round-trip, R60 one-way* ⊙*Hrs vary so it's best to check when you arrive, but usually daily 8:30–7:30.*

NEED A BREAK?

During the warm summer months Capetonians are fond of taking picnic baskets up the mountain. The best time to picnic is after 5, as some say sipping a glass of chilled Cape wine while watching the sun set from Table Mountain is one of life's great joys. The large self-service restaurant called, quite simply, The Restaurant (☎*021/424–8181*) serves great hot breakfasts, light meals, and sandwiches and has a good salad bar. You can also drink local wines here. The Cocktail Bar (☎*021/424–8181*) dishes up a spectacular view along with cocktails and bar snacks from 2 until the last cable car. As you might expect, the place has a good wine list, with local labels predominating.

❸ **Two Oceans Aquarium.** This aquarium is considered one of the finest in ⟳ the world. Stunning displays reveal the marine life of the warm Indian Fodor's Choice Ocean and the icy Atlantic. It's a hands-on place, with a touch pool ★ for children and opportunities for certified divers to explore the vast, five-story kelp forest or the predator tank, where you share the water with a couple of large ragged-tooth sharks (*Carcharias taurus*) and get a legal adrenaline rush (R450, R350 with your own gear). And for something completely different, you can try a copper-helmet dive with antique dive equipment in the predator tank (R650). If you don't fancy getting wet, you can still watch the feeding in the predator tank every day at 3. But there's more to the aquarium than just snapping jaws. Look for the endangered African penguins, also known as jackass penguins because of the awkward braying noise they make; pulsating moon jellies and spider crabs; and, if you're lucky, the strange and elusive sunfish, which is exhibited only when one gets trapped in the harbor. ✉*Dock Rd., Waterfront* ☎*021/418–3823* ⊕*www.aquarium. co.za* ✍*R70* ⊙*Daily 9:30–6.*

WHERE TO STAY

Finding lodging in Cape Town can be a nightmare during peak travel season (December and January), as many of the more reasonable accommodations are booked up. If you arrive in Cape Town without a reservation, head for the Cape Town Tourism office, which has a helpful accommodations desk.

Sip & Spoeg Like an Expert

South Africa currently has more than growing areas that yield a huge selection of very different wines. One of the best ways to find your way around the enormous selection is to buy one of the local magazines, such as the monthly *Wine* magazine (R25), devoted to the subject.

AH, BUT YOUR LAND IS BEAUTIFUL

When it comes to South African terroir, think sun, sea, and soil. While Northern hemisphere farmers work hard to get as much sunlight onto their grapes as possible, local viticulturists have to deal with soaring summer temperatures (this is why the cooling influence of the two oceans is so welcome). South Africa also has some of the world's oldest soil, and there's a mineral element to its wines, a quality that's most prominent in the top-end Sauvignon Blancs like those produced by Cape Point Vineyards, Steenberg, and Springfield.

YOU CAN'T LEAVE WITHOUT TRYING PINOTAGE

In 1920s, a professor at Stellenbosch University decided to create a truly South African varietal. He crossed Pinot Noir (a tricky grape to grow) with Cinsaut (a vigorous and very hardy grape)—he liked the idea combining the drama queen with a pragmatic, nononsense type—and came up with Pinotage. Though it's had its ups and downs, including being accused—by everyone from critics to connoisseurs—of being bitter and rubbery, strides are being made to express the grape's character. One example is the coffee Pinotage. It's been on the market for just a few years and is hugely popular because it's a ballsy, bold wine. There's a distinct mocha flavor to the wine that's a combination of the soil and the winemaking technique. A good example of this is the Diemersfontein Carpe Diem Pinotage, which retails for R120. Other Pinotages to keep an eye out for: Stellenzicht golden triangle Pinotage (R60), Spier Private Collection Pinotage (R108), or Kanonkop Pinotage (R130).

HUNDREDS AND THOUSANDS TO CHOOSE FROM

Wines that have helped put South Africa on the map include Chenin Blanc, Sauvignon Blanc, and Bordeaux-style red blends of Cabernet Sauvignon, Merlot, and Cabernet Franc. South African red blends have done well at international competitions, and the quality rivals some of the world's best producers. Until recently, Chenin Blanc was something of a Cinderella varietal. It accounts for the bulk of South African white wine plantings but, because of its versatility, was largely overlooked. Luckily, this has shifted and there are now more than 100 Chenin Blancs out there demanding attention and commanding top prices.

Good Sauvignon Blancs: Alexanderfontein Sauvignon Blanc (R30), Springfield Estate Life from Stone Sauvignon Blanc (R53), or Cape Point Vineyards Sauvignon Blanc (R110).

Great Red Blends: Stellenrust Timeless (R89), Rustenberg John X Merriman (R115), or Kanonkop Paul Sauer (+/- R175).

Great Chenin Blancs: Kleine Zalze barrel fermented Chenin Blanc (R49), Rudera Robusto Chenin Blanc (R95), or Ken Forrester The FMC Chenin Blanc (R230).

A ROSÉ BY ANY OTHER NAME

Though it legally can't be called champagne, Methode Cap Classique, South Africa's version of the bubbly, is made in exactly the same way. You'd be unwise to pass on an offer of Graham Beck Brut Blanc de Blancs (R89) or Villiera Brut Tradition (R69).

NAME-DROPPING

There are some iconic South African wines you really should try before you leave the country. Of course, the list of such wines varies depending on who you talk to, but keep an eye out for:

- Kanonkop Pinotage (R210) or Paul Sauer (R259)

- Meerlust Rubicon (R219)

- De Toren Fusion V (R220)

- Vergelegen V (R750)

- Steenberg Sauvignon Blanc Reserve (85)

- Hamilton Russell Chardonnay (195) and Pinot Noir (R250)

- Cape Point Isliedh (R130)

- Jordan Chardonnay (R95)

- Springfield Méthode Ancienne Cabernet Sauvignon (R230)

- Boekenhoutskloof Cabernet Sauvignon (R170)

- Boplaas Vintage Reserve Port (R365)

- Potential future icons include Columella and Palladius, both made by Eben Sadie, and Raats Family Vineyard Cabernet Franc.

5

Hotels in the city center are a good option if you're here for only a short stay. During the day the historic city center is a vibrant place. At night, though, it's shut up tight (though this is changing slowly as some office buildings are converted into apartment complexes); night owls may prefer a hotel amid the nonstop action of the Waterfront.

Keep in mind that international flights from the United States and Europe arrive in the morning and return flights depart in the evening. Because most hotels have an 11 AM checkout, you may have to wait for a room if you've just arrived; if you're leaving, you will be hauled kicking and screaming out of your room hours before your flight. Most hotels will try to accommodate you, but they often have no choice in peak season. Some of the larger hotels have residents-only lounges where you can spend the hours awaiting your flight. Note that many small luxury accommodations either do not permit children or have minimum-age restrictions. It's a good idea to inquire in advance if this will be an issue.

Another option is to stay in one of Cape Town's numerous guesthouses or B&Bs, which is what many South Africans do when they travel. There are some very classy and professionally run establishments that offer everything a hotel does but on a smaller, more personal scale. The most reliable source of good B&B establishments is **South African Accommodation** (☎021/794–0030 ⊕*www.bookabed.co.za*). The **Portfolio of Places** (☎021/689–4020 ⊕*www.portfoliocollection.com*) brochure includes guesthouses, B&Bs, villas, and more. **Cape Stay** (☎021/674–3104 ⊕*www.capestay.co.za*) has a wide selection of accommodations to suit different needs.

CITY CENTER

$$$$

Fodor'sChoice

★

Mount Nelson Hotel. This distinctive pink landmark is the grande dame of Cape Town. Since it opened its doors in 1899 to accommodate passengers just off the Union-Castle steamships, it has been the focal point of Cape social life. It retains a traditional charm and gentility that other luxury hotels often lack: afternoon tea is served in the lounge to piano accompaniment, the Planet Champagne Bar is very glam, and the staff almost outnumbers the guests. Rooms are decorated with fine antiques and fresh flowers and have an air of aristocracy about them. The hotel stands at the top of Government Avenue, but, surrounded as it is by 9 acres of manicured gardens, it might as well be in the country. Once a week the head gardener leads a guided tour through the magnificent gardens, and tea is served afterward. Very civilized! For peak season, December–March, it's advisable to book a year in advance. ⊠*76 Orange St., Gardens 8001* ☎*021/483–1000* ⊕*www.mountnelson.co.za* ⌑*145 rooms, 56 suites* ⌂*In-room: a/c, safe, refrigerator, DVD, VCR. In-hotel: 2 restaurants, room service, bar, tennis courts, pools, gym, spa, children's programs, laundry service, concierge, Internet, airport shuttle, parking (no fee), no-smoking rooms* ☰*AE, DC, MC, V* ⊗*BP*.

$$

Townhouse Hotel. Proximity to government buildings, an easygoing atmosphere, and extremely competitive rates make the Townhouse a popular choice. Rooms, decorated in neutral shades, provide a restful retreat from the hubbub of the city. Request a room with a view of the mountain. ✉ *60 Corporation St., Box 5053, Cape Town Central 8000* ☎ *021/465–7050* ⊕ *www.townhouse.co.za* ⇨ *104 rooms* ♿ *In-room: a/c, safe, refrigerator. In-hotel: restaurant, room service, bars, pool, gym, laundry facilities, laundry service, concierge, Internet, airport shuttle, parking (fee), no-smoking rooms* ▤ *AE, DC, MC, V.*

$ ⛶ **Daddy Long Legs Boutique Hotel.** Being voted *House & Leisure*/Visa's
★ best hotel in South Africa in 2006 and one of *Decorex*'s top-10 boutique hotels in South Africa in 2007 puts DDL in a class of its own. Independent travelers with artistic streaks love this place. It was built to represent the creative community of Cape Town, and well-known local artists—including poet-author Finuala Dowling and architect Andre Vorster—were given a budget and invited to decorate a room to their tastes. The results are fantastic. In the Photo Booth room, a huge portrait behind the bed is made up of 3,240 black-and-white photos of Capetonians, while a funky room by the fusion band Freshlyground has a bright red throw, portraits of the band members, and music. But it's not all about show—the amenities are all in place as well. The linen is crisp and clean, the staff is friendly, and the only real drawback is finding parking on Long Street (it's fine after hours, but a crush during the day). ✉ *134 Long St., Cape Town Central 8010* ☎ *021/422–3074* ⊕ *www.daddylonglegs.co.za* ⇨ *13 rooms* ♿ *In-room: no phone, no TV (some). In-hotel: bar, no elevator, laundry service, Internet, no-smoking rooms* ▤ *AE, DC, MC, V.*

WATERFRONT ⛶ **Cape Grace.** The exclusive and well-appointed Cape Grace, at the
$$$$ V&A Waterfront, is a hard act to follow. Built on a spit of land jut-
Fodor's Choice ting into a working harbor, it offers views of seals frolicking in the
★ surrounding waters and seagulls soaring above. Large, elegant guest rooms have harbor or mountain views and are decorated with a combination of French period furnishings and wonderful modern design. The attention to detail throughout is outstanding, from the antique pieces to the fresh flowers in the rooms. There's a wonderful well-stocked library for browsing, and the superb restaurant, one waterfront, serves creative cuisine with a strong South African influence. Add to that a fantastic spa with treatments inspired by the spice route and African traditions. You also have free use of a nearby health club and the hotel's courtesy car for getting into the city and to the main beaches. Make time for at least one drink at Bascule, the hotel's sophisticated watering hole with an incredible selection of single-malt whiskies. ✉ *West Quay Rd., Box 51387, Waterfront 8002* ☎ *021/410–7100* ⊕ *www. capegrace.com* ⇨ *122 rooms* ♿ *In-room: a/c, safe, refrigerator. In-hotel: restaurant, room service, bar, pool, spa, no elevator, laundry service, executive floor, Internet, airport shuttle, parking (no fee), no-smoking rooms* ▤ *AE, DC, MC, V* ⧾⧾*BP.*

WHERE TO EAT

Cape Town is the culinary capital of South Africa. Nowhere else in the country is the populace so discerning about food, and nowhere else is there such a wide selection of restaurants. Western culinary history here dates back more than 350 years—Cape Town was founded specifically to grow food—and that heritage is reflected in the city's cuisine. A number of restaurants operate in historic town houses and 18th-century wine estates, and many include heritage dishes on their menus.

CITY CENTER $$$$ ✕**Haiku.** As this is widely regarded as the best Pan-Asian restaurant in town, it's worth putting up with the waiting lists, multiple seatings, and a complex tomelike menu that you'll probably need the server's help to wade through. The dim sum includes a spicy panfried lamb pot sticker with coriander and green chilies, and from the wok menu you can order salt-pepper calamari fried with five spices. Grills include mint lamb chops served with dry red chilies and garlic. On the sushi menu, the salmon roses, thin sashimi curls filled with mayonnaise and topped with pink caviar, are outstanding. Multiple kitchens mean that cuisine arrives when it's ready, not once all orders for the table are complete. Although this provides the freshest dining experience, it may mean fellow diners watching while you eat, or vice versa. ⊠*33 Burg St., Cape Town Central* ☎*021/424–7000* ⌖*Reservations essential* ⊟*AE, DC, MC, V* ⊗*No lunch Sun.*

$$$–$$$$ ✕**Cape Colony Restaurant.** Tall bay windows, a high-domed ceiling, and a giant trompe-l'oeil mural—an inventive evocation of Table Mountain in days of yore—create a befitting setting for the city's most historic and unashamedly colonial hotel, the Mount Nelson. This is a good place to come for a stylish night out, enhanced by a band. Chef Ian Mancais's menu includes such classic dishes as foie gras *ballentine* with apple-pear chutney and brioche, and lamb's kidney Bercy (with shallots and white wine). But you'll also find Asian-inspired creations such as tomato-and-basil risotto in tomato water with fried dim sum, and Vietnamese black-lacquered roasted rack of lamb with fried bok choy. The Oasis, the hotel's Mediterranean poolside buffet restaurant, is outstanding. ⊠*Mount Nelson Hotel, 76 Orange St., Gardens* ☎*021/483–1000* ⌖*Reservations essential* ⊟*AE, DC, MC, V.*

$–$$$$ ✕**Panama Jack's.** In this raw-timber structure in the heart of the docks, the music is loud, the tables are crowded, and the decor is nonexistent, but nowhere in town will you find bigger crayfish. Your choice, made from large open tanks, is weighed before being grilled or steamed. Expect to pay about R460 per kilogram for this delicacy and a whopping R660 a kilogram for the scarce and endangered wild abalone (but keep in mind that this mollusk is being poached nearly to extinction). Large prawns range in price from R199.50 for 10 to about R30 each for Mozambique langoustines. There is plenty of less expensive seafood as well, and daily specials such as baby squid and local line-caught fish are competitively priced. It can be difficult to find this place at night, so you may want to come for lunch if it's your first visit. ⊠*Royal Yacht Club basin, off Goliath Rd., Docks* ☎*021/447–3992* ⊟*AE, DC, MC, V* ⊗*No lunch Sat.*

$$$ ✕**Africa Cafe.** Tourist oriented it may be, but it would nevertheless be a pity to miss out on this vibrant restaurant in a historic 18th-century former home, with its African decor and city views. Fresh-fruit cocktails accompany a communal feast, with dishes originating from Ethiopia to Zambia, from Kenya to Angola. There are no starters or entrées, but rather a tasty series of patties, puffs, and pastries accompanied by addictive dips, along with dishes like West African shrimp-and-pep-

per salad, ostrich fillet in a cashew-nut sauce, and Ethiopian *doro wat* chicken, cooked in a mild *berbere* (Ethiopian spice mix) paprika sauce. Vegetarian dishes are plentiful, including the Soweto *chakalaka* (a fiery cooked-vegetable relish). The cost of this colorful prix-fixe abundance is R125 per person. Wines from Cape estates are available, or you can ask for *umqomboti* beer, brewed from sorghum or millet. ⊠*Heritage Square, 108 Shortmarket St., Cape Town Central* ☎*021/422–0221* ⊟*AE, DC, MC, V* ⊗*Closed Sun. No lunch.*

$ ✕**Noon Gun Tearoom and Restaurant.** On the slopes of Signal Hill in the colorful Bo-Kaap neighborhood, this eatery is a good place to stop for traditional, home-cooked Malay food. Your entertaining hostess, Miriam Misbach, cooks up a mean curry and *biryani* (a spicy rice-based dished). And her samosas are to die for. The menu is limited, but Miriam's repertoire is anything but; she's chatty and engaging. ⊠*273 Longmarket St., Bo-Kaap* ☎*021/424–0529* ⊟*No credit cards* ⊗*Closed Sun.*

SPORTS & THE OUTDOORS

SCUBA DIVING The diving around the Cape is excellent, with kelp forests, cold-water corals, very brightly colored reef life, and numerous wrecks. An unusual experience is a dive in the Two Oceans Aquarium. CMSA, NAUI, and PADI dive courses are offered by local operators, beginning at about R1,700. **Orca Industries** (☎*021/671–9673* ⊕*www.orca-industries. co.za*) offers dive courses and charters. **Pro Divers** (☎*021/433–0472* ⊕*www.prodiverssa.co.za*) runs dive tours to some of the many ships wrecked at the infamous Cape of Storms. The friendly **Scuba Shack** (☎*021/424–9368 in Cape Town* ☎*021/782–7358 in Kommetjie* ⊕*www.scubashack.co.za*) has two outlets: one in town and one near Kommetjie. **Underwater World** (☎*021/461–8290*) is a city dive shop that offers only NAUI courses.

JOHANNESBURG & CAPE TOWN ESSENTIALS

TRANSPORTATION

BY AIR

For information on air service to Johannesburg and Cape Town, see South Africa Essentials, below.

AIRPORTS South Africa's major airports are in Johannesburg and Cape Town. Most international flights arrive at and depart from Johannesburg International Airport, now called O.R. Tambo, and sometimes abbreviated O.R.T.I.A. by safari companies. It is 19 km (12 mi) from the city. The airport has a tourist information desk, a V.A.T. refund office, and a computerized accommodations service. Several international flights departing from Cape Town are also routed via Johannesburg. O.R. Tambo, though small by international standards, is Africa's busiest airport. The check-in area has not yet been modernized, so it can be a jumble of people going to various destinations squeezed into a tight area at peak departure times—which can add to preflight stress. Expect long lines at check-in counters in the early evening, when many long-distance flights depart; the lines move quickly, however, so you likely won't wait more than a half hour. Baggage claim usually takes about 15 minutes. The airport has its own police station, but security can be a problem: baggage is sometimes stolen either in transit or even within the airport itself. Be vigilant and keep your belongings close and within your sight at all times.

Cape Town International is 20 km (12½ mi) southeast of the city. The domestic and international terminals both have booths run by Cape Town Tourism, which are open from 7:30 AM until the last flight comes in. This is a much smaller airport than O.R. Tambo and is therefore much easier to navigate.

■TIP➔ Note that at both airports there are vast distances between gates, so clear security before stopping for a snack or shopping, as you don't want to scramble for your flight.

If you are traveling to or from either airport, be very aware of the time of day. Traffic can be horrendous between 7 and 9 in the morning and between about 3:30 and 6 in the evening, so if you need to be, say, at Cape Town International at 5, it's better to leave at 3 and spend the extra time reading a book at the airport. It's less stressful than spending the same amount of time in traffic. The morning rush hour does not affect Cape Town International as much—but only if you're traveling from the city center.

International Airports Cape Town International Airport (*CPT* ☎*021/937–1200*). **O.R. Tambo International Airport** (formerly Johannesburg) (*JNB ORTIA* ☎*011/921–6262*).

GROUND   Touch Down Taxis is the only officially authorized airport taxi. Look
TRANSFERS   for the ACSA symbol on the vehicles. Legend Tours and Transfers offers prearranged shared ride transfers; rates start at R260. All major car-rental companies have counters at Cape Town International, and driving to the City Bowl or V&A Waterfront is straightforward in daylight. If your flight arrives after dark, consider prearranging transportation through your hotel or guesthouse. It should cost less than R200 to the V&A Waterfront.

If you're overnighting in Johannesburg, it's well worth the cost to arrange your transfer directly through your hotel or guesthouse after your long flight. Someone will greet you, and escort you to the vehicle. Get the name of the car service from the hotel concierge before leaving home and carry it in your hand baggage, as well as the phone number for where you are staying.

If your hotel or guesthouse does not have a shuttle, ask them to arrange for your transportation with a reliable company. Most lodgings have a regular service they use, so you should have no problem arranging this in advance. If it proves difficult, that is a red flag that you might want to chose a different establishment.

Prices vary, depending on where you are staying, but plan on R350 for a ride from the airport to hotels in the Sandton section of the city, and about R250 or R275 for a hotel or guesthouse in Rosebank or Melrose. Most hotels will allow you to add the charge to your bill, so you needn't worry about paying in cash.

Magic Bus operates a minibus service that connects to all the major hotels in Sandton. It runs all day on the half hour, costs R110, and takes 30 minutes to an hour. Airport Link will ferry you anywhere in Johannesburg in a Toyota Camry or Mercedes minibus for R255 per person. Legend Tours and Transfers offers prearranged shared ride transfers. Rates start at R355. In addition, scores of licensed taxis line up outside the airport terminal. By law they must have a working meter. Expect to pay about R250–R350 for a trip to Rosebank or Sandton.

Cape Town Legend Tours and Transfers (☎ 021/674–7055 ⊕ www.legendtours. co.za). **Touch Down Taxis** (☎ 021/919–2834).

Johannesburg Airport Link (☎ 011/792–2017 ⊕ www.airportlink.co.za). **Legend Tours and Transfers** (☎ 021/674–7055 ⊕ www.legendtours.co.za). **Magic Bus Airport Transfers** (☎ 011/394–6902 or 011/609–1662 ⊕ www.magicbus.co.za).

5

TRANSFERS BETWEEN AIRPORTS The domestic and international terminals at O.R. Tambo and Cape Town are a short stroll away from each other, and luggage trolleys are provided free of charge. There is no need to be too worried about security, but be aware of your surroundings as you would anywhere. Don't talk to strangers. For added peace of mind, you can use a uniformed porter to transit between the two. Be sure to tip him for his services.

In O.R. Tambo, if you are taking a chartered safari flight and do not see your representative, stand near the information kiosk in the middle of the hall and your representative will find you.

BY BUS

In Cape Town, a few shuttle buses operate tourist-friendly routes around the city center. Shuttles to Kirstenbosch (R40 per person) and the Table Mountain cableway (R30) can be obtained from the Waterfront's Cape Town Tourism office. A regular bus runs from the central train station to the Waterfront (R2.50), and there's also service from the Cape Town Tourism Office in the city center.

For information on long-distance bus travel, see South Africa Essentials, below.

BY CAR

If you're only going to be in Johannesburg for a brief period, avoid driving if you can: traffic is a nightmare, and rogue taxis run lights and rarely obey rules of the road. However, a car is by far the best way to get around Cape Town, particularly in the evenings, when public transportation closes down. If you're a member of any organization at home affiliated with Automobile International Travel (AIT), you qualify for basic benefits here, including breakdown service, towing, and transportation to the nearest provincial hospital. AIT's local representative in Cape Town is the Automobile Association (AA); fill in a form at the airport's Imperial Car Rental depot (Imperial has a rental-discount deal with the AA) or at any of the city's three AA auto shops.

Almost all gas stations are open 24 hours, and many have 24-hour convenience stores, some of which sell an impressive range of goods. Where possible, park in designated parking areas in shopping malls and at attractions. Parking attendants organized by municipal authorities and private business networks provide a valuable service. Most wear brightly colored vests; pay them R2–R3 for a short daytime stop and R5–R10 in the evening.

Rental Companies **Aroundaboutcars** (⊠ *Cape Town International Airport, Cape Town* ☎ *021/422-4022* ⊕ *www.aroundaboutcars.com*). **Avis** (⊠ *Cape Town International Airport, Cape Town* ☎ *021/934-0330* ⊕ *www.avis.co.za* ⊠ *123 Strand St., Cape Town* ☎ *021/424-1177* ⊠ *167A Rivonia Rd., Sandton, Johannesburg* ☎ *011/884-2221* ⊠ *O.R. Tambo International Airport, Johannesburg* ☎ *011/394-5433*). **Budget** (⊠ *Cape Town International Airport, Cape Town* ☎ *0861/016-622* ⊕ *www.budget.co.za* ⊠ *Holiday Inn Crowne Plaza, Rivonia Rd. and Grayston Dr., Sandton, Johannesburg* ☎ *011/883-5730* ⊠ *O.R. Tambo International Airport, Johannesburg* ☎ *011/394-2905*). **Europcar** (⊠ *Sandton Holiday Inn Garden Court, Maude and West Sts., Sandton, Johannesburg* ☎ *011/883-8508* ⊕ *www.europcar.co.za* ⊠ *O.R. Tambo International Airport, Johannesburg* ☎ *011/394-8832*). **Hertz** (⊠ *Cape Town International Airport, Cape Town* ☎ *0861/600-136* ⊕ *www.hertz.co.za* ⊠ *Sandton Hilton, Rivonia Rd. at Chaplin St., Sandton, Johannesburg* ☎ *011/322-1598* ⊠ *O.R. Tambo International Airport, Johannesburg* ☎ *011/390-9700*). **Imperial** (⊠ *Cape Town International Airport, Cape Town* ☎ *021/935-8600* ⊕ *www.imperialcarrental.co.za* ⊠ *Strand and Loop Sts., Cape Town* ☎ *021/421-5190* ⊠ *Sandton Sun hotel, 5th St. and Alice La., Sandton, Johannesburg* ☎ *011/883-4352* ⊠ *O.R. Tambo International Airport, Johannesburg* ☎ *011/390-3909*). **Tempest Car Hire** (⊠ *Village Walk, Maude St., Sandton, Johannesburg* ☎ *011/784-3343* ⊕ *www.tempestcarhire. co.za* ⊠ *O.R. Tambo Airport International, Johannesburg* ☎ *011/394-8626*). **Value Car Hire** (⊠ *Cape Town International Airport, Cape Town* ☎ *021/386-7699 or 0800/040-7557* ⊕ *www.valuecarhire.co.za*).

Roadside Assistance **Automobile Association** (☎ *080/001-0101 or 080/011- 1998* ⊕ *www.aasa.co.za*).

BY TRAIN

There's no train service within Johannesburg and its immediate surroundings, but there is in Cape Town. Cape Town's train station is on Adderley Street, in the heart of the city, surrounded by lively rows of street vendors and a taxi stand. The station building and facilities serve local, interprovincial, and luxury lines.

Metrorail, Cape Town's commuter line, offers regular service to the northern, southern, and False Bay suburbs, plus the Winelands towns of Paarl, Stellenbosch, and Franschoek. If you travel on Metrorail during off-peak periods, avoid isolated cars and compartments, and be alert to your surroundings when the train is stopped. Muggers work trains intensively, slipping on and off with ease. Train security is at best erratic. You're safer standing in a cramped third-class car than sitting comfortably in splendid isolation in an empty first-class one, but watch your pockets.

National carrier Shosholoza Meyl runs the *Trans-Karoo* daily between Cape Town and Johannesburg; the trip takes about 26 hours and costs R500 first class, R335 second class, and R200 economy. First- and second-class cars have sleeping compartments. A weekly train from Cape Town to Durban, the *Trans-Oranjia,* takes two days and costs R645 first class. You need to make first- and second-class reservations by phone (bookings open three months before date of travel) and then pay at the station in advance (not just before departure). For a third-class ticket you can pay just before you go. The reservations office at the Cape Town train station is open 8–4 weekdays and 8–10 AM weekends. Transnet's *Union Limited* steam train and Shongololo Express's *Southern Cross* also run through the Karoo and the Garden Route to Johannesburg. The *Southern Cross* is a night ride, so forget about seeing the splendors of the Garden Route along the way.

For more information on long-distance train travel and luxury train trips, see South Africa Essentials, below.

Train Line **Metrorail** (☎ 080/065-6463 ⊕ www.metrorail.co.za). **Shongololo Express** (☎ 011/781-4616 ⊕ www.shongololo.com). **Shosholoza Meyl** (☎ 086/000-8888 ⊕ www.spoornet.co.za/ShosholozaMeyl). **Transnet** (⊕ www.spoornet.co.za).

CONTACTS & RESOURCES

BUSINESS SERVICES & FACILITIES

If you need an office on the fly, you can use your hotel's business center. Or, look for a PostNet South Africa, which is the country's version of Kinko's. It offers a range of business solutions with branches countrywide. But unless you have business in South Africa, we suggest you leave the laptop at home and take memory cards for your vacation photos. You can check e-mail for a few rand either in the comfort of your hotel or at a public Internet café. The Cybercafes Web site lists more than 4,000 Internet cafés worldwide.

Contacts **PostNet South Africa** (☎ 860/767-8638 ⊕ www.postnet.co.za). **Cybercafes** (⊕ www.cybercafes.com).

DAY TOURS IN & AROUND CAPE TOWN

Several companies offer guided tours of the city center, the south peninsula, the Winelands, and anyplace else in the Cape you might wish to visit. They differ in type of transportation used and tour focus.

BIKE TOURS BazBus tours the south peninsula with a trailer full of bikes. You cycle the fun parts and sit in the bus for the rest. It costs about R385. Daytrippers specializes in bike tours but uses all sorts of modes of transportation, from bus to boat to foot, to explore the area.

Tour Operator **BazBus** (☎ 021/439-2323 ⊕ www.bazbus.com). **Daytrippers** (☎ 021/511-4766 ⊕ www.daytrippers.co.za).

BOAT TOURS ■TIP➜ Until the middle of the 20th century, most travelers' first glimpse of Cape Town was from the sea, and that's still the best way to get a feeling for the city's impressive setting, with its famous mountain as a backdrop. The Waterfront Boat Company offers trips on a range of boats, from yachts to large motor cruisers. A 1½-hour sunset cruise from the V&A Waterfront costs about R190, and includes a glass of bubbly. *Tigger 2* and Drumbeat charters both run a variety of trips in the lovely Hout Bay area, ranging from sunset cruises to full-day crayfishing expeditions. A trip from Hout Bay to Seal Island with Drumbeat Charters costs R50 for adults, R20 for kids. ■TIP➔ The only boat trip to actually land on Robben Island is the museum's ferry.

Tour Operators **Drumbeat Charters** (☎ 021/791–4441 or 021/790–4859 ⊕ www.drumbeatcharters.co.za). *Tigger 2* **Charters** (☎ 021/790–5256 ⊕ www. tiggertoo.co.za). **Waterfront Boat Company** (☎ 021/418–0134 ⊕ www.water frontboats.co.za).

BUS & CAR TOURS Large- and small-group bus tours are operated by African Eagle Day Tours, Hylton Ross, Springbok Atlas, and Windward Tours, among many others. Expect to pay R300–R350 for a half-day trip and about R450–R600 for a full-day tour. There's a wide selection of tours to choose from. A day trip might include Cape Town highlights followed by a visit to Stellenbosch for some wine tasting; a half-day trip could involve a visit to a local township. Many of the companies will also tailor private trips to suit your needs.

Hylton Ross also sells tickets for the hop-on/hop-off CitySightSeeing Cape Town bus; a day ticket costs R100, and there are two routes to choose from. The Red Route runs through the city, and you can get on and off at major museums, the V&A Waterfront, Table Mountain Aerial Cableway, Two Oceans Aquarium, and other attractions. The Blue Route takes you farther afield—to Kirstenbosch National Botanic Gardens, Hout Bay, World of Birds, and Camps Bay, to name just a few destinations.

Paradise Touring leads tours all around the Cape Town area. In addition to the usual Winelands and scenic peninsula tours, there are tours specifically designed to keep kids happy. The half-day family tour includes Two Oceans Aquarium, Table Mountain, and the South African Museum, plus time to play miniature golf and feed squirrels. The company also offers a township dinner-and-jazz experience.

Friends of Dorothy leads small group tours of the Winelands, the peninsula, and more for gay travelers. Quite a few cultural tours are also offered. Thuthuka Tours leads music and gospel tours of the townships.

Tour Operators **African Eagle Day Tours** (☎ 021/464–4266 ⊕ www.africa-adventure.org/a/africaneagle). **Friends of Dorothy** (☎ 021/465–1871 ⊕ www. friendsofdorothytours.co.za). **Hylton Ross Tours** (☎ 021/511–1784 ⊕ www. hyltonross.co.za). **Paradise Touring** (☎ 021/713–1020 ⊕ www.paradisetouring. co.za).. **Springbok Atlas** (☎ 021/460–4700 ⊕ www.springbokatlas.com). **Thuthuka Tours** (☎ 021/433–2429 or 083/979–5831). **Windward Tours** (☎ 021/419–3475 ⊕ www.windwardtours.co.za).

HELICOPTER & AIRPLANE TOURS Helicopters fly from the V&A Waterfront for a tour on a three- or four-seater chopper. Most operators charge between R1,300 and R1,800 for a 20-minute trip, and R4,900 to R5,400 for an hour in the air. Civair and NAC/Makana offer tours of the city and surrounding area ranging in length from 20 minutes to several hours. Custom tours can also be arranged, and the price varies according to how many people are flying. Downhill Adventures offers trips in a variety of light aircraft, including helicopters.

Tour Operators **Civair Helicopters** (☎*021/419–5182* ⊕*www.civair.co.za*). **Downhill Adventures** (☎*021/422–0388 or 021/422–1580* ⊕*www.downhilladventures.com*). **NAC/Makana Aviation** (☎*021/425–3868* ⊕*www.nacmakana.com*).

WALKING TOURS Cape Town on Foot offers fun city walking tours lasting 1½–2½ hours. The tours cover major historical attractions, architecture, and highlights of modern-day Cape Town. A separate Bo-Kaap tour is one of the best ways to explore this neighborhood. Expect to pay around R100 for 2½ hours.

Footsteps to Freedom has two really good walking tours—one of the city and its historical sites and the other of the V&A Waterfront. The guides are friendly and well informed, offer a rare insight into the city, and can help you with tours of the Bo-Kaap and townships. They also have great maps of the city, peninsula, and Winelands called *Serious Fun Guides*, which you can pick up at various outlets.

Take some of the mystery out of Table Mountain with a guide who can share information on the incredible diversity of flora and fauna you'll come across. Join walking and climbing tours with Venture Forth International, or tag along on a group walk open to everyone (most are on weekends). Pick up a Cumhike timetable from any Cape Union Mart outdoor store (found in almost every mall). Pamphlets for a self-guided walking tour of city-center attractions can be picked up at Cape Town Tourism. You can book specialized birding walks through Bird-Watch Cape.

Tour Operators **Bird-Watch Cape** (☎*021/762–5059* ⊕*www.birdwatch.co.za*). **Cape Town on Foot** (☎*021/462–4252* ⊕*www.wanderlust.co.za*). **Footsteps to Freedom** (☎*021/426–4260 or 083/452–1112* ⊕*www.footstepstofreedom.co.za*). **Venture Forth International** (☎*0861/106–548* ⊕*www.ctsm.co.za*).

DAY TOURS IN & AROUND JOHANNESBURG

DIAMOND & GOLD TOURS Schwartz Jewellers conducts one-hour tours of its workshops in Sandton by appointment. You can see stone grading, diamond setting, and gold pouring, and, of course, you can buy the finished product. Tours are free and include refreshments, and you need to take your passport along for security reasons.

Tour Operators **Schwartz Jewellers** (☎*011/783–1717* ⊕*www.schwartzjewellers.com*).

GENERAL-INTEREST TOURS Springbok Atlas and Gold Reef City Tours offer two- to three-hour tours of Johannesburg that include visits to the city center, the vibrant Soweto area, the Apartheid Museum, Gold Reef City theme park, and some of the city's more interesting parks and suburbs. Other tours explore Tshwane; Cullinan Diamond Mine, including a working mineshaft; Sun City; and Pilanesberg National Park. Tour fees start around

R350 per person for half-day tours and R150 per person for five-hour game drives. Wilro Tours conducts various tours to Soweto, Johannesburg, and the Pilanesberg. The Johannesburg Tourism Company has customized tours (golf anyone?) that include visits to the Apartheid Museum, the Tswaing Meteorite Crater, and Soweto. The company also has information on the city's accommodations, sights, nightlife, and restaurants. Observer Tours and Charters will do tailor-made, chauffeur-driven tours for one or two people or small groups, costing up to R1,200 for an eight-hour tour of the city. It also has shorter tours to Soweto and Tshwane. JMT Tours and Safaris can arrange trips to Soweto, Sun City, the Lesedi Cultural Village in Magaliesberg, Kruger National Park, and other destinations.

The Adventure Bus is an excellent way to see Johannesburg's main sights in about three hours, with plenty of stops. Tours leave several times a day from Sandton (except Monday). Your ticket is valid for 24 hours, so you can jump on and off as many times as you like.

Africa Explore offers full- and half-day tours of the Cradle of Humankind area; the full package (from R780 per person sharing per day) includes the Kromdraai Gold Mine, Sterkfontein Caves, and Rhino and Lion Park. Palaeo-Tours runs full- and half-day trips to local paleontological sites.

If you choose not to drive around Pilanesberg National Park on your own, you can join a 2½-hour escorted safari with Pilanesberg Mankwe Safaris for R230. Or you can embark on an elephant safari offered by Game Trackers Outdoor Adventures, offered three times daily for R1,090. The outfit also has balloon safaris. No under-five-year-olds are allowed and the maximum number of riders is 10. A one-hour flight (R2,750 per person) includes a game drive, sparkling wine, and a full English breakfast at the Bakubung game lodge. Bookings are essential.

Tour Operators Adventure Bus (☎011/975–9338). **Africa Explore** (☎011/917–1999 ⊕ www.africa-explore.co.za). **Game Trackers Outdoor Adventures** (☎014/552–5020 ⊕ www.gametrac.co.za). **Gold Reef City Tours** (☎011/917–1999). **JMT Tours and Safaris** (☎011/980–6038 ⊕ www.jmttours.co.za). **Johannesburg Tourism Company** (☎011/214–700 ⊕ www.joburgtourism.com). **Observer Tours and Charters** (☎011/609–4752). **Palaeo-Tours** (☎011/726–8788 ⊕ www.palaeotours.com). **Pilanesberg Mankwe Safaris** (☎014/555–7056 ⊕ www.mankwesafaris.co.za) **Springbok Atlas** (☎011/396–1053 ⊕ www.springbokatlas.com). **Wilro Tours** (☎011/789–9688 ⊕ www.wilrotours.co.za).

TOWNSHIP TOURS Tours of Soweto and/or Alexandra (also called Alex) are offered by many of the above operators as well as Jimmy's Face to Face Tours. Information on additional Soweto tours can also be obtained from the Soweto Tourism Association and Soweto.co.za.

Tour Operators Jimmy's Face to Face Tours (☎11/331–6109 ⊕ www.face2face.co.za). **Soweto.co.za** (☎011/326–1600 ⊕ www.soweto.co.za). **Soweto Tourism Association** (☎011/938–3337).

EMERGENCIES

Emergency centers at public hospitals are overworked, understaffed, and underfunded. They deal with a huge number of local people, most of whom cannot afford any alternative. Ambulances are provided by the state, but visitors are advised to use private hospitals, which are open round-the-clock and have ambulances linked to their private hospital group (although these services can transport patients to any health facility).

Most pharmacies close about 6, though there are a few all-night pharmacies. If a pharmacy is closed, it will still usually post emergency numbers. There are also pharmacies in Clicks and Dischem stores, which are located in shopping complexes in both cities.

Emergency Services **Ambulance** (☎*999 or 10177*). **General Emergencies** (☎*10111 from landline, 112 from mobile line*). **Police** (☎*10111*). **Police, Fire, and Ambulance services** (☎*107 from landline*). **Vodacom emergency services** (☎*112 from mobile phone*).

Hospitals in Johannesburg **Milpark Hospital** (✉*9 Guild Rd., off Empire Rd., Parktown* ☎*011/480–5600*). **Sandton Medi-Clinic** (✉*Main St. and Peter Pl., off William Nicol Dr., Lyme Park* ☎*011/709–2000*).

Hospitals in Cape Town **Constantiaberg Medi-clinic** (✉*Burnham Rd., Plumstead* ☎*021/799–2911*). **Panorama Medi-clinic** (✉*Rothchild Blvd., Panorama* ☎*021/938–2111*).

MONEY

You can exchange currency at Johannesburg International Airport or at the larger branches of South Africa's banks, such as ABSA, FNB (First National Bank), Nedbank, and Standard Bank's operations in Rosebank and Sandton. Look for the BUREAU DE CHANGE (exchange counter) signs at these banks. ATMs are all over the city, especially at shopping centers. Be careful when using them, though. Don't let anybody distract your attention, and avoid ATMs in quiet spots at night. Traveler's checks are welcome, but more and more businesses are switching over to credit cards.

In Cape Town, don't even think about changing money at your hotel. The rates at most hotels are outrageous, and the city has plenty of banks and bureaux de change offering better rates. Most suburbs have banks in the main streets and malls with currency-exchange facilities and American Express branches open during business hours (weekdays and Saturday mornings). Rennies Bank's Waterfront branch is open until 9 PM daily. At the airport, Foreign Exchange exchanges currency weekdays 7 AM–11 PM and weekends 8 AM–11 PM.

Exchange Services **American Express** (✉*Ground fl., Thibault House, Thibault Sq., Cape Town Central* ☎*021/425–7991* ✉*Shop 11A, Alfred Mall, Waterfront* ☎*021/419–3917* ⊕*www.amex.co.za*). **Rennies Bank** (✉*2 St. George's Mall, Cape Town Central* ☎*021/418–1206* ✉*Upper Level, Victoria Wharf, Waterfront* ☎*021/418–3744*).

SAFETY

Johannesburg is notorious for being South Africa's most dangerous city, and it is inadvisable to drive yourself in and around the city as certain areas are known carjacking spots. The crimes are so prevalent that there are permanent street signs marking those areas that are most dangerous. Order a car service or transportation from your hotel for trips in and around the city if you are not traveling with a local. That said, the city is generally safe so long as you take reasonable precautions. Don't carry large wads of cash and don't walk in the city center or any of the townships with flashy jewelry or expensive equipment. If you do drive, don't leave bags or valuables visible in a car, and keep the doors locked, even while driving (to minimize the risk of smash-and-grab robberies or being hijacked).

Although overall crime in Cape Town has declined in recent years, certain areas that are perfectly safe during the day, such as the City Bowl's side streets, should be avoided at night. Seek the advice of locals, take taxis directly to and from your destination, and don't walk alone or even in pairs unless a resident has told you that a neighborhood is safe. Despite thousands of safe visits every year, Table Mountain, which couldn't look less threatening, has been the location of several knife-point robberies in daylight. Never be completely off guard.

VISITOR INFORMATION

Cape Town Tourism is the city's official tourist body, providing information on tours, hotels, restaurants, rental cars, and shops. It has a coffee shop, wineshop, and Internet café. The staff also makes hotel, tour, travel, and walking-tour reservations. The office at Burg and Castle streets is open weekdays 8–6, Saturday 8:30–1, and Sunday 9–1. The Waterfront branch is open daily 9–9.

The Johannesburg Tourism Company has an excellent Web site, as does the Soweto Accommodation Association's site, which lists more than 20 lodgings. Interested in making a trip to the Cradle of Humankind? The Maropeng Visitor Centre provides information about the visitor centers in the area.

Contacts **Cape Town Tourism** (⊠ *The Pinnacle, Burg and Castle Sts., Cape Town Central* ☏ *021/487–6800 or 021/405–4500* ⊠ *Clock Tower Centre, South Arm Rd., Waterfront* ☏ *021/405–4500* ⊕ *www.tourismcapetown.co.za*). **Johannesburg Tourism Company** (☏ *011/214–0700* ⊕ *www.joburg.org.za*). **Maropeng Visitor Centre** (☏ *014/577–9000* ⊕ *www.maropeng.co.za*). **Soweto Accommodation Association** (☏ *011/936–8123* ⊕ *www.sowetobedandbreakfast.co.za*).

BEACH ESCAPES

So you've had your fill of exploring the bush, tracking animals and birds, immersing yourself in wilderness. Now maybe you've got time to head for the beach. Summer is the best time to catch a tan, but both Plettenberg Bay and Wilderness, on South Africa's famed Garden Route, are great in winter, too, with plenty to do and see nearby. People also head to Durban in winter as well as in summer.

DURBAN

Though Durban is South Africa's most vibrant city as well as Africa's busiest port, it also has some of the most accessible, beautiful, and safe beaches in the world. The sand and inviting water temperatures extend all the way up the Dolphin (North) Coast and beyond, as well as south from Durban, down the Hibiscus Coast and into the Eastern Cape. Even in winter (April through September), the weather is particularly pleasant and you'll be able swim.

Durban's beachfront extends for about 12 km (7½ mi) from South Beach, at the base of Durban Point, all the way past North Beach and the Suncoast Casino to Blue Lagoon, on the southern bank of the Umgeni River. The section of beachfront between South Beach and the Suncoast Casino is particularly safe, as police patrol often. It's lovely to take a stroll along here early or late in the day, when it's less busy, just don't walk here late at night. Walk out onto one of the many piers and watch surfers tackling Durban's famous waves. Of any place in Durban, the Beachfront most defines the city.

WHAT TO SEE

2 **uShaka Sea World.** The world's fifth-largest aquarium and the largest in
★ ☼ the Southern Hemisphere, Sea World has a capacity of nearly 6 million gallons of water, more than four times the size of Cape Town's aquarium. The innovative design is as impressive as the size. You enter through the side of a giant ship and walk down several stories, past the massive skeleton of Misty, a southern right whale that died near Cape Town after colliding with a ship, until a sign welcomes you to the BOTTOM OF THE OCEAN. Here you enter a "labyrinth of shipwrecks"—a jumble of five different fake but highly realistic wrecks, from an early-20th-century passenger cruiser to a steamship. Within this labyrinth are

massive tanks, housing more than 200 species of fish and other sea life and the biggest variety of sharks in the world, including ragged-tooth and Zambezi sharks (known elsewhere as bull sharks), responsible for more attacks on humans than any other species. Don't expect to see great whites, though; they don't survive in aquariums. While inside the aquarium, try to catch a fish-feeding.

On dry land, 20-minute dolphin and seal shows, held in adjacent stadiums twice a day (three times during busy seasons), are both well worth attending. For the best views of dolphin and seal shows, sit in the middle of the stadium toward the back. ⊠*1 Bell St., Point* ☎*031/328-8000* ⊕*www.ushakamarineworld.co.za* 🖪*R92; R135 with Wet 'n Wild* ⊙*Daily 9–5, weekends 9–6.*

❶ Natal Sharks Board. Most of the popular bathing beaches in KwaZulu-
★ ⓒ Natal are protected by shark nets maintained by this shark-research institute, the world's foremost. Each day, weather permitting, crews in ski boats check the nets, releasing healthy sharks back into the ocean and bringing dead ones back to the institute, where they are dissected and studied. The Natal Sharks Board offers one-hour tours that include a shark dissection (sharks' stomachs have included such surprising objects as a boot, a tin can, and a car license plate!) and an enjoyable and fascinating audiovisual presentation on sharks and shark nets. An exhibit area and good curio shop are also here. You can also join the early morning trip out to sea on a Sharks Board ski boat and watch the staff service the shark nets off Durban's Golden Mile. Depending on the season, you will more than likely see dolphins and whales close at hand. Booking is essential for trips to the shark nets, and a minimum of six people is required. ■TIP➔ Book well in advance for this, it may turn out to be a highlight of your trip. ⊠*1a Herrwood Dr., Umhlanga Rocks* ☎*031/566–0400* ⊕*www.shark.co.za* 🖪*Show R25; boat trips R200* ⊙*Trips to shark nets, 6:30–8:30* AM. *Shark show Tues., Wed., and Fri. 9 and 2 and Sun. at 2. Closed on Sat. and public holidays.*

WHERE TO STAY

BEACHFRONT   🏨 **Suncoast Hotel and Towers.** Durban's newest hotel, opened in Decem-
HOTELS ber 2006, is adjacent to the Suncoast Casino and is a stone's throw from
$–$$$$ the beach. Like the casino, the hotel is designed in the art deco style of the 1930s, in keeping with some of Durban's architectural heritage (the city is still home to a few beautiful art deco apartment buildings). The hotel is furnished in pastel shades and is elegantly minimalist, though the rooms are rather small. The sea views from the higher floors are spectacular (sea-facing rooms are slightly more expensive, but worth it). The hotel mostly attracts businesspeople and gamblers. ⊠*20 Battery Beach, Box 10690, Marine Parade, 4056* ☎*031/314–7878* ⊕*www.southernsun.com* ➴*165 rooms, 36 suites* ⚷*In-room: safe, Wi-Fi. In-hotel: restaurant, room service bar, pool, gym, spa* ▭*AE, DC, MC, V* ▯❙*CP.*

$$$ 🏨 **Southern Sun Elangeni.** One of the best hotels on the beachfront, this 21-story high-rise overlooks North Beach, and is a two-minute drive from the city center. It attracts a mix of business, conference, and leisure travelers. Though all rooms have views of the water, request a

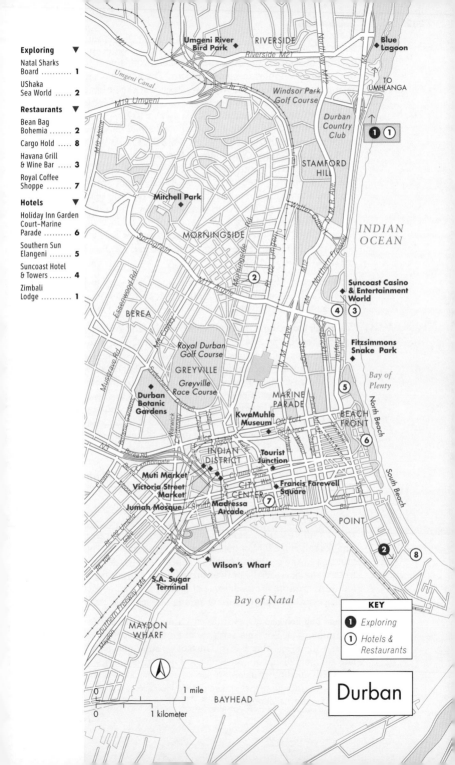

Umgeni River
Bird Park

RIVERSIDE

Blue
Lagoon

Riverside M21

Umgeni Canal

TO
UMHLANGA

Windsor Park
Golf Course

Durban
Country
Club

1 **1**

STAMFORD
HILL

**INDIAN
OCEAN**

Mitchell Park

MORNINGSIDE

2

Suncoast Casino
& Entertainment
World

4 **3**

BEREA

Fitzsimmons
Snake Park

Royal Durban
Golf Course

Bay of
Plenty

GREYVILLE

5

Greyville
Race Course

MARINE
PARADE

Durban
Botanic
Gardens

KwaMuhle
Museum

BEACH
FRONT

6

INDIAN
DISTRICT

Tourist
Junction

Muti Market

CITY
CENTER

Francis Farewell
Square

Victoria Street
Market

7

Jumah Mosque

Madressa
Arcade

POINT

2 **8**

Wilson's Wharf

S.A. Sugar
Terminal

Bay of Natal

KEY	
1	*Exploring*
1	*Hotels &* *Restaurants*

MAYDON
WHARF

1 mile

0

0   1 kilometer

BAYHEAD

Durban

room on an upper floor for a full ocean view. Rooms are small and narrow and have a beachlike seaside feel at odds with the formality of the marbled lobby and public rooms. The hotel has one of the few Japanese restaurants in the city as well as a first-class Indian restaurant. The hotel requires a minimum stay of two nights (price cited is for one night only). ✉ *101 Florida Rd., Berea 4001* ☎ *031/303–5246* ⊕ *www. quarters.co.za* ⇝ *25 rooms* ⚙ *In-room: Ethernet, refrigerator, safe. In-hotel: restaurant* ⊟ *AE, DC, MC, V* ⦿ *BP.*

$ ⬚ **Holiday Inn Garden Court—Marine Parade.** You can't beat the location of this pleasant hotel midway between South and North beaches and a five-minute drive from the city center. Rooms are attractive and modern, each with a small sitting area. All face the sea, but request an upper-floor room for the best views. Views from the pool deck on the 30th floor are superb. ✉ *167 Marine Parade, Box 10809, Beachfront 4056* ☎ *031/337–3341* ⊕ *www.southernsun.com* ⇝ *340 rooms, 6 suites* ⚙ *In-room: refrigerator, safe. In-hotel: restaurant, bar, pool* ⊟ *AE, DC, MC, V* ⦿ *BP.*

UMHLANGA   Pronounced m-*shlang*-gah, this area is one of the key Durban suburbs for surf, sand, and sun. It has a host of good restaurants, movie theaters, and shops.

$$$$ ⬚ **Zimbali Lodge.** One of only two luxury lodges in the province with
★   direct access to the beach, Zimbali's tranquil setting is in one of only a very few remaining coastal forests in the province. The decor is a stylish mix of African and Balinese, with lots of glass, dark wood, and rough woven fabrics. Rooms have an indulgently private and luxurious feel to them, with crisp white linen, wood carvings, large baths, and balconies that look out onto the forest, lake, and sea beyond. It's a wonderful place to laze around, enjoy afternoon tea, play a round of golf, horseback ride, or swim in the private Mauritian-style pool on the beach. The service is friendly and efficient. ✉ *M4, 20 km (12 mi) north of Umhlanga, Box 404, Umhlali 4390* ☎ *032/538–1007* ⊕ *www.sun-international.com* ⇝ *76 rooms, 10 executive forest suites* ⚙ *In-room: Wi-Fi, refrigerator, DVD, safe. In-hotel: room service, golf course, tennis courts, pools, gym, spa* ⊟ *AE, DC, MC, V.*

WHERE TO EAT

Durban offers some superb dining, provided you eat to its strengths. Thanks to a huge Indian population, it has some of the best curry restaurants in the country. Durban's other great gastronomic delight is fresh seafood, especially prawns brought down the coast from Mozambique. Apart from the food, some of the dining locales—including many with spectacular sea views—are among the best in the world.

¢–$$$$ ✕ **Bean Bag Bohemia.** One of the city's most intimate and most popular restaurants, Bohemia serves a mix of cosmopolitan and Mediterranean food. It's abuzz with Durban's young and trendy, especially late at night, when you can get a good meal after movies or the theater. Cocktails and lighter meals are served at the bar downstairs, where live musicians often play jazz or the piano. Up rickety wooden stairs at the main restaurant, a popular starter is the meze platter, with Mediterranean snacks such as hummus, baba ghanoush (an eggplant spread), olives, and pita. ⊠*18 Windermere Rd., Windermere* ☏*031/309–6019* ⊟*AE, DC, MC, V.*

$$–$$$ ✕**Cargo Hold.** You might need to book several months in advance to
★ secure a table next to the shark tank, but if you do, it'll be one of your most memorable dining experiences ever. You can enjoy a trio of carpaccios—smoked ostrich, beef, and salmon—while 13-foot ragged-tooth and Zambezi sharks drift right by your table. Aside from the array of fish dishes like sesame-seared tuna and Kingklip à la Cargo (grilled kingklip topped with mussels poached in a passion fruit and bourbon cream sauce), Cargo Hold also serves meat dishes like oxtail, a South African favorite; and rosemary-and-rock-salt leg of lamb. The restaurant is done up like a shipwreck; of three floors, two have tank frontage (the view of the shark tank from the bottom floor is best, so ask for this when booking). The restaurant is part of the Phantom Ship. Access to the ship costs R20, though this is refunded if you dine in Cargo Hold. ⊠*1 Bell St., Point* ☏*031/328–8065* ⊟*AE, DC, MC, V.*

$–$$$ ✕**Havana Grill & Wine Bar.** The sea views and good food combine to
★ make this one of Durban's finest restaurants, though most dishes are on the pricey side for Durban. It offers spectacular sea vistas (ask for a table with a view when making your reservation) and minimalist Afro-Cuban decor, with upholstered chairs, leather couches, and antelope horns on the walls. Steak—aged on meat hooks in a giant fridge integrated into the decor—and seafood are both specialties. Try Havana's tasting platter for starters (minimum of two people sharing): nachos, crumbed jalapeño poppers stuffed with cheese, grilled calamari, and spring rolls. For mains, consider the Lamb Tanganyika, which is rubbed with toasted cumin and coriander and served with a rich gravy, or line fish (likely sailfish, dorado, or Cape salmon), served in five different ways: grilled with lemon butter, topped with fresh pesto and fettucine, with a coriander dipping sauce and wasabi-infused mash, in a Thai green coconut curry, or in an Asian red curry. There's a good basic wine list as well as a walk-in cellar from which special bottles can be ordered. ⊠*Shop U2, Suncoast Casino & Entertainment World, Beach-front* ☏*031/337–1304* ⊿*Reservations essential* ⊟*AE, DC, MC, V.*

$–$$ ✕**Royal Coffee Shoppe.** Its location in the Royal Hotel makes this a popular meeting place for Durban society and pre- and post-theater crowds. Crystal chandeliers, etched glass, formally dressed staff, and live piano music in the nearby lounge at lunchtime create a rich atmosphere of old-time colonial Durban. The café serves light breakfasts and lunch as well as coffees, teas, cakes, quiches, salads, and sandwiches. ⊠*267 Smith St., City Center* ☏*031/304–0331* ⊟*AE, MC, V.*

PLETTENBERG BAY

☾ Plettenberg Bay is South Africa's premier beach resort, as the empty houses on Beachy Head Road (known as Millionaires' Mile) during the 11 months when it's not beach season will attest. But in December the hordes with all their teenage offspring arrive en masse. Even then you can find yourself a stretch of lonely beach if you're prepared to

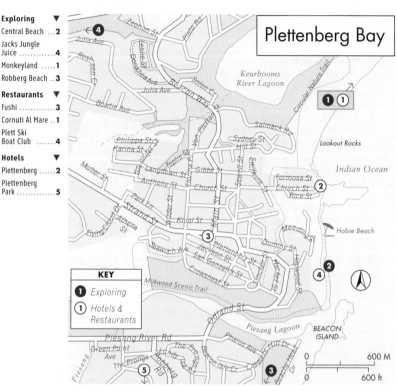

walk to the end of Keurboomstrand. Plett, as it is commonly known, is one of the best places in the world to watch whales and dolphins (peak whale-watching season is July–October). Boat-based trips are run from Central Beach, as are sea-kayaking trips, which, although loads of fun, are not quite as efficient as the big motorboats.

Plett presides over a stretch of coastline that has inspired rave reviews since the Portuguese first set eyes on it in 1497 and dubbed it *Bahia Formosa* (Beautiful Bay). Three rivers flow into the sea here, the most spectacular of which—the Keurbooms—backs up to form a large lagoon. For swimming, surfing, sailing, hiking, and fishing you can't do much better than Plett, although the water is still colder than it is around Durban and in northern KwaZulu-Natal.

WHAT TO SEE

❷ **Central Beach.** All the dolphin-watching boats and kayak trips leave from this beach. A constant stream of tenders going out to the fishing boats moored in the bay makes this area quite busy, but it's still a great beach. Just keep away from the boat-launching area, and swim in the southern section.

❹ **Jacks Jungle Juice.** It's fun to tour this *mampoer* (moonshine) distillery at the Buffalo Hills Game Reserve and Lodge. You can see how mampoer is made, and taste several mampoer-based liqueurs. ⊠*Stofpad, Witte-drif* ☏*044/535–9739* ✉*Free* ☉*Weekdays 9–3.*

❶ **Monkeyland.** Monkeyland is a refuge for abused and abandoned pri-
☺ mates, most of which were once pets or laboratory animals. They now roam in a huge enclosed area of natural forest and are free to play, socialize, and do whatever it is that keeps primates happy. There are lemurs, gibbons, spider monkeys, indigenous vervet monkeys, howler monkeys, and many more. Guided walks are run throughout the day, and the tamer "inmates" often play with guests. ⊠*16 km (10 mi) east of Plettenberg Bay along N2, just before Nature's Valley turnoff* ☏*044/534–8906* ⊕*www.monkeyland.co.za* ✉*R100* ☉*Daily 8–5.*

❸ **Robberg Beach.** Just on the other side of the Beacon Isle, the unmissable hotel at the end of the tombolo, is Robberg, a great swimming beach that continues in a graceful curve all the way to Robberg Peninsula. You can get pretty good sightings of dolphins and whales just behind the back break.

SPORTS & OUTDOOR ACTIVITIES

Fodor'sChoice **Whale-Watching.** Plettenberg Bay is truly one of the best locations
★ worldwide for boat-based whale- and dolphin-watching. Most days visitors see at least two cetacean species and Cape fur seals, as well as a variety of seabirds, including Cape gannets and African penguins. On some days people have seen up to six cetacean species in the course of a few hours.

Two similar operators have you board an open vehicle outside a shop and from there step directly onto a boat at the beach. Boats are fast, safe, and dry. Both operators offer a standard trip (about R300), in which the boat must stay 975 feet from the animals, and a close-encounter trip (about R500) on a boat that is licensed to approach within 162 feet. These trips are limited in order to minimize distur-bance to the whales. **Ocean Blue** (⊠*Hopwood St., Central Beach* ☏*044/533–5083* ⊕*www.oceanadventures.co.za*) runs whale- and dolphin-watching trips from its base on the beach. Based near the beach, **Ocean Safaris** (⊠*Hopwood St., Central Beach* ☏*044/533–4963 or 082/784–5729* ⊕*www.oceansafaris.co.za*) runs regular whale- and dolphin-watching trips.

WHERE TO STAY & EAT

As one of the most sophisticated destinations on the Garden Route, Plett has plenty of fabulous places to eat and overnight.

$–$$ ✕**Fushi.** Plett's slickest, sleekest eatery is all clean surfaces and clas-sical lines. In addition to sushi, there are unusual Pan-Asian dishes such as the deboned, pressed lamb shank with saffron rice, spicy chili sauce, and cucumber-yogurt dressing. The wasabi crème brûlée is a new twist on an old favorite. ⊠*Upper Deck, Marine Dr.* ☏*044/533–4440* ⊟*AE, DC, MC, V* ☉*No dinner Sun.*

¢–$$ ✕**Cornuti Al Mare.** The blue-and-white tiles on the facade of this popu-lar, casual Italian eatery—a favorite with locals that's usually pretty full—give the place a beach-house feel. Try a nice solid pasta, or the thin wood-fired pizzas; the potato pizza is so much tastier than it sounds. In summer, arrive early to get a seat on the veranda. ⊠ *Odd-lands and Perestrello Sts.* ☎ *044/533–1277* ⚲ *Reservations not accepted* ⊟ *AE, DC, MC, V.*

¢ ✕ **Plett Ski Boat Club.** Want to know a secret? Plett fisherfolk, ski-boat skippers, surfers, kayak operators, and other locals frequent this very, very casual eatery. It's right on the beach where the ski boats launch, so there's a great view—especially from the outside tables. It offers really good value for the money; well-cooked, fresh but not fancy seafood; the usual burgers and fries; and full breakfasts. Many locals can be reliably tracked down to the popular bar on weekday afternoons—especially if there is a rugby match on TV. ⊠ *Central Beach* ☎ *044/533–4147* ⚲ *Reservations not accepted* ⊟ *AE, DC, MC, V* ⊘ *No dinner.*

$$$$ ✕🏠 **Plettenberg.** High on a rocky point in Plettenberg Bay, this luxury
★ hotel has unbelievable views of the bay, the Tsitsikamma Mountains, Keurbooms Lagoon, miles of magnificent beach, and, in season, whales frolicking just beyond the waves. Built around an 1860 manor house, the hotel is light and bright, decorated in shades of white and blue. Service is wonderfully attentive, with a front-desk staff that tries to anticipate your every need. Even if you don't stay here, treat yourself to lunch on the hotel terrace. Diners sit under large fabric umbrellas and look out over a pool that seems to extend right into the incredible views. The lunch menu is small: salads, sandwiches, a pasta dish, and the catch of the day. Dinner in the restaurant ($$; reservations essential) is a fancier affair, focusing on local meat and seafood. Villas are self-catering. ⊠ *Lookout Rocks* ⌂ *Box 719, 6600* ☎ *044/533–2030* ⊕ *www.plettenberg.com* ⟿ *24 rooms, 12 suites, 2 villas* ⚲ *In-room: a/c, kitchen (some), refrigerator. In-hotel: restaurant, bar, pools, spa, no elevator, laundry service, airport shuttle, parking (no fee), no kids under 12, no-smoking rooms* ⊟ *AE, DC, MC, V* ⊙❘*BP.*

$$$$ 🏠 **Plettenberg Park.** The setting of this stylish, minimalist lodge—in
★ splendid isolation on a cliff top in a private nature reserve on the western (wild) side of Robberg Peninsula—is one of the best anywhere, and the view of the open ocean across fynbos-clad hills is spectacular. Rooms are decorated in an understated African colonial style in shades of white and cream; those that face the sea have dramatic views, and the others overlook a tranquil lily pond. A steep path leads to a private beach and natural tidal pool. ⊠ *Off Robberg Rd.* ⌂ *Box 167, 6600* ☎ *044/533–9067* ⊕ *www.plettenbergpark.co.za* ⟿ *9 rooms* ⚲ *In-room: safe, refrigerator, VCR. In-hotel: restaurant, room service, bar, pool, gym, spa, beachfront, no elevator, laundry service, concierge, airport shuttle, no kids under 12, no-smoking rooms* ⊟ *AE, DC, MC, V* ⊙❘*BP.*

SHOPPING

Plenty of shops in and around town sell casual beachwear and various crafts, but for a good concentration in a small place, you can't beat **Old Nick** (⊠ *N2, just east of town* ☎ *044/533–1395*). Originally just a pottery and weaving studio, it has grown to include a host of other crafts—so many that you could spend a whole day here. Included are a weaving museum, a shop selling lovely woven goods, a crystal shop, and a few galleries. A handmade-soap factory beckons with the scent of essential oils and fruits, and the **Country Kitchen** competes for your olfactory attention with the heady aroma of freshly brewed espresso.

WILDERNESS

Wilderness is a popular vacation resort for good reason. Backed by thickly forested hills and cliffs, the tiny town presides over a magical stretch of beach between the Kaaimans and Touw rivers, as well as a spectacular system of waterways, lakes, and lagoons strung out along the coast, separated from the sea by towering vegetated dunes.

WHAT TO SEE
Much of the area now falls under the control of **Wilderness National Park,** a 6,500-acre reserve that stretches east along the coast for 31 km (19 mi). This wetlands paradise draws birders from all over the country to its two blinds. Walking trails wend through the park, including the circular 10-km (6-mi) Pied Kingfisher Trail, which covers the best of what Wilderness has to offer: beach, lagoon, marsh, and river. ⊠ *Off N2* ☎ *044/877–1197* ⊕ *www.sanparks.org* ⊠ *R15* ⊙ *Daily 8–5.*

WHERE TO STAY & EAT

¢–$$ ✕ **Pomodoro.** A convenient location in the middle of town, friendly service, great food, and good value are the highlights of this Italian eatery. Pomodoro does breakfasts and throws in the odd burger to keep the masses happy, but the emphasis here is on crispy thin-crust pizzas—the butternut, feta, and rocket (arugula) is a favorite with local herbivores—pastas, and other Italian dishes. Try the fish-fillet parcels with white wine, tomatoes, peppers, and fresh herbs. Even the ubiquitous ostrich is given a Mediterranean twist—grilled with a pancetta, vermouth, and cream sauce. ⊠ *George St.* ☎ *044/877–1403* ⊟ *DC, MC, V.*

$$$–$$$$ ▦ **Xanadu.** Deep-pile carpets, double-volume spaces, spectacular floral arrangements, and voluminous drapes framing the sea-view windows add to the sense of opulence at this beachfront establishment. The classic, slightly over-the-top style—with dramatic shades of terracotta, and rich vibrant fabrics—tells you you're about to be pampered. Rooms are individually decorated, and all have balconies. The beach is just a short hop from the lawns and the saltwater pool. A small kitchenette means you can prepare a snack. ⊠ *43 Die Duin* ⌂ *Box 746, 6560* ☎ *044/877–0022* ⊕ *www.xanadu-wilderness.co.za* ⊠ *6 rooms* △ *In-room: a/c, no phone, DVD. In-hotel: pool, no elevator* ⊟ *AE, DC, MC, V* ⊠ *BP.*

$ ▦ **Wilderness Farm Backpackers.** Horses and cows in the field, a huge vegetable garden, and endless views over the ocean create a sense of space and abundance at this friendly, squeaky-clean hostel set high on a farm above Wilderness. Brothers Riaan and Theo, both qualified tour guides, offer excursions all over the Garden Route, as well as surfboard rentals and regular shuttles to and from Wilderness. You're welcome to use the well-equipped kitchen or barbecue, though you might want to opt to start the day off with a big farm breakfast for R25. ⊠ *291*

Whites Rd. ☎*Box 366, 6530* 🖀*082/838–5944 or 076/338–0512* ⊕*www.wildfarmbackpackers.co.za* ⇨*1 room, 1 dormitory* ☐*In-room: no phone, safe, no TV. In-hotel: bar* ☐*AE, DC, MC, V.*

¢–$ ⊡**Ebb and Flow Restcamp, Wilderness National Park.** Within Wilderness National Park is this rest camp divided into two sections, North and South. The South section is larger and consists of brick family cottages, which sleep up to six, as well as log cabins and forest huts, both of which sleep up to four. The log cabins are prettier than the cottages, but both are bright and pleasant, furnished in a plain but adequate manner with floral or geometric curtains and upholstery; both have bedrooms, kitchens, and bathrooms with balconies. Forest cabins are smaller but cute. Campsites, some of which directly overlook the river, are set on a wide lawn under trees. The much smaller North section has a few grassy campsites and 15 not-particularly-attractive rondawels. The communal bathroom areas are well maintained, clean, and adequate, and there area also on-site laundry facilities. You can fish, hike, and boat here. ⊠*Off N2* 🖀*044/877–1197* ⊕*www.sanparks.org* ⇨*5 cottages; 8 log cabins; 10 2-bed and 10 4-bed forest cabins; 12 rondawels, 10 with bath; 100 campsites* ☐*No elevator* ☐*AE, DC, MC, V.*

SPORTS & THE OUTDOORS

Wilderness National Park and environs provide opportunities for lovely walks, fantastic paddling, and fishing that is more recreational than productive.

★   Based inside Wilderness National Park, **Eden Adventures** (🖀*044/877–0179* ⊕*www.eden.co.za*) offers a canoeing and mountain-biking trip (R220), a kloofing (canyoning) excursion (R250), and abseiling (rappelling) in Kaaimans Gorge (R250). These are all half-day trips and include lunch, but they can be combined to form a full-day trip (R440–R475). You can also rent a two-seater canoe for exploring the wetlands (R120 per day). Eden Adventures also runs a 2 ½ -day guided canoeing and hiking trip in the park. It's fully catered, and accommodation is in either a tented camp or chalets. Prices range from R1,095 to R1,200, and custom tours can be arranged.

HIKING   On the five-day, guided **Garden Route Trail** (🖀*044/883–1015 or 082/213–5931* ⊕*www.gardenroutetrail.co.za*), you start in the Ebb and Flow Restcamp and then head east along the coast, taking in long beach walks and coastal forest, before ending in Knysna. The emphasis is on the natural environment, and knowledgeable guides provide commentary along the way. The trip is catered and portered, and you do some canoeing in addition to hiking. The five-day trail costs R4,200; a three-day trail is also available for R3,100.

PARAGLIDING   Wilderness is one of the best paragliding spots in the country, with
★   loads of launch sites. You can ridge-soar for miles along the dune front, watching whales and dolphins in the sea. If you've never done it before, don't worry: you can go tandem (R350–R450) with an experienced instructor from **Cloudbase Paragliding** (🖀*044/877–1414* ⊕*www.cloudbase-paragliding.co.za*). All you have to do is hang in there.

DURBAN, PLETTENBERG BAY & WILDERNESS ESSENTIALS

TRANSPORTATION

BY AIR

Durban International Airport (DUR) is 16 km (10 mi) south of town along the Southern Freeway, or an easy 20-minute drive. South African Airways (SAA) flies to Durban via Johannesburg. Domestic airlines serving Durban include SAA, BA/Comair, Kulula, 1Time, SA Airlink, and Mango.

The most inexpensive transfer into Durban and back is the Airport Shuttle Service, which costs R30 and departs a half hour after incoming flights arrive and leaves the city center every hour. Its drop-off points include the Hilton and Royal Hotels, but it is likely to drop you anywhere central if you request it first. Call ahead and the bus will pick you up at any hotel in the city; there's no need to reserve for the trip into Durban. If you want to go farther afield, call Magic Bus or Mozzie Cabs.

The only true airport serving the Garden Route is George Airport, 10 km (6 mi) southwest of the town of George (George is about 12 km [7 mi] northeast of Wilderness). George is well served by SAA, Kulula. com, 1time, and Nationwide. SA Airlink sometimes runs one flight a day between Johannesburg and the little airfield in Plett, 6 km (4 mi) west of town. African Ramble runs charters from Plett to Johannesburg and Cape Town, but more commonly to the Eastern Cape game reserves like Addo. These particularly scenic trips start by flying over Robberg and out over the bay (where you may see whales or dolphins) and then hugging the coast up to the small settlement of Nature's Valley before heading inland.

Airports **Durban International Airport** (☎ *031/408–1155*). **George Airport** (*GRJ* ☎ *044/876–9310* ⊕ *www.acsa.co.za*).

Airlines **African Ramble Air Charter** (✉ *Plettenberg Bay airfield* ☎ *044/533–9006* ⊕ *www.aframble.co.za*). **BA/Comair** (☎ *031/450–7000* ⊕ *www.britishairways.com*). **Kulula.com** (☎ *0861/585–852* ⊕ *www.kulula.com*). **Mango** (☎ *0861/162–646* ⊕ *ww6.flymango.com*). **Nationwide Airlines** (☎ *0861/737–737* ⊕ *www.flynationwide.co.za*). **1time** (☎ *0861/345–345* ⊕ *www.1time.co.za*). **SA Airlink** (☎ *0861/359–722 or 011/978–5313* ⊕ *www.saairlink.co.za*). **South African Airways** (☎ *0861/359–722 or 011/978–5313* ⊕ *ww4.flysaa.com*).

Airport Transfers **Airport Shuttle Service** (☎ *031/465–5573*). **Magic Bus** (☎ *031/263–2647*). **Mozzie Cabs** (☎ *0860/669–943*).

BY BUS

Greyhound and Translux Express offer long-distance bus service from Durban to cities all over South Africa. All intercity buses leave from New Durban Station (off N.M.R. Avenue, between Old Fort Avenue and Argyle Road). Nowadays, though, you can often fly for much the same prices as traveling by bus, especially if you book well in advance or find a discount.

Within Durban, Durban Transport operates two types of bus service, but you need concern yourself only with the Mynah buses. These small buses operate from 6 to 11:45 along set routes every half an hour through the city and along the Beachfront and cost a couple of rands per ride. Bus stops are marked by a sign with a mynah bird on it. The main bus depot is on Pine Street between Aliwal and Gardiner streets. You pay as you board; exact change is not required. Route information is also available at an information office at the corner of Aliwal and Pine streets.

Bus Lines Greyhound (☎ *083/915–9000*). **Mynah Bus (Durban City Transport)** (☎ *031/309–5942*). **Translux Express** (☎ *031/361–7670*).

BY CAR

You'll be much freer to explore the Durban area if you have a car. Avis, Budget, EuropCar, Imperial, and Tempest have rental offices at the airport. Durban is relatively easy to find your way around, because the sea is a constant reference point. Parking downtown is a nightmare; head for an underground garage whenever you can. It's pretty safe to park outside of Joe Cool's, between North and South beaches, but it's probably not a good idea to leave your keys with anyone.

Wilderness lies 441 km (273 mi) east of Cape Town along the N2 highway; Plettenberg Bay is an additional 72 km (45 mi) east of Wilderness. The road is in good condition and well signposted. It usually takes about five hours to drive from Cape Town to Wilderness—unless you stop to look at a view, have lunch, or browse in a roadside produce or crafts store. A few words of warning, however: there is a wide shoulder along most of the route, but pull onto it to let faster cars overtake you *only* when you can see a good few hundred yards ahead. ⚠ The area between George and Wilderness is notorious for speed traps, especially in the Kaaimans River Pass, just west of Wilderness. And in case you're continuing east on the N2, keep in mind that the fuel complex at Storms River Bridge is your last eastbound chance to refuel before Port Elizabeth—more than 160 km (100 mi) away.

■ TIP➔ An alternative to the N2 is the less traveled—some say more interesting—inland route, dubbed Route 62, even though some of it is on the R60. From Worcester, in the Breede River valley, traveling on the R60 and R62 to Oudtshoorn provides a great view of the Little Karoo.

Avis, Budget, Europcar, and Hertz all have car-rental offices at George Airport. Avis and Budget also have additional offices in the area. Europcar rentals include a cell phone.

Rental Companies Avis (✉ *Ulundi Pl., City Center, Durban* ☎ *031/304–1741* ⊕ *www.avis.co.za* ✉ *George Airport* ☎ *044/876–9314* ✉ *Plettenberg Bay* ☎ *044/533–1315*). **Budget** (✉ *Durban International Airport* ☎ *031/408–1809* ⊕ *www.budget.co.za* ✉ *George Airport* ☎ *044/876–9204* ✉ *9 Hill House, Main St., Plettenberg Bay* ☎ *044/533–1858*). **Europcar** (✉ *Durban International Airport* ☎ *031/469–0667* ⊕ *www.europcar.co.za* ✉ *George Airport* ☎ *044/876–9070*). **Hertz** (✉ *George Airport* ☎ *044/801–4700* ⊕ *www.hertz.co.za*). **Imperial Car Rental** (✉ *52 Stanger St., Morningside, Durban* ☎ *031/337–3731*). **Tempest Car Hire** (✉ *47 Victoria Embankment, Victoria Embankment, Durban* ☎ *031/469–0660*).

BY RICKSHAW

Colorfully decorated rickshaws are unique to Durban—you won't find them in any other South African city. Though their origins lie in India, these two-seat carriages with large wheels are all over the city and are pulled exclusively by Zulu men dressed in feathered headgear and traditional garb. The rickshaw runners ply their trade all day, every day, mostly along the Golden Mile section of the beachfront. The going rate is R30 for a ride (2 people) for about 15 minutes, and R10 for a photo (don't assume you can take a picture without paying for the privilege). While it's worth doing because it will be memorable and won't have the opportunity anywhere else, beware you aren't charged more because you're a foreigner—negotiate the rate before climbing on.

BY TAXI

Taxis in Durban are metered and start at R5, with an additional R7 per kilometer (per half mile). Expect to pay about R60 from City Hall to North Beach and R200 to the airport. The most convenient taxi stands are around City Hall and in front of the beach hotels. Some taxis display a "for-hire" light, whereas others you simply hail when you can see they're empty. Major taxi companies include Bunny Cabs, Checker Radio Taxis, Deluxe Radio Taxis, and Morris Radio Taxis. Eagle Radio Taxis is a little more expensive than other companies. If you're headed to the Indian Market on a weekend, consider having your taxi wait for you, as it can be difficult to flag a taxi in this neighborhood.

Taxi Companies **Bunny Cabs** (☎ 031/332–2914). **Checker Radio Taxis** (☎ 031/465–1660). **Deluxe Radio Taxis** (☎ 031/337–1661). **Eagle Radio Taxis** (☎ 031/337–8333). **Morris Radio Taxis** (☎ 031/337–2711).

BY TRAIN

The Durban railway station is a huge, ghastly place that is difficult to find your way around in. It's dirty and crowded, and petty theft is a problem. Spoornet's *Trans-Natal* train runs daily between Durban and Johannesburg, stopping at Pietermaritzburg, Estcourt, and Ladysmith. The trip to Jo'burg takes 13 hours and costs about R300 one way.

Train Station **Durban Railway Station** (✉ N.M.R. Ave., City Center, Durban ☎ 031/361–7609).

Train Line **Spoornet** (☎ 031/361–7609 ⊕ www.spoornet.co.za).

CONTACTS & RESOURCES

DAY TOURS

Durban Africa has a series of city walking tours for R40 per person. Tours depart from the Tourist Junction weekdays at 9:45 and return at 12:30, but you need to book in advance as the tour guide only arrives if reservations have been made. The Oriental Walkabout explores the Indian District, including Victoria Market and several mosques. The Historical Walkabout covers the major historic monuments in the city, and the Feel of Durban Walkabout explores some of the city's military past, including the Old Fort, Warrior's Gate, and the original armory. Durban Africa offers other tour options as well; a comprehensive list of tour options is on its Web site.

Sarie Marais Pleasure Cruises and Isle of Capri offer sightseeing cruises around Durban Bay or out to sea. Tours, which last about 90 minutes and cost about R60 per person, depart from the jetties next to the Natal Maritime Museum, on the Victoria Embankment at Aliwal Stand, the Point.

Tour Operators **Durban Africa** (⊠ *Tourist Junction, 160 Pine St., City Center, Durban* ☎ *031/304–4934* ⊕ *www.durban.kzn.org.za*). **Isle of Capri** (☎ *031/337–7751*). **Sarie Marais Pleasure Cruises** (☎ *031/305–2844*).

EMBASSY

United States **U.S. Embassy** (⊠ *Durban Bay House, 333 Smith St., City Center, Durban* ☎ *031/305–7600*).

EMERGENCIES

The best hospitals in central Durban are Entabeni and St. Augustine's, both private hospitals in the Glenwood area with 24-hour emergency rooms. Umhlanga Hospital is the best north of the city. Daynite Pharmacy is open daily until 10:30.

Most towns around Plett and Wilderness have late-night pharmacies, and if they don't, pharmacies usually have an emergency number on the door. Call the general-emergencies number for all emergencies. If you break down while driving, call your car-rental company or the company's designee. You can also call the Automobile Association (AA) for assistance. Call the National Sea Rescue Institute (NSRI) for local marine emergencies.

Emergency Services **Automobile Association** (☎ *083/84322*). **General Emergencies** (☎ *10111 from landline, 112 from mobile phone*). **National Sea Rescue Institute** (⊠ *Plettenberg Bay* ☎ *044/533–2744 or 082/490–6226*).

Hospitals **Entabeni Hospital** (⊠ *148 S. Ridge Rd., Glenwood, Durban* ☎ *031/204–1300*). **George Mediclinic** (⊠ *York St. and Gloucester Rd., George* ☎ *044/803–2000*). **Medsac Private Health Centre** (⊠ *Marine Dr., Plettenberg Bay* ☎ *044/533–0212*). **St. Augustine's** (⊠ *4 Cato Rd., Glenwood, Durban* ☎ *031/268–5000, 031/268–5559 trauma*). **Umhlanga Hospital** (⊠ *323 Umhlanga Rocks Dr., Umhlanga* ☎ *031/560–5500, 080/033–6967 trauma*).

Late-Night Pharmacy **Daynite Pharmacy** (⊠ *West St., City Center* ⊠ *Point Rd., Point, Durban* ☎ *031/368–3666*).

MAIL & INTERNET

The main post offices usually stay open from about 9 to 4:30 on weekdays and on Saturday mornings. There are Internet cafés all over, and most lodgings offer Internet access to their guests. Postnet (www.postnet.co.za) is a franchise that offers business, mail, Internet, and courier services.

MONEY MATTERS

There are plenty of ATMs in and around Durban—at shopping centers, large attractions like Suncoast and uShaka, and even some of the smaller supermarkets. Most bank branches exchange money, and the airport and uShaka have money exchanges, as do Rennies and the

AmEx foreign-exchange bureau. Though you will need cash at the markets, don't carry too much. Use credit cards where you can.

Exchange Services **AmEx foreign-exchange bureau** (⊠ *350 Smith St., City Center, Durban* ☎ *031/301–5541).* **Rennies** (⊠ *Durban Bay House, 333 Smith St., City Center, Durban* ☎ *031/307–2625).*

SAFETY

Durban has not escaped the crime evident in every South African city. Particularly in the city center but also elsewhere, smash-and-grab thieves roam the streets, looking for bags or valuables in your car, even while you're driving, so lock any valuables in the trunk and keep your car doors locked and windows up at all times. While there's no need to be fearful, be observant wherever you go. Don't walk downtown with expensive equipment like cameras clearly visible, and carry only small amounts of cash. Ask your hotel or guesthouse for safety tips about specific areas, because levels of crime can vary within a few streets. The Golden Mile is fairly safe and is regularly patrolled by police, but watch out for the street kids, who sometimes hunt in gangs. If you plan on taking a dip while you're at the beach, ask a neighboring beach-goer or lifeguard to keep an eye on your belongings, or put them in a locker—available between North and South beaches.

VISITOR INFORMATION

Durban's Tourist Junction, in the restored Old Station Building, houses a number of tourist-oriented companies and services, where you can find information on almost everything that's happening in Durban and KwaZulu-Natal. Among the companies represented are Durban Africa, the city's tourism authority; an accommodations service; an intercity train reservations office; a KwaZulu-Natal Nature Conservation Service booking desk; regional KwaZulu-Natal tourist offices; and various bus and transport companies. It is open weekdays 8–5 and weekends 9–2. Sugar Coast Tourism (covering the Umhlanga and nearby Umdloti areas) is open weekdays 8–4:30 and Saturday 9–noon.

The local tourism bureaus in Plett and Wilderness are generally very helpful. In peak season (generally October to April), you may find them open longer than their off-season hours, which are typically weekdays 8 or 8:30 to 5 or 5:30, Saturday 8 or 8:30 to 1 or 1:30. In very quiet periods the staff may close up shop early.

Tourist Office **Plettenberg Bay Tourism Association** (⊠ *Shop 35, Melville's Corner, Marine Dr. and Main St., Plettenberg Bay* ☎ *044/533–4065* ⊕ *www. plettenbergbay.co.za).* **Sugar Coast Tourism** (⊠ *Chartwell Dr., off Lighthouse Rd., Umhlanga 4320* ☎ *031/561–4257).* **Tourist Junction** (⊠ *160 Pine St., City Center, Durban 4001* ☎ *031/304–4934).* **Wilderness Tourism** (⊠ *Milkwood Village, Beach Rd., Wilderness* ☎ *044/877–0045* ⊕ *www.wildernessinfo.co.za).*

SOUTH AFRICA ESSENTIALS

TRANSPORTATION

BY AIR

As a rule, you need to get to the airport an hour before a domestic flight and three hours before an international one. In peak season (midsummer and South African school vacations), it's a good idea to give yourself at least a half hour extra for domestic flights, as the check-in lines can be horrendous—particularly on flights to the coast at the start of vacations and back to Johannesburg at the end. It is not necessary to reconfirm domestic flights if you have a confirmed booking—but it's always a good idea.

If you are returning home with souvenirs, leave time for a V.A.T. inspection before you join the line for your international flight check-in. Baggage carts are widely available at South African airports at no charge.

All domestic flights within South Africa are no-smoking—the longest is only two hours—and all airports are smoke-free except for designated smoking areas.

If you are visiting a game lodge deep in the bush, you will be arriving by light plane—and you really will be restricted in what you can bring. Excess luggage can usually be stored with the operator until your return. Don't just gloss over this: charter operators take weight very seriously, and some will charge you for an extra ticket if you insist on bringing excess baggage.

AIRPORTS   The two major airports in South Africa are Johannesburg's O. R. Tambo and Cape Town International. Most international flights are routed through Johannesburg. *For more information on these two airports, see Johannesburg & Cape Town Essentials above.*

Kruger Mpumalanga International Airport (KMIA), at Nelspruit, and Hoedspruit airport, close to Kruger's Orpen Gate, serve Kruger National Park. KMIA has a restaurant, curio shops, banking facilities, car-rental agencies, VIP lounges, information desks, and shaded parking; Hoedspruit has a restaurant and curio shop.

The airport at Richards Bay is the closest to the Hluhluwe-Umfolozi area—about 100 km (60 mi) south of Hluhluwe-Umfolozi and about 224 km (140 mi) south of Itala. Upington International Airport is 260 km (162 mi) south of Kgalagadi Transfrontier Park; many lodgings provide shuttle service from the airport, or you can rent a car here. The closest airport to Addo Elephant Park and the Shamwari Game Reserve is in Port Elizabeth, about 72 mi (45 mi) away.

Airport Information **Cape Town International Airport** (*CPT* ☎ *021/937–1200*). **Durban International Airport** (☎ *031/408–1155*). **Hoedspruit** *(HDS)* (⊕ *hoedspruit-hds-airport.webport.com*). **Kruger Mpumalanga International Airport (KMIA)** *(MQP)* (☎ *27/13/753–7502* ⊕ *www.kmiairport.co.za*). **O. R. Tambo International Airport** (formerly Johannesburg) (*JNB ORTIA* ☎ *011/921–6262*). **Port Elizabeth Airport** (☎ *041/507–7319* ⊕ *www.acsa.co.za*). **Upington International Airport** (☎ *054/332–2161*).

FLIGHTS When booking flights, check the routing carefully as South Africa–bound flights from U.S. cities have refueling stops en route, and sometimes those stops can be delayed. Don't plan anything on the ground too rigidly after arriving; leave yourself a cushion for a connecting flight to a game lodge. Currently only South African Airways (SAA) and Delta provide direct service from the United States to South Africa, but flights routed through Europe may be more pleasant. First, they allow you to stretch your legs and change planes, or even stop over on the way there or back. Second, most European flights bound for Africa are overnights, so you will arrive in South Africa in the morning, with plenty of time to make connections.

Most major airlines serve Johannesburg. South African Airways (SAA) flies from New York (JFK) and Washington Dulles (IAD) to Johannesburg and Cape Town. Delta flies from Atlanta (ATL) to Johannesburg.

In addition to South African Airways, the major carriers with domestic flights in and out of Johannesburg are British Airways, operated by Comair, and SA Airlink and SA Express. In the past few years, several good quality, low-cost domestic airlines have sprung up, and all are worth flying—they tend to have less legroom and smaller seats, and you will need to pay for snacks on board, but they're usually cheaper than SAA and its affiliates. Kulula.com, 1time, and Mango give travelers more options than ever. Nationwide is also giving the big guys a run for their money by accepting only online bookings. If you know your schedule, be sure to check their fares.

Three airlines—SA Airlink, SA Express, and Nationwide—link Johannesburg to Kruger Mpumalanga International Airport. SA Airlink has daily flights, SA Express flies on weekends, and Nationwide has flights on Wednesday, Friday, and Sunday. SA Airlink also flies directly to Mala Mala airstrip, which serves the Sabi Sands lodges.

SA Express also flies from Johannesburg to Hoedspruit, close to Kruger's Orpen Gate, and from Johannesburg to Richards Bay airport, somewhat near Hluhluwe-Umfolozi and Itala. SA Airlink has daily flights between Johannesburg and Phalaborwa, a mining town on the edge of central Kruger; the airline also operates daily service between Upington and both Johannesburg and Cape Town.

International Airlines **American Airlines** (☎021/440–6440). **British Airways** (☎011/441–8600). **Delta** (☎011/482–4582 in South Africa, 800/241–4141 in U.S. ⊕ www.delta.com). **KLM Royal Dutch Airlines** (☎011/881–9696). **Qantas** (☎011/441–8550). **Singapore Airlines** (☎011/880–8566 ⊕ www.singaporeair.com). **South African Airways** S(☎011/778–1111 in South Africa, 800/521–4845 in U.S. ⊕ www.flysaa.com). **Virgin Atlantic** (☎011/340–3400).

Domestic Airlines **British Airways** (operating as Comair ☎011/921–0222 ⊕ www.comair.co.za). **Kulula.com** (☎0861/585–852 ⊕ www.kulula.com). **Mango** (☎011/359–1222 or 021/936–1061 ⊕ www.flymango.co.za). **Nationwide** (☎011/390–1660 ⊕ www.flynationwide.co.za). **1time** (☎0861/345–345 ⊕ www.1time.co.za). **South African Airways/SA Airlink/South African Express** (☎011/978–1111 ⊕ www.flysaa.com).

Air Travel Resources in South Africa **Airports Company South Africa** (⊕ *www.acsa.co.za*) has detailed information on all of South Africa's airports, as well a form for lodging complaints.

General Information **Flight information** (☏ *086/727–7888*).

BY BUS

Intercape Mainliner serves Cape Town, Johannesburg, Durban, towns in the southwest Cape, and many more towns in South Africa, plus Windhoek in Namibia. Greyhound offers daily overnight service between Cape Town and Johannesburg and Tshwane (also known as Pretoria), but for Western Cape destinations Intercape Mainliner is a better option. Translux runs luxury vehicles between major cities, and its sister company City-to-City serves less-well-serviced destinations like Umtata in addition to mainstream routes. BazBus offers a hop-on/hop-off service and other flexible tours aimed mostly at backpackers who don't want to travel vast distances in one day and can't easily get to train and bus stations. BazBus is more expensive than a regular bus but more convenient for covering distances in short stages. A one-week package costs R850, and a two-week package costs R1,600. It's especially useful if you're planning a long leg followed by a few short ones before returning to your starting point.

Daily overnight service between Cape Town and Johannesburg and Tshwane costs around R450–R500 one way. Cape Town to Windhoek is about R450–R550, to George (near Wilderness and Plettenberg Bay) R150, and to Durban R450–R500. Round-trip tickets are roughly double. A BazBus Durban hopper ticket via the Wild Coast costs about R1,800 one way and R2,310 round-trip; travel cards are R850 for a seven-day pass and R1,600 for a 14-day pass.

Bus Lines **BazBus** (☏ *021/439–2323* ⊕ *www.bazbus.co.za*). **Greyhound** (☏ *083/915–9000* ⊕ *www.greyhound.co.za*). **Intercape Mainliner** (☏ *0861/287–287 or 0861/287–329* ⊕ *www.intercape.co.za*). **Translux/City-to-City** (☏ *0861/589–282* ⊕ *www.translux.co.za*).

BY CAR

The first thing you will have to remember is that South Africans drive on the left-hand side of the road. That may be confusing at first, but having the steering wheel on the right might help to remind you that the driver should be closer to the middle of the road. You'll get used to it very quickly once you start. The most dangerous maneuver is turning onto an empty road, without oncoming traffic to orient you. Be careful not to lapse and veer to the right side.

⚠ **Carjackings can and do occur with such frequency that certain high-risk areas are marked by permanent carjacking signs.** South Africa has a superb network of multilane roads and highways, so driving can be a pleasure. Remember, though, that distances are vast, so guard against fatigue, which is an even bigger killer than alcohol. Toll roads, scattered among the main routes, charge anything from R10 to R60.

In South African parlance, traffic lights are known as "robots," and what people refer to as the "pavement" is actually the sidewalk. Paved roads are just called roads. Gas is referred to as petrol and gas stations are petrol stations.

You can drive in South Africa for six months on any English-language license; otherwise, you need an international license.

GASOLINE ■TIP➜ Credit cards are not accepted anywhere for fueling your tank, but nearly all gas stations are equipped with ATMs. Huge 24-hour service stations are positioned at regular intervals along all major highways in South Africa. There are no self-service stations; attendants pump the gas, check the oil and water, and wash the windows. In return, tip the attendant R2–R3. South Africa has a choice of unleaded or leaded gasoline, and many vehicles operate on diesel—be sure you get the right fuel. Older vehicles run on leaded fuel. Check when booking a rental car as to what fuel to use. Gasoline is measured in liters, and the cost works out to about R20 a gallon. When driving long distances, check your routes carefully, as the distances between towns—and hence gas stations—can be as much as 200 km (125 mi). It's better to fill a half-full tank than to try to squeeze the last drop out of an unfamiliar rental car.

ROAD CONDITIONS South African roads are mostly excellent, but South African drivers tend to be aggressive and reckless, thinking nothing of tailgating at high speeds and passing on blind rises. During national holidays the body count from highway collisions is staggering. The problem is compounded by widespread drunk driving. In towns, minibus taxis can be quite unnerving, swerving in and out of traffic without warning to pick up customers. Stay alert at all times, and expect the unexpected.

ROADSIDE EMERGENCIES If you have an accident or break down, call the AA and/or the car-rental agency. In the case of an accident you should also call the police and—perhaps—an ambulance. (From mobile phones you can call one number for police and ambulance.) When you get your rental car, the agency will give you a detailed outline of what to do in an emergency. Read it.

Emergency Services **Automobile Association** (☎ *0800/01–0101*). **General emergency number** (☎ *112 from mobile phone, 10111 from landline*).

RULES OF THE ROAD South Africa's Automobile Association publishes a range of maps, atlases, and travel guides, available for purchase on their Web site (⊕ *www.aashop.co.za*). Also check with your home automobile club, as many provide international maps and other resources.

The commercial Web site Drive South Africa (⊕ *drivesouthafrica. co.za*) has everything you need to know about driving in the country, including road safety and driving distances in their "Travel South Africa" section.

But the most important thing for Americans and Canadians to remember is to drive left, and look right.

RENTAL CARS The decision to rent a car in a foreign country depends on many factors: whether you get nervous when you get lost or see it as an adventure, and whether you enjoy going off the beaten path, or would rather do the tried-and-true itinerary. You should always ask for the best route, where it's safe to park and, as South African crime can be unpredictable, safety tips and suggested places to stop, if need be. ■ TIP→ Make sure you have your destination's contact information with you, as well as that of the hotel you just left.

In order to rent a car you need to be 23 years or older and have held a driver's license for three years. Younger international drivers can rent from some companies, but will pay a penalty. You need to get special permission to take rental cars into neighboring countries, such as Lesotho, Swaziland, Namibia, or Botswana. You cannot take rental cars into Zimbabwe. Most companies allow additional drivers, but some charge extra. Get the terms in writing before you leave on your trip. ■ TIP→ Make sure that a confirmed reservation guarantees you a car. Agencies sometimes overbook, particularly for busy weekends and holiday periods.

Rates in South Africa are similar to those in most U.S. destinations, and can vary depending on the bells and whistles and where you intend to drive. Some companies even charge more on the weekend, so it's best to get a range of quotes before booking your car. Request car seats and extras such as GPS when you book and ask for details on what to do if you have a mechanical problem or other emergency.

At the time of writing, rates on average began at about R210 per day for unlimited mileage or a slightly cheaper rate for 200 km (125 mi) per day and about R1.50 for each additional kilometer. These prices are for an economy car with a 1,300-cc engine, no air-conditioning, and a stick shift. For a car with automatic transmission and air-conditioning, you'll pay around R400 per day for unlimited kilometers, and slightly less for 200 km (125 mi) per day plus about R3.50 per extra kilometer. When comparing prices, make sure you're getting the same thing. Some companies quote prices with no insurance, some include 80% or 90% coverage, and some quote with 100% protection.

The major international companies (Avis, Budget, Hertz, Europcar) all have offices in tourist cities and at international airports, and their vehicle types are the same range you'd find at home: subcompact choices such as Hyundai Getz, compacts such as Chevy Aveos, VW Golfs, Toyota Corollas, and luxury BMWs and Mercedes. There is generally no need to rent a 4x4 vehicle as all roads are paved, including those in Kruger National Park; in Kgalagadi Transfrontier Park, however, some routes are only accessible by 4x4.

Maui Motorhome Rentals, with offices in Johannesburg, Cape Town, and Durban, offers fully equipped motor homes, camper vans, and 4x4s, many of which come totally equipped for a bush sojourn. Prices start at around R1,100 per day, not including insurance. However, standard insurance coverage may be included or can be added for R140 to R230 per day.

Leave ample time to return your car when your trip is over. You shouldn't feel rushed when settling your bill. Be sure to get copies of your receipt.

Local Agencies **Car Mania** (☎ *021/447–3001 or 021/447–3009* ⊕ *www.carmania. co.za*). **Imperial Car Rental** (☎ *086/113–1000* ⊕ *www.imperialcarrental.co.za*). **Maui Motorhome Rental** (☎ *011/396–1445 or 021/982–5107* ⊕ *www.maui.co.za*). **Value Car Hire** (☎ *021/696–2198* ⊕ *www.valuecarhire.co.za*).

BY TRAIN

Shosholoza Meyl, part of the rail network known as Spoornet, operates an extensive system of passenger trains along eight routes that connect all major cities and many small towns in South Africa. Departures are usually limited to one per day, although trains covering minor routes leave less frequently. Distances are vast, so many journeys require overnight travel. The service is good and the trains are safe and well maintained, but this is far from a luxury option, except in Premier Classe, the luxury service that runs between Cape Town and Tshwane (Pretoria). The old first- and second-class designations have been replaced by referring to the cars as four-sleeper (old first class) and six-sleeper. The only difference between four- and six-sleepers is that the four-sleeper has two double bunks, whereas the six-sleeper has two triple bunks. Don't expect air-conditioning or heat in either class, and in either case you will be using a communal toilet and shower. The compartments have a sink. Bedding can be rented. The dining car serves pretty ordinary food, but it's reasonably well cooked and inexpensive. Third class is now referred to as "sitter class," because that's what you do—up to 25 hours on a hard seat with up to 71 other people in the car, sharing two toilets and no shower. You must reserve tickets in advance for four- and six-sleeper accommodations, whereas sitter-class tickets require no advance booking. You can book up to three months in advance with travel agents, reservations offices in major cities, and at railway stations. Note that though the classes have been officially renamed, most people still refer to them by their old names.

Information **Premier Classe** (☎ *086/000–8888* ⊕ *www.premierclasse.co.za*). **Shosholoza Meyl** (☎ *086/000–8888* ⊕ *www.spoornet.co.za*).

LUXURY TRAIN TRIPS The luxurious and leisurely *Blue Train* has a couple of routes, but the main one runs from Cape Town to Tshwane (Pretoria). It departs once a week, takes two days, and costs around R15,000 one-way during peak season, including meals and excursions. The *Blue Train* also has special packages to Durban from Tshwane and can arrange chartered trips that include stays in luxury lodges. All meals and alcohol are included in the ticket price, which ranges from R17,750 for a double in low season between Cape Town and Tshwane to R30,400 for a deluxe double in high season, one-way. Less frequently, the *Blue Train* runs to Bakubung Game Reserve in Pilanesberg National Park.

Compartments on the *Blue Train* are individually air-conditioned and have remote-operated blinds and curtains, TV, CD player, and a personal mobile phone for contacting your butler/valet or making outgoing calls. The comfortably furnished lounge car offers refreshments and drinks throughout the day and is a good place to meet fellow travelers. There are two trains: the Classic and the African theme, which is decorated with African touches such as faux-animal-skin furniture and somewhat more exotic uniforms for the staff. In the well-appointed dining car, men are required to wear jacket and tie to dinner.

The Rovos Rail *Pride of Africa* runs from Cape Town to Tshwane every Monday and costs R12,195 for the two-day trip in a deluxe suite, up to R16,000 for a royal suite, including excursions, meals, and drinks. There are also biweekly overnight trips that are run between Cape Town and George. Every May a seven-day round-trip between Cape Town and Swakopmund, Namibia, is run; in July there is a two-week round-trip epic from Cape Town to Dar es Salaam, Tanzania. There's also a six-day one-way trip to Victoria Falls, Zimbabwe. Prices per person sharing range from R8,160 for a deluxe suite on the Cape Town–Tshwanee run to nearly R70,000 for the Royal Suite on trip from Cape Town to Victoria Falls. The single-occupancy supplement is 50%. Rovos Rail also has theme trips, such as a golf safari.

Luxury Train Lines **Blue Train** (☏ *011/773–7631* ⊕ *www.bluetrain.co.za*). **Rovos Rail** (☏ *012/323–6052* ⊕ *www.rovos.co.za*).

SPECIALTY TRAIN TRIPS A really fun way to see the country is on the Shongololo Express—a devilishly clever idea. The train is pretty basic, much like the Shosholoza Meyl trains. While you sleep at night, it heads off to a new destination. After breakfast, tour buses are loaded, and you head off to explore the surroundings. In the evening, you climb back on the train, have supper, and sleep while you head off to the next fun destination. Trips include the Dune Adventure (highlighting the dunes of Namibia), the Good Hope Adventure (highlighting Cape attractions), and the Southern Cross Adventure (exploring six African countries). Rates start at about R1,000 per person per night, sharing. By the way, a *shongololo* is a millipede.

Contacts **Shongololo Express** (☏ *011/781–4616* ⊕ *www.shongololo.com*).

CONTACTS & RESOURCES

CUSTOMS & DUTIES

Visitors may bring in new or used gifts and souvenirs up to a total value of R3,000 duty-free. For additional goods (new or used) up to a value of R12,000, a fee of 20% is levied. In addition, each person may bring up to 200 cigarettes, 20 cigars, 250 grams of tobacco, 2 liters of wine, 1 liter of other alcoholic beverages, 50 ml of perfume, and 250 ml of toilet water into South Africa or other Southern Africa Common Customs Union (SACU) countries (Botswana, Lesotho, Namibia, and Swaziland). The tobacco and alcohol allowance applies only to people 18 and over. If you enter a SACU country from or through another in the union, you are not liable for any duties. You will, however, need to complete a form listing items imported.

The United States is a signatory to CITES, a wildlife protection treaty, and therefore does not allow the importation of living or dead endan-

CLOSE UP

Language Barrier

If you are traveling in South Africa, you may want to be aware of a few phrases that may not mean what you think—or logically what they are meant—to mean.

If a South African tells you she will meet you at the restaurant "just now" or "now now," this does not mean that she will meet you immediately. It means she will meet you at some vague point in time in the future, which could be 20 minutes or could be two hours. In other words, you probably want to determine an exact time. Also, if a South African tells you something is "lekker," that's a good

thing: "lekker" can mean anything from cool to sexy.

Another word to note is the term "colored" (spelled "coloured"). While its usage is extremely offensive to Americans, the term is widely used in South Africa to describe South Africans of mixed race, often descended from imported slaves, the San, the Khoekhoen, and European settlers. Over the years the term "coloureds" has lost any pejorative connotations. Most coloureds don't regard themselves as black Africans, and culturally they are extremely different.

5

gered animals, or their body parts, such as rhino horns or ivory. If you purchase an antique that is made partly or wholly of ivory, you must obtain a CITES preconvention certificate that clearly states the item is at least 100 years old. The import of zebra skin or other tourist products also requires a CITES permit.

Information in South Africa **Southern Africa Customs Union** (⊕ *www.dfa.gov. za/foreign/Multilateral/africa/sacu.htm*).

U.S. Information **U.S. Customs and Border Protection** (⊕ *www.cbp.gov*). **U.S. Fish and Wildlife Service** (⊕ *www.fws.gov*).

DISCOUNTS & DEALS

If you're keen to explore South Africa's many wilderness areas, buying a Wild Card from South African National Parks might be worth your while, but be sure to read all the fine print. There are several types of passes covering different clusters of parks for individuals, couples, and families; at this writing an individual pass to all of the parks cost R795.

Contact **South African National Parks** (⊕ *Box 787, Pretoria0001* ☎ *012/343–1991* ⊘ *reservations@sanparks.org* ⊕ *www.sanparks.org*).

ELECTRICITY

The electrical current is 220 volts, 50 cycles alternating current (AC); wall outlets in most of the region take 15-amp plugs with three round prongs (the old British system), but some take the straight-edged three-prong plugs, also 15 amps.

If your appliances are dual-voltage, you'll need only an adapter. In remote areas (and even in some lodges) power may be solar or from a generator; this means that delivery is erratic both in voltage and supply. In even the remotest places, however, lodge staff will find a way to charge video and camera batteries, but you will receive little sympathy if you insist on using a hair dryer or electric razor.

HEALTH

Make sure that you have medical insurance that's good in South Africa before you leave home.

Two important health issues to be aware of in South Africa are malaria and HIV/Aids. *For more information, see Health & Safety in the South Africa Planner, above.* On hot days and days when you are on the move, especially after long flights, try to drink a few liters of water. If you're prone to low blood sugar or have a sensitive stomach, consider bringing along rehydration salts, available at camping stores, to balance your body's fluids and keep you going when you feel listless. Alcohol is dehydrating, so try to limit consumption on hot days or long travel days. The drinking water in South Africa is treated and, except in rural areas, is absolutely safe to drink. Many people filter it, though, to get rid of the chlorine. You can eat fresh fruits and salads and have ice in your drinks.

The sun can be strong in South Africa, so be sure to pack your favorite sunscreen protection and use it generously. That said, most major brands are available in South Africa, so you can pick some up if you forget yours.

As a foreigner, you will be expected to pay in full for any medical services, so check your existing health plan to see whether you're covered while abroad, and supplement it if necessary. South African doctors are generally excellent. The equipment and training in private clinics rivals the best in the world, but stay away from public hospitals, which are overcrowded and underfunded.

On returning home, if you experience any unusual symptoms, including fever, painful eyes, backache, diarrhea, severe headache, general lassitude, or blood in urine or stool, be sure to tell your doctor where you have been. These symptoms may indicate malaria, tick-bite fever, bilharzia, or—if you've been traveling north of South Africa's borders—some other tropical malady.

■ TIP→ If on safari or camping, check your boots and shake your clothes out for spiders and other crawlies before getting dressed.

OVER-THE-
COUNTER
REMEDIES
You can buy over-the-counter medication in pharmacies and supermarkets, and you will find the more general remedies in Clicks, a chain store selling beauty products, some over-the-counter medication, and housewares. Your body may not react the same way to the South African version of a product, even something as simple as a headache tablet, so bring your own supply for your trip and rely on pharmacies just for emergency medication.

SHOTS &
MEDICATIONS
South Africa does not require any inoculations for entry. Travelers entering South Africa within six days of leaving a country infected with yellow fever require a yellow-fever vaccination certificate. The South African travel clinics and the U.S.'s National Centers for Dis-

ease Control and Prevention (CDC) recommend that you be vaccinated against hepatitis A and B if you intend to travel to more isolated areas. Cholera injections are widely regarded as useless, so don't let anyone talk you into having one, but the newer oral vaccine seems to be more effective.

If you are coming to South Africa for a safari, chances are you are heading to a malarial game reserve. Only a handful of game reserves are nonmalarial. Millions of travelers take oral prophylactic drugs before, during, and after their safaris. It is up to you to weigh the risks and benefits of the type of antimalarial drug you choose to take. If you are pregnant, or traveling with small children, consider a nonmalarial region for your safari.

The CDC provides up-to-date information on health risks and recommended vaccinations and medications for travelers to Southern Africa. In most of South Africa you need not worry about any of the above, but if you plan to visit remote regions, check with the CDC's traveler's health line. For up-to-date, local expertise, contact South African Airways Netcare Netcare Travel Clinics.

Health Warnings **National Centers for Disease Control & Prevention** (*CDC* ☎ *877/394–8747 international travelers' health line* ⊕ *www.cdc.gov/travel*). **South African Airways Netcare Travel Clinics** (☎ *0800/002–609 toll-free in South Africa* ⊕ *www.travelclinic.co.za*).

Medical-Assistance Companies **International SOS Assistance, South Africa** (☎ *011/541–1350* ⊕ *www.internationalsos.com/countries/SouthAfrica*).

HOLIDAYS

National holidays in South Africa are New Year's Day (January 1), Human Rights Day (March 21), Good Friday, Easter, Family Day (sometime in March or April), Freedom Day (April 27), Workers Day (May 1), Youth Day (June 16), National Women's Day (August 9), Heritage Day (September 24), Day of Reconciliation (December 16), Christmas Day (December 25), and Day of Goodwill (December 26). If a public holiday falls on a Sunday, the following Monday is also a public holiday. Election days are also public holidays, so check calendars closer to your time of travel for those, which are not on fixed dates.

In Cape Town, January 2 is also a holiday, known as *tweede nuwe jaar* (second new year). School vacations vary with the provinces, but usually comprise about 10 days over Easter, about three weeks around June or July, and then the big summer vacation from about December 10 to January 10.

HOURS OF OPERATION

The most surprising aspect of South Africa's business hours, especially for tourists who come to shop, is that shopping centers, including enclosed secure indoor malls, all close by 6 in the evening. It is rare for a store to remain open after dinner, just when you may be ready to shop! (But cafés in malls stay open late).

Business hours in major South African cities are weekdays from about 9 to 5. Most banks close in midafternoon, usually about 3:30, but dedicated currency exchange offices usually stay open longer. In addition, post offices and banks are open briefly on Saturday morning from about 9, so get there early. In rural areas and small towns things are less rigid. Post offices often close for lunch, and, in very small towns and villages banks may have very abbreviated hours.

Most museums are open during usual business hours, including Saturday morning, but some stay open longer.

MAIL

The mail service in South Africa is reasonably reliable, but mail can take weeks to arrive, and money and other valuables may be stolen from letters and packages. You can buy stamps at post offices, open weekdays 8:30–4:30 and Saturday 8–noon. Stamps for local use only, marked STANDARDISED POST, may be purchased from newsstands in booklets of 10 stamps. PostNet franchises—a combined post office, courier service, business services center, and Internet café—are in convenient places like shopping malls and are open longer hours than post offices.

All overseas mail costs the same. A postcard is about R3.50, and a letter ranges from R4 to about R15, depending on size and weight.

SHIPPING PACKAGES   If you make a purchase, try your best to take it home on the plane with you, even if it means packing your travel clothes and items into a box and shipping those to your home, or buying a cheap piece of luggage and paying the excess weight fees. If you buy something from a store accustomed to foreign visitors, they will likely already have a system for getting your items to you, often in a surprising few weeks' time.

Federal Express and DHL offer more reliable service than regular mail, as do the Fast Mail and Speed Courier services, yet even these "overnight" services are subject to delays. PostNet also offers courier services. A parcel of up to about a pound (half a kilogram) will cost between R300 and R750 to send to the United States, and a 1-kilogram parcel (2.2 pounds) will cost anything from R550 to just over R1,000.

Express Services DHL (☎ *0860/345–000* ⊕ *www.dhl.co.za*). **FedEx** (☎ *021/951–6660, 080/953–9599 toll-free in South Africa* ⊕ *www.fedex.com*). **PostNet** (⊕ *www.postnet.co.za*).

MONEY

ATMS & BANKS   Be sure to bring cash and traveler's checks, because ATMs are hard to come by in the parks, although there are generally plenty of ATMs near the parks. That said, South Africa has a modern banking system, with branches throughout the country and otherwise ubiquitous ATMs, especially at tourist attractions, in gas stations, and in shopping malls. Banks open at 9 in the morning weekdays and close at 3:30 in the afternoon; on Saturday they close at 11 in the morning, and they are closed Sunday. Many banks can perform foreign-exchange services or international electronic transfers. The major South African banks are: ABSA, First National Bank, Nedbank, and Standard.

It is wise to bring two ATM cards for different accounts with you whenever traveling abroad, both in case one is stolen or "eaten" by a machine, and to give yourself an option in case a machine takes only one or the other type. Most ATMs accept Cirrus, Plus, Maestro, Visa Electron, and Visa, and MasterCard.

The best place to withdraw cash is at an indoor ATM, preferably one guarded by a security officer. If you're unsure where to find a safe ATM, ask a merchant. Most machines will not let you withdraw more than the equivalent of about $150 at a time. If anyone approaches you while you're using an ATM, immediately press cancel.

CREDIT CARDS MasterCard, Visa, and American Express are accepted almost everywhere, including in the parks. Diners Club is not quite as widely accepted throughout the country. Discover is not recognized.

CURRENCY & EXCHANGE At this writing, the rand was trading at about R7 to $1, a dramatic change from the days of R14 to $1, when South Africa was truly a bargain. It is still relatively inexpensive given the quality of lodgings, which cost probably two-thirds the price of comparable facilities in the United States.

Note that there is no currency exchange within parks and park lodges, so be sure to change any money before your park visit.

To avoid administrative hassles, keep all foreign-exchange receipts until you leave the region, as you may need them as proof when changing any unspent local currency back into your own currency. You may not take more than R5,000 in cash out of South Africa. For more information you can contact the South African Reserve Bank.

Currency Information South African Reserve Bank (✉ *Box 427, Pretoria 0001* ☎ *012/313–3911* ⊕ *www.reservebank.co.za*).

TRAVELER'S CHECKS Some consider this the currency of the cave man, and it's true that fewer establishments accept traveler's checks these days. Nevertheless, they're a cheap and secure way to carry extra emergency money, particularly on trips to urban areas. Only bring American Express traveler's checks if coming from the United States, as Amex is well known and widely accepted; you can also avoid hefty surcharges by cashing Amex checks at Amex offices. Whatever you do, keep track of all the serial numbers in case the checks are lost or stolen.

Traveler's checks in either rand or other major denominations (U.S. dollars, euros, and sterling) are readily accepted by most lodgings, though most people use credit cards.

PHONES
The country code for South Africa is 27. When dialing from abroad, drop the initial 0 from local area codes.

CALLING WITHIN SOUTH AFRICA Local calls are very cheap, although all calls from hotels attract a hefty premium. South Africa has two types of pay phones: coin-operated phones, which accept a variety of coins, and card-operated phones. Coin-operated phones are being phased out, and there aren't too many left in tourist destinations. Phone cards are the better option; they free you from the hassle of juggling handfuls of coins, and they're available in several denominations. In addition, a digital readout tells you how much credit remains while you're talking. Cards are available at newsstands, convenience stores, and telephone company offices. When making a phone call in South Africa, always use the full 10-digit number, including the area code, even if you're in the same area.

For directory assistance in South Africa, call 1023. For operator-assisted national long-distance calls, call 1025. For international operator assistance, dial 0903. These numbers are free if dialed from a Telkom (landline) phone but are charged at normal cell-phone rates from a mobile—and they're busy call centers. Directory inquiries numbers are different for each cell-phone network. Vodacom is 111, MTN is 200, and Cell C is 146. These calls are charged at normal rates, but the call is timed only from when it is actually answered. You can, for an extra fee, get the call connected by the operator.

CALLING OUTSIDE SOUTH AFRICA When dialing out from South Africa, dial 09 before the international code. So, for example, you would dial 09/1 for the United States (the country code for the United States is 1). Other country codes are 267 for Botswana, 264 for Namibia, 260 for Zambia, and 263 for Zimbabwe.

■ TIP→ If you really want to save on international phone calls, the best advice is to provide a detailed itinerary back home and agree upon a schedule for calls. Even if they call your "free" cell phone, they'll be paying on the other end, so speak quickly or keep in touch via the Internet.

Access Codes **AT&T Direct** (☎ 0800/99-0123 from South Africa). **MCI World-Phone** (☎ 0800/990-011 from South Africa). **Sprint International Access** (☎ 0800/990-001 from South Africa).

MOBILE PHONES The least complicated way to make and receive phone calls is to obtain international roaming service from your cell-phone service provider before you leave home, but this can be expensive. If you have a multiband phone (some countries use different frequencies from what are used in the United States) and your service provider uses the world-standard GSM network (as do T-Mobile, Cingular, and AT&T), you can probably use your phone abroad, but to avoid roaming fees, you must get a SIM card for the country, which will dramatically reduce your rates. ■ TIP→ Verizon and Sprint customers cannot use their phones in Africa. Any phone that you take abroad must be unlocked by your company in order for you to be able to use it.

If you plan on getting a cell phone while you're traveling, know that plans change frequently, so try to gather as many details before leaving to figure out which plan is right for you. Some allow free calls to your number, but charge rates close to landline calls if you call the United States. If you don't text message at home, you'll learn to in Africa, where a simple text message costs a fraction of the cost of making an actual call. This is a handy option for meeting up with friends, but for calling a hotel reservations line, it's best to make the call.

Cell phones in South Africa are ubiquitous and have quite extensive coverage. There are three cell-phone service providers in South Africa—Cell C, MTN, and Vodacom. Vodacom, MTN, and Cell-C SIM cards are in supermarkets, as are airtime cards. Cell phones can be rented by the day, week, or longer from the airport on your arrival, but this is an expensive option.

Contacts **Cell C Rentals** (☎021/934–1452 in Cape Town, 011/390–2922 in Johannesburg ⊕www.cellcrentals.co.za). **Cellucity/Vodashop** (☎021/934–0492 in Cape Town, 011/394–8834 in Johannesburg ⊕www.cellucity.co.za). **MTN** (☎119/912–3000 ⊕www.mtn.co.za). **Vodacom** (☎082–111 from landline, 111 from mobile phone ⊕www.vodacom.co.za) is the country's leading cellular network.

RESTROOMS

All fuel complexes on the major roads have large, clean, well-maintained restrooms. In cities you can find restrooms in shopping malls, tourist attractions, at some gas stations, and in restaurants—most of which are quite happy to allow you to use them. Many have access for people who use wheelchairs. On safari, particularly when you stop for sundowners, you'll be pointed to a nearby bush (which the ranger checks out before you use it). Carry tissues and toilet paper with you, although these are usually available on the vehicle. Bury any paper you may use. If you have an emergency, ask your ranger to stop the vehicle and check out a suitable spot.

SAFETY

South Africa is a country in transition, and as a result experiences growing pains that reveal themselves in economic inequities, which result in high crime rates. While the majority of visitors experience a crime-free trip to South Africa, it is essential to practice vigilance and extreme care.

Crime is a major problem in the whole region, particularly in large cities, and all visitors should take precautions to protect themselves. Do not walk alone at night, and exercise caution even during the day. Avoid wearing jewelry (even costume jewelry), don't invite attention by wearing an expensive camera around your neck, and don't flash a large wad of cash. If you are toting a handbag, wear the strap across your body; even better, wear a money belt, preferably hidden from view under your clothing. When sitting at airports or at restaurants, especially outdoor cafés, make sure to keep your bag on your lap or between your legs—otherwise it may just quietly "walk off" when you're not looking. Even better, loop the strap around your leg, or clip the strap around the table or chair.

Carjacking is another problem, with armed bandits often forcing drivers out of their vehicles at traffic lights, in driveways, or during a fake accident. Always drive with your windows closed and doors locked, don't stop for hitchhikers, and park in well-lighted places. At traffic lights, leave enough space between you and the vehicle in front so you can pull into another lane if necessary. In the unlikely event you are carjacked, don't argue, and don't look at the carjacker's face. Just get out of the car, or ask to be let out of the car. Do not try to keep any of your belongings—they are all replaceable, even that laptop with all that data on it. If you are not given the opportunity to leave the car, try to stay calm, ostentatiously look away from the hijackers so they can be sure you can't identify them, and follow all instructions. Ask again, calmly, to be let out of the car.

Many places that are unsafe in South Africa will not bear obvious signs of danger. Make sure you know exactly where you're going. Purchase a good map and obtain comprehensive directions from your hotel, rental car agent, or a trusted local. Taking the wrong exit off a highway into a township could lead you straight to disaster. Many cities are ringed by "no-go" areas. Learn from your hotel or the locals which areas to avoid. If you sense you have taken a wrong turn, drive toward a public area, such as a gas station, or building with an armed guard, before attempting to correct your mistake, which could just compound the problem. When parking, do not leave anything visible in the car; stow it all in the trunk. As an added measure, leave the glove box open, to show there is nothing of value inside (take the rental agreement with you).

Before setting out on foot, ask a local, such as your hotel concierge, or a shopkeeper, which route to take and how far you can safely go. Walk with a purposeful stride so you look like you know where you're going, and duck into a shop or café if you need to check a map, speak on your mobile phone, or recheck the directions you've been given.

Lone women travelers need to be particularly vigilant about walking alone and locking their rooms. South Africa has one of the world's highest rates of rape. If you do attract someone who won't take a firm but polite *no* for an answer, appeal immediately to the hotel manager, bartender, or someone else who seems to be in charge. If you have to walk a short distance alone at night, such as from the hotel reception to your room in a dark motel compound, or back from a café along a main street, have a plan, carry a whistle, or know what you will do if you are grabbed.

TAXES

All South African hotels pay a bed tax, which is included in quoted prices.

In South Africa the value-added tax (V.A.T.), currently 14%, is included in the price of most goods and services, including hotel accommodations and food. To get a V.A.T. refund, foreign visitors must present their receipts (minimum of R250) at the airport and be carrying any purchased items with them or in their luggage. You must fill out Form V.A.T. 255, available at the airport V.A.T. refund office. Whatever you buy, make sure that your receipt is an original tax invoice, containing the vendor's name and address, V.A.T. registration number, and the words "tax invoice." Refunds are paid by check, which can be cashed immediately at an airport bank, or refunded directly onto your credit card, with a small transaction fee. Be sure you visit the V.A.T. refund desk in the departures hall before you go through check-in procedures, and try to organize your receipts as you go, to make for easy viewing. Officials will go through your receipts and randomly ask to view your purchases.

Airport taxes and fees are included in the price of your ticket.

Contacts V.A.T. Refund Office (☎ *011/394–1117* ⊕ *www.taxrefunds.co.za*).

VISITOR INFORMATION

South African Tourism ((☎ *800/782–9772 in U.S., 011/895–3000 in South Africa, 083/123–6789 in South Africa for tourism and accommodation information* ⊕ *www.southafrica.net*)) provides advice and brochures, but no bookings. For a range of accommodation choices and links to maps by region, as well as updated traveler information, try ⊕ *www.sa-venues.com*. The South African National Parks (SANParks) Web site (⊕ *www.sanparks.org*) outlines where the parks are, provides detailed maps, and includes information on accommodations, animals, park activities, and booking.

5

GREEN LODGINGS IN SOUTH AFRICA

Being a "green traveler" means minimizing the negative impact on your surroundings. How can you be sure you're traveling green? We've given you a few places you can stay on safari that are ecoconscious. Of course our list is not exhaustive, but it's a starting place.

CONTACT INFORMATION

Grootbos Private Nature Reserve: 028/384–8000; www.grootbos.com

Hog Hollow Country Lodge: 044/534–8879; www.hog-hollow.com

Vuyatela Bush Lodge: 013/735–5118; www.djuma.com

Only a 15-minute drive from Hermanus and two hours from Cape Town, **Grootbos Private Nature Reserve** is home to the largest private fynbos garden in the world. Set on 2,500 acres of Western Cape landscape overlooking Walker Bay, Grootbos offers up-close observation of Protea, fynbos, milkwood forests, and tropical rainforests as well as aquatic life including penguins, dolphins, seals, and Southern Right Whales in early spring (opposite bottom). There are hiking, horseback riding, and great beaches as well as children's programs. Luxury accommodations include private cottages with fireplaces and sundecks and exquisite cuisine is enhanced by vegetables and herbs grown on the premise. The reserve's foundation works to educate and employee the community with a variety of conservation, research, and sustainable living projects.

Djuma comprises three separate lodges, of which **Vuya-tela Bush Lodge** (opposite) is the most outstanding—and naturally, the most expensive. Djuma has access to more than 22,000 acres in the Sabi Sand Reserve, which is in itself noteworthy. The game-viewing is among the best there are and everything at Vuyatela is owner-run, so attention to detail is paramount. The camp was built with local labor and there was no heavy machinery used, to lessen the impact on the environment. In keeping with their philosophy of community involvement, the owners of Djuma established a day-care center called N'wa Tumberi in the neighboring Shangaan community that has been received favorably. The lodge also includes an aquarium and a boma, as well as the opportunity for walking safaris. *See Luxury Lodges, in Sabi Sands Game Reserve for more information about the camp.*

Just outside Plettenberg Bay, **Hog Hollow Country Lodge** (top right) is a beautiful oasis run by Andy Fermor and Debbie Reyneke, a conscientious couple dedicated to employing local people. The lodge, in a private reserve, has views of the surrounding valleys and Tsitsikamma Mountains. Personalized service is one of the hallmarks of a stay at Hog Hollow. The main lodge and 12 cottages straddle a central dam, creating a serene hideaway that blends with the landscape and indigenous forest. The house includes a pool overlooking the Matjes River gorge, and one of the outdoor lounges has a grand old Fig Tree sprouting up through its wooden deck, providing an excellent perch for birdwatchers. Hike through the surrounding forest or take a quick drive to Keurbooms Beach and Nature's Valley, both just 10 minutes from Hog Hollow.

GREEN QUESTIONS TO ASK YOUR OPERATOR

If you're serious about being an ecotourist, shouldn't the tour operator you pick be ecologically conscious as well? Make sure the tour operator you pick feels as passionate about being green as you do and has the actions to prove it, that is, cooperatives with the local community, a nonprofit partner, etc. How do you find this out? We've got a few question suggestions that should help you find the greenest operator out there.

■ Are the lodges on the itineraries solar powered?

■ Do the safari guides, rangers, and trackers belong to tribes from the region in which you're traveling?

■ Do the chefs and porters hail from the surrounding area?

■ Have local materials been used in building your safari lodge?

■ Does the menu in the dining room where you take meals use local ingredients?

5

Botswana

WELCOME TO BOTSWANA

TOP REASONS TO GO

★ **The Okavango Delta.** Whether you are drifting dreamily in a mokoro through the crystal-clear, papyrus-fringed channels, or walking among ancient trees on one of the many islands, your everyday world is guaranteed to fade from your consciousness.

★ **Big game.** You won't find huge herds as in Serengeti, but you will come face to face with more critters than you ever knew existed. And there won't be hordes of other visitors blocking your view or diluting the experience.

★ **Birding.** Marvel at more than 900 species—many endemic—that crowd the game reserves. A sighting of a Pel's fishing owl, one of the world's rarest birds, will have Audubon twitching in his grave.

★ **Walking with the Bushmen.** Far from being lifeless, deserts are miracles of plenty. You just have to be in the right company—that of the Kalahari Bushmen. Listen to their dissonant music, watch them dance a dance as old as time, and then listen to the stars sing.

1 **The Okavango Delta.** The Okavango Delta is formed by the Okavango River, which descends from the Angolan highlands and fans out over northwestern Botswana. It's made up of an intricate network of channels, quiet lagoons, and reed-lined backwaters. There is big game, but it's more elusive and difficult to approach than in the game reserves.

2 **Moremi Game Reserve.** Here the life-giving waters of the Okavango meet the vast Kalahari. Teeming with game and birds, it is one of Africa's greatest parks, and, unlike the Masai Mara or Kruger Park, has hardly any people. You'll love the Garden of Eden atmosphere even if you do encounter the odd snake or two.

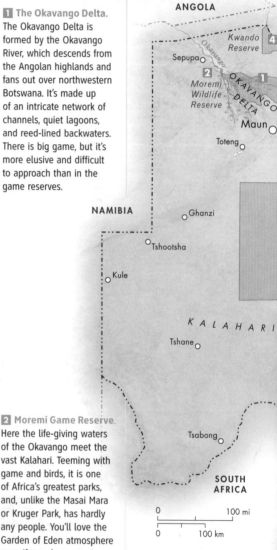

ANGOLA

Kwando Reserve **4**

Sepupa

2 Moremi Wildlife Reserve

1 OKAVANGO DELTA

Maun

Toteng

NAMIBIA

Ghanzi

Tshootsha

Kule

KALAHARI

Tshane

Tsabong

SOUTH AFRICA

0   100 mi
0   100 km

3 **Chobe National Park.** Huge herds of game roam this 11,700-square-km (4,500-square-mi) park that borders the Chobe River in northeast Botswana. Although it's one of Africa's great game reserves, its lack of roads and often almost inaccessible conditions—especially in the rainy season—mean you'll need a 4x4 to tackle it on your own.

4 **Kwando Reserve.** The 2,300-square-km (900-square-mi) private Kwando concession northwest of Chobe and Linyanti has more than 80 km (50 mi) of river frontage. It stretches south from the banks of the Kwando River to the Okavango Delta. It's an area crossed by thousands of ancient game trails still used by wildlife that move freely between the Okavango Delta, Chobe, and the open Namibian wilderness to the north.

GETTING ORIENTED

Botswana is roughly the size of France or Texas, and nearly 18% of its area is reserved for conservation and tourism. The Moremi Game Reserve, the first such reserve in southern Africa created by an African community on its tribal lands, is a major draw. Here you'll see elephants, lions, buffalo, wild dogs, cheetahs, leopards, giraffes, kudus, wildebeests, and hippos. One hundred kilometers (62 mi) west of Victoria Falls in Botswana's northeast corner is Chobe National Park, known for its elephants. The wide and tranquil Chobe River is surrounded by a natural wilderness of floodplain, dead lake bed, sand ridges, and forest. Downstream it joins the mighty Zambezi on its journey through Zimbabwe and Mozambique. Upstream, where it's known as the Linyanti, it forms the border between Botswana and Namibia. In this area the Linyanti Reserve, which borders Chobe National Park, is a huge private concession, as is the Kwando Reserve, to the west.

6

BOTSWANA PLANNER

Fast Facts

Size At 581,730 square km (224,607 square mi), it's roughly the size of France or Texas.

Number of National Parks Six. Chobe National Park (including the Savuti and Linyani areas); Mokolodi Nature Reserve; Moremi Game Reserve; Okavango Delta; Central Kalahari Game Reserve; Kgalagadi National Park.

Number of Private Reserves As new private reserves and concessions are established regularly it's difficult to estimate. Private reserves can be found in all the following areas: Okavango Delta, Moremi Wildlife Reserve, Chobe, Linyanti, Savuti, Selinda, Kwando, Kalahari, the Tuli Block, Makgadikgadi Pans.

Population of Country 1.8 million

Big Five They're all here.

Language The national language is Setswana, but English is the official language and is spoken nearly everywhere.

Time Botswana is on CAST (Central African Standard Time), which is two hours ahead of Greenwich Mean Time and seven hours ahead of Eastern Standard Time.

Health & Safety

There are high standards of hygiene in all the private lodges, and most hotels are usually up to international health standards. But malaria is rife, so don't forget to take those antimalarials. Botswana has one of the highest AIDS rates in Africa (approximately 1 in 3 are HIV positive) but also one of Africa's most progressive and comprehensive programs for dealing with the disease. All the private lodges and camps have excellent staff medical programs; you're in no danger of contracting the disease unless you have sex with a stranger. As in most cities, crime is prevalent in Gaborone, but simple safety precautions such as locking up your documents and valuables, and not walking alone at night, will keep you safe. On safari, there is always potential danger from wild animals, but your ranger will brief you thoroughly on the do's and don'ts of encountering big game.

Important Details

Embassies The American embassy is in Gaborone (⊠ *Government Enclave, Embassy Dr.* ☎ *395–3982*), the country's capital city.

Emergencies Most safari companies include medical insurance in their tariffs, but if not or there's a major problem, you can contact **Medical Rescue International** (☎ *390–1601*), which has 24-hour emergency help.

Money Matters The pula and the thebe constitute the country's currency; one pula equals 100 thebe. You will need to change your money or traveler's checks into pula, as this is the only legally accepted currency. However, most camp prices are quoted in U.S. dollars.

Passports & Visas All visitors, including infants, need a valid passport to enter Botswana for visits of up to 90 days.

Visitor Information The main branch of Botswana's **Department of Tourism** (ᵈ *Private Bag 0047, Main Mall* ☎ *395–3024* ⊕ *www.botswana-tourism.gov.bw*) is located in Gaborone. The staff will help everything from maps, accommodation lists, tour operators, and tourist attractions to general information.

About the Camps & Lodges

Most camps accommodate 12 to 16 people, so the only traffic you'll encounter among the delta's waterways is that of grazing hippos and dozing crocodiles. Even in the northern part of Chobe, where most vehicles are, rush hour consists of buffalo and elephant herds trekking to the rivers. Prices are highest June through October. Check with individual camps for special offers.

A word about terminology: "Land camps" are in game reserves or concessions and offer morning and evening game drives. If you're not in a national park, you'll be able to go out for night drives off-road with a powerful spotlight to pick out nocturnal animals. "Water camps" are deep in the Okavango Delta and often accessible only by air or water. Many camps offer both a land and a true water experience, so you get the best of both worlds.

There is little or no local cuisine in Botswana, so the food is designed to appeal to a wide variety of visitors. Nevertheless, it is very tasty. Most camps bake their own excellent bread, muffins, and cakes and often make desserts such as meringues, éclairs, and homemade ice cream. And you'll find plenty of tasty South African wine and beer. Don't expect TVs or elevators, even at very expensive camps, and air-conditioning is the exception rather than the rule. It's mentioned only when it's present.

Most lodging prices are quoted in U.S. dollars, and you can use dollars as tips wherever you stay. The average price per person per night at private lodges is US$500–US$1,000, which includes accommodations, all meals, soft drinks, and good South African wine. Camps arrange transfers from the nearest airport or airstrip.

■TIP→ It's important to note that there are few budget lodging options available in Botswana, and most of the camps we write about fall into the "luxury" category.

WHAT IT COSTS In U.S. dollars

	¢	$	$$	$$$	$$$$
SAFARI CAMPS & LODGES	under $500	$500–$600	$600–$700	$700–$800	over $800

All prices refer to an all-inclusive per-person rate including tax, assuming double occupancy.

When to Go

The best time to visit Botswana is in the autumn and winter months (April through September), though it's also the most expensive. In the delta during the winter months the water has come in from the Angolan highlands, and the floodplains, channels, lakes, and inland waterways are literally brimming with sparkling fresh water. Elsewhere, as it's the dry season, the grass and vegetation are sparse, and it's much easier to see game, which often have no choice but to drink at available water holes or rivers. But be warned: it can be bitterly cold, particularly early in the morning and at night. Dress in layers (including a thigh-length thick jacket, hat, scarf, and gloves), which you can discard or add to as the sun goes up or down.

During the Green Season (October through February), aptly named as it's when the bush is at its most lush and is populated with lots of baby animals, you'll find great economy deals offered by most of the lodges, but, and this is a big but, it's very hot—temperatures can reach up to 35°C (95°F). If you're a birder (Botswana has more than 400 species of birds), this is the best time to visit, because all the migratory birds have returned. Unless you're in a lodge with air-conditioning, can stand great heat, or are a keen bird-watcher stick with fall and winter.

6

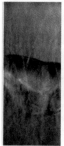

By Kate
Turkington

Half a century ago Botswana was a Cinderella among nations. Then the Fairy Godmother visited and bestowed upon her the gift of diamonds. The resulting economic boom transformed Botswana into one of Africa's richest countries (as measured by per capita income). In 1966 the British Protectorate of Bechuanaland was granted independence and renamed Botswana, and the first democratic President, the internationally respected Sir Seretse Khama, guided his country into a peaceful future.

Where other nations' celebrations quickly turned sour, Botswana's independence brought an enduring tide of optimism. The country sidestepped the scourge of tribalism and factional fighting that cursed much of the continent and is considered one of Africa's most stable democracies.

Botswana's infrastructure is excellent and it's a very safe country. You will certainly come across four-legged predators during your safari, but very unlikely to find two-legged ones lurking outside your tent. Another big bonus is that nearly everybody speaks English—a legacy from when Botswana was a British colony.

Although cities such as Gaborone (pronounced *ha*-bo-ronee), the capital, have been modernized, Botswana has little in the way of urban excitement. But outside the cities it's a land of amazing variety: the Kalahari Desert is in stark contrast to the lush beauty of the Oka-

A MODEL MOTSWANA

The Batswana (singular: Motswana) are renowned for their courtesy and dignity. A perfect role model is the now world-famous Motswana lady detective, Patience Ramotswe of *The No. 1 Ladies' Detective Agency* series by Alexander McCall Smith, who introduced millions of readers all over the world to the unchanging wisdom of a solid, traditional society. The series is now being made into a major motion picture.

vango Delta, one of Botswana's most magnificent and best-known regions. Botswana is passionate about conservation and its legendary big game goes hand-in-hand with its admirable conservation record. Once a hunting mecca for the so-called Great White Hunters (i.e., Ernest Hemingway), most shooting now is with cameras, not rifles. A few proclaimed hunting areas still exist, but they are strictly and responsibly government-controlled.

> **TIPPING TIPS FOR BOTSWANA**
>
> Though the national currency is the pula, you can use U.S. dollars or euros as tips at lodges and camps. Your information folder at each lodge will give helpful suggestions on whom and what to tip.

Botswana's policy of low-impact, high-cost tourism ensures the wilderness remains pristine and exclusive. Nearly 18% of this very flat country's total land area is proclaimed for conservation and tourism. The Moremi Game Reserve, for example, was the first such reserve in southern Africa to have been created by an African community (the Batawana people) on its own tribal lands and has game galore.

Speaking of game galore, the great rivers—the Chobe, the Linyanti and the Kwando—are teeming with herds of elephants and packs of wild dogs, otherwise knows as the elusive "painted wolves" of Africa. The Savuti Channel, where once a mighty river flowed, has now been dry for decades, but among its golden grasses huge prides of lions hunt under skies pulsing with brilliant stars. Then there are the vast white pie-crust surfaces of the Makgadikgadi Pans (the nearest thing on earth to the surface of the moon), once a mega inland lake where flamingoes still flock to breed and strange prehistoric islands of rock rise dramatically from the flaky, arid surface.

If you're interested in meeting some of the most fascinating people, the stark and desolate Central Kalahari Game Reserve is home to the fastest-disappearing indigenous population on earth, the Kalahari Bushmen. They say you can hear the stars sing…listen.

MUST-SEE PARKS

You'd probably like to see all of Botswana, but we know that's not always possible. So we've broken down the chapter by **Must-See Parks** (Okavango Delta, The Moremi Game Reserve, Chobe National Park, and Kwando Reserve) and the **If You Have Time Parks** (Linyanti and Central Kalahari Game Reserves) to help you better organize your time. We suggest though, that you read about all of them and then choose which one is best for you.

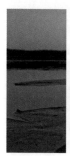

THE OKAVANGO DELTA

Game
★★★★★

Park Accessibility
☆☆★★★

Ease of Getting
Around
☆★★★★

Accommodations
★★★★★

Scenic Beauty
★★★★★

There's no place on earth like the Okavango. The world's largest inland delta, the Okavango was formed by the Okavango River, which floods down from the Angolan highlands once a year and fans out into northwestern Botswana in a meandering complex network of papyrus-lined channels, deep still pools (where crocodiles and hippos lurk), secret waterways (where reeds and grasses almost meet over your head), palm-fringed islands, and natural lagoons.

This watery network covers an area of more than 15,000 square km (5,791 square mi), think a little smaller than Israel or half the size of Switzerland. The lily-studded crystal-clear water is so pure that you can drink it.

This vast area is sometimes referred to as the Swamps, but this gives a false impression because there are no murky mangroves or sinister everglades here. It's just open, tranquil waters where you'll discover an unparalleled experience of being in one of the world's last great wilderness areas. Often, the only way to get around this network of waterways is by boat.

The *mokoro* boat, synonymous with the Okavango, was introduced to the delta in the mid-18th century, when the Bayei tribe (the river bushmen) moved down from the Zambezi. The Bayei invented the mokoro as a controllable craft that could be maneuvered up- or downstream. These boats were traditionally made from the trunks of the great jackalberry, morula, and sausage trees. Today, because of the need to protect the trees, you may find yourself in the modern equivalent: a fiberglass canoe. Either way, a skilled poler (think gondolier) will stand or sit at the rear of the narrow craft guiding you through the delta's waterways—he will be on full alert for the ubiquitous and unpredictable hippos but may be a bit more laid back when it comes to the mighty crocs that lie in the sun. (Powerboats are an option in deeper waters.) Bird-watching from these boats is a special thrill: the annual return of thousands of gorgeous carmine bee-eaters to the Delta in August and September is a dazzling sight, as is a glimpse of the huge ginger-color Pel's fishing owl, the world's only fish-eating owl and one of its rarest birds. ■TIP→ Don't miss the chance to go on a guided walk on one of the many islands.

> ## A HAZARDOUS HERBIVORE
>
> They may look cute and harmless, but it's been said that hippos are the cause of more human deaths than any other large animal in Africa. Though they are not threatening creatures by nature and quickly retreat to water at any sign of danger, the trouble occurs when people get between a hippo and its water.

Although most camps are now both land- and water-based, in a water camp—usually an island surrounded by water—you'll almost certainly see elephants, hippos, crocs, and red lechwes (a beautiful antelope endemic to the Swamps), and you may catch a glimpse of the rare, aquatic sitatunga antelope. You'll almost certainly hear lions but may not always see them; if you're very lucky, you may see a pride swimming between islands. On the other hand, if you are in a land- andwater camp you will see lots of game. Remember that you'll see plenty of animals elsewhere in Botswana. You're in the Delta to experience the unforgettable beauty.

WHERE TO STAY

LUXURY LODGES

$$$$ 🏠**Jao Camp.** Spectacular Jao (as in "now"), a pure Hollywood-meets-Africa fantasy, is on a densely wooded island in a private concession bordering the Moremi Wildlife Reserve. Land and water activities are available, depending on the seasonal water levels, so you can take a day or night game drive in an open 4x4, glide in a mokoro through rippling meadows of water lilies, chug along hippo highways in a motorboat, or go on a guided walk. You'll see lots of predators, especially lions, which live here in the highest concentration in the country, according to a recent wildlife census. Accommodations are individual spacious tree houses with superb views over the vast floodplains. Private bath facilities include an indoor and outdoor shower, flush toilet, and Victorian claw-foot tub. Rare African artifacts decorate the wood, multitiered interior of the main building. The food is delicious and the standard of service is superb. ⌑ *Wilderness Safaris, Box 5219, Rivonia 2128, South Africa* 🕾*11/807–1800* ⊕*www.wilderness-safaris.com* ⌑*8 chalets* ⌂*In-hotel: bar, pool* ⊟*MC, V* ⎮⊙⎮*FAP.*

$$ 🏠**Vumbura Plains.** If it's old-style African safari ambience you're looking for, then this camp is not for you. These state-of-the-art buildings are all about space, shape, light, and texture on a grand scale. Public areas are decorated with rag rugs, beaded beanbag chairs, fiberglass coffee tables (that resemble giant pebbles), and some exquisite indigenous African artwork. The art deco–styled carved wooden bar divides the lounge area from the dining area, which is decorated with dry hol-

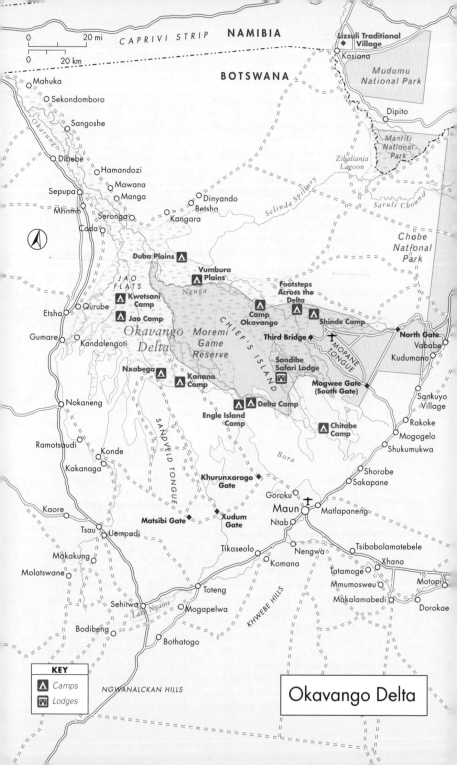

low palm trunks and hanging lamps that mimic the local "sausage" trees. Sip your coffee or after-dinner drinks in deep padded armchairs by firelight on the deck as frogs pipe and fireflies dance. ⚠ **There are many steps and long up-and-down boardwalks between the widely spaced rooms. If this seems a bit challenging, you may want to stay someplace else.** Each en-suite room has a huge wooden outside deck, with comfortable lie-out chairs, a sala (thatched, outdoor, daybed area), and plunge pool, and the enclosed living spaces have floor-to-ceiling windows and mesh doors that capture every source of light, from the early rays of dawn to the blazing sunset. Curl up with a book in your cushioned, sunken lounge, snooze in your king-size bed, or cool off in the emperor-size, leaf-patterned shower. Softly blowing gauzy white curtains divide the sleeping, living, and bathroom areas, and the decor of cream, grey, soft browns, and moss green echoes the pebble and stone theme of the main lodge. ■ **TIP→ Don't miss out on the superb curio shop; it's one of the best in Botswana.** 🗐 *Wilderness Safaris, Box 5219, Rivonia 2128, South Africa* ☎*11/807–1800* ⊕*www.vumbura.com* 🛏*2 7-room camps* ⚐*In-hotel: bar, pool* ▤*MC, V* ⫯⬥*FAP.*

$ 🛏**Delta Camp.** This enchanting camp is set deep on an island in the
☾ Okavango. Reed chalets, each with a private bathroom, are furnished with wood furniture and upturned mokoros; they look like something straight out of *The Swiss Family Robinson.* Each chalet faces northeast to catch the first rays of the sun as it rises above the palm trees, and below your windows are shallow, bird-filled pools, with deep waterways only paces from your front door. Family-owned for many years, the camp has an intimate, relaxed atmosphere; the goal here is to experience the tranquility of the environment. Activities include guided mokoro trails into the maze of waterways and game walks on adjacent islands with a professional licensed guide. A major conservation plus for Delta Camp: motorboats are not used as the emphasis is on preserving the pristine purity of the environment. This adds immeasurably to the relaxed, peaceful atmosphere that pervades this lovely camp. 🗐*Lodges of Botswana, Box 39, Maun, Botswana* ☎*686–1154* ⊕*www.lodgesofbotswana.com* 🛏*7 chalets* ▤*MC, V* ⫯⬥*FAP.*

$ 🛏**Kwetsani Camp.** Perched on high wooden stilts amid a forest canopy on a small island surrounded by enormous open plains, Kwetsani is one of the loveliest of the delta camps. The public areas overlooking the floodplains are built around huge, ancient trees, with a giant jackalberry dominating the bar. Each spacious room, made of canvas, wood, and slatted poles, is set like a child's building block in the middle of a large wooden deck built high into the trees. Polished wooden floors; coir mats; cane armchairs; butlers' tables with tea, coffee, and biscuits; billowing mosquito nets; twinkling ostrich-egg lamps; and indoor and outdoor showers all contribute to a warm, homey atmosphere. After enjoying a game drive or mokoro trip, end your day with a sundowner (cocktail) party by the lagoon lighted by flickering lanterns, with entertainment by the best in local talent—snorting hippos, whooping hyenas, roaring lions, and keening waterbirds. 🗐 *Wilderness Safaris, Box 5219, Rivonia 2128, South Africa* ☎*11/807–1800* ⊕*www.kwetsani. com* 🛏*5 chalets* ⚐*In-hotel: bar, pool* ▤*MC, V* ⫯⬥*FAP.*

6

$ ⊞ **Sandibe Safari Lodge.** A land and water camp run by CC Africa, San-
★ dibe clings to the edge of a pristine channel. Go fishing, take a mokoro
ride through tunnels of interlacing papyrus, walk on a palm-studded
island, or track big game in an open-sided vehicle. Watch out for some
Okavango-specific animals: the aquatic tsessebe antelope—the fastest
antelope—and the secretive sitatunga. The camp has a fairy-tale feel, as
if a giant fashioned an idyllic tiny village out of adobe and thatch and
set it down amid an enchanted forest full of birds. It'll be difficult to
tear yourself away from your honey-color cottage with its huge carved
bed covered with a woven leather bedspread, to walk to the main lodge
with its "curtains" of tattered russet bark wafting in the breeze. After a
splendid dinner, enjoy a nightcap around a crackling fire under a star-
studded sky. ⊞ *CC Africa, Private Bag X27, Benmore 2010, South
Africa* ☎ *11/809–4300* ⊕ *www.sandibe.com* ⇆ *8 cottages* ⌂ *In-hotel:
bar, pool* ⊟ *MC, V* ⑩ *FAP.*

PERMANENT TENTED CAMPS

$$$ ⊞ **Duba Plains.** This tiny camp deep in the delta is nestled upon an island
FodorśChoice shaded by huge trees and surrounded by horizon-touching plains that
★ are seasonally flooded—usually from late April to early October. When
the water is high, the game competes with the camp for dry ground,
and lions and hyenas become regular dusk-to-dawn visitors. You can
watch hundreds of buffalo, leopards, lions, cheetahs, elephants, hippos,
lechwes (a type of antelope), and the most beautiful of all the ante-
lopes—the sable—from one of only two 4x4 open game vehicles in the
reserve. The Duba lion prides are among the few to hunt by day—they
have a taste for buffalo—and if you're really lucky, you might find
yourself and your vehicle bang in the middle of one of these spectacu-
lar hunts. The area is also a birder's paradise, with an abundance of
waterfowl. En-suite tents with ceiling fans and gleaming Rhodesian
teak furniture complement stupendous views. There's a comfy lounge
and small bar in the public area and a poolside gazebo as well as a bird
blind tucked behind the camp. ⊞ *Wilderness Safaris, Box 5219, Rivo-
nia 2128, South Africa* ☎ *11/807–1800* ⊕ *www.dubaplains.com* ⇆ *6
rooms* ⌂ *In-hotel: bar, pool* ⊟ *MC, V* ⑩ *FAP.*

$$$ ⊞ **Eagle Island Camp.** You'll find this camp deep in the central delta on
Xaxaba (pronounced ka-*ka*-ba) Island, which is surrounded by pris-
tine waterways, tall palm trees, and vast floodplains. At dawn and
dusk hippos chortle, birds call, and hyenas whoop. Activities here are
water-based. You'll glide through high, emerald-green papyrus tunnels
in a mokoro; go powerboating on wide lagoons; or enjoy sundowners
as you float silently in your mokoro on crystal-clear water as the sun
sets in a blaze of red and gold. Or have a front-row seat for the same
nightly spectacle—a sunset—in the Fish Eagle Bar, which juts out over
the water. Large walk-in tents are decorated in traditional African style
with four-poster beds and lamps fashioned out of Botswana baskets
and carved African pots. Sit out on your huge veranda, or snooze in
the inviting canvas hammock. Dine in style in the elegant dining room
where old photographs add to the classic safari ambience. The main
viewing deck overlooks vast expanses of water complete with dozing
hippos. ⊞ *Orient-Express Safaris, Box 786432, Sandton 2146, South*

Africa ☎*11/481–6052* 🌐*www.orient-express-safaris.com* *15 tents* *In-hotel: bar, pool, a/c* *MC, V* *FAP.*

$$$ **Shinde Camp.** Ker & Downey's oldest camp, and possibly its loveliest, lies in a vast palm-dotted area in the heart of the northern delta. Surrounded by lagoons and waterways encrusted with white, yellow, and purple water lilies, and home to hundreds of birds, it's also home to lots of game. Your large tent, outfitted with cane and Rhodesian teak furniture, has polished wooden floors both inside and outside on your viewing deck. Spacious bathrooms have flower-painted ceramic sinks, and a sturdy door leads to a separate outside toilet. A spiraling wooden ramp connects the dining area, built high in the trees at the top of the lodge, with a lookout deck and lounge in the middle and a boma under huge old trees at the bottom. If you want even more exclusivity and private pampering, opt for Shinde Enclave, which accommodates up to six guests with a private guide and waiter. *Ker & Downey, Box 27, Maun, Botswana* ☎*686–0375* 🌐*www.kerdowney.com* *9 tents* *In-hotel: bar, pool* *MC, V* *FAP.*

$$ ★ **Camp Okavango.** Most people involuntarily draw a breath when they walk from the airstrip into this sprawling campsite. Its location on remote Nxaragha (Na-*ka*-ra) Island in the heart of the permanent delta makes it accessible only by plane or water. Built by an eccentric American millionaire many years ago (she used to jet off to Los Angeles to get her hair done), this water camp combines style, comfort, and a year-round water wilderness experience. Huge trees arch over an outdoor lounge with sweeping lawns leading down to the water, where hippos snort all night. Your tent, with private bathroom, is built on a raised wooden platform that overlooks the delta. It's set among groves of ancient trees and is so well separated that you might believe you're the only one in camp. Common areas with worn flagstones have comfortable colonial-style furniture, and elegant dinners are served in the high-thatch dining area, where an original sycamore fig mokoro is suspended over the long wooden dining table. A camp highlight: chilled drinks from a bar set up in the middle of a lagoon tended by a wading barman. *Desert & Delta Safaris, Box 130555, Bryanston 2125, South Africa* ☎*11/706–0861* 🌐*www.desertdelta.co.za* *11 tents* *In-hotel: bar, pool* *MC, V* *FAP.*

$$ **Kanana Camp.** The simple natural charm of Kanana makes you feel part of the delta, not cocooned away from it. Game drives, mokoroing, boating, and bush walks (there are resident Pel's fishing owls on nearby islands) are all part of the experience, but a visit to the Thapagadi Lagoon is a must. The lagoon is home to a fantastic heronry, where open-billed maribou and yellow-billed storks nest with all kinds of herons, cormorants, pelicans, darters, and egrets—you'll never forget the sounds of this avian community. Safari tents (where tea and coffee are brought at dawn by a cheerful staff member) with wooden decks overlook dense reed beds and a papyrus-thick floodplain. Cane furnishings and dark-wood cabinetry are complemented by colorful rugs and a white curtain, which separates the gaily decorated bathroom from the bedroom. You'll fall asleep to the sound of hippos munching, squelching, and splashing outside your tent and awake to tumultuous

birdsong. Public areas are built around a massive ancient fig tree, where green pigeons feast as you enjoy imaginative food on the dining deck. ⌂*Ker & Downey, Box 27, Maun, Botswana* ☎*686–0375* ⊕*www. kerdowney.com* ⇆*8 tents* ♿*In-hotel: bar* ▤*MC, V* ⦿*FAP.*

$ ⊡ **Chitabe Camp.** Bring lots of film to this exclusive reserve that borders the Moremi Wildlife Reserve; you'll want to take pictures of everything. Spacious, comfortable tents on stilts are connected by raised wooden walkways that put you safely above the ground and give you a Tarzan's-eye view of the surrounding bush. You'll sleep in a luxurious, East African–style tent with wooden floors, two comfortable single beds, woven palm furniture, wrought-iron washstands, and a private bath. A separate thatch dining room, bar, and lounge area, also linked by wooden walkways, looks out over a floodplain. Unfortunately there are no vistas of water. The camp lies within the Botswana Wild Dog Research Project's research area, which has up to 160 dogs in packs of 10 to 12, so you're almost certain to see these fascinating "painted wolves." The area has a variety of habitats, from marshlands and riverine areas to open grasslands and seasonally flooded plains. Although it's on one of the most beautiful islands in the delta, it's not really a water camp because it doesn't offer water activities. ⌂ *Wilderness Safaris, Box 5219, Rivonia 2128, South Africa* ☎*11/807–1800* ⊕*www.wilderness-safaris.com* ⇆*8 tents at Main Camp, 4 tents at Trails Camp* ♿*In-hotel: bars, pool* ▤*MC, V* ⦿*FAP.*

$ ⊡**Nxabega Okavango Safari Camp.** Renowned for its beauty, Nxabega (pronounced *na*-becka) is in the very heart of the delta and offers both a water and a land experience. Because it's a private concession, you can take a night drive in an open vehicle and spot big predators as well as the small nocturnal ones like civets (black-and-white badger-looking creatures), bush babies (similar to furry, flying squirrels), and genets (small spotted cats). There's a resident naturalist to complement the team of knowledgeable and friendly CC Africa–trained guides. En-suite safari tents are on raised teak platforms, each with a private veranda overlooking the water and bush. The main lodge is made of thatch and wood; the high-roofed and paneled dining room has an almost medieval banquet-hall feel. The food is excellent but don't worry, you'll lose some of those extra calories by taking a guided walk on one of the nearby islands to track game and spot birds. There are also game drives and water excursions. ⌂*CC Africa, Private Bag X27, Benmore 2010, South Africa* ☎*11/809–4300* ⊕*www.ccafrica.com* ⇆*9 tents* ♿*In-hotel: bar, pool, curio shop* ▤*MC, V* ⦿*FAP.*

MOBILE TENTED CAMPS

$ ⚠**Footsteps Across the Delta.** This is the ultimate back-to-nature experience. The emphasis is on learning the secrets of the Okavango—on foot and by mokoro. Because this is a mobile camp that moves with the seasons, there is no electricity, but you'll be more than rewarded for the lack of luxury by the surrounding bird and animal life. The night sounds are awesome, from roaring lions to the ghostly screams of the Pel's fishing owl. Walking with outstanding guides who will answer all of your questions about the surrounding bush is the main activity, but there are also game drives, night drives, boat trips, and fishing oppor-

Vumbura Plains

Kwetsani

Jao

Botswana's Tribes

Bayei local people act as guides punting tourists around in mokoros canoes in the marshes of the Okavango delta

TSWANA

The largest tribal group in Botswana, the Tswana comprise just over half the country's population and mainly live in the eastern part of the country; many Tswana also live in South Africa. Also known as the Batswana, they live mainly in thatched roof rondavels made of mud and cow dung. They are pastoralists and are tied to the land and their cattle, which are used in negotiating marriages and other rites of passage. Though the tribal structure of the Tswana has changed in modern times, they remain family-oriented and still live in villages with the kgosi (chief), as the primary decision-maker. As Botswana has prospered from diamond mining, Tswana society has become more modernized, with many tribe members leaving the family at a young age to seek work in the cities. A large number of Tswana also speak English in addition to their tribal language.

BAYEI (RIVER BUSHMEN)

The Bayei, also known as the River Bushmen, live along the tributaries of the Okavango and Chobe rivers in northern and central Botswana. African oral history states that the Bayei came to the region in the 18th century from Central Africa. One of the tribe's great leaders then married one of the women of the San tribe, perhaps as a means of negotiating peace or perhaps to incorporate the tribe into the matrilineal society.

The Bayei are experts fishermen and they use nets and traps to fish along the waterways and floodplains. The mokoro, a dug-out canoe carved from tree trunks, is also an important part of their daily life, serving as both transportation along the rivers and an important tool for fishing. The Bayei also farm tobacco and wild corn.

tunities. You'll sleep in one of only three tents with insect-proofing and sewn-in floors, where two iron bedsteads, some wooden shelves, and a small table are the only furnishings. You'll wash in a canvas washstand outside your tent (where there are also two canvas chairs), and your bathroom consists of a bush toilet and an overhead bucket shower. ⊕*Ker & Downey, Box 27, Maun, Botswana* ☎*686–0375* ⊕*www. kerdowney.com* ⊲*3 tents* ⊘*In-hotel: bar* ☰*MC, V* ⍟*FAP*.

6

MOREMI WILDLIFE RESERVE

Game	
★★★★★	
Park Accessibility	
☆☆★★★	
Ease of Getting Around	
☆★★★★	
Accommodations	
★★★★★	
Scenic Beauty	
☆★★★★	

Prolific wildlife and an astonishing variety of birdlife characterize this reserve, which has become well-known because it's the first in southern Africa to be proclaimed by the local people (the Batawana) themselves. As there are no fences, the big game—and there's lots of it—can migrate to and from the Chobe Park in the north.

Sometimes it seems as if a large proportion of Botswana's 70,000 elephants have made their way here, particularly in the dry winter season. Be prepared to check off on your game list lions, cheetahs, leopards, hyenas, wild dogs, buffalo, hippos, dozens of different antelopes, zebras, giraffes, monkeys, baboons, and more than 400 kinds of birds. If you're a birder, choose the hot summer months (November–April) because dozens of returning migrants flock here in their thousands. The return of the Carmine bee-eaters and Woodland kingfishers is a dazzling sight, as are the hosts of wading water birds, from storks of all kinds, to elegant little sandpipers. Although during the South African school vacations (July and December) there are more vehicles than normal, traffic is mostly light, and in the Moremi, unlike many of Africa's other great reserves, you'll often be the only ones watching the game. Winter (May–October) is the best game viewing time as the vegetation is sparse and it's easier to spot game. Also, because there's little or no surface water, animals are forced to drink at the rivers or permanent waterholes. However, during the other months—known as the "Green Season"—you'll often get fantastic offers by individual lodges, with greatly reduced rates. But be warned, summer temperatures can soar to the mid-30s centigrade and over, so make sure your lodge of choice has a pool and a/c, or at least a fan. Self-driving is possible in the Moremi, but a 4x4 is essential because road conditions are poor (sometimes impassable in the rainy season), distances from cities are long, and national park lodging consists of very rustic non-serviced camping sites with no electricity. If you're an overseas visitor, we suggest you stick to the private lodges. They might be pricey, but they're worth every penny.

WHERE TO STAY

LUXURY LODGING

$$$$ 🏨 **Mombo Camp and Little Mombo.** On Mombo Island, off the northwest ★   tip of Chief's Island, this legendary camp is surrounded by wall-to-wall game. Although there is plenty of surface water in the area (marshes and floodplains), it's strictly a land-activity camp. The camp has exclusive use of a large area of Moremi, so privacy is assured. Its great wildlife, including all of the large predators, has made this area one of Botswana's top wildlife documentary locations—*National Geographic* and the BBC have both filmed here. The stunning camp has identical guest rooms divided into two distinct camps: Mombo has nine rooms, Little Mombo only three. These camps are among the best known, most expensive, and most sought after in Botswana, so be sure to book months in advance. Each spacious room is built on a raised wooden platform with wonderful views over the open plains (you're almost guaranteed to see game as you sit there), and although the en-suite rooms have a tented feel, they are ultra luxurious. The dining room, lounge, and bar are also built on big wooden decks overlooking the magnificent animal-dotted savanna. The atmosphere is friendly, and the personal attention, food, and guides all excellent. 🖎 *Wilderness Safaris, Box 5219, Rivonia 2128, South Africa* 🕾*11/807–1800* 🌐*www. mombo.co.za* 🛏*12 rooms* 🛆*In-hotel: bar, pool* 🗖*MC, V* ¶O¶*FAP.*

$ 🏨 **Xigera Camp.** The cry of the fish eagle permeates this exceptionally ☾   lovely camp (pronounced *kee*-jer-ah), which is set on the aptly named ★   Paradise Island amid thickets of old trees in one of the most beautiful parts of the reserve. Spacious rooms of timber and canvas are built on a high wooden platform overlooking a floodplain. Reed walls separate the sleeping area from the spacious dressing room, which in turn leads into a reed-floored shower and separate toilet; you can also shower under the stars. Raised wooden walkways connect rooms to the main lodge, which sprawls beside a lagoon where a small wooden bridge joins the island to the mainland. At night this bridge becomes a thoroughfare for lions and hyenas, and it's not uncommon to see one of these nocturnal visitors walk by as you sip your postprandial drink by the blazing fire. The food is varied and excellent, and the staff is ultra-friendly and attentive. 🖎 *Wilderness Safaris, Box 5219, Rivonia 2128, South Africa* 🕾*11/807–1800* 🌐*www. xigera.com* 🛏*5 rooms* 🛆*In-hotel: bar, pool* 🗖*MC, V* ¶O¶*FAP.*

PERMANENT TENTED CAMPS

$$ 🏨 **Camp Moremi.** You get the best of both water and land at Camp Moremi. You'll see lions, elephants, giraffes, zebras, all kinds of ante-

> ## WORD OF MOUTH
>
> "Moremi is such an amazing place, with such variety, that you won't be able to get around it in a day. You'll be so busy driving that you won't get to see animals because you won't have time to stop. If you're going all that way, you need more than one or two days."
>
> –WildDogs

lopes, and often the elusive leopard, cheetah, and wild dog. The rare
Pel's fishing owl regularly plummets down to the shallow pool below the
Tree Lodge to snag a fish and carry it away. Bird-watching is excellent
throughout the year; ask for a powerboat ride to the heronries on nearby
lagoons. Huge African ebony trees, home to two-legged, four-legged,
winged, and earthbound creatures, dominate the campsite on the edge
of a lovely lagoon. From the high viewing platform in the trees you can
look out on a limitless horizon as the sun sets orange and gold over the
smooth, calm waters. Tastefully decorated, comfortable tents are well
spaced to ensure privacy. Camp Moremi's attractive timber-and-thatch
tree lodge has a dining area, bar, main lounge, small library, and sundeck
with great views of Xakanaxa Lagoon. ⌨*Desert & Delta Safaris, Box
130555, Bryanston 2125, South Africa* ☎*11/706–0861* ⊕*www.desert-
delta.co.za* ⟿*11 tents* ⌂*In-hotel: bar, pool* ▭*MC, V* ⎺⎺*FAP.*

$ 🏨**Khwai River Lodge.** As you sit on the wooden deck jutting out over the
clear delta waters, munching brunch or just chilling out, you may just
forget the outside world. Floating water lilies, tiny bejeweled kingfishers dipping and swooping in front of you, and the sounds of gently lapping water relax even the most driven work junkie. Bigger than some
of the other safari lodges and one of the oldest, Khwai is renowned for
its personal attention and friendly service. The location, 8 km (5 mi)
northwest of the north gate of the Moremi Wildlife Reserve, means

Mombo Camp

6

Mombo

Xigera

that you will see lots of game, not only on your drives but also from the lodge itself. The excitement of seeing a hippo or elephant stroll past the viewing deck outside your deluxe tent is not something you'll easily forget. The lodge is also the stuff of bird-watchers' dreams. ⌖ *Orient-Express Safaris, Box 786432, Sandton 2146, South Africa* ☎*11/481–6052* ⊕*www.orient-express-safaris.com* ⤺*15 tents* ⚒*In-hotel: bar, pool* ▭*MC, V* ⧦*FAP.*

$ 🔆**Xakanaxa Camp.** For a genuine bush camp experience—no bells and
☾ whistles or unnecessary frills—it would be hard to beat this old-fashioned camp (pronounced ka-*kan*-ah-ka). From the moment you walk through the rustic reception area, a feeling of unpretentious warmth and relaxation envelops you; it's no wonder that visitors return again and again. Each spacious tent has wooden floors, plenty of storage space, a huge comfy bed, handy reading lamps for making those journal notes, a megasize bathroom under the stars (read: no roof), and a viewing deck. Lighting at night is au naturel (candles, hurricane lamps, and flashlights), although there's electricity during the day. The ultra-experienced staff, many with more than 10 years of experience, gets everything right from their attentive service to the superb, wholesome, home-cooked food. Even the resident croc, who sunbathes under her very own sign BEWARE CROCODILE, has been here since she was a tiny whippersnapper. Wooden-decked public areas sprawl along the water, and elephants and hippos wander past your tent most nights. ⌖ *Lodges of Botswana, Box 39, Maun, Botswana* ☎*686–1154* ⊕*www.lodge-sofbotswana.com* ⤺*12 tents* ▭*MC, V* ⧦*FAP.*

6

CHOBE NATIONAL PARK

Game
☆★★★★

Park Accessibility
☆★★★★

Ease of Getting Around
☆★★★★

Accommodations
★★★★★

Scenic Beauty
☆★★★★

This 12,000-square-km (4,500-square-mi) reserve is the second largest national park in Botswana and it has four very different eco-systems: Serondela in the extreme northwest with fertile plains and thick forests; the dry Savuti Channel in the west; the Linyanti Swamps in the northwest; and the arid hinterland in between.

The whole area, however, is home to a shifting migratory population of more than 40,000 elephants. In addition to spotting Chobe's great pachyderm herds, you should see lions, leopards, hyenas, wild dogs, impalas, waterbucks, kudus, zebras, wildebeests (gnus), giraffes, and warthogs. Watch closely at the water holes when prey species come down to drink and are most vulnerable—they are so palpably nervous that you'll feel jumpy, too. Lions in this area are often specialized killers; one pride might target giraffes, another zebras, another buffalo, or even young elephants. But lions are opportunistic killers, and you could see them pounce on anything from a porcupine to a lowly scrub hare. Birdlife along the river is awesome and the major must-sees are the slaty egrets, rock pratincoles, pink-throated longclaws, and lesser gallinules.

The northern section of the park comprises riverine bush devastated by the hordes of elephants coming down to the perennial Chobe River to drink in winter. Fortunately, the wide sweep of the Caprivi floodplains, where hundreds of buffalo and elephants graze silhouetted against almost psychedelic sunsets, softens this harsh, featureless landscape where it faces neighboring Namibia.

Chobe can be crowded, unlike the rest of Botswana, because there are simply too many vehicles on too few roads, particularly in the dry season. One of the quieter parts of the park is around the Ngwezumba River, an area of forests and pans in the more remote middle of the park; the drawback here is that game is harder to find.

In the southwestern part of the park lies the fabled Savuti (also spelled Savute) area, famous for its predators. Savuti offers a sweeping expanse of savanna brooded over by seven rocky outcrops that guard a relic marsh and the dry Savuti Channel, Africa's Stolen River of myth and legend. (It's "stolen" because it mysteriously disappeared in the early 1980s and has never returned.) You may see wild dogs hunting where only a few decades ago crocodiles swam and basked on the channel banks.

A SUNSET CRUISE

A sunset sundowner cruise on the Chobe River is an unforgettable experience. If your own lodge offers this experience, you'll most likely be in a smallish boat, but if they don't, try to avoid the big, noisy "Booze Cruise" excursions sold by the travel companies in the area. Instead, opt for a smaller boat with an experienced local guide and boatman.

Savuti is dramatically different from elsewhere in Botswana; there are open spaces, limitless horizons, wide skies, and unending miles of waving tall grass punctuated by starkly beautiful dead trees—the legacy of the relentless drought. Like Chobe National Park overall, Savuti is famed for its elephants, but the female of the species is less often seen here, for Savuti is the domain of the bull elephant: old grandfathers, middle-aged males, and feisty young teenagers. The old ones gaze at you with imperturbable dignity, but it's the youngsters who'll make your adrenaline run riot as they kick up the dust and bellow belligerently as they make a mock charge in your direction.

And while you're in the Savuti area looking for leopards and the tiny acrobatic klipspringer antelopes, be sure to pay a visit to the striking rock paintings, early humans' attempts to represent the wildlife all around. In summertime thousands of migrating zebras and wildebeests provide the equivalent of fast food for the lion prides, hungry hyenas, and cheetahs which follow the herds. The Cape buffalo herds also arrive in summer along with thousands of returning bird migrants. The raptors are spectacular. You'll see falcons, eagles, kestrels, goshawks, ospreys, and sparrow hawks. In the northwest of the park are the Linyanti Swamps, also famous for their game concentrations, and in particular wild dogs.

WHERE TO STAY

LUXURY LODGES

$$$$ 📷 **Chobe Chilwero River Lodge.** Easily ⏱ accessible from both the Zimbabwe and Zambian side of the Vic Falls, this lodge is perched on a small hill on the border of Chobe National Park (Chilwero means "high view" in Setswana, the national language). Its 15 spacious thatch cottages are the ultimate in luxury: en-suite bathrooms with sunken baths, pri-

WORD OF MOUTH

"We cruised up the Chobe River to watch the elephants coming down to drink and bathe. There were about 100 of them in one herd. The elephants frolicked and played together, some totally submerging themselves and using their trunks as snorkels, and the babies were rolling over and over."

–Tropical_gal

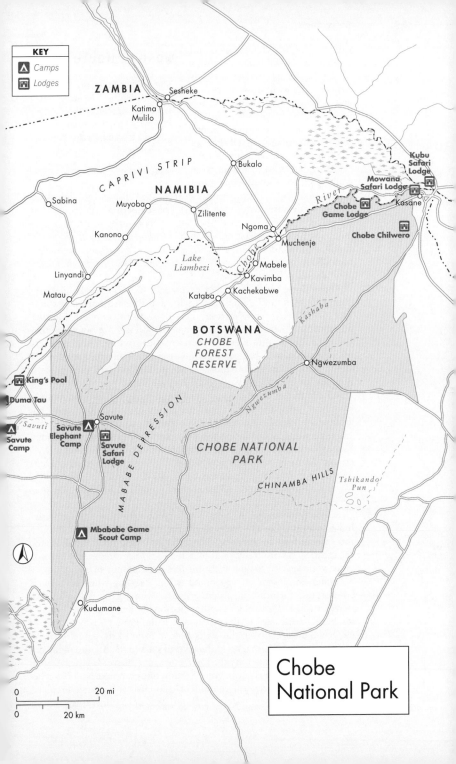

KEY
⛺ *Camps*
🏠 *Lodges*

ZAMBIA

Sesheke

Katima
Mulilo

CAPRIVI STRIP

Bukalo

Sabina

Muyoba

NAMIBIA

Zilitente

Kanono

Ngoma

Muchenje

Chobe River

**Kubu
Safari
Lodge**

**Mowana
Safari Lodge**

Kasane

**Chobe
Game Lodge**

Chobe Chilwero

*Lake
Liambezi*

Mabele

Linyandi

Kavimba

Matau

Kataba

Kachekabwe

BOTSWANA
*CHOBE FOREST
RESERVE*

Kashaba

Ngwezumba

King's Pool

Duma Tau

Savuti

⛺ **Savute
Camp**

Savute

⛺ **Savute
Elephant Camp**

🏠 **Savute
Safari Lodge**

M B A B A B E   D E P R E S S I O N

Ngwezumba

**CHOBE NATIONAL
PARK**

CHINAMBA HILLS

*Tshikando
Pun*

⛺ **Mbababe Game
Scout Camp**

Kudumane

0 ⟶ 20 mi

0 ⟶ 20 km

Chobe
National Park

vate gardens with hammocks, and viewing decks with stunning vistas of the Chobe River. The decor is African chic, with browns, creams, and ochres predominating. Catch up on the real world (if you can bear to!) in the communications center, or pamper yourself with an in-room beauty treatment. All the Chobe activities are available, from walking safaris and fishing to game

drives, canoeing, day trips to the nearby Vic Falls, and the must-not-miss sunset cruises. Although you're not really in a wilderness area, the privacy and exclusivity of the lodge will persuade you that you are miles away from civilization. ⌂ *Chobe Chilwero Lodge, Box 782607 Sandton 2146, South Africa* 🕾 *11/787–7658* ⊕ *www.sanctuarylodges. com* 📻 *15 cottages* ⚴ *In-room: a/c, safe, fan. In-hotel: bar, pool, curio shop, laundry, Internet* ▭ *MC, V* ⏏*FAP.*

$$ 🔲 **Chobe Game Lodge.** The only permanent lodge in Chobe National
◐ Park, this grand old dame—Liz Taylor and Richard Burton got married for the second time here in the '70s—still offers one of Botswana's most sophisticated stays, although the feel is more hotel-like than lodgelike. Terra-cotta tiles, Rhodesian teak furniture, tribal artifacts, and the ubiquitous beautiful handwoven Botswana baskets give the feel of Africa. The solid Moorish-style buildings—with their graceful high arches and barrel-vaulted ceilings—insulate the not-so-intrepid traveler from too-close encounters of the animal kind: baboon mothers have been known to teach their young how to turn a doorknob! The gorgeous gardens are a riot of color and attract lots of small fauna. There's a well-stocked curio shop with great clothes and wildlife books. Don't miss out on the well-run daily activities from game drives to river cruises. An early-morning canoe ride is also a must. ⌂ *Desert & Delta Safaris, Box 130555, Bryanston 2125, South Africa* 🕾 *11/706–0861* ⊕ *www.desertdelta.co.za* 📻 *46 rooms, 4 suites* ⚴ *In-hotel: bar, pool* ▭ *MC, V* ⏏*FAP.*

$$ 🔲 **Savute Safari Lodge.** As your small plane arrives at this attractive lodge, you can see the wide swath the dry riverbed makes through the surrounding countryside. The exterior of the main building and the safari suites are traditional thatch and timber; however, when you enter your spacious suite, it's a bit like walking out of Africa into a Scandinavian design center—blond wood, dazzling white bed linens, comfortable furniture in bright primary colors, gaily colored handwoven rugs, and lots of glass. Outside on your spacious wooden deck it's back to Africa; by full moon watch the gray, ghostly shapes of elephants drinking from the water hole in front of the camp, or if the moon is not yet full, marvel at the myriad stars in the African night sky. When you're not watching the abundant game, there's a large, elegant dining room where you can enjoy scrumptious late-morning brunches and candlelight silver-service dinners, a lounge with a huge fireplace, and an upstairs viewing deck. ⌂ *Desert & Delta Safaris, Box 130555,*

Bryanston 2125, South Africa ☎*11/706–0861* ⊕*www.desert delta.co.za* ⟿*12 suites* ⚂*In-hotel: bar, pool, a/c* ⊟*MC, V* ⦿*FAP.*

$ ☉ 🖵**Kubu Safari Lodge.** If you want to escape the real world for a while, then this small, quiet attractive lodge on the banks of the Chobe, which prides itself on its seclusion is right for you; it has no phones, radios, or TV. Situated where Botswana, Namibia, Zimbabwe, and Zambia meet, the 11 en-suite thatch chalets are on stilts and are unpretentiously but comfortably furnished in earth tones. After your Chobe National Park game drive or boat cruise, come back and take a leisurely saunter around the Kubu Lodge Nature Trail—be on the look-out for dozens of birds and the endemic Chobe bushbuck—or go next door to the Crocodile Farm and eyeball Nelson, one of the oldest and biggest crocs in captivity. ⌂*Kubu Safari Lodge Chobe, Botswana* ☎*No phone* ⊕*www.afrizim. com* ⟿*11 chalets* ⚂*In-room: fan. In-hotel: bar, pool, restaurant, wine cellar, curio shop* ⊟*MC, V* ⦿*FAP.*

¢ ☉ 🖵**Mowana Safari Lodge.** Built round an 800-year-old baobab tree situated among lovely private gardens on the banks of the Chobe River, you'll find this lodge just 8 km (5 mi) from the entrance to Chobe National Park. Like its older sister, Chobe Safari Lodge farther downstream, this lodge is more like a hotel than a proper safari lodge. That's not to say that you still won't get your full safari experience, you'll just be a bit cocooned away from the actual wilderness. Pleasantly decorated with an ethnic African theme, all 104 air-conditioned rooms overlook the river, on which you'll probably spend a fair amount of time boating, birdwatching, game-viewing, canoeing, and fishing. Morning, evening, and night drives are available, but because the river roads are few and many game vehicles use the same roads, your game viewing can become rather crowded. You can take a short flight or helicopter ride over the nearby Vic Falls, go white-water rafting on the Zambezi, or try a host of other activities. Children under 12 stay free if sharing with parents. Plus, you'll feel quite presidential: this is where Bill Clinton and his entourage stayed a few years ago. ⌂*Mowana Safari Lodge, Box 266, Kasane, Botswana* ☎*625–0300* ⊕*www.afrizim.com* ⟿*104 rooms* ⚂*In-room: a/c, minibar, safe. In-hotel: bar, pool, shop* ⊟*MC, V* ⦿*FAP.*

PERMANENT TENTED CAMPS

$$$ 🖵**Savuti Camp.** This intimate camp has only seven walk-in tents, which are raised on stilts above the Savuti Channel, a once flowing, but now dry channel. If you have an elephant phobia, don't even think about coming here, because all day and often all night long, elephants crisscross in front of the camp and in front of the tents on their way to and from the waterhole that's directly in front of the thatch dining area, pub, plunge pool, and viewing decks. This camp is also home to the legendary "woodpile hide"—a small enclosure right at the waterhole, which you hide in to literally eyeball the pachyderms a few feet away.

You will feel part of the herd and fell protected from it. It's an amazing thrill to run be nose-to-knee with elephants galore. Because the waterhole is the only permanent water in the area, there's superb game viewing all year round—particularly in winter—with lions, leopards, cheetahs, wild dogs, and hyenas. You'll have a good chance of also seeing roan and sable antelopes—perhaps the most stately and beautiful of all the species. Your comfortable tent has a bathroom and shower, hand basin and flush toilets, and is attractively furnished in wood and cane. If an elephant wanders past your tiny viewing deck (and one will), just stay still and enjoy the view, because it may be the best you ever get at such close quarters, and the best photograph, too. 🖂 *Wilderness Safaris, Box 5219, Rivonia 2128, South Africa* ☎*11/807–1800* 🌐*www.wilderness-safaris.com* 🛏*7 tents* ⛵*In-hotel: bar, pool* ▭*MC, V* ⅩⅠ*FAP.*

$ 🏕 **Savute Elephant Camp.** In the semiarid Savuti region, splendid, spacious, air-conditioned, twin-bedded tents are elegantly furnished with cane and dark-wood furniture, an impressive overhead bed canopy with attendant mosquito net, woven rugs in creams and browns, white linen bedspreads, and a roomy bathroom with his-and-her sinks. For those cold winter mornings and evenings, there's even a built-in heater. Your private viewing deck overlooking one of the busiest elephant water holes in the world has comfortable chairs and an inviting hammock. As the camp is in Chobe National Park, night drives and walking are against regulations, but you'll still see plenty of game and birds during the day. If you can manage to be here at full moon, the sight of hundreds of great, gray shapes gleaming in the moonlight, jostling, rumbling, and coming and going at the water hole is truly unforgettable. 🖂*Orient-Express Safaris, Box 786432, Sandton 2146, South Africa* ☎*11/481–6052* 🌐*www.orient-express-safaris.com* 🛏*12 tents* ⛵*In-hotel: bar, pool, a/c* ▭*MC, V* ⅩⅠ*FAP.*

6

Savuti Camp

Savuti Camp

Savuti Camp

KWANDO RESERVE

Game
★★★★★

Park Accessibility
☆☆★★★

Ease of Getting Around
☆★★★★

Accommodations
☆☆★★★

Scenic Beauty
☆☆★★★

The 2,300-square-km (900-square-mi) private Kwando conces-sion has more than 80 km (50 mi) of river frontage. It stretches south from the banks of the Kwando River, through huge open plains and mopane forests to the Okavango Delta.

It's an area crisscrossed by thousands of ancient game trails traversed by wildlife that move freely between the Okavango Delta, Chobe, and the open Namibian wilderness to the north. As you fly in to the reserve, you'll see this web of thousands of interlacing natural game trails—from hippo highways to the tiny paths of smaller animals. This should clue you in to Kwando's diverse animal life: wall-to-wall elephants, crowds of buffalo, zebras, antelope of all kinds including roan and sable, wild dogs, lions, and wildebeests. Participants on one night drive came upon a running battle between a pack of 14 wild dogs and 2 hyenas who had stolen the dogs' fresh kill. The noisy battle ended when a loudly trumpeting elephant, fed up with the commotion, charged the wild dogs and drove them off. There's a sheer joy in knowing you are one of very few vehicles in a half-million acres of wilderness.

If you'd like to take a safari with children, there's no better place than Kwando, where under care of top rangers you'll not only have a memo-rable time but learn lots about the bush. The safari starts with a safety briefing, and kids get their own tents next to mom and dad (or you can share). Kids learn to track and take plaster casts of spoor, sit up in the tracker's seat on the vehicle to follow game, cook marshmallows over the boma fire, tell stories, catch and release butterflies, and make bush jew-elry. Kids can eat on their own or with you, and if you want an afternoon snooze, they'll be supervised in a fun activity. This program is available at both Kwando camps; the price is the same per night as for an adult.

WHERE TO STAY

LUXURY LODGING

$$$ ⬚ **Kwando Lagoon Camp.** The camp perches on the banks of the fast-
⟳ flowing Kwando River, quite literally in the middle of nowhere. Com-
★ fortable walk-through tents with private bathrooms and verandas

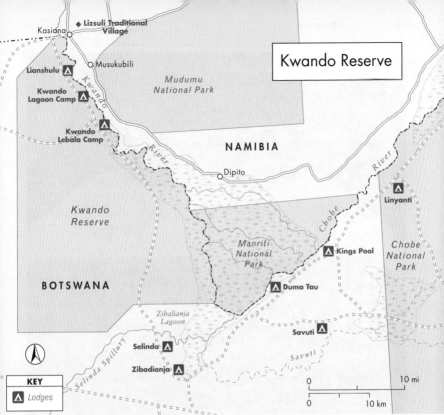

Kwando Reserve

nestle on grassy slopes under the shade of giant jackalberry trees that are hundreds of years old. After a night spent next to one of these mighty trees, a major source of natural energy, people say you wake up rejuvenated, your body buzzing with new life. From the thatch dining and bar area you can watch herds of elephants only yards away as they come to drink and bathe, or hippos snoozing in the sun. You might also spot a malachite kingfisher darting like a bejeweled minijet over the water. Go for a morning or evening game drive, drift along the river in a small boat, or go spinner- or fly-fishing for tiger fish and bream. The emphasis in the camp is on informality, simplicity, and soaking up the wilderness experience. ⌂ *Kwando Wildlife Experience, Box 550, Maun, Botswana* ☎ *686–1449 or 686–4388* ⊕ *www.kwando.co.za* ⌱ *6 tents △ In-hotel: bar, pool ⊟DC, MC, V ⊺⊙⊺FAP.*

$
☾
★
Kwando Lebala Camp. Lebala Camp is 30 km (18 mi) south of Lagoon Camp and looks out over the Linyanti wetlands. The secluded tents, built on raised teak decks, are magnificent. All have private bathrooms with Victorian claw-foot tubs. If you want to get even closer to nature, bathe in your own outdoor shower or just sit on your sundeck and look out at the endless vistas. On morning or evening game drives you'll see loads of game, and if you fancy a freshly caught fish supper, try your hand at spinner fishing. ⌂ *Kwando Wildlife Experience, Box 550, Maun, Botswana* ☎ *686–1449 or 686–4388* ⊕ *www.kwando. co.za* ⌱ *8 tents △ In-hotel: pool ⊟DC, MC, V ⊺⊙⊺FAP.*

Kwando Lebala Camp

Kwando Lebala Camp

Kwando Lagoon Camp

IF YOU HAVE TIME

By all means, do your Big Five–big park thing, but if you can make or take the time, these following parks and areas will entice you into their quite unforgettable uniqueness.

THE CENTRAL KALAHARI GAME RESERVE

One of the biggest conservation areas in the world, this huge area has its own unique beauty, that's only enhanced by its vastness, emptiness, grandeur, and desolation. You won't see the prolific game of Chobe or Moremi, but there's unusual wildlife such as the elusive brown hyena, the stately gemsbok, elegant kudus, African wild cats, leopards, and porcupines. And if you're very lucky, you may spot the huge, black-maned Kalahari lions, which dwarf their bush counterparts. Deception Valley—so-called because from a distance a dry riverbed appears to run deep and full—lies on the northern border of the reserve.

WHERE TO STAY

$$ ★ ⊞ **Deception Valley Lodge.** This striking thatch-and-stone lodge is the only lodge in the Central Kalahari, and is worth visiting for this reason alone. Built entirely by hand by the desert-dwelling Naru people, the main lounge has deep red sofas and kilims, with wooden sliding doors leading out onto a wraparound deck, which faces a busy water hole. You'll sleep in a large thatch bungalow where the roomy lounge has polished wooden floors, more kilims, wrought iron, and wood chairs, a deep comfy sofa, and framed genuine bushman memorabilia. Your bedroom will have a hand-carved headboard, crisp white linens, and plump duvets. There's a separate en-suite bathroom with a claw-foot bath and outside shower. Enjoy delicious food (try the tender oryx fillet marinated in Worcestershire sauce, olive oil, and herbs) including homemade bread and rolls, before sitting out under the blazing desert stars for a nightcap. Although you'll be taken on game drives and birding expeditions, the absolute highlight of your stay at this unique lodge will be a walk with the Bushmen themselves. Dressed in skins and thong sandals, with their bows and arrows over their shoulders, and carrying a spear and a digging stick, they'll lead you through the dry grass and bush on a three-hour walk through one of the most remote areas on earth. You'll be shown how to trap a bird or animal, how to make fire, which plants and trees will heal and sustain you, and at the end of the walk, they will dance and sing for you. This is pure magic. ⬚*Islands in Africa Safaris, Box 70378, Bryanston 2021, South Africa* ☎*11/706–7207* ⊕*www.islandsinafrica. com* ⬚*5 chalets* ⬚*In-hotel: pool* ⊟*DC, MC, V* ⦿*FAP.*

THE MAKGADIKGADI PANS

These immense salt pans in the eastern Kalahari—once the bed of an African superlake—provide some of Botswana's most dramatic scenery. Two of these pans, Ntetwe and Sowa, the largest of their kind in the world, have a flaky, pastrylike surface that might be the nearest thing on earth to the surface of the moon. In winter these huge bone-dry surfaces, punctuated by islands of grass and lines of fantastic palm trees, dazzle and shimmer into hundreds of dancing mirages under the beating sun. In summer months the last great migration in southern Africa takes place here: more than 50,000 zebras and wildebeests with predators in their wake come seeking the fresh young grass of the flooded pans. Waterbirds also flock here from all over the continent; the flamingoes are particularly spectacular.

You can see game elsewhere in Botswana (although not in these numbers) so you should visit May through September to find out why this place is unique. You can see stars as never before, and if you're lucky, as the San/Bushmen say, even hear them sing. Grab the opportunity to ride 4x4 quad bikes into an always-vanishing horizon; close your eyes and listen as an ancient San/Bushman hunter tells tales of how the world began in his unique language—the clicks will sound strange to your ears—or just wander in wonder over the pristine piecrust surface of the pans.

WHERE TO STAY

LUXURY LODGING

$$$ 🖵 **Jack's Camp.** If you're bold-spirited, reasonably fit, and have kept
★   your childlike sense of wonder, then Jack's is for you. A cross between a Fellini movie, a Salvador Dalí painting, and Alice in Wonderland, this camp doesn't offer the cocooned luxury of some of the Okavango camps; it offers a more rugged, pioneer feel reminiscent of a 1940s-style safari. East African safari tents on wooden decks set in a palm grove have ancient Persian rugs, antique brass-hinged storage boxes, teak and canvas furniture, hot and cold running water, a flush toilet and indoor and outdoor showers. Meals are taken under a huge acacia tree or in a large, open-sided pagodalike tent. The camp's highly qualified rangers are respected throughout Botswana and beyond for their love and commitment to this amazing area. You won't find the Big Five here, but you will find unique desert-adapted animals and plants like the brown hyena, meerkats, salt bushes, and desert palms. Remember though, this is the Kalahari Desert. It's hot, hot, hot in summer, and freezing cold in winter. ✑ *Wilderness Safaris, Box 5219, Rivonia 2128, South Africa* ☎ *11/807–1800* ⊕ *www.wilderness-safaris.com* ➪ *8 tents* ⚒ *In-hotel: bar.* ☰ *MC, V* ❘◎❘ *FAP.*

THE TULI BLOCK

This ruggedly beautiful corner of northeastern Botswana is very easily accessible from South Africa and well worth a visit. Huge, striking red-rock formations, unlike anywhere else in Botswana, mingle with acacia woodlands, riverine bush, hills, wooded valleys, and open grassy plains. Be sure to visit the Motloutse ruins where ancient baobabs stand sentinel over Stone-Age ruins that have existed here for more than 30,000 years, as majestic black eagles soar overhead.

Still relatively unknown to foreign travelers, the Tuli Block is home to huge elephant herds, the eland—Africa's largest and highest-jumping antelope—zebras, wildebeests, leopards, and prolific bird life. Try to catch a glimpse of the elusive and diminutive klipspringer antelope perching on top of a rock zealously guarding his mountain home. Gareth Patterson, southern Africa's "Lion Man," lived here alone with three young lions over a period of years, successfully reintroducing them to the wild after having brought them down from Kenya after George "Born Free" Adamson was brutally murdered there by poachers.

GETTING HERE & AROUND

Mashatu is an easy five-hour drive from Johannesburg and Gaborone. You'll be met at Pont Drift, the South African/Botswana border post, where you leave your car under huge jackalberry trees at the South African police station before crossing the Limpopo River by 4x4 vehicle or cable car—depending on whether the river is flooded.

If you'd rather fly, South African Airlink (☎011/978–1111 ⊕www. flyairlink.co.za) flies daily from O.R. Tambo International Airport, Johannesburg, to Polokwane, where you can pick up a self-drive or chauffeur-driven car from Budget Rent a Car (☎011/398–0123) for the just-under-two-hour drive to Pont Drift, the South African/ Botswana border post.

6

MASHATU GAME RESERVE

Mashatu offers a genuine wilderness experience on 90,000 acres that seem to stretch to infinity on all sides. There are wall-to-wall elephants—breeding herds often with tiny babies in tow—as well as aardvarks, aardwolves (a type of hyena), lots of leopards, wandering lions, and hundreds of birds. All the superb rangers are Batswana—most were born in the area and some have been here for more than 15 years. Their fund of local knowledge seems bottomless.

LUXURY
LODGING
¢
★

WHERE TO STAY

▦ **Mashatu Main Camp.** A sister camp to South Africa's world-famous Mala Mala Camp, the professionalism of the staff here is so unobtrusive you only realize later how superbly and sincerely welcomed, entertained, and informed you have been during your stay. Accommodations range from attractive old-style rondawels (round huts) to tasteful suites where Jacobean-patterned fabrics pick up and enhance the terra-cotta floor tiles. Furniture of natural basket weave, russet-and-cream handwoven wool rugs, and pine-paneled ceilings promote the overall atmosphere of quiet good taste. Comfort is assured by heaters in the cold winter months and air-conditioning in the hot summer ones. The thatched outdoor dining area overlooks a large water hole where elephants, zebras, wildebeests, and other Mashatu regulars drink. ✉Box 55514, Northlands 2116, South Africa ☎011/442–2267 ⊕www.mashatu.com ⇩14 suites ⌂In-hotel: bar, pool, curio shop ☰AE, DC, MC, V ⏅FAP.

PERMANENT
TENTED
CAMPS
¢

△ **Mashatu Tent Camp.** This small and intimate camp offers the same excellent service as Main Camp but with a firsthand bush experience. The camp is deep in the wilderness, and as you lie in your tent and listen to a lion's roar, a hyena's whoop, or a leopard's cough, you'll feel part of the heartbeat of Africa. Seven spacious tents with carpeted floors, each with a tiny veranda overlooking the surrounding bush, provide an unparalleled back-to-nature feeling. A fenced walkway leads to an en-suite bathroom where the stars are your roof. Knowledgeable, longstanding local rangers will open your ears and your eyes to the environment: on one night game drive guests saw a male leopard up a tree jealously guarding his impala kill from a female leopard who was hoping for a slice of the action, while a hopeful hyena lurked nearby. There's plenty of water in the vicinity, so the game is particularly plentiful—once two guests were trapped in their tent when a pride of lions killed a zebra outside it. This camp may not be for everyone; but for something truly different, real, and very special, a stay here won't soon be forgotten. ⌂ *Box 55514, Northlands 2116, South Africa* ☎ *011/442–2267* ⊕ *www.mashatu.com* ⇌ *8 tents* ☐ *In-hotel: bar, pool, curio shop.* ☐ *AE, DC, MC, V* ☺*FAP.*

LINYANTI AREA

The Linyanti Reserve, which borders Chobe National Park, is one of the huge concession areas leased to different companies by the Department of Wildlife and National Parks and the Tawana Land Board; concessions can be leased for up to 15 years. It's a spectacular wildlife area comprising the Linyanti marshes, open floodplains, rolling savanna, and the Savuti Channel. Because it's a private concession, open vehicles can drive where and when they like, which means superb game-viewing at all hours of the day.

Basic choices for viewing wildlife are game drives (including thrilling night drives with spotlights), boat trips, and walks with friendly and knowledgeable Motswana guides. Even in peak season there is a maximum of only six game vehicles driving around at one time, allowing you to see Africa as the early hunters and explorers might have first seen it. The Savuti Channel, once a huge river, but dry now for more than two decades, has starred in several *National Geographic* documentaries, and it's not hard to see why. Take lots of pictures, and for once you won't bore your friends with the results: hundreds of elephants drinking from pools at sunset, hippos and hyenas nonchalantly strolling past a pride of lions preparing to hunt under moonlight, and thousands of water and land birds everywhere.

PERMANENT **WHERE TO STAY**

TENTED 📷 **King's Pool.** The centuries-old giant leadwood tree, which dominates
CAMPS the spacious main deck that overlooks the Linyanti River gives you a
$$ clue about your classic, yet understated, Out-of Africa–like accommo-
★ dation. Everything about this camp is on a regal scale—a modern-day tribute to the European royalty who used to hunt in this area. Old photographs of tribal leaders and Batswana maidens watch over the carved wooden furniture, comfortable wing chairs with beaded throws, inviting wooden bar with high leather-and-wood bar stools, soft furnishings in earth colors, and the open-sided dining room. There's even a small gym facing the river where you can work off some of the yummy food before taking a river cruise (only when the water is high), a guided

bush walk, a fishing trip, or a visit to the sunken blind (a must in the dry season) where you're eyeball-to-eyeball with splashing elephant feet. The massive hand-carved door of your megasize thatch-and-canvas-ceiling chalet leads into an entrance hall, bedroom with four-poster bed, a sitting area with earth-color couches and armchairs

> **WORD OF MOUTH**
>
> "King's Pool is in a great game viewing area. You should have great general game viewing and have high chances of seeing both cheetah and wild dogs."
>
> –Kavey

splashed with orange and red cushions, and a huge bathroom with his-and-her basins and tiled showers. Don't miss the fascinating curio shop with classy artifacts from all over Africa. ⌕ *Wilderness Safaris, Box 5219, Rivonia 2128, South Africa* ☎ *11/807–1800* ⊕ *www.wilderness-safaris.com* ↩ *9 chalets* ⚒ *In-hotel: bar, pool* ▭ *MC, V* ⚓ *FAP.*

$ ⌕ **Duma Tau.** This classy camp, with imaginatively decorated and furnished raised tent chalets under thatch and overlooking the water, lies at the very heart of the concession. The spacious chalets have African fabrics; clever cane furniture decorated with plaited reeds, brass, and local beadwork; wood floors with handwoven rugs; an indoor shower and another one on your outside deck so you can wash as you view; and personal touches such as a guinea-fowl feather or dried seedpod placed artistically among your towels. The lounge and dining area of the main lodge are open on all sides (a bit cold in winter); the toilet at the end of the deck must have the best view of any in the world. The food is simple but superb. Before you set out on your early morning game drive, try a plate of piping hot porridge, a Danish straight from the oven, or a freshly baked muffin. ⌕ *Wilderness Safaris, Box 5219, Rivonia 2128, South Africa* ☎ *11/807–1800* ⊕ *www.dumatau.com* ↩ *8 chalets* ⚒ *In-hotel: bar, pool* ▭ *MC, V* ⚓ *FAP.*

GATEWAY CITY

Many visitors to Botswana will find themselves with a layover in Johannesburg before or after their safari. It's a massive metropolitan area—more than 1,300 square km (800 square mi)—that epitomizes South Africa's paradoxical make-up—it's rich, poor, innovative, and historical all rolled into one. Most of the sights and many of the city's good hotels and major malls are in the northern suburbs: Melville (closest to the city center), Greenside, Parkhurst, Sandton, and Rosebank, among many others. Some notable destinations for food include Melrose Arch, Parkhurst, Sandton, the South (for its Portuguese cuisine), Melville, and Chinatown in the CBD (Central Business District).

For some ideas and suggestions to help determine where you should stay, eat, and if you have time, some sights to visit, *See Gateway City in Chapter 5 South Africa.*

BEACH ESCAPES

Looking for a little R&R after your safari? Botswana may not be a coastal country, but it's close proximity to South Africa's coast provides many opportunities for sun, sand, and smiles.

DURBAN

Just 474 mi (762 km) southeast from Botswana's capital Gaborone, Durban's accessible, beautiful, and safe beaches make it a great escape for this landlocked country (as well as for South Africa). Plus, there are daily flights between Gaborone and Durban, though you will probably have to do a stopover in Johannesburg, making it a quick escape as well.

The city's beachfront stretches for about 12 km (7 ½ mi) from South Beach, at the base of Durban Point, to Blue Lagoon on the southern bank of the Umgeni River. Even in winter (April though September), the weather is particularly pleasant and you will be able to swim.

See Beach Escapes in Chapter 5 South Africa for information on places to eat, stay, and visit.

MAPUTALAND COASTAL RESERVE

If Robinson Crusoe had washed ashore on the pristine coastline of Maputaland, he wouldn't have found anybody to call Friday—and he certainly wouldn't have cared what day of the week it was. It's that empty and that magnificent. No other buildings lie within 16 km (10 mi) of Rocktail Bay Lodge, tucked away in South Africa's Maputaland Coastal Reserve, a narrow strip of wilderness that stretches from Greater St. Lucia Wetland Park all the way to Mozambique. If you love exploring untouched beaches, fishing, scuba diving, snorkeling, and walking, coming here will be the perfect beach getaway after your safari. Rocktail Bay is not a game lodge, it's the quintessential small private beach lodge—the only animals you're likely to see are loggerhead and leatherback turtles. It's accessible by road or air, but lies far from any other major tourist destination and operates much like a game lodge. Besides glorious beaches, its major attraction is the annual arrival of giant loggerhead and leatherback turtles to lay their eggs. The beaches here are one of the few known egg-laying areas of these endangered animals, and the season extends from the November through early March. During these months rangers lead after-dinner drives and walks down the beach to look for turtles, and you can expect to cover as much as 16 km (10 mi) in a night. From a weather standpoint, the best times to visit the lodge are probably spring (September and October) and autumn (March–May). In summer the temperature regularly soars past 38°C (100°F), and swimming during winter is a brisk proposition. August is the windiest month, and it's in summer that the turtles come ashore to dig their nests and lay their eggs—an awesome spectacle.

Continued on page 436

(top) Weaving pandanu vegetal carpets. (bottom) Botswana basket.

AFRICAN ARTS & CULTURE

by Kate Turkington

African art is as diverse as its peoples. If you're a collector, an artist, or just an admirer, you'll find everything from masks and carvings to world famous rock art, hand-painted batiks, and hand-woven cloths.

African art is centered on meaning. Its sculptures, carvings, and masks symbolize the powerful spirit world that underpins most African societies. Christianity and the Westernization of many African communities has stifled much of the traditional craftsmanship by imposing new themes and, in the past, denigrating traditional religions. Fortunately, wooden masks—some genuine, some not, some beautiful, some seriously scary—wire and bead tribal necklaces, beadwork, woven baskets, and much, much more continue to be big sellers all over Southern and East Africa.

If you're looking for something a little funky or unique, check out the handmade bead-and-wire animals, birds, cars, and mobiles for sale along South Africa's roads and in Tanzania's markets.

TYPES OF CRAFTS AND ART

High-quality crafts abound, from handwoven cloths in East Africa, to stunning soapstone and wood carvings at Victoria Falls, hand-woven baskets in Botswana and Zululand, leatherwork, pottery and embroidery in Namibia, and jewelry just about everywhere.

BOTSWANA BASKETS

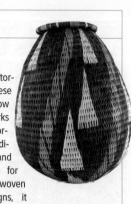

Once used for storage purposes, these baskets are now sought-after works of art that incorporate many traditional designs and patterns. Known for the intricately woven geometric designs, it can take up to six weeks to make a basket. Zulu baskets, from South Africa's KwaZulu province, can be made of brightly colored wire or grass and palm coils. For either type, expect to pay anywhere from US$20 to US$300.

MASKS

Masks were often worn by tribal elders in rites of passage (birth, initiation, weddings, and funerals) and can range from frightening depictions of devils and evil spirits, to more gentle and benign expressions. A few dollars will buy you a readily available tourist mask; an authentic piece could run you hundreds, sometimes thousands of U.S. dollars.

BEADWORK

Each color and pattern has meaning. Green is for grass or a baby, red is for blood or young women, and white are for purity. By looking at a women's beadwork you can tell how many children she has (and what sex), how old she is or how long she's been married. Beading is used in headdresses, necklaces, rings, earrings, wedding aprons, barrettes, and baskets. Expect to pay US$10 for a Zulu bracelet or US$200 for a Masai wedding necklace.

WEAVING

The striking red handmade robes of East Africa's Masai people are a fine example of a centuries-old African weaving tradition. Fabrics, like kekois and Masai cloaks, are usually made of cotton. Handpainted or batik cloths are more expensive than factory printed ones. A cotton kekoi will cost you US$15, a red Masai cloth US$20, a batik US$30.

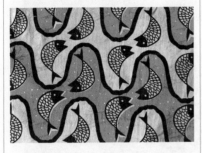

ROCK ART

Engravings (made by scratching into a rock's surface), paintings, and finger paintings are found all over sub-Saharan Africa, particularly in South Africa. The rock paintings in the Drakensburg Mountains in Kwa-Zulu Natal, are regarded as the world's finest. Central Namibia has the world's largest open-air art gallery at Twyfelfontein where thousands of paintings and engravings line the sides of the rocks and mountain. Materials came from the immediate environment: ocher (red iron-oxide clay) for red, charcoal for black, and white clay for white. Most images illustrate the activities and experiences of the African shamans. The shamans believed that when an image was drawn, power was transferred to the people and the land.

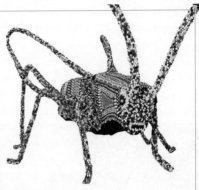

WIRECRAFT FIGURES

Wire-and-bead animals and all kinds of previously unimagined subjects are now contemporary works of art. First made and sold in South Africa, you can now buy them just about anywhere. A palm-sized critter usually sells for US$10, but a nearly-life-sized animal can cost up to US$450; you'd pay three times more in a European or U.S. gallery. Tip: Beaded key rings (US$5) make great easy-to-pack gifts.

PAINTING

Painting in acrylics is a fairly recent medium in Africa. Keep an eye out for Tinga Tinga paintings (above) at curio shops or stalls in Kenya and Tanzania. Prices range from $10 to $50; you can expect to pay upwards of $100 online. The semi-impressionistic wildlife paintings of Keith Joubert are particularly sought-after. The Everard Read Gallery (☎ 021/418–4527 in Cape Town, 011/788–4805 in Johannesburg ⊕ www.everardread.co.za) specializes in wildlife paintings and sculpture, including the work of Joubert.

SMART SHOPPING TIPS AND WHERE TO SHOP

So where should you buy all of this amazing handiwork? And what do you do when you've found that piece you want to take home? Read on for helpful tips and locations across our Safari coverage.

KENYA

What Nairobi lacks in safety and charm, it makes up for in its abundance of curios. The widest and best selection is at the curio stalls around the city market on Muindi Mbingu St. Bargain for masks, drums, carvings of all kinds, batiks and the famous brightly-colored kekoi cloths. Semiprecious stones can be found at Kimathi Jewellers (⊠ Norwich Union House, Kimathi St. ☎ 02/224–754). Adelphi Leather Shop (E Jubilee Insurance Exchange Bldg., Kaunda St. ☎ 02/228–925) specializes in exclusive handcrafted articles using local leather. In Mombasa, Malindi, and Lamu, ask at your accommodation where the best markets are.

TANZANIA

For some of the best Masai jewelry, batiks, Tinga Tinga paintings and Makonde carvings, check out the curio shops between the clock tower and India Rd in Arusha. One of the city's largest dealers in tanzanite, Cultural Heritage (⊠ Dodoma Rd. ☎ 27/250–8698), has in-house artisans producing beautiful jewelry plus souvenirs galore. If you're in Dar es Salaam, head to the Slipway (⊠ Slipway Road Junction ☎ 22/260–0893 ⊕ www.slipway.net), a converted boatyard on the Msasani Bay that has four restaurants and a traditional market. Get

AFRICAN BEADS

Small discs, dating from 10,000 B.C., made from ostrich eggshells are the earliest known African beads. The introduction of glass beads came with the trade from around 200 B.C. Subsequently, European and Arab traders bartered beads for ivory, gold, and slaves. In many African societies, beads are still highly prized for both everyday and ceremonial ornamentation.

ready to bargain for everything from beaded leather sandals and wire animals to jewelry and carved figures. There are plenty of shopping opportunities in Zanzibar as well. If you're in Stone Town, head to Kenyatta Road which has numerous shops including Memories of Zanzibar (☎ 24/223–9376 ⊕ www.memories-zanzibar.com) and Zanzibar Secrets (☎ 24/223–4745). Memories has great deals on tanzanite jewelry, kangas, carved wooden animals, and all sort of gifts that make great souvenirs and presents. The shopping at Zanzibar Secrets is a little more unique as its clothing, jewelry, beaded purses, and beautiful lighting fixtures won't be found at many other places on the island.

SOUTH AFRICA

Art lovers should make sure to include Johannesburg in their trip. Excellent galleries abound, including the Everard Read Gallery (⊠ 6 Jellicoe Ave., Rosebank ☎ 011/788–4805), which specializes in wildlife paintings and sculpture; the Kim Sacks Gallery (⊠ 153 Jan Smuts Ave., Rosebank ☎ 011/447–5804), which has a superb collection of authentic African art; and Rural Art (⊠ Mutual Gardens, Rosebank ☎ 011/788–5821), which sells Ndebele and Xhosa beadwork, jewelry, and fabrics. Cape Town's V&A Waterfront is a shopper's paradise, and you can buy some of the best wine in the world along the Cape Winelands.

BOTSWANA

Handmade woven baskets are the best buy here. Find them in your safari lodge shop or at the Gaborone Mall (⊠ Queen's St., Gaborone), in the middle of the city.

NAMIBIA

Windhoek's Post Street Mall has an impressive array of crafts and curios (check out the irresistible Herero dolls) as does the Namibia Craft Centre (⊠ 40 Tal St., Windhoek ☎ 061/242–2222), next to the Warehouse Theatre. You'll have gemstones on the soles of your shoes if you visit House of Gems (E 131 Stübel St., Windhoek ☎ 061/225–202), where you can see gemstones sorted, cut, faceted, and polished. Tourmalines, a local specialty,

TIPS

■ Local markets, roadside stalls, and cooperatives often offer the cheapest, most authentic crafts.

■ Safari lodge shops can be pricey, but stock really classy souvenirs (often from all over Africa) and cool safari gear.

■ A universal rule for bargaining is to divide the seller's first price by half, then up it a bit.

■ If possible, carry your purchases with you. Try to get breakables bubble-wrapped and pack securely in the middle of your main suitcase. Pack smaller purchases in your carry-on.

■ Mail your dirty clothes home or donate them to a local charity so you'll have more room for purchases.

■ Only ship home if you've bought something very big, very fragile, or very expensive.

are a best buy item here. Or treat yourself to a stunning Namibian karakul leather jacket or coat at Nakara, which has locations in Windhoek and Swakopmund (☎ 061/224–209 in Windhoek, 064/405–907 in Swakopmund ⊕ www.nakara-namibia.com). If you do go to Windhoek, head to Independence Avenue. It's a major shopping destination and where you'll find Nakara.

VIC FALLS

If you're staying on the Zambian side of the Falls, be sure to cross the historic bridge over the Zambezi to visit the craft market on the Zimbabwe side. You'll find some of Africa's finest carvings here, from masks and tableware to chess sets and soapstone sculptures. The market opens at 9 am and stays open late; it's just behind Livingstone Way, the town's main street. Bargaining is essential and U.S. dollars are eagerly accepted. Make sure you have small bills ($1, $5, $10); you do not want to get change in Zimbabwe banknotes.

Maputaland
Coastal Reserve

MOZAMBIQUE Zitundo

Catuane Manhoca 201

Ndumo
Wilderness Camp
Ndumo
Game Reserve

Tembe
Elephant
Game
Reserve

Kosi Bay Coastal
Forest Nature
Reserve

Lake
Kosi
eMangusi

Ndumo

SWAZILAND Ingwavuma

Sihangwane

Rocktail
Bay Lodge

Maputaland
Marine
Reserve

Hluthi

Lavumisa

Golela

Kingholm

Mseleni

Lake
Sibaya

HULLY POINT

Ponglola

Ponglola

Itala Game
Reserve R66

Candover

Magudu R69

R69 Nkonkoni

Ubombo

Tshongwe

Jozini

Mbazwana

Sodwana Bay
Lodge

Sodwana Bay

JESSER POINT

Louwsburg

Mahlangasi

Mkuze

Mkuze
Game
Reserve

Sodwana Bay
National Park

Mkuze

Ngome

R618

Bayala

Msundozi

Phinda
Private
Reserve

LEVEN POINT

Nongoma

R66

0   20 mi

0   20 km

R618 Hilltop
Mtwazi

Hluhluwe

Lake
St. Lucia

Greater St Lucia
Wetland Park

Fanie's Island

KEY

▲ Camps

🏠 Lodges

GETTING HERE & AROUND

Visitors fly into Richard's Bay from Johannesburg and are picked up by
lodge, which will make all the flight and pickup arrangements. If you'd
like to drive instead of fly, the lodge can arrange a car service to get you
to and from Johannesburg. You could drive yourself, but it's really an
unnecessary waste of time as you won't be able to use the vehicle once
you are at the lodge. Plus, you'd need to rent a 4x4 as the last part of
the road is a very bumpy, muddy bush road.

WHERE TO STAY

$ 🏠 **Rocktail Bay Lodge.** The lodge lies in a swale formed by enormous
Fodor'sChoice dunes fronting the ocean. Walkways tunnel through the dune forest to
★ a golden beach that sweeps in a gentle arc several miles to the north.
There are no lifeguards or shark nets, but the swimming and snorkeling are fabulous. The lodge consists of simple A-frame chalets raised
on wooden platforms above the forest floor. Wood and thatch create
a rustic ambience, complemented by solar lighting and basic furnishings. A large veranda and adjoining thatch bar provide the backdrop
for alfresco meals under a giant Natal mahogany tree. Activities include
great surf fishing (tackle provided), snorkeling, and walking through
the forest or along the beach. Rangers lead excursions to see hippo
pools, the rich bird-life of Lake Sibaya, and Kosi Bay, where the local

Tembe people catch fish using the age-old method of basket netting, and Tsonga descendants also use ancient woven fish traps. For many people, though, a trip to Rocktail Bay is a chance to kick back and just soak in the atmosphere of an unspoiled coastal wilderness. ⌕ *Box 78573, Sandton 2146, South Africa* ☎*011/883–0747* ⊕*www.rocktailbay.com* ⇘*10 chalets* ♿*In-hotel: bar, pool* ▭*AE, DC, MC, V* ⬚*FAP.*

BOTSWANA ESSENTIALS

TRANSPORTATION

BY AIR

In this huge, often inaccessible country, air travel is the easiest way to get around. Sir Seretse Khama Airport, 15 km (9½ mi) from Gaborone's city center, is Botswana's main point of entry. Kasane International Airport is 3 km (2 mi) from the entrance to Chobe National Park, and small but very busy Maun Airport is 1 km (½ mi) from the city center of this northern safari capital. All three are gateways to the Okavango Delta and Chobe; they're easy to find your way around in and rarely crowded.

Air charter companies operate small planes from Kasane and Maun to all the camps. Flown by some of the youngest-looking pilots in the world, these flights, which your travel agent will arrange, are reliable, reasonably cheap, and average between 25 and 50 minutes. Maximum baggage allowance is 12 kilograms (26 pounds) in a soft sports/duffel bag (no hard cases allowed), excluding the weight of camera equipment (within reason). Because of the thermal air currents over Botswana, and because most flights are around midday, when thermals are at their strongest, flights can sometimes be very bumpy—take air-sickness pills if you're susceptible to motion sickness; then sit back and enjoy the fabulous bird's-eye views. You're sure to spot elephants and hippos from the air.

Air Botswana has scheduled flights from Johannesburg to Gaborone and Maun on a daily basis, and from Cape Town to Maun on Monday, Wednesday, and Friday, returning to Cape Town Tuesday, Thursday, and Sunday. The airline also flies Johannesburg to Kasane on Thursday and Sunday. SA Express Airways also has daily flights between Johannesburg and Gaborone.

Mack Air, Northern Air, Sefofane Air, Swamp Air, and Delta Air/Synergy Seating fly directly between Johannesburg's Grand Central Airport and Maun on private charters.

6

Airports Kasane International Airport (☎ *625–0161*). **Maun Airport** (☎ *686–0762*). **Sir Seretse Khama Airport** (☎ *391–4518*).

Airlines Air Botswana (☎ *390–5500 or 395–1921* ⊕ *www.airbotswana.co.bw*). **Delta Air/Synergy Seating** (☎ *686–0044*). **Mack Air** (☎ *686–0675*). **Northern Air** (☎ *686–0385*). **SA Express Airways** (☎ *11/978–5577 in South Africa or 397–2397 in Botswana*). **Sefofane Air** (☎ *686–0778*). **Swamp Air** (☎ *686–0569*).

BY CAR

All the main access roads from neighboring countries are paved, and cross-border formalities are user-friendly. Maun is easy to reach from South Africa, Namibia, and Zimbabwe, but the distances are long and not very scenic. Gaborone is 360 km (225 mi) from Johannesburg via Rustenburg, Zeerust, and the Tlokweng border post. Driving in Botswana is on the left-hand side of the road. The "Shell Tourist Map of Botswana" is the best available map. Find it at Botswana airports or in airport bookstores.

Forget about a car in the Okavango Delta unless it's amphibious. Only the western and eastern sides of the delta panhandle and the Moremi Wildlife Reserve are accessible by car; but it's wisest to always take a 4x4 vehicle. The road from Maun to Moremi North Gate is paved for the first 47 km (29 mi) up to Serobe, where it becomes gravel for 11 km (7 mi) and then a dirt road.

It's not practical to reach Chobe National Park by car. A 4x4 vehicle is essential in the park itself. The roads are sandy and/or very muddy, depending on the season.

CONTACTS & RESOURCES

ELECTRICITY

To use electric-powered equipment purchased in the United States or Canada, bring a converter and adapter. If your appliances are dual-voltage, you'll need only an adapter. The electrical current is 220 volts, 50 cycles alternating current (AC); wall outlets usually take 15-amp plugs with three round prongs, but some take the straight-edged three-prong plugs, also 15 amps. Most of the lodges and camps have their own generators, so you're able to charge your cameras and other electronic equipment. Bring a reading light if you intend to read in bed at night, as tent and chalet lights tend to be dim.

MONEY MATTERS

There are no restrictions on foreign currency notes brought into the country as long as they are declared. Travelers can carry up to P10,000 (about US$1,600), or the equivalent in foreign currency, out of the country without declaring it. Banking hours are weekdays 9–3:30, Saturday 8:30–11. Hours at Barclays Bank at Sir Seretse Khama International Airport are Monday–Saturday 6 AM–10 PM.

TELEPHONE NUMBERS

Botswana numbers begin with the 267 country code, which you don't dial within the country. (There are no internal area codes in Botswana.)

TRAVEL AGENCIES

Visit Botswana Tourism's Web site for tour operator and travel agency information. To be listed on the Web site, these organizations must satisfy and adhere to the high standards demanded by Botswana Tourism.

Contacts **Botswana Tourism** (⊕ *www.botswana-tourism.gov.bw*). **Harvey World Travel** (⌂ *Box 1950, Gaborone, Botswana* ☎ *390–4360* ⊕ *www.harveyworld.co.za*). **Travel Wise** (⌂ *Box 2482, Gaborone, Botswana* ☎ *390–3244*).

6

GREEN LODGINGS IN BOTSWANA

Botswana's fragile ecosystem of more than 15,000 square km of waterways must be protected and preserved. How can you make sure you're doing your part to preserve it? Check into an eco-conscious lodge. Of course our list of options is not exhaustive, but it's a start.-

CONTACT INFORMATION

Chief's Camp: 11/438–4650; www.sanctuary lodges.com

Duba Plains: 11/807–1800; www.dubaplains.com

Nxabega Okavango Safari Camp: 11/809–4300; www.ccafrica.com

Chief's Camp (opposite top) is in the exclusive Mombo Concession of the Okavango Delta's Moremi Game Reserve. The area is home to the rare white rhino and is the only area in Botswana where these animals can be seen in their natural environment. The main lodge sits under a canopy of Jack-alberry, Sausage, and Rain trees. The lodge was built with wood from commercially grown forests using the skills of local builders. Also, the limited number of suites is part of the camp's commitment to low-impact tourism. Chief's Camp works in partnership with the non-profit Friends of Conservation in an effort to involve the local community in the running of the camp.

Arguably the Okavango Delta's most remote camp, **Duba Plains** (above) is built on an island that can only be reached by plane. Shaded by ebony, fig, and garcinia trees and surrounded by vast plains, which are flooded from about May to early October, depending on the rains, the camp is ideal for true wilderness buffs. The camp is in the Kwedi Reserve, a massive wildlife sanctuary that has been ceded by the Botswana Government and the Tawana Land Board to the people who live in the north of the delta. The aim is that the local people benefit from the wildlife that tourists come to see in their "backyard," so to speak. Annual payments are made to a trust called the Okavango Community Trust, which represents the interests of all the people living in the five villages to the north of the Okavango. *See Permanent Tented Camps, in the Okavango Delta for more information about the camp.*

Set on the edge of the Okavango Delta in a private wildlife concession on the southwestern border of the Moremi Wildlife Reserve, **Nxabega Okavango Safari Camp** (below) is made up of nine classic safari tents on raised platforms with private verandas. The camp overlooks wetlands, delta channels, and grassy floodplains, which host lion, leopard, elephant, and buffalo, as well as several unique bird species; African Ebony and strangler figs shade the main camp. Boat excursions and bush walks are offered and the staff will even arrange wilderness picnics or breakfast in bed. CC Africa, which runs Nxabega Camp, promotes sustainable development in the region through the nonprofit Africa Foundation. Projects include building classrooms, libraries, and clinics as well as offering jobs to the local Tswana people. *See Permanent Tented Camps, in the Okavango Delta for more information about the camp.*

BE SENSITIVE TO CULTURES & CUSTOMS

■ Remember that you are in Africa and, in general, things occur at a slower pace than elsewhere in the world. You'll often receive service with a smile, but service with speed is an altogether different story.

■ It's important to be clear on the tipping protocol of your chosen tour operator and/or lodges before you travel. Paying too little or even too much can be viewed as disrespectful of a person's work ethic and way of life.

■ Don't take photos without asking first (if it's of locals) or making sure there's adequate distance between you and the subject (if it's of wildlife).

■ Don't wear revealing clothing, especially in African cities, as this is offensive to the Muslim majority.

■ When visiting religious sites, behave appropriately.

■ If you're in the bush, binoculars are a natural accessory, but be aware of your surroundings before you whip out a pair when traveling in cities or near military personnel or national landmarks.

Namibia

WELCOME TO NAMIBIA

TOP REASONS TO GO

★ **The world's oldest living desert.** The Namib is everything you might imagine a "real" desert looks like.

★ **A memorable drive.** The road from Swakopmund to Walvis Bay is one of the most beautiful and unusual routes in the world.

★ **Water-hole wonders.** Arm yourself with binoculars, drinks, a picnic, and patience. Open your car windows and wait for the game to come. You won't be disappointed.

★ **Ride the Desert Express.** During this three-day train journey between Windhoek and Swakopmund, you'll stop to walk in the desert, visit the world's biggest outdoor rock-art gallery, watch lions being fed, and view a spectacular desert sunset (or sunrise).

★ **Etosha National Park.** One of Africa's largest and most spectacular game parks, Etosha has cheap and cheerful self-catering accommodations, an excellent road network, and superb game-viewing, including the Big Five.

1 **Namib Naukluft Park.** At nearly 50,000 square km (19,300 square mi) and bigger than Switzerland, this park, which contains the oldest desert in the world, is one of the largest national parks in Africa. Expect classic desert scenery (including towering sand dunes) plus windswept gravel plains, rocky outcrops and inselbergs, and some of the earth's strangest living things, from plants and insects to mammals and reptiles.

GETTING ORIENTED

ZAMBIA

Katima Mulilo

CAPRIVI STRIP

Grootfontein

KAUKAUVELD

2 Damaraland. Situated in northwest Namibia, Damaraland is a different desert from Namib. It's barren and inhospitable, but there is life and plenty of it, including Welwitschia mirabilis, reputed to be the world's longest-living plant; colorful lichen fields; camelthorn trees; candelabra euphorbias; salt bushes; and the ubiquitous shepherd's tree. And of course there are the amazing desert elephants.

3 Etosha National Park. Regarded as one of Africa's great national parks, Etosha is dominated by Etosha Pan: a landscape of white salty plains. The numerous water holes make this park ideal for game-viewing. If you plan to do a self-drive, this is the place for it—the roads are good, and there are plenty of affordable accommodations.

Gobabis

BOTSWANA

NAMALAND

SOUTH AFRICA

Karasburg

0   100 mi

0   100 km

Namibia is a big country, four times as large as the United Kingdom and bigger than Texas, but its excellent road network means you can get around very easily. The country is bordered by the icy Atlantic on the west, the Kalahari Desert on the east, the Kunene River to the north, and the Orange River to the south. Although South Africa, Botswana, and Angola are its immediate neighbors, if you're traveling by road it's easiest to access Namibia from South Africa.

By all means drive yourself, but punctuate this self-drive with a fly-in safari into one of the more remote lodges on the Skeleton Coast or Damaraland. This way you'll get to see Namibia's true vastness and remoteness.

7

NAMIBIA PLANNER

Fast Facts

Size. Namibia covers 824,292 sq km (318,259 sq mi).

Number of National Parks. Eight: Ai-Ais & Fish River Canyon, Etosha National Park, Kaudom National Park, Mamili National Park, Mudumu National Park, Namib-Naukluft National Park, Skeleton Coast Park, Waterberg National Park.

Number of Private Reserves. There are numerous private reserves.

Population of Country. Slightly more than 2 million.

Big Five. In Etosha you can see all of the Big Five.

Language. English is the official language, but it's usually spoken as a second language. Afrikaans is spoken by many residents of various races, and there is a large population of German-speaking people. The most widely spoken indigenous languages are Kwanyama (a dialect of Owambo), Herero, and a number of Nama (San) dialects.

Time. Namibia, like Botswana, is on CAST (Central African standard time), which is two hours ahead of Greenwich Mean Time. That makes it seven hours ahead of North American eastern standard time (six hours ahead during eastern daylight saving time).

Health & Safety

Malaria is endemic in the east, north, and northeast, so antimalarials are essential. Take the African sun and heat seriously: always use sunscreen and a hat, and drink plenty of water. AIDS is a major problem, as elsewhere in Africa; do not have sex with a stranger. In towns, don't walk alone at night, and lock your valuables, documents, and cash in the hotel or lodge safe. In game areas, never walk after dark unless accompanied by an armed guide. Because there is comparatively little traffic, self-driving visitors are often tempted to speed. Don't. Gravel roads can be treacherous.

Important Details

Embassies. The **American Embassy** (✉ 14 Lossen St., Box 12029 ☎ 061/22–1601) is in Windhoek.

Emergencies. For a general emergency, dial **International SOS** (☎ 112 from mobile phone ☎ 061/23–0505 Windhoek ☎ 064/40–0700 Swakopmund ☎ 081/28–5501 Tsumeb ☎ 064/20–0200 Walvis Bay). Call **Netcare** (☎ 061/22–3330) for any medical emergencies.

Money Matters. Namibia's currency is the Namibian dollar, which is linked to the South African rand. (Namibia's currency cannot be used in South Africa, except unofficially at border towns.)

Passports & Visas. All non-nationals, including infants, need a valid passport to enter Namibia for visits of up to 90 days. Business visitors to Namibia need visas.

Visitor Information. Namibian Tourism (✉ Sanlam Centre, Independence Ave., Windhoek ☎ 061/290–6000 ⊕ www.namibiatourism.com.na) can provide details on camps, a free map, and a free copy of Welcome to Namibia—Official Visitors' Guide, which gives lots of useful information plus accommodation lists. It's open weekdays 8–1 and 2–5. **Namibia Wildlife Resorts** (✉ Independence Ave., opposite Zoo Park, Windhoek ☎ 061/23–6975 ⊕ www.nwr.com.na) dispenses information on the national parks. You can also book national park accommodations here.

About the Camps & Lodges

Namibia's private camps, lodges, and other accommodations are often up to high international standards. Even deep in the desert, at tented camps, there are en-suite bathrooms and private verandas, but don't expect TV. Air-conditioning is the exception and is mentioned in reviews only when it is present. Most prices at private lodges are all-inclusive (Full American Plan), including transfers, meals, activities, and usually drinks. Camps offer at least two activities a day.

At the national park camps, self-catering (with cooking facilities) accommodations are basic, clean, comfortable, and much cheaper than private lodges outside the park. Plus you're in the midst of big-game action. In Etosha each camp has a restaurant with adequate food; a shop selling basic foodstuffs and curios; a post office; a gas station; and a pool. Most rooms have private toilets, baths or showers, air-conditioning, a refrigerator, and a *braai* (barbecue). Linens are provided. Some bigger bungalows have a full kitchen.

You won't find much truly Namibian food (although local venison, seafood, and Namibian oysters are superb); cuisine is mainly European, often German. Lodges usually serve good home-style cooking—pies, pastries, fresh vegetables, lots of red meat, mouthwatering desserts, and the traditional braai. Because of its past as a German colony, Namibia is known for its lager. South African wine, which is excellent, is readily available.

WHAT IT COSTS In Namibian dollars

	¢	$	$$	$$$	$$$$
SAFARI CAMPS AND LODGES	under N$400	N$400–N$700	N$700–N$1,000	N$1,000–N$1,500	over N$1,500
RESTAURANTS	under N$50	N$51–N$75	N$76–N$100	N$101–N$125	over N$125
HOTELS	under N$500	N$501–N$1,000	N$1,001–N$2,000	N$2,001–N$3,000	over N$3,000

All prices refer to an all-inclusive per-person rate including tax, assuming double occupancy.

When to Go

Namibia has a subtropical desert climate with nonstop sunshine throughout the year. It's classified as arid to non-arid, and, generally speaking, it gets wet only in the northwest and then only during the rainy season (October–April), which is the hottest season. The south is warm and dry, although temperatures vary dramatically between night and day, particularly in the desert, where the air is sparkling, and pollution practically unheard-of. Days are crystal clear and perfect for traveling. Elsewhere the weather is clear, dry, crisp, and nearly perfect, averaging 25°C (77°F) during the day, but in the desert areas it can drop to freezing at night, especially in winter. (Bring warm clothes for after the sun goes down.)

The climate can be breathtakingly varied along the Skeleton Coast because of the Atlantic and its cold Benguela current, which makes the night cool and damp and brings thick morning coastal fog. Days are usually bright and sunny, and during the summer, extremely hot, so dress in layers.

Etosha's best season is winter (May–September), when the weather is cooler, the grass shorter, and game easier to see. But if you can stand the heat, consider a summer visit to see the return of thousands of waterbirds, as well as the tens of thousands of animals to the lush feeding grounds around Okuakuejo.

By Kate
Turkington

Look northwest of South Africa and you'll find the wide-open spaces of Namibia. Deserts that stretch to an ever-vanishing horizon, jagged mountain peaks, flat gravel plains glistening with garnets cannot fail to stir your soul. In the Great White Place of Etosha National Park, your camera will likely click nonstop as golden lions pad over white sand, crimson-breasted shrikes flit among dry trees, and herds of black-faced impalas slake their thirst at water holes in the heat of day, watched by a crouching leopard.

Many countries in Africa boast teeming wildlife and gorgeous scenery, but few others, if any, can claim such limitless horizons; such huge, untamed wilderness areas; such a pleasant sunny climate; so few people (fewer than two per square mile); the oldest desert in the world; a wildly beautiful coastline; one of Africa's greatest game parks; plus—and this is a big bonus—a well-developed infrastructure and tourist facilities that are among the best in Africa. But you'll find all these and more in Namibia.

A former German colony, South West Africa, as it was then known, was a pawn in the power games of European politics. Although the Portuguese navigators were the first Europeans to arrive, in 1485, they quickly abandoned the desolate and dangerous Atlantic shores of the "Coast of Death," as they called it. By the late 1700s British, French, and American whalers were using the deepwater ports of Lüderitz and Walvis (Whalefish) Bay, which the Dutch, now settled in the Cape, then claimed as their own. A few years later, after France invaded Holland, England seized the opportunity to claim the territory together with the Cape Colony. Then it became Germany's turn to throw its hat into the ring. In the wake of its early missionaries and traders, it claimed the entire country as a German colony in 1884, only to surrender it to South African forces, who were fighting on the Allied side during World War I. South Africa was given a League of Nations mandate to administer the territory after the war, and despite a 1978 UN resolution to revoke the mandate, South Africa held on to Namibia for an additional stormy 10 years. A bitter and bloody bush war with SWAPO (South West African People's Organization) freedom fighters raged until Namibia finally won its independence on March 21, 1990, after 106 years of foreign rule. Although most of the earlier colonial influences have now vanished, everywhere you go in Namibia today you'll find traces of the German past—forts and castles, place-names, cuisine, and German efficiency.

Often called the "Land God Made in Anger" because of its stark, surreal landscapes, untamed wilderness, harsh environment, and rare beauty, Namibia was carved out by the forces of nature. The same savage, continuous geological movements produced not only spectacular beauty but also great mineral wealth: alluvial diamonds, uranium, platinum, lead, zinc, silver, copper, tungsten, and tin—still the cornerstone of Namibia's economy. Humans have lived here for thousands of years; the San (Bushmen) are the earliest known people, although their hunting-gathering way of life is now almost extinct. Today most Namibians are employed in the agricultural sector, from subsistence farms to huge cattle ranches and game farms.

Namibia prides itself on its conservation policies and vision. More and more, wildlife conservation is symbiotically linked with community development; in many conservation areas, local communities, the wildlife, and the environment have been successfully integrated, with benefits for all. Wilderness Damaraland Camp, for example, is an internationally acclaimed role model in linking tourism with community development projects. Hunting, a controversial issue for many people, is carefully controlled so that the impact on the environment is minimal the revenue earned is substantial and can often ploughed back into sustainable conservation.

MUST-SEE PARKS

Unfortunately, you probably won't be able to see all of Namibia in one trip. So we've broken down the chapter by **Must-See Parks** (Namib Naukluft Park, Damaraland, Etosha National Park) and the **If-You-Have-Time Parks** (the Skeleton Coast, the Caprivi Strip, Waterberg Plateau Park) to help you better organize your time. We suggest that you read about *all* of them and then choose for yourself.

NAMIB NAUKLUFT PARK

Game

☆☆☆★★

Park Accessibility

☆★★★★

Ease of Getting
Around

☆★★★★

Accommodations

★★★★★

Scenic Beauty

★★★★★

Namib Naukluft Park, south of Walvis Bay, is the fourth-largest national park in the world, and is renowned for its beauty, isolation, tranquillity, romantic desert landscapes, and rare desert-adapted plants and creatures.

Covering an area of 12.1 million acres, it stretches 400 km (248 mi) long and 150 km (93 mi) wide, along the southern part of Namibia's coastline from Walvis Bay to Lüderitz, and accounts for a tenth of Namibia's surface area. The Namib Desert is considered the world's most ancient desert, at more than 55 million years old. To examine the park properly, it's best to think of it as five distinct areas: the Northern Section—between the Kuiseb and Swakops rivers—synonymous with rocky stone surfaces, granite islands (inselbergs), and dry riverbeds; the Middle Section, the 80-million-year-old heart of the desert and home of Sesriem Canyon and Sossusvlei, the highest sand dunes in the world; Naukluft (meaning "narrow gorge"), some 120 km (74½ mi) north-west of Sesriem, which has wall-to-wall game and birds and is the home of the Kuiseb Canyon; the Western Section, with its lichen-covered plains, prehistoric plants, and bird sanctuaries of Walvis Bay and Sandwich Harbour; and the Southern Section, where, if you're traveling up from South Africa by road, it's worth having a look at Duwisib Castle, 72 km (45 mi) southwest of Maltahöhe beside the D286—an anachronistic stone castle built in 1909 by a German army officer who was later killed at the Somme. The park's southern border ends at the charming little town of Lüderitz.

The kind of wildlife you'll encounter will depend on which area of the park you visit. In the north look out for the staggeringly beautiful gemsbok (oryx), the quintessential desert antelope, believed by some to be the animal behind the unicorn myth. These animals are amazingly well adapted for the desert; they obtain moisture from roots, tubers, and wild melons when water is scarce, and although oryx body temperatures can soar, specialized blood vessels in their nostrils keep their brains cool. Also visible are springboks, spotted hyenas, black-backed jackals, and the awesome lappet-face vultures, the biggest in Africa.

In Naukluft you'll see the most game, more than 50 species of mammals, including leopards, caracals, Cape and bat-eared foxes, aardwolves, and klipspringers. There are almost 200 species of birds, from the startlingly beautiful crimson-breasted boubou shrike to soaring falcons and buzzards. You'll notice huge haystacks weighing down tall trees and telephone poles. These are the condominiums of the sociable weavers, so called because they nest communally, sometimes with thousands of fellow weavers.

You'll be able to observe some of the earth's strangest creatures in the sand dunes: the dune beetle, which collects condensed fog on its back into a single droplet that it then rolls down its back into its mouth; the golden mole (thought until recently to be extinct), which "swims" beneath the sand, ambushing beetles and grubs on the surface; the sidewinding adder; a sand-diving lizard that raises one foot at a time above the hot sand in a strange stationary dance.

Don't overlook the amazing desert-adapted plants. Ask your guide to point out a dollar bush (so called because its leaves are dollar size) or an ink bush, both of which can survive without rain for years; the gold, frankincense, and myrrh of the Commiphora plants; the Namib's magic plant, the nara melon, still harvested and eaten by the locals; and the baffling geophytes, plants that disguise themselves as stones. Watch for withered-looking desert lichens—if you pour a tiny drop of water onto one it will seemingly rise from the dead. Last, but by no means least, is the mind-boggling *Welwitschia mirabilis,* the Namib's most famous, and the world's oldest, living plant.

SESRIEM & SOSSUSVLEI

Even if you're not a romantic, the Sossusvlei's huge, star-shape desert dunes, which rise dramatically 1,000 feet above the surrounding plains and sprawl like massive pieces of abstract sculpture, are guaranteed to stir your soul and imagination. The landscape has continuously shifting colors—from yellow-gold and ocher to rose, purple, and deep red—that grow paler or darker according to the time of day. The dunes have their own distinctive features, ranging from the crescent-shape barchan dunes—which migrate up to 2 or 3 yards a year, covering and uncovering whatever crosses their path—to the spectacular, stationary star-shape dunes, formed by the multidirectional winds that tease and tumble the sands back and forth. Park gates open an hour before sunrise, so if you can, try to be among the dunes as the sun comes up—it's a spectacular sight. If you're in good shape, you can hike to the top of Big Daddy, the highest sand dune in the world. But it's tough going: more than an hour of very hot trudging and wading through ankle- and sometimes knee-deep sand to climb the major route up to Dead Vlei (where ghostly skeletons of ancient trees jut up from a flat, sandy, dried-up lake) and Big Daddy (the hub of Sossusvlei) from the parking area. If you don't feel up to any physical exertion at all, then sit in the

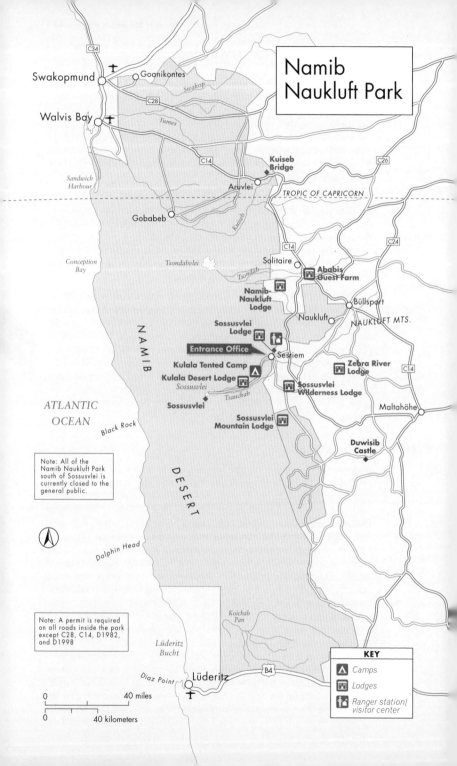

shade of camelthorn trees at the bottom of the dunes and watch the birdlife, or focus your binoculars on the distant climbers.

About 4 km (2½ mi) from Sesriem Gate, your entry point to Sossusvlei, is Sesriem Canyon, named after the six *rieme* (thongs) that were tied to the buckets of the early Dutch settlers when they drew up water from the canyon. If you have time, cool off in the pools, easily reached by steps in the rock. If you're fairly fit, it's well worth climbing the towering Elim Dune, the nearest sand dune to Sesriem, about 5 km (3 mi) away; it will take you more than an hour, but the superb views of the surrounding desert and gravel plains are infinitely rewarding. Be warned: dune climbing is exhausting, so make discretion the better part of valor. If you're driving yourself, check with your car-rental company for distances and times, which can vary according to the state of the roads. Keep in mind that a 4x4 will give you more access and better viewing, and with a 4x4 you can park just below Dead Vlei.

WHERE TO STAY

LUXURY LODGES

$$$$ ⚑**Kulala Desert Lodge.** In the heart of the Namib and bordering Namib Naukluft Park, this lodge offers magnificent views of the famous red dunes of Sossusvlei, superb mountain scenery, and vast open plains. Tented, thatch-roofed chalets (*kulala*) have a wooden platform overlooking the dry riverbed. In summer you can move your mattress onto a private star-gazing platform on your rooftop to sleep under the stars. The veranda at the main lodge overlooks a water hole and is the perfect place to watch or photograph the magnificent desert sunset. Activities include desert excursions, morning and evening game drives, trips to Sossusvlei, birding, and guided walks. For an additional fee you can splurge on a hot-air balloon trip over the desert—a once-in-a-lifetime opportunity. ⌂ *Wilderness Safaris, Box 5219, Rivonia 2128, South Africa* ☎*27/11/807–1800 South Africa* ⊕*www.wilderness-safaris. com* ⌂*12 chalets* ⌂*In-hotel: bar, pool* ☰*AE, DC, MC, V* ⓄⅠ*FAP.*

$$$$ ⚑**Sossusvlei Lodge.** If you want to be on the spot when the park gates open at first light, then this hotel right at the Sesriem entrance is the right choice for you. Its decor in shades of terra-cotta, burnt sienna, and apricot blends perfectly with the desert surroundings. You may feel like a well-to-do bedouin in your spacious and luxurious tented room, imaginatively constructed of concrete, ironwork, canvas, and leather. After a hot, dusty day in the desert, it's wonderful to wallow in the swimming pool, which faces the dunes, and later gaze at the dazzling brilliance of the night skies. There's a good restaurant serving light meals. ⌂ *Box 6900, Windhoek, Namibia* ☎*063/69–3223* ⊕*www.sossusvleilodge.com* ⌂*45 rooms* ⌂*In-room: safe. In-hotel: restaurant, bar, pool* ☰*AE, MC, V* ⓄⅠ*MAP.*

$$$$ ⚑**Sossusvlei Mountain Lodge.** This gorgeous lodge has a spectacular setting in the NamibRand Nature Reserve. Its ultraluxurious desert villas, facing a vast golden-yellow plain with misty mountains on the horizon, are built of natural rock and look out over a plain ringed by peaks. Huge desert-facing suites have private patios and sundecks and big

open fireplaces to keep you warm on chilly desert nights. Shower in your megasize bathroom (even your toilet has an incomparable view) or outside in your own little walled garden. You can lie in bed and watch the stars through the skylight overhead or climb up to the observatory behind the lodge. It has its own state-of-the-art telescope through which an astronomer-ranger will guide you through the heavens. The food is as creative as the lodge itself—try tandoori-baked *kingklip* (a delicious southern African fish) served with mango salsa—and there's a super wine cellar. You can explore the area on an ecofriendly quad bike, go for guided nature walks or drives, spot some native desert birds and animals, or just sit and gaze at the incredible views. ⏎ *Africa Leisure Travel, Swakopmund, Namibia* ☎064/46–3812 *or* 064/46–3813 ⊕*www.ccafrica.com* ⊷*10 villas* ⚭*In-room: a/c. In-hotel: pool* ☐*AE, DC, MC, V* ❖*FAP.*

$$$$ ⛺**Sossusvlei Wilderness Camp.** In one of the most dramatic settings in Africa, exquisitely appointed rock, timber, and thatch bungalows cling to the side of a mountain with spectacular views of the desert as it stretches away to the horizon. After the bumpy 20-km (12½-mi) drive to the dunes, you'll enjoy breakfast under spreading camelthorn trees at the foot of Sossusvlei before returning to camp at midday via the Sesriem Canyon. You can then cool off in your private plunge pool as you watch the sun set over awesome desert scenery to the calls of barking geckos. ⏎ *Wilderness Safaris, Box 5219, Rivonia 2128, South Africa* ☎27/11/807–1800 *South Africa* ⊕*www.sossusvleicamp.com* ⊷*9 bungalows* ⚭*In-room: a/c. In-hotel: restaurant, bar, pool* ☐*AE, DC, MC, V* ❖*FAP.*

PERMANENT TENTED CAMPS

$$$$ ⛺**Kulala Tented Camp.** Although this small, stylish camp calls itself a "tented" camp, only the walls of your chalet are actually made of canvas: your roof is thatch and your floor and elevated viewing deck are made of wood. As the camp faces west, don't miss the opportunity to sit out on your personal deck to watch a spectacular Namibian sunset. You won't find much big game here, but spotting springbok and ostrich skittering over the stark landscape, catching a glimpse of the dramatic desert oryx, and listening to the barking geckos as the sun goes down are all memorable experiences. Take a guided trip to Sossusvlei, go walking with a knowledgeable guide in the surrounding desert, or treat yourself (go on; it's expensive but the experience of a lifetime) to a dawn hot-air balloon ride. ⏎ *Wilderness Safaris, Box 5219, Rivonia 2128, South Africa* ☎27/11/807–1800 *South Africa* ⊕*www.wilderness-safaris.com* ⊷*9 tented chalets* ⚭*In-hotel: bar, pool* ☐*AE, DC, MC, V* ❖*FAP.*

MOBILE TENTED CAMPS

⛺ **Wilderness Safaris.** The cost of these mobile safaris in Sossusvlei are comparable to what you'd pay for a luxury lodge, but these mobile camps are usually even more remote than the usual lodges and generally accommodate fewer than seven guests. Spacious walk-in dome tents, erected before you reach camp, are used, with separate flush toilets and bucket-shower enclosures. ⏎ *Wilderness Safaris, Box 5219,*

Kulala Desert Lodge

7

Sossusvlei Wilderness

Sossusvlei Mt Lodge

Rivonia 2128, South Africa ☎*27/11/807–1800 South Africa* ⊕*www. wilderness-safaris.com* ☰*AE, DC, MC, V* ❖*FAP.*

BUDGET ACCOMMODATIONS

$$ ⊡ **Namib Naukluft Lodge.** Resembling children's building blocks set down by a giant hand in the middle of nowhere, this pinkish-brown desert-toned lodge sits in the midst of a wide plain of desert. Awesome views go with the territory. You can choose to sit on your private veranda and watch the fiery desert sunset, sip a sundowner by the pool, or enjoy a meal in the open-air restaurant. The lodge will arrange outings and activities for you—don't miss out on an easy walk in the world's oldest desert. ⊡*African Extravaganza, Box 22028, Windhoek, Namibia* ☎*063/69–3381* ⊕*www.namib-naukluft-lodge.com* ⬧*16 rooms* ⚒*In-hotel: restaurant, bar, pool* ☰*AE, DC, MC, V* ❖*FAP.*

$ ⊡ **Ababis Guest Farm.** Ostriches and cows rub unlikely shoulders at this intimate, historic guesthouse at a farm on the northern side of the Naukluft Mountains, near the tiny town of Solitaire. It was established in 1898 as an outpost of the German Imperial Stud Farm at Nauchas. Today it's an ideal base for exploring the area, whether on foot or by 4x4—although it's a day-long trip to Sossusvlei and back. With long hikes and short strolls around the farm, the area is ideal for hikers. There are five en-suite rooms with private verandas, and the English-and-German-speaking hosts will escort you on game drives, to nearby San paintings, or to the Naukluft plateau. You'll dine well on home-cooked food, and there's a surprisingly good wine selection. ⊡*Box 1004, Maltahöhe, Namibia* ☎*063/29–3362* ⊕*www.ababis-gaestefarm.de* ⬧*5 rooms* ⚒*In-hotel: bar, pool* ☰*MC, V* ❖*FAP.*

$ ⊡ **Zebra River Lodge.** From this delightful lodge, where personal attention and friendly service are outstanding (the lodge gets lots of repeat visitors), you can drive yourself to Sesriem and Sossusvlei (90 km [56 mi] to the gate) or to Naukluft, or take a full-day excursion with Rob Field, the friendly and knowledgeable owner (book this when you reserve your room). All activities cost extra. The comfortable and unpretentious lodge has its own canyon, hiking trails, perennial springs, and superb cooking. The seven guest rooms all have views of the plunge pool and green garden. ⊡*Box 11742, Windhoek, Namibia* ☎*063/69–3265* ⊕*www.zebrariver.com* ⬧*7 rooms, 1 cottage* ⚒*In-hotel: bar, pool* ☰*MC, V* ❖*FAP.*

NATIONAL PARKS ACCOMMODATIONS

¢ ⊡ **Naukluft Campsite.** This lovely campsite is 12 km (7½ mi) from the Naukluft entrance, 10 km (6 mi) south of Büllsport. The eight shady campsites ringed by mountains are strictly for camping. There's an ablution block, but that's all—other than firewood and water, you must bring all your own supplies. During peak holiday times, you can stay for only three nights, and it's essential to book in advance at MET in Windhoek. ⊡*Ministry of Wildlife, Conservation and Tourism (MET), Private Bag 13306, Windhoek 9000, Namibia* ☎*061/23–6975* ⊕*www.met.gov.na* ⬧*8 campsites* ☰*DC, MC, V.*

Continued on page 462

The Sossusvlei salt pans.

THE NAMIBIA DUNES

by Kate Turkington

Be prepared for sand like you've never seen it before: in dunes that roar, rumble, and ramble. We guarantee the sight will stir your soul and imagination.

Namibia's dunes, which rise dramatically more than 1,000 meters (3,281 feet) above the surrounding plains, are said to be the world's highest. But don't think that if you've seen one sandy ridge you've seen them all. Expect great variety here. There are crescent-shaped dunes that migrate up to 2 or 3 meters (7 to 10 feet) a year, covering and uncovering whatever's in their path. There are also fossil dunes made of ancient sand that solidified millions of years ago, and star-shaped dunes formed by multidirectional winds teasing and tumbling the sand.

Amid this unique landscape live some of the world's strangest, most well-adapted creatures. The golden mole, for instance, spends its life "swimming" under the sand, popping up to the surface to grab unwary insects. Certain types of beetles collect condensed droplets of water on their backs and then roll the liquid down to their mouths; still other beetles dig trenches to collect moisture. As its name suggests, the side-winding adder moves itself from side to side over the sand, while, contrary to its name, the sand-diving lizard stands motionless, one foot raised, as if in some ancient ritual dance. And then there's the quintessential desert antelope: the beautiful gemsbok (oryx), which is believed by some to be the animal behind the unicorn myth.

WHERE DID THE DUNES COME FROM?

The formation and structure of sand dunes is extremely complex, but basically there are three prerequisites for dunes: plenty of loose sand, plenty of wind, and a flat surface with no obstacles like trees or mountains to prevent dunes building up. Namibia has these three things in abundance.

A MILLION GRAINS OF SAND FOR YOU TO EXPLORE

SKELETON COAST

NAMIBIA

Big Daddy Dune
Dead Vlei Vally

Walvis Bay

Sossusvlei

NAMIB NAUKLUFT PARK

Luderitz

Gemsbok in the desert dunes of Namib-Naukluft Park.

WHERE ARE THE DUNES?

Enormous Namib-Naukluft Park—renowned for its isolated, romantic desert scapes—stretches 400 km (250 mi) along the southern part of Namibia's coastline, from Walvis Bay to Lüderitz, and accounts for a tenth of the country's surface area. Sossusvlei, the 80-million-year-old heart of the desert, is in the middle section of the park. It's a great entry point from which you can start your adventures. This desert is thought to be the oldest desert in the world. Although its geological base area is relatively stable, the dunes themselves are continuously sculpted by the desert winds.

DUNE EXPLORER

Sure, you could explore the dunes on your own, but you really can't beat the know-how of an experienced guide; ask your lodge to arrange this. Look to climb "Big Daddy," a dune that's as tall as a seven-story building, or Dune 7 (about 1,256 feet) or Dune 45 (557 feet). You could also just climb to the halfway point of Big Daddy or simply sit in the shade at the bottom of a dune and watch the distant climbers exert themselves.

WHEN TO GO

Sunset and sunrise are the best times to visit (be at the gates of Sesriem when it opens at 5 AM or camp in the park), because the colors of the dunes change in spectacular fashion from yellow-gold and ocher to rose, purple, and deep red. Keep in mind that midday temperatures can peak at over 40°C (104°F) in summer.

THE SLOW PACE

Sip sundowners as the sun sinks, go hot-air ballooning at dawn, or simply marvel at the life that is found in this harsh environment. You won't see big game, but you will see a wealth of unique birds, insects, plants, and geological formations. Whatever you do, make sure you take a moment to appreciate the soul-searing and soul-searching silence.

ADRENALINE JUNKIES WELCOME

(top) Preparing to sandboard. (bottom) Sandboarding.

Looking for some excitement? Adrenaline junkies can try their hand (or feet) at skydiving, dune-buggying, paragliding, sandboarding or dune-boarding (for the more advanced). The less adventurous (but romantic) can take day, moonlight, sunrise or sunset horseback or camel rides through the riverbeds and up into the moonlike landscape.

If you have time for just one thing, make it sandboarding because it will certainly get your heart pumping. Once you are ferried up the dunes by quad bike, your operator will arm you with the necessary equipment: a sandboard—a flat piece of hardboard, a safety hat, gloves, and elbow guards. It's also a good idea to wear long pants and long sleeves to avoid a sandburn. Beginners should head to the smaller dunes to practice (i.e. sliding down on your stomach) to get the feel of it. As you get better and more adventurous, head to the top of a high dune, but be advised, you can reach speeds of up to 80 kph (50 mph). Once you get the hang

of this, try standing up. Hey, if Cameron Diaz survived, so will you.

If you get really advanced, there's always dune-boarding. You use all the same gear as sandboarding, except your board is similar to a regular surfboard on which you stand up and "surf" down the dunes.

DAMARALAND

Game	☆☆★★★
Park Accessibility	☆☆☆☆★
Ease of Getting Around	☆☆☆★★
Accommodations	☆☆☆★★
Scenic Beauty	★★★★★

Stretching 600 km (370 mi) from just south of Etosha to Usakos in the south and 200 km (125 mi) from east to west, this stark, mountainous area is just inland from Skeleton Coast National Park.

You can drive into Damaraland from the park via the Springbokwater Gate, or drive from Swakopmund to Uis, where you can visit the Daureb Craft Centre and watch the craftspeople at work, or make it part of your customized safari. A good base for touring southern Damaraland is the little town of Khorixas. From here you can visit the Organ Pipes, hundreds of angular rock formations, or watch the rising or setting sun bathe the slopes of Burnt Mountain in fiery splendor. You'll find yourself surrounded by a dramatic landscape of steep valleys; rugged cliffs of red, gray, black, and brown; and towering mountains, including Spitzkoppe (Namibia's Matterhorn, which towers nearly 2,000 feet above the plains), where Damara guides will show you the Golden Snake and the Bridge—an interesting rock formation—and the San (Bushman) paintings at Bushman's Paradise. There are more spectacular rock paintings at the Brandberg Mountain, especially the famous White Lady of Brandberg, at Tsisab Gorge, whose depiction and origin have teased the minds of scholars for decades. (Is she of Mediterranean origin? Is "she" really a "he" covered in white initiation paint?)

Other stops of interest are the Petrified Forest, 42 km (25 mi) west of Khorixas, where the corpses of dead trees lie forever frozen in a bed of sandstone. Twyfelfontein, 90 km (56 mi) west of Khorixas, is the biggest outdoor art gallery in the world, where thousands of rock paintings and ancient rock engravings are open to the sky. It's extremely rare for this many paintings and engravings to be found at the same site. As you approach, you'll see scattered boulders everywhere—a closer examination will reveal thousands of rock paintings and engravings. Get yourself a local knowledgeable guide when you arrive, and try to give yourself a full day here; start early (it's hard to pick out some of the art in full sunshine), bring binoculars, wear sturdy shoes, and bring water (at least a gallon) and a hat.

Northern Damaraland consists of concession areas that have been set aside for tourism, with many tourist operators working hand in hand with the local communities. This is a desert of a different kind from the classic sand dunes of the Namib. It's a landscape of almost unsurpassed rugged beauty formed by millions of years of unending geological movement. Vivid brick-red sediments complement gray lava slopes punctuated by black fingers of "frozen" basaltic rock creeping down from the jagged rocky horizons. Millions of stones, interspersed with clumps of silvery-gray shrubs and pioneer grasses, litter the unending slopes, hillsides, and mountain faces. There seem to be as many rocks, huge and small, as there are grains of sand on the beaches of the windswept, treacherous Skeleton Coast, some 90 km (56 mi) to the west. But there is life, and plenty of it, in this seemingly inhospitable landscape, including dozens of *Welwitschia mirabilis* plants that can live for up to 1,000 years. Stop at a 500-year-old "youngster" and consider that when this plant was a newborn, Columbus was sailing for the New World and the Portuguese to Namibia.

The landscape is also dotted with colorful lichen fields, dark-green umbrella-shape camelthorn trees, candelabra euphorbias raising their prickly fleshy arms to the cloudless sky, saltbushes, and the ubiquitous shepherd's tree. Also here is the *moringa* tree—the "enchanted" tree, so-called because according to San legend, the god of thunder, not wanting moringa trees in heaven, pulled them all up and threw them out. They fell upside down into the earth, looking like miniature baobab trees. In the middle of this rocky desert rubble is Slangpost, a small verdant oasis in the middle of what seems to be nowhere (not even the mountains have a name in this part of the world; they're referred to simply as the "no-name" mountains). Look out for traces of the amazing desert elephants (sometimes called the desert-adapted elephants), their huge footprints trodden over by the healthy herds of goats and sheep belonging to the local Damara farmers. Your best chance of seeing the elephants is along the surprisingly green and fertile dry Huab River bed, where they browse on the large seedpods of the Ana tree and whatever else they find edible. To see the great gray shapes silhouetted against the dry river's sandy mounds ringed by mountains and sand dunes is an incredible sight.

The Kaokoveld, north of Damaraland, although enticing because it is pristine and rarely visited, is also inhospitably rugged. Self-drives are for the really intrepid, do-it-yourself explorer.

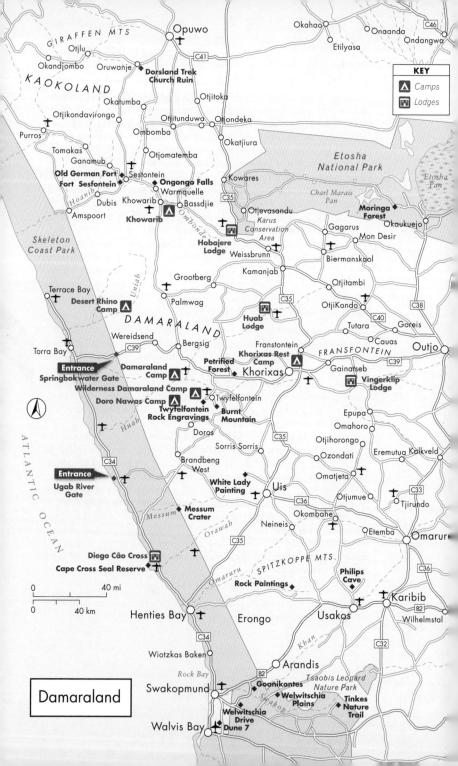

WHERE TO STAY

LUXURY LODGES

$$$$ **Doro Nawas Camp.** Set amid stony slopes, rugged boulders, the distant Entendeka Mountains, and the pink and russet sandstone cliffs of Twyfelfontein to the south (where you can visit some of the most famous San rock paintings and engravings in the world), this is classic Damaraland. What's more, this camp may be your best bet to see the long-legged desert elephants. You'll stay in a sturdy en-suite stone, canvas, and thatch chalet with an indoor and outdoor shower; it's great to snuggle into bed at night and hear the desert wind blowing eerily outside. You can relax in the pool after a day's activities, or climb up to the roof area of the main building to sip sundowners or watch the blazing stars. *Wilderness Safaris, Box 5219, Rivonia 2128, South Africa* 27/11/807–1800 South Africa *www.wilderness-safars.com* 16 chalets In-hotel: pool AE, DC, MC, V FAP.

PERMANENT TENTED CAMPS

$$$$

Fodor'sChoice

★

Desert Rhino Camp. If it's rhinos you're after, especially the rare black rhino, then this remote tented camp, formerly Palmwag Rhino Camp, in the heart of the private 1-million-acre Palmwag Reserve is a must. Because there are freshwater springs everywhere, you'll see not only the desert-adapted black rhino, but plenty of other game, too, including desert elephants, giraffes, zebras, kudu, and possibly lions, leopards, and cheetahs. The camp collaborates with the Save the Rhino Trust, and one of the highlights of your stay will be tracking the rare black rhino on foot. (If this is not your idea of fun, go tracking in an open vehicle instead.) You'll likely feel very close to the desert in your spacious tent with en-suite bathroom, flush toilet, and hot water on demand for your bucket shower. *Namibia Tracks & Trails, Box 339, Swakopmund, Namibia* 064/40–4459 *www.namibia-tracks-and-trails.com* 8 tents In-hotel: bar MC, V FAP.

$$$$ **Wilderness Damaraland Camp.** A joint community venture with the local *riemvasmakers* (thong makers), this desolate camp is on the Huab River in central Damaraland, midway between Khorixas and the coast. From your large walk-in tent you can look out over a landscape of craggy beauty formed by millions of years of unending geological movement. You'll drive with an experienced ranger in an open 4x4 to see the famous *Welwitschia* and track desert elephants. After a day in the desert, cool off in the natural rock pool and watch the desert birds. *Wilderness Safaris, Box 5219, Rivonia 2128, South Africa* 27/11/807–1800 South Africa *www.damaraland.com* 8 tents In-hotel: bar, pool AE, DC, MC, V FAP.

BUDGET ACCOMMODATION

$$ **Vingerklip Lodge.** In a dramatic locale in Damaraland's Valley of the Ugab Terraces, this lodge is set against the backdrop of a mighty stone finger pointing toward the sky. Take time while you're here to listen to the silence. The 360-degree views from the Sundowner Terrace are magnificent. The friendly and knowledgeable staff organizes tours to the well-known sights in the vicinity such as the petrified forest, a Himba

village, and the rock engravings at Twyfelfontein. Bungalows cling to the side of a rocky hill and are clean and comfortable, but it's the remarkable views that you'll always remember. ⌂*Box 11550, Windhoek, Namibia* ☎*061/25–5344* ⊕*www.vingerklip.com.na* ⤳*11 bungalows* ⌂*In-hotel: restaurant, bar, pool* ☐*MC, V* ⍾*MAP.*

¢   ⊡**Khorixas Rest Camp.** Grayish stone-and-tile bungalows, some of which face a seasonally flowing river, are scattered among trees and flowering shrubs. Although this spot is hardly the last word in luxury, it is clean, inexpensive, unpretentious, and very handy for exploring the major attractions of the area. ⌂*Box 2, Khorixas, Namibia* ☎*067/33–1196* ⊕*www.namibiareservations.com* ⤳*38 bungalows, campsite* ⌂*In-hotel: restaurant, bar, pool* ☐*MC, V* ⍾*BP.*

TIPPING

Tipping is tricky and depends on where you are staying and what services you have received. Your in-room lodge-information package often makes tipping suggestions. Tips can be given in U.S. or Namibian dollars, or South African rand. Most lodges suggest US$10 per person per day for your guide and US$5 per person per day for your tracker. Since tipping is so highly subjective, tip what you feel comfortable with.

Doro Nawas

7

Vingerklip Lodge

Damaraland Camp

ETOSHA NATIONAL PARK

Game
★★★★★
Park Accessibility
★★★★★
Ease of Getting Around
★★★★★
Accomomdations
★★★★★
Scenic Beauty
★★★★★

This photogenic, startlingly beautiful park takes its name—meaning Great White Place—from a vast flat depression that was a deep inland lake 12 million years ago. The white clay pan, also known as the Place of Mirages, covers nearly 25% of the park's surface.

Although it is usually dry, in a good rainy season it floods and becomes home to many waterbirds, including tens of thousands of flamingoes that feed on the blue-green algae of the pan. Although the park is never crowded with visitors like some of the East African game parks, the scenery here is no less spectacular: huge herds of animals that dot the plains and gather at the many and varied water holes, the dust devils and mirages, and terrain that changes from densely wooded thickets to wide-open spaces and from white salt-encrusted pans to blond grasslands.

The game's all here—the Big Five—large and small, fierce and gentle, beautiful and ugly. But one of Etosha's main attractions is not the numbers of animals that you can see (more than 114 species), but how easily you can see them. The game depends on the natural springs that are found all along the edges of the pan, and as the animals have grown used to drinking at these water holes for decades, they are not put off by vehicles or game-seeking visitors. On the road from the Von Lindequist Gate, the eastern entrance to Etosha, to the well-restored white-wall German colonial fort that is now Namutoni Rest Camp, look out for the smallest of all African antelopes, the Damara dik-dik. If you see a

PARK ESSENTIALS

The park gates are open from sunrise to sunset, and the daily entrance fee is N$80 for foreign visitors and N$10 for a passenger vehicle with fewer than 10 seats. You pay for your vehicle entry permit at the gate and for any balance remaining on your pre-booked accommodations (which include personal entry fees) at the reception area.

diminutive Bambi sheltering under a roadside bush, that's it. The Namutoni area and the two Okevi water holes—Klein Namutoni and Kalkheuwel—probably provide the best chances to see leopards. Don't miss the blackface impala, native to Etosha, one of the rarest of antelopes and an endangered species. Bigger and more boldly marked than its smaller cousin, the impala, you'll find it drinking in small herds at water holes all over the park.

WORD OF MOUTH

"Etosha is the best area in Namibia for game-viewing. This is definitely a place where you can sit by a waterhole and watch animals come to you. There are private concessions adjacent to the park (similar to the Sabi Sands at Kruger), where you can do off-road driving and night driving, such as the Ongava Reserve."

–jasher

The real secret of game-watching in the park is to settle in at one of the many water holes, most of which are on the southern edges of the pan, and wait. And wait. Each water hole has its own unique personality and characteristics. Even if the hole is small and deep, like Ombika, on the western side, you'll be amazed at what may arrive. Old Africa hands maintain that you should be up at dawn for the best sightings, but you can see marvelous game at all times of day; one visitor was lucky enough to see a leopard and her cubs come to drink at high noon. The plains, where you'll likely spot cheetahs, are also home to huge herds of zebras and wildebeests, and you may see the silhouettes of giraffes as they cross the skyline in stately procession. Watch out for herds of springbok "pronking"—pronking is when these lovely little antelopes bounce and bound high into the air as they run. Zoologists argue over the reason for this behavior. Some say it is to avoid predators, others that it is to demonstrate agility, strength, and stamina; most visitors like to believe that pronking is just for fun. Salvadora, a constant spring on the fringe of Etosha Pan near Halali, is a favorite watering point for some of these big herds. Watch out also for the stately eland, Africa's largest antelope. As big as a cow, although more streamlined and elegant, this antelope can jump higher than any other African antelope—amazing when you consider its huge size. And where there's water, there's always game. Predators, especially lions, lurk around most of the water holes looking for a meal. Plan to spend at least half a night sitting on a bench at the floodlighted Okaukuejo water hole. You really are within spitting distance of the game. Bring a book, write in your journal, or just sit while you wait. You may be amazed at the variety of animals that come down to drink: black and white rhinos, lions, jackals, and even the occasional leopard. This is a particularly good place to look out for black rhinos, which trot purposefully up to drink and in so doing scare all but the bravest of other game away. Groot Okevi waterhole, close to Namutoni, is also good for black rhinos.

Don't overlook the more than 340 dazzling varieties of birds—the crimson-breasted boubou is particularly gorgeous—and watch for ostriches running over the plains or raptors hunting silently overhead. There are

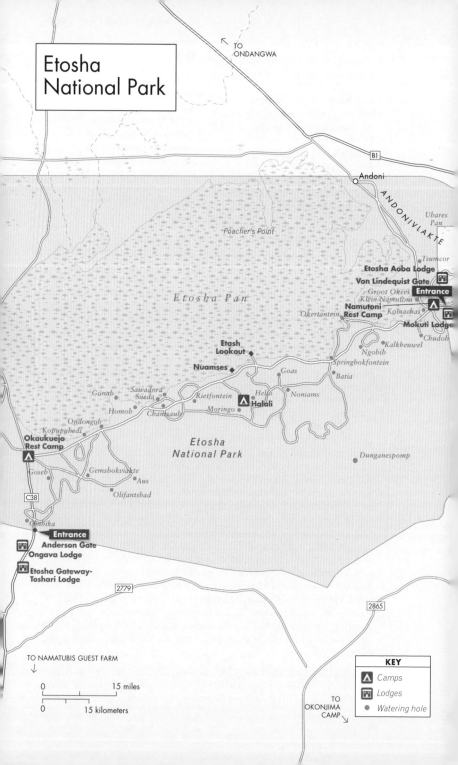

many endemics, including the black-faced and bare-cheeked babblers, violet woodhoopoe (look for them in Halali camp), Rüppell's parrot, Bradfield's swift, and the white-tailed shrike (which you can see hopping happily around on the lawns at Namutoni camp).

The park is huge—22,270 square km (8,598 square mi), 300 km (186 mi) wide and 110 km (68 mi) long—and it's currently undergoing renovation of its infrastructure. The western part is still mostly undeveloped (you need a special permit to visit), so stick to the other parts; there's plenty to see. If you prefer to visit the park on one of the many safaris offered by various tour companies, make sure you choose one with an open vehicle or pop-top with few passengers—you probably don't want to find yourself in an air-conditioned 75-seater bus. That said, the best way to see the park is to drive yourself so you can stop at your leisure (don't exceed the 60 kph speed limit, and stick to marked roads). A two-wheel-drive car is fine, as the roads are good, but the higher up you sit, the better your view, so opt for the more expensive *combis* (vans) or 4x4s if possible. In addition to patience, you'll need drinks, snacks, field guides to the animals and birds, binoculars, and your camera. There are more than 40 water holes, with Rietfontein, Okaukuejo, Goas, Halali, Klein Namutoni, and Chudob regarded as the best for game-watching and taking pictures, but nothing is certain in the bush. Keep your eyes and ears open, and you may come across game at any time, in any place. Arm yourself with the MET map of Etosha (available in the camps), which shows the names and locations of the water holes and indicates which roads are open.

Be aware of the trees, shrubs and plants as well. Just east of Okaukuejo is the legendary Haunted or Ghost Forest where moringa trees have morphed into twisted, strange and grotesque shapes: you may feel as if you are in Snow White's forest or deep in Middle Earth.

WHERE TO STAY

If you wish to stay inside Etosha itself you can lodge at one of the government rest camps (book months in advance, especially for the peak periods of July–September and around Christmas and Easter, though you may want to avoid the crowds at these times). The rest camps of Halali, Namutoni, and Okaukuejo are all self-catering. All have pools, grocery-curio-liquor stores, gas stations, and restaurants serving breakfast, lunch, and dinner (just don't expect a gourmet meal). There are also more expensive, more luxurious full-service private lodges and guest farms near the park.

LUXURY LODGES

$$$$ ★ **Ongava Lodge.** On the southern boundary of Etosha close to the Anderson Gate, the lodge has its own surrounding game reserve as well as its own entrance into the park. It's one of Namibia's most luxurious lodges, with accommodations in private, spacious thatch chalets with handmade wood furniture—and gold faucets in the bathrooms. Chalets also have wood decks, which cling to the side of a steep, rocky outcrop overlooking a couple of busy water holes. The stunning main

area has stone floors and sweeping thatch roofs, as well as myriad spots from which to gaze at the never-ending plains beyond. Take a guided walk and sneak up on some zebras and wildebeests, or sit in the bird blind just before sunset and listen to the soft twittering calls of hundreds of sand grouse as they come to drink. Lions often stray in from Etosha and join the evening party. If you want to be more on the wild side, you can stay at Ongava Tented Camp, a small, intimate site nestled deep in the bush. You'll sleep in a walk-in tent on a slate base under a thatch awning with a private bathroom. After a day spent game-watching (tracking rhinos on foot is a highlight), it's great to cool off in the outside shower or in the plunge pool. If you want even more exclusivity and luxury, opt for Little Ongava, which has three gorgeous suites all with their own plunge pool and *sala* (outdoor covered deck). ☐ *Wilderness Safaris, Box 519, Rivonia 2128, South Africa* ☎ *27/11/807–1800 South Africa* ⊕ *www.ongavalodge.com* ✆ *10 chalets, 6 tents, 3 suites* ⌂ *In-room: a/c. In-hotel: restaurant, bar, pool* ⊟ *AE, DC, MC, V* ⎮⚋⎮ *FAP.*

BUDGET LODGINGS

$$$ ☖ **Etosha Aoba Lodge.** This small, family-owned, ultrafriendly lodge is 10 km (6 mi) east of the Von Lindequist Gate—about a 30-minute drive from the park. After a hot, dusty day in the park, you can slip into crisp, white bed linens in your cool, thatch chalet, or sip a cocktail on your mini-veranda while listening to the noises of the night. The owners emphasize excellent cuisine made with fresh, local produce; you'll dine under the thatch roof of the main building. Most visitors have their own vehicles, but the lodge can arrange trips into the park for you. The lodge gets lots of repeat visitors. ☐ *Box 21783, Windhoek, Namibia* ☎ *061/22–9106* ⊕ *www.etosha-aoba-lodge.com* ✆ *10 chalets* ⌂ *In-room: a/c. In-hotel: restaurant, bar, pool, no kids under 13* ⊟ *MC, V* ⎮⚋⎮ *BP.*

$$$ ☖ **Mokuti Lodge.** Since this lodge is in its own park a stone's throw
☪   from the Von Lindequist Gate, you may well wake up and find an antelope or warthog munching the grass outside your room. This was Namibia's first lodge, and it is also its largest, and the experience is obvious in the impeccable service and good food. The smallish rooms are rather sparsely furnished, but you'll be out most of the day game-spotting. You can take a walk, either guided or on your own, and be quite safe. Follow the paths, and you may come face-to-face with a giraffe or any number of gorgeous birds. Don't miss the amazing reptile park, where you can meet pythons, scorpions, tortoises, and the odd crocodile. To catch sight of the bigger game, take an early-morning or afternoon tour into Etosha from the lodge. Air Namibia flies to and from Mokuti five days a week. ☐ *Namib Sun Hotels, Box 2862, Windhoek, Namibia* ☎ *064/40–0315* ⊕ *www.namibsunhotels.com.na* ✆ *92 rooms, 8 suites, 8 family units* ⌂ *In-room: a/c, safe, refrigerator. In-hotel: restaurant, bar, tennis court, pool* ⊟ *MC, V* ⎮⚋⎮ *BP.*

$$ ☖ **Etosha Gateway Lodge—Toshari Inn.** Situated 25 km (15½ mi) south
☪   of Etosha's Anderson Gate, this pleasant, affordable, owner-managed lodge makes a great base for exploring the park. If you're fed up with self-driving, then let an experienced guide take you on the lodge's 7½-

hour drive in an open game vehicle with a great picnic included (10 people maximum). Cheerful well-appointed double rooms with fans and mosquito nets are set among green lawns and old trees. The restaurant serves excellent home-cooked food and has a good wine

WORD OF MOUTH

"My kids loved Etosha Park. In fact, our love for African wildlife has its origins right there!"

–Fabio

list specializing in fine Cape wines. You can also dine in the *boma* (a traditional open-air enclosure) under the unbelievably brilliant Namibian stars. Kids ages 3–11 stay free with their parents. 🖭 *Box 164, Outjo, Namibia* ☏ *065/48–3702* ⊕ *www.etoshagateway-toshari.com* 🛏 *16 chalets* ⚐ *In-hotel: restaurant, bar, pool, laundry facilities* ▤ *AE, DC, MC, V* ⦿ *BP.*

$$ 🖭 **Okonjima Camp.** Located 130 km (80 mi) north of Okahandja, this is an excellent stopover point on your way to Etosha. Nestled among the Omboroko Mountains, this lovely, but very busy lodge is also home to the environmental-award-winning Africat Foundation (⊕ www.africat. org), which has rehabilitated and cared for leopards and cheetahs for many years. You can get a close look at these magnificent cats feeding, and there are also guided San and Bantu walking trails. A bonus is the spacious hide, within walking distance of your thatched room, where you can sit and watch some of the smaller animals and hundreds of birds. In addition to lodging in the farmhouse, there's a bush camp comprising eight thatched African-style chalets with a canvas "front wall" that can be lifted during the day so you can enjoy the view. If you're looking for ultimate exclusivity, treat yourself to the gorgeous bush suite. 🖭 *Box 793, Otjiwarongo, Namibia* ☏ *067/68–7032, 067/68–7034, or 067/68–7035* ⊕ *www.okonjima.com* 🛏 *10 rooms* ⚐ *In-room: a/c (some). In-hotel: restaurant, bar, pool, no kids under 12* ▤ *AE, DC, MC, V* ⦿ *MAP.*

$ 🖭 **Namatubis Guest Farm.** About 15 km (9 mi) from Outjo on the Okuakuejo road to Etosha, Namatubis is an oasis in the surrounding dry countryside. You'll find pastel-color chalets with tile floors and Namibian rugs surrounded by green lawns and multicolor carpets of flowers and shrubs. The food is good farm-style cooking; choose either the superb steak, venison, chicken pie, or a decadent brandy pancake. You can also take day excursions from the lodge to the Vingerklip rock formation, Twyfelfontein, or the Petrified Forest and still be back in time for dinner. 🖭 *Box 467, Outjo, Namibia* ☏ *067/31–3061* ⊕ *www. namatubis-guestfarm.com* 🛏 *23 chalets* ⚐ *In-room: refrigerator. In-hotel: restaurant, bar, pool* ▤ *AE, DC, MC, V* ⦿ *MAP.*

NATIONAL PARKS ACCOMMODATIONS

$–$$$ 🖭 **Halali.** Etosha's smallest national park self-catering camp, and often the quietest, is rather barracklike and dusty, but if you're a bird-watcher, it merits a giant check mark on your list. Rare violet woodhoopoes and bare-cheeked babblers frequent the camp, and if you walk up the rocky path to the pleasant floodlighted water hole and are prepared to sit and wait, there's a good chance you'll spot lions, elephants, and black rhinos. Halali, which is roughly halfway between Okuakuejo and Namutoni, is in the only area of the park with hills. ⊠*Namibia Wildlife Resorts, Independence Ave., opposite Zoo Park, Windhoek, Namibia* ☎*061/23–6975 or 061/23–6978, 067/22–9400 Halali* ⊕*www.nwr. com.na* 🛏*60 huts, 2 cottages* ⚐*In-room: a/c. In-hotel: restaurant, pool* ☰*MC, V* ⊗*Closed Nov.–mid-Mar.*

$–$$$ 🏨**Namutoni Rest Camp.** On the eastern edge of the park and resembling something out of the novel and films *Beau Geste*, this restored colonial fort with its flying flag and graceful palm trees is the most picturesque of the national-park camps. Hearing the bugle call from the watchtower at sunrise and sunset, you almost expect to see the French Foreign Legion come galloping over the horizon. The historic rooms are tiny—the troops didn't live all that well—so if it's comfort rather than history you're after, don't choose a fort room; opt instead for one of the fully equipped bungalows, built at a respectful distance from the fort so as not to destroy the ambience. Directly behind the fort is a floodlighted water hole for game-viewing. ⊠*Namibia Wildlife Resorts, Independence Ave., opposite Zoo Park, Windhoek, Namibia* ☎*061/23–6975 or 061/23–6978, 067/22–9800 Namutoni* ⊕*www.nwr.com.na* 🛏*18 bungalows, 10 rooms, 1 apartment, 4 cottages, 4 dormitories* ⚐*In-room: a/c, refrigerator. In-hotel: restaurant, pool* ☰*MC, V.*

$–$$$ 🏨**Okaukuejo.** On the western side of Etosha, this is the biggest and noisiest national-park camp (the noise comes from the staff quarters), and the staff could certainly do with a few workshops on how to deal with the public in a pleasant way. But its floodlighted water hole—regarded as one of the finest in Africa—more than makes up for any inconvenience. Climb the spiral staircase to the top of the round tower for a good view of the surrounding countryside, and then settle down to an all-night game-watching vigil. Pleasantly furnished, spotlessly clean accommodations range from basic two-bed huts with communal facilities to large, fully equipped eight-bed cottages. There are mail facilities at the camp as well as a place to fill up the tank and a store to stock up on provisions. ⊠*Namibia Wildlife Resorts, Independence Ave., opposite Zoo Park, Windhoek, Namibia* ☎*061/23–6975 through 061/23–6978, 067/22–9800 Okaukuejo* ⊕*resafrica.net/ okaukuejo* 🛏*70 chalets, 40 double rooms* ⚐*In-room: a/c, kitchen (some), refrigerator. In-hotel: restaurant, pool* ☰*MC, V.*

Ongava Lodge

Halali

Namutoni

Namibia's Tribes

HERERO

The Herero came to Namibia during the 17th century from East Africa. They are traditionally pastoralists; cattle playing a major role in their nomadic lifestyle. Today, though, most Herero are farmers, merchants, or professionals in Namibia's urban hubs. Herero women (pictured above) are known for full-length colorful gowns and unique, wide-brimmed hats. Ironically, this style of dress was adopted from missionaries that introduced German colonial rule in the early part of the 20th century. The Herero-German War (1904–07) was a cruel episode in the history of Southern Africa as German military policy was to annihilate or confine Herero to labor camps so Europeans could establish farms. Issues regarding the treatment of the Herero during this time are still being battled out in the legal system: the German government has issued an official apology, but the Herero feel they deserve more for the death of an estimated 65,000 people, and are seeking financial reparations through the international courts.

HIMBA

A matriarchal tribe closely related to the Herero, the Himba are famous for covering their faces and hair with a light mixture of ochre, herbs, and animal fat to shield them from the hot sun. They wear very little clothing due to the harsh desert climate. The tribe lives mainly in the Kunene region of northern Namibia and like the Herero, the Himba are a nomadic people who breed cattle as well as goats. Himba women do most of the work in the tribe—they bear children, take care of the children, tend to the livestock, and even build homes. In the 1980s and '90s, Himba culture was endangered due to severe draught and the war in nearby Angola. Recently they've had to battle modernization with the proposed hydro-electric dam, which threatens to flood their homesteads and destroy their pastures. However, with help from the international community, the Himba have been successful at blocking the dam and have managed to maintain control of their land and their traditions.

IF YOU HAVE TIME

While we've gone into great detail about the must-see parks in Namibia, there is one other spot worth exploring if you have time.

THE SKELETON COAST

This wildly beautiful but dangerous shore, one-third of Namibia's western coastline, stretches from the Ugab River in the south to the Kunene River, the border with Angola, in the north. The Portuguese seafarers who explored this area in the 15th century called this treacherous coast with its cold Benguela current and deadly crosscurrents the "Coast of Death." Its newer, no-less-sinister name, the Skeleton Coast, testifies to innumerable shipwrecks, to lives lost, to bleached whale bones, and to the insignificant, transient nature of puny humans in the face of the raw power of nature. Still comparatively unknown to tourists, this region has a stark beauty and an awesomely diverse landscape—gray gravel plains, rugged wilderness, rusting shipwrecks, desert wastes, meandering barchan dunes, distant mountains, towering walls of sand and granite, and crashing seas. You'll rarely see more than a handful of visitors in this inaccessible and rugged coastal area. This is not an easy ride, as distances are vast, amenities scarce or nonexistent, and the roads demanding. Don't exceed 80 kph (50 mph) on the gravel roads, and never drive off the road on the ecologically vulnerable salt pans and lichen fields. It takes decades for them to regenerate.

Skeleton Coast National Park extends along this rugged Atlantic coast and about 40 km (25 mi) inland; the 200-km (125-mi) stretch of coast from Swakopmund to the Ugab River is named National West Coast Tourist Recreational Area. You can drive along a coastal road right up to Terrace Bay, and for the first 250 km (155 mi) from Swakopmund north to Terrace Bay you'll find not sand dunes, but glinting gravel plains and scattered rocks. Stop and sift a handful of gravel: you may well find garnets and crystals among the tiny stones. In other places the plains are carpeted with lichens—yellow, red, orange, and many shades of green. In the early morning these lichen fields look lushly attractive, but during the heat of midday they seem dried up and insignificant. But don't whiz by. Stop and pour a drop of water on the lichens and watch a small miracle as they unfurl and come alive. If you're a birder, then the salt pans on the way from Swakopmund to Henties Bay are worth a visit; you might spot a rare migrant wader there. The famous Namibian oysters are farmed here in sea ponds—don't leave Namibia without tasting these. The surreal little seaside holiday town of Henties Bay is like a deserted Hollywood back lot in winter, but in summer is full of holidaying Namibian fisherfolk from Swakopmund, Windhoek, and Tsumeb hoping to catch kabeljou and steenbras.

PARK ESSENTIALS

If you are only passing through, you can buy a permit (N$20 per adult, N$20 per car) at the gate. For a longer trip you must obtain a permit in advance from Namibia Wildlife Resorts (⊕ *www.nwr.com.na*).

You'll smell the hundreds of thousands of Cape fur seals (*Arctocephalus pusillus pusillus*) at the Cape Cross seal colony, north of Henties Bay, long before you get there, but stifle your gags and go goggle at the seething mass on land and in the water. If you visit in late November or early December, you can ooh and aah at the furry baby seal pups, as well as the marauding jackals looking for a fast-food snack. Farther north the dunes begin, ending only in the north at the Kunene River, Namibia's border with Angola. This northern stretch of coast from the Ugab River to the Kunene River is managed by the government as a wilderness area and accounts for one-third of Namibia's coastline. But if it's lush green pastures and abundance of game you want, then this raw, rugged, harsh, and uncompromising landscape is not for you. What you will find are dramatically different scenery—big skies and unending horizons—an absence of tourists ("crowds" around here means one or two vehicles), and some wildlife: brown hyenas, springbok, oryx, jackals, and, if you're really lucky, a cheetah or rhino. The sight of a majestic oryx silhouetted against towering sand dunes or a cheeky jackal scavenging seal pups on the beaches is extremely rewarding. The best activity, however, is just concentrating on the freedom, beauty, and strange solitude of the area. You can drive (a 4x4 gives you more flexibility) from Swakopmund north through Henties Bay via the Ugab Gate, with its eerie painted skulls and crossbones on the gates, or from the more northerly Springbokwater Gate. You must reach your gate of entry before 3 PM. Always stick to the marked roads and avoid driving on treacherous salt pans. Look out for an unusual wreck lying next to the road between the Ugab River and Terrace Bay; it's an abandoned 1960s oil rig, now home to a huge colony of cormorants.

The Uniab River valley, between Torra Bay and Terrace Bay, is your best chance of spotting big game such as rhino and occasionally elephants. Once you get to Terrace Bay, 287 km (178 mi) north of Henties Bay, that's the end of your car trip. It's the last outpost. If you want to explore further, then a fly-in safari is your only option.

WHERE TO STAY

LUXURY LODGES

$$$$ 🏕 **Serra Cafema.** This astonishingly different and dramatically sited
Fodor'sChoice   camp in the extreme northwest of Namibia, on the Angolan border, is
★   the most remote camp in Southern Africa. After a dry, dusty, but magnificently beautiful drive from the airstrip, you are guaranteed to gasp with awe as you first catch sight of the camp from a high sand dune. Built amid a grove of ancient albida trees on the banks of the wide Kunene River, it seems like a desert mirage. Only the nomadic Himba people share this area, and a visit to a local village is an eye-opening experience and one of the highlights of a stay here. Another day, ride a quad bike over the billowing sand dunes and spot the Atlantic from a high vantage point. Although tents (on raised platforms) are ultraluxurious and have private bathrooms, don't come here if you aren't tough. The flight from Windhoek is long and bumpy, and the terrain harsh and demanding, but the experience—staying by a wide river in the midst of the oldest desert in the world—is almost surreal. This is one-of-a-

CLOSE UP

From Portugal to the Skeleton Coast

More than 500 years ago, a daring little band of Portuguese sailors, inspired by the vision of their charismatic leader, Prince Henry the Navigator—who, contrary to what you might expect from his name, never left his native land—set sail from the School of Navigation at Sagres, the farthest western point of Europe, to find fame, fortune, and new lands for the Crown. Facing unknown dangers and terra incognita (the maps of the time were little more than fanciful sketchbooks filled with dragons and warnings that "here be monsters"), the intrepid sailors pushed back the edges of the known world nautical mile by mile until they entered the waters of the southwest coastline of Africa on tiny,

frail caravels. In 1485, Captain Diego Cão and his battered crew finally dropped anchor off a desolate beach thousands of miles from home and safety. There, on the lonely windswept sands, they erected a cross both in honor of their heavenly king, whom they credited with protecting and directing them during their arduous journey, as well as to King John I, their earthly monarch. North of Swakopmund, as you marvel at thousands upon thousands of the Cape fur seals at Cape Cross, you can see a replica of that cross (the original is in the Berlin Oceanographic Museum). Sadly, the courageous Captain Cão never made it home: he is buried nearby on a rocky outcrop.

kind Africa. Stay for three nights to make the most of the experience: go walking, boating, birding, or quad biking; do a nature drive; or just sit by the rushing river and contemplate. ⌂ *Wilderness Safaris, Box 5219, Rivonia 2128, South Africa* ☎*27/11/807–1800 South Africa* ⊕*www.wilderness-safaris.com* ⇄*8 tents* ⌂*In-hotel: bar, pool* ⊟*AE, DC, MC, V* ⧖*FAP.*

PERMANENT TENTED CAMPS

$$$$ ▣ **Skeleton Coast Camp.** If you long for a remote wilderness area, con-
★ sider a three-night safari into this desolate camp in 660,000 acres of the northern part of Skeleton Coast National Park. You sleep under canvas in an elegantly furnished tent with your own small deck and awesome desert view and eat in the open-air dining room under an ancient lead-wood tree. You visit an authentic Himba settlement, picnic beside the crashing Atlantic, and drive through oryx-studded plains and shifting sand dunes with their desert birds. The days are long—you leave camp after breakfast as the morning mists drift from the coastline and don't return until after sunset—but they are packed so full of excitement and beauty that your head will still be spinning as you fall into your comfortable bed after a splendid dinner. Departures are from Windhoek every Wednesday and Saturday. ⌂ *Wilderness Safaris, Box 5219, Rivonia 2128, South Africa* ☎*27/11/807–1800 South Africa* ⊕*www. wilderness-safaris.com* ⇄*5 tents* ⊟*AE, DC, MC, V* ⧖*FAP.*

NATIONAL PARKS ACCOMMODATION

$$$ ▣ **Terrace Bay.** An isolated outpost and government resort and the northernmost point in the park to which you can drive, this may well be the most remote spot on earth you ever visit. Surrounded by gravel

plains, it's a popular spot for anglers and people who want to get to know the desert. Don't miss the surprising Uniab River delta—a lush green oasis in a miniature canyon a couple of miles from Terrace Bay. It's also a good stop if you're going on into Damaraland. The accommodations, once part of a diamond-mining operation, are simple and basic, though each bungalow has a refrigerator, shower, and toilet. The four-room Presidential Suite has all the modern conveniences, including air-conditioning and a fully equipped kitchen. All meals are provided, and there's a small shop that stocks basics. The resort does not accommodate day visitors. ⊠*Namibia Wildlife Resorts, Independence Ave., opposite Zoo Park, Windhoek, Namibia* ☎*061/23–6975 or 061/23–6978* ⊕*www.nwr.com.na* ♿*In-room: a/c (some), refrigerator. In-hotel: restaurant, bar* ☐*MC, V* ⦿*FAP.*

BUDGET ACCOMMODATION

¢   🔭**De Duine Country Hotel.** Gleaming white in the harsh sun, the low flat buildings of this holiday lodging in Henties Bay suggest a Foreign Legion fort rather than a family hotel, although the minute you hear the crashing surf you'll know this is not the Sahara. The small basic rooms are comfortable, but the big attraction here is the coastline, reputed to offer some of the best deep-sea fishing in the world. Some of Namibia's top tourist attractions are all within easy reach: Brandberg, Spitzkoppe, the Cape Cross seal colony, and farther south, Swakopmund. The hotel will organize excursions for you if you don't want to drive yourself. During peak holiday season, the public bar jumps with locals and tourists making the most of the billiard table and slots. The à la carte restaurant serves some of the finest seafood anywhere—try the legendary crayfish—and on Sunday there's a sumptuous lunch buffet. ⊠*34 Duine Rd., Henties Bay* ⬠*Box 1, Henties Bay, Namibia* ☎*064/50–0001* ⊕*www.namibialodges.com* ⤸*20 rooms* ♿*In-hotel: room service, bar, pool* ☐*MC, V* ⦿*BP.*

CAPRIVI STRIP

This lovely unspoiled area—one of Namibia's best-kept secrets—lies in northeast Namibia (and is sometimes simply referred to as northeast Namibia) at the confluence of the Zambezi and Chobe rivers and serves as a gateway to Zimbabwe's Victoria Falls and Botswana's Chobe National Park. Because it's relatively unknown as a tourist area, you'll get the feeling here that you are truly alone with nature.

Think of the Caprivi Strip as a long finger of land at the top of the country pointing eastward for 450 km (280 mi) toward Zimbabwe and Zambia; in many ways, because of its rivers, marshes, and forests, the area is much more like those countries than the rest of Namibia. This part of Namibia is the closest thing to Botswana's Okavango Delta, and it shelters much of the same game: elephants, the aquatic lechwe and the rare sitatunga antelope, the uncommon roan and sable antelopes, and, hardly ever seen in Namibia, big buffalo herds. However, you're unlikely to see predators.

This corridor of land became strategically important when Germany annexed South West Africa (now Namibia) in 1884. The British, concerned about further German colonial expansion up into Africa, struck a deal with Khama, a local Bechuana king, and formed the British Protectorate of Bechuanaland (now Botswana). The Caprivi Strip was part of the deal. It was then shuttled back and forth between Britain and Germany until it finally passed into the hands of South Africa at the end of World War II. However, its troubles were far from over, and during the Namibian struggle for independence, the area became the scene of bitter fighting between Sam Nujoma's freedom fighters (Sam Nujoma became the first president of Namibia in 1990) and the South African Defence Force (SADF). Today, the game that was scared away is back, the area is once again peaceful, and it's a relatively little-known and little-visited destination by overseas tourists. If you've seen your Big Five and your classic desert and are looking for somewhere offbeat, then this is a great destination.

You've got to be fairly determined to get here because the journey can be circuitous, to say the least. You can fly in to Katimo Mulilo, the vibey little main town (which is closer to Gaborone, Botswana, or Lusaka, Zambia, then it is to Windhoek), pick up a vehicle, and drive. Visit the Caprivi Art Centre near the African market where you'll find beautifully crafted baskets, carvings, and handmade pottery. There's a main road across the strip, the B8 (euphemistically called the Golden Highway), but it's often crowded with commercial traffic to and from Zambia and Botswana. Or you can fly into Livingstone in Zambia, cross the border post into Botswana, and then go by road and river to your chosen lodge. (To give you some idea: to get to Susuwe Island Lodge, you fly from Johannesburg into Livingstone, then take a small plane to the Namibian immigration post at Katimo Mulilo, then fly to the Immelman airstrip nearby, the once infamous Doppies SADF forward base, and travel by road and river to the lodge.) However you get here, the destination is well worth every last mile for a remote, water-wilderness experience. Your best bet is to choose a lodge and then let it make all your travel arrangements for you.

Neither the Caprivi Strip's Mudumu National Park or Mahango National Park is particularly accessible—particularly in the wet season—but if you're a do-it-yourself adventure type, you might enjoy a visit to either park. The best time to visit is July–October. You'll see plenty of game, including hippos, elephants, buffalo, roan and sable antelope, kudu, zebra, and maybe even wild dogs. Mahango is great for bird-watching, with more species than any other Namibian park.

WHERE TO STAY

LUXURY LODGES

$$$$ ⬚ **Chobe Savanna Lodge.** This luxury lodge lies on the banks of the Chobe River, overlooking Chobe National Park. Each North Africa–inspired stone-and-thatch cottage has a private deck and bathroom. Cream-textured linen, vases of dried grasses, polished wooden floors, handcrafted furniture, and handwoven cream-and-brown rugs provide a comfortable and elegant haven. Cruise the wide river game-spotting,

bird-watching, or just soaking up an awesome sunset; take a guided game walk through the unspoiled bush; or just sit on the viewing deck, with its magnificent views of the floodplains and river, and watch scores of elephants and buffalos mooching about. *Desert & Delta Safaris, Box 130555, Bryanston 2125, South Africa* ☎*27/11/706–0861 South Africa* ⊕*www.desertdelta.co.za* ➲*12 cottages* ⚴*In-room: a/c. In-hotel: bar, pool* ▤*MC, V* ¶OI*FAP.*

$$$$ ⬚ **Lianshulu Lodge.** This lovely old lodge, which sprawls under huge jackalberry and mangosteen trees along the banks of the Kwando River, bordering Botswana, was one of the first private lodges to be built inside a national park—Mudumu National Park. Considered for many years one of the best lodges in Namibia, it offers a splendid water-wilderness experience—from chugging down the Kwando in a double-decker pontoon, sipping sundowners as the boat dodges hippos and crocs, to tiger-fishing, game cruises, and superb birding with more than 400 recorded species. A night cruise on the river is particularly exciting. Accommodation is in en-suite A-frame thatch-and-brick chalets; the food is outstanding (there's a resident chef), and the personal service memorable. You can visit the nearby Lizauli traditional village, built and managed by the local community. Because an immigration official lives at the lodge, you can easily cross into Botswana. *Box 142, Katimo Mulilo, Namibia* ☎*065/48–3702* ⊕*www.lianshulu.com. na* ➲*10 chalets, 1 family unit* ⚴*In-hotel: restaurant, bar, pool* ▤*AE, DC, MC, V* ¶OI*FAP.*

$$$ ⬚ **Impalila Island Lodge.** At the crossroads of four countries—Namibia, Botswana, Zambia, and Zimbabwe—this all-inclusive lodge is famous for its hospitality, accommodations, food, and activities. Raised wood-and-thatch chalets, furnished with polished local mukwa wood, open onto wide verandas overlooking the Mambova Rapids at the confluence of the Zambezi and Chobe rivers. The main thatched dining and bar area is built around two huge baobab trees. After your day's activities, relax on the wooden deck and boast about your tiger-fishing skills, or tick off your mammal and bird lists. Don't miss a guided boat trip to the banks of Botswana's Chobe National Park for game-viewing, or a tranquil *mokoro* (canoe) trip in the papyrus-fringed channels. *Islands in Africa Safaris, Box 70378, Bryanston 2021, South Africa* ☎*27/11/706–7207 South Africa* ⊕*www.islandsinafrica.com* ➲*8 chalets* ⚴*In-hotel: pool* ▤*DC, MC, V* ¶OI*FAP.*

$$$ ⬚ **Ntwala Island Lodge.** East of Susuwe Island Lodge is the breathtaking,
★ daringly beautiful Ntwala Island Lodge. Only 80 km (50 mi) upstream from Victoria Falls, the four art deco–meets-Africa chalets are built on an untouched Namibian cluster of small islands linked by floating wooden walkways. You can fly in from Namibia or Botswana, but there's also a road option. Drive to Kasane in Botswana, and then board a small boat that skirts rapids and dodges hippos as it takes you to your very own Treasure Island. A gray, mosaic-edge, kidney-shape pool surrounded by white sand shimmers outside your cream-color, tile-roof chalet, just a couple of yards from the rushing Zambezi. The braying of trumpeter hornbills, the liquid notes of the robins, and the startled calls of francolins greet you. The chalets are spectacular by any stan-

dard, with huge rooms, circular wooden canopies echoing the circular bed platforms, carved half-moon chests, handwrought light fittings of metal feathers, and bathrooms big enough to host a party. Freestanding canvas and wooden screens are topped by metal Prince-of-Wales's feathers, matching the metal curlicued towel rails and bath accessories trolley. Try your hand at tiger-fishing, marvel at the industry of the reed cormorants as they continuously crisscross the sky carrying nesting material to their heronry, or watch the sunset herds of elephants and buffalo, the unique Chobe bushbuck, a group of impala, and if you're really lucky, in the dry season, some thirsty lions. 🖉 *Islands in Africa Safaris, Box 70378, Bryanston 2021, South Africa* ☎ *27/11/706–7207 South Africa* ⊕ *www.islandsinafrica.com* ⇔ *6 chalets* ⚲ *In-hotel: pool* ⊟ *DC, MC, V* ⦿ *FAP.*

$$$ 🏠 **Susuwe Island Lodge.** This is classic Africa, a solid structure of wood and stone built before the designer-chic lodge invasion. This six-chalet lodge is at the eastern end of the Caprivi Strip (before the strip broadens and widens on its way to Botswana) on a small island in a teak forest. Here, the deep, clear waters of the Kwando River lap the island's edges, and swamp boubous whistle their melodious calls. Take the time to climb to the highest viewing deck—up in that bird-rich canopy your inner spirit will be restored. A brass lizard, frozen in time, scurries up a wooden stair rail, while a long-lashed giraffe with bead earrings adorns the outside of one door. Two mokoros act as bookcases; a tiny, tiled elephant watches you from a corner of the stone floor; and in your emperor-size chalet, you'll find candles in carved logs, faded kilims, and a personal plunge pool beside the rushing river. This river trip is one you won't likely forget. Though elephants are around, this is not Big Five country; it's a place to unwind, which is a perfect way to end a safari. 🖉 *Islands in Africa Safaris, Box 70378, Bryanston 2021, South Africa* ☎ *27/11/706–7207 South Africa* ⊕ *www.islandsinafrica. com* ⇔ *6 chalets* ⚲ *In-hotel: pool* ⊟ *DC, MC, V* ⦿ *FAP.*

BUDGET LODGINGS

$$ 🏠 **Zambezi Lodge.** Just 2 km (1 mi) from Katimo Mulilo, this is the area's best hotel, where the rooms spread along the banks of the Zambezi River amid colorful bougainvillea bushes and flame trees. But far from the traditional sounds of Africa, the sounds you are most likely to hear are rap, hip-hop, and hard rock from the radios in the Zambian riverside villages just across the river. It's a convenient stopover offering clean, comfortable, tiled rooms with windows and double doors facing the river. (Look for the Cape clawless otters playing in the river.) Food is quick and palatable, but don't hold your breath for something special. Short cruises on the river are available. There's an interesting floating bar, but it's only open 4–7 PM. 🖉 *Box 2061, Katima Mulilo, Namibia* ☎ *66/25–3149* ⊕ *www.proteahotels.com* ⇔ *27 chalets* ⚲ *In-room: a/c. In-hotel: pool* ⊟ *DC, MC, V* ⦿ *BP.*

WATERBERG PLATEAU PARK

This lovely game reserve, established in 1972 when several rare and endangered species were introduced from other areas of Namibia and South Africa, is one of the most peaceful and relatively unknown wilderness areas in Namibia. About 91 km (56 mi) east of Otjiwarongo, it's also an ideal stopover on the way from Windhoek to Etosha. The plateau is a huge, flat-top massif rising abruptly from the surrounding plain and offering superb views of the park, the outstanding rock formations, and the magnitude of the plateau itself. Edged with steep-sided, rugged, reddish-brown cliffs, the plateau is covered with red Kalahari sand that supports a range of dry woodland vegetation, from the red syringa trees and Kalahari apple leaf to the kudu bush. You're not allowed to drive yourself, but game-viewing tours operate every morning and evening from the beautifully landscaped Bernabé de la Bat Rest Camp (book in advance; you can join a tour even if you're not a guest of the camp). Although you won't see the big numbers of game that you'll find in Etosha, you could spot the rare roan and sable antelope, Cape buffalo, white and black rhinos, giraffes, hyenas, leopards, and cheetahs. But game-spotting is not an exact science, so there are no guarantees. The park is a wonderful place to hike, whether on the much-sought-after three-day accompanied Waterberg Wilderness Trail (book through Bernabé de la Bat Rest Camp in advance) or on a short 3-km (2-mi) walk round camp.

WHERE TO STAY

NATIONAL PARKS ACCOMMODATIONS

$ ⚏ **Bernabé de la Bat Rest Camp.** Located on the escarpment's wooded slopes, you can take a dip in the camp's natural-spring-fed swimming pool at the foot of the towering sandstone cliffs, then relax in front of your bungalow and watch the sun set over the plateau. Surrounding the camp is one of the largest varieties of plant species in Southern Africa. It's best to book accommodations in advance at MET in Windhoek, although you can take a chance (particularly in the low season) and book when you arrive at the park office between 8 AM and sunset. ⌂ *Ministry of Wildlife, Conservation and Tourism (MET), Private Bag 13306, Windhoek 9000, Namibia* ☎ *061/23–6975* ⊕ *www.met.gov.na* ➴ *35 bungalows* ⌂ *In-hotel: restaurant, pool* ⊟ *DC, MC, V.*

GATEWAY CITY

It's very likely that you'll have to take a connecting flight through Windhoek, Namibia's capital city, on route to your safari destination. In fact you may have to spend an overnight here. The following information will help you plan where to stay and eat and what to visit.

WINDHOEK

The pleasant little capital city of Windhoek lies almost exactly in the center of the country and is surrounded by the Khomas Highland and the Auas and Eros Mountains. It is much more European than African in feel, with lots of colonial architecture, sidewalk cafés, and friendly bars. Settled by the Germans in the 1890s, it's an easy town to explore on foot, and there are several places of interest near one another—and only a few easy hills to climb. The city has a population of about 200,000 and growing and it's home to the country's brewing industry—a holdover from its days as a German colony.

WHAT TO SEE

1 Christuskirche. The Lutheran Christ Church is German colonial architecture at its best—a mixture of art nouveau and neo-Gothic dating from 1896. Although the church is generally locked, you can obtain a key from the nearby church office at 12 Fidel Castro Street (down the hill from the church). ⊠ *Robert Mugabe Ave.* ☎ *061/288–2627* ⊙ *Church office weekdays 7:30–1.*

3 Namibia Crafts Centre. On Tal Street in the old breweries building behind the Kalahari Sands and Casino hotel, the Namibia Crafts Centre has dozens of stalls showcasing the work of more than 1,500 rural craftspeople. Look for striking and original handmade African outfits, beautifully woven baskets, distinct Caprivian pots, wood carvings, exquisite embroidery, jewelry, marula oils and soaps, and much more. ⊠ *Tal St.* ☎ *061/242–2222* ⊙ *Weekdays 9–5:30, Sat. 9–1:30.*

2 Post St. Mall. At this open-air market known for its colorful sidewalk displays of curios, crafts, and carvings of all kinds, international tourists and businesspeople rub shoulders with Herero women in full traditional Victorian dress. Keep an eye out for the meteorites mounted on slender steel columns. These meteorites hit the earth during the Gibeon meteorite shower, which rained down some 600 million years ago, the heaviest such shower known on earth. ⊠ *Post St.* ⊙ *Mon.–Sat. 9–5* .

WHERE TO STAY & EAT

¢–$$$$ ✕ **Fürstenhof Restaurant.** Some of Windhoek's best food is served at this restaurant, where the chef combines German and French nouvelle techniques with local ingredients. Try Namibian saddle of springbok or any of the chef's specials, followed by homemade cheesecake. Light lunches and breakfast are served in the casual yet elegant bistro. A jacket and tie are appropriate for dinner (although they are not required). The restaurant is in Hotel Fürstenhof, which is a five-minute walk from Windhoek's business district. The 33 rooms ($$) have a/c and en-suite bathrooms, and there's a pool in the hotel. ⊠ *Corner of Bulow St. and Hosea Kutako Dr., Windermere* ☎ *061/23–7380* ⊕ *www.proteahotels. com* ⌂ *Reservations essential* ⊟ *AE, DC, MC, V.*

¢–$$$$ ✕ **Joe's Beerhouse.** Tuck into generous portions of superb German and
☾ Namibian food at this popular Windhoek landmark. Venison is a specialty (try the kudu steak or gemsbok fillet), but if the Teutonic urge strikes, opt for the sauerkraut and pork fillet. Vegetarian food is also available. Although the interior is fun-filled with Joe's personal collection of memorabilia, it's also pleasant to sit outside in the boma by a roaring fire and quaff *glüwein* (mulled wine) or a local lager. There's a great play area for kids. ⊠ *160 Nelson Mandela Ave.* ☎ *061/23–2457* ⊕ *www.joesbeerhouse.com* ⌂ *Reservations essential* ⊟ *AE, DC, MC, V.*

$ ▦ **Kalahari Sands and Casino.** Known locally as the Sands, this is where England's Queen Elizabeth and Prince Philip stayed in 1990, the year of Namibia's independence. That said, the rooms are pleasant but bland (it's one of those hotels where you could be anywhere in the world), but it's the hotel's central location that wins it brownie points. ⊠ *22 Independence Ave., Windhoek, Namibia* ☎ *061/22–2300* ⊕ *www.sunin-ternational.com* ⇌ *167 rooms, 5 suites* ⌂ *In-room: a/c, safe. In-hotel: restaurant, bar, pool, gym, Internet* ⊟ *AE, DC, MC, V* ⏵*BP.*

$ ▦ **The Hilltop House.** Perched on a hill up a quiet winding road in the pleasant suburb of Klein Windhoek, this lovingly restored colonial-style home has splendid views of Windhoek and the surrounding mountains. The spacious rooms are stylishly furnished with handcrafted Knysna blackwood furniture, cream fabrics, African artifacts, and wildlife paintings. Choose between the health-conscious breakfast or a full English one served in the comfort of your own room or on the pool patio. Light lunches and dinners are available on request. ⊠ *12 Lessing St., Klein Windhoek, Namibia* ☎ *061/24–9116* ⇌ *6 rooms* ⌂ *In-room: a/c, refrigerator. In-hotel: bar, pool* ⊟ *AE, DC, MC, V* ⏵*BP.*

$ ▦ **Hotel Heinitzburg.** This is your chance to stay in a turn-of-the-20th-century castle, a white fort with battlements set high on a hill and commissioned by a German count for his fiancée in 1914. The spacious interiors, handmade furniture, and antiques will transport you to a stylish bygone age, and the hotel has amazing views over the city. The excellent food and wine are what you might expect of a Relais & Château property. Book well in advance, as this is the most sought-after

CLOSE UP

Windhoek's Historic Buildings

You'll find several historic buildings very close by Christ Church. Walk along the tree-lined avenue behind the church to the handsome, circa-1912 **Tintenpalast** (*Palace of Ink* ✉*Robert Mugabe Ave.* ☎*061/ 288–2583*), which is fronted by beautiful formal gardens. Formerly the administration offices of the German colonial government, the two-story building now houses the National Assembly. One-hour tours are given weekdays at 9, 10, and 3. Next to the Tintenpalast is the **Office of the Prime Minister**, attractively decorated in indigenous woods, marble, and copper. The Parliament Gardens are a few minutes' walk away on the same

street. As you stroll around Parliament Gardens look out for the Yebo Gallery in the **John Muafangejo Art Centre** (John Muafangejo was Namibia's most famous artist), where young artists work; the center is open weekdays 9–5. The 1890 **Alte Feste Museum**, with its Foreign Legion charm and historical displays on Namibia, is the oldest building in the city; it once garrisoned the first contingent of German colonial troops. To get here from the John Muafangejo Art Centre, walk up the hill along Robert Mugabe Avenue. ✉*Robert Mugabe Ave.* ☎*061/293– 4362* 🎟*Free* ☾*Weekdays 9–6, weekends 10–12:30 and 3–6.*

hotel in the city. ✉*22 Heinitzburg St., Windhoek, Namibia* ☎*061/24– 9597* ⊕*www.heinitzburg.com* ⇆*16 rooms, 1 suite* ⎈*In-room: a/c, safe. In-hotel: restaurant, bar, pool, gym, spa, Internet* ⊟*AE, DC, MC, V* ⊠*BP.*

WINDHOEK ESSENTIALS

TRANSPORTATION

BY AIR Namibia's main point of entry is Hosea Kutako International Airport. It's a small, bustling, modern airport that's a splendidly scenic 45-km (28-mi) drive from Windhoek. The smaller Eros Airport handles local flights and charters. Once in the country you can make use of scheduled flights or charter flights that service all domestic destinations.

There's frequent bus service from Hosea Kutako International Airport to Windhoek's city center; the pickup and drop-off point is opposite the Kalahari Sands and Casino, on Independence Avenue. Expect to pay N$100 each way. Many larger hotels run a courtesy shuttle service to and from the airport. Taxis are available, but negotiate the price before you get in. Check on current fares at the airport information counter.

For information on air service to Windhoek, see Namibia Essentials, below.

Airports Eros Airport (☎*061/23–8220*). **Hosea Kutako International Airport** (☎*062/54–0271*).

BY BUS Intercape Mainliner runs buses between Windhoek and Swakopmund.

Bus Line Intercape Mainliner (☎*064/20–2867* ⊕*www.intercape.co.za*).

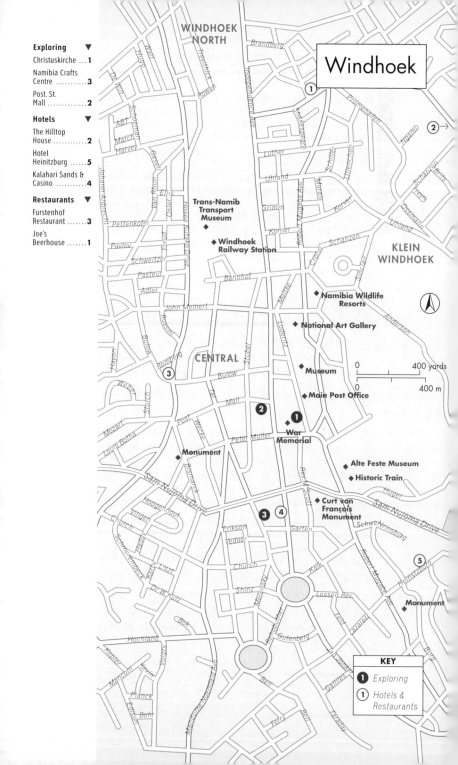

Windhoek

**WINDHOEK
NORTH**

**KLEIN
WINDHOEK**

CENTRAL

Trans-Namib
Transport
Museum

Windhoek
Railway Station

Namibia Wildlife
Resorts

National Art Gallery

Museum

Main Post Office

War
Memorial

Monument

Alte Feste Museum

Historic Train

Curt von
François
Monument

Monument

0   400 yards

0   400 m

KEY

❶ *Exploring*

① *Hotels &
Restaurants*

BY CAR If you're only in Windhoek for 24 hours or so, you won't need a car. It's an easy city to walk around, and taxis are available everywhere. Always negotiate with the driver before getting into the taxi. Hotels also provide shuttle service.

That said, if you plan to drive to Swakopmund or any of the parks, you can rent a car here. Gas is on sale in all towns, but if you are planning a long journey between towns, fill up in Windhoek before you leave.

Rental Companies Avis (☎ *061/233–166* ⊕ *www.avis.co.za*). **Budget** (☎ *061/228–720* ⊕ *www.budget.co.za*). **Hertz** (☎ *061/255–4115* ⊕ *www.hertz.co.za*).

BY TRAIN If you've got three days or so to spare and you're headed to or from the coastal resort of Swakopmund, then consider traveling on the Desert Express. The train departs from Windhoek on Tuesday and Friday, and from Swakopmund on Wednesday and Saturday. Your first stop on the outward journey from Windhoek is Okapuka Ranch, where you'll watch lions being fed, after which you get back on the train and enjoy a splendid dinner yourself. The train parks in a siding for the night, then leaves early in the morning so you can catch a spectacular sunrise over the desert. Later, you get a chance to walk in the Namib when the train stops in the dunes between Swapkopmund and Walvis Bay. If you do the return journey, you'll be taken to see the San rock paintings at Spitzkoppe. The train has 24 air-conditioned, small but comfortable cabins with en-suite facilities. Longer journeys to Etosha and Lüderitz are available.

7

Train Information **Desert Express** (✉ *Windhoek Railway Station, Bahnhof St.Windhoek* ☎ *061/298–2600* ⊕ *www.desertexpress.com.na*).

CONTACTS & RESOURCES

BUSINESS SERVICES & FACILITIES The Kalahari Sands and Casino hotel has a business center, and most of the bigger hotels have wireless Internet. Hotel staff can also direct you to the nearest Internet café. The main post office is next to the clock tower on Independence Avenue. Sending packages from Windhoek is cheap, easy, and reliable.

DAY TOURS African Extravaganza specializes in shuttle services, scheduled safaris, charter tours and fly-ins, self-drive options, day excursions, and transfers. But as Windhoek is a small town, easy to walk around in, your best bet is to stay in the city and see what's going on there. Ask your hotel concierge or guesthouse owner for up-to-date information.

Tour Operator **African Extravaganza** (☎ *061/37–2100* ⊕ *www.african-extravaganza.com*).

EMERGENCIES If you need medical attention in Windhoek, consider the Medi-Clinic, an excellent private clinic, or the Catholic Mission Hospital. Ask at your accommodation for the nearest pharmacy.

Hospitals **Catholic Mission Hospital** (✉ *92 Stubel St.* ☎ *061/23–7237*). **Medi-Clinic** (✉ *Heliodoor St., Eros Park* ☎ *061/22–2687*).

HOURS OF OPERATION *See Namibia Essentials, below, for information on business hours.*

MONEY *See Namibia Essentials, below, for information on money.*

RESTROOMS Stick to hotel restrooms.

SAFETY Pickpockets work the city center, particularly the markets and the Post Street Mall. Lock your valuables away in the hotel safe, and carry only what you need. Never travel with expensive jewelry. Don't walk alone at night, and stick to well-lighted areas.

VISITOR INFORMATION Namibia Tourism has information on Windhoek as well as the rest of Namibia. It's open weekdays 8–1 and 2–5.

The Tourist Information Bureau at the Post Street Mall can provide information on Windhoek and environs; it's open weekdays 7:30–1 and 2–4:30. The bureau operates a kiosk on Independence Avenue opposite the Kalahari Sands and Casino.

Contacts **Namibia Tourism** (⊠ *Sanlam Centre, Independence Ave., Windhoek* ☎ *061/290–6000* ⊕ *www.namibiatourism.com.na*). **Tourist Information Bureau** (⊠ *Post St. Mall* ☎ *061/290–2092 or 061/290–2058* ⊕ *www.cityofwindhoek.org. na* ⊠ *Independence Ave., opposite Kalahari Sands and Casino*).

BEACH ESCAPE

You don't come to Namibia for beaches, but if you do fancy a dip in the sea, Swakopmund, the country's only real beach resort, is your best bet.

SWAKOPMUND

Although the desert continues to sweep its remorseless way toward the mighty Atlantic and its infamous Skeleton Coast, humans have somehow managed to hang on to this patch of coastline, where Swakopmund clings to the edge of the continent. The first 40 German settlers, complete with household goods and breeding cattle, arrived here with 120 German colonial troops on the *Marie Woermann* in the late 19th century. Today, instead of the primitive shelters that the early settlers built on the beach to protect themselves from sand and sea, stands Swakopmund, or Swakops, as the resort town is affectionately known. There's something surreal about Swakops. On the one hand, it's like a tiny European transplant, with its seaside promenade, sidewalk cafés, fine German colonial buildings, trendy bistros, friendly and neat-as-a-pin pensions, and immaculate boarding houses and hotels. On the other hand, this little town is squashed between the relentless Atlantic and the harsh desert, in one of the wildest and most untamed parts of the African continent—something you might understandably forget while nibbling a chocolate torte or sipping a good German beer under a striped umbrella.

Swakops makes for a different, unique beach escape because of its history and surreal surroundings. It's one of the top adventure centers in Africa, second only to Victoria Falls in Zimbabwe. Adrenaline junkies can try their hand (or feet) at skydiving, sandboarding, jet skiing, kayaking, dune-buggying, paragliding, or wave-skipping in a light aircraft. The less adventurous (but romantic) can take day, moonlight, sunrise, or sunset horseback or camel rides through the riverbeds and up into the moonlike landscape.

There are also lots of curio shops and commercial art galleries, making Swakops great for shopping. But if you really want some sand and sun time, head to the Mole, Swakops's most popular beach. Keep in mind that this is not Mauritius or the Caribbean and the weather can

7

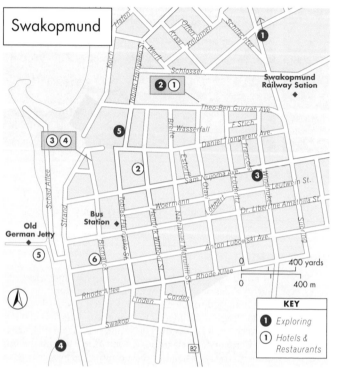

be treacherous. The Mole's a short walk from the center of town and there are numerous cafés and restaurants along the beach to stop for a quick drink or bite to eat. Since the beach is sheltered by a breakwater, its calm waters attract crowds, especially on the weekends; if you do swim out beware of the strong currents just off the breakwater. There's a paved walkway that heads north along the beach if you need to stretch your legs. You can also head to the jetty at the southern end of the beach for a stroll. The southern side of the jetty is for walkers, while the northern side is reserved for fishing.

Keep in mind that the town is packed with vacationing Namibians at Christmas, New Year's, and Easter, so avoid these times if you can.

WHAT TO SEE

❶ **Karakulia.** Although this crafts center has a shop on the Nedbank Arcade, off Sam Nujoma Avenue, if you have a car it's worth driving to the workshop itself. Handmade rugs, carpets, curtains, and wall hangings woven and spun from karakul wool are for sale, and you can even have a design made to order. The center will ship your purchases home for you. ⊠ *Rakotoka St.* ☎ *064/461–415* ⊕ *www.karakulia.com.na* ☼ *Weekdays 9–5, Sat. 9–1.*

❹ **National Marine Aquarium.** The small, attractive aquarium showcases great displays of marine life in its 20 tanks, including a huge main tank that is crossed by an underground walkway. Catch the action when the big fish are hand-fed by divers at 3 on Tuesday and weekends. ⊠ *Opposite the Strand* 📞 *064/410–1000* 💳 *N$30* 🕐 *Tues.–Sun. 10–4.*

2 **Old Station Building.** No trip to Swakops would be complete without a visit to its most notable landmark, the gorgeous, historic Old Station Building, built in 1901. Declared a national monument in 1972, this magnificent example of German colonial architecture came to life again in the early 1990s, when it was restored and renovated in a style evoking the charm and nostalgia of the old railway days. Don't miss the huge bustling lobby—a remnant of the building's former life as a railway station. Today, the building houses the Swakopmund Hotel and Entertainment Centre. ⊠ *2 Theo-Ben Gurirab Ave.*

5 **Peter's Antiques.** This store has been described as the best shop in Africa for its superbly eclectic collection of pieces from all over sub-Saharan Africa. If it's genuine antique Africana books you seek, this is the place. ⊠ *24 Tobias Hainyeko St.* 📞 *064/405–624* ⊕ *www.peters-antiques. com* 🕐 *Weekdays 9–1 and 3–6, Sat. 9–1 and 5–6, Sun. 5–6.*

3 **Sam Cohen Library.** As in Windhoek, there are lots of historic German buildings dating to the turn of the 20th century, most of them in perfect condition. The railway station, the prison, the Woermann House, the Kaserne (barracks), the Lutheran Church, and the District Court look more like illustrations from some Brothers Grimm fairy tale than the working buildings they once were. You can pick up a map and detailed information from the Sam Cohen Library, which is worth a visit for its impressive collection of Africana books alone; it's next to the Transport Museum. ⊠ *Sam Nujoma and Windhuker Sts.* 📞 *064/402–695* 💳 *Free* 🕐 *Weekdays 9–1 and 3–5, Sat. 10–12:30.*

WHERE TO STAY & EAT

¢–$$$$

FodorsChoice

★

✕ **Café Anton.** Here, at one of the town's visitor institutions, you can sit on the palm-shaded terrace overlooking the lighthouse and the sea and watch the world go by while you eat a breakfast of scrumptious home-baked cake or pastry. The chocolate-drenched Florentiner cookies are divine, and the Black Forest cake is made exactly as it is in Germany. Lunch packs are available on request. In the early evening the menu changes for dinner: try a fresh seafood platter, the line fish of the day, or grilled prawns. ⊠ *Schweizerhaus Hotel, 1 Bismarck St., overlooking the Mole* 📞 *064/40–2419* 💳 *AE, DC, MC, V.*

¢–$$$$

✕ **Hansa Hotel Main Restaurant.** If you're looking for a special-occasion dinner and you appreciate good, rich food such as venison, steak, and Namibian seafood delicacies, then you can't do better than this rather formal, highly rated restaurant with an excellent wine list. Start with the game consommé with marrow dumplings before moving on to the giant prawns in honey-lemon butter or springbok loin. Your surroundings are a perfectly restored 1905 German colonial building (the hotel itself has earned plenty of accolades). ⊠ *3 Hendrik Witbooi St.* 📞 *064/41–4200* ⊕ *www.hansahotel.com.na* 🍽 *Reservations essential* 💳 *AE, DC, MC, V.*

¢–$$$$

✕ **The Tug.** As its name suggests, this restaurant is actually an old tugboat that has been raised up and moored next to the jetty. Have a drink out on the deck or sit inside at a colorful table—each tabletop has been hand-painted by a different local artist. Swakops is known for its fresh seafood, which is particularly good here; if you're not in the mood for something fishy, opt for the venison or ostrich stir-fry. Try to reserve a corner table so you can watch the crashing ocean just a few yards away. ⊠*The Strand* ☎*064/40–2356* ⌖*Reservations essential* ▤*AE, DC, MC, V.*

$$$$ 🏨**Swakopmund Hotel and Entertainment Centre.** At this hotel within the ☾ 1901 Old Station Building, the huge bustling lobby is a reminder of the building's previous incarnation as a railway station. It's a very popular place, so be prepared for lots of tour groups milling around. Victorian-style rooms look out over a central courtyard and pool area, and there are lots of facilities, including a game room. You can dine formally at the Platform 1 restaurant (which serves breakfast, lunch, and light meals) or opt for the Captain's Tavern restaurant, which specializes in fresh fish, oysters, and shellfish. The hotel can also arrange a "Desert Evening," during which you eat in the desert under a star-studded sky. ⊠*2 Theo-Ben Gurirab Ave.* ☎*064/410–5200* ⊕*www.legacyhotels. co.za* ⟰*90 rooms* ⌖*In-room: a/c, safe, refrigerator. In-hotel: restaurant, bar, pool, gym* ▤*AE, DC, MC, V* ⋔*BP.*

$$ 🏨**Hotel Schweizerhaus.** This small hotel with great sea views has been owner-run by the Anton family since 1965 and is a Swakops tradition—full of character and ideally set beside the sea, yet only minutes from the city center. It has quaint, comfortable, German-style rooms, most with a balcony and sea view. Don't forget to greet the parrots and other colorful birds in the hotel courtyard. Its Café Anton is probably the most famous restaurant in Namibia. ⊠*1 Bismarck St.* ☎*064/400– 331 or 064/400–333* ⊕*www.schweizerhaus.net* ⟰*34 rooms* ⌖*In-hotel: restaurant, bar* ▤*MC, V* ⋔*MAP.*

$ 🏨**Hotel Europa Hof.** For a taste of Europe in the middle of Africa, try the Europa, which looks like a combination of Bavarian Gothic, Swiss chalet, and fairy-tale gingerbread house. Once inside you may find it hard to believe you're not in Germany. The accommodations are solidly comfortable, the location very central, and the restaurant serves both traditional German food and local delicacies such as springbok and crocodile. Try an oyster, venison, or seafood platter. ⊠*39 Bismarck St.* ☎*064/40–5061 or 064/40–5062* ⊕*www.europahof.com* ⟰*35 rooms* ⌖*In-room: safe. In-hotel: restaurant, bar* ▤*MC, V* ⋔*MAP.*

SPORTS & THE OUTDOORS

The **Desert Explorers Adventure Centre** (⊠*Nathaniel Maxuilili St.* ☎*064/40–5038* ✉*desertex@iafrica.com.na*) houses most of Swakopmund's small adventure companies for activities like sandboarding, rappelling, kayaking, skydiving, and quadbiking. **Alter-Action Ltd.** (☎*064/40–2737*) arranges sandboarding. **Dare Devil Adventures** (☎*064/20–9532* ✉*daredev@iway.na*) runs various adventure excursions. **Namib Quad Rentals** (☎*081/129–5794 mobile phone* ✉*longbeachlodge@iway.na*) rents ATVs. Among the half- and full-day excursions offered by **Tommy's Tours & Safaris** (☎*064/46–1038* ⊕*www. tommys.iway.na*) is a 4x4 tour that focuses on desert wildlife.

SWAKOPMUND ESSENTIALS

TRANSPORTATION

BY AIR   Walvis Bay, which handles domestic flights, is the nearest airport for Swakopmund. *For information on air service, see Namibia Essentials, below.*

Airport Walvis Bay Airport (☎ *064/20–2867*).

BY BUS   Intercape Mainliner runs buses between Windhoek and Swakopmund. There are no reliable bus services within Swakopmund for visitors.

Bus Line Intercape Mainliner (☎ *064/20–2867* ⊕ *www.intercape.co.za*).

BY CAR   If you have the time, it's worth renting a car to drive from Windhoek to Swakopmund. It's a very scenic and easy drive, about 368 km (228 mi) on the B1, a good paved road. Once in Swakopmund, it's easy to find your way around. With a car, you'll also be able to visit the Cape Cross seal colony and drive farther north toward the Skeleton Coast, or drive 30 km (19 mi) south to Walvis Bay. A two-wheel-drive vehicle is fine, but if you intend visiting Sossusvlei in Namib Naukluft Park, then a 4x4 will give you more access and better viewing.

If you arrange to rent a car in advance at any of the reliable agencies, you'll be met at Walvis Bay Airport.

Rental Companies Avis (✉ *Swakopmund Hotel and Entertainments Centre, 2 Theo-Ben Guribab Ave.* ☎ *064/40–2527*). **Hertz** (✉ *GIPF Building, Sam Nujoma Ave.* ☎ *064/46–1826*). **Namib 4x4** (✉ *Sam Nujoma Ave.* ☎ *064/40–4100*).

BY TRAIN   *For information on train travel between Windhoek and Swakopmund, see Windhoek Essentials, above.*

CONTACTS & RESOURCES

BUSINESS SERVICES & FACILITIES   Your hotel will most likely have business services; if not, ask the staff to direct you to the nearest Internet café.

DAY TOURS   Namib Tours runs all kinds of tours, including desert trips and day trips to Spitzkoppe and Cape Cross.

Okakambe Trails has daytime, moonlight, sunrise, and sunset horseback rides.

Local guide Bruno Nebe of Turnstone Tours is renowned for his indepth one-day desert tours. He also runs trips farther afield to Sandwich Harbour, with its rich birdlife, and inland trips from the coast.

Namib Tours (☎ *064/40–4072*). **Okakambe Trails** (☎ *064/40–2799*). **Turnstone Tours** (☎ *064/40–3123* ⊕ *www.turnstone-tours.com*).

EMERGENCIES   Bismarck Medical Centre is a private clinic. Ask at your accommodation about the nearest pharmacy.

Emergency Contacts Ambulance/Hospital (☎ *064/40–5731*). **Police** (☎ *064/10111*).

Hospital Bismarck Medical Centre (✉ *17 Sam Nujoma Ave.* ☎ *064/40–2575 or 064/40–5894*).

HOURS OF OPERATION	*See Namibia Essentials, below, for information on business hours.*
MONEY	*See Namibia Essentials, below, for information on money.*
RESTROOMS	Stick to hotel restrooms in the city.
SAFETY	Swakops is a very safe little town, but you should still always be aware of potential pickpockets. Lock your valuables away in the hotel safe, and carry only what you need. Never travel with expensive jewelry. Don't walk alone at night, and stick to well-lighted areas.
VISITOR INFORMATION	Namib I, the tourist information center, provides excellent national and local information, maps, and more.

Contact **Namib I** (✉ *Kaiser Wilhelm and Roon Sts.* ☎ *064/40–4827* ⊕ *www. namibi.org*).

NAMIBIA ESSENTIALS

TRANSPORTATION

BY AIR

Namibia's main point of entry is Hosea Kutako International Airport, near Windhoek. The smaller Eros Airport handles local flights and charters. Once in the country you can make use of scheduled flights or charter flights that service all domestic destinations. Walvis Bay is the nearest airport for Namib Naukluft and the Skeleton Coast and has daily flights from Windhoek.

The national carrier is Air Namibia, which operates international flights between Windhoek and London, Frankfurt, Johannesburg, and Cape Town, and internal flights to most of Namibia's major tourist destinations. South African Airways (SAA) operates links to Johannesburg and Cape Town. Air Botswana links Maun with Windhoek, and SA Express Airways flies between Johannesburg and Walvis Bay.

All camps in Etosha National Park have their own landing strip. Have your tour operator arrange charters or fly-in safaris for you. Air Namibia flies directly to Mokuti on the regularly scheduled flight between Windhoek and Victoria Falls. Chartered flights and fly-in safaris also use the Ongava airstrip.

Airlines Air Botswana (☎ *27/11/390–3070 Johannesburg* ⊕ *www.airbotswana.co.bw*). **Air Namibia** (☎ *061/298–2605* ⊕ *www.airnamibia.com*). **SA Express Airways** (☎ *27/11/978–5577 Johannesburg*). **South African Airways** (☎ *27/11/778–1111 Johannesburg* ⊕ *www.flysaa.com*).

BY CAR

Driving to Namibia from South Africa is possible, and there's an excellent road network for all in-country tourist attractions, but be warned that the trip is tiring and time-consuming because of the huge distances involved. The Trans-Kalahari Highway links Johannesburg to Windhoek and Gaborone. From Johannesburg to Windhoek on this road is 1,426 km (884 mi). To allow free access to game, there are no fences in the Kalahari, so don't speed, and look out for antelope as well as donkeys and cows on the road. You can also drive from Johannesburg to Windhoek (1,791 km [1,110 mi]) via Upington, going through the Narochas (Nakop) border post (open 24 hours). This is a good route if you want to visit the Augrabies Falls and Kgalagadi Transfrontier Park in South Africa first. You can also drive from Cape Town to Namibia along the N7, an excellent road that becomes the B1 as you cross into Namibia at the Noordoewer border post (open 24 hours). It's 763 km (473 mi) from Cape Town to Noordoewer, 795 km (493 mi) from Noordoewer to Windhoek. Border posts are efficient and friendly—make sure you have all your paperwork to hand over. You will need a current international driver's license.

To reach Etosha National Park you can drive from Windhoek, via Otjiwarongo and Tsumeb, and arrive at the park on its eastern side by the Von Lindequist Gate (near Namutoni Rest Camp), 106 km (66 mi) from Tsumeb and 550 km (341 mi) north of Windhoek. Alternatively, you can drive from Windhoek via Otjiwarongo and Outjo and come in the Anderson Gate, south of Okaukuejo, 120 km (74½ mi) from Outjo, 450 km (279 mi) north of Windhoek. The latter is the more popular route. Both drives are long, hot, and dusty, so you might want to fly to your camp's landing strip if you're short on time. Travel time will depend on your driving and choice of vehicle, so check with your car-rental company.

If you're not staying at a private lodge that provides transportation, you will need to rent your own vehicle. Air-conditioning is a must at any time of the year, as are spare tires in good condition. You can pick up rental cars at the town nearest whichever park you are visiting or at Etosha itself, but it's better to book them before you leave home. For driving on the main roads, a two-wheel-drive vehicle is fine. In some areas, though, including parts of the Namib Naukluft Park and Damaraland, four-wheel drive is essential. In Etosha a two-wheel-drive car is fine (although you get better views in a van or SUV because you sit higher up); don't exceed the speed limit of 60 kph (37 mph). Always check the state of the roads with the nearest tourist office before you set off, and never underestimate the long distances involved. Don't drive at night unless you absolutely have to. Roads are unlighted, and animals like to bed down on the warm surfaces. If you hit an animal, even a small one, it could be the end of you and your vehicle. Never speed on gravel roads (80 kph [50 mph] is reasonable), which can often be very slippery. It's very easy to skid or roll your vehicle—at least one tourist per year is killed this way. And make sure you have plenty of water and *padkos,* Afrikaans for "road food." Finally, keep in mind that gas stations only accept cash.

Automobile Associations **Automobile Association of Namibia (AAN)** (⊠ *Windhoek* ☎ *061/22–4201).*

BY TRAIN

The Desert Express travels between Windhoek, the capital of Namibia and Swakopmund, the country's premier coastal resort. The train departs from Windhoek on Tuesday and Friday and from Swakopmund on Wednesday and Saturday. Longer journeys to Etosha and Lüderitz are also available.

Train Information **Desert Express** (✉ *Windhoek Railway Station, Bahnhof St., Windhoek* ☎ *061/298–2600* ⊕ *www.desertexpress.com.na*).

CONTACTS & RESOURCES

CUSTOMS & DUTIES

You may bring up to 200 cigarettes, 20 cigars, 250 grams of tobacco, 2 liters of wine, 1 liter of other alcoholic beverages, 50 ml of perfume, and 250 ml of toilet water into Namibia or other Southern Africa Common Customs Union (SACU) countries (South Africa, Botswana, Lesotho, and Swaziland). The tobacco and alcohol allowance applies only to people 18 and over. If you enter a SACU country from or through another in the union, you are not liable for any duties. You will, however, need to complete a form listing items imported.

ELECTRICITY

To use electric-powered equipment purchased in the United States or Canada, bring a converter and adapter. If your appliances are dual-voltage, you'll need only an adapter. The electrical current is 220 volts, 50 cycles alternating current (AC); wall outlets usually take 15-amp plugs with three round prongs, but some take the straight-edged three-prong plugs, also 15 amps. The more inaccessible lodges have their own generators, but if you want to read at night in your tent, bring a good reading light.

EMERGENCIES

Be sure you have comprehensive medical insurance before you leave home. There's a high standard of medical care in Namibia. Consult your hotel about particular doctors or consult the white pages of the telephone directory under medical practitioners. If you get sick, go to a private clinic rather than a government-run one.

Windhoek and Otjiwarongo both have excellent private clinics. Both cities have a Medi-Clinic, and Windhoek also has the Catholic Mission Hospital.

Hospitals **Catholic Mission Hospital** (✉ *92 Stubel St., Windhoek* ☎ *061/23-7237*). **Medi-Clinic** (✉ *Heliodoor St., Eros Park, Windhoek* ☎ *061/22-2687* ✉ *Son St., Otjiwarongo* ☎ *067/30-3734 or 067/30-3735*).

HEALTH

Never venture into the desert without water, a sun hat, and sunblock.

Malaria, HIV/AIDS, and the power of the heat and sun are the main health concerns in the country. *For more information, see Health & Safety in the Namibia Planner, above.*

HOURS OF OPERATION

Shops in Windhoek and Swakopmund are generally open 9–5. Banking hours are 8–1 and 2:30–5 Monday–Saturday. Restaurants vary but usually operate noon–3 and 6–10, although cafés frequently stay open all day. Nightclubs stay open late; the closing hour usually depends on the number of customers. Even on public holidays many shops will be open—only banks, government offices, and business premises will close.

MONEY

There are main branches of major banks near or in the city center of Windhoek and Swakopmund, plus several easy-to-find ATMs. Ask at your accommodation for more information. Major credit cards are accepted everywhere but street markets. South African rand are accepted everywhere.

Namibia's currency is the Namibian dollar, which is linked to the South African rand. (Namibia's currency cannot be used in South Africa, except unofficially at border towns.) At this writing, the Namibian dollar was trading at about N$6.8 to US$1. *Bureau de change* offices at the airports often stay open until late.

In more rural or remote areas, carry Namibian dollars or South African rand. In Windhoek, Swakopmund, and the larger towns there are plenty of banks and ATMs. Visa cards are best for drawing cash from ATMs. Credit cards can be used almost everywhere; MasterCard and Visa are preferred by business owners to American Express because of substantial charges levied by the latter to proprietors. Traveler's checks can be cashed only at banks. Note that gas stations only take cash.

PHONES

The country code for Namibia is 264. When dialing from abroad, drop the initial 0 from local area codes.

Namibian telephone numbers vary and are constantly changing; many have six digits (not including the area and country code), but some have fewer or more digits.

You can use public phones for direct international calls. Buy Telecards from post offices or supermarkets for N$10, N$20, or N$30. There's cell phone reception in all major towns. Enable your own for international roaming before you leave home, or buy a local SIM card when you arrive (a much cheaper option).

SAFETY

For more information, see Health & Safety in the Namibia Planner, above.

GREEN LODGINGS IN NAMIBIA

Plenty of lodges and camps in Namibia are eco-conscious, but we've chosen a few properties to help you start your search. We hope reading about these places will help you on your path towards green travel.

CONTACT INFORMATION

Skeleton Coast Camp: 27/11/807–1800 in South Africa; www.wilderness-safaris.com

Wilderness Damaraland Camp: 27/11/807–1800 in South Africa; www.damaraland.com

The Wolwedans Private Camp: 061/230–616; www.wolwedans.com

Skeleton Coast Camp (opposite bottom) hosts fly-in safaris in one of the most remote wilderness areas in Africa. Visitors to the camp—built on an island just a few miles in from the coast—are privy to 660,000 acres of pristine, uninhabited coastline. Many areas are accessible only on foot as vehicle tracks can damage the natural environment. Nature hikes are a large part of any stay at Skeleton Coast Camp, and include views of unique plants like lithops and Welwitschia. Wilderness Safaris, which runs the camp, also operates the Wilderness Wildlife Trust. The trust has some interesting projects, including the Skeleton Coast Lichen Research Project which assesses the long-term impact of human activity on the Namib Desert's lichen communities and aims to increase recovery rates; lichen is vital to the Skeleton Coast's ecology. *See Permanent Tented Camps in the Skeleton Coast under If You Have Time for more information about the camp.*

Located in the serene and secluded NamibRand Nature Reserve, **Wolwedans Private Camp** (opposite) is built of simple wood and canvas giving its guests up-close access to the surrounding desert habitat. The reserve is a reflection of the diversity of the Namib Desert with its steep mountain ranges, vast savannahs, glorious red sand dunes, and clay pans. Here you might possibly see the oryx, as well as more than 100 bird species including the rare dune lark. The reserve is sparsely developed and off-limits to large vehicles such as tour buses and 4x4s. What's more, a percentage of your park entry fee goes directly into conserving the integrity of the reserve.

Set on Namibia's Skeleton Coast between Khorixas and Torra Bay, this beautiful 10-tent camp manages to integrate conservation and community development with the tourist mission of the camp. With the assistance of the Integrated Rural Development & Nature Conservation (IRDNC), the World Wildlife Fund (WWF), and other sustainable development organizations, **Wilderness Damaraland Camp** has included local indigenous tribes in the protection and management of wildlife and the land surrounding the camp, giving them an income, training, and the feeling of ownership in the community. The nearby Brandberg Mountain (Namibia's highest) provides natural eye candy, while wildlife migrate to the area based on their desert survival needs. Elephant, black rhinoceros, Oryx, kudu, springbok are just a few species that might be spotted at Damaraland Camp. There are also opportunities to visit the nearby Twyfelfontein engravings, one of the most unique rock art sites in Southern Africa, which provide evidence of human habitation of life at Twyfelfontein more than 6,000 years ago. *See Permanent Tented Camps, in Damaraland in for more information about the camp.*

YOUR FOOTPRINT

How can you make sure that your personal footprint is as minimal as possible?
- Never litter.

- Think small. Stay in a B&B or locally owned accommodation that benefits the community.

- Don't buy shells or pieces of coral from street vendors. It encourages ocean destruction.

- Purchase local products.

- Use water sparingly.

- Turn off lights when not in use.

- Don't feed wild animals.

- Don't leave anything behind when you leave your campsite. Also, use biodegradable soap or toothpaste.

- Don't take anything with you from the environment, whether it's a flower, a rock, or impala horns you've found lying in the bush.

- Above all, remember that you're a guest. The people and creatures you see were here long before you arrived and they will be here long after you depart.

Victoria Falls

WELCOME TO VICTORIA FALLS

TOP REASONS TO GO

★ **The phenomenon.** Not only can you experience Victoria Falls and the Batoka Gorge from up, down, and even inside—the sheer size still allows for the experience to have an exclusive feel.

★ **Fundamental adrenaline.** Looking for an adventure to get your heart pounding? From bungee jumping to elephant back riding and skydiving, Victoria Falls has it all.

★ **Ultimate relaxation.** Massages are offered on the banks of the Zambezi River, sumptuous food is served wherever you turn, and there is nothing like having a gin and tonic while the spray of the Falls fades in the evening light to end the perfect day.

★ **Africa central.** With direct flights from London to Livingstone you'll be within spitting distance of the Okavango Delta and the Big Five in record time.

1 Livingstone, Zambia. Livingstone, named after the famous Dr. David Livingstone, was established in 1900, 10 km (6 mi) north of the falls, in an attempt to avoid malaria, believed to be caused by the swampy Zambezi. Its main street, Mosi-oa-Tunya Road, is lined with colonial buildings. The current political climate in Zimbabwe has led many tourists to choose Livingstone as their base instead of Victoria Falls.

2 Victoria Falls, Zimbabwe. The town of Victoria Falls lies west of the falls on the southern bank of the Zambezi. The view from here is said to be the best of the falls and the gorge. At one time, the town was the principle tourist destination for the area, but the tyrannical rule of President Mugabe has left inhabitants struggling to cope with limited access to basics such as bread and milk. Although the town is perfectly safe, the atmosphere can be uncomfortable.

Sankaia

Zambezi National Park

Mosi-oa-Tunya National Park

Zambezi River

ZIMBABWE

Kazungula Rd.

0   2 miles

0   2 kilometers

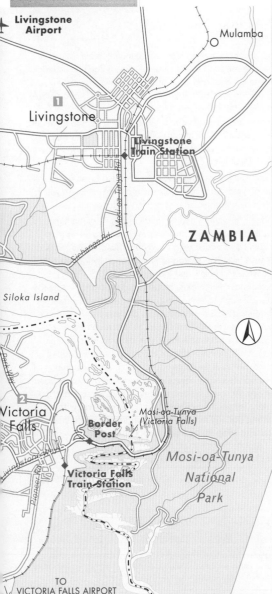

GETTING ORIENTED

Victoria Falls is in Southern Africa on the border of Zambia and Zimbabwe. Each country has a national park that surrounds the falls (Mosi-oa-Tunya National Park in Zambia and Victoria Falls National Park in Zimbabwe), as well as a town (Livingstone in Zambia and Victoria Falls in Zimbabwe) that serves as the tourist center. The fissure containing the falls stretches over a mile, roughly from southwest to northeast. Livingstone lies to the north and the town of Victoria Falls to the south. The border between the countries, which is at the falls, is within walking distance of the compact town of Victoria Falls. The stretch between the falls border and town center should not be attempted on foot, because of the dangers of wandering elephants, the African sun, and the occasional opportunistic thief.

8

VICTORIA FALLS PLANNER

Health & Safety

It's always a good idea to leave ample space in your luggage for common sense when traveling to Victoria Falls. Wild animals abound throughout this area and must be given a lot of room and respect. You must also remember that Zimbabwe and Zambia are relatively poor. Both countries have tourism police, but opportunistic thieving still happens occasionally. Although crime is generally nonviolent, losing your money, belongings, or passport will result in spending the remainder of your trip with various officials in stuffy, badly decorated offices instead of sitting back on the deck of your sunset cruise, drink in hand.

As for the water, it is always advisable to drink bottled water, although the tap water in Zambia is generally considered safe. Should you develop any stomach upset, be sure to contact a physician, especially if you are running a fever, in order to rule out malaria or a communicable disease.

Finally, confirm that your insurance covers you for a medical evacuation should you be involved in a serious accident, as the closest intensive-care facilities of international standard are in South Africa.

Eat Right, Sleep Well

In Zimbabwe, game meat can be found on almost any menu, but it's something of a delicacy in Zambia; superior free-range beef and chicken are available everywhere. The local bream, filleted or whole, is quite good, and the staple starch, a thick porridge similar to polenta— *sadza* in Zimbabwe and *nsima* in Zambia—is worth a try; use the finger bowl to eat it. Adventurous? Try *macimbi* or *vinkuvala* (sun-dried mopane worms) and, in the flood season, *inswa* (flash-fried flying ants).

Meals are taken at regular hours, but during the week, restaurants close around 10. Dress is casual, although you'll never be out of place in something more formal.

Lodge reservations can be made at any time, but flight availability can be a problem, especially traveling from and to South Africa on a Friday and Sunday. Lodges tend to have inclusive packages; hotels generally include only breakfast. All hotels and lodges quote in U.S. dollars, but accept payment in other currencies at unfriendly exchange rates. Though hotels in Zimbabwe have set rates, they are currently desperate for business, and you can bargain in many instances. It's best though to take an all-inclusive package tour because meals can be exorbitantly expensive. A 10% service charge is either included or added to the bill (as is the value-added tax) in both countries, which frees you to include an extra tip only for exceptional service. Although air-conditioning can be expected in the hotels, lodges tend to have fans. ■TIP➔ Travel with a sarong (locally available as a *chitenge*), which you can wet and wrap around you for a cooler siesta.

WHAT IT COSTS In U.S. dollars

	¢	$	$$	$$$	$$$$
DINING	under $5	$5–$10	$10–$15	$15–$25	over $25
LODGING	under $50	$50–$100	$100–$200	$200–$350	over $350

Restaurant prices are per person for a main course at dinner, a main course equivalent, or a prix-fixe meal. Lodging prices are for a standard double room in high season, including 12.5% tax.

Coming & Going

You'll need a valid passport and visa to enter **Zambia**, but it's simple to purchase a visa when you enter the country. The Zambian immigration department is currently revising its visa fees. At press time a standard U.S. entry visa costs US$135, and a single-entry or transit visa is not necessary provided you do not leave the airport terminal. Day-trip visas cost US$20 (often included in the cost of prebooked activities, so check with your booking agent). If you plan to leave Zambia and return, you'll need a multiple entry visa or will have to buy another visa upon your return.

You can buy point-of-entry visas for **Zimbabwe** for US$65 for a single entry. If you leave Zimbabwe for more than 24 hours, you will need to buy another to reenter (unless you bought a double-entry visa for US$80), so think before you travel. To cross the border into Zambia for a day, you'll need to purchase a Zambian day visa for US$10, unless you have booked an activity that includes this cost. Visas can be purchased from an embassy before departure, but it will almost certainly be more trouble and generally cost more than buying them at the border.

When in Rome . . .

Fearing a few weeks without your Budweiser? No worries. There are a couple great local brews for you to try on both sides of the falls: Mosi in Zambia and Zambezi in Zimbabwe. Both are crisp, light, and thirst-quenching beers. What about after your meal? Order an Amarula on ice. Not unlike Baileys Irish Cream, this liquor is made from the fruit of the marula tree, a well-documented delicacy for elephants.

When to Go

If you are at all sensitive to heat and humidity, visit from May through August, when it is dry and cool, with pleasant days and cool to cold nights. Although the bush can resemble a wasteland, with short brown stubble and bare trees, it does improve game viewing, and most other adventure activities are more comfortable in the cooler weather. This is also the time when the mosquitoes are less active, although it remains a malaria area year-round, and precautions should always be taken.

The rainy season starts sometime around late October and generally stretches well into April. With the first rains also comes the "time of the bugs," with tsetse flies, mosquitoes, and the harmless but aptly named stink bug seemingly running the show for a couple of months. Of course, the abundance of insect life also leads to great bird-watching. Although the rain showers tend to be of the short and spectacular kind, they can interfere with some activities, especially if your visit is a short one. Try to arrange your activities for the early hours, as the rain generally falls in the late afternoon.

Peak flow is achieved in late April and May, when rafting and visiting Livingstone Island might not be possible. Make sure your visit does not coincide with school vacations in South Africa, as the area tends to get very full.

8

VICTORIA FALLS PLANNER

Getting Info

Although the Zambia National Tourist Board (⊠ *Tourist Centre, Mosi-oa-Tunya Rd.* ☎ *213/32–1404* ⊕ *www.zambiatourism. com*), open weekdays 8–1 and 2–5, Saturday 8–noon, is very helpful and friendly, you might be better off visiting the Zigzag coffee house (⊠ *The Warehouse, Mosi-oa-Tunya Rd.* ☎ *213/32–2814* ⊕ *www.zigzagzambia.com*) for serious unbiased advice. It's open daily 8–8.

In Zimbabwe, the Victoria Falls Publicity Association (⊠ *412 Park Way* ☎ *013/4–4202* ✑ *vfpa@mweb.co.zw*) is fairly well stocked with brochures. It's open weekdays 8–1, 2–4 and Saturday 8–1. It's also a good idea to seek advice from the many safari companies in town.

Languages

Zambia has more than 70 dialects, but there are only four main languages: Lozi, Bemba, Nyanja, and Tonga. English is the official language and is widely spoken, read, and understood.

Zimbabwe's official language is English. Chishona and Sindebele and their dialects are widely spoken.

Money Matters in Zambia

Kwacha and U.S. dollars are welcome everywhere. It's a good idea to travel with plenty of small U.S. bills for tips and small purchases. Make sure you have only "big head" dollars, as the older, "small head" ones are no longer accepted. International banks, along Mosi-oa-Tunya Road, have ATMs and exchange services. Banking hours are generally weekdays 8–2 (although some do open the last Saturday of the month). Bank ATMs accept only Visa.

⚠ **You may be invited to do a little informal foreign exchange by persuasive street financiers.** Resist the temptation—it's not worth the risk of being ripped off or arrested. There are many reputable exchange bureaus throughout town, though they are sometimes flooded with dollars and low on kwacha, generally toward the end of the month. MasterCard and Visa are preferred by business owners and banks to American Express or Diners Club. Business owners always prefer cash (or traveler's checks) to credit cards, and some smaller hotels levy fees up to 10% to use a credit card. Traveler's checks are also widely accepted, but your change is likely to be in kwacha.

Money Matters in Zimbabwe

If you limit your visit to Vic Falls, it's not absolutely necessary to change money into Zimbabwean dollars, because everyone accepts foreign currency. However, you will be given change in Zimbabwean dollars—probably at a pretty bad exchange rate.

It's advisable to stick to U.S. dollars for all activity payments to both the Zimbabwean and the Zambian based operators. Credit card facilities are not readily available, but traveler's checks are accepted.

It's illegal to change money on the black market, so do so only at banks located around Livingstone Way and Park Way, which are generally open only in the morning. All official *bureaux de change* have been closed down by the government. Beware of street vendors. They'll try to rip you off in ways you'd never have believed possible.

Updated by
Sanja Cloete-
Jones

ROMANCE, INTRIGUE, MYTH, decadence, awe, and terror: the largest curtain of falling water known to humankind reveals itself like an irresistible read. Roughly 1,200 km (750 mi) from its origin as an insignificant spring, the Zambezi River has grown more than a mile wide. Suddenly there's a bend to the south, the current speeds up, and a few miles downstream the entire river is forced into a fissure created in the Jurassic age by the cooling and cracking of molten rock. Nearly 2½ million gallons of water disappear over a vertical drop 300 feet high in a matter of seconds. The resulting spray is astounding, the force splashing drops of water up into the air to form a smokelike cloud that is visible 40 miles away on a clear day.

Dr. David Livingstone, a Scottish medical doctor and missionary, visited the area in 1855 and is widely credited with being the first European to document the existence of this natural wonder. He named it Victoria Falls in honor of his queen, although the Makololo name, Mosi-oa-Tunya (literally, "the Smoke that Thunders"), remains popular.

Livingstone fell madly in love with the falls, describing them in poignant prose. Other explorers had slightly different opinions. E. Holub could not contain his excitement and spoke effusively of "a thrilling throb of nature," A. A. de Serpa Pinto called them "sublimely horrible" in 1881, and L. Decle (1898) expected "to see some repulsive monster rising in anger." The modern traveler can explore all of these points of view. There is so much to do around the falls that your only limitations will be your budget and sense of adventure (or lack of sense!).

The settlements of Livingstone, Zambia and Victoria Falls, Zimbabwe, both owe their existence to the falls. In different countries and intriguingly diverse in character, they nevertheless function like two sides of one town. Crossing the border is a formality that generally happens with minimum fuss. Although the Zimbabwean town of Victoria Falls remains perfectly safe and far away from the documented strife, Livingstone, on the Zambian side, is currently the favored destination.

Not only are the visitors spoiled with choices in Zambia, which has a plethora of top-class safari lodges along the Zambezi, but strong competition places the emphasis on individualized service, which enables you to tailor your visit. In Zimbabwe, the general mood is not always upbeat, but the absence of throngs of travelers is lovely, and it currently provides excellent value for money. The region deserves its reputation as an adventure center and offers adrenaline-inducing activities by the bucketful. The backdrop for any of these is stunning, and the safety record superb.

8

DID YOU KNOW . . .

The first uttering of the popular phrase "Dr. Livingstone, I Presume?" may never have happened. Although Livingstone did meet John Rowlands (the assumed utterer of the phrase) in Tanzania in 1871, the famous quote is widely considered a figment of Rowlands's imagination. Another figment of Rowlands's imagination: his American parentage under the name Henry Stanley.

LIVINGSTONE, ZAMBIA

This marvelous old town has a wealth of natural beauty and a surplus of activities. It was the old colonial capital, but after a few decades of neglect it has recast itself as Zambia's tourism and adventure capital. There is a slight air of the past here: historic buildings outnumber new ones, and many inhabitants live a life not unlike that of 100 years ago. Livingstone handles the surge of tourists with equal parts grace, confidence, African mischief, and nuisance.

Many visitors to this side of the falls opt to stay in one of the secluded safari-style lodges on the Zambezi River. The Zambian experience offers a tranquil respite from the compact Victoria Falls town across the border in Zimbabwe, which can easily be busy and noisy.

WHAT TO SEE

Numbers in the margin correspond to numbers on the Livingstone map.

❺ The **Batoka Gorge,** just below the falls, is split between Zambia and Zimbabwe and is more than 120 km (75 mi) long and 600 meters (2,000 feet) deep. It lies mostly within the Hwange Communal Land and is covered with mopane and riparian forests that are interspersed with grassland. On the Zambian side, the gorge is surrounded by the Mosi-oa-Tunya National Park, which contains a tropical rain forest that thrives on the eternal rainfall from the falls. Victoria Falls National Park in Zimbabwe surrounds the other side of the gorge.

Operators from both countries offer excursions to what is reputed to be the world's best one-day white-water rafting, with commercial rapids Class 6 and down (amateurs can only do Class 5 and down) that have been nicknamed "The Ugly Sisters" and "Oblivion." If you're *lucky*

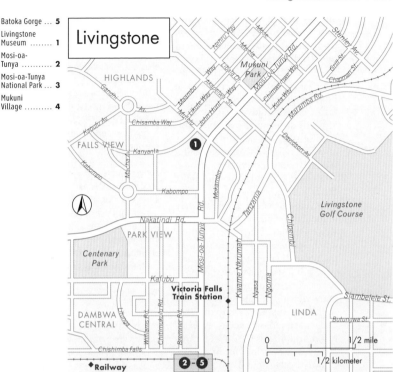

enough to experience what locals call a "long swim" (falling out of the raft at the start of a rapid and body surfing through), your definition of the word *scary* will surely be redefined. The walk in and out of the gorge is quite strenuous on the Zimbabwe side, but as long as you are reasonably fit and looking for adventure, you need no experience. On the Zambian side though, operators use the Ecolift to transport you from the bottom of the gorge to your waiting transportation (and beverage) at the top.

❶ Livingstone Museum. The country's oldest and largest museum contains history, ethnography, natural history, and archaeology sections and includes materials ranging from newspaper clippings to photographs of Queen Elizabeth II dancing with Kenneth Kaunda (Zambia's first president) to historical information dating back to 1500. Among the priceless David Livingstone memorabilia is a model of the mangled arm bone used to identify his body and various journals and maps from the period when he explored the area and claimed the falls for his queen. ✉*Mosi-oa-Tunya Rd., between civic center and post office* ☎*213/32–0495* 💴*US$5* 🕐*Daily 9–4:30.*

❷ Mosi-oa-Tunya. Literally translated as "The Smoke that Thunders," the Fodor'sChoice falls more than live up to its reputation as one of the world's great-★ est natural wonders. No words can do these incredible falls justice, and it's a difficult place to appreciate in just a short visit, as it has many moods and aspects. Though the Zimbabwean side may offer more panoramic views, the Zambian side—especially the **Knife Edge** (a sharp headland with fantastic views)—allows you to stand virtually suspended over the Boiling Pot (the first bend of the river after the falls), with the deafening water crashing everywhere around you. From around May to August the falls are a multisensory experience, though you'll get absolutely drenched if you venture onto the Knife Edge, and there may be too much spray to see the bottom of the gorge. If you get the sun behind you, you'll see that magic rainbow. A network of paths leads to the main viewing points; some are not well protected, so watch your step

A THREE-HOUR TOUR

Many park guides are knowledgeable, but the ultimate Mosi-oa-Tunya National Park experience is the three-hour guided walking safari offered by **Livingstone Safaris** (☎ 213/32-2267 ✉ gecko@zamnet.zm). Not only can you see the endangered white rhino and other plains game, but your professional guide and park scout will impart detailed information on birding, flora, and the modern use of plants by local people. Walks are conducted early in the morning and late in the afternoon and cost US$65, including transfers within Livingstone. Hopefully, your trip won't turn out like Gilligan's.

and wear good, safe shoes, especially at high water, when you are likely to get dripping wet. You will have dramatic views of the full 1½ km (1 mi) of the ironstone face of the falls, the Boiling Pot directly below, the railway bridge, and Batoka Gorge. At times of low water it is possible to take a guided walk to Livingstone Island and swim in the **Devils Pool,** a natural pond right on the lip of the abyss. ✉ *Entrance off Mosi-oa-Tunya Rd., just before border post* ☎ *No phone* 🗠 *US$10* ☉ *Daily 6–6, later at full moon.*

❸ **Mosi-oa-Tunya National Park.** This park is a quick and easy option for
☾ viewing plains game. In fact, you are almost guaranteed to spy white rhinos. You can also visit the Old Drift graveyard, as the park includes the location of the original settlement here. The park's guides are knowledgeable, but you can visit without one, though the roads get seriously muddy in the rainy season, and a guide who knows where to drive becomes a near-necessity. ✉ *Sichanga Rd., off Mosi-oa-Tunya Rd., 3½ km (2 mi) from Livingstone* 🗠 *US$10* ☉ *Daily 6 AM–6 PM.*

❹ **Mukuni Village.** Fascinated by the history, customs, and traditions of
☾ the area? Local guides can escort you on an intimate visit inside a local house and explain the customs of the village. This is not a stage set but a very real village, so your tour will be different depending on the time of the day you go. For example, at mealtimes you can see how local delicacies are prepared. It is customary to sign in the visitor book and to pay a small fee to your guide. Bushtracks (⇨ *Livingstone and Zambia Essentials, below*) conducts organized visits. ☉ *Daily 6–6.*

WHERE TO STAY & EAT

$$$$ ✕**Livingstone Island Picnic.** Available throughout the year except for a
Fodor's Choice couple of weeks when the water level is too high, this is a spectacular,
★ romantic dining option. Livingstone Island is perched right on the edge
of the abyss, where you'll sit around a linen-decked table while being
plied with a delicious buffet lunch (with salads) and drink by liver-
ied waiters. You get there by boat (two engines, just in case). Brunch
and afternoon tea are US$47 and US$63, respectively, and lunch is
US$99, including transfers. The trips are run by Tongabezi Lodge, and
there is a maximum of 12 guests. ⊠*Livingstone Island* ⌂*Box 31*
☎*213/32–7450* ⊟*MC, V* ⊗*Closed a couple of months around Feb.–
June, depending on water level. No dinner.*

$–$$ ✕**Kamuza.** The Moghuls themselves might declare a meal here a feast.
Spicy but not hot, the curries are lovingly prepared from ingredients
imported from India. The chicken Tikka Masala is a house specialty,
and the handmade saffron Kulfi is a great way to end a hot day in
Africa. ⊠*Ngolide Lodge, Mosi-oa-Tunya Rd.* ☎*213/32–1091* ⊟*MC,
V* ⊗*No dinner Mon.*

¢–$ ✕**Funky Munky.** Cheap and cheerful, this small pizzeria's reputation
keeps spreading. On offer find thin-crust pizzas baked in a traditional
wood-fired oven and named after primates. Try the popular bacon and
mushroom Baboon, the Chimpancheese four-cheese extravaganza, or
build your own. If you seek lighter fare, have a fresh French baguette
stuffed with various traditional lunch fillings. And on those unbear-
ably hot summer days pop in for Shave Ice that might make you forget
you are about as far from Hawaii as possible! ⊠*Mosi-oa-Tunya Rd.*
☎*213/32–0120* ⊟*No credit cards.*

$$$$ ✕▦ **Royal Livingstone.** This high-volume, high-end hotel has an incredibly gorgeous sundowner deck, arguably on the best spot on the river,
just upstream from the falls. The attractive colonial safari-style buildings are set amid sweeping green lawns and big trees and have fantastic
views, but passing guest traffic makes for a lack of real privacy. The
decor of the guest rooms and the public rooms is deliberately ostenta-
tious. This resort is tremendously popular and can be extremely busy,
especially during peak times, but the staff is always friendly and helpful. Unfortunately, the volume of people can lead to problems, omissions, and errors with service standards struggling to match the high
costs. ⚠Vervet monkeys are an entertaining nuisance, so hang on to your
expensive cocktail. ⊠*Mosi-oa-Tunya Rd.* ☎*213/32–1122* ⊕*www.
suninternational.co.za* ⇆*173 rooms* ⭢*In-hotel: restaurant, room service, bar, pool, no elevator* ⊟*AE, DC, MC, V* ⑩*CP.*

$$$$ ✕▦ **Zambezi Sun.** Part of the same complex as the Royal Livingstone,
☾ this hotel is less expensive, less pretentious, and a whole lot more welcoming than its pricier cousin. The design borrows freely from a variety
of (mostly African) cultures and is vibrantly colorful, sparkly, and fun.
Buildings are earth red and round cornered, blending in with the surroundings. Rooms are decorated with bright primary-color murals, and
the spacious bathrooms have colorful tiles and handmade sinks. The
hotel is child-friendly, with family rooms and a play center. The buffet
breakfasts and dinners are gastronomic feasts, but all food and drink

8

Zambia's Tribes

Women dance during a Chewa initiation ceremony.

BEMBA

The Bemba originally came from the Democratic Republic of the Congo, but now live mainly in Zambia's northern provinces and the Copperbelt, an industrial area around Ndola, Kitwe, and Chinjola that has many copper mines. Also known as the forest people, they account for 3.1 million or about 20% of the country's population. The Bemba traditionally used bark as loin cloths but today they wear mainly western-style clothing. There are over two dozen Bemba clans and they will often name themselves after regional flora and fauna such as the Royal Crocodile Clan whose main chief is called "The Great Tree." Folklore is a large part of Bemba culture, and many Bemba legends incorporate a belief in the supernatural or magical powers of the Bemba God. The Bemba believe that this god lives in the sky and that he controls things such as weather and fertility. The Bemba are a matrilineal society and live largely off the land, farming the soil with maize until it is infertile and then moving on to another location where they can start anew. Bemba women oversee agriculture while Bemba men are often involved in trade or the running of the village. Most Bemba live in grass-roofed huts in villages comprised of several generations of extended family.

CHEWA

You'll find Chewa tribes in Zambia, Malawi, and Zimbabwe, though the original tribe is thought to have come from Nigeria and Cameroon by way of the Democratic Republic of the Congo. Most engage in tobacco and maize farming. They are a matrilineal society and have a strong sense of community. Known for their secret societies, or Nyau, the Chewa men often dress as animals or mask themselves as ancestors and participate in dance ceremonies in which they enter a trance and perform difficult movements.

are exorbitantly priced. Although the Zambezi Sun doesn't share the Livingstone's fantastic view, it's even closer to the falls—within walking distance. ⊠ *Mosi-oa-Tunya Rd.* ☎ *213/32–1122, 27/11/780–7444 reservations (South Africa)* ⊕ *www.suninternational.co.za* ⇨ *208 rooms, 4 suites* ⅏ *In-hotel: 2 restaurants, bar, pool, children's programs (all ages), no elevator* ▤ *AE, DC, MC, V* ¶⊙¶ *CP.*

$$ ✕⊞ **Waterfront.** There's a hive of happy activity here ranging from opportunistic monkeys relieving unsuspecting tourists of their lunch to serious late-night boozing to adventure enthusiasts (hangover optional) being whisked off to do their thing at all hours of the day. Curiously, the spacious rooms where families can stay can be reached only via a steep exterior wooden staircase, but this is also a popular spot for camping. Restaurant service is notoriously slow and mediocre. ⊠ *Sichanga Rd., just off Mosi-oa-Tunya Rd.* ☎ *213/32–0606* ⊕ *www.safpar.com* ⇨ *21 chalets, 24 adventure village tents, campsites accommodating 86 campers* ⅏ *In-hotel: restaurant, bars, pools, no elevator* ▤ *MC, V* ¶⊙¶ *BP.*

$–$$ ✕⊞ **Zig Zag Coffee House.** First came the coffee shop, which still serves ⟳ the best coffee in town, including a choice of flavored espresso and cappuccino. Then its owners added the Warehouse complex, with a swimming pool, crafts market, children's play area, and B&B ($). Meals are simple and good—soups, ciabatta bread, nachos, muffins, and all-day breakfasts, which you can eat while catching up on all the scandalous gossip Livingstone town can provide. ⊠ *Mosi-oa-Tunya Rd.* ☎ *213/32–2814* ⊕ *www.zigzagzambia.com* ⇨ *12 rooms* ⅏ *In-hotel: pool, no elevator* ▤ *No credit cards* ¶⊙¶ *BP.*

¢ ✕⊞ **Fawlty Towers.** Centrally located to town, this old textile factory was named after the popular British comedy from the 1970s and has become the most popular backpacker's lodge in the area. There's a big lawn with a pool and a popular restaurant and bar. Very comfortable rooms with private bath are available, as are dorm rooms, but they have communal baths. Unfortunately, the origin of the lodge's name is unknown. Sorry Basil. ⊠ *Mosi-oa-Tunya Rd.* ☎ *213/32–3432* ⊕ *www. adventure-africa.com* ⇨ *23 rooms, 6 dormitories* ⅏ *In-hotel: restaurant, bar, pool, no elevator* ▤ *MC, V* ¶⊙¶ *EP.*

$$$$ ⊞ **River Club.** With split-level rooms that cling to the edge of the great ★ Zambezi, the River Club puts a modern spin on a Victorian house party. The view from the infinity pool seems unbeatable, until you watch the sun set from your claw-foot tub. Clever cooling mists of water draw flocks of birds to the massage tent, and the library begs for a glass of port and a serious book. History clings to the structure, built to the plans of the original house, but decorations have been lovingly collected from past and present. You could spend an entire day reading interesting anecdotes, old maps, *Punch* cartoons, and updates about the River Club's support of the local village. A candlelight dinner is followed by croquet on the floodlighted lawn before you retire to your partially starlighted room. You approach the lodge from the river—purely for the spectacular effect—but it necessitates negotiating some steep stairs. If you think you'll struggle, ask to be transferred by vehicle. ⌂ *Box 60469* ☎ *213/32–3672* ⊕ *www.wilderness-safaris.com* ⇨ *10 rooms* ⅏ *In-hotel: pool, no elevator* ▤ *MC, V* ¶⊙¶ *FAP.*

8

$$$$ ⊡ **Tongabezi and Sindabezi Island.** If you're looking for a truly African
Fodor'sChoice experience, Tongabezi and Sindabezi, its satellite island 4 km (2½ mi)
★ downriver, won't disappoint. Never formal but flagrantly romantic,
they are the frame around the picture, so to say, and do not upstage
the reason you have come: the flora and fauna. At Tongabezi, standard
rooms are spacious cream-and-ocher *rondawels* (round thatch huts)
featuring private verandas that can be enclosed in a billowing mosquito
net. Three suites are built into a low cliff and incorporate the original
riverine forest canopy. King beds set in tree trunks and covered by curtains of linen netting, oversize sofas in the sitting area, and giant bathtubs on the private decks are all unashamedly romantic. Every room
has a local guide who acts as a personal valet and caters to your every
whim. Room service is ordered via antique telephones, and the lodge
has an in-house holistic therapist. Small **Sindabezi Island,** which has
a 10-guest maximum, is separated by a stretch of river from Zambezi
National Park. Each of the island's huts has an open front with a private view, and your every need is anticipated, but there's no electricity
and hot bucket showers are by demand only. If your party takes Sindabezi for itself, the guide, boat, and land vehicle are at your disposal.
Dinner is served by lantern and candlelight on a sandbank under the
stars. ⬛*Box 31* ☎*213/32–7450 or 213/32–7468* ⊕*www.tongabezi.
com* ➡*5 suites, 5 cottages* ⚒*In-hotel: pool* ▤*MC, V* ⑩*FAP.*

¢ ⊡ **Bovu.** The vibe of California and Marrakesh in the '60s and '70s is
alive and well at this collection of thatched huts and campsites along
the banks of the Zambezi, 52 km (32 mi) upstream of the falls. This
is the place to chill out. Take a good book or an excellent companion.
Accommodations are basic but somehow quite perfect, each with gorgeous river views, and there are hot showers and flush toilets. The
food is good and the coffee better than most of the upscale lodges
serve. You can swim in a shallow section of small rapids naturally
protected from crocodiles or hippos (or this is the theory). Warning:
"island time" operates here and anything goes, so the staid or conservative are likely to find it unsuitable.Return transfers cost US$50 and
include a guided sunset cruise in a *mokoro* (an African canoelike boat)
and village walks. Meals are provided but cost extra. Don't forget to
check out the hat collection behind the bar in the main camp and add
your own to the mix. ⬛*Box 61122* ☎*213/32–3708* ⊕*www.jungle
junction.info* ➡*8 huts* ⚒*In-hotel: bar, no elevator.*

SPORTS & THE OUTDOORS

Livingstone can compete with the best as far as indulging the wildest
fantasies of adrenaline junkies and outdoor enthusiasts goes. You can
reserve activities directly with the operators, let your hotel or lodge
handle it, or book through a central booking group. **Safari Par Excellence** (☎*213/32–1629* ⊕*www.safpar.net*) offers elephant back safaris, game drives, river cruises, canoeing, kayaking, and rafting as well
as trip combinations, which are a good option if your time is limited
or you just want to go wild, such as the Raft-Heli, which offers a
spectacular view of the gorge at the conclusion of a hard day's rafting (you can substitute tandem kayaking or river boarding for raft-

ing) or the Heli-Jet that involves no strenuous walking as you helicopter in, go wild in a jetboat, and then helicopter out. Prices for combinations are available on request. **Livingstone's Adventure** (☎ *213/32–0058* ⊕ *www.livingstonesadventure.com*) offers a central booking service as well as operating Batoka Sky, *African Queen*, and Livingstone Quad Company.

WORD OF MOUTH

"[If you are visiting Livingstone] with kids, an elephant safari would be a hit. You can do raft trips that are not in the rapids too. A couple of days there would make sense."

–atravelynn

ATV-ING

Riding a quad through the mopane forest, seeing local villages, and playing in Batoka Gorge is possible courtesy of **Livingstone Quad Company** (☎ *213/32–0058* ⊕ *www.livingstonesadventure.com*). A one-hour ecotrail adventure costs US$65. The minimum age is 16, but even absolute beginners are welcome.

BOATING

Truly the monarch of the river, the *African Queen* (no relation to the movie except in name) (☎ *213/32–1513* ✎ *african.queen@thevictoriafalls.co.zm*) is an elegant colonial-style riverboat. Sunset cruises offer the maximum style and splendor. Costs start at US$37 for a 1½-hour lunch cruise. **Victoria Falls River Safaris** (☎ *213/32–1513* ✎ *riversafaris@zamnet.zm*) operates a doubly silenced, propeller-free, water-turbine boat (from US$65), which can access areas no other boats can get to. It's excellent for game and bird-spotting.

BUNGEE JUMPING

Bungee jumping off the 340-foot-high Victoria Falls Bridge with **African Extreme** (☎ *213/32–4231* ✎ *bungi@zamnet.zm*) is a major adrenaline rush, with 65 feet and three seconds of free fall and a pretty spectacular view. The jump costs from US$90, but it's worth getting the US$40 video, complete with *Top Gun* music track.

CANOEING

A gentle canoeing trip on the upper Zambezi is a great opportunity to see birds and a variety of game. Many of the lodges upriver have canoeing as an inclusive activity, but trips are also run by a number of companies, which are all reputable and provide similar value for your money. **Safari Par Excellence** is the longest running outfitter in the area and offers custom-made canoe trips that range from half-day outings to multiday excursions with costs starting at US$85.

ELEPHANT-BACK RIDING

Elephant Back Safaris. Fancy the idea of meandering through the bush courtesy of your own ellie? Not only does this operation keep clients happy enough to forget their sore thighs the next day, it also has the elephants happy enough to keep having babies! Trips with **Safari Par Excellence** start at US$60 for a meet and greet to US$140 for a ride.

8

FLYING

Livingstone Air Safaris (✉ *Office 20 Livingstone International Airport* ☎ *213/32–3147* ⊕ *No web*) will introduce you to the falls from a fixed wing aircraft. ■TIP→ Consider having the right hand door removed for excellent photographic conditions. Twenty-minute flights start at US$76. They also provide charters and seat rates throughout Zambia and Botswana and introductory flying lessons in various small aircraft including a Tiger Moth.

Batoka Sky (☎ *213/32–0058* ⊕ *www.livingstonesadventure.com*) offers weight-shift Aerotrike twin-axis microlighting (flying jargon for what resembles a motorized hang glider) and helicopter flights over the falls and through the gorges. There's a minimum of two passengers for helicopters. For microlighting you are issued a flightsuit (padded in winter) and a helmet with a headset, but you may not bring a camera for safety reasons. Batoka Sky has been operating since 1992, and has a 100% microlighting safety record. Flights are booked for early morning and late afternoon, and are dependent on the weather. Prices run US$90–US$190, depending on length of flight and aircraft. Your transfer and a day visa, if you are coming from Victoria Falls, are included. The Helicopter Gorge picnic (US$265) includes lunch and drinks for a minimum of six people.

HORSEBACK RIDING

You can take a placid horseback ride through the bush along the banks of the Zambezi with **Chundukwa Adventure Trails** (☎ *213/32–7452* ✑ *chundukwa@zamnet.zm*). If you are comfortable enough to keep your riding cool while a herd of elephants approach, you may want to watch game from horseback or do a multiday trail ride. Costs are U$60 for 1½ hours to a full day including lunch and drinks for US$137.50.

JETBOATING

If you want some thrills and speed but rafting seems a bit daunting, or you can't face the walk in and out, you'll probably enjoy jetboating with **Jet Extreme** (☎ *213/32–1375* ✑ *jetextremetony@microlink.zm*). A new cable-car ride, included in the cost of the jetboat ride (US$95 for 30 minutes), will mean no more strenuous walking out of the gorge. Jetboating can be combined with a rafting excursion, as the jetboat starts at the end of the rafting run, or with a helicopter trip out of the gorge. ■TIP→ The rafting and heli must be booked separately, although big operators like Safari Par Excellence and Livingstone's Adventure offer combinations. Children over seven can jetboat if they are accompanied by an adult.

KAYAKING

If you're feeling brave, try tandem kayaking. You do the same stretch of river as the rafting trips but in a two-seat kayak with a guide. Although you don't need previous experience, you have to be a fast study, as it entails getting a crash course in steering a kayak through serious Class 5 rapids. It's not for the faint of heart or, strangely, the big and macho—there's a weight limit of 175 pounds. The trip costs US$150 and is run by **Safari Par Excellence**.

RAPPELLING & SWINGING

For something completely different, **Abseil Zambia** (☎*213/32–1188* ✉*theswing@zamnet.zm*) has taken some specially designed heavy-duty steel cables, combined them with various pulleys and rigs, one dry gorge, and a 100% safety record to entertain both the fainthearted and the daring. The full day (US$115) is a great value, as it includes lunch, refreshments, and as many repeats of the activities as you like. △ Keep in mind that you will have to climb out following the gorge swing and the rappel; there's no Ecolift here. A half day (US$95) is advised during the hot months of October–December. Work up an appetite for more daring drops by starting on the zip line (or flying fox). You run off a ramp while attached to the line, and the sensation is pure freedom and surprisingly unscary, as you are not moving up or down. Next rappel down into the 175-foot gorge, and, after you climb out, try it again facing forward. It's called a rap run. You're literally walking down the cliff face. End the day with the king of adrenaline activities, a whopping 175-foot, 3½-second vertical free-fall swing into the gorge (US$60 for one swing). Three-two-one-hoooo-ha!

RAFTING & RIVER BOARDING

Safari Par Excellence offers rafting excursions to Batoka Gorge that cost US$120 to US$135 for either a half- or full-day trip, including a one-day visa if you're crossing the border to do it. The new Ecolift transports rafters out of the gorge, so you only have to climb down. You can also do a combination helicopter-and-rafting trip. Bring secure shoes, dry clothes for the long drive home, a baseball cap to wear under your helmet, and plenty of sunscreen. You can also decide to try river boarding (from US$145), in which you hop off the raft onto a body board and surf suitable rapids.

SHOPPING

If you fall in love with the furniture in your lodge, visit **Kubu Crafts** (✉*133 Mosi-oa-Tunya Rd.* ☎*213/32–0320* ⊕*www.kubucrafts.com*), a stylish home decor shop. Locally made furniture in hardwood and wrought iron is complemented by a selection of West African masks and weavings and the work of numerous local artists, including the fantastic oil paintings of Stephen Kapata. Prices can be ridiculously inflated. It's worth having a look through Mukuni Park before you buy the same article at a 500% markup. Kubu Crafts also sells tea, coffee, and cakes to enjoy in the garden.

Although the park at the entrance to the falls has stalls where you can find stone and wood carvings and simple bead and semiprecious-stone jewelry, the real gem of an African bazaar lies in the center of town, at **Mukuni Park Market** (✉*Mosi-oa-Tunya Rd. and Libala Dr.* ☎*No phone*). ■ TIP➔ This is the place to bargain. You'll be quoted top dollar initially, but shop around and watch the prices drop to roughly one-third of the original quote. Walk through the entire market before you commence buying. This will not only ensure that you get the best price but will give you the opportunity to gauge the level of craftsmanship that can be expected. Look out for individual and unusual pieces, as it is occasionally possible to find valuable antiques. The market is open daily approximately 7–6.

LIVINGSTONE & ZAMBIA ESSENTIALS

TRANSPORTATION

BY AIR

Nationwide, South African Airways, and Comair/British Airways fly regularly from Johannesburg into Livingstone International Airport, 5 km (3 mi) out of town. The flight is a comfortable hop, just under two hours, and the airport is small and friendly, with helpful staff to speed you on your way. ■TIP➔ If at all possible, do not check your luggage through from Johannesburg International, and always lock suitcases securely, as luggage theft in South Africa is an everyday occurrence.

Airlines **Comair/British Airways** (☎ 01/25–4444 or 01/25–4473 ⊕ www.british-airways.com). **Nationwide** (☎ 213/32–2251 ⊕ www.flynationwide.co.za). **South African Airways** (☎ 01/25–4350 ⊕ www.flysaa.com).

BY CAR

There is a perfectly reasonable traffic code in Zambia. Unfortunately, not many people have ever heard of it. You would do well to leave the driving to your guides or negotiate an all-inclusive rate with a taxi driver recommended by your hotel or lodge for the duration of your stay. Note that taxis are generally not allowed to cross the border, so if you want to visit Zimbabwe, you will have to book a tour that includes transfers. Once at the border, it is feasible to walk into and around Victoria Falls town, or rent a bicycle.

If you insist on renting a car, you should know that some of the roads have more potholes than tar. You don't necessarily need a 4x4, but it's not a bad idea, especially if you want to off-road it a bit. Imperial Car Rental operates from the offices of Voyagers at the Day Activity Center near the Zambezi Sun lodge. Hemingways rents out Land Rovers, fully equipped with tents and other camping equipment, you can even hire a driver! Costs start from US$180 for an unequipped vehicle.

Rental Companies **Hemingways** (☎ 213/32–0996 or 097/86–6492 ⊕ www.hemingwayszambia.com). **Imperial Car Rental** (☎ 213/32–3454 ⊕ www.voyagerszambia.com).

> ### PERUSING THE MARKETS
>
> Original African art is hard to come by in curio markets and unfortunately, most of the pieces are crude replications. Explore the markets with an open mind and simply buy a piece that tickles your fancy. Don't buy anything until you've walked the length of the market. This will give you a sense of what's on offer and the standard of workmanship. Look for objects carved from one solid piece of wood. Those made from more than one piece of wood are stuck together using very dodgy processes. Within a year you could find your beloved treasure in pieces.

CONTACTS & RESOURCES

CURRENCY EXCHANGE

Zambia's currency is the Zambian kwacha, which comes in denominations of ZK20, ZK50, ZK100, ZK500, ZK1,000, ZK5,000, ZK10,000, and ZK50,000 bills, necessitating carrying huge wads of notes. The kwacha is theoretically divided into 100 ngwees, but as you can buy nothing for one kwacha, an ngwee exists in name only and any bill including ngwees will simply be rounded off. At time of writing the conversion rate was about ZK5,000 to the US$1.

ELECTRICITY

To use electric-powered equipment purchased in the United States or Canada, bring a converter and adapter. If your appliances are dual voltage, you'll need only an adapter. The electrical current is 220 volts, 50 cycles alternating current (AC); wall outlets in most of the region take 15-amp plugs with three straight-edge prongs. ⚠ Power outages are a way of life in Livingstone. Do not leave anything plugged in that can be damaged by a power outage or fluctuating current.

> ### WORD OF MOUTH
>
> "The border crossing was very easy from Zambia to Zimbabwe. We walked across the bridge and watched the bungee jumpers. A few words of advice: Arrive as early as possible, not only for the photographic light but because of the heat; I would guess at least 100F in early October. Make sure to bring water on the walk. While there was almost no water on the Zambia side, there was plenty on the Zim side. Our walk along the trail which connects a string of viewpoints took a bit over an hour. We had the company of many monkeys...."
>
> –ekscrunchy

EMBASSIES

United States **U.S. Embassy** (⊠ *United Nations Ave. and Independence Rd., Box 31617, Lusaka* ☎ *01/25–0955* ✎ *ConsularLusaka@state.gov* ⊕ *zambia.usembassy.gov*).

EMERGENCIES

For minor injuries, a test for malaria, or the treatment of non–life-threatening ailments, you can go to the Rainbow or Southern medical centers or the Shafik clinic. For serious emergencies, contact SES (Specialty Air Services). Musamu Pharmacy is open weekdays 8–8, Saturday 8–6, and Sunday 8–1.

Emergency Services **General emergency** (☎ *999*). **Police** (☎ *991*). **Fire** (☎ *993*). **SES** (☎ *213/32–2330 land line, 097/74–0307 mobile phone*).

Hospitals **Rainbow Medical Centre** (⊠ *192 Kabila St.* ☎ *213/32–3519*). **Shafik clinic** (⊠ *Akapelwa St.* ☎ *213/32–1130*). **Southern Medical Centre** (⊠ *House 9, 1967 Makombo Rd.* ☎ *213/32–3547*).

Pharmacy **Musamu Pharmacy** (⊠ *Mosi-oa-Tunya Rd.* ☎ *09/65–88219 mobile phone*).

8

GAY & LESBIAN TRAVELERS

Homosexuality is technically illegal in Zambia, although it is widely accepted and presents no real problem.

INTERNET

Zigzag is open 8 to 8 and has free broadband and wireless.

Internet Access **Zigzag** (⊠ *The Warehouse, Mosi-oa-Tunya Rd.* ☏ *213/32–2814* ⊕ *www.zigzagzambia.com*).

TAXES

Zambia has a 17.5% V.A.T. and a 10% service charge, which is included in the cost or itemized on your bill.

TELEPHONES

Telephone rates in Zambia are much cheaper and more stable than those in Zimbabwe. Check numbers very carefully, as some are Zimbabwean mobile phones. Zambia and Zimbabwe now both have cell coverage, and there are certain areas where the networks overlap and mobile telephones work in both countries. If you have any trouble dialing a number, check with a hotel or restaurant owner, who should be able to advise you of the best and cheapest alternative. International roaming on your standard mobile phone is also an option, as coverage is quite extensive. Alternatively you could purchase a local Sim card with pay-as-you-go fill-ups. Pay phones are not a reliable option, and the costs of all telephone calls out of the country can be exorbitant.

The country code for Zambia is 260. When dialing from abroad, drop the initial 0 from local area codes. Note that all telephone numbers are listed as they are dialed from the country that they are in. Although the number for operator assistance is 100, you will be much better off asking your local lodge or restaurant manager for help.

TIME

Zambia operates on CAST (Central African Standard Time), which is two hours ahead of Greenwich Mean Time. That makes it seven hours ahead of North American eastern standard time (six hours ahead during eastern daylight saving time).

TIPPING

Tipping is less common in Zambia since service charges are included, but it's appreciated. Small notes or 10% is appropriate. Gas station attendants can be tipped, but tip a taxi driver only on the last day if you have used the same driver for a number of days.

TOURS

If it is serious game viewing you desire, join a one-day excursion to Chobe National Park in Botswana with **Bushtracks** (☏ *213/32–3232* ⊕*www.gotothevictoriafalls.com*). The trip costs US$170 and includes transfers from Livingstone, a game drive, a boat cruise, and all meals. Bushtracks is also your best bet for a visit to the Mukuni Village (US$32). Reservations must be in writing and prepaid for both.

Continued on page 528

Victoria Falls

VICTORIA FALLS

by Kate
Turkington

Expect to be humbled by the sheer power and majesty. Expect to be deafened by the thunderous noise, drenched by spray, and overwhelmed at the sight. Expect the mighty swath of roaring, foaming Victoria Falls—spanning the entire 1-mile width of the Zambezi River—to leave you speechless.

On a clear day the spray generated by the falls is visible from 31 mi (50 km) away—the swirling mist rising above the woodland savanna looks like smoke from a bush fire inspiring their local name, Mosi-Oa-Tunya, or the "Smoke that Thunders." The rim of the Falls is broken into separate smaller falls with names like the Devil's Cataract, Rainbow Falls, Horseshoe Falls, and Armchair Falls.

The Falls, which are more than 300 feet high, are one of the world's seven natural wonders and were named a UNESCO World Heritage Site in 1989. Upon seeing Victoria Falls for the first time Dr. David Livingstone proclaimed, "Scenes so lovely must have been gazed upon by angels in their flight." Truer words were never spoken.

WATCH OUT

Unlike other great waterfalls, the Zambezi has no rapids to warn of the approaching drop. One moment you'll be in calm placid waters; the next you'll be hurtling over the edge.

FALLS FACTS

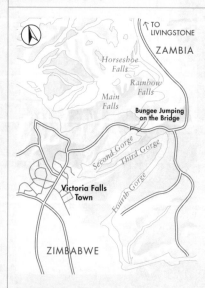

FORMATION OF THE FALLS

A basaltic plateau once stood where the falls are today. The whole area was once completely submerged, but fast-forward to the Jurassic Age and the water eventually dried up. Only the Zambezi River remained flowing down into the gaping 1-mile-long continuous gorge that was formed by the uneven cracking of the drying plateau.

WHEN TO GO

The Falls are spectacular at any time, but if you want to see them full, visit during the high water season (April–June) when more than 2 million gallons hurtle over the edge every second. The resulting spray is so dense that, at times, the view can be obscured. Don't worry though, the frequent gusts of wind will soon come to your aid and your view will be restored. If you're lucky to be there during a full moon, you might be able to catch a moonbow (a nighttime version of a rainbow) in the spray.

TO ZIM OR TO ZAM

Sorry Zambia, but the view from your side just doesn't stack up to the view from the Zimbabwean side. Only on the Zim side do you see infamous Devil's Cataract racing through the gorge; the entire width of the world's most spectacular waterfall; and the most rainbows dancing over the rapids—a bronze statue of Dr Livingstone's first sight of the falls is also here. You'll also get to walk through the glorious rain forest that borders the cliff edges, where wild flowers glow from greenery and monkeys chatter in ancient trees. This is also where accessible, flat-stone pathways—found immediately after you pass through the Zimbabwe entrance to the Falls—will take even the most unfit, tottery, or wheelchair-bound visitor right up to all the viewpoints. You don't need a map or a guide, as each path to the viewpoints is clearly marked.

CROSSING THE FALLS

Built in 1905, Victoria Falls Bridge is a monument to explorer, adventurer, empire-builder and former South African Prime Minister Cecil Rhodes's dream of creating a Cape-to-Cairo railway. Though the line was never completed, steam-powered trains still chug over the bridge, re-creating a sight seen here for over a century. From the bridge you get a knockout view of the falls, as well as the Zambezi River raging through Batoka Gorge. An added bonus: watching adrenaline junkies hurl themselves off the 364-foot-high Victoria Falls Bridge.

GREAT SCOT!

The first European to set eyes on the falls was the Scots explorer and missionary Dr. David Livingstone in the mid-1850s. Overcome by the experience he named them after his queen, Victoria.

EXTREME SPORTS

Bungee jumping off Victoria Falls Bridge above the Zambezi River

Victoria Falls is renowned for the plethora of adventure activities that can be organized on either side. It's best to arrange activities through your hotel, or a safari adventure shop, but if you want to go it alone, know that some operators only serve one side of the falls and operators have a tendency to come and go quickly.

■ Bungee jumping with **African Extreme** (☎ 213/32–4231 ✉ bungi@zamnet.zm) is a major adrenaline rush, with 65 feet and three seconds of free fall and a pretty spectacular view.

■ If you fancy an elephant-back safari on your own elephant for a couple of hours in the morning or evening then **Safari Par Excellence** (☎ 213/1-4424 ⊕ www.safpar. com) will put you on board.

■ **Livingstone Air Safaris** (☎ 213/32–3147) will take you over the falls in a fixed-wing aircraft while **Batoka Sky** (☎ 213/32–0058 ⊕ www.livingstones adventure.com) will put you in a helicopter or microlight plane.

■ If you are comfortable enough to keep your cool while a herd of elephants approaches, go horseback riding along the banks of the Zambezi with **Chundukwa Adventure Trails** (☎ 213/32–7452 ✉ chundukwa@zamnet.zm).

■ If you want some thrills and speed but rafting seems a bit daunting, go jetboating with **Jet Extreme** (☎ 213/32–1375 ✉ jetextremetony@microlink.zm). A cable-car ride, included in the cost of the jetboat ride, will save strenuous walking out of the gorge.

■ Big operators like Safari Par Excellence and **Shearwater Adventures** (☎ 213/4–5806 ⊕ www.shearwatersadventures.com) can satisfy your every adventure whim with their combination packages that include jet-skiing, kayaking, rappelling, swinging, and of course, white-water rafting, reputed to be the best in the world with Class-6 rapids and down.

VICTORIA FALLS, ZIMBABWE

The town of Victoria Falls started with a little curio shop and slowly expanded until the 1970s, when it became the preferred falls destination. The political problems following independence have been well documented in the world press and have certainly taken their toll.

There has been significant poaching in the Zambezi National Park to the northwest. (If you really want to have the African game experience, take a day trip to Chobe National Park, 70 km [44 mi] away in Botswana; ⇨ *Livingstone and Zambia Essentials, above.*) Regardless, the town enjoys the happy coincidence of being a shopper's paradise inside a national park. This means you can buy an elephant carving while watching the real McCoy march past the shop window. The town is extremely compact. Almost all the hotels are within walking distance, and the falls themselves are only 10 minutes away on foot. The main road that runs through town and goes to the falls in one direction and to the airport in the other is called Livingstone Way. Park Way is perpendicular. Most of the shops, banks, and booking agents can be found on these two streets, and this part of town is also where most of the hawkers operate. ■ TIP➔ Give them a clear berth, as their wares are cheap for a reason (the boat cruise is substandard, it is illegal to change money, etc.)

WHAT TO SEE

Numbers in the margin correspond to numbers on the Victoria Falls (town) map.

❻ **Falls Craft Village.** The village consists of 35 life-size constructions, typi-
☾ cal of six main ethnic groups living in Zimbabwe in the 19th century. All artifacts are genuine. A free pamphlet and on-site guide explain the living arrangements, various crafts, and the uses of different tools. At the back of the village you can watch artisans carving the stone and wood sculptures that are sold in the adjoining shop. For a small fee you

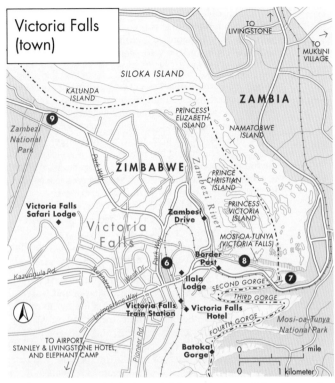

Victoria Falls
(town)

TO LIVINGSTONE

TO MUKUNI VILLAGE

SILOKA ISLAND

KALUNDA ISLAND

ZAMBIA

PRINCESS ELIZABETH ISLAND

NAMATOBWE ISLAND

Zambezi National Park

ZIMBABWE

PRINCE CHRISTIAN ISLAND

Zambezi River

PRINCESS VICTORIA ISLAND

Victoria Falls Safari Lodge ◆

Victoria Falls

Zambesi Drive

MOSI-OA-TUNYA (VICTORIA FALLS)

 9

Park Way

Park Way

6

Border Post

8

7

Kazungula Rd.

West Dr.

Ilala Lodge ◆

SECOND GORGE

THIRD GORGE

Livingstone Way

Reynard Rd.

Victoria Falls Train Station

Victoria Falls Hotel ◆

FOURTH GORGE

Mosi-oa-Tunya National Park

Pioneer Rd.

TO AIRPORT, STANLEY & LIVINGSTONE HOTEL, AND ELEPHANT CAMP

Batoka Gorge ◆

0 ——— 1 mile

0 ——— 1 kilometer

8

can have a *n'anga* (witch doctor) "throw the bones" to tell your fortune. There is traditional dancing every night (about US$30). ✉ *Stand 206, Soper's Crescent, off Livingstone Way, behind banks* ☎ *013/4–4309* ✎ *cvillage@mweb.co.zw* 💲 *US$20* ⏱ *Daily 8:30–5.*

NEED A BREAK?

The River Cafe (✉ *Landela Centre, off Livingstone Way* ☎ *No phone*) is a popular venue with travelers and locals in need of a fuss-free and relatively speedy lunch. Inside a little shopping mall it provides quick, easy meals including burgers and the *peri peri* (a chile-based sauce) chicken, which is particularly good.

7 **Victoria Falls Bridge.** A monument to Cecil Rhodes's dream of completing a Cape-to-Cairo rail line, this graceful structure spans the gorge formed by the Zambezi River. It would have been far easier and less expensive to build the bridge upstream from the falls, but Rhodes was captivated by the romance of a railway bridge passing over this natural wonder. A net was spanned across the gorge under the construction site, whereupon the construction workers went on strike for a couple of days. They resumed work only when it was explained that they would not have to leap into it at the end of every workday. Although the workers did not share the current adrenaline-fueled obsession with jumping into the abyss, the net probably had a lot to do with the miraculous fact that only two people were killed during construction. The bridge was completed in only 14 months, and the last two cross-girders were defiantly joined on April 1, 1905.

To get onto the bridge, you first have to pass through Zimbabwean immigration and customs controls, so bring your passport. Unless you decide to cross into Zambia, no visa is necessary. Depending on crowds, the simple procedure can take from five minutes to a half hour. The border posts are open daily from 6 AM to 10 PM, after which the bridge

> **A NATURAL HIGH**
>
> As the second-highest bungee jump in the world, the 340-foot leap from the Victoria Falls Bridge is a major magnet for adrenaline junkies. The view, if you can stomach it, is pretty spectacular, too. A jump with **Shearwater Adventures** (☎ *013/4–5806* ⊕ *www.shearwateradventures. com*) costs US$90, and you must produce your passport to get a bridge pass.

is closed to all traffic. From the bridge you get a knockout view of the river raging through Batoka Gorge as well as a section of the falls on the Zambian side. An added bonus is watching the bungee jumpers disappear over the edge. ⊠ *Livingstone Way.*

⑧ Victoria Falls National Park. Plan to spend at least two hours soaking in the splendors of this park. Bring snacks and water, and supervise children extremely well, as the barriers are by no means safe. Babies and toddlers can be pushed in a stroller. If you visit the falls during the high-water peak, between April and June, you'd do well to carry a raincoat or umbrella (you can rent them at the entrance) and to bring along a waterproof, disposable camera, because you *will* be drenched in the spray from the falls, which creates a permanent downpour. Photo opportunities are very limited due to the mist. ■ TIP→ Leave expensive cameras, cell phones, and wristwatches in your hotel or lodge safe.

The constant drizzle has created a small rain forest that extends in a narrow band along the edge of the falls. A trail running through this dripping green world is overgrown with African ebony, Cape fig, Natal mahogany, wild date palms, ferns, and deep red flame lilies. A fence has been erected to keep non-fee-paying visitors at bay. Clearly signposted side trails lead to viewpoints overlooking the falls. The most spectacular is **Danger Point,** a perilous rock outcropping that overlooks the narrow gorge through which the Zambezi River funnels out of the **Boiling Pot,** but be careful, as this viewpoint is hazardously wet and precarious. In low-water months (September–November) most of the water goes over the falls through the **Devil's Cataract,** a narrow and mesmerizingly powerful section of the falls visible from **Livingstone's statue.** Around the full moon the park stays open late so you can see the lunar rainbow formed by the spray—a hauntingly beautiful sight. Early morning and late afternoon are popular visiting times, as you can see the daylight rainbows then. A booklet explaining the formation and layout of the falls is available from the Victoria Falls Publicity Association for a small fee. ⊠ *Off Livingstone Way* ☎ *No phone* 🖙 *US$20* ⊙ *Daily 6–6, later around full moon.*

❾ Zambezi Wildlife Sanctuary. Originally a crocodile farm, this place also
☺ has several wildcats in cages as well as ostriches, making it an interesting stop. During late December you can watch baby crocodiles
hatch—an almost continuous process. Feeding times are 11:15 AM and
3:45 PM for the crocs and 4 PM for the lions. Drive down a short bush
track about 200 feet before the entrance to the sanctuary, where you
can spy large numbers of vultures preying on the leftovers from the
croc feedings. The sanctuary also has a tea garden. ⊠ *325 Park Way
Dr.* ☎ *013/4–3576 or 013/4–4604* ⊘ *znscroc@africaonline.co.zw*
⊒ *US$5* ☉ *Daily 8–5.*

WHERE TO STAY & EAT

It's important to know that inflation caused by the current political climate is causing prices to constantly rise. Getting an all-inclusive package tour is by far the best bet to this area.

$$ ✕ **Mama Africa Eating House.** Painted a wild lime green, Mama Africa
wraps you in her vibrantly colored bosom and stimulates your senses.
Funky sculptures abound, and a live township quartet provides toe-
tickling local jazz from 7 until late. Humorously named for its size,
the Elephant Turd T-Bone Steak competes with Sadza Ndiuraye ("the
meal that kills you") and other dishes from all over Africa, many
served in traditional black cast-iron, three-legged pots. Ground nuts,
mild Mozambique peri-peri, and slow-cooked local sadza flavor the
air. Game meat is available in individual portions cooked to order.
Alternatively, have a selection on a platter with the evening barbecue.
Mama Africa provides a courtesy shuttle, which you can book when
you make your reservation. ⊠ *Back of Trading Post Shopping Centre,
Livingstone Way* ☎ *013/4–1725* ⊘ *mamaafrica@africaonline.co.zw*
⊛ *Reservations essential* ⊟ *No credit cards.*

$$$$ ✕ ⊡ **Victoria Falls Hotel.** Hotels come and go, but this landmark built
Fodor's Choice in 1904 has retained its former glory as a distant, stylish outpost in
★ empire days, while pandering to today's modern tastes, needs, and
wants. Such grandeur can be a little overwhelming, and especially sur-
prising if you've just been on safari. The hotel's manicured lawns are
perched on the falls' edge, with a view of the bridge, and soothing
sounds permeate the gardens (and the rooms if you leave the windows
open). Cool cream walls form the backdrop for elegant mahogany and
wicker furniture. In the bathroom an old-fashioned drench shower will
wash away the most stubborn African dust. Halls are filled with sepia-
tone photos from throughout the hotel's history and animal trophies
so old they are going bald. After checking your e-mail in the E-Lounge
and visiting the salon, you can dine and dance at the elegant Living-
stone Room ($$$$). Two far less formal restaurants include the Terrace
($–$$$), with an à la carte menu, daily high tea, and a beautiful view
of the bridge, and Jungle Junction (US$30), which has a huge barbecue
buffet and traditional dancers. ⊠ *Mallet Dr., Box 10* ☎ *013/4–4751
or 013/4–4760* ⊕ *www.victoriafallshotel.com* ⊿ *143 rooms, 18 suites*
⊘ *In-hotel: 3 restaurants, room service, bar, tennis court, pool, no elevator* ⊟ *V* ⊙ *BP.*

8

$$$–$$$$ ✕⊡**Victoria Falls Safari Lodge.** Award-winning architecture, superb service, beautiful decor, and a magnificent view all set this lodge apart. About 4 km (2½ mi) outside town, it sits on a hilltop overlooking Zambezi National Park. A water hole below the lodge attracts herds of game, including buffalo and elephants. Soaring thatch roofs, huge wooden beams, and reed ceilings envelop you in a luxurious African atmosphere. The sides of the lodge are completely open to admit cooling breezes. All rooms face out, and you can fold back the glass-and-wood screens leading to your private veranda. The Makuwa-Kuwa Restaurant ($–$$$) makes full use of the view. Carnivorous options include prime Zimbabwe beef, warthog, and ostrich grilled to perfection. For dessert, dare to resist the Mosi Mousse, which has a chocolate band that spans a cascade of fruit and chocolate mousse. The Boma, also on the premises, offers prix-fixe dining (US$35). There is a courtesy shuttle to and from Victoria Falls. ⊠ *Off Park Way, 4 km (2½ mi) from Victoria Falls* ⌂ *Box 29* ☎ *013/4–3211 or 013/4–3220* ✉ *saflodge@saflodge.co.zw* ⇆ *72 rooms, 6 suites* ♿ *In-room: no TV. In-hotel: 2 restaurants, room service, bar, pools, no elevator* ⊟ *AE, MC, V* �†◎⊟ *BP.*

$$$ ✕⊡**Ilala Lodge.** Near the center of town, this small gem is 10 minutes
★   from the falls on foot. Thatch roofs give the lodge an elegant yet African look. Dining outside under the night sky at the Palm Restaurant ($$), with the falls thundering 300 feet away, is a particularly enticing way to while away a Zimbabwean evening. The Palm also serves a great terrace lunch overlooking the bush. Guest rooms are hung with African paintings and tapestries and filled with delicately caned chairs and tables and with dressers made from old railroad sleepers. French doors open onto a narrow strip of lawn backed by thick bush. Unlike most hotels in town, Ilala Lodge has no fence around it, so at night it's not uncommon to find elephants browsing outside your window or buffalo grazing on the lawn. ⊠ *411 Livingstone Way, Box 18* ☎ *013/4–4737* ⊕ *www.ilalalodge.com* ⇆ *32 rooms, 2 suites* ♿ *In-hotel: restaurant, room service, bar, pool, no elevator* ⊟ *V* †◎⊟ *BP.*

$$$$ ⊡**Masuwe Lodge.** Tucked away on the Masuwe estate, this tented en-suite lodge, a 10-minute drive from Victoria Falls, is redolent of East African camps. Tents are well appointed and spacious with private viewing decks. Game drives, elephant rides, and lion walks are all available. Transfers to and from Victoria Falls make this an appealing retreat and base to plan your safari. ☎ *013/4–4424* ⊕ *www.safpar.net* ⇆ *10 rooms* ♿ *In-room: no a/c, no TV. In-hotel: bar, pool, no elevator* ⊟ *V* †◎⊟ *FAP.*

$$$$ ⊡**Stanley and Livingstone at Victoria Falls.** This painstakingly composed small hotel is on its own 6,000 acres of game reserve 10 minutes out of town. Public rooms are furnished with some spectacular antiques and have verandas overlooking a water hole where elephants and other animals come to drink. Spacious suites are decorated with dark wood, and bathrooms are a stylish study in white tile, green marble, and gold trim. All suites share the view of the water hole. The rate includes game drives and all on-site activities except elephant rides and transfers to the airport or to town. ⌂ *Box 160* ☎ *013/4–1003 or 013/4–1009* ⊕ *www.*

stanley-livingstone-hotel.com ⇆*15 suites* ⌂*In-hotel: restaurant, bar, pool, no elevator, no children under 12* ▭*AE, MC, V* ⦶*FAP.*

$ ⌸**Jingle Bells.** A comfortable and spacious bed-and-breakfast type that owes its name to the time of year it originally opened, Jingle Bells is a great option for a quiet stay in Victoria Falls. Decor is fresh and simple. Mariolina De Leo, the very friendly and helpful host, is fluent in Italian, English, and French. Of the rooms, two have double beds and nine have twins; all have private bathrooms. The entire house can be rented fully serviced with a cook and cleaners. ⊠*591 Manyika Rd., Box 289* ☎*013/4–3242* ✉*marcla@mweb.co.zw* ⇆*11 rooms* ⌂*In-hotel: pool, no elevator* ▭*No credit cards* ⦶*BP.*

$ ⌸**Victoria Falls Backpackers.** Rooms at this inexpensive and jolly backpacker's lodge are named after animals, with decor to match. The owners have created a child-friendly environment (the pool has a small fence, for example), offer great booking services, and claim to get the best activity prices in town. Overland trucks are not allowed. ⊠*357 Gibson Rd., Box 151* ☎*013/4–2209 or 013/4–2248* ⊕*www.victoria-fallsbackpackers.com* ⇆*6 rooms* ⌂*In-hotel: bar, pool* ▭*No credit cards* ⦶*CP.*

SPORTS & THE OUTDOORS

You can book all the adventures listed below (and many others) through your hotel or one of the major booking offices along Park Way:

Safari Par Excellence (☎*013/4–4424* ⊕*www.safpar.com*). **Shearwater Adventures** (☎*013/4–4471* ⊕*www.shearwateradventures.com*). **Wild Horizons** (☎*013/4–4571* ⊕*www.wildhorizons.co.za*).

BOATING

A cruise on the Upper Zambezi is a relaxing way to take in game and scenery. Hippos, crocs, and elephants are spied fairly regularly, and your captain will stop and comment whenever something noteworthy rears its head. **Shearwater Adventures** has a sunset cruise (US$35). Shearwater also offers a 30-minute white-water jetboat ride below the falls. This activity is a great adventure for the not so bold, since all you do is hang on. Children over seven can jetboat if accompanied by an adult. Beer and other cold drinks are included in the price (US$80).

CANOEING

Shearwater Adventures offers half- and full-day canoe trips and a very gentle Wine Route trip on which you don't even paddle (US$70). **Wild Horizons** leads canoe trips on the Zambezi River above the falls. The river here is mostly wide and flat. You might view crocodiles, hippos, or elephants. The one-hour game drive through Zambezi National Park to reach the launch point is an added bonus. Most trips provide a bush breakfast, a coffee break, and a casual lunch. You can select a half- or full-day trip or two- to three-night expeditions. No experience or physical prowess is required. Expect to pay US$85 for a half day and US$105 for a full day.

8

CLOSE UP

Zimbabwe's Tribes

Traditional Shangaan dancer wearing animal skins during a performance.

NDEBELE

The Ndebele people (called Matabele by the British who could not pronounce Ndebele), are distant cousins of the Zulu. Ndebele women are known for their colorful beaded dress in striking geometric patterns and contrasting colors. Beaded ornamentation on female Ndebele symbolizes their status in society; the older a woman gets, the more ornamentation she wears. The Isingolwani, a colorful necklace made of grass and cotton, is the typical ornamentation of married women and has been incorporated into western designs. The Ndebele have struggled to keep their heritage alive. They live in wards, with the chief, or ikozi, holding authority over each ward. Extended families make up the umuzi, or residential unit. Initiation into adulthood for Ndebele women entails being secluded in the home and taught to be a homemaker. This is followed by a coming-out ceremony where the woman displays herself wearing traditional dress. This is also how Ndebele women prepare for the marriage ceremony.

SHANGAAN

Although about 6 million Shangaan people live in various regions across Southern Africa, a large concentration reside in eastern southern Zimbabwe. They live in rondavels and are a largely agricultural society. Shangaan society is patrilineal, with many men taking more than one wife, and the extended family living together. When minerals were discovered in Southern Africa, many Shangaan became laborers in the diamond and gold mines. This shift has caused the rural traditions of the tribe to fade somewhat. With the introduction of Christianity to Africa, many Shangaan converted, though some still practice the animist worship of their ancestors. This can involve the practice of animal sacrifice or ritual offerings, especially in rural settlements. There are as many as five variants of the language of the Shangaan, called Xichangana.

ELEPHANT-BACK RIDING

The **Shearwater Elephant Company** (☎*013/4–5806* ⊕*www.shearwater adventures.com*) has morning and evening rides accompanied by breakfast or snacks and sunset drinks (US$100). **Wild Horizons** offers elephant rides (US$100), including transfers and either a full breakfast or drinks and snacks.

FLYING & PARASAILING

Flying over the falls, called the Flight of Angels, is a better option from the Zambian side, as the Vic Falls airport is a long way from the Zimbabwean side of the falls. Still, there are some options available. **Shearwater Adventures** runs a helicopter flight from the Elephant Hills Hotel and gets you over the falls in a couple of minutes. It costs US$95 for 12–13 minutes. **Zambezi Parasailing** (☎*013/4–2209* ⊕*www. victoriafallsbackpackers.com*) provides 10-minute parasails for US$50, including transfers from anywhere in town.

HORSEBACK RIDING

Safari Par Excellence is the booking agent for **Zambezi Horse Trails** (☎*091/21–3270* ✉*zamhorse@mweb.co.zw*), run by Alison Baker, a Vic Falls legend. She knows the bush, rides hard, and can shoot straight (and knows how to avoid having to). Experienced riders may go on game-viewing rides ranging from three hours to five days. Novices can go for two hours but will not be allowed close to animals such as elephants and lions. Costs range from US$55 for two hours to US$100 for a full day, including lunch, drinks, and park fees. Multiday rides are available by request.

RAFTING & RIVER BOARDING

Safari Par Excellence specializes in multiday trips to Batoka Gorge as well as the standard half- and full-day adventures. Rafting starts at US$105. **Shearwater Rafting** (☎*013/4–5806* ⊕*www.shearwateradventures.com*) runs a full-day trip for US$110—lunch, drinks, and transfers included. Half-day trips are available. **Wild Horizons** leads full- and half-day rafting trips, as well as a 2½-day trip, starting at US$95.

RAPPELLING & SWINGING

Wild Horizons lets you swing off steel cables in the gorge. Take your pick from the flying fox, rap jump, abseil (rappel), or the big gorge swing. *For descriptions of what these crazy activities are, see Rappelling & Swinging under Livingstone, Zambia, above.* The cost is from US$30 for a single activity to US$115 for the full day adrenalin package.

8

SHOPPING

Several curio and crafts shops lie beyond the Falls Craft Village, including the stylish **Elephant Walk Mall** (✉*Sopers Crescent, behind banks and post office*). At the sprawling **Trading Post** (✉*Livingstone Way*) you can buy a variety of crafts. There is an international shipping agent between the shops.

VICTORIA FALLS & ZIMBABWE ESSENTIALS

TRANSPORTATION

BY AIR

Victoria Falls Airport (VFA) lies 22 km (14 mi) south of town. South African Airways, Air Zimbabwe, and British Airways all fly direct between Johannesburg and Victoria Falls daily.

Airport Victoria Falls Airport (✉ *Livingstone Way* ☎ *013/4-4250*).

Airlines Air Zimbabwe (☎ *013/4-4316* ⊕ *www.airzimbabwe.com*). **British Airways-Comair** (☎ *013/4-2053 or 013/4-2388* ⊕ *www.british-airways.com*). **South African Airways** (☎ *04/738-922* ⊕ *www.flysaa.com*).

BY BUS

Most hotels send free shuttle buses to meet incoming flights and provide free transfers for departing guests; book in advance. The cheapest way to get to and from the airport is to book a shuttle bus with Falcon Safaris or Travel Junction in the Trading Post. A one-way transfer is US$10 per person.

Shuttles Falcon Safaris (☎ *013/4-2695* ⊕ *www.falconsafaris.com*). **Travel Junction** (☎ *013/4-41480* ⊕ *www.victoriafallsbackpackers.com*).

BY CAR

Attractions in town tend to be within walking distance or just a short taxi ride away, so a rental is not worth it.

BY TAXI

Taxis are cheap and convenient. You can pay in local or foreign currency, but fares fluctuate drastically. Hotels can summon reputable taxis quickly and advise you on the cost. Tipping is not mandatory, but change is always appreciated.

CONTACTS & RESOURCES

CURRENCY EXCHANGE

Zimbabwe's currency is the Zimbabwe dollar. Bearer cheques, as the bills are known since they are promissory notes not official legal tender, are in denominations that range from Z$1 to Z$100,000. ⚠ Stay away from Zimbabwe money and carry US$ in small denominations. Zimbabwe's currency remains particularly volatile, with the daily exchange rate rising by the thousands.

ELECTRICITY

To use electric-powered equipment purchased in the United States or Canada, bring a converter and adapter. If your appliances are dual voltage, you'll need only an adapter. The electrical current is 220 volts, 50 cycles alternating cur-

> ### GOOD SOUVENIRS
>
> Shona stone carvings from Zimbabwe, woven baskets from Botswana and Zambia, and soapstone from Zambia and Zimbabwe make great souvenirs. Make sure you pack these things carefully, especially the soapstone, as it's all extremely fragile.

rent (AC); wall outlets in most of the region take 15-amp plugs with three square prongs.

EMBASSIES

United States **U.S. Embassy** (✉ *172 Herbert Chitepo Ave., Box 4010, Harare* ☎ *04/25-0593* ✎ *consularharare@state.gov* ⊕ *harare.usembassy.gov*).

EMERGENCIES

MARS (Medical Air Rescue Services) is on standby for all emergencies. Dr. Nyoni is a trauma specialist and operates a hospital opposite the Shoestring lodge. Go to Victoria Falls Pharmacy for prescriptions.

Emergency Services **Police** (☎ *013/4-4206 or 013/4-4681*). **MARS** (✉ *West Dr., opposite Shoestring* ☎ *013/4-4646*).

Hospital **Dr. Nyoni** (✉ *West Dr., opposite Shoestring* ☎ *013/4-3356*).

Pharmacy **Victoria Falls Pharmacy** (✉ *Phumula Centre, off Park Way* ☎ *013/4-4403*).

GAY & LESBIAN TRAVELERS

Homosexuality is not illegal in Zimbabwe but can be a practical problem. Attitudes are improving, but it's advisable to be extremely circumspect.

INTERNET

As telephone rates continue to climb, so do Internet prices. The average cost at time of writing is between US$1 and US$2 for 15 minutes.

Internet Access **E-world** (✉ *Victoria Falls Hotel* ☎ *013/4-4751*). **Shearwater** (✉ *Park Way* ☎ *013/4-5806*).

TELEPHONE

The country code for Zimbabwe is 263. When dialing from abroad, drop the initial 0 from local area codes. Operator assistance is 962 for domestic and 965 for international inquiries, but it's better to ask a hotel or restaurant owner.

Zimbabwe has card-operated pay phones. Phone cards are available in several denominations, and a digital readout tells you how much credit remains. Telephone cards are available at newsstands and convenience stores.

TIME

Zimbabwe operates on CAST (Central African Standard Time), which is two hours ahead of Greenwich Mean Time. That makes it seven hours ahead of North American eastern standard time (six hours ahead during eastern daylight saving time).

GREEN LODGINGS IN ZIMBABWE & ZAMBIA

Staying green in this area is a no-brainer. Check out these three places as a starting point for your research.

ZIMBABWE GREEN LODGE

About 25 mi upstream from Victoria Falls is **Matetsi Safari Camp,** (above) which is at the center of Matetsi Game Reserve, the largest private game reserve in Zimbabwe and the single biggest rangeland for Africa's surviving elephants. The camp has 12 tents and access to about 8 mi of the Zambezi River waterfront. The lodge employs local people and works with them on an ongoing project to catalog the traditional use of plants. Guided bush walks and game drives offer exclusive access to buffalo, kudu, sable antelope, and even the endangered wild dog. You can also have a special dinner in the bush, as prepared by the kitchen staff. The fact that there are no fences between Matetsi and bordering Botswana's Chobe National Park and the Okavango Delta means that wildlife can roam freely across borders, which creates a rich sanctuary here for all manner of creatures.

CONTACT INFORMATION

ZAMBIA
Chiawa Camp: 01/26–1588; www.chiawa.com

Islands of Siankaba: 03/32–7490 or 01/26–0279; www.siankaba.net

ZIMBABWE
Matetsi Safari Camp: 443/552–3325; www.ccafrica.com

ZAMBIA GREEN LODGES

You'll find **Islands of Siankaba** (right) about 30 mi upstream from Victoria Falls. Awarded the Environmental Certificate by the Environmental Council of Zambia in 2002, shortly before its opening, the lodge is on two forested islands in the Zambezi River. A suspension bridge links the two islands and leads to an overhead walkway in the tree canopy that connects the elevated chalets to the lodge's restaurant. The walkways are in place to protect the islands' delicate riverine environment. In fact, the construction of the lodge was built mainly with commercially grown, non-indigenous pine. When local wood was used, the lodge planted hardwood saplings to replace them. Electricity is drawn from the Victoria Falls hydroelectric plant and river water is recycled and treated on-site for use in the camp. Local tribes are employed by the lodge, where sunset cruises, mokoro rides, guided nature walks, white-water rafting, and bungee jumping are all on the menu. Guests can also opt to fly over Victoria Falls in a microlight plane.

Chiawa Camp, (below) a family-owned and -managed property in Zambia, supports the surrounding Lower Zambezi area through conservation, wildlife education, and community involvement. The camp has undertaken the project of reintroducing wild cheetahs and the ground hornbill to the Lower Zambezi National Park, and it contributes school supplies for AIDS orphans in surrounding communities annually. These are just a few of Chiawa's projects, so while you relax in one of five classic safari tents under a grove of Mahogany trees, you will know that you are not only enjoying the beauty of the Zambezi River Valley but helping to preserve it as well.

OFFSET YOUR FOOTPRINT

Everyone needs to do their part to help ease the environmental impact on our planet. A good place to start is by offsetting your carbon footprint. To do this, look into offsetting greenhouse gas emissions. If you have a choice, take trains over flying. If you must fly, try to take a nonstop flight. You can calculate your CO_2 footprint using several online tools. Atmosfair (⊕ *www.atmosfair.de*), Better World Club (⊕ *www.betterworldclub.com*), NativeEnergy (⊕ *www.nativeenergy.com*) all have CO_2 calculators that will calculate your emissions for individual flights, as well as provide you with ideas on how to offset them.

8

On Safari

By Andrew Barbour, Julian Harrison, and David Bristow Updated by Kate Turkington

Mention Africa and most of us conjure up visions of wild-life—lions roaring as night falls, antelope cantering across the plains, a leopard dangling languidly from a tree. The images never fail to fascinate and draw us in, and once you experience them in the flesh, you're hooked. The look, the feel—the dusty smell—of the African bush seep into your soul, and long after you've gone, you find yourself missing it with an almost physical longing.

Do everyone a favor, though, and pass up the impulse to rush out and buy khakis and a pith helmet. The oldtime safari is dead. Hemingway and the great white hunters took it to their graves, along with thousands upon thousands of equally dead animals. Indeed, too many wildlife documentaries have conditioned foreign visitors into thinking that Africa is overrun with animals. The truth is far less romantic—and much safer—especially in South Africa, where fences or rivers enclose all major reserves. The African bush is no Disney-choreographed show, however; this wilderness is a real one.

In choosing to take a safari, you'll embark on one of the biggest travel adventures of your life. It's a big investment of both time and money—and planning well is crucial to ensure you have a good time. Even a basic question like "what should I wear?" is extremely important. In this safari section, we'll cover all the special considerations and lingo you'll need, with plenty of insider tips along the way.

GETTING STARTED

It's never too soon to start planning your safari. There are many factors to consider just regarding the destination: geography, animal migrations, weather, visa requirements, and inoculations. You must also weigh some personal factors: your budget, schedule, fitness level, and comfort requirements. Most people start planning a safari six to nine months in advance, which allows time to set a spending limit, choose an itinerary, and organize travel documents. You can wait and plan the trip over a few weeks, but doing so greatly increases your chances of being closed out of the places you really want to see. In fact, planning your trip 12 months in advance isn't unreasonable, especially if you want to travel during peak season—November through February in South Africa, July through October elsewhere—and have your heart set on a particular lodge.

TELEPHONE COUNTRY CODES

- Botswana: 267
- Kenya: 254
- Namibia: 264
- South Africa: 27
- Tanzania: 255
- Zambia: 260
- Zimbabwe: 263

Deciding where you want to go and choosing the safari operator in whose hands you'll place your trip are the most important things you need to do. Start planning for your safari the way you would any trip. Read travel books about the areas that most interest you. Talk to people who have been on a similar trip; word-of-mouth advice can be invaluable. Surf the net. Get inspired. Line up your priorities. And find someone you trust to help plan your trip.

THE PAPER TRAIL

A valid passport is a must for travel to any African country. If you don't have a passport, apply immediately, because the process takes approximately five to six weeks. For a greatly increased fee, the application process can be shortened to as little as one week, but leaving this detail to the last minute can be stressful. If you have a passport, check the expiration date; if it's due to expire within six months of your return date, you need to renew your passport at once. ⚠ Certain countries, such as South Africa, won't let you enter with a soon-to-expire passport; you also need two blank pages in your passport to enter South Africa.

Check on what immunizations are required for the countries you're visiting. *See our chart below for what you'll need for each country.* Some countries may demand an inoculation certificate if you arrive directly from a tropical area or have traveled to one prior to your safari trip.

If you're taking a self-driving safari or will be renting a car in countries other than South Africa and Namibia, you'll need an international driver's license. These licenses are valid for one year and are issued at any American Automobile Association (AAA) office in the United States; you must have a current U.S. driver's license. You need to bring two passport-type photographs with you for the license. A valid U.S. driver's license is accepted in South Africa and Namibia.

■TIP➔ If you're planning a honeymoon safari, make sure the bride's airline ticket, passport, and visas all use the same last name. Any discrepancies, especially between a passport and an airline ticket, will result in your trip being grounded before you ever take off. Brides may want to consider waiting to change their last name until after the honeymoon. And be sure to let the lodge know in advance that you are on your honeymoon. You'll get lots of special goodies and extra-special pampering thrown in.

TRAVEL INSURANCE

Get a comprehensive travel-insurance policy in addition to any primary insurance you already have. Travel insurance incorporates trip cancellation; trip interruption or travel delay; loss or theft of, or damage to, baggage; baggage delay; medical expenses; emergency medical transportation; and collision damage waiver if renting a car. These policies are offered by most

DOCUMENT CHECKLIST

- Passport
- Visas, if necessary
- Airline tickets
- Proof of yellow-fever inoculation
- Accommodation and transfer vouchers
- Car-rental reservation forms
- International driver's license
- Copy of information page of your passport
- Copy of airline tickets
- Copy of medical prescriptions

travel-insurance companies in one comprehensive policy and vary in price based on both your total trip cost and your age.

It's important to note, especially in light of recent events in Kenya, Bali, etc. that travel insurance does not include coverage for threats of a terrorist incident or for any war-related activity. It's important that you speak with your operator before you book to find out how they would handle such occurrences. For example, would you be fully refunded if your trip was canceled because of war or a threat of a terrorist incident? Would your trip be postponed at no additional cost to you?

■ TIP→ Purchase travel insurance within seven days of paying your initial trip deposit. For most policies this will not only ensure your trip deposit, but also cover you for any preexisting medical conditions and default by most airlines and safari companies. The latter two are not covered if your policy is purchased after seven days.

Many travel agents and tour operators stipulate that travel insurance is mandatory if you book your trip through them. This coverage is not only for your financial protection in the event of a cancellation but also for coverage of medical emergencies and medical evacuations due to injury or illness, which often involve use of jet aircraft with hospital equipment and doctors on board and can amount to many thousands of dollars.

If you need emergency medical evacuation, most travel-insurance companies stipulate that you must obtain authorization by the company prior to the evacuation. Unfortunately, many safari camps and lodges are so remote that they don't have access to a telephone, so getting prior authorization is extremely difficult if not impossible. You should check with your insurance company before you leave to see whether it has this clause and if so, what can be done to get around it. Good travel agents and tour operators are aware of the issue and will address it.

MONEY MATTERS

Most safaris are paid for in advance, so you need money only to cover personal purchases and gratuities. (The cash you take should include small denominations, like US$1, US$5, and US$10, for tips.) If you're not on a packaged tour and are self-driving, you need to carry more money. Credit cards—MasterCard, Visa, and, to a much lesser extent, American Express and Diners Club—are accepted throughout South Africa (American Express and, for the most part, Diners Club are not accepted in Botswana) and at most group-owned lodges and hotels, but not much elsewhere. Always check in advance whether your preferred card is accepted at the lodge. If you're self-driving, note that many places prefer to be paid in the local currency, so make sure you change money where you can.

Throughout this guide, the following abbreviations are used: **AE**, American Express; **DC**, Diners Club; **MC**, MasterCard; and **V**, Visa.

■TIP➜ It's a good idea to notify your credit-card company that you'll be traveling to Africa, so that unusual-looking transactions aren't denied.

HEALTH ISSUES

If you stick to cities and safari lodges, you won't be at an exaggerated health risk for most diseases. The real danger is malaria, but by taking the necessary precautions you should be well protected.

MALARIA
Malaria is the most common parasitic infection in the world. It occurs throughout the tropics and in adjacent hot and low-lying areas and infects 300 to 500 million people each year in some 90 countries, killing between 1.5 million and 3 million. Malaria infects about 10,000 returning travelers each year, killing about 1% of them. However, malaria is preventable and shouldn't prevent you from going on safari.

The disease is spread by the female Anopheles mosquito, who "feeds" between dusk and dawn, usually after midnight when you are most soundly asleep. If you have been bitten by an infected mosquito, you can expect to feel the effects anywhere from 7 to 90 days afterward. Typically you will feel like you have the flu, with worsening high fever, chills and sweats, headache, and muscle aches. In some cases this is accompanied by abdominal pain, diarrhea, and a cough. If it's not treated you could die. It's possible to treat malaria after you have contracted it, but this shouldn't be your long-term strategy for dealing with the disease.

⚠ If you feel ill even several months after you return home, tell your doctor that you have been in a malaria-infected area. The onset of flulike symptoms—aching joints or headache—is often the first sign that you have contracted either tick-bite fever (a bacterial infection transmitted

FEAR FACTOR

The recent volatile situation in Kenya has reminded us all how politically unstable this part of the world still is. While we can not tell you what to do about your plans for the once-in-a-lifetime trip that you've been planning for months, we can strongly suggest that you do your homework and be fully aware of the situation before making your final decision. The following sources will help you determine just what you'll face and help you make that call.

Centers for Disease Control (www.cdc.gov/travel). The CDC has information on health risks associated with almost every country on the planet, as well as what precautions to take. If you're planning a cruise, check out the CDC's Green Sheet—a list of cruise ships and their health-inspection scores.

World Health Organization (www.who.int). The WHO, the health arm of the United Nations, has information by topic and by country. Its clear, well-written publication "International Travel and Health," which you can download from the Web site, covers everything you need to know about staying healthy abroad.

Central Intelligence Agency (www.cia.gov). The CIA's online "World Factbook" has maps and facts on the people, government, economy, and more for countries from Afghanistan to Zimbabwe. It's the fastest way to get a snapshot of a nation. It's also updated regularly and, obviously, well researched.

World-Newspapers.com. There's nothing like the local paper for putting your finger on the pulse. This site has links to English-language newspapers, magazines, and Web sites in countries the world over.

U.S. State Department (travel.state.gov). The State Department's advice on the safety of a given country is probably the most conservative you'll encounter. That said, the information is updated regularly, and nearly every nation is covered. Just try to parse the language carefully. For example, a warning to "avoid all travel" carries more weight than one urging you to "avoid nonessential travel," and both are much stronger than a plea to "exercise caution." A travel warning is more permanent (though not necessarily more serious) than a so-called public announcement, which carries an expiration date.

AllSafeTravels.com. In one Web site you can check the official travel warnings of several nations (for a more rounded picture), catch up on relevant news articles, and see what other travelers have to say. The site covers not only safety and security concerns, but also weather hazards and health issues. For a small fee you can receive e-mail updates and emergency notifications for specific destinations.

ComeBackAlive.com. The Web site of author, filmmaker, and adventurer Robert Young Pelton is, as its name suggests, edgy, with information on the world's most dangerous places. Finding safety information on other, seemingly safer places requires a little more fiddling around. There are forums where danger junkies share tips, and there links to other relevant sites.

by ticks with symptoms including fever, severe headache, and a rash consisting of small red bumps) or malaria. Take it very seriously and go for a blood test immediately.

The first malarial protection method is to practice "safe safari"—that is, avoid getting bitten in the first place. Start your precautions by treating your clothes with a mosquito-repellent spray or laundry wash before you leave home. Most of these last approximately 14 days and through several washings and contain the active ingredient permethrin, which is sold as Permanone and Duranon. This spray is specifically for clothes and shouldn't be used on skin. You can find it at camping and outdoor stores such as Eastern Mountain Sports. Bring a mosquito-repellent spray that contains DEET and light-colored clothing, as mosquitoes (and tsetse flies) are attracted to dark surfaces, where they're hard to detect. *For more tips on what to do once you're on safari, see the malaria section of Health on Safari, below.*

There's no vaccine against malaria, but there are several medications you can use to protect yourself from getting the disease. It's vital that you take the prescribed dosage and the full course of the antimalarial medication because the incubation period for malaria can last up to four weeks after your return. Not taking even the last tablet of a multi-week course can mask the disease for several months; when it does erupt it will be more advanced and harder to detect than if you had followed the full regimen. Medication improves all the time, so consult your doctor or travel clinic for up-to-date information.

Where children are concerned, you cannot be too safe. The Center for Disease Control and Prevention or CDC (☎877/394–8747 international travelers' health line ⊕*www.cdc.gov/travel*) recommends that parents of children traveling to a malarial area see a doctor four to six weeks prior to the trip. Make sure you find out which prescription antimalaria drugs are approved for use by children. Malaria's effects on young children are much worse than they are on older people, and both the effects of malaria and the side effects of malarial prophylactics put strain on young kidneys. For this and other health reasons, it's best not to visit malarial areas with children under age 10 unless you practice stringent nonchemical preventive measures. Another, easier option is to choose a nonmalarial safari destination, including the Waterberg, Pilanesberg and Sun City, or the Eastern Cape in South Africa, or Etosha National Park in Namibia.

OTHER HEALTH ISSUES

Yellow fever isn't inherent in any of the countries discussed in this book. Southern countries may, however, require you to present a valid yellow-fever inoculation certificate if prior to arrival you traveled to a region infected with yellow fever, so it's always best to carry one.

Hepatitis A can be transmitted via contaminated seafood, water, or fruits and vegetables. According to the CDC, hepatitis A is the most common vaccine-preventable disease in travelers. Immunization consists of a series of two shots received six months apart. You need have

Pills & Vaccinations

	Yellow Fever	Malaria	Hepatitis A	Hepatitis B	Typhoid	Rabies	Polio	Other
Kenya	●	●	●	●	●	●	●	Meningitis
Tanzania	●	●	●	●	●	●	●	
South Africa	◑	●	●	●	●	●	●	
Botswana	◑	●	●	●	●	●	●	
Namibia	◑	●	●	●	●	●	●	
Zambia	◑	●	●	●	●	●	●	
Zimbabwe	◑	●	●	●	●	●	●	

KEY: ● = Necessary
● = Recommended
◑ = The government requires travelers arriving from countries where yellow fever is present to have proof that they got the vaccination

received only the first one before you travel. This should be given at least four weeks before your trip.

The CDC recommends vaccination for hepatitis B only if you might be exposed to blood (if you are a health-care worker, for example), have sexual contact with the local population, stay longer than six months, or risk exposure during medical treatment. As needed, you should receive booster shots for tetanus-diphtheria (every 10 years), measles (you're usually immunized as a child), and polio (you're usually immunized as a child).

The Web site, Travel Health Online (⊕ *www.tripprep.com*), is a good source to check out before you travel because it compiles primarily health and some safety information from a variety of official sources, and it's done by a medical publishing company.

VACCINATIONS

Traveling overseas is daunting enough without having to worry about all the scary illnesses you could contract. But, if you do your research and plan accordingly, there will be no reason to worry.

Check out the extremely helpful and informative Web site (www.cdc.gov) for the Centers for Disease Control and Prevention (CDC). You can find out country-by-country what you'll need. Remember that the CDC is going to be extremely conservative, so it's a good idea to meet with a trusted health care professional to decide what you'll really need, which will be determined on your itinerary. We've also included the basic information on the countries we cover in the preceding chart.

Keep in mind that there is a time frame for vaccines. You should see your health provider 4–6 weeks before you leave for your trip. Also keep in mind that vaccines and prescription could run you anywhere from $1,000 to $2,000. It's important to factor this into your budget when planning, especially if you're plans include a large group.

You must be up-to-date with all of your routine shots such as, measles/mumps/rubella (MMR) vaccine, diphtheria/pertussis/tetanus (DPT) vaccine, etc. If you're not up-to-date, usually a simple booster shot will bring you up to par. If you're traveling to Northern Kenya December through June, don't be surprised if you're doctor advises you to get inoculated against meningitis as this part of the continent tends to see an outbreak during this time.

We can't stress enough the importance of taking malaria prophylactics. But be warned that all malaria medications are not equal. Chloroquine is NOT an effective antimalarial drug. And halofantrine (marketed as Halfan), which is widely used overseas to treat malaria, has serious heart-related side effects, including death. The CDC recommends that you do NOT use halofantrine.

WHAT TO PACK

If you're flying to safari destinations with regular airports where large airplanes are used—Hoedspruit or Nelspruit's Kruger Mpumalanga International Airport, both in South Africa—normal international airline baggage allowances apply. Otherwise, access to game-viewing areas is often by light aircraft, on short sandy landing strips; therefore, luggage weight restrictions are strictly enforced. You'll be allowed one duffel-type bag, approximately 36 inches by 18 inches, so that it can be easily packed into the baggage pods of a small plane. One small camera and personal-effects bag can go on your lap. Keep all your documents and money in this personal bag.

Do yourself a favor and leave breakables and valuables at home. If you'd be heartbroken if an item was broken or lost, it probably doesn't belong on a safari.

■ TIP➔ At O.R. Tambo International Airport in Johannesburg you can check bags at Lock-Up Luggage, one level below international departures. The cost is approximately US$7 per bag per day.

CLOTHING

You should need only three changes of clothing for an entire trip; almost all safaris include laundry as part of the package. If you're self-driving you can carry more, but washing is still easy and three changes of clothes should be ample if you use drip-dry fabrics that need no ironing. On mobile safaris you can wear tops and bottoms more than once, and either bring enough underwear to last a week between lodges, or wash as you go in the bathroom sink. Unless there's continual rain (unlikely), clothes dry overnight in the hot, dry African air.

■ TIP→ In certain countries—Botswana and Tanzania, for example—the staff won't wash underwear because it's against cultural custom.

For game walks, pack sturdy but light walking shoes or boots—in most cases durable sneakers suffice for this option. For a walking-based safari, you need sturdy, lightweight boots. Buy them well in advance of your trip so you can break them in. If possible, isolate the clothes used on your walk from the remainder of the clean garments in your bag. Bring a couple of large white plastic garbage bags for dirty laundry.

TOILETRIES & SUNDRIES

Most hotels and game lodges provide toiletries such as soap, shampoo, and insect repellent, so you don't need to overpack these items. In the larger lodges in South Africa's national parks and private game reserves, stores and gift shops are fairly well stocked with clothing, film, and guidebooks; in self-drive and self-catering areas, shops also carry food and drink. In Botswana, lodges that belong to groups such as Wilderness Safaris or Gametrackers have small shops with a limited selection of books, clothing, film, and curios. Elsewhere in Africa you're not likely to find this type of amenity on safari.

On a canoe safari you're in the relentless sun every day and have to protect your legs, especially the tops of your thighs and shins, from sunburn. Bring a towel or, even better, a sarong, and place it over your legs. Sunscreen of SPF 30 or higher is de rigueur.

⚠ The African sun is harsh, and if you're even remotely susceptible to burning, especially coming from a northern winter, don't skimp on sunscreens and moisturizers. Also bring conditioner for your hair, which can dry out and start breaking off.

PLUGGING IN

Most of Southern Africa is on 220/240 volt alternating current (AC). The plug points are round. However, there are both large 15-amp three-prong sockets (with a ground connection) and smaller two-prong 5-amp sockets. Most lodges have adapter plugs, especially for recharging camera batteries; check before you go, or purchase a universal plug adapter before you leave home.

Safari hotels in the Serengeti, the private reserve areas outside Kruger National Park, and the less-rustic private lodges in South Africa are likely to provide you with plug points and plugs, and some offer hair dryers and electric-razor sockets as well (check this before you go). Lodges on limited generator and solar power are usually able to charge camera batteries, as long as you have the right plug.

Continued on page 554

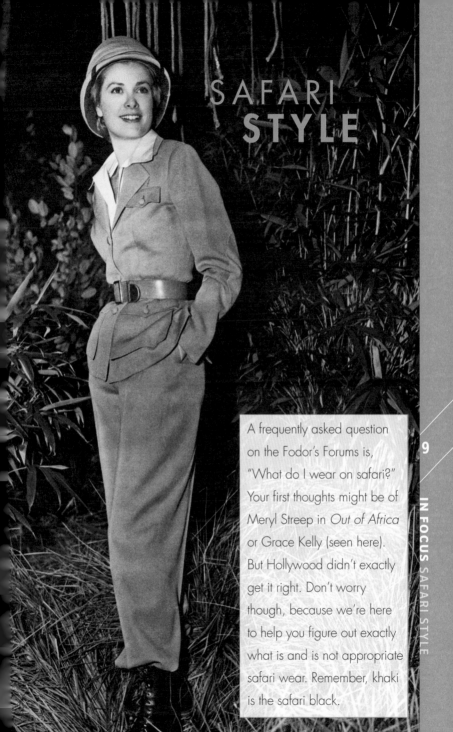

SAFARI
STYLE

A frequently asked question on the Fodor's Forums is, "What do I wear on safari?" Your first thoughts might be of Meryl Streep in *Out of Africa* or Grace Kelly (seen here). But Hollywood didn't exactly get it right. Don't worry though, because we're here to help you figure out exactly what is and is not appropriate safari wear. Remember, khaki is the safari black.

WHAT TO WEAR

SUNGLASSES: The sun is bright here, and good UV protection is a must. Glasses also keep flying debris (like sand) out of your eyes. Plus you never know when you might see a spitting cobra—they aim for the eyes.

INSECT REPELLENT: Make sure yours has at least 20% DEET and is sweat resistant. We suggest OFF! Active. It has 25% DEET and comes in a 3-ounce pump spray bottle—perfect for those Transportation Security Administration (TSA) restrictions.

HAT: This is a must to keep off the sun and keep you in the shade. Make sure it has a brim all the way around and is packable and breathable. The Tilley hat (www.tilley.com) has been highly recommended in the Fodor's Forums.

CLOTHES: Make sure your clothes are cotton (read: breathable). Also we suggest you wear long pants in light earth colors—khaki and brown are best. Pants keep the bugs off, help prevent sunburn, and protect your legs from thorny bushes. Another thing to keep in mind: If you don't want to lug a bag, cargo pants are great for storage.

WALKING SHOES: The key words here are "sturdy," "support," and "traction." Though you probably won't be walking miles, you will be in and out of your vehicle and might be able to go on a walking safari. Hi-Tec (www.hi-tec.com) is an excellent brand with styles for all occasions.

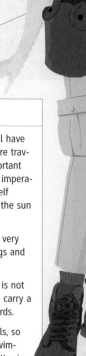

HOT...

■ Usually your guide will have water for you, but if you're traveling alone it's very important that you bring water. It's imperative that you keep yourself hydrated when you're in the sun and heat.

■ Bring layers. It can be very cold in the early mornings and late evenings.

■ A photographer's vest is not a bad idea if you plan to carry a lot of film or memory cards.

■ Most lodges have pools, so make sure you pack a swimsuit and a sarong. The latter is important to use as a cover-up.

WHAT NOT TO WEAR

LOTS OF MAKEUP:
Your daily regime should consist of slathering on sunscreen and spraying insect repellent, not applying blush or foundation.

DESIGNER OUTFITS:
We think this goes without saying, but one never knows. Leave the fancy threads at home. They're bound to get ruined if you bring them.

CAMOUFLAGE: This is a big no-no. Warring factions in Africa wear camouflage, and you don't want to be confused with the military or appear to be making fun of the situation.

LEAVE THE BLING AT HOME: A safari is not a fashion show, and though you may get "dressed up" for dinner, there's no need for gold bracelets or diamonds. The shininess, not to mention the clinking of jewelry, will alert the animals to your presence. And when you're in the major cities, why invite trouble? You can live without your bling for a few days.

ANYTHING WITH HEELS: Prada or Gucci? Try L.L. Bean or EMS. You need sturdy, practical footwear. Again, a safari is not a fashion show. It's all about being comfortable and enjoying the experience.

...OR NOT

■ Don't wear clothes in any variation of blue or black, especially if you're traveling to tsetse-fly areas. These colors attract the pesky sleeping-sickness transmitters.

■ Don't wear perfume. Animals have an incredible sense of smell and will sense your arrival immediately and be gone before you can say "Greater Kudu."

■ Don't wear white. It reflects sunlight and startles animals.

■ Don't overpack. Most of the small airplanes you'll be taking to your camps have luggage-weight limits.

PACKING CHECKLIST

Light, khaki, or neutral-color clothes are universally worn on safari and were first used in Africa as camouflage by the South African Boers, and then by the British army that fought them during the South African War. Light colors also help to deflect the harsh sun and, unlike dark colors, are less likely to attract mosquitoes. Do not wear camouflage gear. Do wear layers of clothing that you can strip off as the sun gets hotter and put back on as the sun goes down.

- Three cotton T-shirts
- Two long-sleeve cotton shirts
- Two pairs shorts or two skirts in summer
- Two pairs long pants (three pairs in winter)
- Optional: sweatshirt and pants, which can double as sleepwear
- Optional: a smart/casual dinner outfit
- Underwear and socks
- Walking shoes or sneakers
- Sandals
- Bathing suit
- Warm thigh-length padded jacket, and sweater, in winter
- Lightweight jacket in summer
- Windbreaker or rain poncho
- Camera equipment, plenty of film, and extra batteries
- Contact lenses, including extras
- Eyeglasses
- Binoculars
- Small flashlight
- Personal toiletries
- Malaria tablets
- Sunscreen and lip balm with SPF 30 or higher, moisturizer, and hair conditioner
- Antihistamine cream
- Insect repellent
- Basic first-aid kit (aspirin, bandages, antidiarrheal, antiseptic cream, etc.)
- Tissues and/or premoistened wipes
- Warm hat, scarf, and gloves (for winter)
- Sun hat and sunglasses (Polaroid and UV-protected ones)
- Documents and money (cash, traveler's checks, credit cards), etc.
- A notebook and pens
- Travel and field guides
- A couple of large white plastic garbage bags
- U.S. dollars in small denominations ($1, $5, $10) for tipping

BINOCULARS

Binoculars are essential and come in many types and sizes. You get what you pay for, so avoid buying a cheap pair—the optics will be poor and the lenses usually don't stay aligned for long, especially if they get bumped, which they will on safari. Whatever strength you choose, pick the most lightweight pair, otherwise you'll be in for neck and shoulder strain. Take them with you on a night drive; you'll get great visuals of nocturnal animals and birds by the light of the tracker's spotlight. Many people find that when they start using binoculars and stop documenting each trip detail on film, they have a much better safari experience.

CAMERA SMARTS

All the safaris included in this book are photographic (game-viewing) safaris. That said, if you spend your entire safari with one eye closed and the other peering through a camera lens, you may miss all the other sensual elements that contribute to the great show that is the African bush. And more than likely, your pictures won't look like the photos you see in books about African safaris. A professional photographer can spend a full year in the field to produce a book, so you are often better off just taking snaps of your trip and buying a book to take home.

■ TIP→ No matter what kind of camera you bring, be sure to keep it tightly sealed in plastic bags while you're traveling to protect it from dust. (Dust is especially troublesome in Namibia.) Tuck your equipment away when the wind kicks up. You should have one or more cloth covers while you're working, and clean your equipment every day if you can.

Learning some basics about the wildlife that you expect to see on your safari will help you capture some terrific shots of the animals. If you know something about their behavior patterns ahead of time, you'll be primed to capture action, like when the hippos start to roar. Learning from your guide and carefully observing the wildlife once you're there will also help you gauge just when to click your shutter.

9

PHOTOGRAPHY POINTERS

The trick to taking great pictures has three components: first is always good light. An hour after sunrise and before sunset are the magic times, because the light is softer and textures pop. For the few hours of harsh light each side of midday, you might as well put your camera away. The second component is framing. Framing a scene so that the composition is simple gives an image potency; with close-ups, fill the frame for maximum impact. Using objects of known size in the foreground or middle ground will help establish scale. The third component is capturing sharp images: use a tripod or a beanbag to rest the camera on while in a vehicle. When using a long lens (upward of 200mm), you cannot hand-hold a steady shot; you must have some support if you want your photos to be clear.

DIGITAL CAMERAS

Good digital cameras and their memory cards or sticks may be more expensive than basic 35mm cameras, but the benefits of being able to preview shots, select what you want and delete what you don't, store them, and then adjust them on a computer can outweigh the initial cost. The resolution of nonprofessional digital images is approaching that of good film. Cameras with eight megapixels of resolution can print high-quality, smooth A4 or letter-size prints; images with five-megapixel resolution are fine as well.

Invest in a telephoto lens to shoot wildlife, as you tend to be too far away from the animals to capture any detail with the zoom lens generally built into most point-and-shoot digital cameras. This may mean upgrading to a more robust camera. A tripod or beanbag is another must-have; it will stabilize your camera, especially when a zoom lens is extended.

Buy or borrow as many memory cards as you can—you'll use them. You may want to use multiple smaller memory cards to minimize the risk of losing an entire card's worth of images. And, as always, bring extra batteries.

VIDEO CAMERAS

Video cameras these days are almost universally digital. The benefits of video are threefold: it's much easier to get basically pleasing results with moving images than with still photography; video cameras are much more light-sensitive than still cameras, so you can shoot in much lower light conditions; and you can edit your footage and show them on your DVD or computer at home. There's also the added benefit of the zoom-lens capability on most video cameras, which can give you almost as close a look at large animals as with binoculars (the zoom doesn't work as well with smaller, far-off subjects). Video cameras are hungry for batteries, however, and you may run into recharging problems in remote safari destinations.

Another problem with video cameras (but not for the person behind the lens) is that persistent videographers can become annoying to the other people in a group, so be sensitive about this. Don't go everywhere with your camera glued to your eye while simultaneously issuing non-stop commentary. Eventually someone is going to tell you to plug it, or worse. Resist poking your lens close to strangers' faces—it looks great through the lens but these are not paid actors, and they'll appreciate being given their own space.

ON SAFARI

The pieces are falling into place, but your idea of what life is like on safari may still be a golden-tinged haze. The whos, whats, and hows still need to come into focus. If you have questions like, Where's the best place to sit in a game-drive vehicle? and Can you get near a honey badger? then read on.

GAME-VIEWING

This is the heart of a safari, and it has certain similarities regardless of the safari destination you've chosen. First, there's the overwhelming primeval atmosphere. You realize that you are the transient visitor in an ancient tableau of nature that has been going on since the dawn of time. Then there are the animals, from tiny rodents to the largest of land mammals, all going about their daily business: feeding, killing or avoiding being killed, and engaging in the never-ending territorial disputes that have evolved between species to ensure the maximum reproductive success of each animal group. The species you see are selected by time and nature; they are supremely adapted to their unforgiving habitats. You can move through the scene in dreamlike wonderment, but the strong scents of the bush, the birdsong, the bellows, and the roars remind you that you are very much awake, and alive.

GAME RANGERS & TRACKERS

Game rangers (sometimes referred to as guides) tend to be of two types: those who have come to conservation by way of hunting and those who are professional conservationists. In both cases they have vast experience with and knowledge of the bush and the animals that inhabit it. Rangers work in conjunction with trackers, who sit in a special seat on the front of the 4x4, spot animals, and advise the rangers where to go.

For better or worse, the quality of your bush experience depends most heavily on your guide or game ranger and tracker. A ranger wears many hats while on safari: he's there to entertain you, protect you, and put you as close to the wilderness as possible while serving as bush mechanic, first-aid specialist, and host. He'll often eat meals with you, will explain animal habits and behavior while out in the bush, and, if you're on foot, will keep you alive in the presence of an excitable elephant, buffalo, hippo, or lion. This is no small feat, and each ranger has his particular strengths. Because of the intensity of the safari experience, with its exposure to potentially dangerous animals and tricky situations, your relationship with your guide or ranger is one of trust, friendliness, and respect. Misunderstandings may sometimes occur, but you're one step closer to ensuring that all goes well if you know the protocols and expectations.

Wondering how to treat your ranger? Acknowledge that your guide is a professional and an expert in the field, and defer to his knowledge. Instead of trying to show how much you know, follow the example of the hunter, which is to walk quietly and take notice of all the little signs

9

CLOSE UP

Safari Tipping

■ TIP→ Gratuities are a fact of life on safari. If possible, tip in U.S. currency. Plan to give the local equivalents of about US$10 per person per day to the ranger and not much less to the tracker; an additional tip of US$25 for the general staff would be sufficient for a couple staying two days. Tips are presented as a lump sum at the end of the trip. Mark Harris, managing director of Tanzania Odyssey, a London-based tour operator, suggests that tipping roughly $15 a day (per couple) into the general tip box and approximately $15 a day to your specific driver is generous.

If you have a guide, Sarah Fazendin, president of the Fazendin Portfolio, a Denver-based company that represents tour operators, lodges, and safari experiences, suggests tipping them at least US$5 per person per day.

It's also a good idea to bring some thank you cards with you from home to include with the tip as a personal touch. Fodor's Forum member atravelynn adds, "Put bills in an envelope for your guide and in a separate envelope with your name on it for the camp staff. Sometimes the camps have envelopes, but bringing some from home is also a good idea."

---

around you. Save social chatter with the guide for when you're back at camp, not out on a game drive. Rangers appreciate questions, which give them an idea of your range of knowledge and of how much detail to include in their animal descriptions. However, if you like to ask a lot of questions, save some for later, especially as several other people are likely to be in the safari vehicle with you. Carry a pocket notebook on game drives and jot down questions as they occur; you can then bring them up at dinner or around the campfire, when your ranger has more time to talk and everyone can participate in the discussion.

Wondering how your ranger will treat you? You can expect your ranger or guide to behave with respeckkelieve a show-off guide or gung-ho ranger is speaking down to you, a quiet word with him should be enough to change his demeanor. (The safari world is small; a guide's reputation is built by word of mouth and can be eroded in the same fashion.)

Don't let your ranger get away with rote guiding, or "guiding by numbers"—providing only a list of an animal's attributes. Push him by politely asking questions and showing you'd like to know more. Even the best guides may experience "bush burnout" by the end of a busy safari season with demanding clients, but any guide worthy of the title always goes out of his way to give you the best possible experience. If you suspect yours has a case of burnout, or just laziness, you have a right to ask for certain things. There's never any harm in asking, and you can't expect your guide to read your mind about what you like. If, for example, you have a preference for birds, insects, or whatever, ask your guide to spend time on these subjects. You may be surprised by how happy he is to oblige.

GAME-VIEWING WITH A RANGER

When you're in the care of a professional guide or ranger, you're unlikely to be placed in a dangerous situation. If you're going for a walk or ride in risky territory, your guide will first brief you about all the possible dangers and tell you how to behave in the unlikely event of an emergency. Listen to all the safety briefings and adhere to them strictly.

At most southern African camps and lodges, open vehicles with raised, stepped seating—meaning the seats in back are higher than the ones in front—are used for game drives. There are usually three rows of seats after the driver's row; the norm at a luxury lodge is to have two people per row. In the front row you'll have the clearest conversations with the ranger, but farther back you'll have a clearer, elevated view over the front of the car. Try not to get stuck in the very back, though; in that row you spend a lot of time ducking thorny branches, you're exposed to the most dust, you feel the most bumps, and communicating with your ranger is difficult because of the rows between you. In closed vehicles, which are used by private touring companies operating in Kruger National Park, sit as close to the driver-guide as possible so you can get in and out of the vehicle more easily and get the best views.

The tracker will be busy searching out animal tracks, spoor, and other clues to nearby wildlife while the guide drives and discusses the animals and their environment. As described in Luxury Lodge–Based Safaris, *see Chapter 1 for more information,* rangers often communicate with each other via radio when someone has a good sighting.

Guided bush walks vary, but usually a maximum of eight guests walk in single file with the armed ranger up front and the tracker at the back. A bush walk is a more intimate experience than a drive. You are up close with the bush and with your fellow walkers and guides. Your guide will brief you thoroughly about where and how to walk, emergency procedures, and the like. If you are in a national park, you will most likely have to pay an additional fee to have an armed park ranger escort you on your walk.

GAME-VIEWING ON A SELF-DRIVE SAFARI

Although most animals in popular parks are accustomed to vehicles with humans in them and will carry on unperturbed in many cases, a vehicle should still approach any animal carefully and quietly, and the driver should "feel" the response. This is for your own and the animals' safety. A delicate approach also gives you a better chance of getting as close as possible without alarming the animal. Be conservative and err on the side of caution, stopping as soon as circumstances suggest.

Human presence among wild animals never goes unnoticed. Don't get out of the vehicle, even if the animals appear friendly, and don't feed the creatures. Animals don't associate people in a vehicle with the potential food source or possible threat that they are when out of the vehicle. But for this ruse to work you must be quiet and still. The smell of the exhaust fumes and noise of a vehicle mask the presence of the human cargo, so when the engine is off you need to exercise extra caution.

This is especially true when closely viewing lions and elephants—the only two animals likely to attack a vehicle or people in a vehicle. When approaching lions or elephants, never leap out of your seat or talk loudly; you want to be able to get as close as possible without scaring them off, and you want to avoid provoking an attack.

It does take time to develop your ability to find motionless game in thick bush. On the first day you're less likely to spot an animal than to run it over. All those fancy stripes and tawny colors really do work. Slowly, though, you learn to recognize the small clues that give away an animal in the bush: the flick of a tail, the toss of a horn, even fresh dung. To see any of this, you have to drive *slowly*, 15–25 kph (10–15 mph). Fight the urge to pin back your ears and tear around a park at 50 kph (30 mph) hoping to find something big. The only way to spot game at that speed is if it's standing in the road or if you come upon a number of cars already at a sighting. But remember that being the 10th car at a game sighting is less exciting than finding the animal yourself. Not only do the other cars detract from the experience, but you feel like a scavenger—a sort of voyeuristic vulture.

The best time to find game is in the early morning and early evening, when the animals are most active, although old Africa hands will tell you that you can come across good game at any time of day. Stick to the philosophy "you never know what's around the next corner," and keep your eyes and ears wide open all the time. If your rest camp offers guided night drives on open vehicles with spotlights—go for it. You'll rarely be disappointed, seeing not only big game, but also a lot of fascinating little critters that surface only at night. Book your night drive in advance or as soon as you get to camp.

HEALTH ON SAFARI

Of all the horror stories and fantastic nightmares about meeting your end in the bush—being devoured by lions and crocodiles; succumbing to some ghastly fever like Ernest Hemingway's hero in *The Snows of Kilimanjaro*—the problem you're most likely to encounter will be of your own doing: dehydration. Also be wary of malaria, motion sickness, and intestinal problems. By taking commonsense precautions, your safari will be uneventful from a health perspective but memorable in every other way.

DEHYDRATION & OVERHEATING
The African sun is hot and the air is dry, and sweat evaporates quickly in these conditions. You might not realize how much bodily fluid you are losing as a result. Wear a hat, lightweight clothing, and sunscreen—all of which will help your body cope with high temperatures.

Drink at least two to three quarts of water a day, and in extreme heat conditions as much as three to four quarts of water or juice. Drink more if you're exerting yourself physically. If you overdo it at dinner with wine or spirits or even caffeine, you need to drink even more water to recover the fluid lost as your body processes the alcohol. Antimalar-

A COMMON SAFARI AFFLICTION

In addition to the health hazards described in the "Health on Safari" section, there's a safari disease that's as well known as malaria: "khaki fever." Though this fever may not kill you, it can wreak havoc upon your sensibilities and your heart. In fact, it is part of the plotline in the 1953 film *Mogambo,* in which the married society girl (Grace Kelly) falls for the rugged, tanned game ranger (Clark Gable), who's already carrying on with a wild American (Ava Gardner).

When you're on safari, a magical world quite unlike the one to which you're accustomed reveals itself. When it does, a perpetual good mood might strike and with it, a feeling of euphoria and romance. We can't blame you. The campfire can be very seductive and the bush is full of bewitching, sensual stimuli—a full moon hovers above the trees, a lion roars in the distance, a nightjar fills the velvety night with its trilling call. Then there's the tanned, knowledgeable ranger protecting you from the wilds of Africa, chauffeuring you around, and seemingly delivering your every wish.

Hey, heavenly things can happen… but if they do, just make sure you're prepared for the earthbound realities. AIDS in Africa is rife; if there's even the remotest chance of having a sexual encounter on safari, carry condoms. Better still, abstain.

ial medications are also very dehydrating, so it's important to increase your water intake while you're taking this medicine.

Don't rely on thirst to tell you when to drink; people often don't feel thirsty until they're a little dehydrated. At the first sign of dry mouth, exhaustion, or headache, drink water, because dehydration is the likely culprit.

■ TIP➔ To test for dehydration, pinch the skin on the back of your hand and see if it stays in a peak; if it does, you're dehydrated. Drink a solution of ½ teaspoon salt and 4 tablespoons sugar dissolved in a quart of water to replace electrolytes.

Heat cramps stem from a low salt level due to excessive sweating. These muscle pains usually occur in the abdomen, arms, or legs. When a child says he can't take another step, investigate whether he has cramps. When cramps occur, stop all activity and sit quietly in a cool spot and drink. Don't do anything strenuous for a few hours after the cramps subside. If heat cramps persist for more than an hour, seek medical assistance.

MALARIA

See the malaria section *under* Getting Started, *above,* for details on antimalarial drugs.

If you're on safari in a malarial zone, be vigilant about protecting yourself. In the morning and evening cover exposed skin with strong insect repellent; dress in long pants, long-sleeve shirts, and shoes and socks; and wear clothes you've treated with a mosquito-repellent spray or laundry wash. Forget fashion statements and tuck your pants into your socks so your ankles aren't exposed. Spray insect repellent on your shoes, socks, and legs up to your knees, even if you're wearing pants, before you set off for a game walk or evening drive. Wear light-color clothing, since mosquitoes (as well as tsetse flies) are attracted to dark surfaces. Spray all exposed skin with an up-to-date mosquito-repellent spray or use a cream or roll-on. Most private safari lodges provide insect repellents in your room. Citronella and other natural bug repellents can be used, but don't work half as well. If you've been out on a walk it's a good idea to take a hot shower and soap your entire body when you return.

When you go to bed, make sure you turn on any fan that's over or facing your bed, since mosquitoes can't fly well in moving air; keep it on while you sleep. Use mosquito coils and sprays in your room (especially if you're traveling with children), and sleep under mosquito nets. If you are 100% vigilant, these tactics should work.

■TIP→ Sleeping under a mosquito net or in an insect proof tent is customary, but it can stifle airflow. If you can't sleep, wet a sheet or towel, wring it out, and lie under it: you'll fall asleep before you know it.

MOTION SICKNESS

If you're prone to motion sickness, be sure to examine your safari itinerary closely. Though most landing strips for chartered planes are not paved but rather grass, earth, or gravel, landings are smooth most of the time. If you're going on safari to northern Botswana (the Okavango Delta, specifically), know that small planes and unpaved airstrips are the main means of transportation between camps; these trips can be very bumpy, hot, and a little dizzying even if you're not prone to motion sickness. If you're not sure how you'll react, take motion-sickness pills just in case. Most of the air transfers take an average of only 30 minutes and the rewards will be infinitely greater than the pains.

■TIP→ When you fly in small planes, take a sun hat and a pair of sunglasses. If you sit in the front seat next to the pilot, or on the side of the sun, you will experience harsh glare that could give you a severe headache and exacerbate motion sickness.

INTESTINAL UPSET

Microfauna and -flora differ in every region of Africa, so if you drink unfiltered water, add ice to your soda, or eat fruit from a roadside stand, you might get traveler's diarrhea. All reputable hotels and lodges have filtered, clean tap water or provide sterilized drinking water, and nearly all camps and lodges have supplies of bottled water. If you're traveling outside organized safari camps in rural Africa or are unsure of local water, carry plenty of bottled water and follow the CDC's advice for fruits and vegetables: boil it, cook it, peel it, or forget it. If you're going on a mobile safari, ask about drinking water.

VOCABULARY

African countries are far less homogenous in language than most North American or European countries. In Namibia, Afrikaans, Ovambo, German, Herero, and English are widely spoken and understood. South Africa has 11 official languages, although English is the lingua franca except in the deepest rural areas. Zimbabwe and Botswana each have two or three prevalent local languages, but English is the official one and widely understood. Zambia, Kenya, and Tanzania have many local languages, but again English is the most widely used and spoken, with Swahili being the common local lingo.

For the purpose of safaris, mastering the basics of just two foreign languages, Zulu and Swahili, should make you well equipped for travel through much of the region. Zulu is the most common of the Southern African Nguni family of languages (Zulu, Shangaan, Ndebele, Swazi, Xhosa) and is understood in South Africa and Zimbabwe. Swahili is a mixture of Arabic and Bantu and is used across East Africa. In Namibia, Botswana, and Zambia your best bet initially is to stick with English.

SAFARI SPEAK

The following words and terms are used throughout the book.

Ablution blocks: public bathrooms

Banda: bungalow or hut

Big Five: buffalos, elephants, leopards, lions, and rhinoceros, collectively

Boma: a fenced-in open-air eating area, usually circular

Braai: barbecue

Bush or bushveld: general safari area in South Africa, usually with scattered shrubs and trees and lots of game; also referred to as the bush or the veld

Camp: used interchangeably with lodge

Campground: a place used for camping that encompasses several campsites and often includes some shared facilities

Campsite: may or may not be part of a campground

Concession: game-area lease that is granted to a safari company and gives it exclusive access to the land

Game guide: used interchangeably with ranger; usually a man

Hides: small, partially camouflaged shelters from which to view game and birds; blinds

Kopje/Koppies: hills or rocky outcrops

Kraal: traditional rural settlement of huts and houses

9

Lodge: accommodation in rustic-yet-stylish tents, rondawels, or lavish suites; prices at lodges usually include all meals and game-viewing

Marula: tree from which amarula (the liquor) gets its name

Mobile or overland safari: usually a self-sufficient, camping affair set up at a different location (at public or private campgrounds) each night

Mokoro: dugout canoe; plural *mekoro*

Ranger: safari guide with vast experience with and knowledge of the bush and the animals that inhabit it; used interchangeably with game guide

Rest camp: camp in a national park

Rondawel/rondavel: a traditional, round dwelling with a conical roof

Sala: outdoor covered deck

Self-catering: with some kind of kitchen facilities, so you can store food and prepare meals yourself

Self-drive safari: budget-safari option in which you drive, and guide, yourself in a rented vehicle

Sundowner: cocktails at sunset

Tracker: works in conjunction with a ranger, spotting animals from a special seat on the front of the 4x4 game-viewing vehicle

Veld: a grassland; see bushveld

Vlei: wetland or marsh

SOUTH AFRICAN WORDS & PHRASES

BASICS

Abseil: rappel

Bakkie: pickup truck (pronounced "bucky")

Berg: mountain

Boot: trunk (of a car)

Bottle store: liquor store

Bra/bru/my bra: brother (term of affection or familiarity)

Buck: antelope

Burg: city

Chommie: mate, chum

Dagga: marijuana, sometimes called *zol*

Djembes: drums

Dorp: village

Fanagalo: a mix of Zulu, English, Afrikans, Sotho, and Xhosa

Highveld: the country's high interior plateau, including Johannesburg

Howzit?: literally, "how are you?" but used as a general greeting

Indaba: literally, a meeting but also a problem, as in "that's your indaba."

Ja: yes

Jol: a party or night on the town

Kloof: river gorge

Kokerbooms: quiver trees

Lekker: nice

Lowveld: land at lower elevation, including Kruger National Park

Mopane: nutrient-poor land

Moppies: vaudeville-style songs

More-ish: so good you will want more, mouthwatering

Muthi: traditional (non-Western) medicine

Plaas: farm

Petrol: gasoline

Robot: traffic light

Sangoma: traditional healer or mystic

Shebeen: a place to drink, often used for taverns in townships

Sis: gross, disgusting

Sisi or usisi: sister (term of affection or respect)

Spaza shop: an informal shop, usually from a truck or container

Spar: name of grocery market chain in Africa

Stoep: veranda

Takkie: (pronounced tacky) sneaker

FOOD & DRINK

Biltong: spiced air-dried (not smoked) meat, made of everything from beef to kudu

Bobotie: spiced minced beef or lamb topped with savory custard, a Cape Malay dish

Boerewors: Afrikaaner term for a spicy farmer's sausage, often used for a braai (pronounced "*boo*-rah-vorse")

Bredie: a casserole or stew, usually lamb with tomatoes

Bunny chow: not a fancy name for salad—it's a half loaf of bread hollowed out and filled with meat or vegetable curry

Chakalaka: a spicy relish

Gatsby: a loaf of bread cut lengthwise and filled with fish or meat, salad, and fries

Kabeljou: one of the varieties of line fish

Kingklip: a native fish

Koeksister: a deep-fried braided, sugared dough

Malva: pudding

Melktert: a sweet custard tart

Mogodu: beef or ox tripe

Moroho: mopane worms

Pap: also called *mielie pap,* a maize-based porridge

Peppadews: a patented vegetable, so you may see it under different names, usually with the word *dew* in them; it's a sort of a cross between a sweet pepper and a chili and is usually pickled.

Peri-peri: a spicy chili marinade, Portuguese in origin, based on the searing hot *piri-piri* chili; some recipes are tomato-based, others use garlic, olive oil, and brandy

Potjie: pronounced "*poy*-key" and also called *potjiekos,* a traditional stew cooked in a three-legged pot

Rocket: arugula

Rooibos: an indigenous, earthy-tasting red-leaf tea

Samp: corn porridge

Snoek: a barracuda-like fish, often smoked, sometimes used for *smoorsnoek* (braised)

Sosaties: local version of a kebab, with spiced, grilled chunks of meat

Waterblommetjie: water lilies, sometimes used in stews

Witblitz: moonshine

SWAHILI ESSENTIALS

ANIMALS
Baboon: Nyani

Buffalo: Nyati

Cheetah: Duma

Crocodile: Mamba

Elephant: Tembo

Giraffe: Twiga

Hippo: Kiboko

Impala: Swala

Leopard: Chui

Lion: Simba

Rhino: Kifalu

BASICS
Yes: ndio

No: hapana

Please: tafadhali

Excuse Me: samahani

Thank you (very much): asante (sana)

Welcome: karibu

Hello: jambo

Beautiful: nzuri

Goodbye: kwaheri

Cheers: kwahafya njema

FOOD & DRINK
Food: chakula

Water: maji

Bread: mkate

Fruit(s): (ma)tunda

Vegetable: mboga

Salt: chumvi

Sugar: sukari

Coffee: kahawa

Tea: chai

Beer: pombe

USEFUL PHRASES
What is your name?: Jina lako nani?

My name is…: Jina langu ni…

How are you?: Habari?

Where are you from?: Unatoka wapi?

I come from…: Mimi ninatoka…

Do you speak English?: Una sema kiingereza?

I don't speak Swahili.: Sisemi kiswahili.

I don't understand.: Sifahamu.

9

How do you say this in Kiswahili?: Unasemaje kwa kiswahili

How much is it?: Ngapi shillings?

May I take your picture?: Mikupige picha?

Where is the bathroom?: Choo kiko wapi?

I need...: Mimi natafuta...

I want to buy...: Mimi nataka kununua...

No problem.: Hakuna matata.

ZULU ESSENTIALS

BASICS
Yes: yebo

No: cha

Please/Excuse Me: uxolo

Thank you: ngiyabonga

You're welcome: nami ngiyabonga

Good morning/hello: sawubona

Goodbye: sala kahle

Do you speak English?: uya khuluma isingisi?

FOOD & DRINK
Food: Ukudla

Water: Amanzi

Bread: Isinkwa

Fruit: Isthelo

Vegetable: Uhlaza

Salt: Usawoti

Sugar: Ushekela

Coffee: Ikhofi

Tea: Itiye

Beer: Utshwala

USEFUL PHRASES

What is your name?: Ubani igama lakho?

My name is…: Igama lami ngingu…

Do you speak English?: Uya khuluma isingisi?

I don't understand.: Angizwa ukuthi uthini.

How much is it?: Kuyimalini lokhu?

May I take your picture?: Mikupige picha?

Where is the bathroom?: Likuphi itholethe?

I would like…: Ngidinga…

I want to buy…: Ngicela…

9

Africa

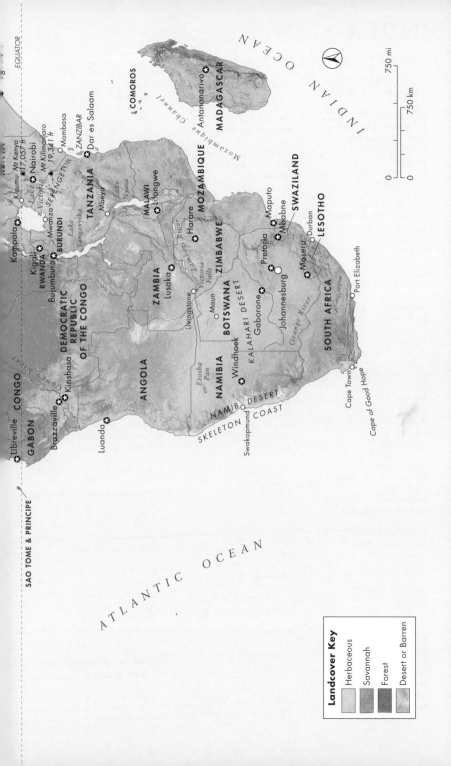

EQUATOR

INDIAN OCEAN

ATLANTIC OCEAN

Mozambique Channel

MADAGASCAR
Antananarivo ✪

COMOROS

Mombasa
ZANZIBAR
Dar es Salaam

Mt Kenya
17,057 ft
Kisumu Nairobi
Lake Mt Kilimanjaro
Victoria 19,341 ft
Kampala ✪ SERENGETI
Mwanza
BURUNDI TANZANIA
Kigali Mbeya Lake
RWANDA Nyasa
Bujumbura MALAWI MOZAMBIQUE
Lilongwe ✪
Lake SWAZILAND
Tanganyika Harare ✪
DEMOCRATIC Zambezi River Maputo
REPUBLIC ZAMBIA ZIMBABWE Mbabane ✪
OF THE CONGO Lusaka ✪ LESOTHO
Victoria Durban
Libreville ✪ Falls Pretoria ✪ Maseru ✪
CONGO Livingstone Port Elizabeth
GABON Maun Johannesburg
Brazzaville ✪ BOTSWANA Orange River
Kinshasa Gaborone ✪ SOUTH AFRICA
ANGOLA KALAHARI DESERT
Luanda Etosha Windhoek ✪
Pan NAMIBIA Cape Town
NAMIB DESERT Cape of Good Hope
SAO TOME & PRINCIPE Swakopmund
SKELETON COAST

Congo River

750 mi

750 km

0

0

Landcover Key

Herbaceous

Savannah

Forest

Desert or Barren

INDEX

PHOTO CREDITS

1, *Ingrid van den Berg/age fotostock*. 2-3, *Tibor Bognar/Alamy*. 5, *Juniors Bildarchiv/age fotostock*. **Chapter 1: Your Safari:** 10-11, *Fritz Poelking/age fotostock*. 12 (top), *Tim Graham/Alamy*. 12 (bottom), *Namibia Tourism Board*. 13 (top), *Peter Malsbury/iStockphoto*. 13 (bottom) and 14, *Marion Granberry*. 15 (left), *Mike Hill/Alamy*. 15 (right), *Dave Humphreys/Namibia Tourism Board*. 16, *Sabi Sands Game Reserve*. 17 (left), *Frantisek Staud/Alamy*. 17 (right), *CC Africa*. 18, *Marion Granberry*. 19 (left), *Torsten Karock/iStockphoto*. 19 (right), *Almero Olwagen/age fotostock*. 20, *nomad-tanzania.com*. 21 (left), *Maurizio Borgese/age fotostock*. 21 (right), *Morales/age fotostock*. 22, *Selous Safari Camp*. 23, *sanparks. org*. 24, *Guy Upfold*. 26, *Chiawa Camp*. 27 (left), *Thanda Private Game Reserve*. 27 (right), *CC Africa*. 28, *sanparks.org*. 29 (left), *Siankaba*. 29 (right), *Wilderness Safaris*. 31 (top), *Martin Harvey/Alamy*. 31 (bottom), *N. Joy Neish/Shutterstock*. 32-33 (top), *Jack Barker/Alamy*. 32 (center), *Dana Allen/Wilderness Safaris*. 32 (bottom), *Maximilian Weinzierl/Alamy*. 33 (center), *CC Africa*. 33 (bottom), *Images of Africa Photobank/Alamy*. 34 (top), *Chad Ehlers/Alamy*. 34 (bottom), *Ariadne Van Zandbergen/Alamy*. 35 (top), *Charles Sturge/Alamy*. 35 (center), *Mike Myers/Wilderness Safaris*. 35 (bottom), *David Hopson/Alamy*. 36, *Catherine Hugo/iStockphoto*. 37 (left and right), *Gibb's Farm*. 38, *CC Africa*. 39 (left), *Bruce van Niekerk/Wilderness Safaris*. 39 (right), *Karsten Wrobel/Alamy*. 40, *Steve Hynes/Alamy*. 41 (left), *Images of Africa Photobank/Alamy*. 41 (right), *Dave Humphreys/Namibia Tourism Board*. 42, *Images of Africa Photobank/Alamy*. 43 (left), *Robert Caputo/Aurora Photos*. 43 (right), *Ute von Ludwiger/Namibia Tourism Board*. **Chapter 2: Flora & Fauna:** 44-45, *Frank Krahmer/age fotostock*. 48, *Werner Bollmann/ age fotostock*. 49, *Karl Ammann/age fotostock*. 50-51, *Singita Lebombo Lodge*. 52-53, *Martin Harvey/ Alamy*. 54-55, *Juniors Bildarchiv/age fotostock*. 56-57, *Kenya Tourist Board*. 58 (top), *F. Poelking/ ARCO/age fotostock*. 58 (bottom), *Nigel Dennis/age fotostock*. 59 (top right), *Chris Burt/Shutterstock*. 59 (top left), *Ingrid van den Berg/age fotostock*. 59 (center right), *Ariadne Van Zandbergen/Alamy*. 59 (bottom left), *Antonio López Román/age fotostock*. 59 (bottom right), *Werner Bollmann/age fotostock*. 60 (left), *Holger Ehlers/Alamy*. 60 (right), *Peter Malsbury/iStockphoto*. 61 (left), *Robert Harding Picture Library Ltd/Alamy*. 61 (top right), *David Tipling/Alamy*. 61 (bottom right), *Frank Krahmer/age fotostock*. 62 (left), *Nigel Dennis/age fotostock*. 62 (top right), *Natural Visions/Alamy*. 62 (bottom right), *Nigel Dennis/age fotostock*. 63 (left), *Richard Du Toit/South African Tourism*. 63 (top center), *Christina Krutz/ age fotostock*. 63 (top right), *Brendon Boyes/age fotostock*. 63 (bottom right), *tanzaniaodyssey.com*. 64 (left), *Jill Sneesby/South African Tourism*. 64 (top right), *Winfried Wisniewski/age fotostock*. 64 (bottom right), *Johan Swanepoel/iStockphoto*. 65 (top left), *blickwinkel/Alamy*. 65 (bottom left), *C. Hütter/ ARCO/age fotostock*. 65 (right), *Nigel Dennis/age fotostock*. 66 (left), *Tim Graham/Alamy*. 66 (center), *Herbert Hopfensperger/age fotostock*. 66 (right), *Nigel Dennis/age fotostock*. 67 (top left), *J & C Sohns/ age fotostock*. 67 (bottom left), *AfriPics.com/Alamy*. 67 (right), *J & C Sohns/age fotostock*. 68 (top left), *Casey K. Bishop/Shutterstock*. 68 (bottom left), *Piotr & Irena Kolasa/Alamy*. 68 (right), *Robert Preston Photography/Alamy*. 69, *Nigel Dennis/age fotostock*. **Chapter 3: Kenya:** 70-71, *R. Schmid/SIME/eStock Photo*. 72 (top), *Mark Eveleigh/Alamy*. 72 (bottom), *Ripani Massimo/SIME/eStock Photo*. 73, *Kevin O'Hara/age fotostock*. 76, *Jones Huw/SIME/eStock Photo*. 78, *Martin Harvey/Alamy*. 86 (top), *Ol Seki Mara*. 86 (bottom left), *Mara Explorer*. 86 (bottom right), *CC Africa*. 90, *Mike Hill/Alamy*. 95 (top), *Martin Harvey/Alamy*. 95 (bottom left), *Camp ya Kanzi*. 95 (bottom right), *Ol Donyo Wuas*. 98, *D. Damschen/ARCO/age fotostock*. 103 (top and bottom right), *Galdessa*. 103 (bottom left), *Tina Manley/ Africa/Alamy*. 107, *SuperStock*. 111 (top and bottom left), *Sabuk*. 111 (bottom right), *Il Ngwesi*. 117, *blickwinkel/Alamy*. 118-19, *Steve Bloom Images/Alamy*. 121, *Werner Bollmann/age fotostock*. 124, *Terry Wall/Alamy*. 126, *SIME s.a.s/eStock Photo*. 136, *Ripani Massimo/SIME/eStock Photo*. 168, *Cottars*. 169 (left), *Il Ngwesi*. 169 (right), *porini.com*. **Chapter 4: Tanzania:** 170-71, *Doug Scott/age fotostock*. 172 (top), *Vera Bogaerts/Shutterstock*. 173, *Joaquin Ayllon Perez/Shutterstock*. 176, *Emilio Suetone/ age fotostock*. 179, *Fritz Poelking/age fotostock*. 184-85 (all), *CC Africa*. 189, *Winfried Wisniewski/age fotostock*. 195 (all), *Gibb's Farm*. 196, *CC Africa*. 198, *Tibor Bognar/Alamy*. 203 (top and bottom), *CC Africa*. 204, *blickwinkel/Alamy*. 211 (top), *nomad-tanzania.com*. 211 (bottom left), *Ian Cumming/age fotostock*. 211 (bottom right), *Alexis Kelly*. 212, *MJ Photography/Alamy*. 217, *Martin Harvey/Alamy*. 218-19 and 221, *WorldFoto/Alamy*. 222 (top, second from top, third from top, and fourth from top), *Debra Bouwer*. 222 (bottom), *blickwinkel/Alamy*. 223, *Debra Bouwer*. 229, *SuperStock*. 236, *Robert Eilets/Tanzania Tourism Board*. 239, *URF/age fotostock*. 256, *CC Africa*. 257 (top), *Manolo Yllera*. 257 (bottom), *Craig Zendel*. **Chapter 5: South Africa:** 258-59, *David Paynter/age fotostock*. 260, *Photosky 4t com/Shutterstock*. 261, *Nicolaas Weber/Shutterstock*. 264, *Etienne Rothbart/age fotostock*. 266, *Images of Africa Photobank/Alamy*. 279, *Walter Schmitz/Bilderberg/Aurora Photos*. 280 (top), *Singita Lebombo Lodge*. 280 (bottom left and bottom right), *Sweni Lodge*. 281 (top), *Protea Hotel*. 281 (bottom), *Rhino Post Plains Camp*. 282, *Adrian Bailey/Aurora Photos*. 293 (top), *Leopard Hills/Sabi Sands Game Reserve*. 293 (bottom left), *Bush Lodge/Sabi Sands Game Reserve*. 293 (bottom right), *David*

Braun. 294, *Eric Nathan/Alamy.* 305 (top and bottom right), *Hilltop Camp/Hluhluwe Game Reserve.* 305 (bottom left), *Impala Camp/Hluhluwe Game Reserve.* 306 (all), *CC Africa.* 307, *Nigel Dennis/age fotostock.* 313, *Ann and Steve Toon/Alamy.* 325 (top), *Saez Pascal/SIPA/Newscom.* 325 (bottom) and 326 (left), *Lebrecht Music and Arts Photo Library/Alamy.* 326 (top right), *Reimar/Alamy.* 326 (bottom right), *JTB Photo Communications, Inc./Alamy.* 327 (top left), *Images of Africa Photobank/Alamy.* 327 (bottom left), *blickwinkel/Alamy.* 327 (top right), *Perry Correll/Shutterstock.* 327 (center right), *Miguel Cuenca/Alamy.* 327 (bottom right), *Timothy Large/iStockphoto.* 328 (top left), *Bernard O'Kane/Alamy.* 328 (bottom left), Eric Miller/PDI/Newscom. 328 (right), *AFP/Getty Images/Newscom.* 329 (top), *Siphiwe Sibeko/Reuters.* 329 (bottom), *Adrian de Kock/Pierre Tostee/Zuma Press/Newscom.* 330, *Bruno Perousse/ age fotostock.* 344, *EcoPrint/Shutterstock.* 359, *Nicholas Pitt/Alamy.* 390, *Djuma Game Reserve.* 391 (top), *Hog Hollow Country Lodge.* 391 (bottom), *Grootbos Private Nature Reserve.* **Chapter 6: Botswana:** 392-393, *Wilderness Safaris.* 394, *Sharon Maritz/age fotostock.* 395, *Alan Compton/age fotostock.* 398, *Andoni Canela/age fotostock.* 400, *Adrian Bailey/Aurora Photos.* 407 (all), *Wilderness Safaris.* 408, *Des Curley/Alamy.* 410, *Trevor Lovegrove/Alamy.* 413 (all), *Wilderness Safaris.* 415, *P. Narayan/age foto-stock.* 421 (all), *Wilderness Safaris.* 422, *Russell Johnson/Alamy.* 424 (all), *Wilderness Safaris.* 431 (top), *Sylvain Grandadam/age fotostock.* 431 (bottom), *Meredith Lamb/Shutterstock.* 432 (left), *Bill Bachmann/ Alamy.* 432 (top right), *Meredith Lamb/Shutterstock.* 432 (bottom right), *Tom Grundy/Shutterstock.* 433 (top left), *J Marshall- Tribaleye Images/Alamy.* 433 (bottom left), *Rick Matthews/age fotostock.* 433 (top right), *Sylvain Grandadam/age fotostock.* 433 (bottom right), *Ulrich Doering/Alamy.* 434, *Neil Moultrie/South African Tourism.* 440, *Dana Allen/Wilderness Safaris.* 441 (top), *Sanctuary Lodges & Camps.* 441 (bottom), *CC Africa.* **Chapter 7: Namibia:** 442-43, *Werner Bollman/SuperStock.* 444, *Karsten Wrobel/Alamy.* 445, *Chris Mattison/age fotostock.* 448, *LaTerraMagica/ARCO/age fotostock.* 450, *Wilderness Safaris.* 455 (top and bottom left), *Wilderness Safaris.* 455 (bottom right), *CC Africa.* 457, *Gianluca Basso/age fotostock.* 458-59, *Images of Africa Photobank/Alamy.* 458 (top and bottom insets), *Namibia Tourism Board.* 458 (second and third from top insets), *Dave Humphreys/Namibia Tourism Board.* 460, *Roine Magnusson/age fotostock.* 461 (top), *Charles Sturge/Alamy.* 461 (bottom), *Richard Wareham Fotografie/Alamy.* 462, *Karsten Wrobel/Alamy.* 467 (top and bottom right), *Wilder-ness Safaris.* 467 (bottom left), *Vingerklip Lodge.* 468, *Patrick Frischknecht/age fotostock.* 475 (top), *Wilderness Safaris.* 475 (bottom left and bottom right), *Namibia Wildlife Resorts.* 476, *Morales/age fotostock.* 485, *Rainer Kiedrowski/age fotostock.* 491, *World Travel/Alamy.* 500, *Herbert Breuer/ NamidRand Safaris Ltd.* 501 (top), *CC Africa.* 501 (bottom), *Dana Allen/Wilderness Safaris.* **Chapter 8: Victoria Falls:** 502-03, *Berndt Fischer/age fotostock.* 504 (top), *Kord.com/age fotostock.* 504 (bottom), *Siankaba.* 505 and 510, *Sue Cunningham Photographic/Alamy.* 514, *JTB Photo Communications, Inc./Alamy.* 523-27, Victoria Falls. 528, *CC Africa.* 534, *Lebrecht Music and Arts Photo Library/Alamy.* 538, *CC Africa.* 539 (top), *Siankaba.* 539 (bottom), *Chiawa Camp.* **Chapter 9: On Safari:** 540-41, *Bob Handelman/Alamy.* 542, *Kenya Tourist Board.* 551, *Everett Collection.* 552-53, *William Wu.*

NOTES

NOTES

NOTES

The Great Migration — Grumeti
River

Kwazulu-Natal Park —
South Africa —
black rhino

Gombe Stream —
Tanzania —
Chimpanzee

NOTES

ABOUT OUR WRITERS

Kate Turkington is one of South Africa's best-known journalists and broadcasters. Her live Sunday-night talk show on Radio 702/Cape Talk, *Believe It or Not,* is the longest-running radio show in South Africa. During World War II she was evacuated from London to the fens and marshes of East Anglia, a region of eastern England, and she has traveled ever since. Her beat is the world, but her heart and home are in Africa, where she lives in Johannesburg, surrounded by a large family. She's been held up by Ethiopian tribesmen armed with Kalashnikovs in the Rift Valley, ridden astride dolphins in Cuba's Caribbean, broken bread with Buddhist monks in Tibet's oldest monastery, white-water rafted down the Ganges, and sipped coffee surrounded by a million and a half migrating wildebeest in the Serengeti. She worked on the Kenya, Tanzania, South Africa, Namibia, and Botswana chapters, as well as the What to Expect, Arts & Culture, Music & Dance, Namibia Dunes, Great Migration, and Victoria Falls features.

Kristan Schiller has walked the Serengeti for weeks with nothing but a fold-up tent and a Masai guide, tracked lions at night in the most remote reaches of the Okavango Delta, and trawled for crayfish off the coast of Kommetjie, South Africa. She has a master's degree in African studies from the University of London's School of Oriental and African Studies. She is currently at work on a book about environmental crime during Apartheid. She worked on the Flora & Fauna chapter as well the eco-lodge spreads, the Big Five feature, the tribes' pieces, and the Changing Continent information.

SOUTH AFRICA CONTRIBUTORS

Brian Berkman lives in Cape Town and covered dining for his fair city. Karena du Plessis wrote about wine, the Winelands, and Cape Town, and Debra A. Klein helped with the South Africa Essentials chapter. Cape Town–based travel writer Jennifer Stern covered the beach destinations of Plettenburg Bay and Wilderness. Tara Turkington, a journalist from Johannesburg, covered her hometown as well as Durban.

VICTORIA FALLS CONTRIBUTOR

Sanja Cloete-Jones lives in Zambia and worked on the Victoria Falls chapter.